KEY MATHS

AQA (Modular) Specification B Module 5

- **David Baker**
  The Anthony Gell School, Wirksworth
- **Jim Griffith**
  The Bishop of Hereford's Bluecoat School, Hereford
- **Paul Hogan**
  St. Wilfrid's Church of England High School, Blackburn
- **Chris Humble**
  Gillotts School, Henley-on-Thames
- **Barbara Job**
  Christleton County High School, Chester
- **Peter Sherran**
  Weston Road High School, Stafford

Series Editor: **Paul Hogan**

First published in 1998 by:
Stanley Thornes (Publishers) Ltd

This edition published in 2002 by:
Nelson Thornes Ltd
Delta Place
27 Bath Road
CHELTENHAM
GL53 7TH
United Kingdom

02 03 04 05 06 / 10 9 8 7 6 5 4 3 2 1

A catalogue record for this book is available from the British Library.

ISBN 0-7487-6736-3

Illustrations by Maltings Partnership, Peters and Zabransky, Oxford Illustrators, Clinton Banbury
Page make-up by Tech Set Ltd

Printed and bound in China by Midas Printing International Ltd.

Acknowledgements
The publishers thank the following for permission to reproduce copyright material: Alton Towers: 417, 426; Art Directory: 117 (bottom); Bruce Coleman: 242 (Mark Carwardine); Eye Ubiquitous: 163 (T Futter), 181 Getty Images: 240 (Tony Stone Images/S Lowry/Univ. of Ulster), 85 (top – Tony Stone Images/Kristian Hilsen), 86; Image Bank: 235 (Leo Mason); John Walmsley Photography: 133, 139, 155, 211, 217; Leslie Garland Picture Library: 115 (top), 116, 117 (top, top middle), 395 (Vincent Lowe); Martyn Chillmaid; 47 (top), 48, 50, 85 (bottom), 104, 275, 276, 277, 278, 291, 359, 369, 386; Rex Features: 216 (Vic Thomasson); Skyscan Balloon Photography: 99; Still Pictures: 211 (top – David Hoffman), 212 (David Hoffman); Topham Picturepoint; 47 (botom – Press Association), 53, 78; TRIP: 117 (bottom middle – J Stanley), 118 (Dinardia)
All other photographs Nelson Thornes Archive.

The publishers have made every effort to contact copyright holders but apologise if any have been overlooked.

Contents

16 Formulas and equations

CORE

1 Finding a formula
Formulas for sequences using times tables
Two part formulas for sequences
Finding formulas for patterns with shapes

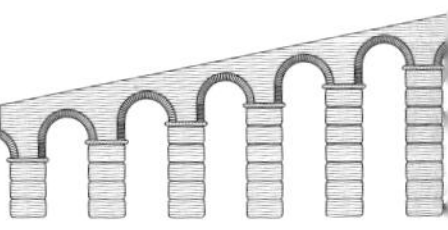

2 Solving equations
Solving one step equations
Solving two step equations

3 Trial and improvement
Solving equations with integer solutions
Solving equations to 1 dp and 2 dp

QUESTIONS

EXTENSION

TEST YOURSELF

1 Finding a formula

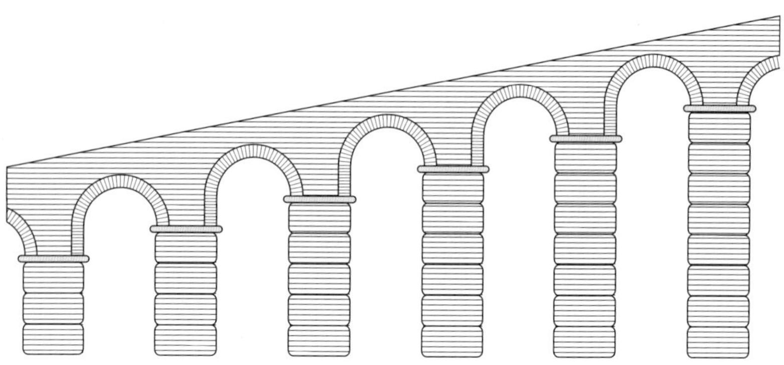

The blocks in the pillars give the sequence 3, 4, 5, 6, 7, 8, …
Sequences are often found in investigational work.
You can find a formula for sequences.

Look at the sequence	5	10	15	20	…
Term number	1	2	3	4	n

The rule is '**add 5**'.

5 →(+5) 10 →(+5) 15 →(+5) 20 →(+5) $5n$

This is the 5 times table.

The first term is	$5 \times 1 = 5$	because the term number is 1
The second term is	$5 \times 2 = 10$	because the term number is 2
The third term is	$5 \times 3 = 15$	because the term number is 3

nth term The term in the sequence with term number $\boldsymbol{n}$ is called the **nth term**.

So the nth term is $5 \times \boldsymbol{n} = 5\boldsymbol{n}$ because the term number is $\boldsymbol{n}$

If you know the nth term you can work out **any** term with a function machine.
You put the 5 from $5\boldsymbol{n}$ in the function machine.

Term number → × 5 → 1st term
1 → × 5 → 5

You can do more than one term at a time.

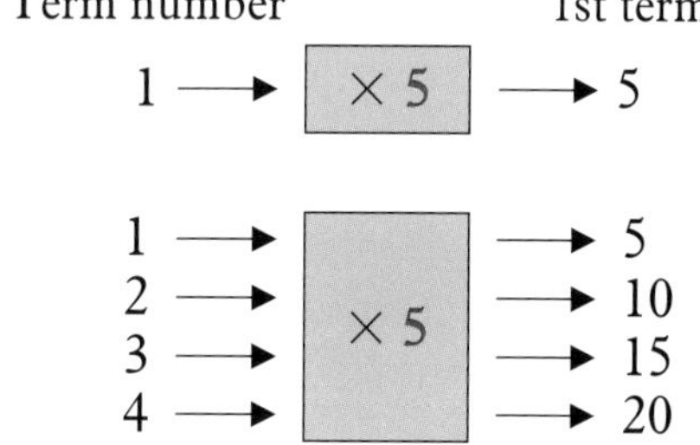

Exercise 16:1

1 The nth term of this sequence is $6n$. The 6 is used in the function machine. Copy the function machine. Fill in the missing numbers.

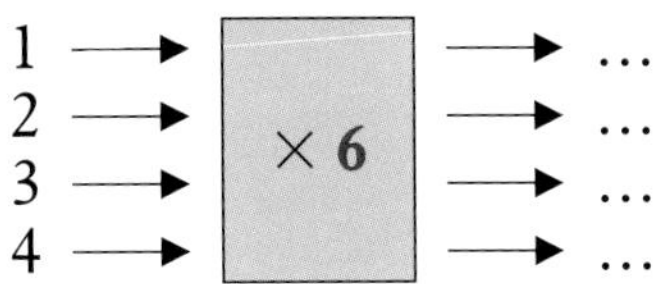

2 These are the nth terms of some sequences.
Use function machines to work out the first 4 terms.

a $8n$ $\boxed{\times 8}$
b $9n$ $\boxed{\times 9}$
c $10n$ $\boxed{\times \ldots}$
d $20n$ $\boxed{\times \ldots}$
e $100n$ $\boxed{\times \ldots}$
● **f** $2.5n$ $\boxed{\times \ldots}$

3 These are the nth terms of some sequences.
Work out the 5th, 6th, 7th and 8th terms for each one.

a $2n$ $\boxed{\times 2}$
b $3n$ $\boxed{\times 3}$
c $4n$ $\boxed{\times \ldots}$
d $6n$ $\boxed{\times \ldots}$
e $22n$ $\boxed{\times \ldots}$
f $100n$ $\boxed{\times \ldots}$

You can use a formula to find any term in a sequence.

Example Find the 25th term in the sequence whose formula is $4n$

Term number 25 → $\boxed{\times 4}$ → 100 (25th term)

---

4 Work out the 20th term for each of these sequences.
Use the function machines given.

a $2n$ $\boxed{\times 2}$
b $3n$ $\boxed{\times 3}$
c $4n$ $\boxed{\times \ldots}$
d $6n$ $\boxed{\times \ldots}$
e $22n$ $\boxed{\times \ldots}$
f $100n$ $\boxed{\times \ldots}$

You can write a formula which gives you any term in the sequence.
It is the same as the formula for the nth term.

Look at the sequence	3	6	9	12	...	
Term number	1	2	3	4	...	n

The rule is '**add 3**'

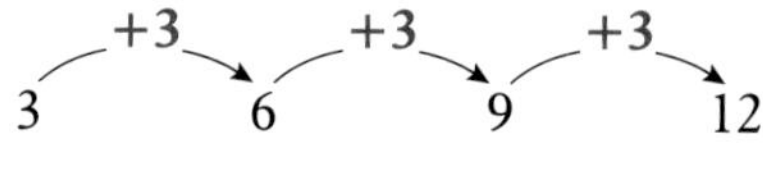

... $3n$

This comes from	3×1	3×2	3×3	3×4		$3 \times n$

So:

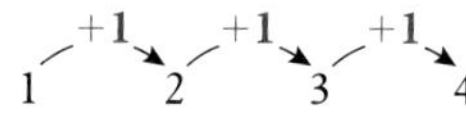

The formula for the **1** times table is $\mathbf{1}n$
(but $\mathbf{1}n$ is always written as n)

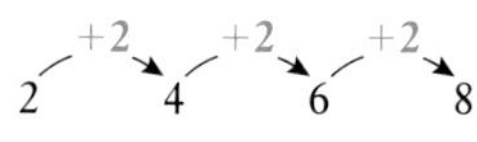

The formula for the 2 times table is $2n$

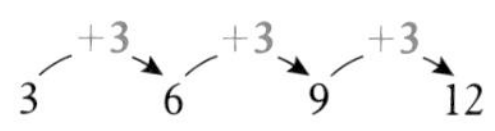

The formula for the 3 times table is $3n$

Example Write down the formula for this sequence 7, 14, 21, 28, ...

Term number	1	2	3	4	...	n

The rule is '**add 7**'

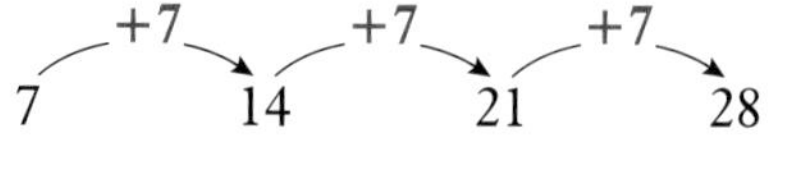

... $7n$

This comes from	7×1	7×2	7×3	7×4		$7 \times n$

These are the multiples of 7
So the formula for the sequence is $7n$.

You can check the formula by using it to find one of the terms in the question.
You could check the third term. This is when $n = 3$
So $7n = 7 \times 3 = 21$
This is the same as the third term in the question, so the formula is correct.

Exercise 16:2

For questions **1–10**:

a Copy down the sequence.
b Write down the rule.
c Write down a formula for each sequence.
d Check the formula by finding the third term.

1 4, 8, 12, 16, …

2 5, 10, 15, 20, …

3 6, 12, 18, 24, …

4 10, 20, 30, 40, …

5 20, 40, 60, 80, …

6 8, 16, 24, 32, …

7 100, 200, 300, 400, …

8 9, 18, 27, 36, …

9 22, 44, 66, 88, …

10 90, 180, 270, 360, …

11 **a** Copy these boxes.
b Connect each pair of boxes that match with an arrow.

Terms	Formula
2, 4, 6, 8, …	$9n$
30, 60, 90, 120, …	$11n$
11, 22, 33, 44, …	$8n$
8, 16, 24, 32, …	$100n$
12, 24, 36, 48, …	$7n$
7, 14, 21, 28, …	$12n$
100, 200, 300, 400, …	$30n$
9, 18, 27, 36, …	$2n$

Formulas with two parts

Look at this sequence. It is not the 5 times table!

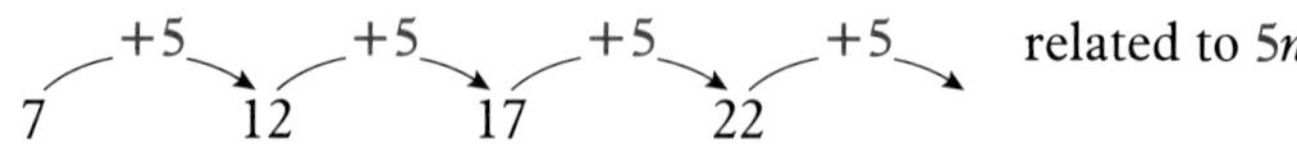

The rule for this sequence is **add 5**,
so it must have something to do with the 5 times table.
You can write related to 5*n* to help you.
The formula for the 5 times table is 5*n*.
Write the sequence 5*n* underneath. Compare the two sequences.

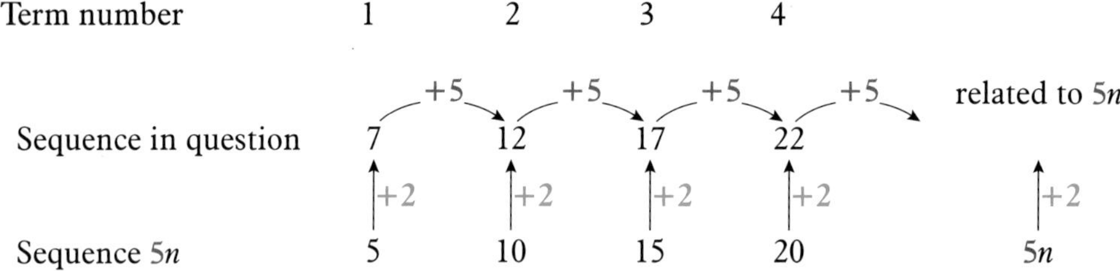

This is called a sequence diagram.

You need to add 2 to every term in 5*n* to make the new sequence.
So the formula for the new sequence is 5*n* + 2

Exercise 16:3

1 **a** Copy the sequence diagram below. Fill in the missing numbers.

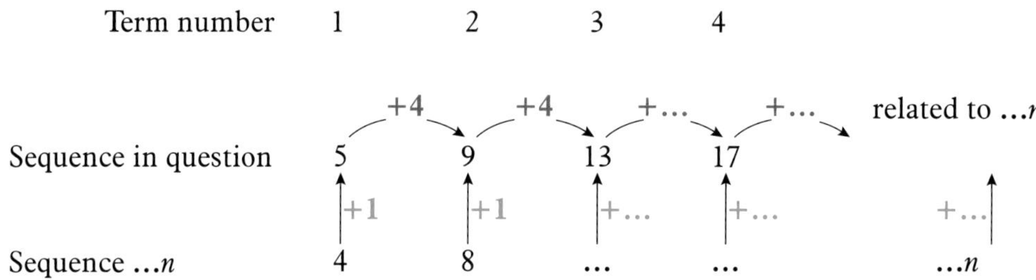

b Write down the formula for the new sequence.

2 **a** Copy the sequence diagram below.
b Fill in the missing numbers.
c Write down the formula for the sequence.

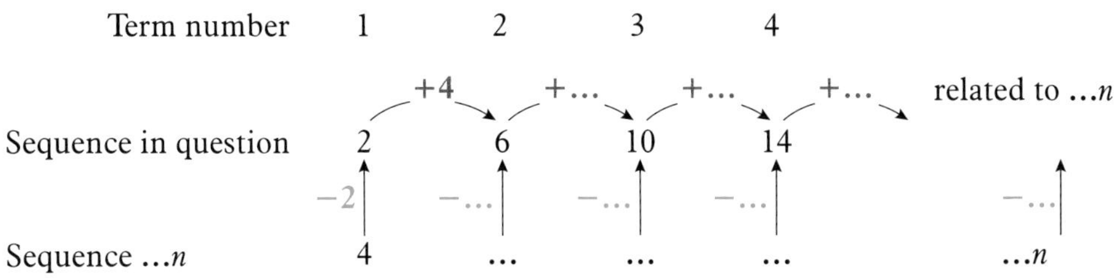

Term number	1	2	3	4	
	+4 →	+… →	+… →	+… →	related to …n
Sequence in question	2	6	10	14	
	−2 ↑	−… ↑	−… ↑	−… ↑	−… ↑
Sequence …n	4	…	…	…	…n

3 For each of these sequences:
(1) draw diagrams (2) find the formula

a 7, 11, 15, 19, …
b 7, 10, 13, 16, …
c 7, 12, 17, 22, …
d 5, 7, 9, 11, …
e 3, 5, 7, 9, …
f 3, 8, 13, 18, …
g 11, 17, 23, 29, …
h 9, 15, 21, 27, …
● **i** 27, 29, 31, 33, …
● **j** 5.5, 8, 10.5, 13, …

4 **a** Copy these boxes.
b Connect each sequence to the correct formula with an arrow.

Sequence	Formula
9, 15, 21, 27, …	$7n + 3$
3, 8, 13, 18, …	$5n - 2$
10, 17, 24, 31, …	$6n + 3$

● **5** These 2 sequences are both based on $2n$.
They have different formulas. Find the formula for each one.

a 3, 5, 7, 9, … **b** 1, 3, 5, 7, …

● **6** For each of these sequences:
(1) draw diagrams
(2) find the formula

a 21, 19, 17, 15, … **b** 95, 90, 85, 80, …

You can work out the terms for sequences like $2n + 3$ using function machines.

You need a function machine to work out $2n$ | × 2 |

You need another function machine to get from $2n$ to $2n + 3$ 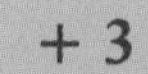

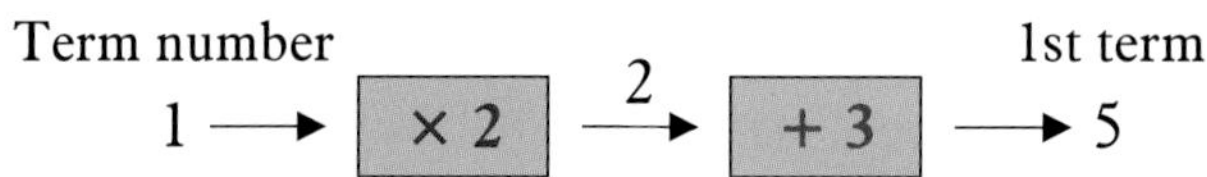

This is also useful for checking that formulas are correct.
Remember, you can do more than one term at a time!

Term				Output
1 →	× 2	→	+ 3	→ 5
2 →		→		→ 7
3 →		→		→ 9
4 →		→		→ 11

Exercise 16:4

1 Work out the first four terms for each sequence.
Show your working out.

a	$2n + 4$	× 2	+ 4		**e**	$n + 5$	× 1	+ …
b	$3n + 1$	× 3	+ 1		**f**	$2n - 3$	× …	− …
c	$3n - 2$	× 3	− 2		**g**	$6n - 5$	× …	− …
d	$4n + 5$	× 4	+ 5	•	**h**	$2.5n + 0.5$	× …	+ …

2 Work out the 5th, 6th, 7th and 8th terms for each sequence.
Show your working out.

a	$2n + 1$	× 2	+ 1		**d**	$6n + 2$	× …	+ …
b	$3n + 4$	× 3	+ 4		**e**	$22n - 10$	× …	− …
c	$4n - 4$	× …	− 4	•	**f**	$100n - 200$	× …	− …

You can use a formula to find any term in a sequence.

Example Find the 22nd term in the sequence whose formula is $4n - 3$

Term number					22nd term
22 →	× 4	88 →	− 3	→	85

3 Work out the 20th term for each of these sequences.

a $2n + 3$ **d** $6n + 5$ **g** $10n + 5$
b $3n + 7$ **e** $8n - 4$ **h** $2n - 36$
c $7n - 2$ **f** $7n - 3$ ● **i** $8n - 200$

4 For each sequence:
(1) Find the formula.
(2) Check your formula by finding the fourth term.
(3) Work out the 100th term.

a 6, 10, 14, 18, … **b** 7, 16, 25, 34, … ● **c** 12, 23, 34, 45, …

Game: It could be you!

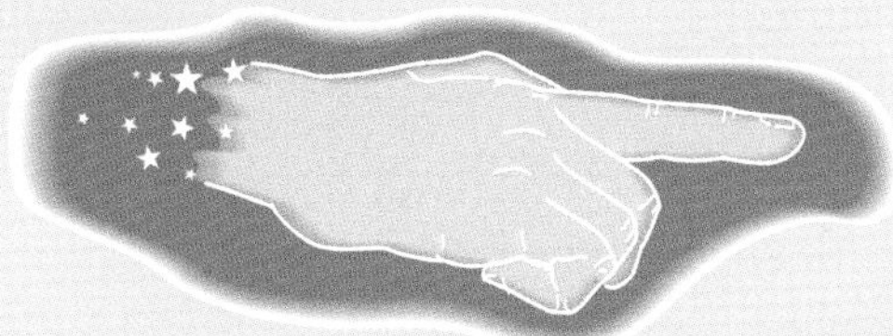

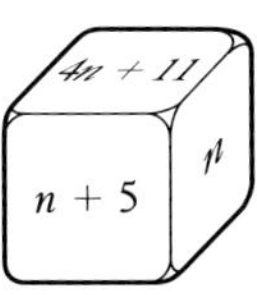

This is a game for 2 players.
Both of you need to write down this list of numbers:

1 3 4 6 7 9 10 15 16 27

You need two dice. One is an ordinary dice numbered from 1 to 6.
You will need to put these formulas on the other dice:

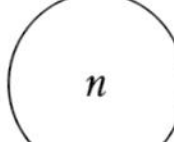

$2n + 10$ $3n - 2$ $4n + 11$ $6n - 3$

Take it in turns to throw both dice.
The ordinary dice tells you the term number.
The other dice tells you the formulas that you need to use.

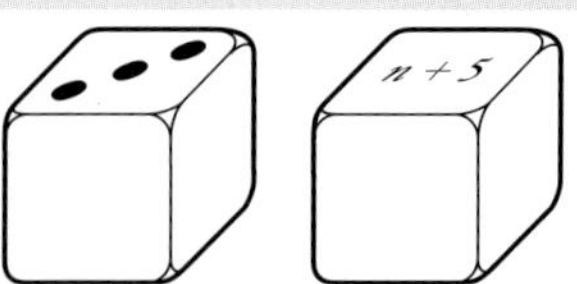

Katriona and Rhodri play the game.
Here is Katriona's throw.

Katriona works out the 3rd term for the formula $n + 5$.

She scores 8. As 8 is not on her list of numbers she cannot cross it out.

Rhodri then has his turn. He throws a '4' and '$4n + 11$'. He scores 27.
As 27 is on his list of numbers, he crosses 27 out.

The winner is the first player to match any six of the scores in their list.

Patterns with shapes

Look at these pillars.
Count the blocks for each pillar.
There is a sequence.

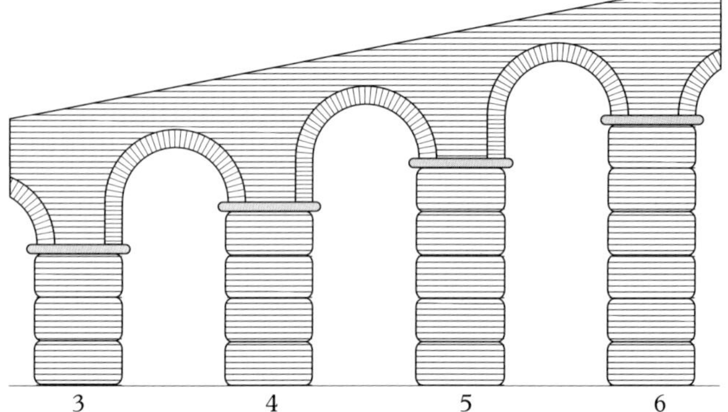

You can work out the formula for the sequence.

The sequence is	3	4	5	6	…
Term number	1	2	3	4	n

	+1 →	+1 →	+1 →	+1 →	related to $\mathbf{1}n$
Sequence in question	3	4	5	6	
	↑ +2	↑ +2	↑ +2	↑ +2	↑ +2
Sequence $1n$	1	2	3	4	$\mathbf{1}n$

So the formula is $\mathbf{1}n + 2$. Write this as $n + 2$.

Exercise 16:5

1 **a** Write the shape sequence as a number sequence.
b Use a sequence diagram to work out the formula.

The sequence is … … … … …

2 **a** Write the shape sequence as a number sequence.
b Use a sequence diagram to work out the formula.

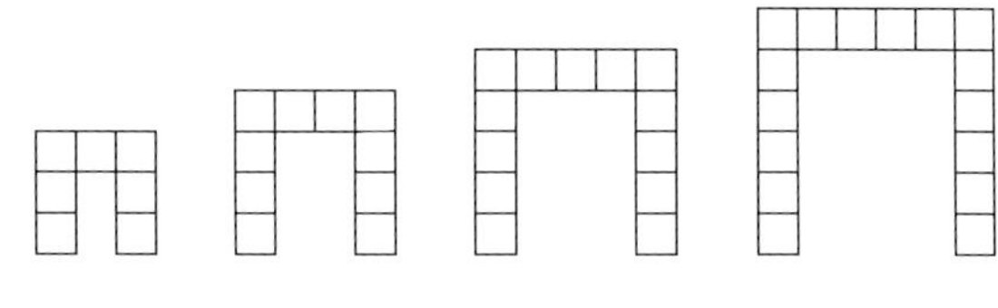

The sequence is … … … …

3 Luciana has some patterns on her wall made from tiles.
a Work out the formula for the sequence.
b How many tiles would you need for the 8th pattern?

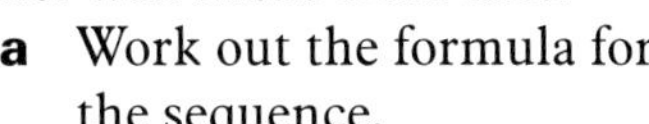

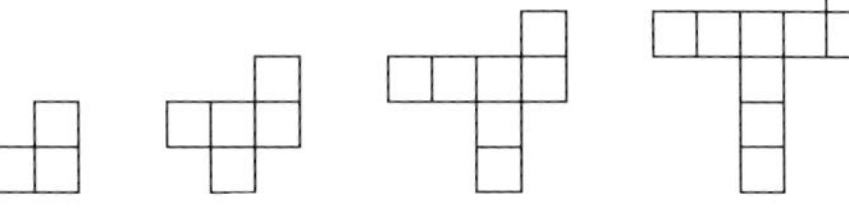

4 The aliens are coming!
a Write down how many are in the next group in the pattern.
b Work out the formula for their flying formation.

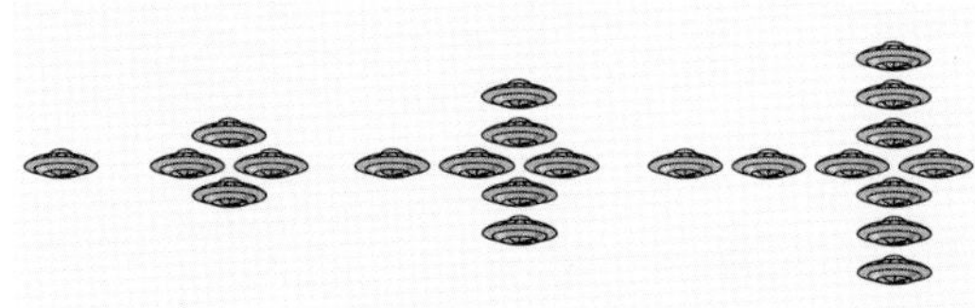

5 These penguins were seen on an ice floe watching RAF aircraft.
a How many are in the next group in the pattern?

b Work out the formula for their formation.

2 Solving equations

Dale, Vincent and Charlene are brothers and sister.

Dale is the youngest. Vincent is three years older than Dale. Charlene is three years older than Vincent.

Their ages add up to 39.
How old are Dale, Vincent and Charlene?

Problems like this can be solved using linear equations.

Linear equations

Equations with simple letters and numbers are called **linear equations.**
Linear equations must not have any terms like x^2, x^3 or $\frac{1}{x}$ in them.

When you solve an equation, you are trying to work out the value of a letter.
You solve it by getting the unknown letter on to one side of the equation.

Example

Solve these equations:

a $x + 5 = 12$ **b** $2x = 7$ **c** $\frac{x}{6} + 3 = 5$

a To solve $x + 5 = 12$, notice that x has 5 added to it.
To leave x by itself, take 5 from each side of the equation.

$$x + 5 - 5 = 12 - 5$$
$$x = 7$$

b In the equation $2x = 7$, the x has been multiplied by 2.
To solve this equation, divide both sides by 2.

$$\frac{2x}{2} = \frac{7}{2}$$

$$x = 3.5$$

c You need to do two things to solve $\frac{x}{6} + 3 = 5$

The x has been divided by 6 and then 3 has been added.
To solve this, subtract the 3 then multiply by the 6.
This means doing the opposite operation in the opposite order.

$$\frac{x}{6} + 3 - 3 = 5 - 3$$

$$\frac{x}{6} \times 6 = 2 \times 6$$

$$x = 12$$

Exercise 16:6

1 Solve these equations.

a $x + 4 = 16$

b $3x = 18$

c $x + 6 = 19$

d $x - 12 = 14$

e $x - 4 = 14$

● **f** $2x = -3$

g $\frac{x}{5} = 6$

h $\frac{x}{7} = 4$

i $\frac{x}{3} = 9$

j $3x + 1 = 16$

k $4x - 3 = 13$

l $5x + 6 = 11$

m $7x - 6 = -13$

n $5x - 6 = 12$

● **o** $0.5x + 2 = 6$

p $\frac{x}{3} + 2 = 10$

q $\frac{x}{4} - 1 = 12$

r $\frac{3x}{2} + 5 = 26$

Some equations have letters on both sides.
To solve them, you need to change them so that they only have the letter on one side.

Example

Solve $5x = 3x + 14$

Look to see which side has least x.
In this example, the right-hand side (RHS) has only $3x$.

Subtract $3x$ from each side	$5x - 3x = 3x - 3x + 14$
You now have x on just the LHS	$2x = 14$
Divide both sides by 2	$x = 7$

Exercise 16:7

1 Solve these equations.

a $5x = 3x + 8$

b $7x = 3x + 24$

c $12x = 7x + 35$

d $3x = x + 19$

• **e** $9x - 8 = 7x$

f $11x = 8x - 6$

g $3.5x = 2.5x + 8$

• **h** $5x = 2x - 12$

i $4.5x = 2x + 10$

j $15x = 8x + 147$

Sometimes, the side with the least x will be the left-hand side (LHS).
You can still solve the equations in the same way.

Example Solve $4x + 9 = 7x$

Take $4x$ from both sides	$4x + 9 - 4x = 7x - 4x$
You now have x on just the RHS	$9 = 3x$
Divide by 3	$3 = x$
Usually you write this the other way around:	$x = 3$

---

2 Solve these equations.

a $6x + 4 = 7x$

b $4x + 7 = 11x$

c $2x - 13 = 4x$

d $3x + 9 = 6x$

• **e** $4x - 6 = 6x$

f $4x - 21 = 11x$

g $3x = 7x - 4$

• **h** $1.5x + 9 = 3.5x$

i $3x - 6 = 5x$

j $2x + 4.5 = 4x$

k $5x - 3 = 7x$

l $23x = 29x + 6$

3 Solve these equations.

a $4x - 12 = 2x$

b $7x + 4 = 5x$

c $3x - 9 = 5x$

d $6x = 4x - 10$

• **e** $4.5x = 6x - 9$

f $4x - 9.5 = 5x$

Some equations have letters and numbers on both sides.
To solve these, change the equation so that it has x on only one side.
Then solve it as before.

Example

Solve $11x + 20 = 6x - 15$

The RHS has least x.

Take $6x$ from each side $\quad 11x - \mathbf{6x} + 20 = 6x - \mathbf{6x} - 15$

$$5x + 20 = -15$$

Now remove the numbers from the side with the x.
Take 20 from each side $\quad 5x + 20 - 20 = -15 - 20$

$$5x = -35$$

Divide both sides by 5 $\quad x = -7$

Exercise 16:8

1 Solve these equations.

a $4x + 4 = 2x + 10$

b $2x - 7 = x + 3$

c $6x - 13 = 4x + 5$

d $8x + 9 = 4x + 13$

e $4x + 6 = 6x + 2$

f $7x + 21 = 3x + 5$

g $3x - 15 = x - 4$

• **h** $6x + 2 = 17 + x$

i $9x - 1 = 5x + 7$

j $12x + 7 = 12 + 2x$

• **k** $3.5x - 15 = x + 5$

l $5x + 25 = 3x + 25$

The method does not change if you have a minus sign in front of one of the letters.
A minus number is always less than a positive number.

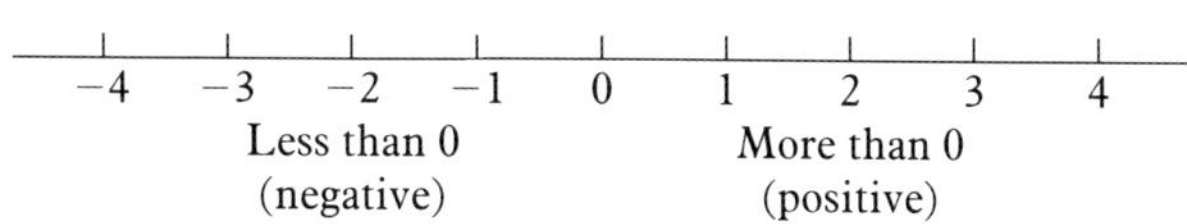

This means that the side with the minus sign has the least x.
To remove the x from this side, add the same number of xs on to each side.

Example Solve $4x + 5 = 20 - x$

First, remove the $-x$ from the RHS.
To do this, add x to each side $4x + 5 + x = 20 - x + x$
$5x + 5 = 20$
Subtract 5 from each side $5x + 5 - 5 = 20 - 5$
$5x = 15$
Divide both sides by 5 $x = 3$

---

2 Solve these equations.

a $6x + 6 = 20 - x$
b $5x + 7 = 21 - 2x$
c $x + 2 = 10 - x$
d $10x - 7 = 17 - 2x$
e $8x - 3 = 27 - 2x$
• **f** $-6x - 9 = 3 - 8x$
g $2.8x - 20 = 22 - 1.4x$
• **h** $7 - 3x = 4 + 2x$

Some equations have brackets in them.
To solve them, first multiply out the brackets.

Example Solve $3(2x + 1) = 27$

Multiply out the bracket $3 \times 2x + 3 \times 1 = 27$
$6x + 3 = 27$
Now solve the equation as usual $6x = 24$
$x = 4$

Exercise 16:9

1 Solve these equations.

a $3(2x + 1) = 21$
b $4(7x - 4) = 40$
c $6(2x - 7) = 42$
d $5(8x - 1) = 35$
e $10(2x - 10) = 40$
f $9(3x - 5) = -18$
g $3(x - 1) = 2x - 2$
h $2(2x - 1) = x + 7$
i $2(x + 1) + 5 = 3(2x + 1)$
• **j** $3(x - 2) - 2(x + 1) = 5$
k $6(7x - 2) = 6(5x + 3)$
l $10(3x - 4) = 5(6 - x)$

You have already seen equations with a divide sign in them such as $\frac{x}{6} = 5$

Sometimes, the x is on the bottom of the fraction.
To solve the equation, you need to get the x back on the top.
To do this, multiply both sides of the equation by x.

Example

Solve the equation $\frac{3}{x} = 6$

First multiply both sides of the equation by x:

$$\frac{3}{x} \times x = 6 \times x$$

This gives

$$3 = 6x$$

Now divide both sides by 6:

$$0.5 = x$$

So, the solution to the equation is $x = 0.5$

Exercise 16:10

1 Solve these equations.

a $\frac{10}{x} = 2$ **c** $\frac{15}{x} = 3$ **e** $\frac{12}{3x} = -2$ ● **g** $\frac{-12}{x} + 1 = 4$

b $\frac{12}{x} = 4$ **d** $\frac{11}{2x} = 2$ **f** $\frac{4}{x} = -1$ ● **h** $\frac{1}{x} - 1 = 4$

3 Trial and improvement

You have seen a formula in the last section that tells you how to solve any quadratic equation using the coefficients of the terms.

Evariste Galois (1811–1832) was a French mathematician who was killed in a duel at the age of only 20. The night before the duel he stayed up and wrote down all of his ideas. It took mathematicians more than 100 years to deal with what he wrote down in one night!

Galois proved that there is no formula for solving an equation using the coefficients (as there is for a quadratic) when the highest power of x is 5 or more.

You need a different way of solving these equations.
You can use trial and improvement.
You can also use trial and improvement for easier equations if you are told to do so.

Example

Solve $x^4 = 104\,976$ using trial and improvement.

Value of x	Value of x^4	
10	10 000	too small
20	160 000	too big
18	104 976	correct

Answer $x = 18$.
This is only part of the answer.
You may need to think about negative values.

Value of x	Value of x^4	
-10	10 000	too small
-20	160 000	too big
-18	104 976	correct

So $x = -18$ as well.

Exercise 16:11

Solve these equations using trial and improvement.
Draw a table to help you set out your working.

1 **a** $x^4 = 531\,441$
b $x^4 = 74\,120.0625$

2 **a** $x^3 = 216$ There is only one answer for this equation.
b $x^3 - 3x = 488$ There is only one answer for this equation.
● **c** $x^3 - 4x^2 + x + 6 = 0$ There are three answers for this equation.

3 The length of this cuboid is x cm.

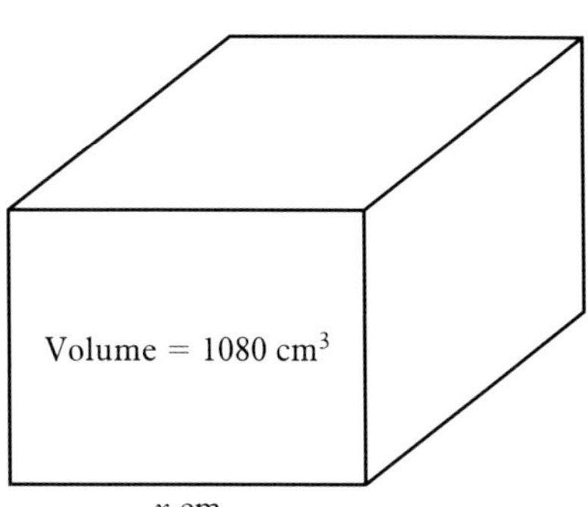

a The width is 2 cm less than the length.
Write down an expression for the width.
b The height is 3 cm less than the length.
Write down an expression for the height.
c The volume of the cuboid is 1080 cm^3.
Show that x satisfies the equation

$$x^3 - 5x^2 + 6x = 1080$$

d Solve the equation $x^3 - 5x^2 + 6x = 1080$ using trial and improvement.
e Write down the length, width and height of the cuboid.

Sometimes answers do not work out exactly.
When this happens you may have to give your answer correct to 1 dp.

Example Solve $x^3 = 135$

Value of x	Value of x^3		
5	125	too small	
6	216	too big	x is between 5 and 6
5.5	166.375	too big	x is between 5 and 5.5
5.1	132.651	too small	x is between 5.1 and 5.5
5.2	140.608	too big	x is between 5.1 and 5.2
5.15	136.590 875	too big	x is between 5 and 5.15

this value is halfway between 5.1 and 5.2

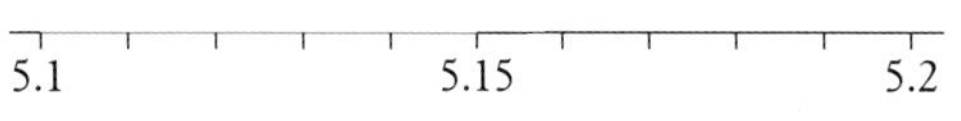

x must be somewhere in the green part of the number line.
Any number in the green part rounds down to 5.1 to 1 dp.
Answer: $x = 5.1$ to 1 dp.

Exercise 16:12

Solve these equations by trial and improvement.
Draw a table to help you find each solution.
Give all of your answers to 1 dp.

1 $x^3 = 250$

2 $x^5 = 21\,892$

3 $x^3 + x = 45$

4 $x^3 + 4x = 70$

5 Solve these equations using trial and improvement.
You need to rearrange the equations to get all the xs on the same side.
Part **a** has been rearranged for you.
All of these equations only have one answer.
Give your answers to 1 dp.

a $x^2 + 1 = \frac{1}{x}$ This is the same as $x^2 + 1 - \frac{1}{x} = 0$

b $x^3 = \frac{1}{x}$

c $\sqrt{x} = \frac{1}{x} + 5$

d $x^3 = \frac{1}{x} + 3$

You can give greater accuracy than 1 dp in your answers.
$x^2 = 135$ gives $x = 11.6$ to 1 dp but you can carry on to get the answer to 2 dp.

Value of x	Value of x^2	
11.6	134.56	too small
11.7	136.89	too big
11.65	135.7225	too big
11.61	134.7921	too small
11.62	135.0244	too big
11.615	134.908 225	too small

x is between 11.6 and **11.7**
x is between 11.6 and **11.65**
x is between 11.61 and **11.65**
x is between 11.61 and **11.62**
x is between 11.615 and **11.62**

this value is halfway between 11.61 and 11.62

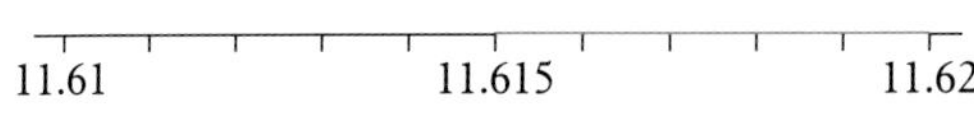

x must be somewhere in the green part of the number line.
Any number in the green part rounds up to 11.62 to 2 dp.
Answer: $x = 11.62$ to 2 dp.

---

6 **a** Solve the equation in question **3** giving your answer to 2 dp.
● **b** Solve the equation in question **4** giving your answer to 3 dp.

1 Write down the formula for each of these.
a 11, 22, 33, 44, 55, …
b 7, 14, 21, 28, 35, …
c 13, 26, 39, 52, 65, …
d 15, 30, 45, 60, 75, …

2 Find the 20th term in the sequence whose formula is:
a $3n$ **b** $5n$ **c** $12n$

3 Work out a formula for each of these.
a 5, 7, 9, 11, 13, …
b 3, 7, 11, 15, 19, …
c 12, 22, 32, 42, 52, …
d 10, 17, 24, 31, 38, …

4 Work out the 3rd, 4th, 5th and 6th terms for the sequence.
a $3n + 2$ **b** $5n - 1$ **c** $7n + 4$

5 Find the 20th term in the sequence whose formula is:
a $2n + 6$ **b** $n - 5$ **c** $8n - 25$

6 **a** Write this pattern of shapes as a number sequence.
b Use a sequence diagram to work out the formula.

7 **a** Write this pattern of shapes as a number sequence.
b Use a sequence diagram to work out the formula.

8 **a** Write this pattern of shapes as a number sequence.
b Use a sequence diagram to work out the formula.

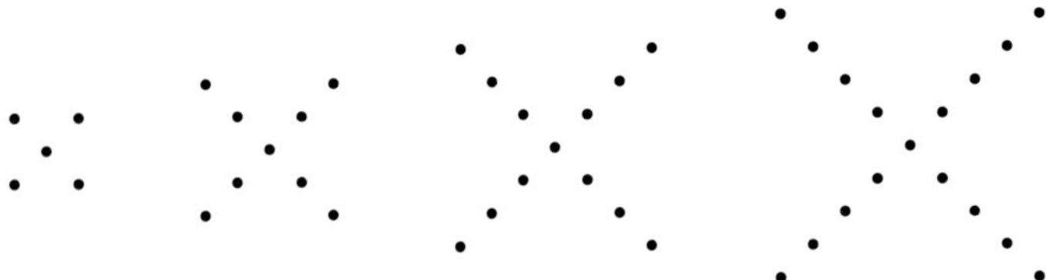

9 **a** Write this pattern of shapes as a number sequence.
b Use a sequence diagram to work out the formula.

10 Solve these equations.

a $2x + 3 = 15$

b $3x - 6 = 12$

c $5x + 3 = 2x - 6$

d $3x - 4 = 8x - 29$

11 Solve these equations.

a $\frac{x}{3} = 6$

b $\frac{x}{4} = -7$

c $\frac{x}{2} + 3 = 14$

d $\frac{x}{4} + 3 = 10$

e $\frac{y}{5} - 4 = 8$

f $\frac{y}{6} - 6 = 12$

12 Solve these equations.

a $4x + 4 = 13 + x$

b $6 - x = 14 - 3x$

c $2x + 1 = 7 - 4x$

d $1 + 4x = 25 - 2x$

e $17 - 3x = 11 - x$

f $5 + 2x = 8 - 4x$

13 Solve these equations.

a $\frac{3x}{4} + 2 = 14$

b $\frac{2x}{3} + 4 = 16$

c $\frac{x}{2} + 3 = \frac{x}{4} + 12$

d $\frac{x}{4} + 1 = \frac{x}{3} - 3$

14 Solve these equations.

a $2(2x + 3) = 18$

b $3(3x - 4) = 15$

c $4(3x - 7) = 32$

d $3(3x - 4x) = -15$

15 Solve these equations by trial and improvement.
For each part:
(1) Copy the table.
(2) Fill it in.
(3) Add more rows until you find the answer.
There are two answers for each part.

a $x^3 = 3375$

Value of x	Value of x^3	
10	…	…
…	…	…

b $x^3 - 4x = 2688$

Value of x	Value of $x^3 - 4x$	
15	…	…
…	…	…

16 Solve these equations by trial and improvement.
Give your answers to 1 dp.

a $x^3 - 26 = 37$

b $x^3 + x = 19$

17 Solve the equation $x^3 - 4 = \frac{1}{x}$ by trial and improvement.
You need to rearrange the equation so that all the xs are on the same side.
Give your answer to 1 dp.

1 A formula for a sequence is $4n - 2$.
Which term has the value:
a 26 **b** 42 **c** 18 **d** 58?

2 A sequence has the formula $2n - 5$.
Which of these numbers belong to the sequence:
a 14 **b** 17 **c** 43 **d** 55?

3 **a** Find the formula for the sequence 2, 5, 8, 11, …
b Find the formula for the sequence 4, 7, 10, 13, …
c Add the two formulas together. Simplify your answer.
d Add the two sequences together to get the new sequence
$2 + 4, 7 + 5,$ ……
6, 12, ……
Find the formula for the new sequence.
e Compare your answers to parts **c** and **d**.

4 Jim is 5 years older than his brother Alan.
Their ages add up to 23.
a Let Alan's age be x.
Write down Jim's age in terms of x.
b Write down an equation in x.
c Solve your equation.
d Write down the ages of the two boys.

5 Tina buys 6 m of fencing to make a run for her rabbit.
She wants to make the run 0.75 m wide.
a Write down an equation for the perimeter of the run.
b Solve the equation to find the length of the run.

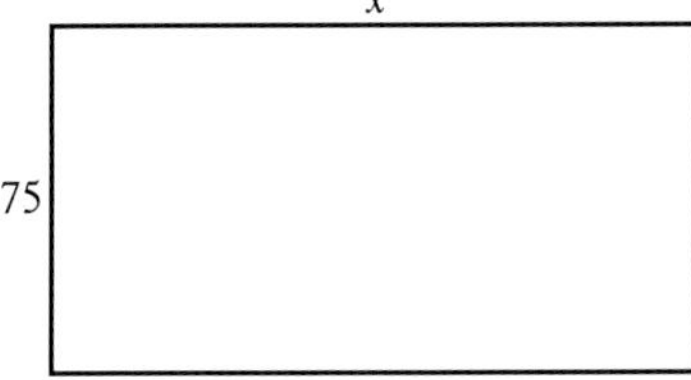

6 A square's sides are $3x$ m long.
A rectangle has a length of $4x$ m and a width of 2 m.
a Write down the perimeter of the square in terms of x.
b Write down the perimeter of the rectangle in terms of x.
c The perimeters of the two shapes are equal.
Write down an equation in x.
d Find the perimeter of each shape.

1 The nth term of a sequence is $11n$.
Write down the first 5 terms of the sequence.

2 Write down the formula for each of these sequences.

a 6, 12, 18, 24, 30, …

b 9, 18, 27, 36, 45, …

3 These two sequences are based on $5n$.
They have different formulas.
Find the formula for each one.

a 6, 11, 16, 21, 26, …

b 2, 7, 12, 17, 22, …

4 Look at this sequence:

11 17 23 29

a Draw a sequence diagram.

b Find the formula for the sequence.

5 Look at these patterns of triangles.

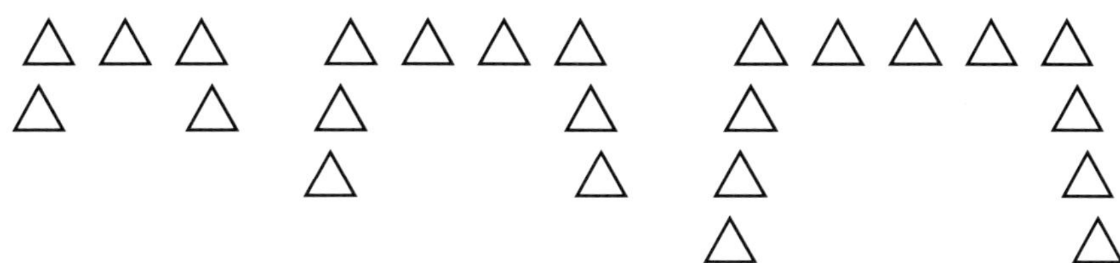

a Draw the next pattern in this sequence.

b Write this pattern of triangles as a number sequence.

c Use a sequence diagram to work out the formula.

6 The formula for a sequence is $6n - 5$

a Find the first 3 terms.

b Find the 20th term.

c Which term has the value 55?

7 A formula for a sequence is $3n + 4$.
Which term has the value

a 10 **b** 19 **c** 28 **d** 304?

8 Solve these equations.

a $4g - 3 = 21$

b $\frac{x}{5} + 6 = 10$

c $8x = 5x - 12$

d $3a + 13 = 5a$

e $14s - 5 = 9s + 20$

f $\frac{24}{x} = 8$

g $6d + 8 = 29 - d$

h $7(3x - 12) = 42$

9 **a** Write down the perimeter of this triangle in terms of x.

b The perimeter of the triangle is 34 cm. Write down an equation in x.

c Use your equation to find the value of x.

d Write down the length of the three sides of the triangle.

e What is the special name of the triangle?

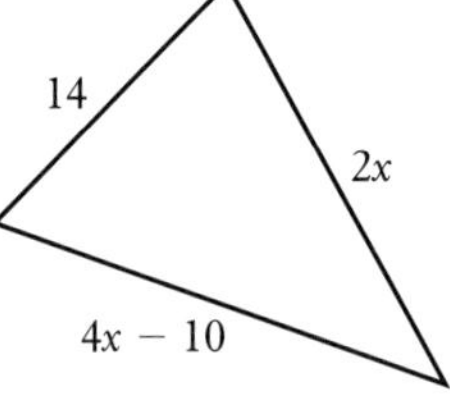

10 Solve the equation $x^3 - 9x = 850$ using trial and improvement.
Use this table to help you.
Give your answer to 2 dp.

Value of x	Value of $x^3 - 9x$	
5	80	too small
12	1701	too big

17 Transformations

CORE

1 Co-ordinates
Using co-ordinates to locate a point
Finding equations of horizontal and vertical lines
Finding the mid-point of a line

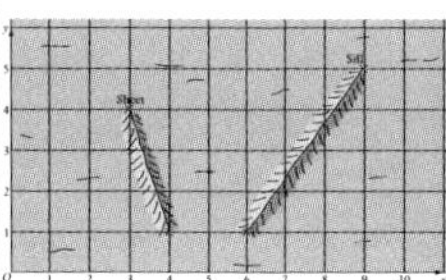

2 Single transformations
Describing translations
Drawing reflections
Drawing rotations
Drawing enlargements

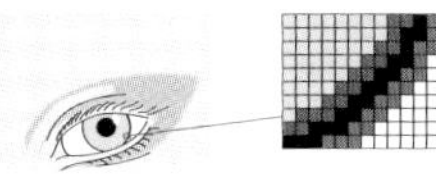

3 Combined transformations
Showing the effect of two successive transformations
Replacing two transformations by a single transformation

QUESTIONS

EXTENSION

TEST YOURSELF

1 Co-ordinates

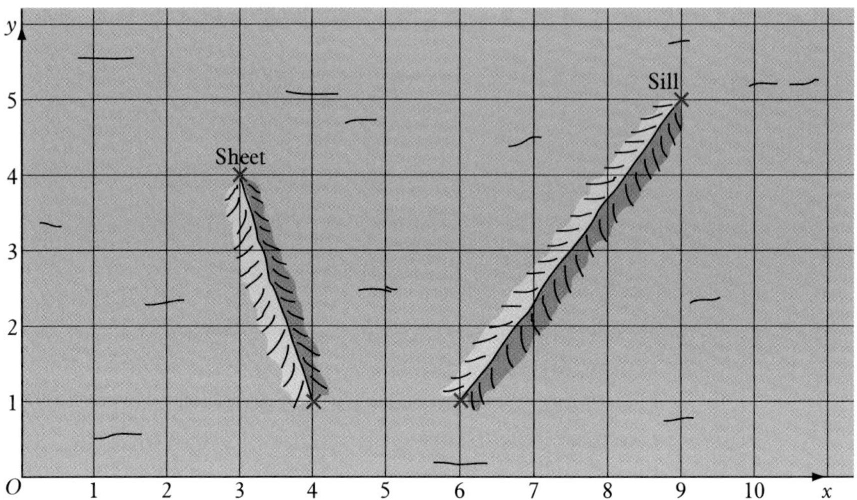

The diagram shows some features found on the surface of the Earth.

Wasim is studying geology.
He has to write a report on what can be seen in the diagrams.
He needs to describe the position of special features in his report.

He decides to use co-ordinates to do this.

This is part of his report:

> 'I will use co-ordinates to identify features on the diagrams.
> The first number is the x co-ordinate. It gives the **horizontal** distance.
> The second number is the y co-ordinate. It gives the **vertical** distance.
>
> Both the sheet and the sill are bodies of rock.
> The sheet starts at (3, 4) and stops at (4, 1).
> The sill starts at (6, 1) and stops at (9, 5).'

Exercise 17:1

1 This is a page of another report.
There are some mistakes with the co-ordinates.

a Write down the features that have the wrong co-ordinates.

b Write down the correct co-ordinates for these features.

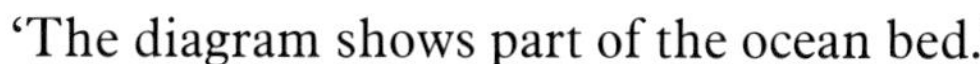

'The diagram shows part of the ocean bed.'

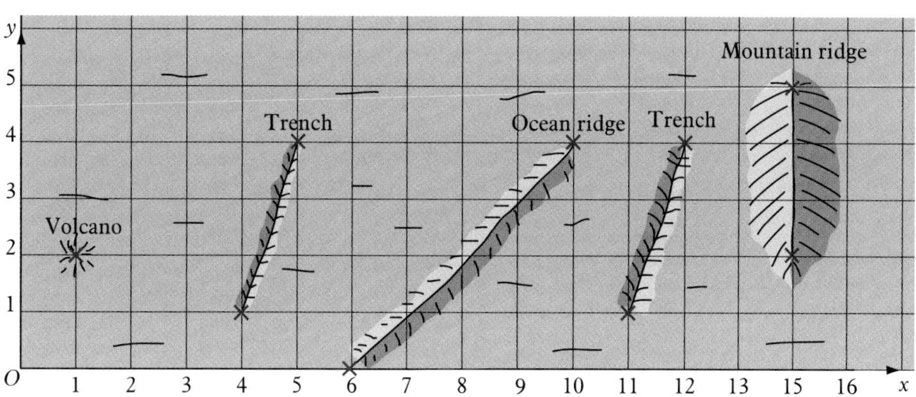

'The left-hand trench goes from (4, 0) to (5, 4).
The right-hand trench goes from (1, 11) to (12, 7).
The ridge of mountains goes from (15, 2) to (15, 5).
The ocean ridge goes from (7, 1) to (4, 10).
There is a volcano at (7, 2).'

2 Use the diagram to write down the co-ordinates of each of these:

a left-hand tuft
b right-hand tuft
c country rock
d crater sediment
e top of blind intrusion
f base of dyke

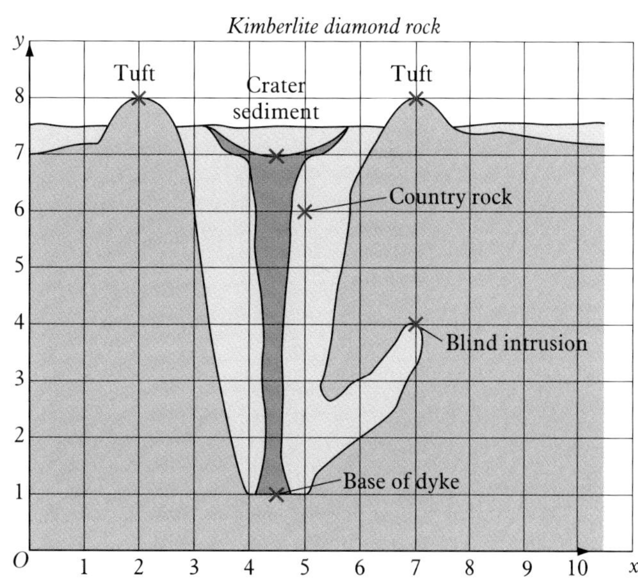

The picture shows the cross section of a mine.

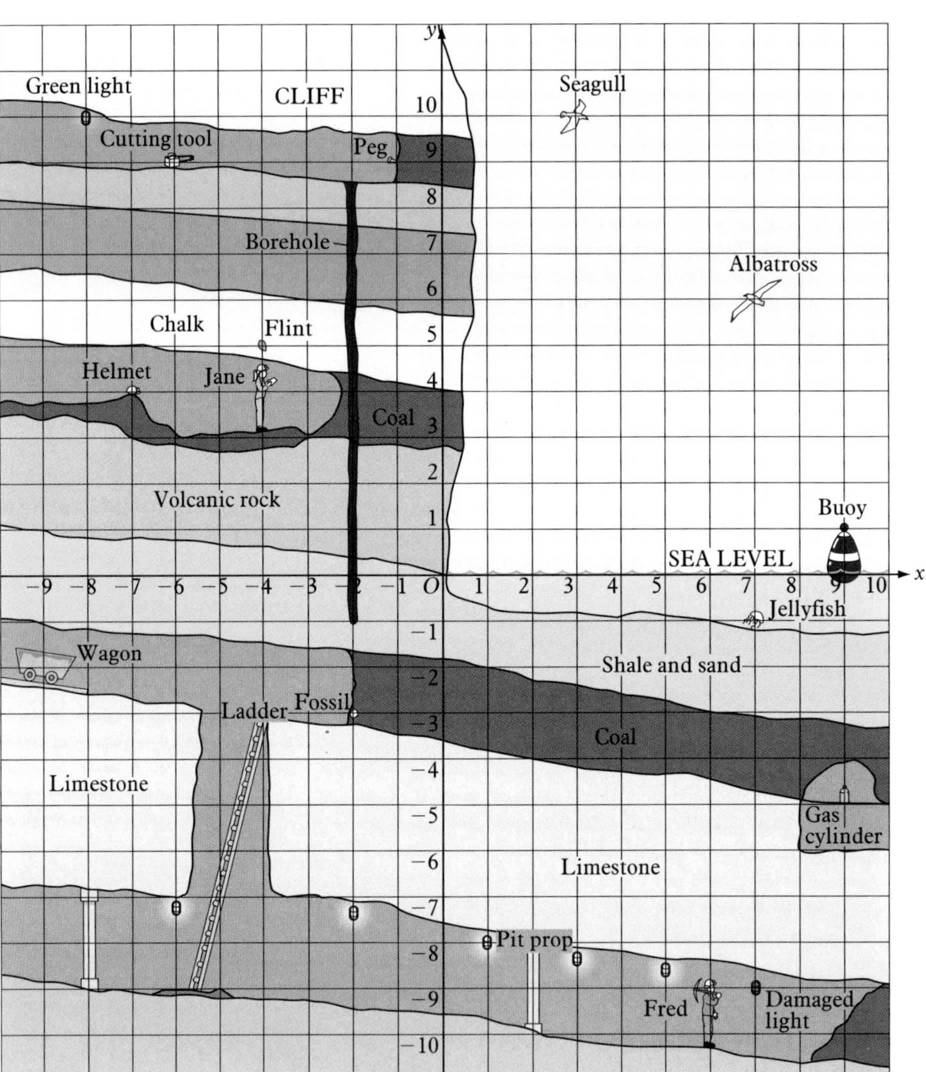

3 What is at each of these co-ordinates?

a (9, 1) **d** (−4, 4) **g** (−4, −3)

b (3, 10) **e** (2, −8) **h** (−9, −2)

c (−1, 9) **f** (6, −9) **i** (7, −9)

4 Write down the co-ordinates of each of these:

a albatross **d** green light **g** jelly fish

b cutting tool **e** gas cylinder **h** flint

c helmet **f** fossil

Wasim wants to describe the position of the layers (strata) in the diagram.

These points all lie on the black line:
(0, 10) (1, 10) (2, 10), (5, 10)
The y co-ordinate is always 10.
This tells you that the equation of the line is $y = 10$.

This is what Wasim has written:

'The wall rock lies between 2 lines.
Both lines are horizontal.
The top horizontal line crosses the y axis at 10. This line is called $y = 10$.
The bottom horizontal line crosses the y axis at 9.
This line is called $y = 9$.
The wall rock lies between $y = 10$ and $y = 9$.'

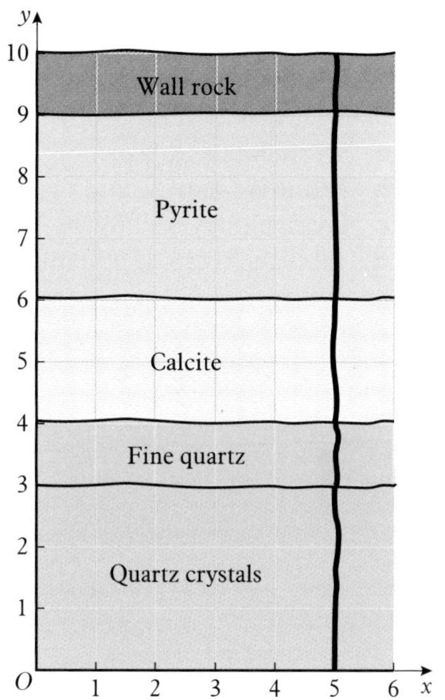

Exercise 17:2

1 Write down the equation of the line between:
  a calcite and pyrite
  b fine quartz and calcite
  c quartz crystals and fine quartz

2 Each unit of the grid represents 1 m.
Write down the thickness of each layer (stratum).

3 There is a vertical crack in the diagram.
  a Write down the co-ordinates of 5 points on this crack.
  b What do you notice about the x co-ordinates of these points?
  c Copy and fill in:
  The crack lies on a vertical line.
  The equation of this line is $x = \dots$

4 These lines have been drawn on a set of axes.

Write down the equation of each line.

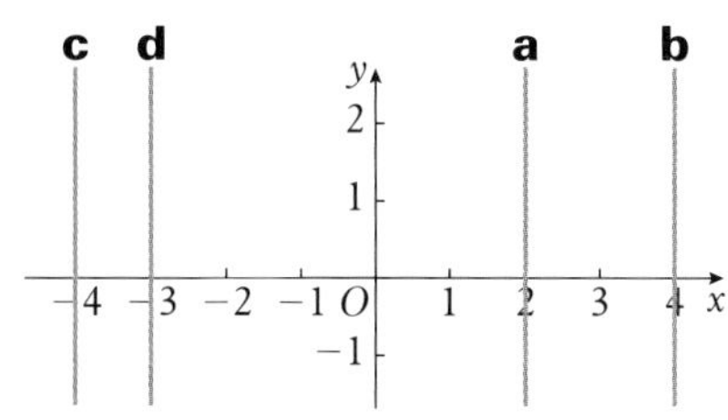

5 The diagram shows the strata under the sea bed.

Write down the equation of the line between:

a sediments and lavas
b primitive mantle and mantle
c lavas and layer of dykes
d gabbroic rocks and mantle

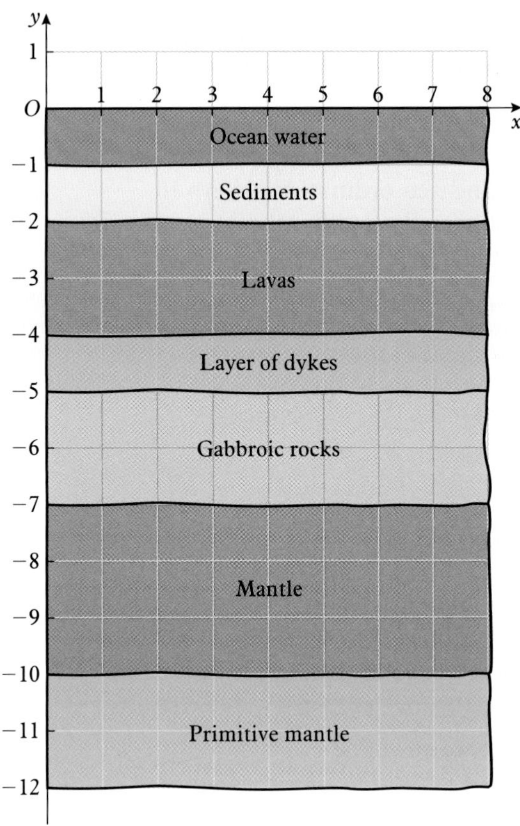

6 These lines have been drawn on a set of axes.
Write down the equation of each line.

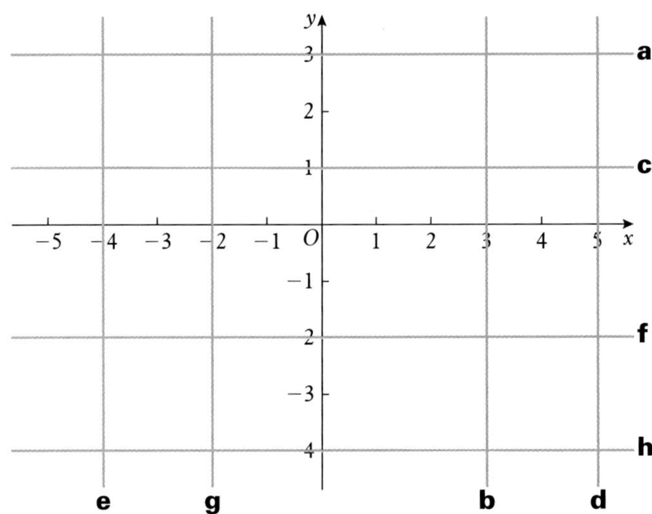

ABC are three vertices of a rectangle.
The length of the rectangle = 5 − 2 = 3 units.
The height of the rectangle = 3 − 1 = 2 units.
You can find the co-ordinates of the 4th vertex, D.

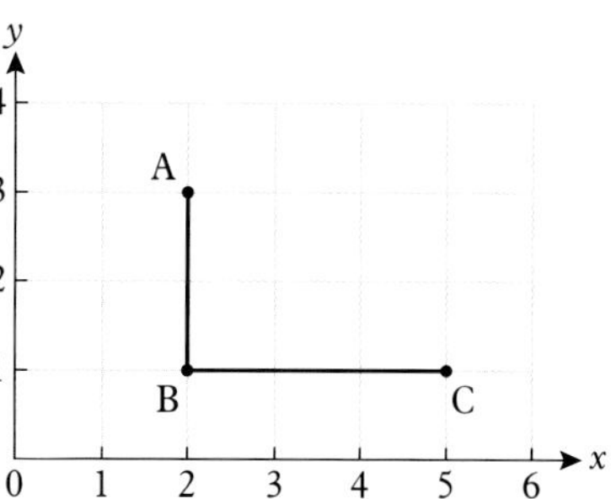

D must be vertically above C, so it must have the same x co-ordinate as C.
D must also be on the same horizontal line as A, so it must have the same y co-ordinate as A.
So the co-ordinates of D are (5, 3).

PQR are three vertices of a parallelogram.
You can find the co-ordinates of the 4th vertex S.
Moving from Q to R you move 2 units horizontally and 3 units vertically.
You use the same movement to go from P to S.
So the x co-ordinate of S = 5 + 2 = 7.
And the y co-ordinate of S = 2 + 3 = 5.
S is the point (7, 5).

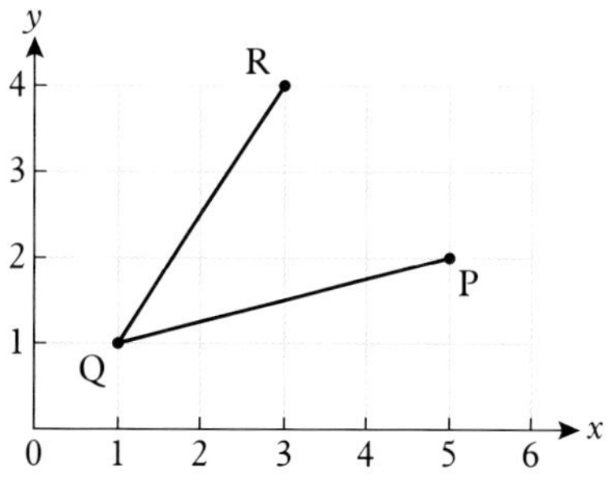

Exercise 17:3

1 ABCD is a parallelogram.
Write down the co-ordinates of the vertex D.

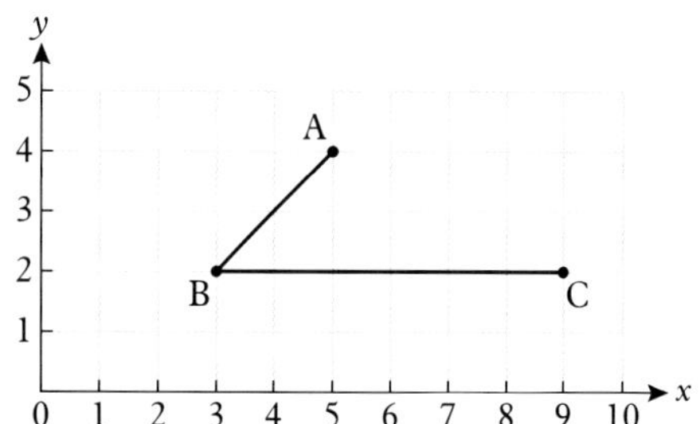

2 WXYZ is a parallelogram.
Write down the co-ordinates of the vertex X.

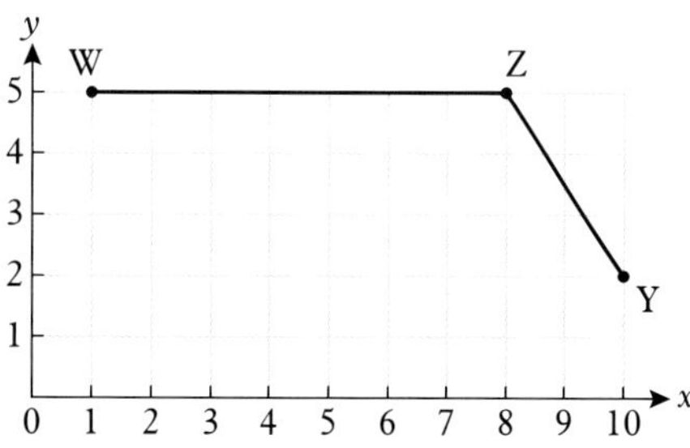

3 KLMN is a square.
The co-ordinates of 3 vertices are K(5, 8) L(5, 3) M(10, 3).
Write down **a** the co-ordinates of N
b the length of the side of the square.

3 EFGH is a square of side 3 units.
E is the point (7, 4).
EFGH can be in 4 possible positions.
Write down the co-ordinates of the 4 vertices for each of the 4 positions.

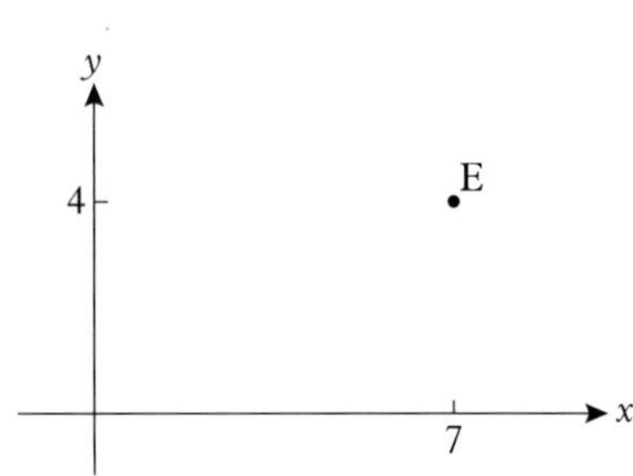

A is the point (1, 2) and B is the pont (5, 9).
M is the mid-point of the line AB.

To find the co-ordinates of M.

Add the two x co-ordinates and divide by 2.
$1 + 5 = 6 \quad 6 \div 2 = 3$

Add the two y co-ordinates and divide by 2.
$2 + 9 = 11 \quad 11 \div 2 = 5.5$

The co-ordinates of M are (3, 5.5).

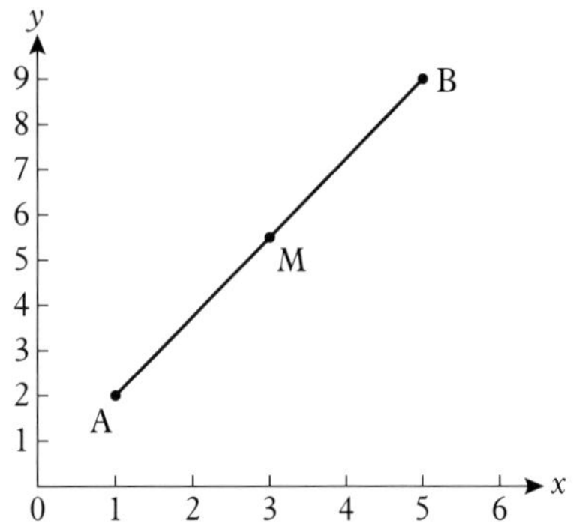

---

5 Find the co-ordinates of the mid-point of the line joining
a D(3, 4) and E(5, 12)
b P(0, 1) and Q(6, 7)
c M(1, 9) and N(6, 1)
d Y(2, 12) and Z(3, 0).

6 ABC is an isosceles triangle.
The base is AB. A is the point (1, 2) and B is the point (5, 2).
a Draw a set of axes and plot the points A and B.
b Find the co-ordinates of M, the mid-point of AB.
c The point C is vertically above M and the height of the triangle is 6 units. Write down the co-ordinates of C.

2 Single transformations

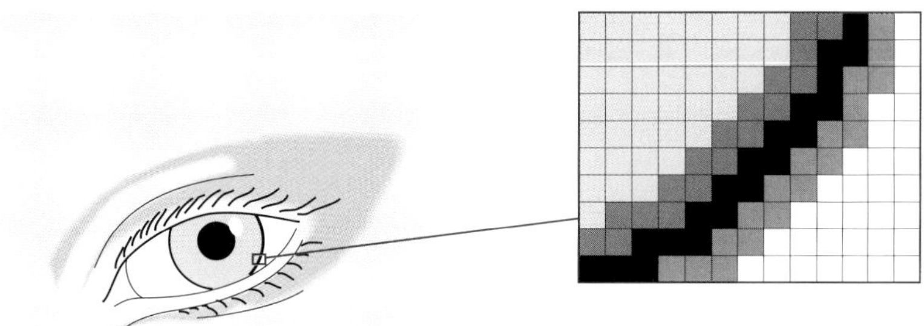

Pictures shown on a computer screen are made up of tiny squares. Each tiny square is called a **pixel**. Storage of pictures based on single pixels can use too much memory.
Patterns of pixels are often repeated in a picture.
Details of how these patterns relate to each other are stored as transformations. This saves memory.

Transformation A **transformation** can change the size, shape or position of an object.

Translation A **translation** is a movement in a straight line.

The movement shown is a translation of 3 places to the right and 2 places down.

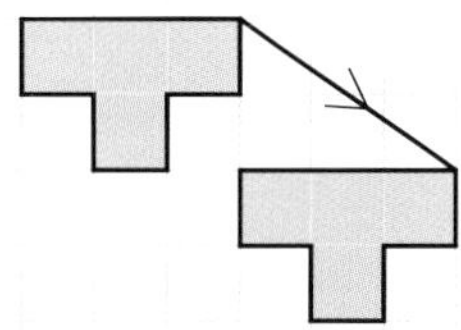

The arrow represents the movement.

The translation can be written as $\begin{pmatrix} 3 \\ -2 \end{pmatrix}$

This is called a **column vector**.

The sign of each number in a column vector gives the *direction* of movement.
This matches the way that axes are labelled.

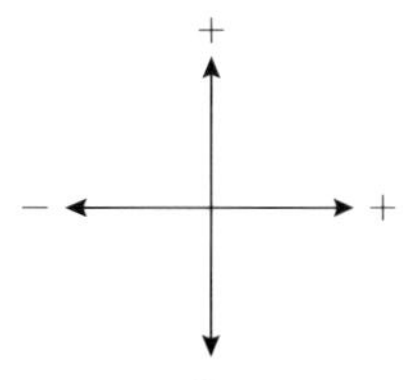

Exercise 17:4

1 Copy and fill in the column vectors for these translations.

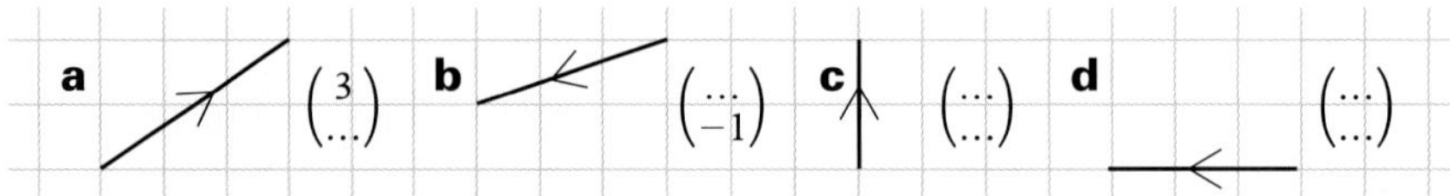

2 Use column vectors to describe these translations.

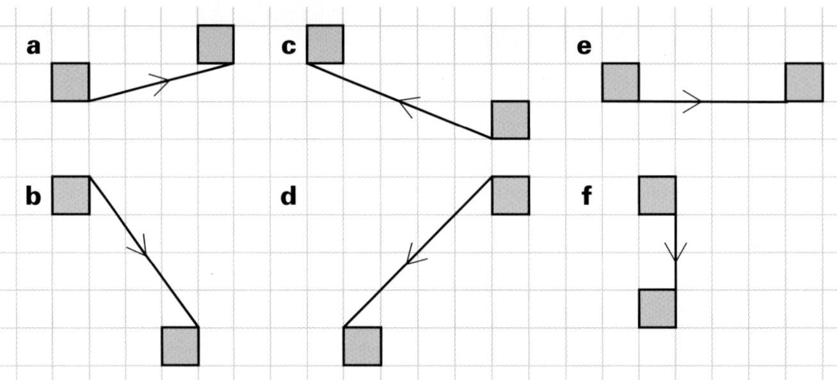

You can describe the translations of single points in the same way as translations of shapes.

3 Give the translations from **P** to each of the other points in turn.
Use column vectors.

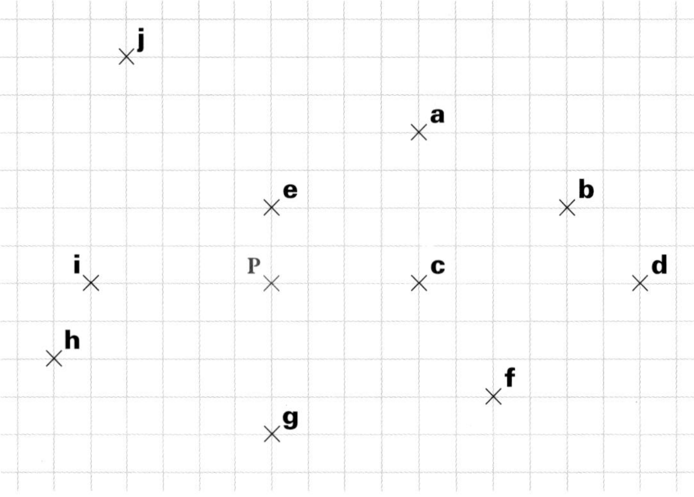

Inverse

A transformation that *undoes* the effect of another is called its **inverse**.

The inverse of 'move 5 places up' is 'move 5 places down'.

The inverse of  $\begin{pmatrix} 2 \\ -1 \end{pmatrix}$ is 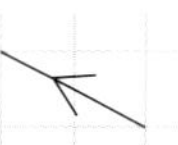 $\begin{pmatrix} -2 \\ 1 \end{pmatrix}$

4 Write down the inverse of each of these.

a 3 places right
b 2 places down
c 4 places left
d 1 place up
e 2 places right and 3 places down
f 3 miles north
g 6.1 miles south
h 0.8 km east
i 5 miles north east
j 5 km west and 3 km north

5 These column vectors represent translations.
Write down the column vector of the inverse of each one.

a $\begin{pmatrix} 4 \\ 1 \end{pmatrix}$
b $\begin{pmatrix} -5 \\ 2 \end{pmatrix}$
c $\begin{pmatrix} 3 \\ -1 \end{pmatrix}$
d $\begin{pmatrix} -6 \\ -4 \end{pmatrix}$
e $\begin{pmatrix} -5 \\ 0 \end{pmatrix}$
f $\begin{pmatrix} 0 \\ 7 \end{pmatrix}$

6 In Logo, instructions are given to control the movement of the **turtle**.

Instruction	Meaning
fd 50	move forward 50 units
bk 30	move back 30 units
rt 90	turn to the right through 90°
lt 60	turn to the left through 60°

Write down the inverse of each of the following Logo instructions.

a fd 60
b rt 20
c bk 350
d lt 125

Object The shape you start with is called the **object**.

Image The transformed shape is called the **image**.

Reflection The diagram shows the image of the object pattern after **reflection** in the line AB.

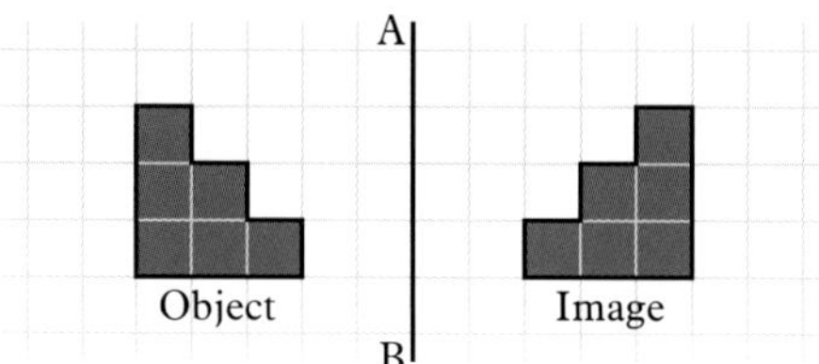

Exercise 17:5

1 **a** Copy the diagram. Reflect shape A in the line PQ. Label the image B.

b Reflect shape A in the line RS. Label the image C.

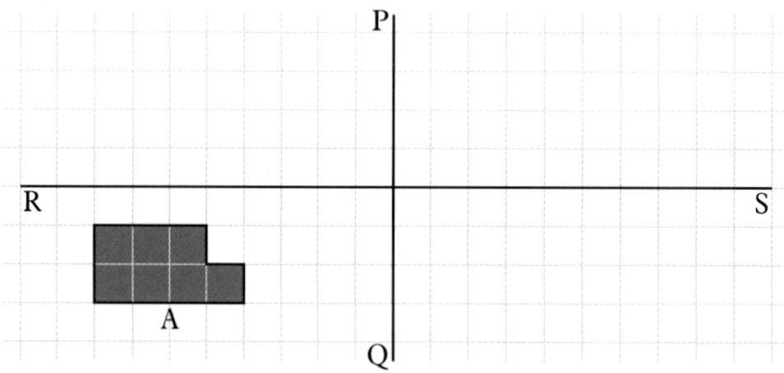

2 Copy the diagram. Reflect the labelled points in the line $y = 1$. Label the image of point A as A′, the image of B as B′ and so on.

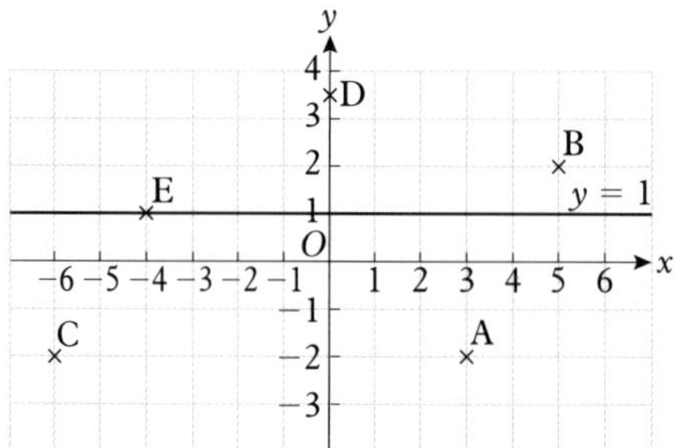

● **3** **a** Draw x and y axes labelled from -3 to 3.
b Plot the points A(2, 3), B(-1, -1) and C(3, -2). Draw triangle ABC.
c Reflect triangle ABC in the line $x = 1$. Label the image A′B′C′.

The image of (2, 1) after reflection in the line $x = 4$ is (6, 1).
You can write this as (2, 1) → (6, 1) or (2, 1) **maps to** (6, 1).

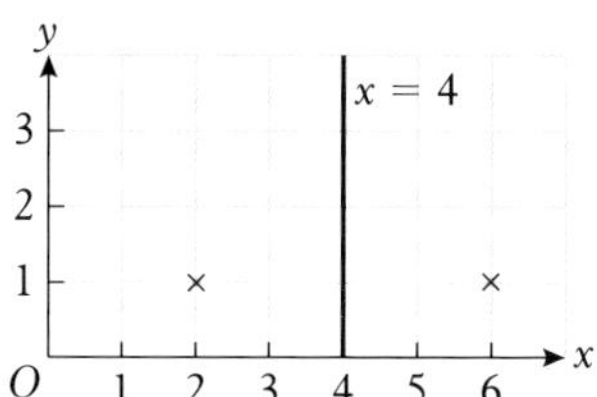

The same reflection maps (6, 1) to (2, 1).

Inverse of a reflection

A second reflection, in the same line, always undoes the effect of the first. The **inverse of a reflection** is the same reflection.

Mirror line

The line that you use to reflect an object is called the **mirror line**.

---

4 Melissa is exploring the effect of repeating reflections in the same mirror line.

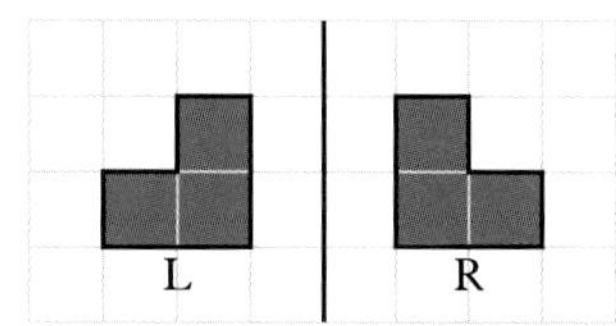

She finds that:
The image of L after one reflection is R.
The image of L after two reflections is L.

Write down the image of L when the number of reflections is:
a 5 **b** 18 **c** 47 **d** even **e** odd
f a prime number that is bigger than 2

Rotation

A **rotation** turns a shape about a fixed point. This point is called the **centre of rotation.**

When you describe a rotation you must give these three things:
(1) the angle
(2) the direction (clockwise or anticlockwise)
(3) the centre.
In the diagram, A is mapped on to B by a rotation of **90° clockwise** with centre (0, 0)

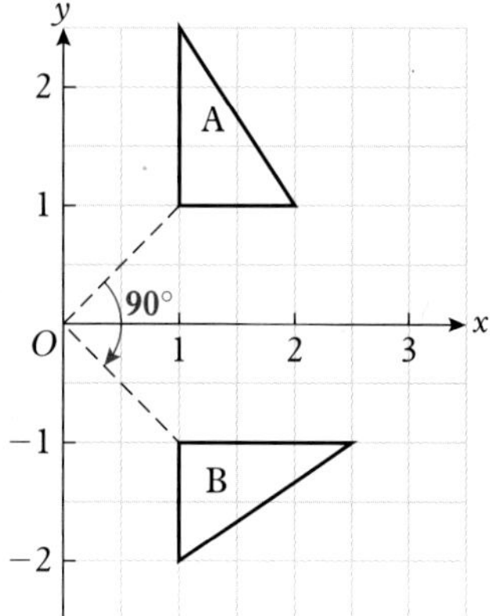

Exercise 17:6

1 You are going to draw the image of C after a rotation of 90° clockwise about (0, 0).

a Copy the diagram.

b Place a piece of tracing paper on the diagram. Trace the shape C and the red cross at the origin.

c Put the point of your pencil on the origin to hold the tracing paper firmly in place.

d Turn the tracing paper through 90° clockwise. Use the cross at the origin to help you.

e Copy the new position of C on to your axes.
This is the image of C after a rotation of 90° clockwise about (0, 0).
Label it D.

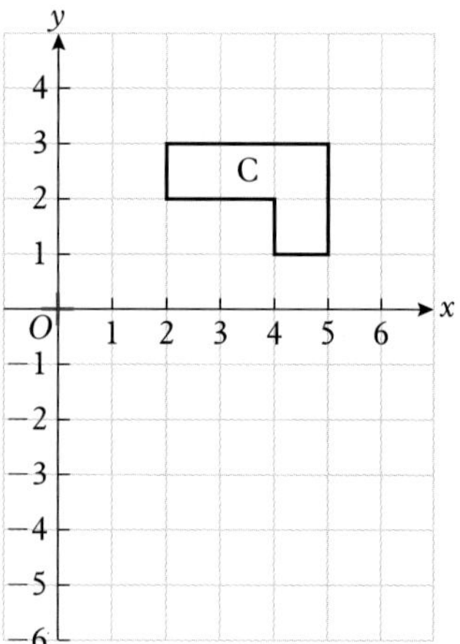

2 **a** Copy the diagram.
b Draw the image of F after a rotation of 90° anticlockwise about (2, 2).
Label the image G.
c Rotate G through 180° clockwise about (2, 2).
Label the image H.
d What is the single clockwise rotation that would map F on to H?

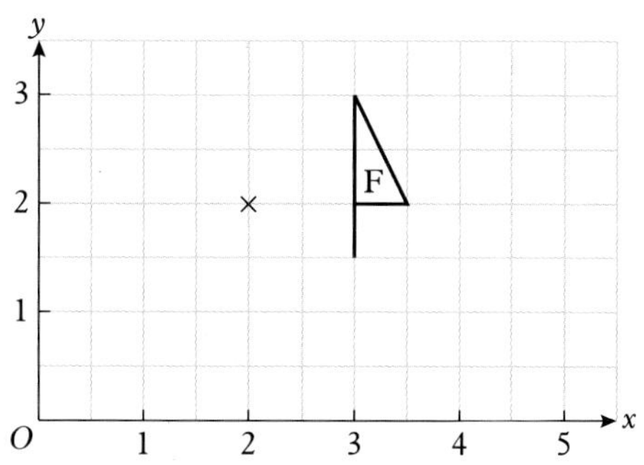

3 Describe these rotations. Remember to give the angle, the direction and the centre.
a P on to Q
b Q on to R
c P on to R
d Q on to S
e S on to Q
f R on to P

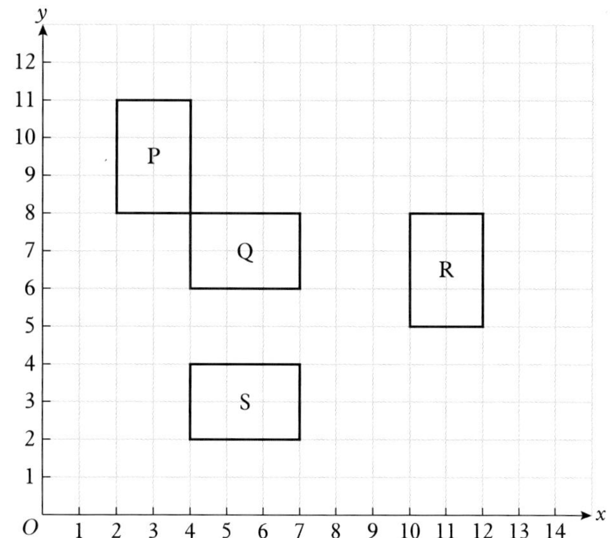

4 The diagram shows a regular hexagon ABCDEF with centre at O.
a Find the smallest angle of rotation about O so that A → B.
b What is the order of rotational symmetry of a regular hexagon?

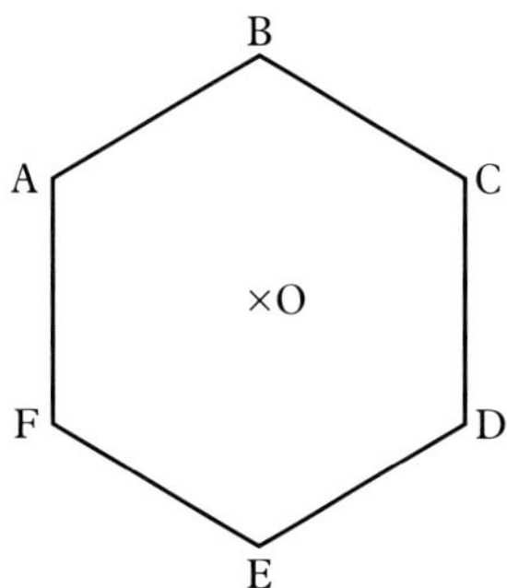

Inverse of a rotation

The **inverse of a rotation** is also a rotation. The angle and the centre are the same but the turn is in the opposite direction.

Example

The inverse of a rotation of 60° **clockwise** about (5, 7) is a rotation of 60° **anticlockwise** about (5, 7).

5 Write down the inverse of each of these:

a 90° clockwise about (8, 1)

b 27° anticlockwise about (−3, 5)

c 48° anticlockwise about (−7, −10)

d 123° clockwise about (11, −6)

● **6** **a** Copy the diagram. Rotate P through 90° clockwise about (3, 3). Label the image Q.

b Rotate Q through 90° anticlockwise about (5, 3). Label the image R.

c Describe the single transformation that would map P on to R.

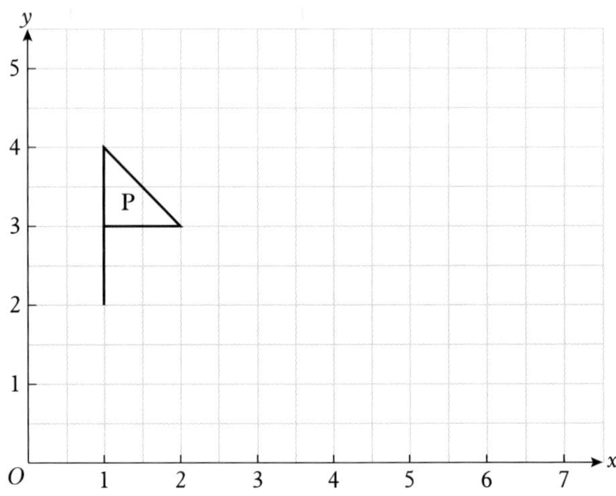

Enlargement

An **enlargement** changes the size of an object.
When you describe an enlargement you must give these two things:

(1) the centre

(2) the scale factor

Example

Enlarge triangle ABC with scale factor 2 and centre O.

(1) Join OA and extend.

(2) Measure OA.

(3) $OA' = OA \times 2$
$= 3$ cm

(4) Measure 3 cm from O.
Label this point A′.

(5) Do the same for point B.

(6) Do the same for point C.

(7) Draw the triangle A′B′C′.

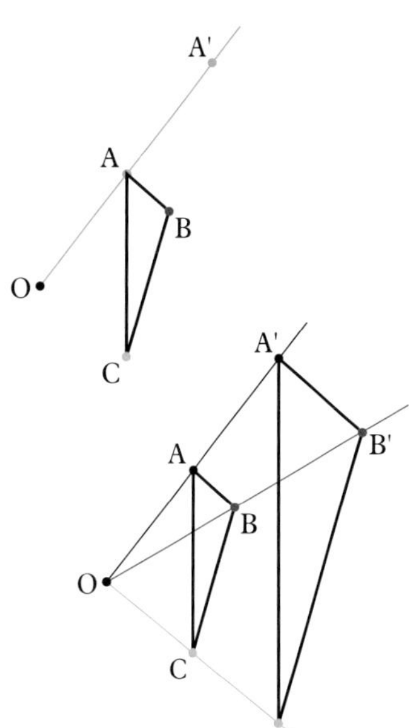

Triangle A′B′C′ is an enlargement of triangle ABC.
A and A′, B and B′ and C and C′ are pairs of corresponding points.

Centre of enlargement

Lines drawn through corresponding points pass through the **centre of enlargement**.

Scale factor

The **scale factor** tells you how many times bigger the enlargement is.

You multiply an object length by the scale factor to get the corresponding image length.
So $A'B' = AB \times 2$

Exercise 17:7

1 **a** Measure the lengths of PQ and P′Q′.
b Use your answers to find the scale factor of the enlargement.

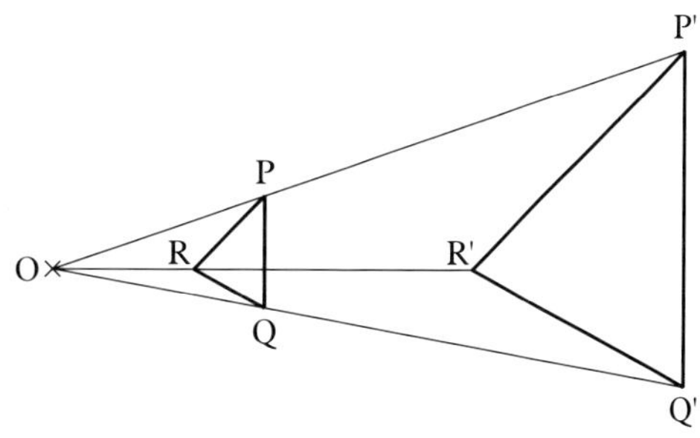

2 Jim has started to enlarge the rectangle with centre at O.
Find the scale factor of the enlargement.

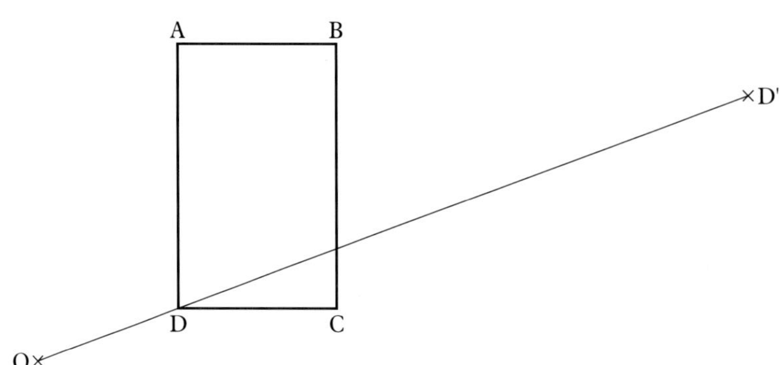

For enlargements with centre at the origin:
co-ordinates of object × scale factor = co-ordinates of image

Example

Find the image of P(3, 1) under an enlargement with scale factor 3, centre at the origin.

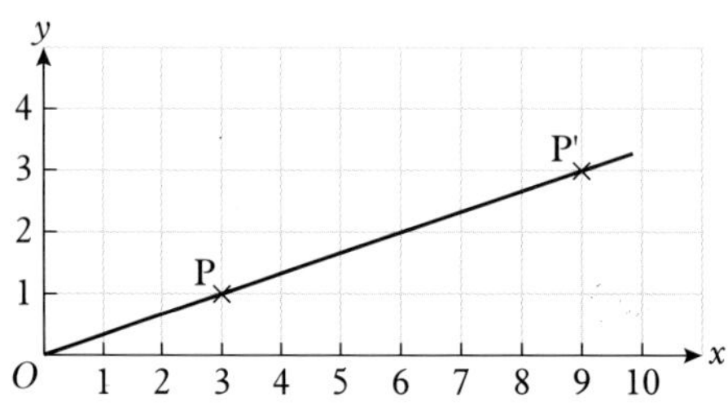

The image of P(3, 1) is P′(9, 3).
The co-ordinates of P have been multiplied by 3.

3 Find the image of these points under an enlargement with scale factor 4 and centre at the origin.

a (3, 2)
b (1, 7)
c (2, −3)
d (−3, 0)
e (0, −6)
f (−3, −5)
g (2.5, 3)
h (−3.5, 1.25)

3 Combined transformations

The three Great Pyramids do not lie in a straight line.
If you draw the position of the three stars in Orion's belt, then enlarge and rotate the diagram, it will fit exactly over the positions of the Great Pyramids.

Combination of transformations

You can often describe a movement by a **combination of transformations**.

Shape A is moved to B by a combination of two transformations.

The first transformation is a **translation** 5 units across and 4 units up.
The second transformation is a **rotation** 90° clockwise, about the point O.

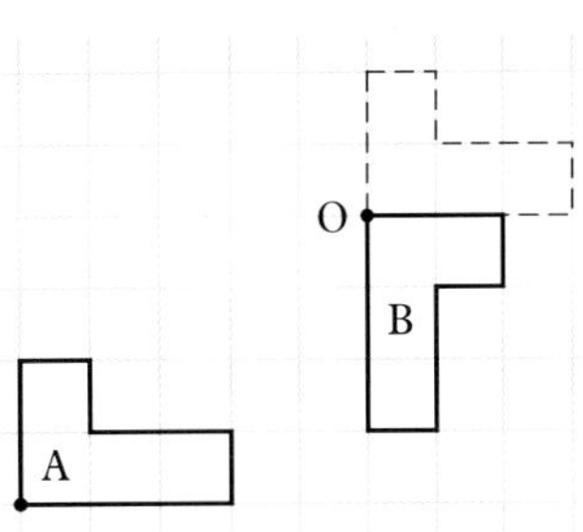

Exercise 17:8

1 These shapes have been moved by a translation followed by a rotation.

For shape S:

a Write down the translation that moves the point A to A′.

b Write down the rotation that has been used.

For shape T:

c Write down the translation that moves the point B to B′.

d Write down the rotation that has been used.

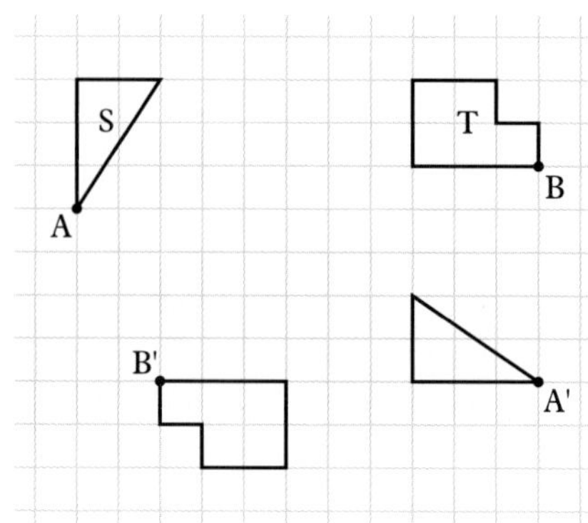

2 The shape T is moved by a translation followed by a rotation to shape B.
Point P is translated to P′.
Write down:

a the translation

b the rotation

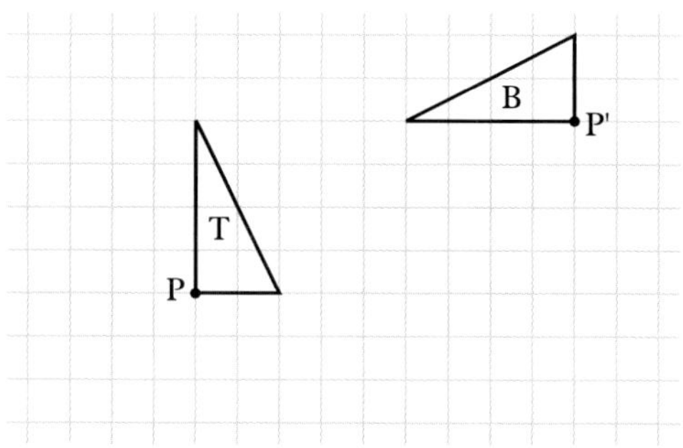

3 Part of a picture has been enlarged to give this pattern of pixels.
A block of 4 pixels appears in the corner at the origin.
You can transform this block to make the patterns at A, B and C.

a Give the translation for A.

b Give the rotation for B.

c Give the translation, to combine with a rotation of 180°, centre (1, 1) for B.

d Give the reflection for C.

e Give the translation to combine with reflection in $y = 2$ for C.

f Give the rotation to map A to C.

g B is given a translation $\begin{pmatrix} 0 \\ -4 \end{pmatrix}$

Give the rotation so that the image maps to A.

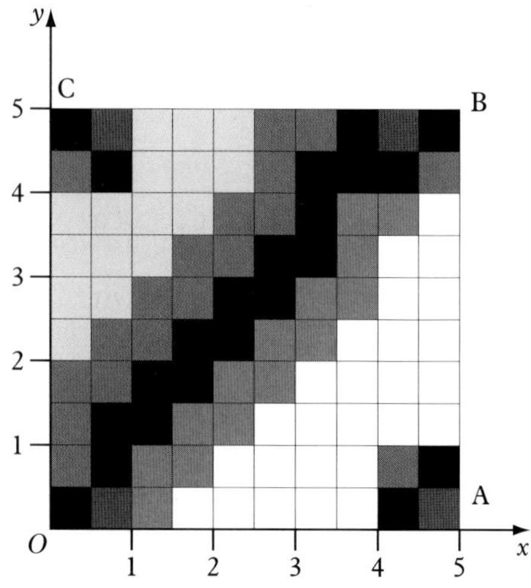

Sometimes a combination of transformations can be replaced by a single transformation.

Shape A is reflected in the y axis to give the image B.

Shape B is rotated 180° anticlockwise about the origin to give the image C.

There is a single transformation that maps shape A onto shape C.
The transformation is a reflection in the x axis.

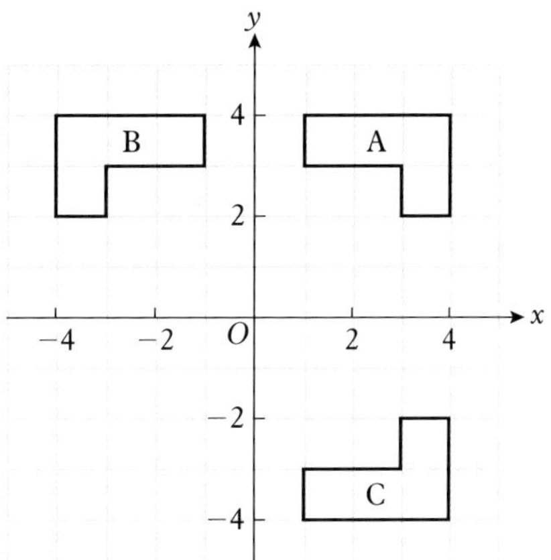

Exercise 17:9

1 **a** Copy the axes and the shape A onto squared paper.
b Reflect A in the x axis.
Label the image B.
c Reflect B in the y axis.
Label the image C.
d Write down the single transformation that maps A to C.

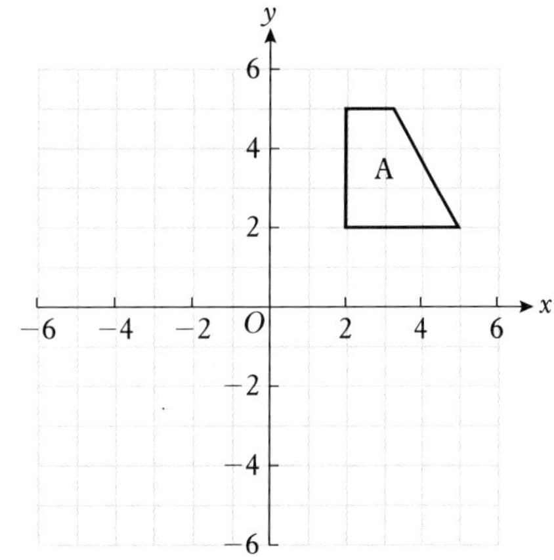

2 **a** Draw another set of axes like those in question **1**.
b Draw the triangle with the vertices (−4, 2), (−2, 2) and (−4, 6).
Label the triangle P.
c Rotate triangle P 180° clockwise about the origin.
Label the image Q.
d Reflect triangle Q in the y axis.
Label the image R.
e Write down the single transformation that maps triangle P to triangle R.

3 **a** Copy the axes and triangle P on to squared paper.
b Reflect triangle P in the y axis. Label the image Q.
c Reflect triangle Q in the line $y = x$. Label the image R.
d Write down the single transformation that maps triangle P to triangle R.

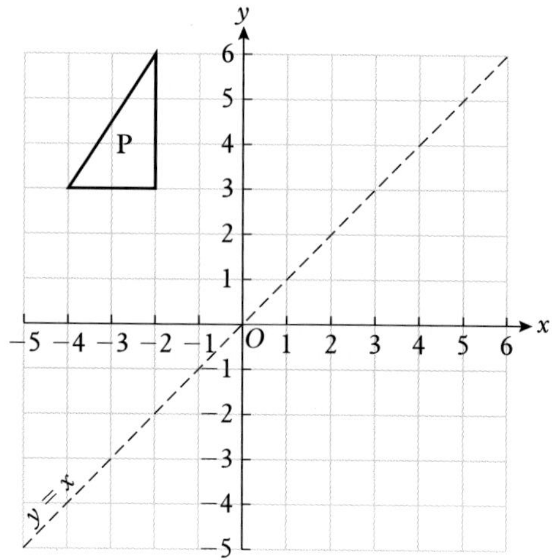

4 **a** Draw a set of axes with x and y from -6 to 6. Draw the triangle with vertices (2, 1), (3, 1) and (2, 4). Label this triangle A.
b Use triangle A to check if the following statement is true:

A reflection in the x axis followed by a rotation of 90° anticlockwise about the origin	is the same as	a rotation of 90° anticlockwise about the origin followed by a reflection in the x axis.

5 **a** Draw a set of axes and triangle A as in question **4**.
b Use triangle A to check if the following statement is true:

A reflection in the x axis followed by a reflection in the y axis	is the same as	a reflection in the y axis followed by a reflection in the x axis.

6 Here are some Logo instructions.
Write down the instructions that would return you to the starting point in each part.
a fd 80
b rt 45
c fd 30 rt 60
d fd 50 lt 30 fd 80
e fd 50 rt 90 fd 50 rt 90 fd 50 rt 90

1 **a** Write down the co-ordinates of each point.

b Write down the co-ordinates of the mid-point of
(1) HF (2) AF (3) GH

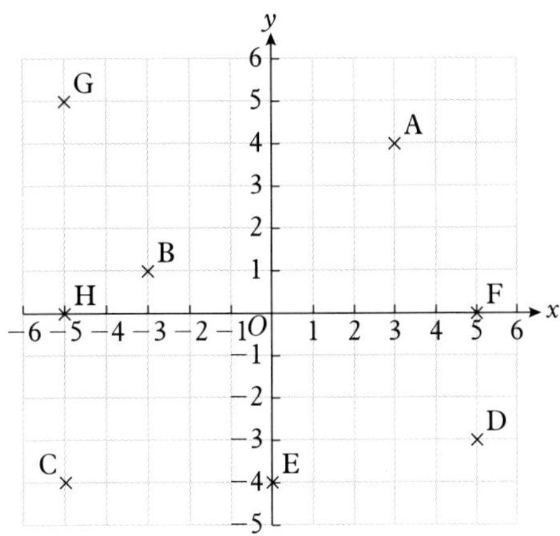

2 Write down the equation of each line.

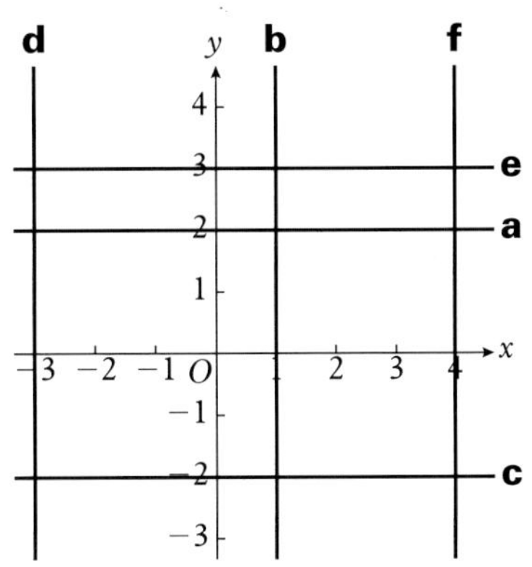

3 These arrows represent translations. Write down the column vectors for each one.

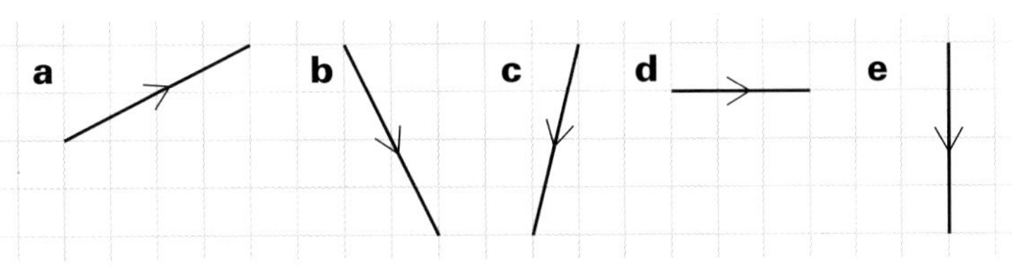

4 Give the translations from **P** to each of the other points.

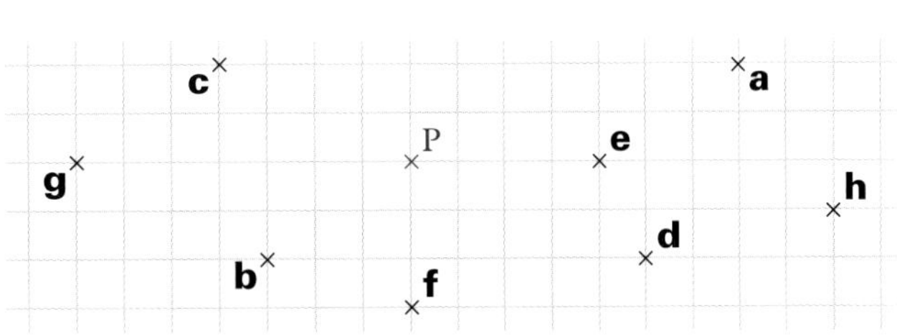

5 Reflect these shapes in the mirror lines.

a

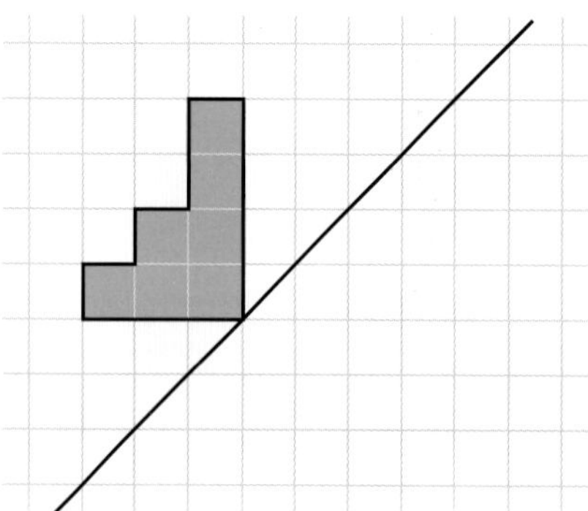

b

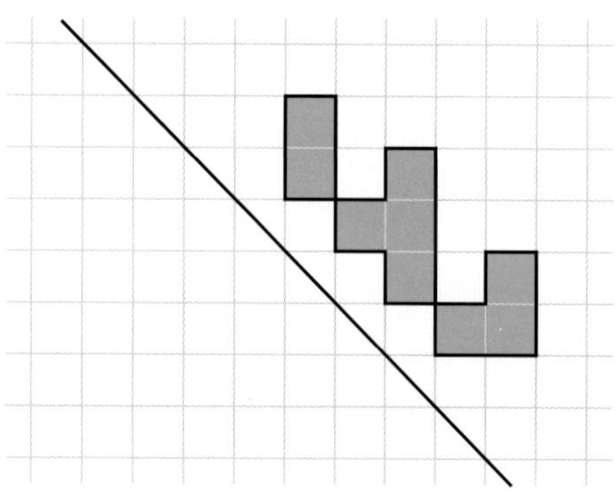

6 Which of these shapes cannot be mapped on to P by a rotation?

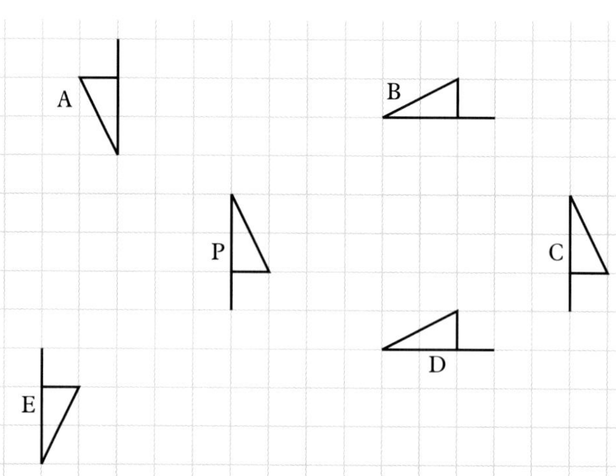

7 Each shape can be mapped on to L by a single transformation. Describe each transformation fully.

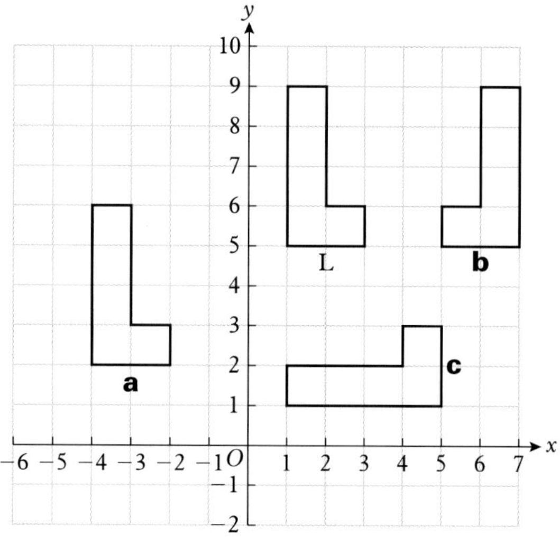

8 **a** The rectangle PQRS is reflected in the line $y = x$ to give rectangle P′Q′R′S′. What are the co-ordinates of S′?

b The rectangle PQRS is enlarged with scale factor 2, centre the origin to give P″Q″R″S″. What are the co-ordinates of Q″?

c The rectangle PQRS is rotated 90° clockwise about (0, 0) to give rectangle P‴Q‴R‴S‴. What are the co-ordinates of R‴?

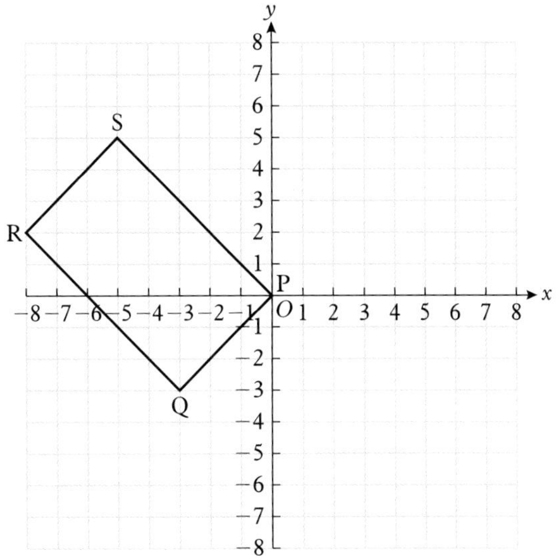

9 **a** Copy the axes and shape A.

b Reflect shape A in the line $y = 4$. Label the shape B.

c Rotate the shape A 180° clockwise about the origin. Label the shape C.

d Reflect shape A in the x axis. Label the shape D.

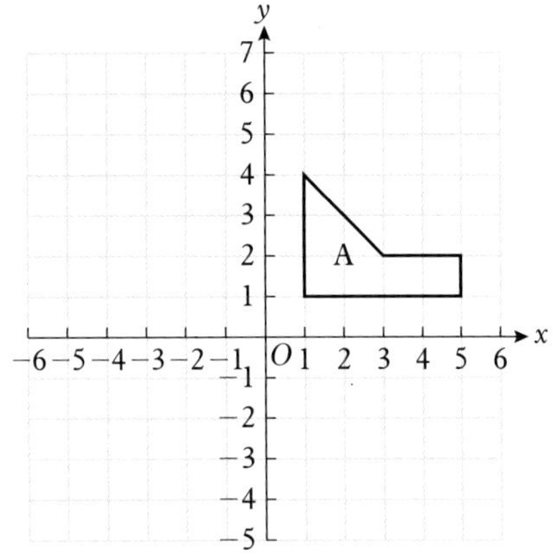

10 **a** Draw a set of axes on to squared paper. Use values of x and y from -8 to 8.

b Plot the points $(1, -1)$, $(3, -1)$ and $(3, -4)$. Join them up with straight lines. Label the triangle P.

c Reflect the triangle in the line $y = x$. Label this triangle Q.

d Reflect triangle Q in the x axis. Label this triangle R.

e Which single transformation maps triangle P onto triangle R?

1 **a** Copy the diagram.
b Translate shape A 5 units to the left and 2 units up. Label the image B.
c Reflect shape A in the line $y = -x$. Label the image C.
d Rotate shape A through 450° clockwise about $(-1, -1)$. Label the image D.

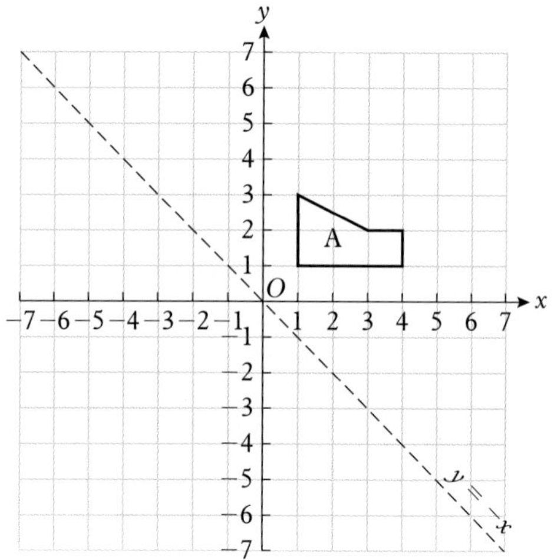

2 Describe the translation that maps (3, 5) to the point:
a (6, 9) **b** (3, 5) **c** (0, −2) **d** (−3, 6)

3 **a** Draw a set of axes on to squared paper. Use values of x and y from −6 to 6.
b Plot the points (1, 0), (0, 3) and (3, 4). Join them up. Label the triangle A.
c Reflect triangle A in the x axis. Label the image B.
d Reflect triangle B in the line $y = x$. Label the image C.
e Write down the single transformation that maps triangle A to triangle C.

4 **a** Draw a set of axes on to squared paper. Label the x and y axes from −8 to 8.
b Draw the line $y = x$.
c Reflect these points in $y = x$.
A (4, 5) C (−3, 2) E (−1, 0)
B (2, 6) D (0, −4) F (−2, −1)
Label the image points A′, B′, etc.
d Use your answers to part **c** to describe what happens to the co-ordinates of a point when it is reflected in the line $y = x$.
e Investigate what happens to co-ordinates of points when they are reflected in:
(1) $y = -x$ (3) $y = 1$ (5) $x = 2$
(2) $y = 3$ (4) $x = 1$ (6) $x = 4$

1 **a** Write down the co-ordinates of the points A, B, C, D and E.
b Write down the equations of the lines P, Q, R and S.
c Write down the equation of
(1) the x axis
(2) the y axis.
d Write down the co-ordinates of the mid-point of EB.

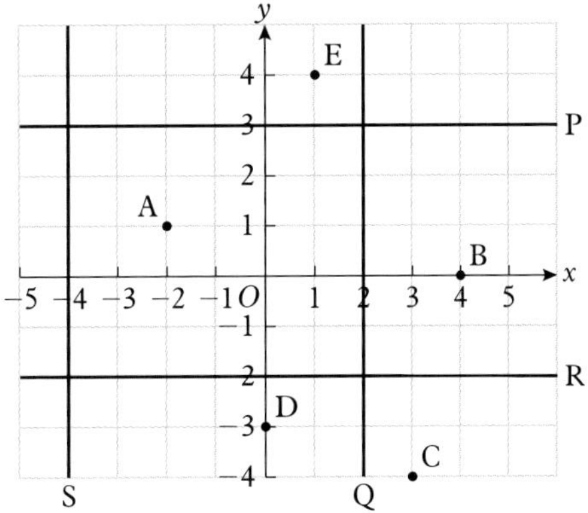

2 **a** Use words to describe this translation.

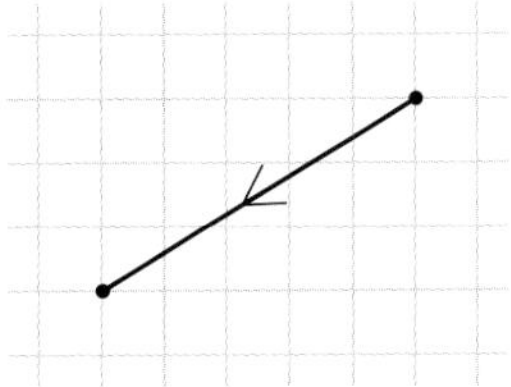

b Draw a line to show the translation:

(1) $\begin{pmatrix} -3 \\ 4 \end{pmatrix}$ (2) $\begin{pmatrix} 0 \\ -2 \end{pmatrix}$

3 **a** Copy the diagram.
b Reflect the shape in the y axis. Label the new shape b.
c Rotate the shape 90° anticlockwise about (0, 0). Label the new shape c.

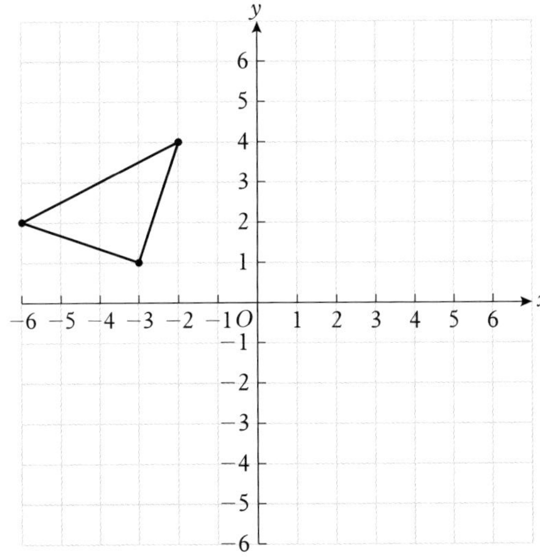

4 Write down the inverse of each of these:

a a translation 3 squares up and 2 squares to the left

b a translation of $\begin{pmatrix} 3 \\ -4 \end{pmatrix}$

c a rotation of 270° clockwise about the point (2, −3)

5 **a** Copy the diagram.

b Enlarge the triangle with scale factor 3, centre (1, 2).

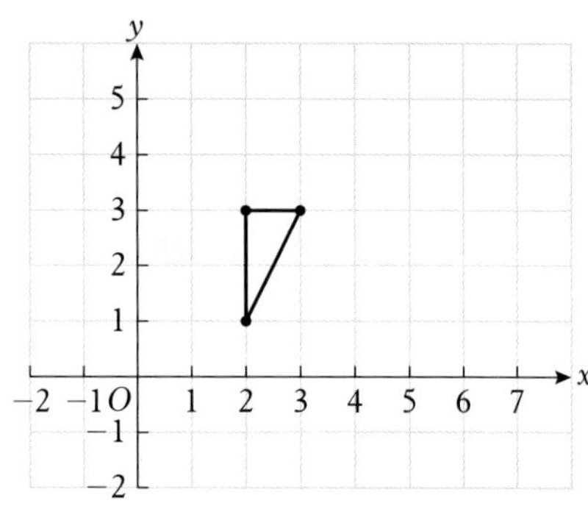

6 **a** Copy the diagram.

b Reflect shape T in the y axis. Label the image B.

c Rotate shape T 90° clockwise with centre the origin. Label the image C.

d Write down the single transformation that maps B onto C.

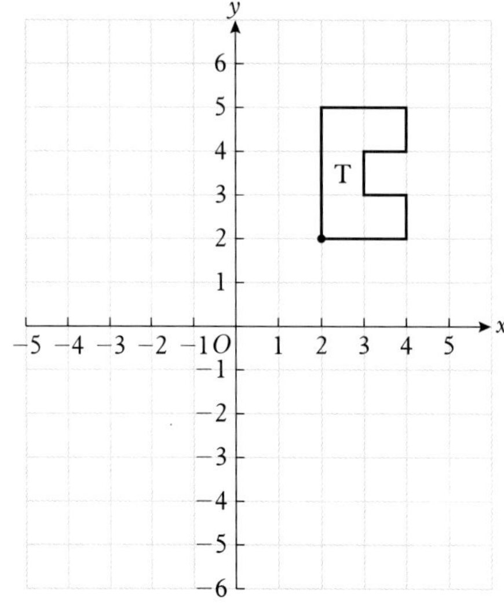

18 Graphs: a bit steep

1 Gradients
Looking at slopes of lines
Naming lines that go through the point (0, 0)
Lines that slope downwards

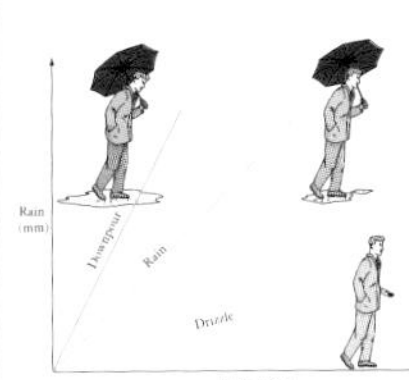

2 Straight lines
Naming lines that don't go through the point (0, 0)
Knowing when lines are parallel
Using graphs to solve problems

3 Linear equations
Spotting equations that make straight lines
Finding equations

CORE

QUESTIONS

EXTENSION

TEST YOURSELF

1 Gradients

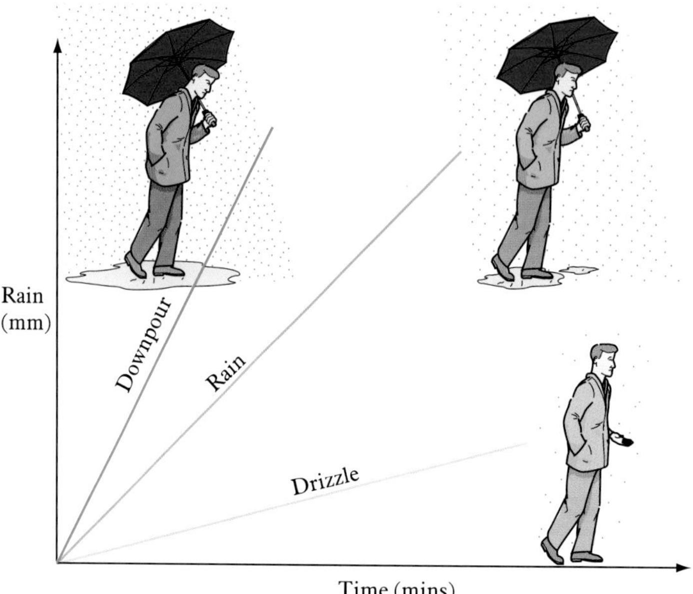

This graph shows different types of rainfall.
The heavier the rain, the steeper the line.

This graph shows the number of pages in a magazine and its cost.
The magazines are *Computer World*, *Your Car* and *Pop Scene*.

The steeper the line the more pages you get per £1.

The best value magazine is *Computer World*.
You get about 320 pages for £1.
This magazine gives the most pages per £1.

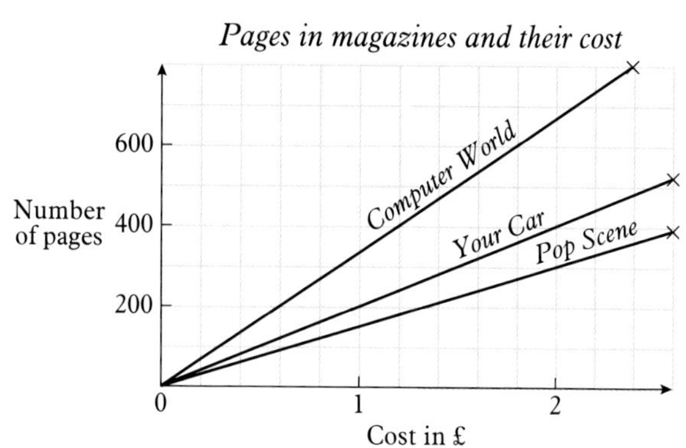

Exercise 18:1

1 Use the graph above to estimate the number of pages you get for £1 with:
a *Pop Scene* **b** *Your Car*

2 This graph shows the rates of climb on take off for some planes.

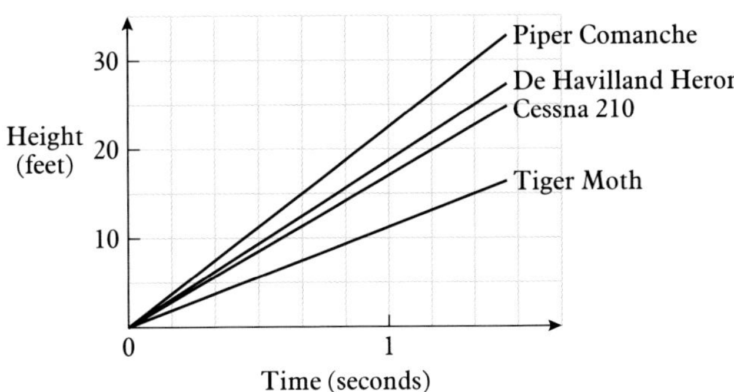

a Which plane takes off at a rate of 11 feet per second?
b Estimate the rate of climb for the other three planes.
c Which plane climbs the fastest?

Sometimes you need to know exactly how steep the line is.

Gradient

The **gradient** of a line tells you how steep the line is.

To find the gradient of a line choose two points on the line as far apart as possible.

You need to be able to read the co-ordinates of the points accurately.

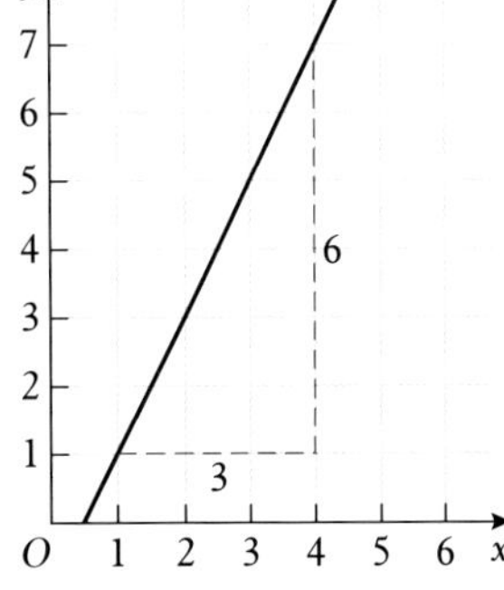

$$\text{Gradient} = \frac{\text{vertical change}}{\text{horizontal change}}$$

$$= \frac{7-1}{4-1}$$

$$= \frac{6}{3}$$

$$= 2$$

The gradient of the line is 2.

For each of these lines:

a Choose two points on the line whose co-ordinates you can read.
b Write down the vertical change between the two points.
c Write down the horizontal change between the two points.
d Find the gradient of the line.

3

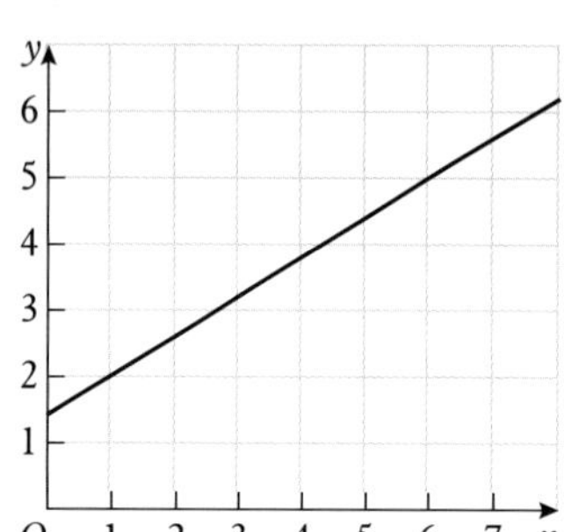

4

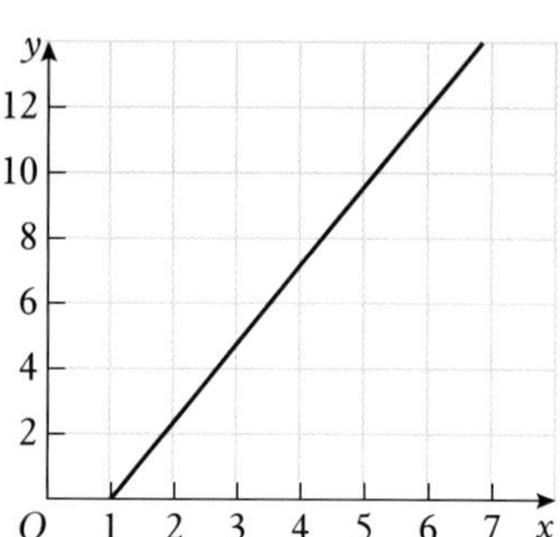

Work out the gradient of the line in questions **5–7**.

5

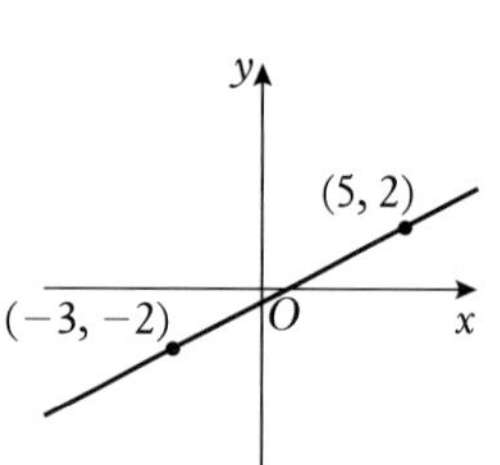

6

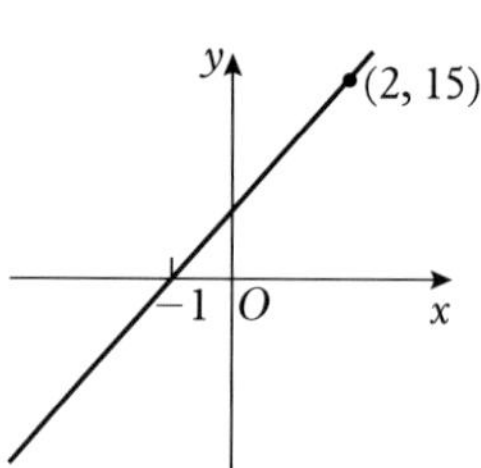

7

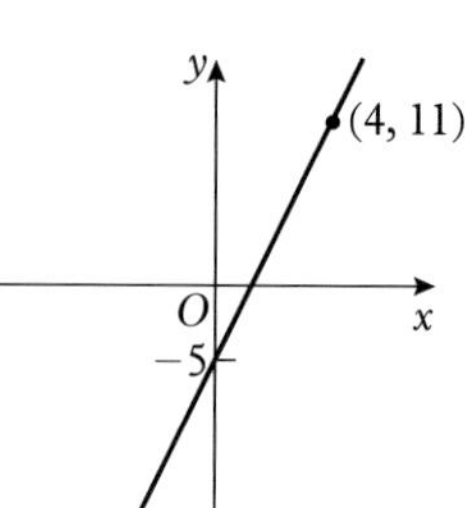

8 Find the gradient of the line passing through the points:

a (2, 3) and (4, 11)
b (5, 0) and (7, 14)
c (1, 4) and (2, 5)
d (0, 3) and (5, 28)

A shop expects to sell 5 computers per day on average.
If d is the number of days, the number of computers sold $= 5d$

If n is the number of computers sold then
$n = 5d$

$n = 5d$ is called a formula. You can draw a graph for this formula.

When $d = \mathbf{1}$, $n = 5 \times \mathbf{1} = 5$
When $d = \mathbf{2}$, $n = 5 \times \mathbf{2} = 10$
When $d = \mathbf{3}$, $n = 5 \times \mathbf{3} = 15$

These values can be put into a table:

d	1	2	3
n	5	10	15

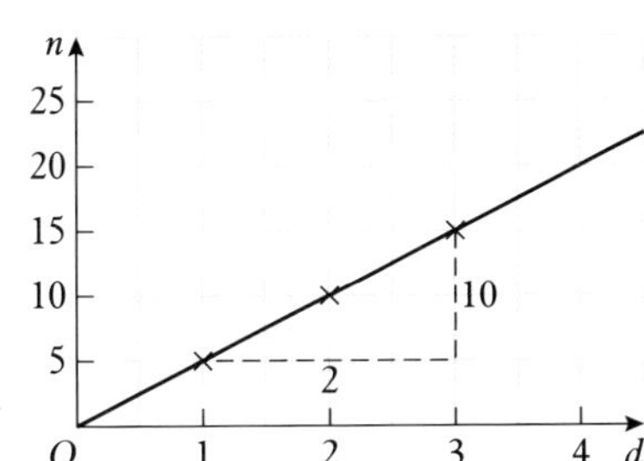

Plot the points (1, 5) (2, 10) (3, 15)
Join them up.
You get a straight line.

$$\text{gradient} = \frac{15-5}{3-1} = \frac{10}{2} = 5$$

$n = 5d$ is the equation of the straight line.
The gradient of the line is 5.

Exercise 18:2

1 This formula gives the average $n$umber of telephone calls received by a firm each $h$our: $n = 8h$

a On average how many calls does the firm get each hour?

b Copy this table.
Fill it in.

h	1	2	3
n	…	…	…

c Draw the straight line with equation $n = 8h$

d What is the gradient of this line?

e Use your graph to find how many calls the firm gets on average in 4 hours.
Draw a dotted line to show your method.

2 Ruth uses a graph to change £s into French Francs. She knows that £1 is the same as 10 French Francs.

a How many French Francs are the same as
(1) £2 (2) £3?

b Copy the axes.

c Use your answers to part **a** to draw a line on the axes.

d Write down the gradient of this line.

e Use the graph to convert £2.80 into French Francs.

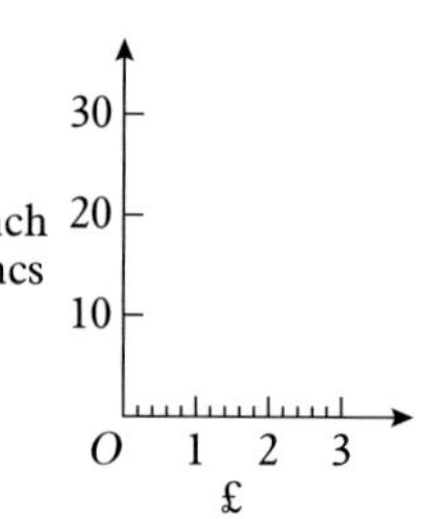

3 This table is for the formula $y = 2x$.

a Copy the table.
Fill it in.

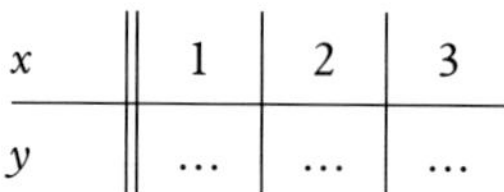

x	1	2	3
y	…	…	…

b Copy these axes.

c Plot the graph of $y = 2x$.

d Draw a triangle to find the gradient of the line.

e What do you notice about the gradient and the formula?

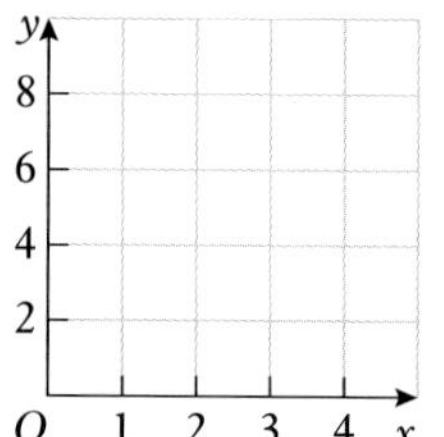

4 This table is for the formula $y = 3x$.

a Copy the table.
Fill it in.

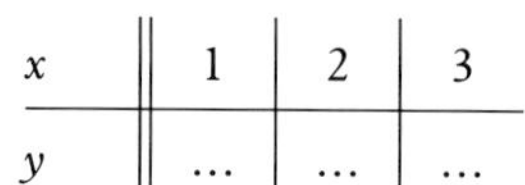

x	1	2	3
y	…	…	…

b Copy these axes.

c Plot the graph of $y = 3x$.

d Draw a triangle to find the gradient of the line.

e What do you notice about the gradient and the formula?

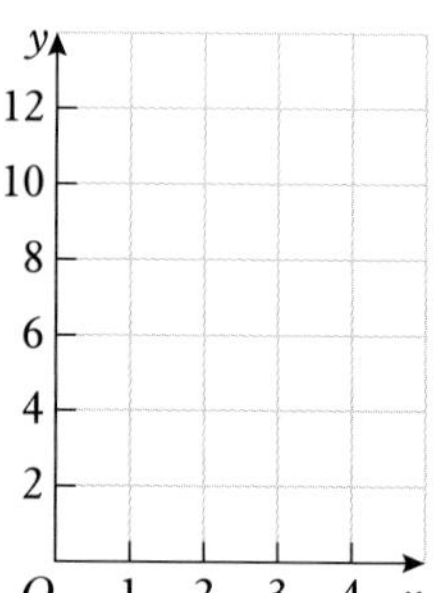

You sometimes use the word 'equation' instead of 'formula'.
If a line goes through the origin, there is an easy way to get its equation.

This graph shows a straight line.
The gradient is 7.

The equation of this line is $y = 7x$.
The number multiplying the x is the gradient.

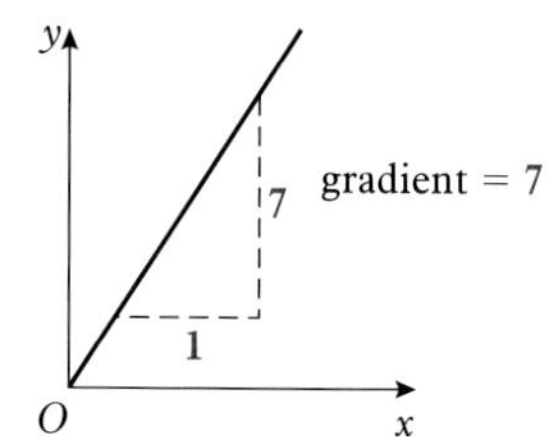

Exercise 18:3

1 Write down the gradient of each of these lines.

a $y = 5x$ **b** $y = 4x$ **c** $n = 7h$

2 Write down the equation of each of these lines.

a

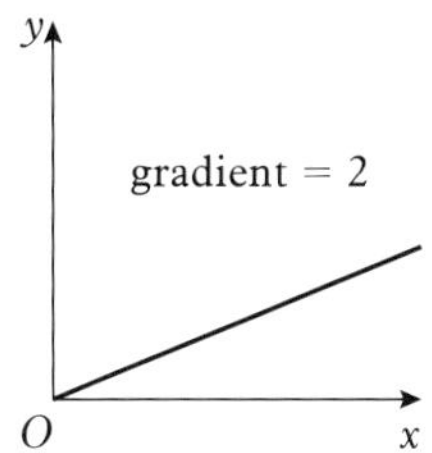

b

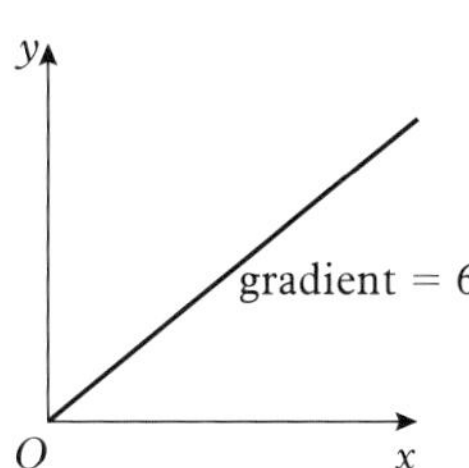

c

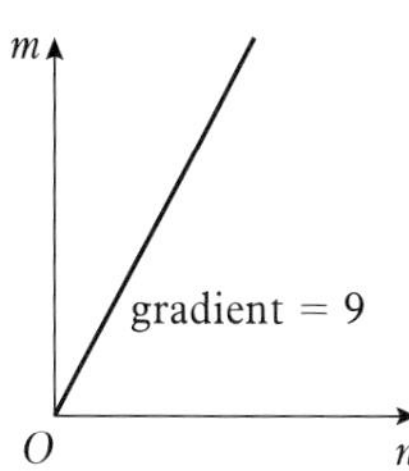

This line has a negative gradient.
As you move along the line from A to B you go down 8.
The vertical change is negative. It is -8.

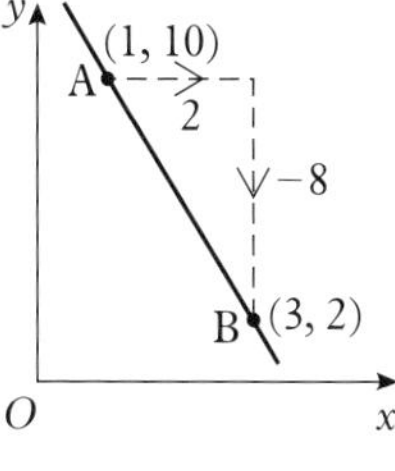

$$\text{Gradient} = \frac{\text{vertical change}}{\text{horizontal change}}$$

$$= \frac{-8}{2}$$

$$= -4$$

The gradient is -4.

A line with a positive gradient slopes uphill.

A line with a negative gradient slopes downhill.

Exercise 18:4

1 These lines all have different gradients.

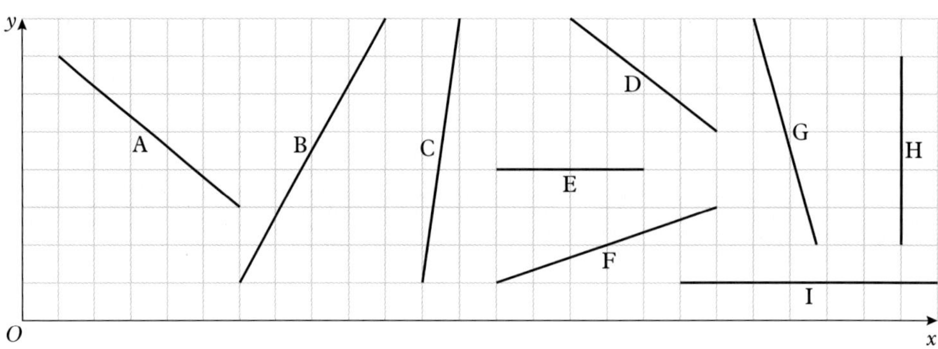

Write down the letters of lines

a with positive gradients
b with negative gradients
c which have neither positive nor negative gradients.

2 Find the gradient of each of these lines.

a

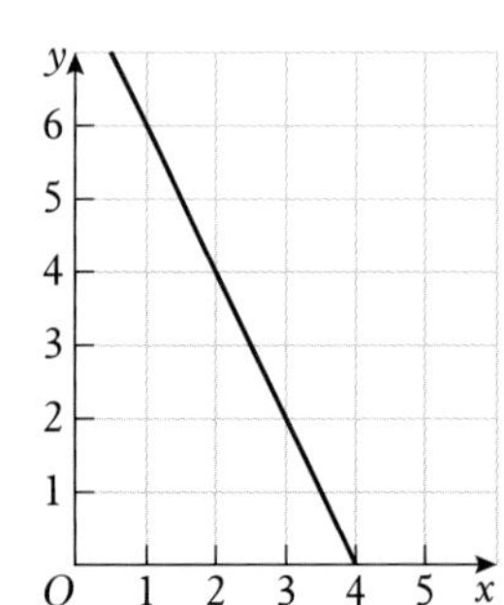

b

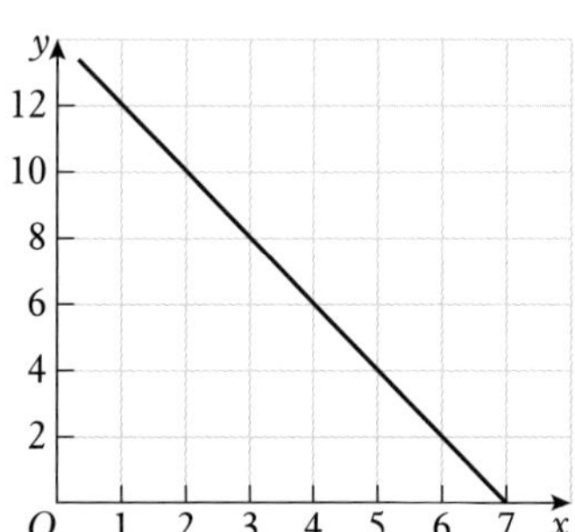

3 Work out the gradient of each of these lines.

a

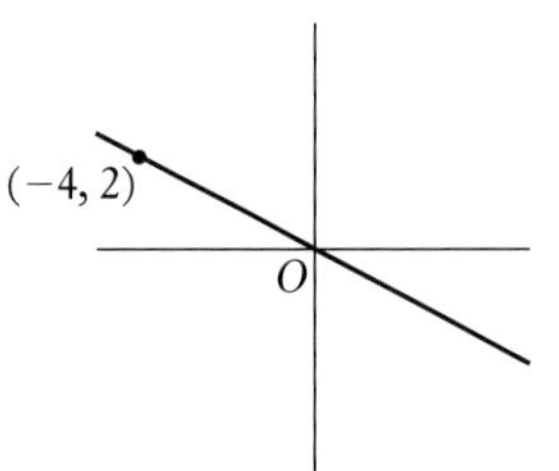

b

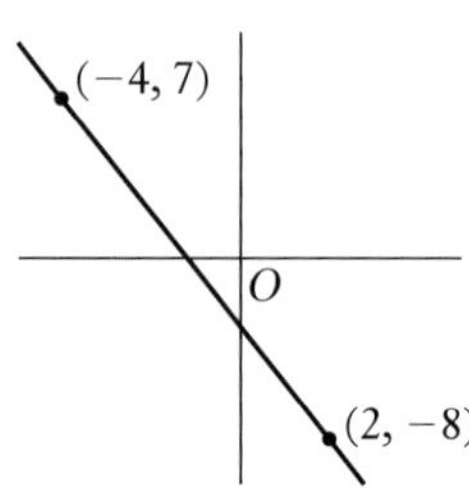

c

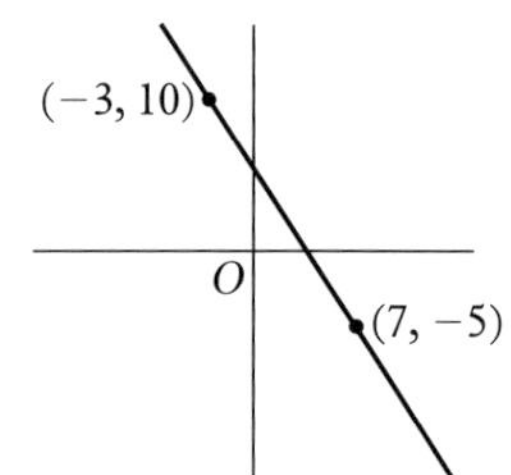

4 Find the gradient of each line.

a

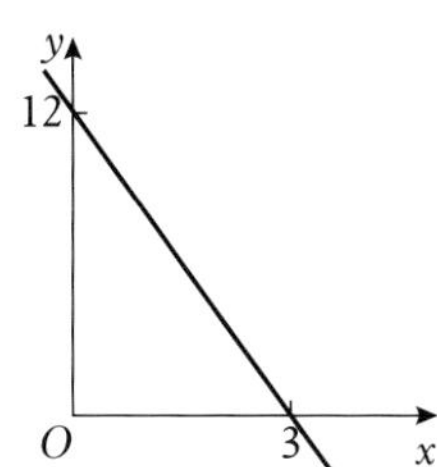

b

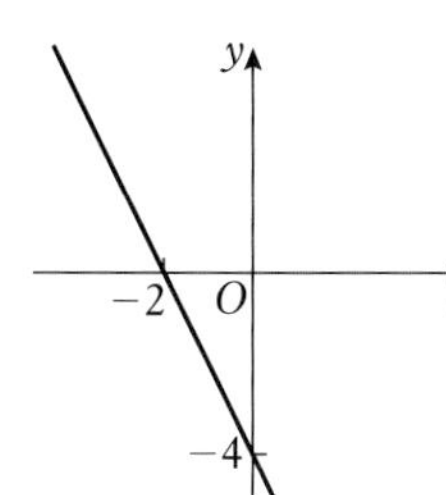

5 Find the gradient of the line passing through these pairs of points. Draw a sketch to help you to see if the line has a positive or negative gradient.

a (1, 1) and (6, 16)
b (2, 9) and (4, 5)
c (−2, −12) and (4, 6)
d (−3, 0) and (0, 12)
e (−5, 4) and (−3, 10)
f (−5, −14) and (−1, 4)

6 Write down the gradient of each of these lines.

a $y = -6x$ **b** $y = -3x$ **c** $y = -x$

7 These lines pass through the origin.
Find the equation of each line.

a

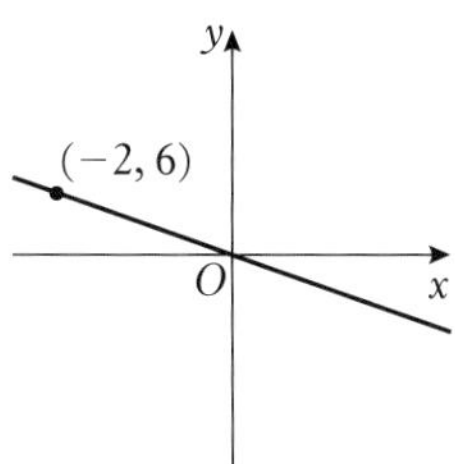

b

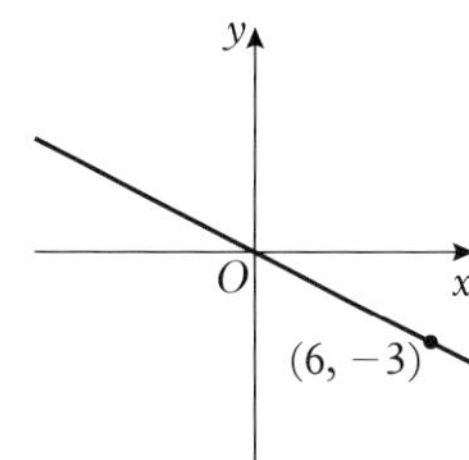

2 Straight lines

Both sides of this bridge are at the same angle.
As you travel from left to right the left side has a positive gradient and the right side has a negative gradient.

Exercise 18:5

1 **a** Copy this table for $y = 2x + 1$.
Fill it in.

x	1	2	3
y	...	...	...

b Copy these axes.
c Plot the line $y = 2x + 1$.
Label the line.
d Draw a table for $y = 2x + 2$.
Plot the line on the same set of axes.
Label the line.
e Draw a table for $y = 2x - 1$.
Plot the line on the same set of axes.
Label the line.
f What do you notice about all three lines?
g Can you see a link between the equations and where the lines cut the y axis?
Write down what you think it is.

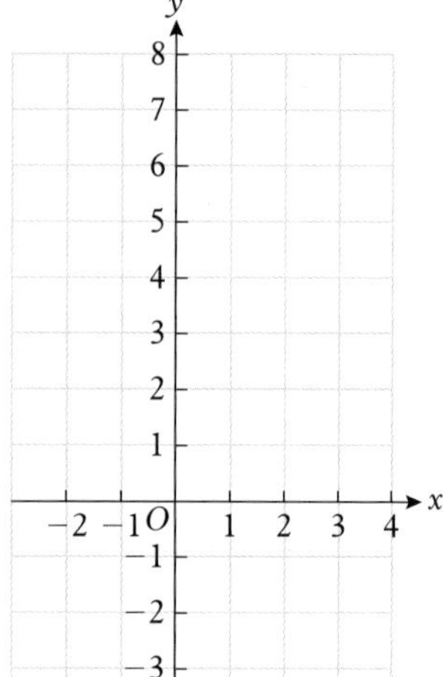

The equation of this line is $y = 4x - 2$.

The gradient of the line is 4.
The line crosses the y axis at -2.

If the equation of a straight line is $y = mx + c$ then the line has a gradient m and cuts the y axis at c.

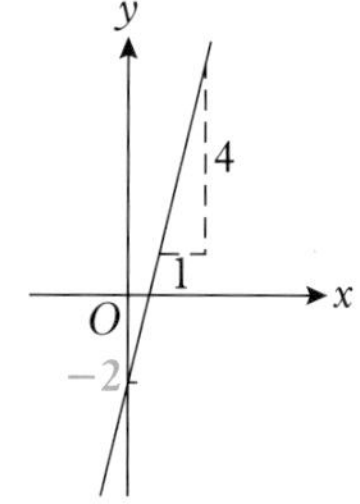

Parallel lines have the same gradient.

Exercise 18:6

1 Write down the gradient of each of these lines.

a $y = 4x + 2$ **b** $y = 2x - 4$ **c** $y = 3x - 1$ **d** $y = -2x + 3$

2 Write down where each of the lines in question **1** crosses the y axis.

3 Write down the equations of the pairs of parallel lines from these:

$y = 2x - 3$ $y = 3x + 2$ $y = 3x - 3$ $y = 2x + 1$

4 **a** Copy this table for $y = -2x + 2$.
Fill it in.

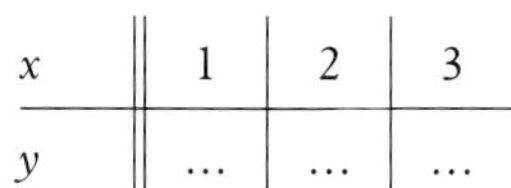

x	1	2	3
y	…	…	…

b Copy these axes.

c Plot the line $y = -2x + 2$.
Label the line.

d Draw a table for $y = -2x$.
Plot the line on the same set of axes.
Label the line.

e Draw a table for $y = -2x - 1$.
Plot the line on the same set of axes.
Label the line.

f What do you notice about all three lines?

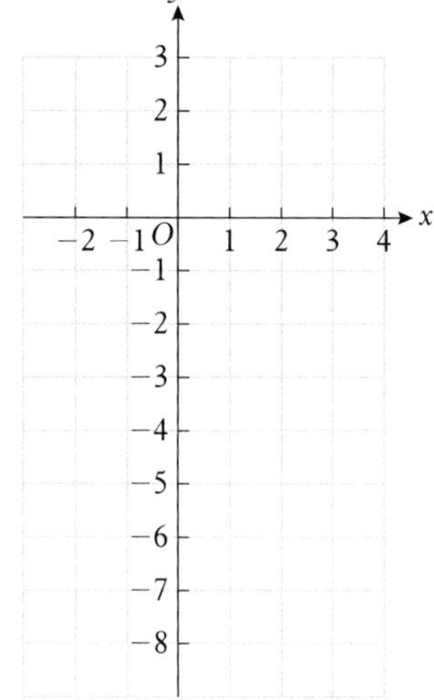

The equation of this line is $y = -3x + 2$.

The gradient of the line is -3.
The line crosses the y axis at 2.

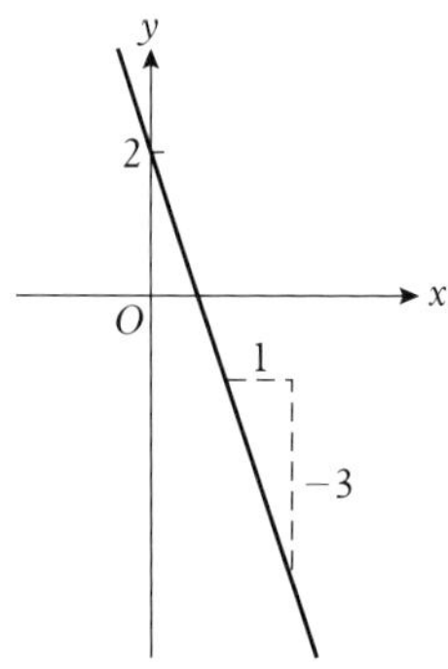

These are the lines $y = -2x + 4$ and $y = -2x - 2$.

These two lines have the same gradient -2. They are parallel.

$y = -2x + 4$ can be written $y = 4 - 2x$. The order of the last two terms has been changed. This makes no difference to the line.

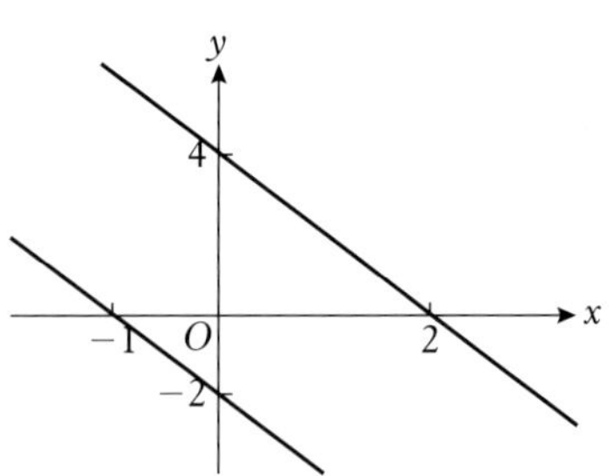

Exercise 18:7

1 Write down the gradients of each of these lines.

a $y = -5x + 3$ **b** $y = -x - 4$ **c** $y = 6 - 3x$ **d** $y = 7 + x$

2 Write down where each of the lines in question **1** crosses the y axis.

3 Write down the equations of the pairs of parallel lines from these:

$y = -x - 3$ $y = -2x + 2$ $y = 5 - x$ $y = 1 - 2x$

4 Write down the equation of the line with:

a gradient 2 y intercept 5 **c** gradient -7 y intercept -2

b gradient -5 y intercept 1 **d** gradient 1 y intercept -3

5 Write down the equations of these lines.

a

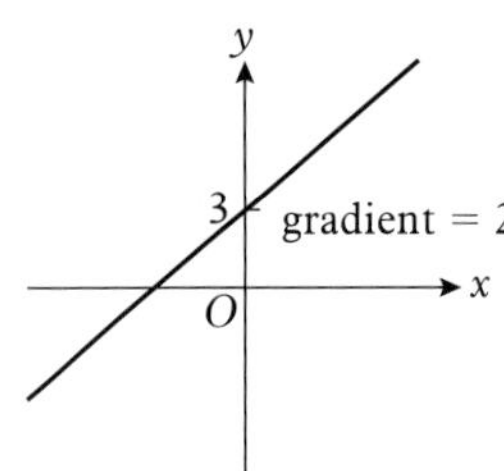

c

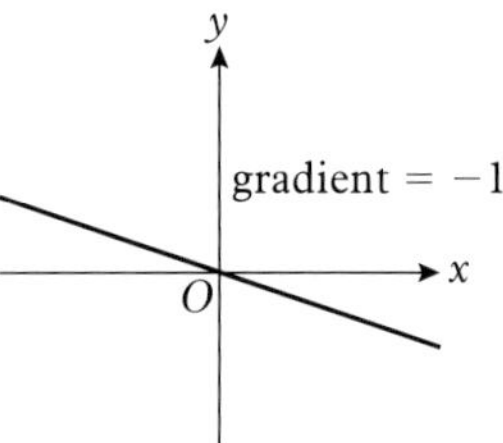

e

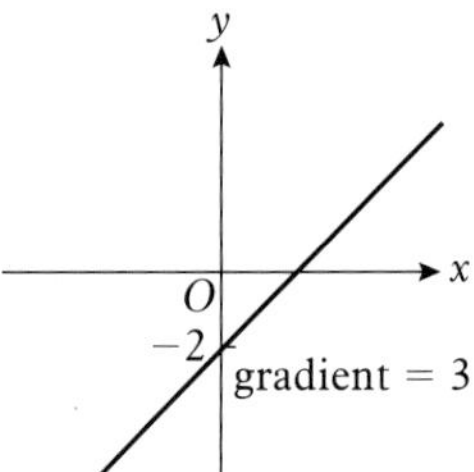

b

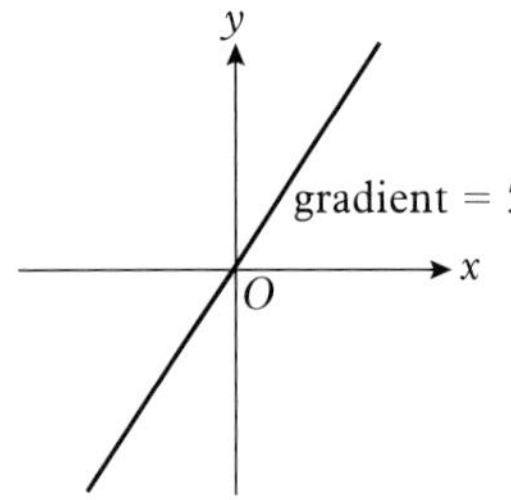

d

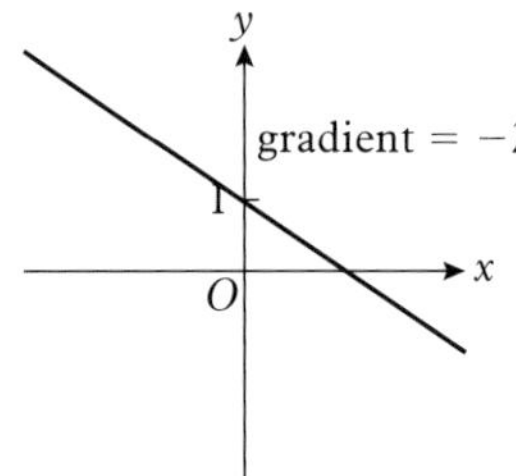

f

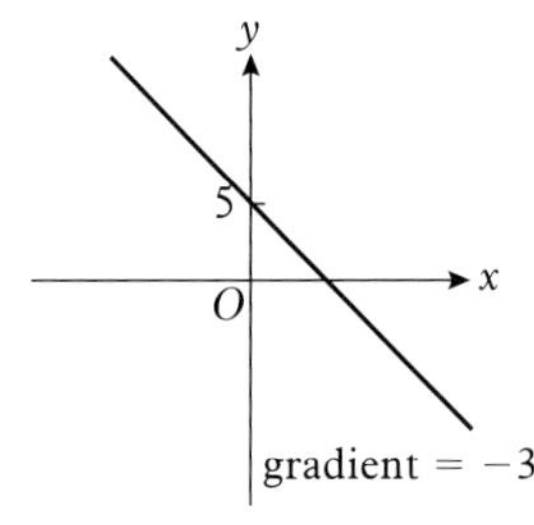

6 Write down the equation of the red line in each part.

a

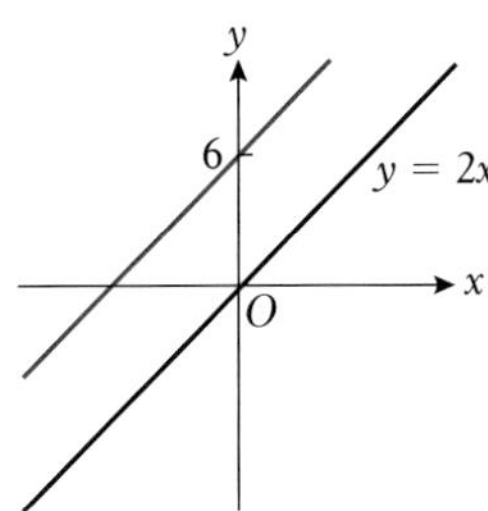

b

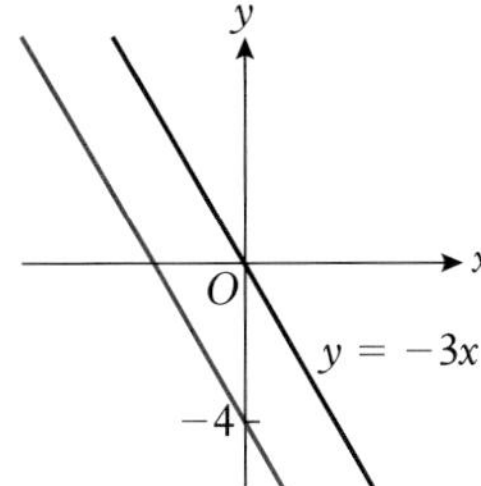

c

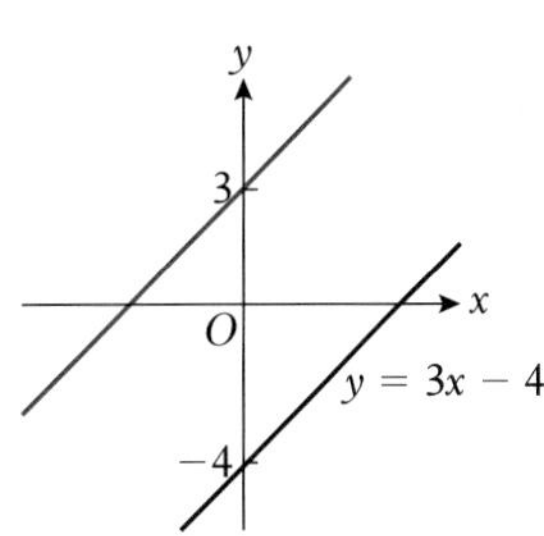

Example Does the point (5, 17) lie on the line $y = 3x + 4$?

Substitute the value of x into the equation

$$y = 3 \times 5 + 4$$
$$= 15 + 4$$
$$= 19$$

When $x = 5$ the value of y is 19 not 17.
The point (5, 17) does not lie on the line $y = 3x + 4$

---

7 Which of these points lie on the line $y = 2x - 3$?

a (1, 5) **b** (2, 1) **c** (5, 7) **d** (−1, −5) **e** (0, 3)

8 These points lie on the line $y = 5x + 2$.
Copy the points and fill in the missing co-ordinates.

a (4, …) **b** (…, 7) **c** (−3, …) **d** (…, −3) **e** (…, −11)

The graph shows the cost of hiring a car.
The cost is made up of a fixed charge and a daily rate.
The cost, C, is given by the formula

$$C = a + bn$$

where n is the number of days.

You can use the graph to find the values of a and b.

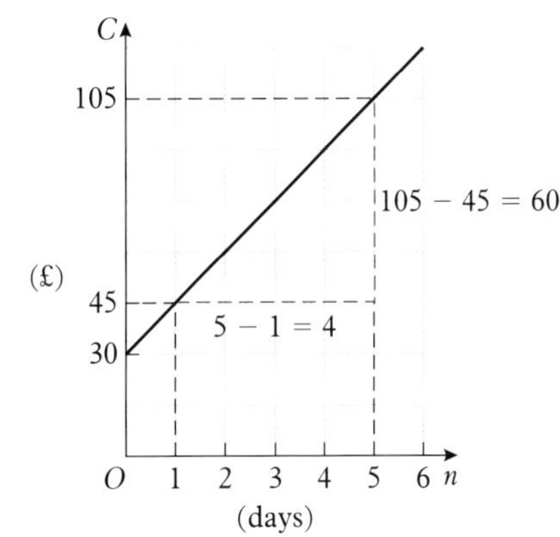

The fixed charge is the point where the line cuts the vertical axis.
This is a.
The fixed charge is £30.
The daily rate is the gradient of the line.
This is b.
The daily rate is $\frac{60}{4}$ = £15

Exercise 18:8

1 This graph shows the cost, C, of a holiday.
The formula is $C = a + bn$
where n is the number of days.
- **a** Find the values of a and b.
- **b** Write down the fixed charge and the daily rate for the holiday.

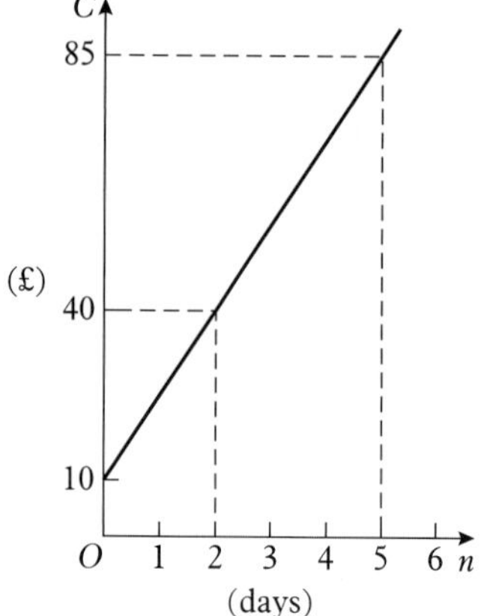

2 The graph shows how the speed of a car changes.

The formula for the speed is
$v = u + at$
where v is the speed and t is the time.
- **a** Find the value of the acceleration a.
- **b** Write down the value of u.

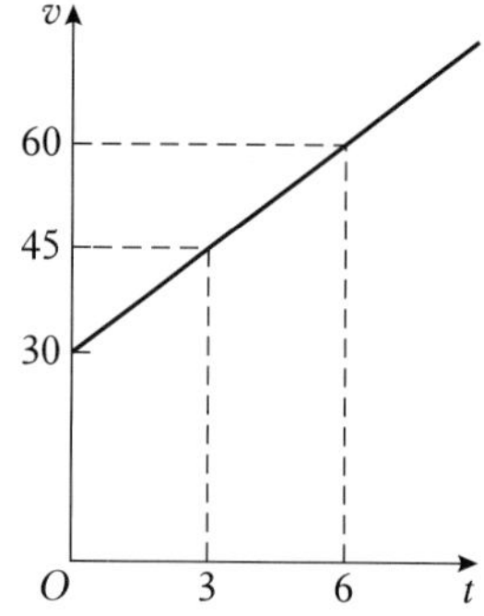

3 Chris is given a fixed amount of money to spend on holiday. He spends the same amount each day.
This is shown on the graph.
- **a** Write down the equation of the line.
- **b** Find the amount of money that he is given.
- **c** How much does he spend each day?
- **d** How many days did the holiday last?

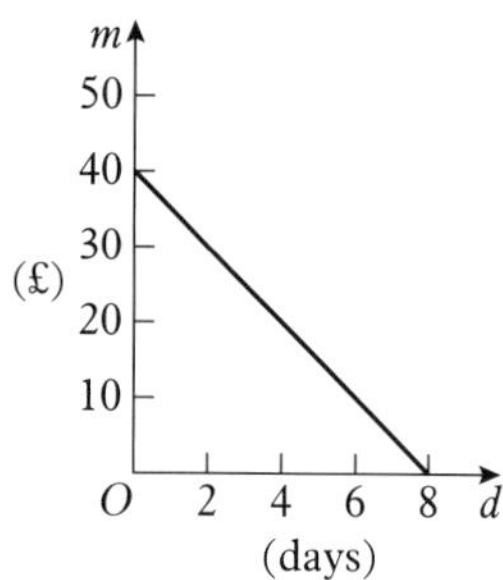

3 Linear equations

There are lots of different ways of spending your money at a fairground.

James has £10 to spend at the fair. He plans to spend it all on the dodgems and waltzers. Each ride costs £1. He spends £d on the dodgems and £w on the waltzers.

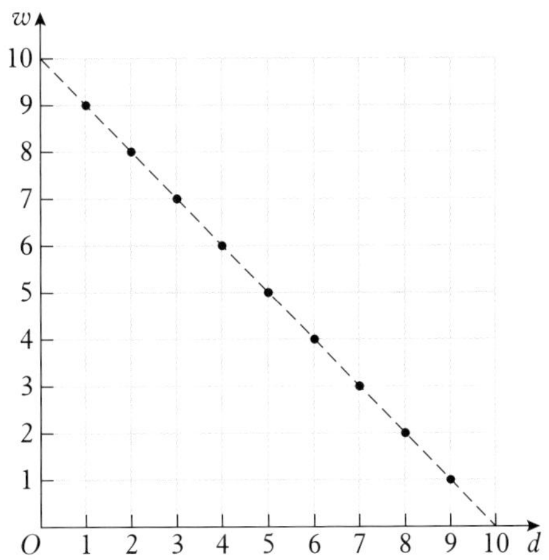

The plotted points show the different ways that James can spend his money. These points lie on a straight line.

The co-ordinates add up to 10 at each point. This means that $d + w$ is 10.

The equation of the line is $d + w = 10$.

Exercise 18:9

1 Vicky has £7 to spend on the waltzers and the dodgems.

  a Plot the points to show how she can spend her money.

  b Join the points with a straight line. Write down its equation.

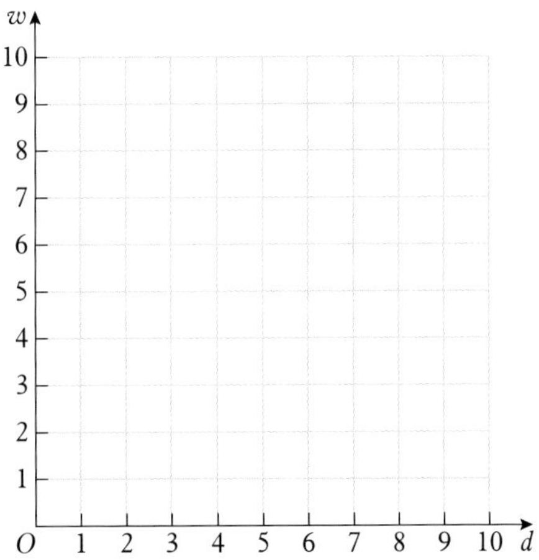

2 **a** Draw x and y axes labelled from 0 to 8.
b Draw a straight line passing through 5 on each axis.
c Write down the co-ordinates of three points on the line.
d Find the value of $x + y$ at each of your three points.
e Write down the equation of the line.

3 **a** Copy the diagram.
b Draw a straight line through P, Q and R.
c Where does this line cross the x axis?
d Where does this line cross the y axis?
e Add the x and y values together at:
(1) P (2) Q (3) R
f Write down the equation of the line.

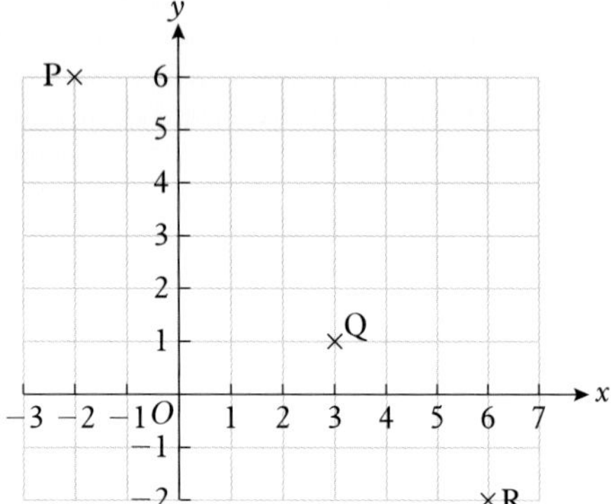

The line $x + y = 6$ crosses both axes at **6**.

The line $x + y = 2$ crosses both axes at 2.

The line $x + y = -4$ crosses both axes at -4.

The line $x + y = \boldsymbol{a}$ crosses both axes at $\boldsymbol{a}$.

All of these lines are parallel.
They all have gradient -1.

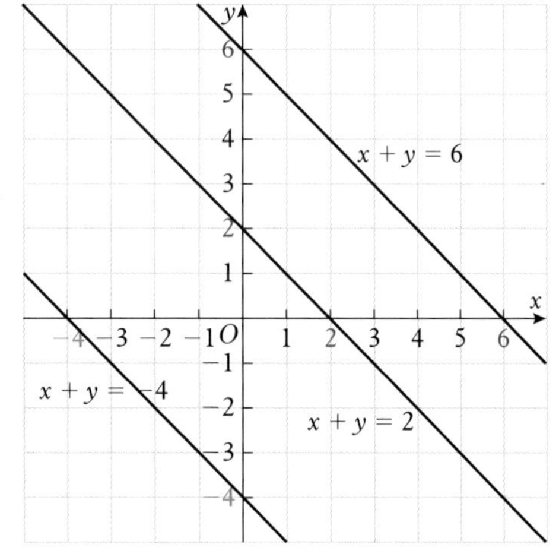

Exercise 18:10

1 A straight line crosses the x and y axes at 8.
a Write down its equation.
b Copy these co-ordinates of points on the line. Fill in the missing values.
(5, …) (…, 7) (−2, …) (11, …)

2 A straight line crosses the x and y axes at -5.
a Write down its equation.
b The point P (3, …) lies on the line. Write down the co-ordinates of P.

3 **a** Find the value of $x + y$ at these points.
(1) A (4, 3) (2) B (8, −1)
b Write down the equation of the straight line through A and B.
c Which of these points lie on the line AB?
P (2, 5) Q (−2, 9) R (−5, −2) S (10, −3) T (−6, 1)
d Copy these co-ordinates of points on AB. Fill in the spaces.
(1) (1, …) (2) (2.5, …) (3) (…, 3.5) (4) (−3, …) (5) (…, −1.5)

4 **a** Where does this line cross the x axis?
b Where does this line cross the y axis?
c Write down the equation of the line.
d Write down the equation of a parallel line passing through:
(1) (1, −5) (2) (−8, 0) (3) (−4, −6)

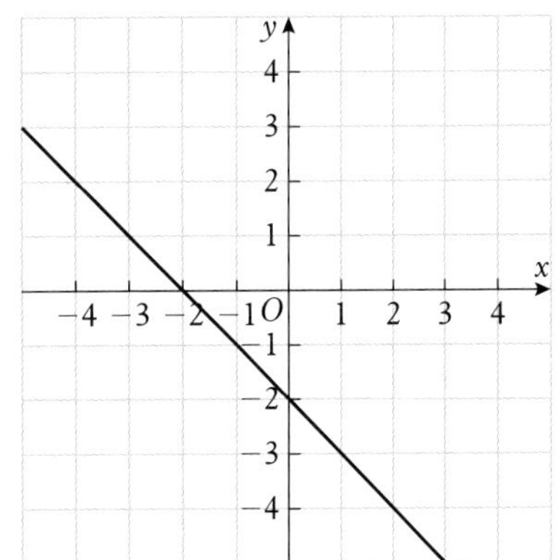

Linear equation

An equation that can be written as $ax + by = c$ is called a **linear equation**; a, b and c are numbers.

$x + y = 4$ is a linear equation with $a = 1$, $b = 1$ and $c = 4$.
$x = 5$ is a linear equation with $a = 1$, $b = 0$ and $c = 5$.

$y = x^2 + 9$ and $y = \frac{4}{x} - 2$ are not linear.

If an equation is linear then you know that its graph will be a straight line.

Exercise 18:11

1 Look at these equations. Write down if each equation is linear or not linear.

a $y = x^2 + 3x$ **d** $y = \frac{2}{x} + 7$ **g** $y = \frac{2x}{3} - 5$

b $y = 5x - 2$ **e** $y = 1.4x + 2$ **h** $x^2 + 3y = 12$

c $y = 3 - 4x$ **f** $x + 3y = 10$ **i** $2y - 1.7x = 11$

Example Draw the graph of the equation $2x + 3y = 6$.

The equation is linear so the graph is a straight line.
This means that you only need to find the co-ordinates of two points on the line.

The easiest points to find are when x and y are zero.

When $x = 0$: $(2 \times 0) + 3y = 6$
so $3y = 6$
so $y = 2$

The point (0, 2) lies on the line.

When $y = 0$: $2x + (3 \times 0) = 6$
so $2x = 6$
so $x = 3$

The point (3, 0) lies on the line.

The line goes through (0, 2) and (3, 0):

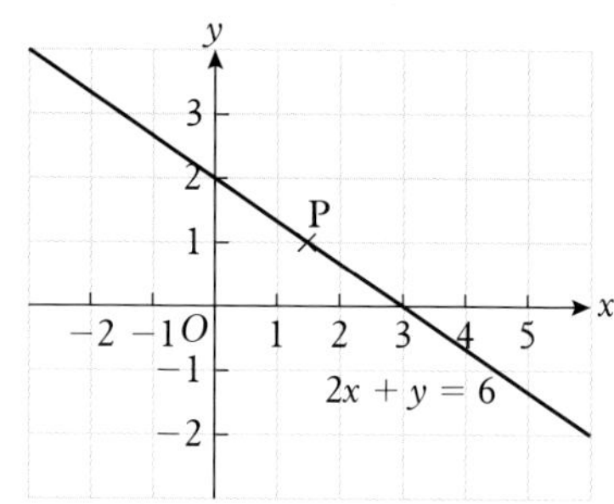

The equation $2x + 3y = 6$ works for all points on the line.
Check: At P (1.5, 1) $(2 \times 1.5) + (3 \times 1) = 6$ ✓

2 **a** Draw x and y axes from -5 to 5.
b Find two points on the line $x + 2y = 7$.
c Plot the points.
d Draw the graph.
e Check that the equation works for another point on the line.

3 **a** Draw x and y axes from -8 to 8.
b Find two points on the line $2x - y = 6$.
c Plot the points.
d Draw the graph.
e Check that the equation works for another point on the line.

4 The points, P, Q, R and S lie on the line $3x + y = 15$.
Copy these co-ordinates. Fill in the spaces.
P (…, 0) Q (2, …) R (6, …) S (…, −6)

5 In the diagram, the line crosses the x and y axes at P and Q.

a Write down their co-ordinates.

b Find the value of $x + 2y$ at P.

c Find the value of $x + 2y$ at Q.

d Write down the equation of the line.

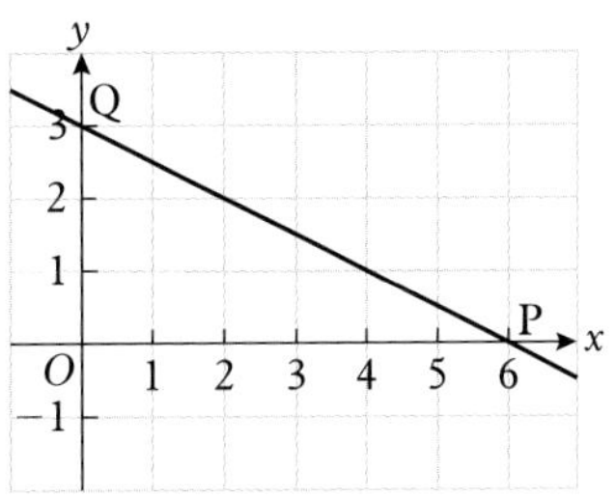

6 Match each of these equations with its graph.

a $y = 2x - 1$ **b** $x + y = 5$ **c** $3x + y = 9$ **d** $\frac{x}{2} + 3y = 6$

(1)

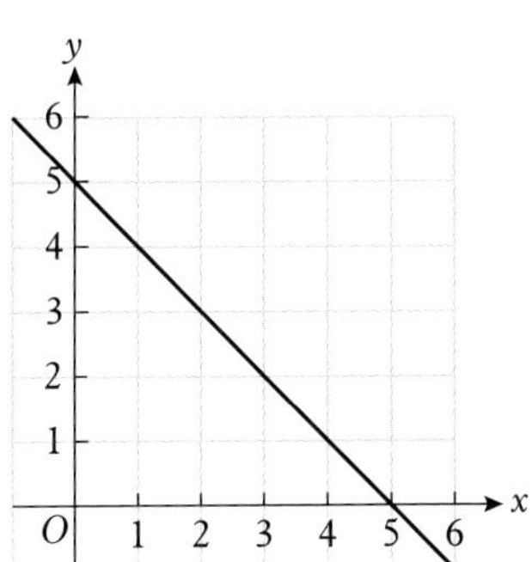

(3)

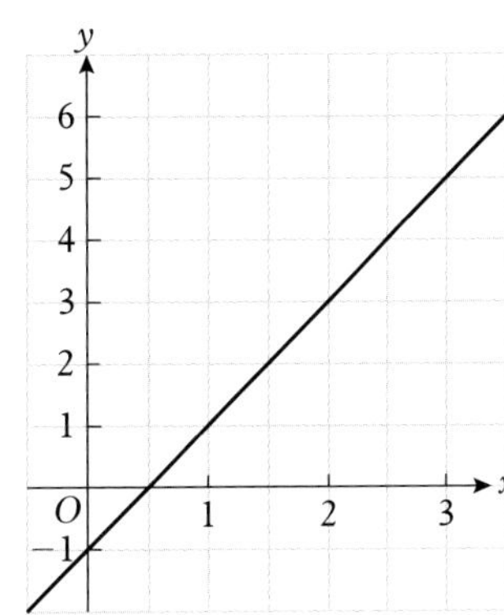

(2)

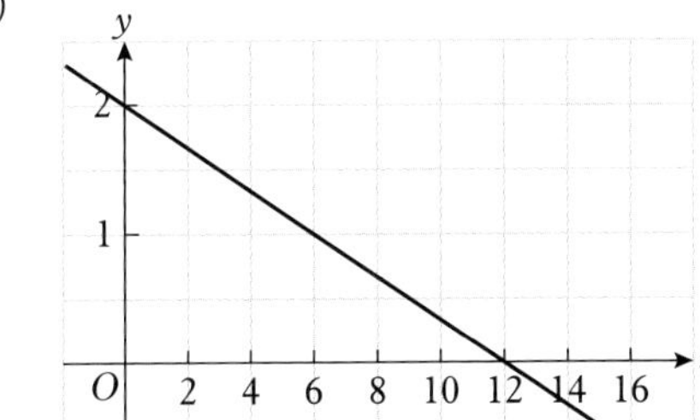

(4)

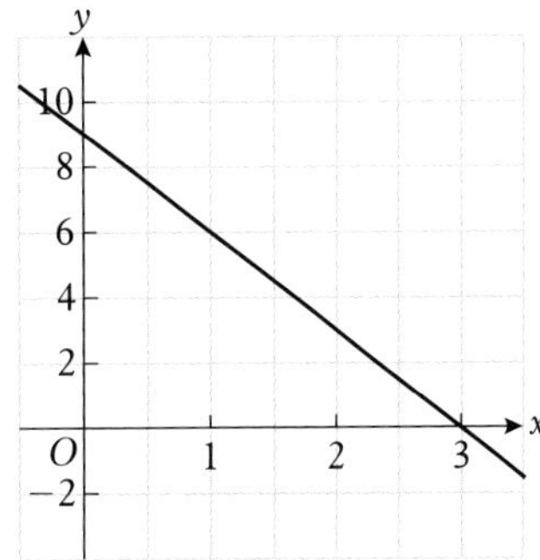

● **7** **a** Which of these points lie on the line $3x - y = 24$?

P (10, 4) Q (10, 6) R (5, −9) S (−7, −3)

b Where does the line cross the x axis?

c Where does the line cross the y axis?

d Write down the co-ordinates of the point where the line $3x - y = 24$ crosses the line (1) $x = 12$ (2) $y = 1.5$ (3) $x = 4$

1 Write down the gradient of each of these lines.

a $c = 4d$ **b** $y = 3x$ **c** $d = -2t$

2 Find the gradient of each of these lines.

a

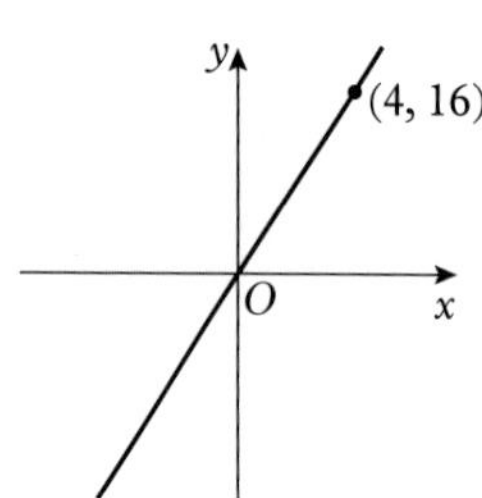

b

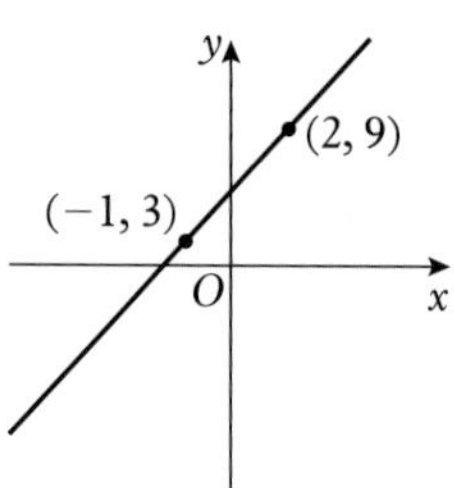

c

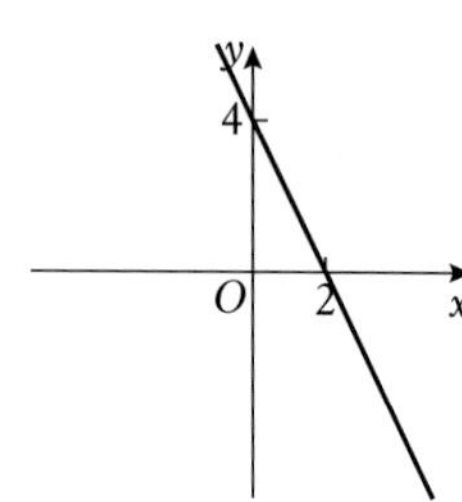

3 Where will these lines cross the y axis?

a $y = 5x + 7$ **b** $y = 2x - 4$ **c** $y = 6x$

4 Which two of these lines are parallel?

$y = 4x + 1$ $y = 3x - 4$ $y = 3x + 4$ $y = x - 4$

5 Which two of these lines are parallel?

$x + 2y = 9$ $x + y = 9$ $2x + y = 11$ $x + y = 11$

6 The line PQ is parallel to the line $3x + y = 12$. The point (6, 2) lies on PQ. Write down its equation.

7 A straight line passes through -4 on each axis. What is its equation?

8 L has co-ordinates (0, 5) and M has co-ordinates (3, 11)

a Draw a diagram to show the line LM.
b Find the gradient of the line.
c Write down its equation.
d Find the equation of a parallel line passing through (1, 10)

9 Find the equation of the line passing through the points:

a (0, 7) and (4, 11)
b (0, −4) and (4, 0)
c (0, 8) and (8, 0)
d (0, 6) and (3, 0)

10 **a** Find the gradient of the line shown.
b Write the equation of the line in the form $y = mx + c$
c Use your equation to find the value of y when $x = 25$
d What value of x gives a y value of -4?

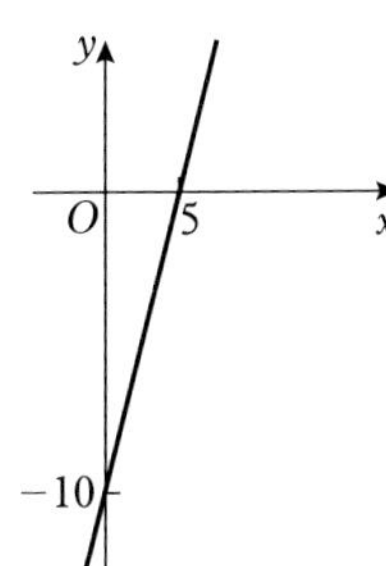

11 Ian is doing an experiment to find the value of m in the equation $F = ma$.

These are his results:

a	2.3	4.1	5.9	6.4
F	28	52	70	77.5

a Plot the values of a and F as co-ordinates.

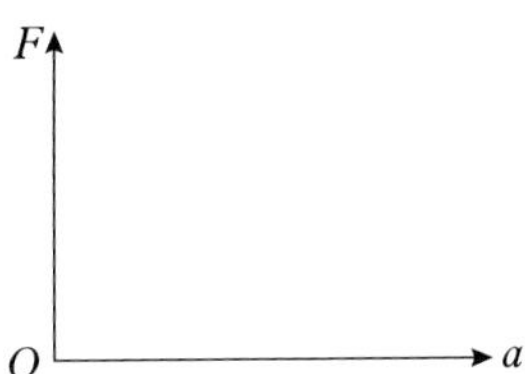

b Join the points with a straight line through the origin.
c Use the graph to find the value of m to the nearest whole number.

12 The table shows the co-ordinates of some points on a line.

x	1	3	5
y	5	11	17

The line has equation $y = mx + c$
a Plot the points and join them up with a straight line.
b Use your graph to find the values of m and c.
c Use the equation of the line to find the value of y when $x = 20$.

1 The table shows the co-ordinates of some points on a line.

x	1	3	5
y	−5	−9	−13

The line has equation $y = mx + c$.

a Plot the points and join them up with a straight line.

b Use your graph to find the values of m and c.

c Use the equation of the line to find the value of y when $x = 20$.

2 The graph shows the time taken to cook a turkey.
The formula is $T = mw + c$.
w is the weight in pounds.
T is the time in minutes.

a Find the value of m.
What does this value tell you?

b Write down the value of c.
Explain what c is.

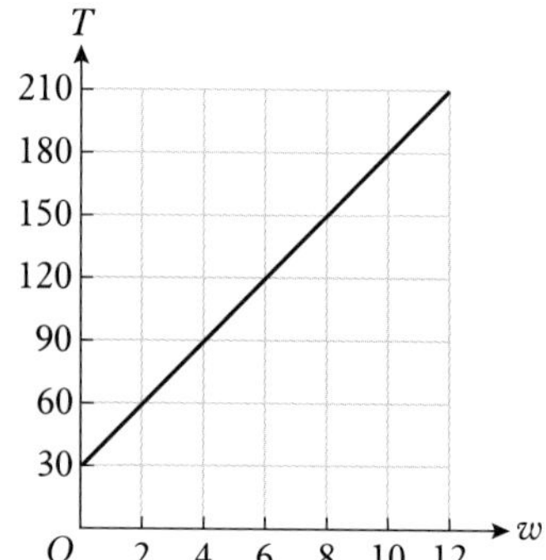

3 Dale uses a graph to change kilometres to miles.
He knows that 8 km is the same as 5 miles.

a Copy the diagram.

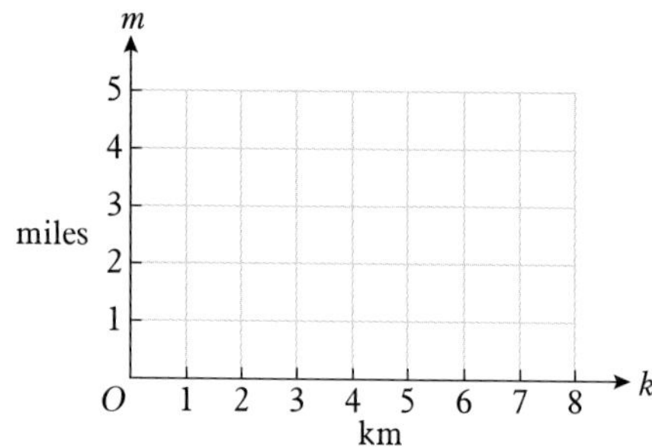

b Use Dale's information to plot a point on the graph.

c Explain why the graph must go through (0, 0). Draw the graph.

d Dale travels 3.6 miles to work. How far is this in kilometres?

e Write down the equation of the graph.

f Use the equation to convert 400 miles to kilometres.

1 Find the gradient of each of these lines.

a

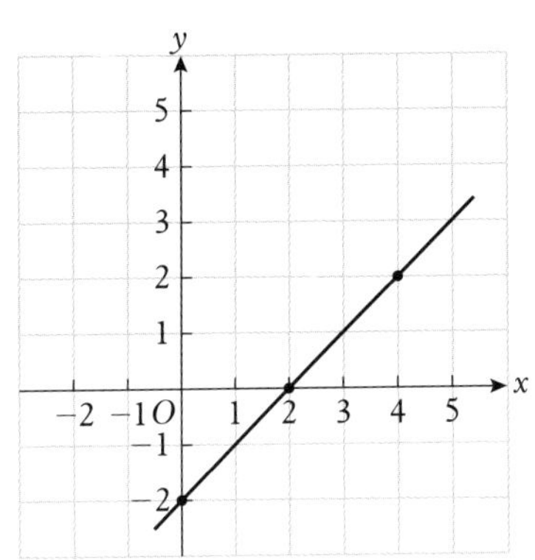

b

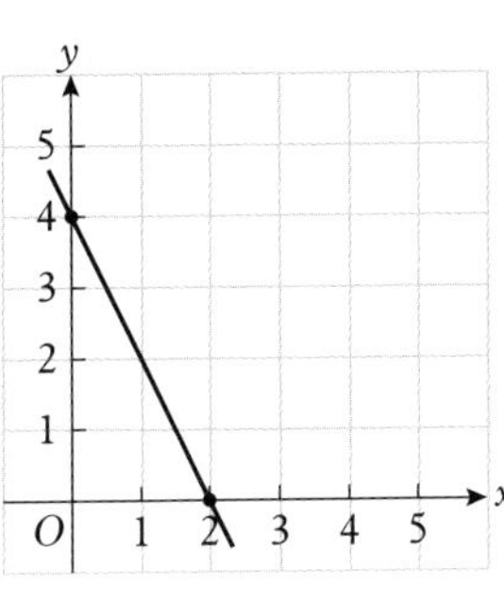

2 Find the gradient of the line passing through each pair of points.

a (2, 3) and (4, 11)

b (0, 9) and (2, 3)

3 Write down the equation of each of these lines.

a

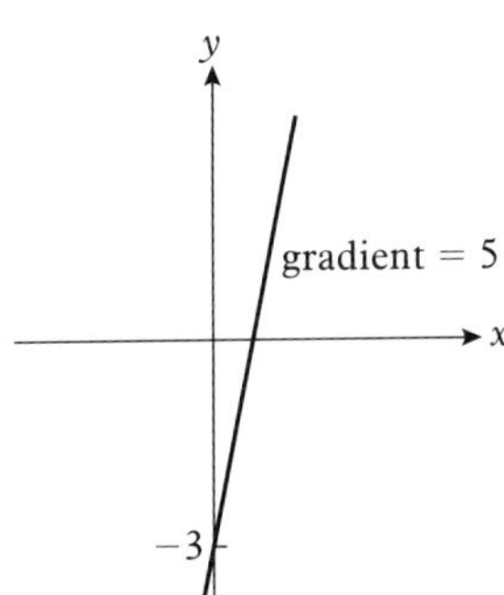

b

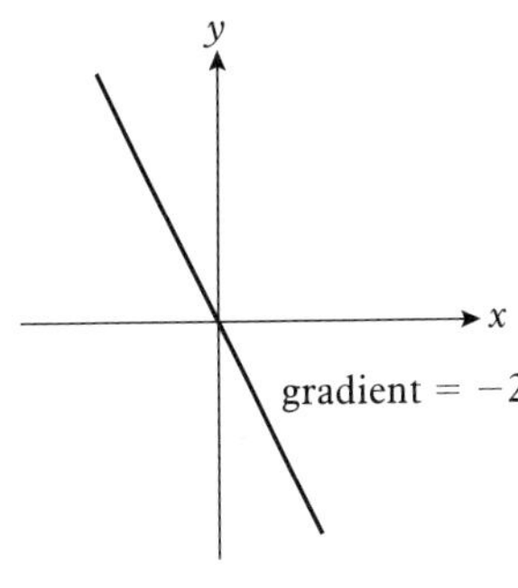

4 Write down the gradients of these lines.

a $y = 3x - 7$

b $y = x + 1$

c $y = -6x$

5 Write down where each line in question **4** crosses the y axis.

6 Write down the equation of a line that is parallel to $y = 7x - 8$.

7 Write down the equation of the **red** line in each part.

a

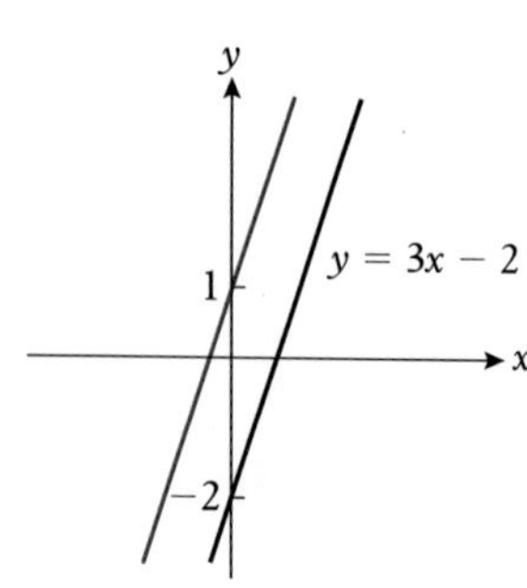

b

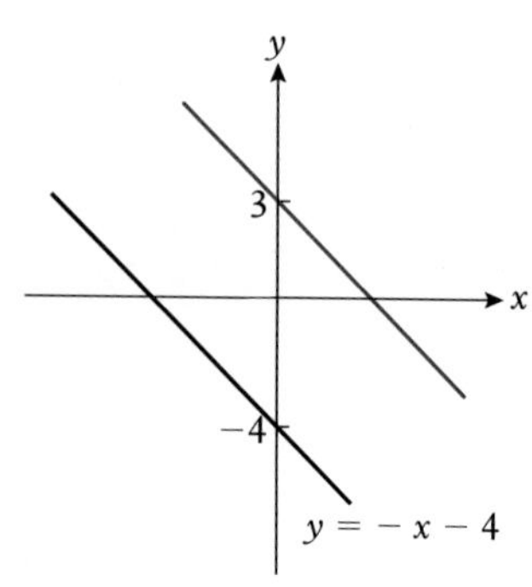

8 The graph shows the cost of printing posters.
The cost, C, is given by the formula

$$C = a + bn$$

where n is the number of posters.
C, a and b are all in £s.

Use the graph to find

a the fixed charge, a.
b the price per poster, b.

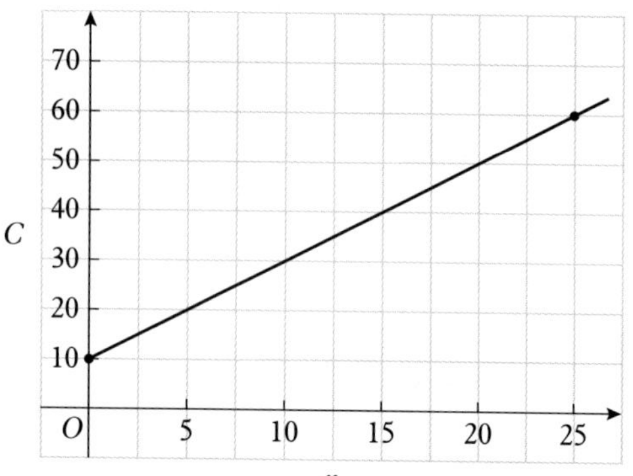

9 Draw the graph of $5x - 2y = 10$.

10 Write down whether each equation is linear or not linear.

a $y = x^2 - 5$ **b** $y = 7 - 2x$ **c** $y = \frac{4}{x} + 3$

19 The bigger picture

CORE

QUESTIONS

EXTENSION

TEST YOURSELF

1 Enlargements

Jo is visiting London.
She thinks the tube train looks very small from a distance.
It is only when it is much closer that she realises how big it is.
She thinks the railway lines are like construction lines for an enlargement.

This is how to enlarge a shape using a scale factor 2.

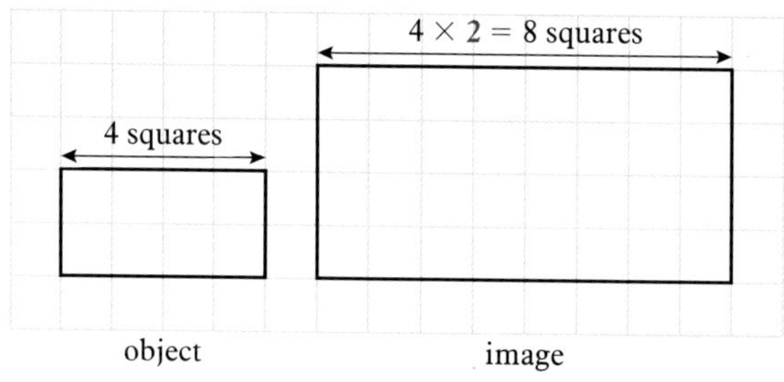

You multiply all the lengths by 2.
The enlargement is 2 times as long and 2 times as high as the object.

Exercise 19:1

1 Copy these shapes on to squared paper.
Enlarge each shape using a scale factor of 2.

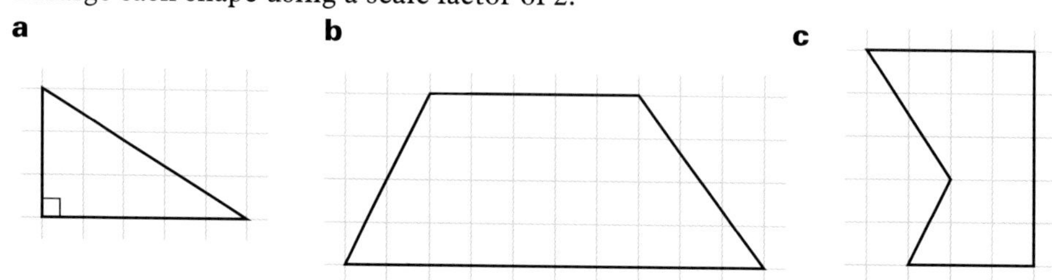

2 Enlarge the shapes in question **1** using a scale factor of 3.

If you have a centre of enlargement, you multiply distances from the centre of enlargement by the scale factor.

Example Enlarge triangle RST with scale factor 2 and centre X.

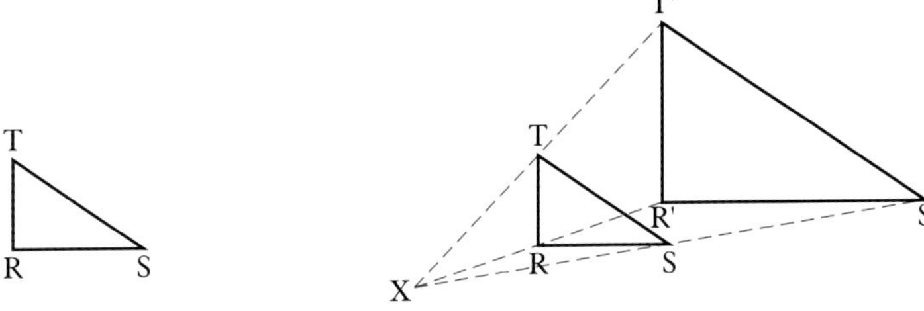

Draw lines from X through R, S and T.
Mark the point R' so that XR' $= 2 \times$ XR
Mark the point S' so that XS' $= 2 \times$ XS
Mark the point T' so that XT' $= 2 \times$ XT
Draw triangle R'S'T'

3 Trace these shapes.
Use X as the centre of enlargement each time.
Enlarge each shape using a scale factor of 4.

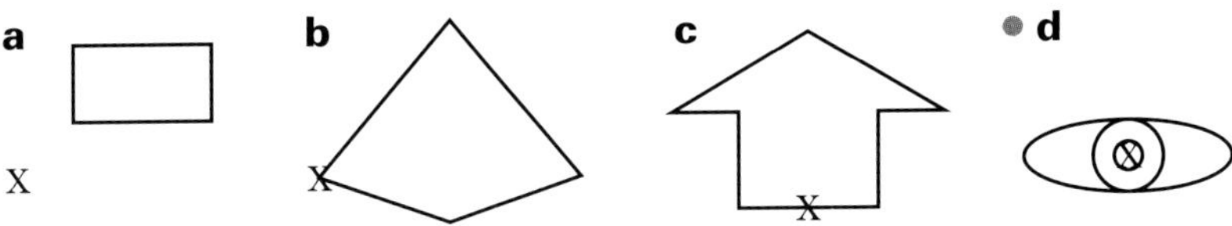

The scale factor of an enlargement may be a fraction.
The diagram shows a parallelogram enlarged using a scale factor of $2\frac{1}{2}$

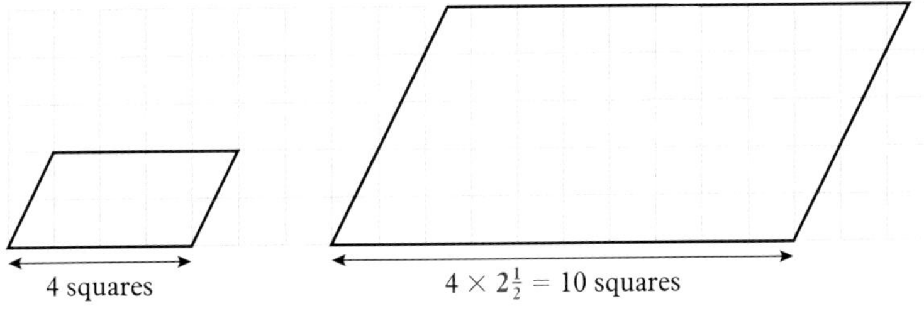

All the lengths are $2\frac{1}{2}$ times longer.

4 Enlarge each of the shapes in question **1** using a scale factor of $2\frac{1}{2}$.

5 Trace these shapes.

a Enlarge this shape using a scale factor of $1\frac{1}{2}$

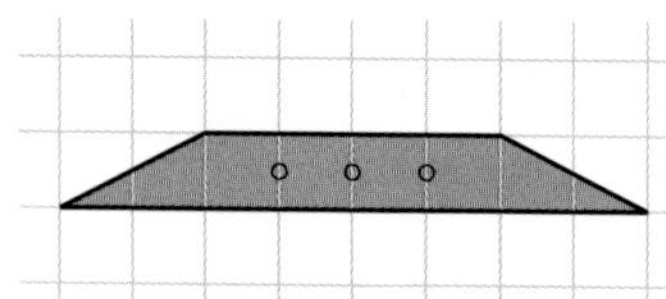

● **b** Enlarge this shape using a scale factor of 1.6

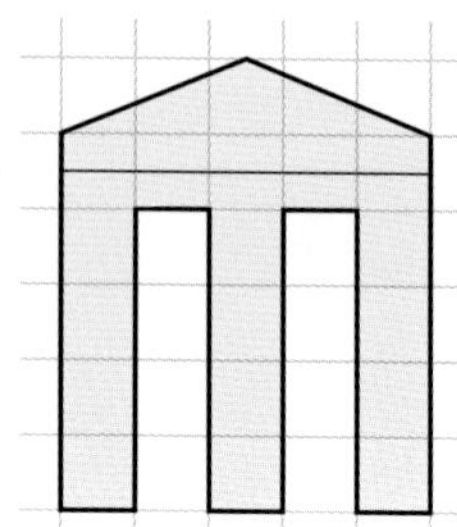

You can use enlargements to make shapes smaller.
These enlargements have a scale factor smaller than 1.
This diagram shows a rectangle enlarged using a scale factor of $\frac{1}{2}$

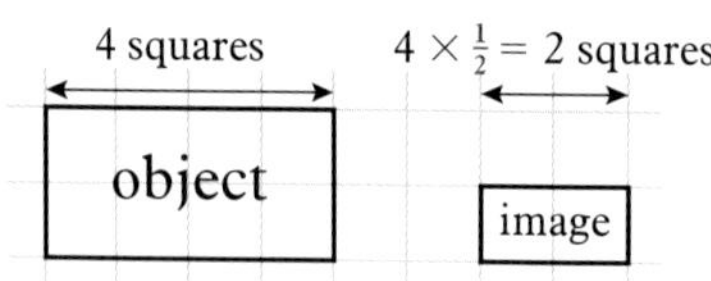

object lengths $\times \frac{1}{2} =$ image lengths

Exercise 19:2

1 For each pair of shapes write down the scale factor for the enlargement from (1) P into Q (2) Q into P.
Make any measurements that you need to do this.

a

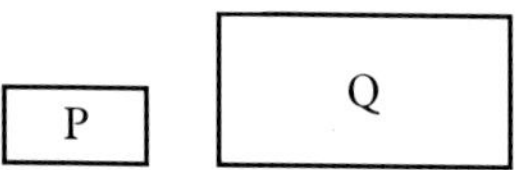

b

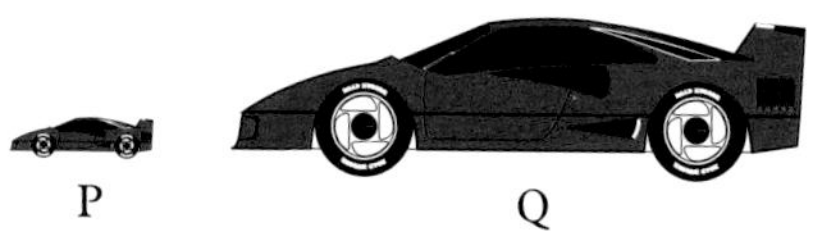

c

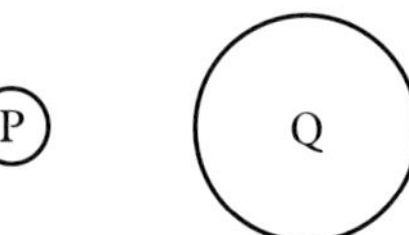

d

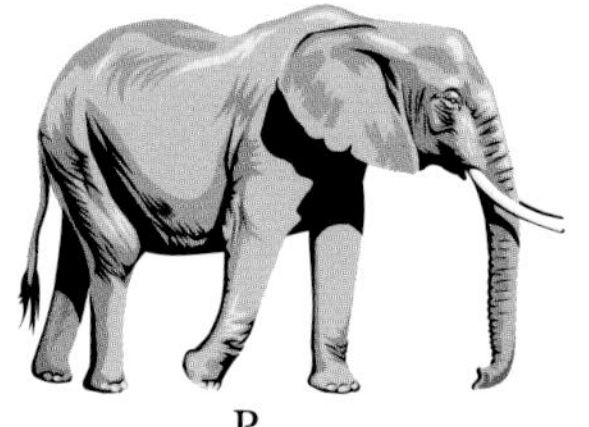

2 Copy these shapes on to squared paper.
Enlarge each shape using a scale factor of (1) $\frac{1}{2}$ (2) $\frac{1}{4}$

a

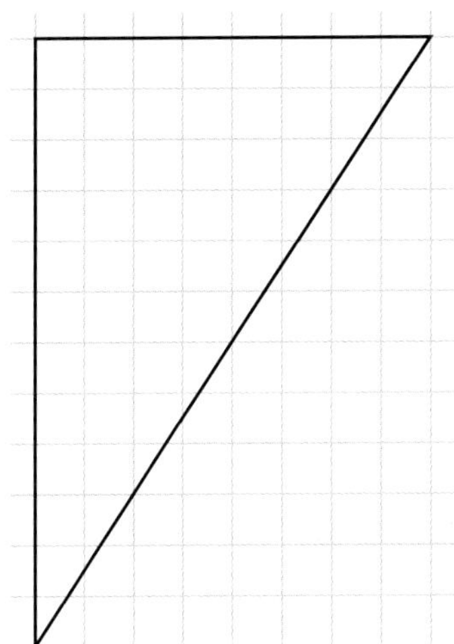

b

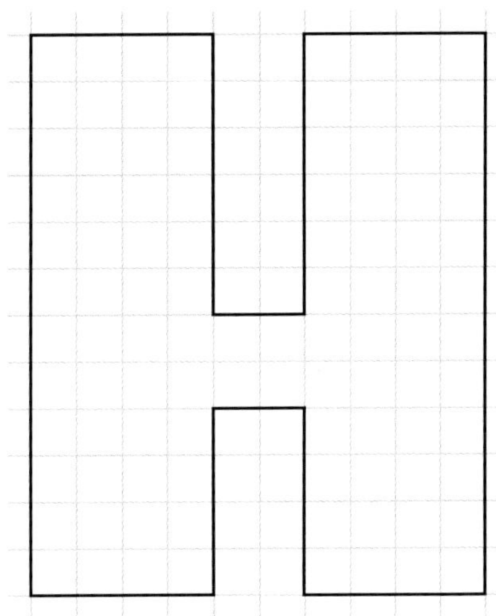

3 Trace these shapes. Use C as the centre of enlargement each time.
Enlarge each shape using a scale factor of $\frac{1}{3}$.

a

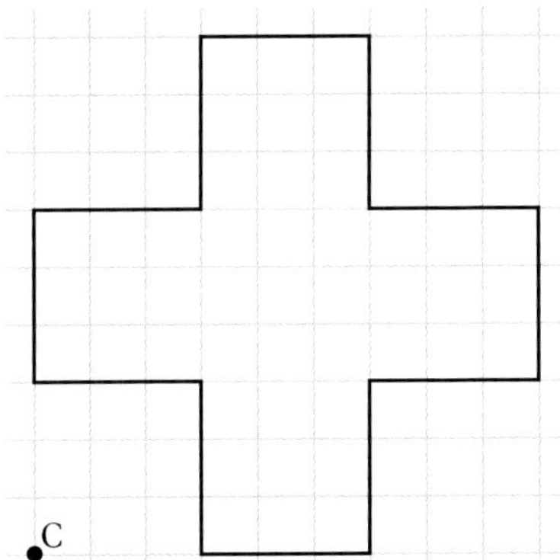

b

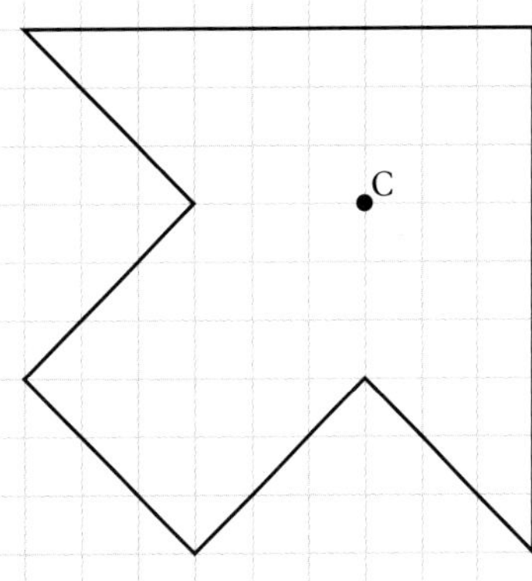

4 Trace these shapes. Use X as the centre of enlargement each time.
Enlarge each shape using a scale factor of (1) $\frac{1}{5}$ (2) $\frac{2}{5}$

a

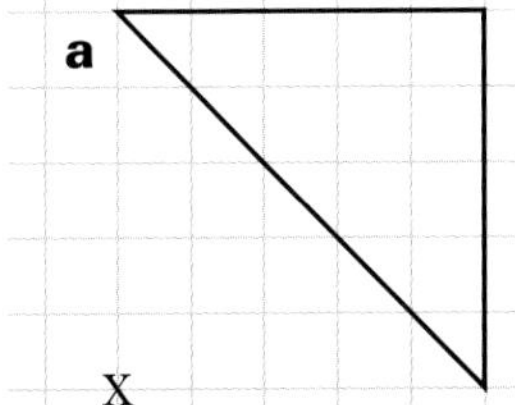

b

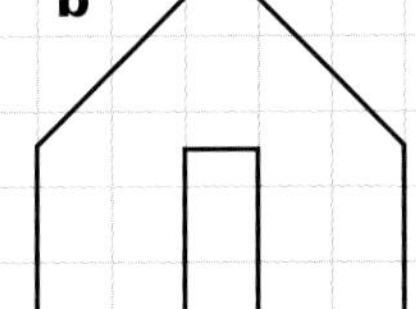

c

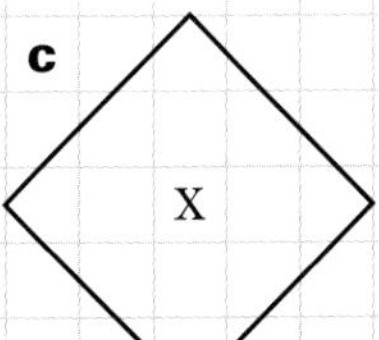

Enlargements with co-ordinates

If you have a centre of enlargement **at the origin** then:
co-ordinates of object × scale factor = co-ordinates of image

Example Find the image of P (3, 6) after an enlargement with these scale factors, centre the origin: **a** 2 **b** $2\frac{1}{2}$ **c** $\frac{1}{3}$

a The image of P (3, 6) is $(3 \times 2, 6 \times 2) = (6, 12)$
b The image of P (3, 6) is $(3 \times 2\frac{1}{2}, 6 \times 2\frac{1}{2}) = (7\frac{1}{2}, 15)$
c The image of P (3, 6) is $(3 \times \frac{1}{3}, 6 \times \frac{1}{3}) = (1, 2)$

When you enlarge a shape, you always join up the vertices of the image.

Exercise 19:3

1 Find the image of these points using an enlargement with scale factor 2, centre the origin.

a (1, 2) **c** (3, 8) **e** $(2\frac{1}{2}, 4)$ **g** (−1, 4)
b (2, 2) **d** (0, 6) **f** (0, 0) **h** (−2, −5)

2 Find the image of these points using an enlargement with scale factor $\frac{1}{3}$, centre the origin.

a (3, 3) **c** (9, 12) **e** $(1\frac{1}{2}, 7\frac{1}{2})$ **g** (−9, 15)
b (6, 6) **d** (0, 9) **f** (0, 0) **h** (−12, −3)

3 The points A, B, C have co-ordinates A (1, 1), B (2, 1) and C (1, 2).

a Copy these axes.
Plot the points A, B and C.
Join them up to get a triangle.

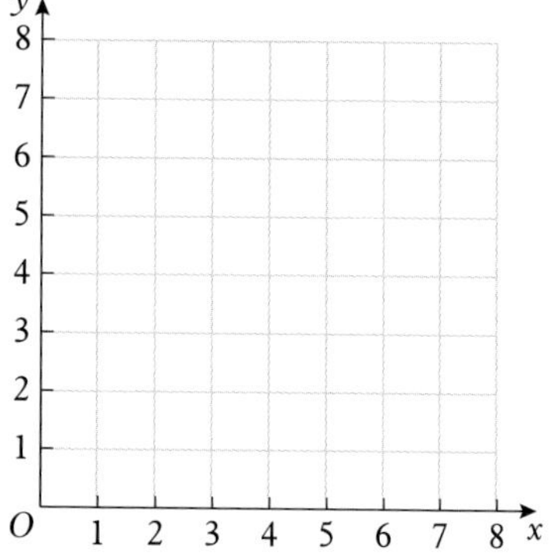

b Measure the lengths of AB, BC and AC.
c Find the new co-ordinates if the triangle is enlarged using a scale factor of 4, centre the origin.
d Check these new co-ordinates are correct by drawing the enlargement.
Show your construction lines.
Label the image A' B' C'.
e Measure the lengths of A'B', B'C' and A'C'.
How do these lengths show if your enlargement is correct?

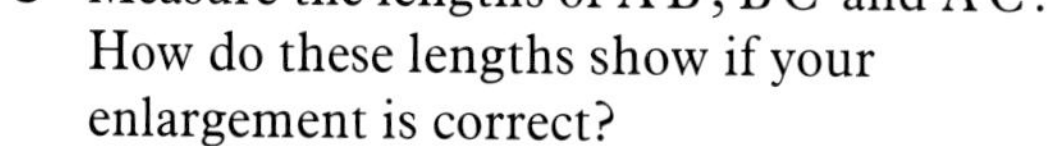

f Measure all the angles on the object.
g Measure all the angles on the image.
h Write down what you notice about angles in corresponding positions on the object and the image.

4 The points Q, R, S, T have co-ordinates:
Q (4, 4), R (4, 8), S (12, 8) and T (12, 4).

a Copy these axes. Plot the points Q, R, S and T. Join them up to get a rectangle.

b Measure the lengths of QR and RS.

c Find the new co-ordinates if the rectangle is enlarged using a scale factor of $\frac{1}{4}$, centre the origin.

d Check these new co-ordinates are correct by drawing the enlargement.
Show your construction lines.
Label the image Q'R'S'T'.

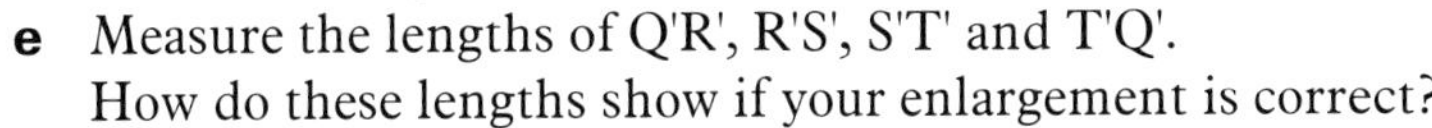

e Measure the lengths of Q'R', R'S', S'T' and T'Q'.
How do these lengths show if your enlargement is correct?

f Measure all the angles on the object.

g Measure all the angles on the image.

h Write down what you notice about these angles.

Similar

Two diagrams are **similar**, if one is an enlargement of the other. They have the same shape but different sizes.

If an object and its image are the same shape, all their angles in corresponding positions will be equal.
You can use the scale factor to find missing lengths.

Flags A and B are similar. Find the missing lengths.

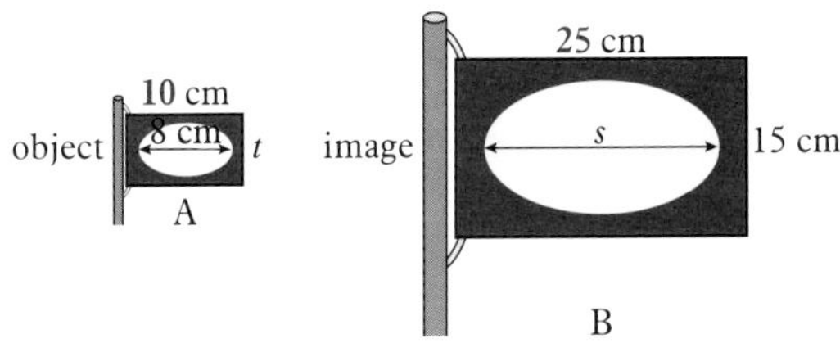

Now use common sense. Flag B is bigger than flag A so the scale factor going from left to right is **more than 1**.

So from flag A to flag B, the scale factor $= \frac{25}{10} = 2.5$

So the length s is $8 \times 2.5 = 20$ cm

Flag A is smaller than flag B,
so the scale factor going from right to left is **less than 1**.

So from flag B to flag A, the scale factor $= \frac{10}{25} = 0.4$

So the width t is $15 \times 0.4 = 6$ cm

Exercise 19:4

1 All circles are similar and all squares are similar.
Not all rectangles are similar.
Explain why the two statements are true.

Each of questions **2–6** in this exercise has a pair of similar shapes.

a Write down the corresponding lengths on the object and image. These lengths are shown in red in questions **1** and **2**.

b Use these lengths in each part to work out the scale factor.

c Use the scale factor to find the sides marked with letters.

2

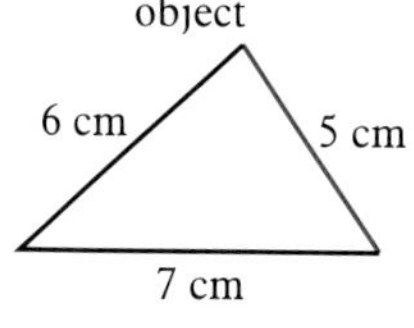

3

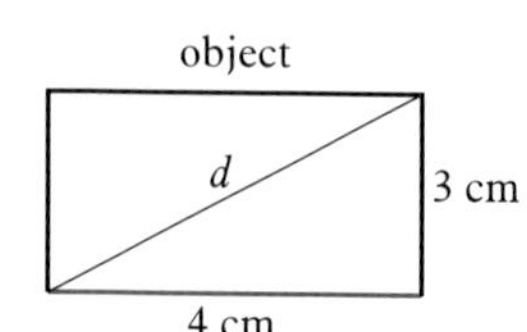

4

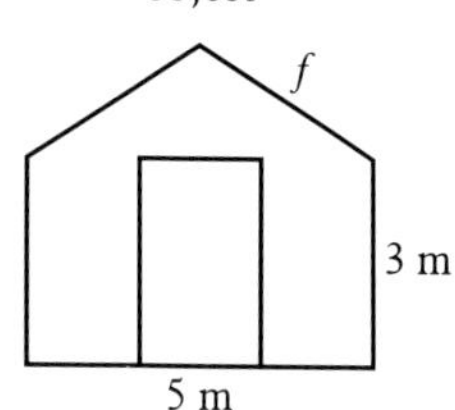

5 The picture shows a section from a bridge with a model alongside.

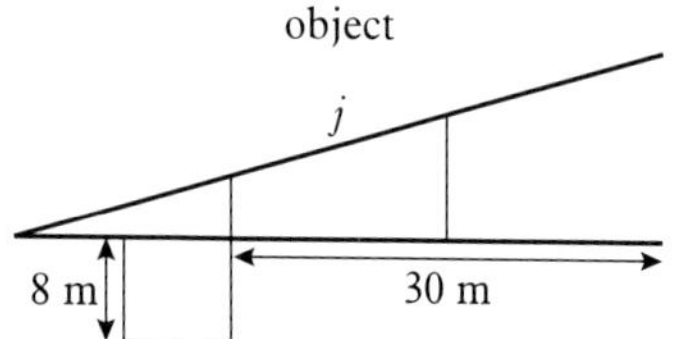

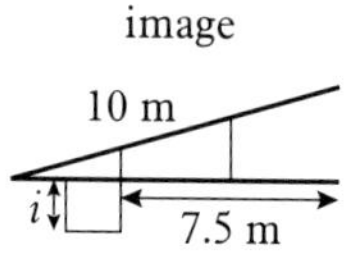

● **6**

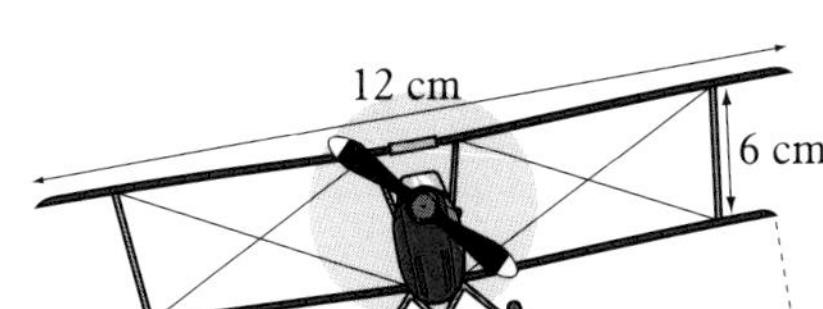

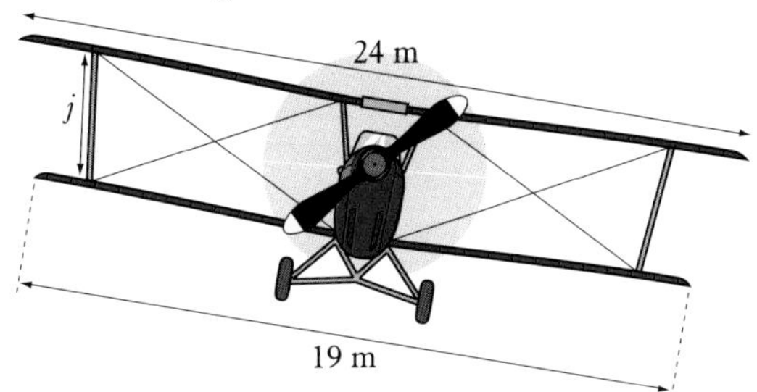

Exercise 19:5

1 **a** Copy this shape onto squared paper.
b Work out the perimeter of the shape.
c Enlarge the shape using a scale factor 2. Use C as the centre of enlargement.
d Work out the perimeter of the new shape.
e Write down what has happened to the perimeter of the shape when it has been enlarged

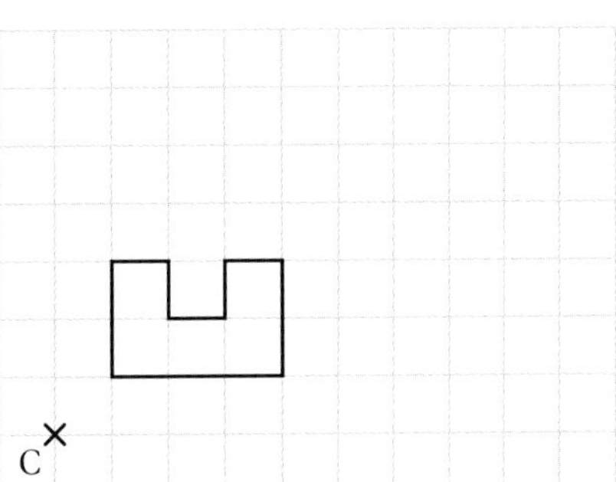

2 **a** Copy this shape onto squared paper.
b Work out the perimeter of the shape.
c Enlarge the shape using a scale factor 0.5
Use C as the centre of enlargement.
d Work out the perimeter of the new shape.
e Write down what has happened to the perimeter of the shape when it has been enlarged.

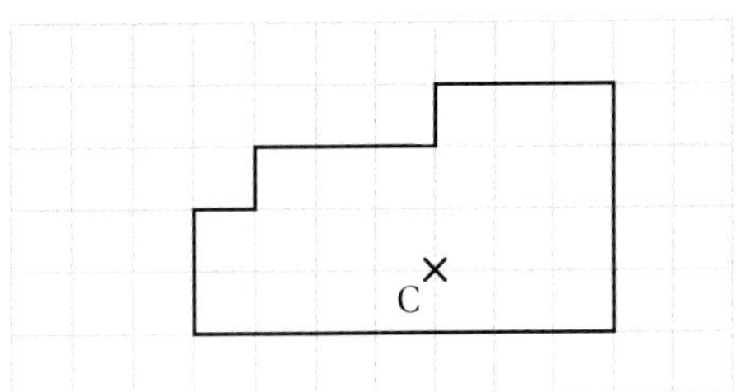

If a shape is enlarged by a scale factor n then the perimeter will also be enlarged by a factor of n.

---

3 A shape has a perimeter of 12 cm.
The shape is enlarged by a scale factor of 4.5
Write down the perimeter of the new shape.

4 A shape is enlarged by a scale factor of 2.5
The perimeter of the enlarged shape is 46.25 cm.
What is the perimeter of the original shape?

If the centre of enlargement of an object is not at the origin then the easiest way to find the co-ordinates of the image is by drawing.

Exercise 19:6

1 **a** Copy the diagram.

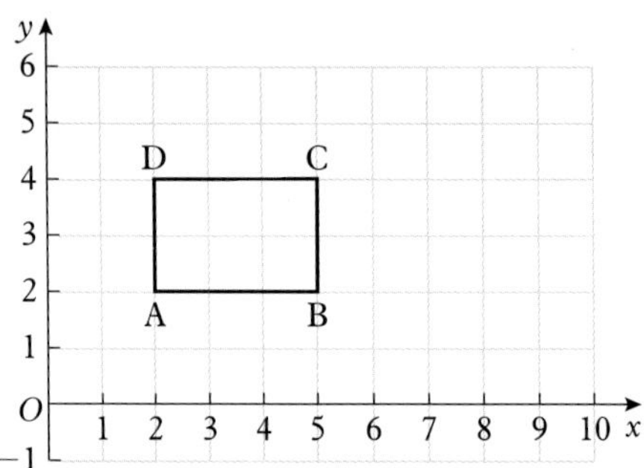

b Find the new co-ordinates by drawing if the shape is enlarged using a scale factor of 2, centre (1, 3).
c Show your construction lines.
d Label your image $A_1B_1C_1D_1$.
e Is the image similar to the object? Write down your reasons.

2 The points V, W, X, Y, Z have co-ordinates:
V (3, 1), W (5, 1), X (6, 3), Y (4, 4) and Z (2, 3).
a Copy these axes. Plot the points. Join them up to get a pentagon.
b Find the new co-ordinates by drawing if the pentagon is enlarged using a scale factor of 3, centre (1, 2).
c Show your construction lines.
d Label your image $V_1W_1X_1Y_1Z_1$.
e Is the image similar to the object? Write down your reasons.

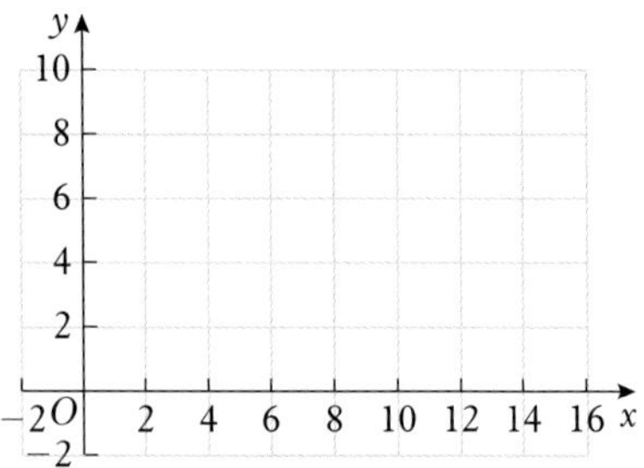

3 **a** Repeat question **2a**. Use another copy of the same set of axes.
b Find the new co-ordinates by drawing if the pentagon is enlarged using a scale factor of $1\frac{1}{2}$, centre (4, 2).
c Show your construction lines.
d Label your image $V_2W_2X_2Y_2Z_2$.
e Is the image similar to the object? Write down your reasons.

Finding the centre of enlargement

To find the centre of enlargement:
(1) Join points on the image to their corresponding points on the object.
(2) Extend all the lines so that they meet at the centre.

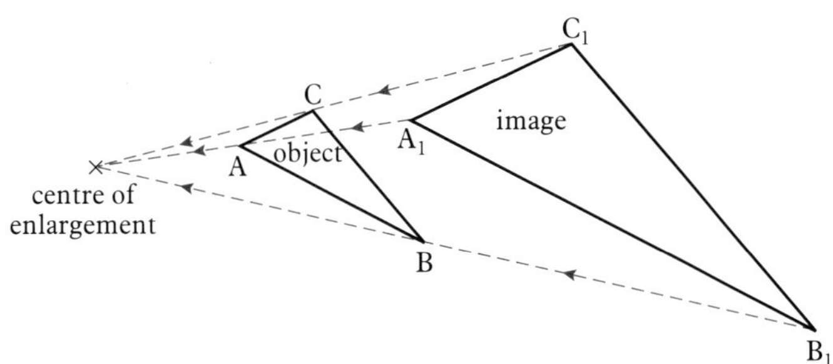

4 Trace these shapes.
Find the centre of enlargement. Show your construction lines.

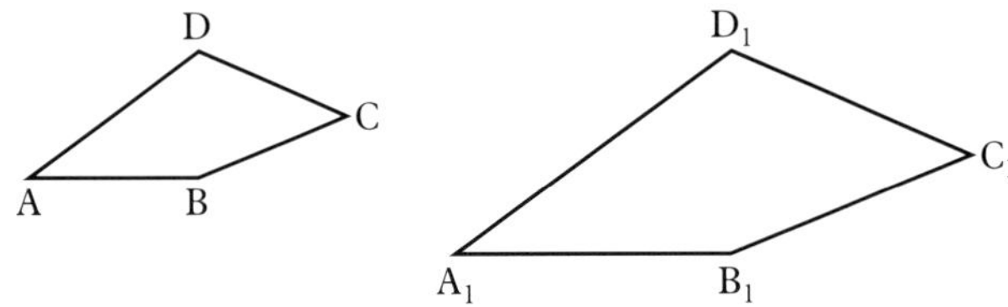

5 Copy the diagrams on to squared paper.
Find the centres of enlargement. Show your construction lines.

a

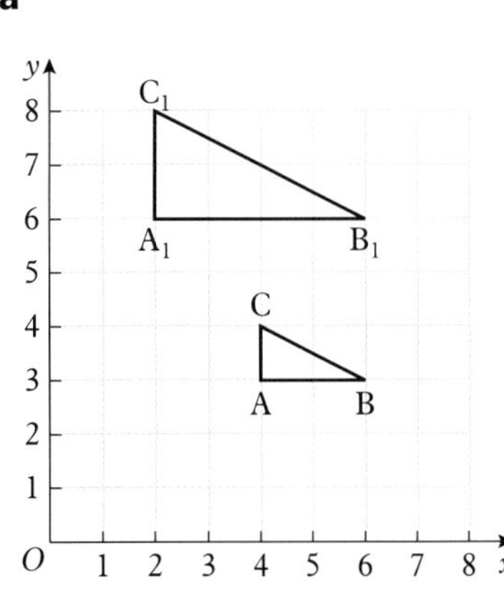

b

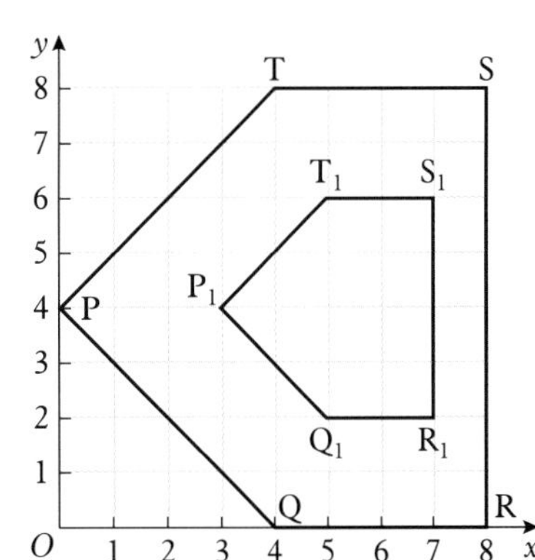

Inverse of an enlargement

The **inverse of an enlargement** with scale factor k is an enlargement with scale factor $\frac{1}{k}$.

To find the inverse of an enlargement:
(1) Write the scale factor as a fraction.
(2) Turn the fraction upside down.
The centre of enlargement does not change.

You can write scale factor 2 as scale factor $\frac{2}{1}$.
So the inverse of an enlargement with scale factor 2 is an enlargement with scale factor $\frac{1}{2}$

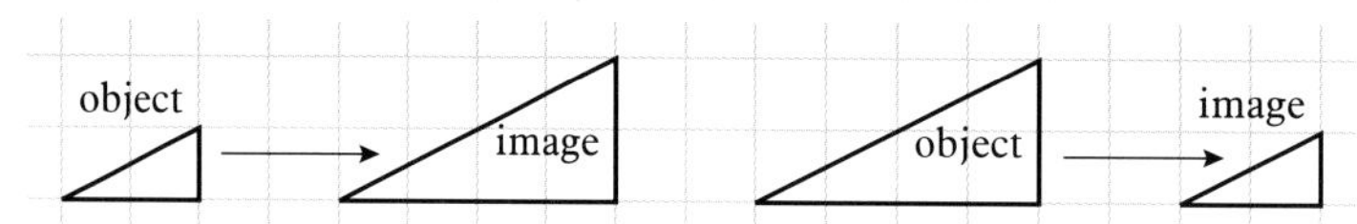

This is an enlargement scale factor 2 This is an enlargement scale factor $\frac{1}{2}$

So you get back to the shape you started with by using the inverse.

Example An enlargement has scale factor **a** 4 **b** $\frac{1}{3}$
Find the scale factor of the inverse for each one.

a 4 is $\frac{4}{1}$, so turn it upside down to get $\frac{1}{4}$
The scale factor of the inverse is $\frac{1}{4}$
b Turn $\frac{1}{3}$ upside down to get $\frac{3}{1}$
The scale factor of the inverse is 3

6 These numbers are the scale factors of enlargements.
Write down the scale factor of the inverse of each one.

a 2 **c** 5 **e** $\frac{1}{4}$ ● **g** 1.6
b 3 **d** $\frac{1}{2}$ **f** $2\frac{1}{2}$ ● **h** $\frac{a}{b}$

7 **a** Find the scale factor of the enlargement from A to B.
b Write down the scale factor of the inverse.

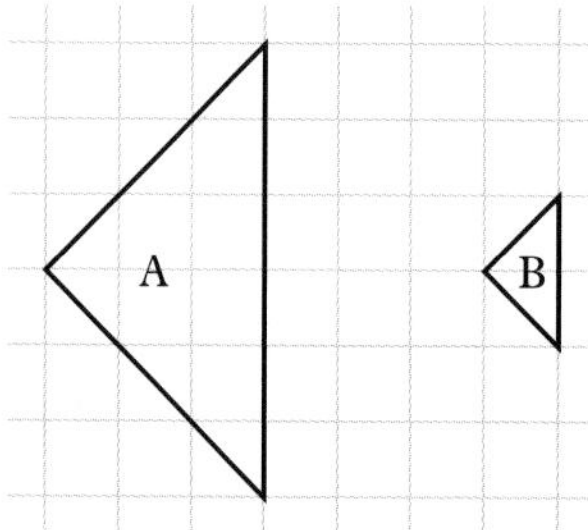

● **8** Find the scale factors for the inverses of each part of question **5**.

2 Scale drawing

This is a photo of the model village at Torquay.

The model village is an exact copy of the real village but it is much smaller!

The scale of the model is 1 to 12.

Models, scale drawings, plans and maps are all exact copies of something drawn to a smaller scale.
Maps can be used to find distances. Plans can be used to find lengths of rooms in a building or to plan the layout of houses or whole housing estates.

Scale

A **scale** tells you what the length on a map or plan represents in real life.

The scale on a house plan could be 1 cm = 1 m.
The scale on a road map could be 1 inch = 1 mile.

Exercise 19:7

1 Read through this list of plans and the list of scales.
Match up the plan with the correct scale.
Write down the correct pairs.

Plan	**Scale**
Plan of a bedroom	1 cm = 10 m
Plan of a housing estate	2 cm = 1 mile
Walkers' map showing footpaths	1 cm = 100 miles
Road atlas	1 cm = 1 m
Plans for a house	1 cm = 5 m
Map of Europe	5 cm = 1 km

This map of a theme park is drawn to scale.
The scale is 1 cm = 100 m.

Example How far is it from the Rollercoaster to the Log Flume?

On the map the distance is 6 cm.
The scale is 1 cm = 100 m.
So in the park it is 6×100 m = 600 m.

---

2 **a** How far is it on the map from the Rollercoaster to the Runaway Train?
b How far is it in the park from the Rollercoaster to the Runaway Train?
c How far is it on the map from the Rapids to the Café?
d How far is it in the park?
e How far is it in the park from the Café to the Ghost Train?
f William has a day out at the theme park.
He walks from the entrance to the Log Flume and then to the Runaway Train. He then walks to the Rollercoaster.
How far has William walked altogether?

3 Mark's bedroom is a rectangle 6.5 m long and 4.5 m wide.
a Draw a scale plan of Mark's bedroom. Use a scale of 1 cm = 1 m.
Mark has a wardrobe which is 2.5 m long and 1 m wide.
He also has a desk which is 1.2 m long and 0.8 m wide.
b Mark these in on your diagram. It does not matter where you put them.

4 This is part of a Derby street map.
The scale is 4 inches = 1 mile.

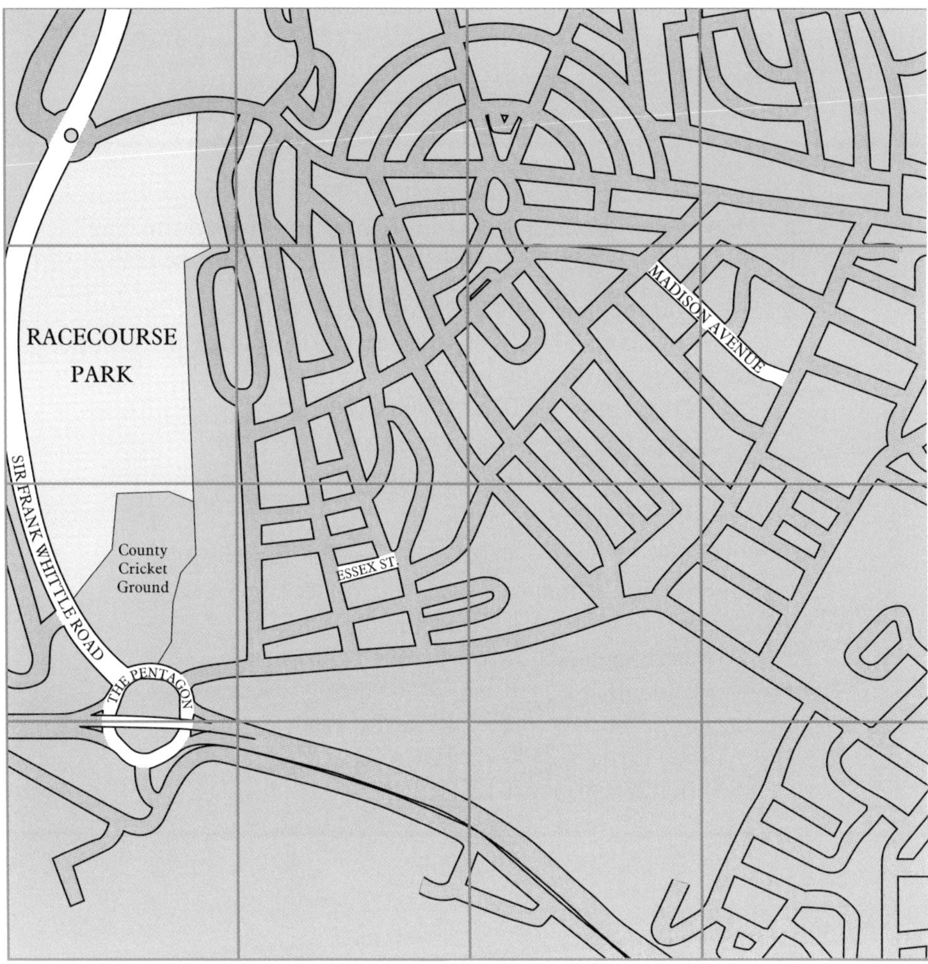

a What distance does 2 inches on the map represent?
b What distance does 1 inch represent?
c About how long is Racecourse Park on the map?
d About how long is the real Racecourse Park?
e How long is Madison Avenue on the map?
f How long is the real Madison Avenue?
g How long is the real Essex Street?
h What is the diameter of the Pentagon roundabout?
i Estimate the length of Sir Frank Whittle Road.
j The width of this section of map is about 5 inches.
What length does this represent?
● **k** The map shown is a square.
What area of Derby is shown on the map?

You can write a map scale as a ratio.
You do not put any units in when you do this.
The ratio tells you what 1 unit on the map represents in the real world.
A scale of 1 : 1000 means that 1 unit on the map is 1000 of those units in the real world.

Example A road map is drawn to the scale 1 : 30 000

a How many kilometres are represented by 3 cm on the map?
b How many miles are represented by 3 inches on the map?

a 1 unit on the map = 30 000 units in the real world.
3 cm on the map = 3 × 30 000 cm = 90 000 cm on the ground.
To change centimetres to metres, divide by 100:
90 000 cm = 90 000 ÷ 100 m = 900 m
To change metres to kilometres, divide by 1000:
900 m = 900 ÷ 1000 km = 0.9 km
So 3 cm represents 0.9 km.

b 1 unit on the map = 30 000 units in the real world.
3 inches on the map = 3 × 30 000 inches
= 90 000 inches
To change inches to yards, divide by 36:
90 000 inches = 90 000 ÷ 36 yards = 2500 yards
To change yards to miles, divide by 1760:
2500 yards = 2500 ÷ 1760 miles = 1.42 miles (2 dp)
So 3 inches represents 1.42 miles.

Exercise 19:8

1 A map is drawn to the scale 1 : 30 000.
a How many kilometres are represented by 1 cm on the map?
b How many kilometres are represented by 5 cm on the map?

2 A map is drawn to the scale 1 : 20 000.
a How many kilometres are represented by 1 cm on the map?
b How many kilometres are represented by 3 cm on the map?

3 Canfield School has a rectangular playing field.
The field measures 800 m by 700 m.
The Deputy Head draws a plan of the field. He uses a scale of 1 : 25 000.
What size should the field be on the plan?

4 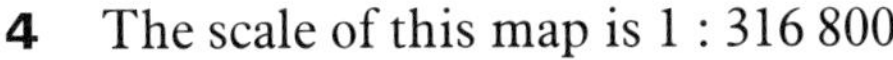 The scale of this map is 1 : 316 800

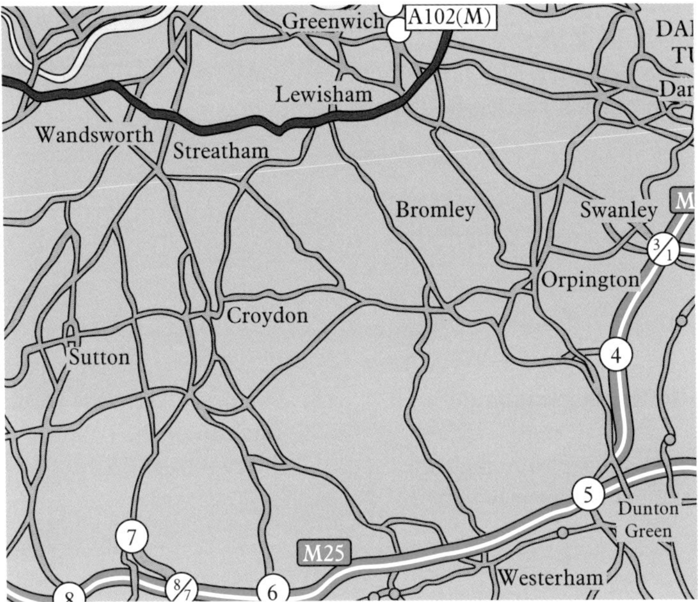

a What distance does 1 inch on the map represent?

b About how far is it between junctions 5 and 6 on the M25?

c About how far is it from Lewisham to Swanley along the A20?

5  The scale of this map is 1 inch = 250 yards.

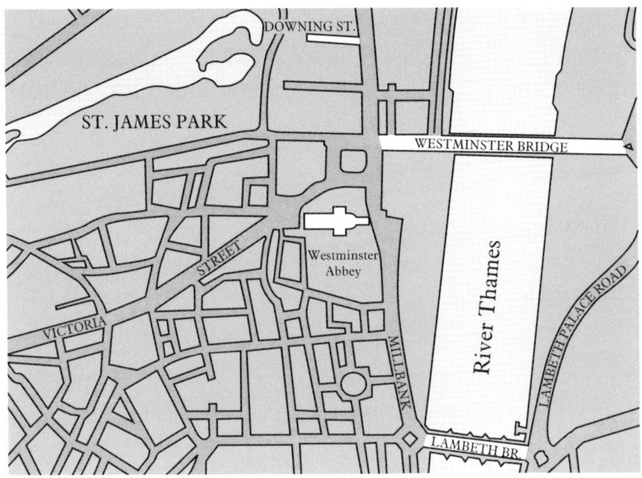

a Convert 250 yards into inches.

b Write the scale of the map as a ratio.

c About how far is it down the river from Westminster Bridge to Lambeth Bridge?

d About how far is it from Downing Street to Westminster Abbey?

There are other types of scale drawing.
Lots of people draw plans so that they can see what the real thing will look like.
Lizzy is a garden designer. She runs a busy company. She draws a plan of each garden before she plants it.

Here is a sketch of one of Lizzy's gardens.

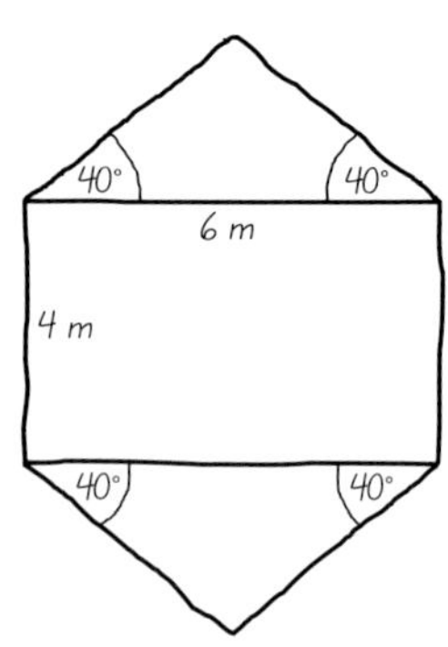

Lizzy wants to draw a scale plan of the garden.

She decides on a scale of 1 cm = 1 m.

(1) First she draws the rectangular section.
She uses a set square to make sure that the corners are exactly 90°.

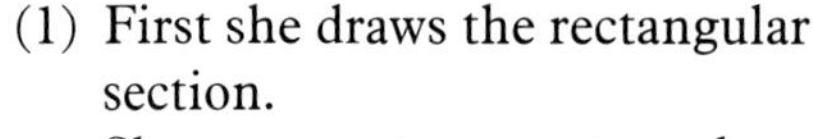

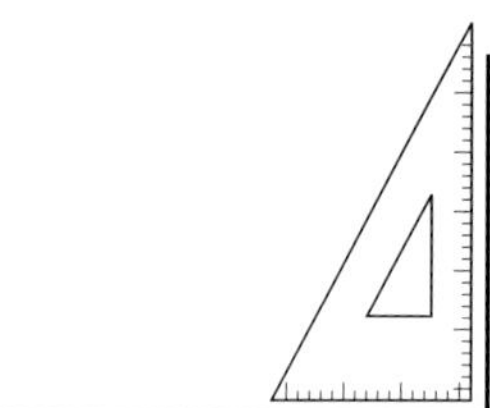

(2) Lizzy uses a protractor to measure the angles of the triangle.

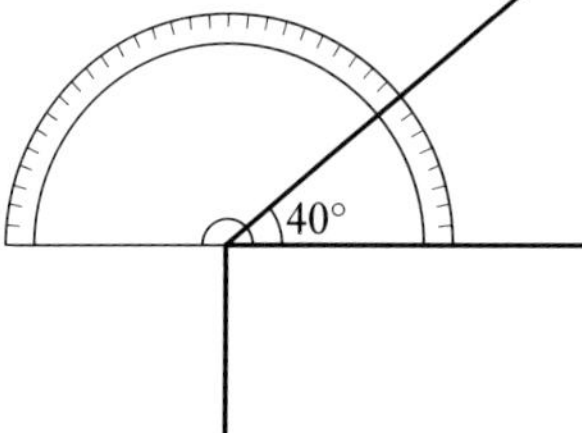

(3) She draws one line from each side.
The top of the triangle is where the two lines cross.

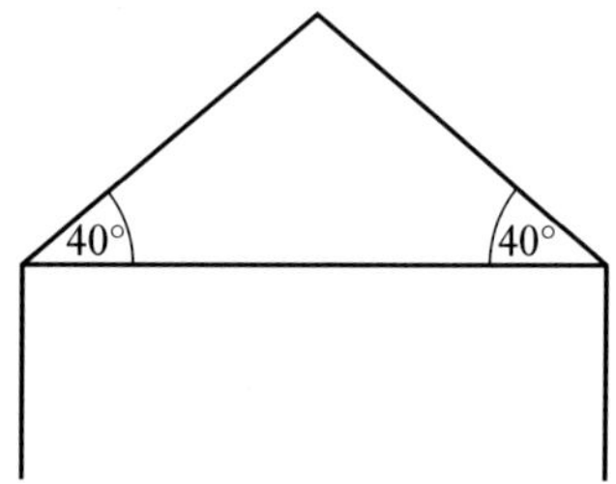

(4) She does the same for the other triangle to finish the plan.

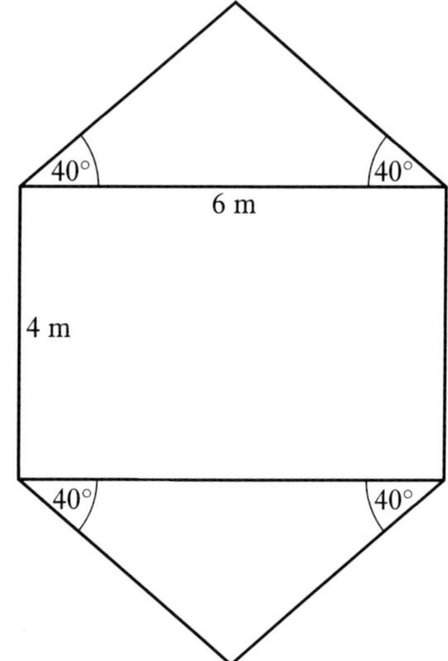

Exercise 19:9

1 Make a copy of Lizzy's plan.
Use a scale of 1 cm = 1 m.

2 Here is a sketch of another garden that Lizzy is designing.

a Draw the centre line.
Use a scale of 1 cm = 1 m.

b Draw the top triangle.
Use a protractor to measure the angles.

c Turn your diagram upside down.
Draw the other triangle to finish the plan.

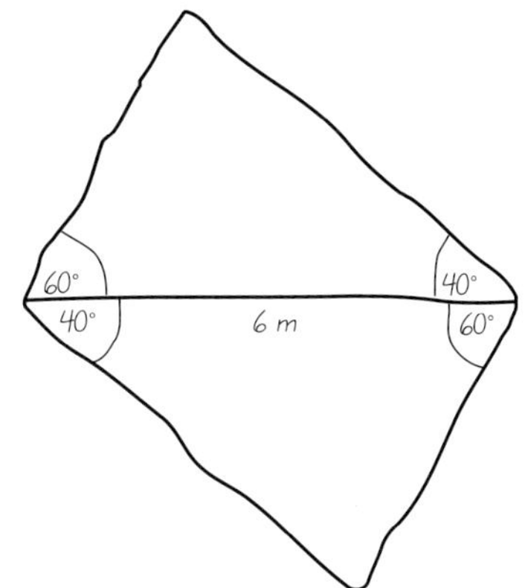

3 This is a sketch of a school playing field.

a Make a scale drawing of the field.
Use a scale of 1 cm = 5 m.

b Measure the sides of your drawing in centimetres.

c What is the perimeter of your drawing?

d What is the perimeter of the real field?

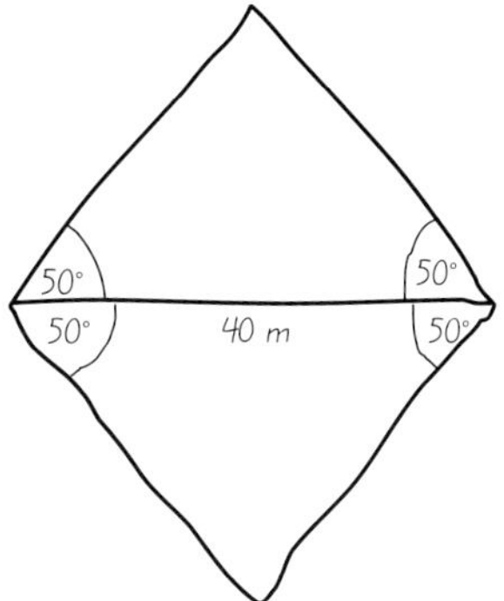

4 Lee is building a bird table with a nesting box on top.
Here is the sketch that he has made for it.

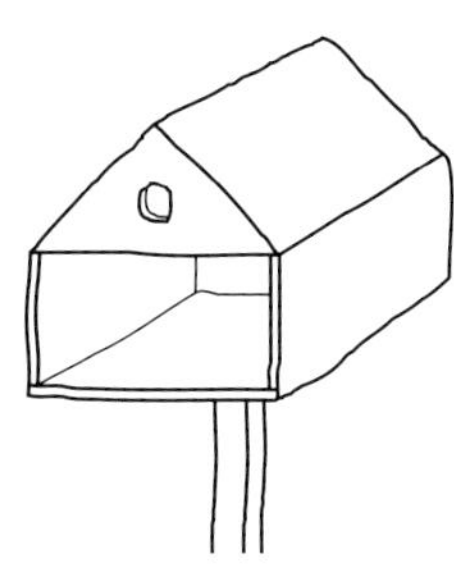

The end pieces look like this.
Make a scale drawing of the end piece.
Use a scale of 1 cm = 5 cm.

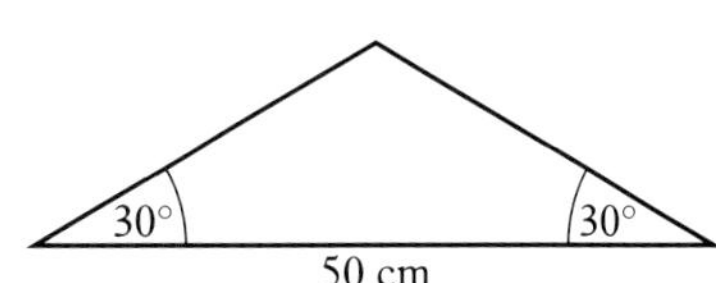

You can also draw triangles using compasses and a ruler.
To do this you need to know the lengths of all three sides.

Example Draw a triangle with sides 8 cm, 6 cm and 4 cm.

(1) Draw the 8 cm side with a ruler.
Leave space above it for the other sides.

8 cm

(2) Set your compasses to 6 cm.
Draw an arc from one end of your line.

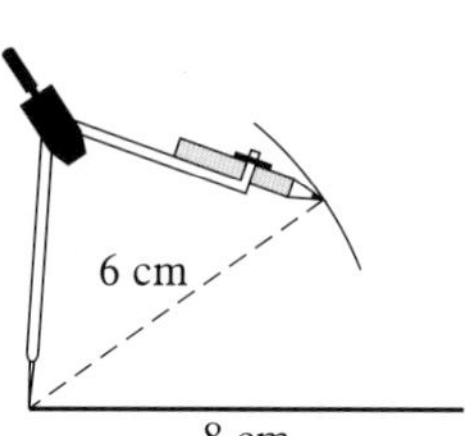

(3) Set your compasses to 4 cm.
Draw an arc from the other end of your line.
The two arcs should cross.
This is the third corner of the triangle.

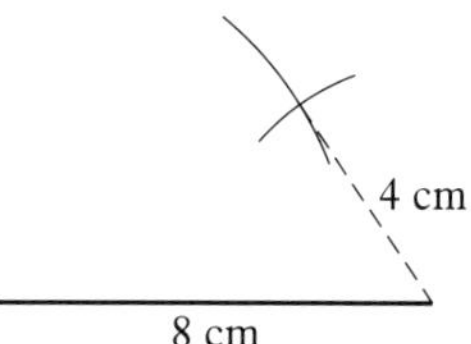

(4) Join the ends of your line to the crossing point.

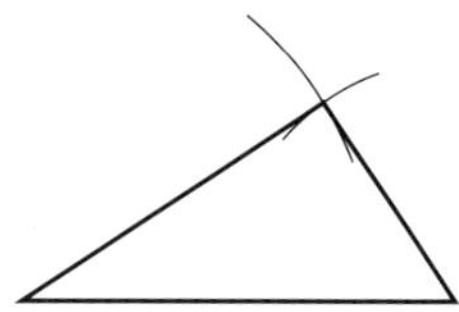

(5) Do not rub out your construction lines.
In an exam, these show your method.

Exercise 19:10

1 Use compasses to draw a triangle with sides 8 cm, 5 cm and 6 cm.

2 Draw an equilateral triangle with sides of 6 cm.

3 Construct each of these shapes.

a

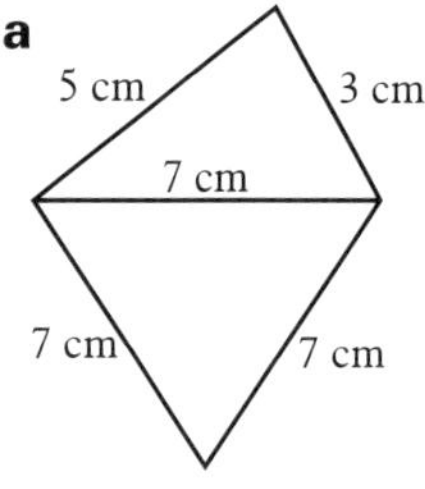

b

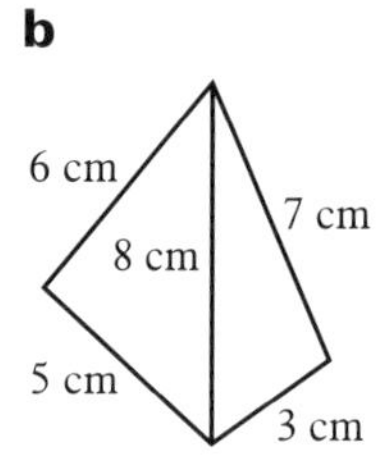

c

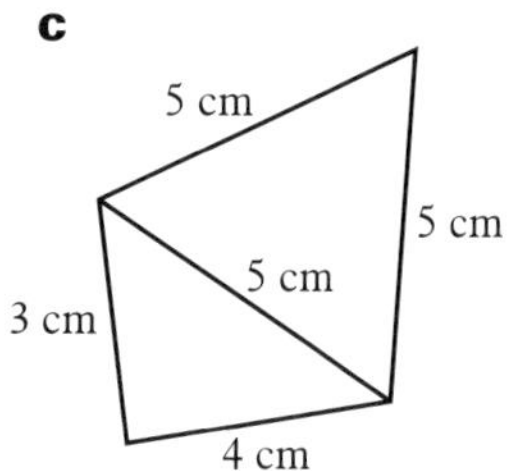

1 **a** Copy these shapes on to squared paper.
b Enlarge each shape using a scale factor of 3.

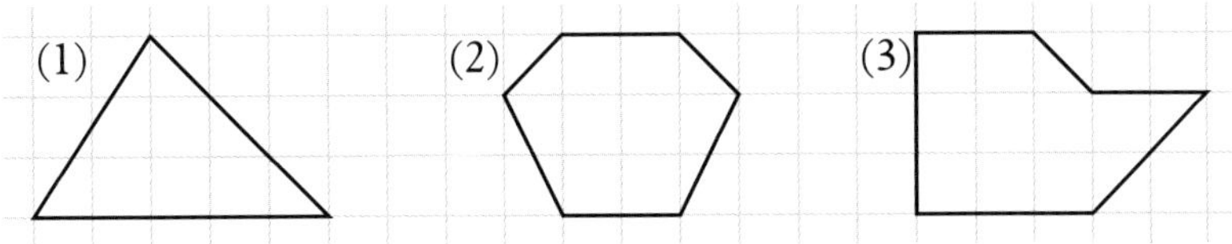

2 **a** Trace these shapes.
Use the red dot as the centre of enlargement each time.
b Enlarge each shape using a scale factor of $\frac{1}{2}$.

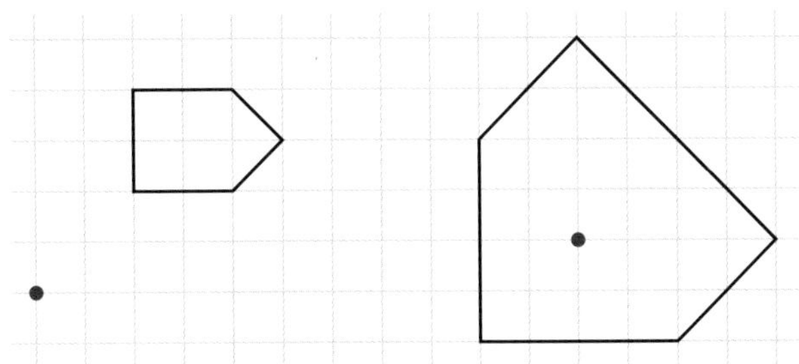

3 ABCD is a kite.

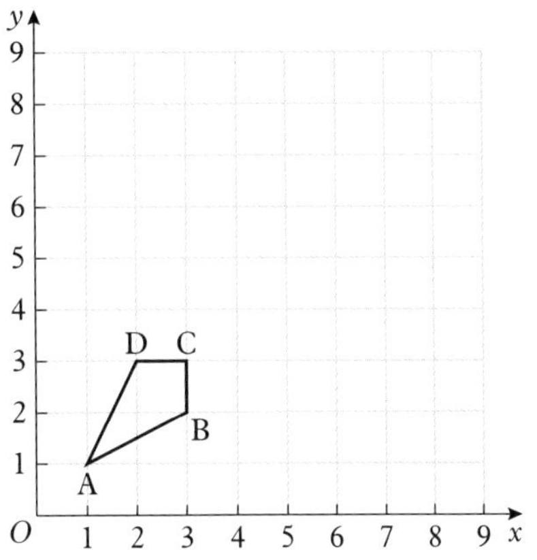

a Copy the diagram. Write down the co-ordinates of A, B, C and D.
b Measure the lengths of AC and BD.
c Find the new co-ordinates if the kite is enlarged by scale factor 3, centre (0, 0).
d Check these new co-ordinates are correct by drawing the enlargement. Show your construction lines. Label the image $A_1B_1C_1D_1$.
e Measure the lengths of A_1C_1 and B_1D_1. How do these lengths show if your enlargement is correct?
f Draw the new shape if $A_1B_1C_1D_1$ is enlarged by scale factor $\frac{1}{3}$, centre (0, 9). Label the image $A_2B_2C_2D_2$.
g Write down the scale factor of the inverse of the last enlargement.
h Is $A_1B_1C_1D_1$ similar to $A_2B_2C_2D_2$? Write down your reasons.

4 Sophie's bedroom is a rectangle 5.3 m long and 5.2 m wide.
a Draw a scale plan of Sophie's bedroom. Use a scale of 1 cm = 1 m.
b Sophie has a dressing table which is 1.8 m long and 1 m wide. She also has a computer desk which is 1.4 m long and 1.1 m wide. Mark these in on your diagram. It does not matter where you put them.

5 A map is drawn to the scale 1 : 25 000.
a How many kilometres are represented by 1 cm on the map?
b How many kilometres are represented by 4 cm on the map?

6 A map is drawn to the scale 1 : 30 000.
a How many miles are represented by 1 inch on the map?
b How many miles are represented by 6 inches on the map?
Round your answers to 2 dp when necessary.

7 This is a sketch of a park.
a Make a scale drawing of the park. Use a scale of 1 cm = 5 m.
b What is the perimeter of the real park?

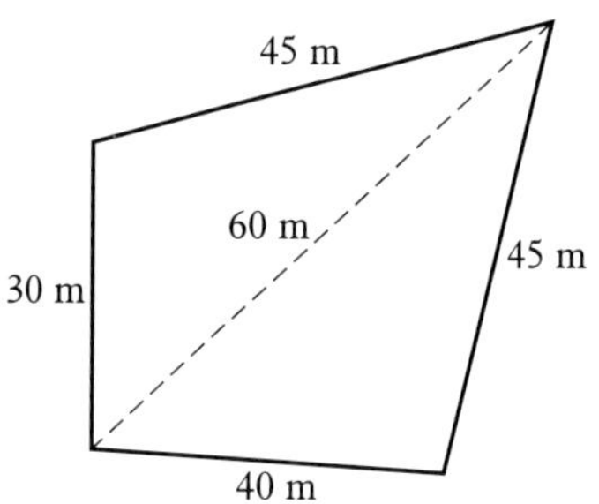

8 This is the sketch of part of a net of a square based pyramid. Draw an accurate net for this pyramid.

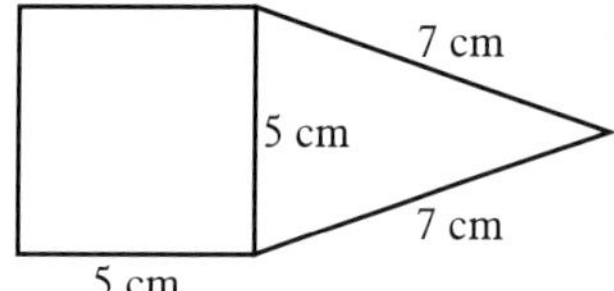

9 A model steam train is built to a scale of 1 : 150.
a The height of the funnel on the model is 0.5 cm. What is the height of the real funnel?
b The length of the real train is 12 m. What is the length of the model train?

1 A map is drawn to a scale of 1 : 25 000.

a Find the length represented by 1 cm on the map.

b Find the area represented by 1 cm^2 on the map.

2 The diagram shows a sketch of a map. It is not to scale.
When the map is drawn to scale, the distance between A and B is 28 cm.
Work out the scale of the map.
Give your answer in the form 1 : n where n is an integer.

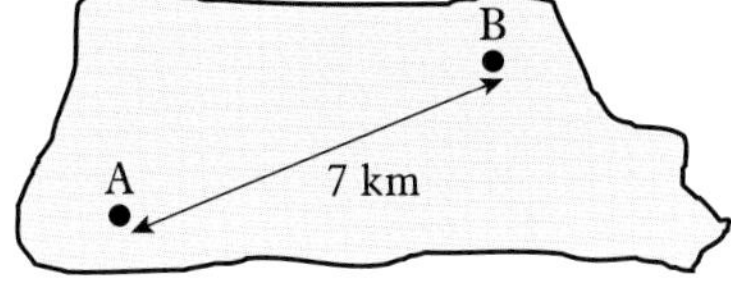

3 Howard wants to work out how far away a tower is on the other side of the river.
He measures a distance of 100 m along the side of the river.
He then measures the angles from the ends of his lines to the base of the tower.

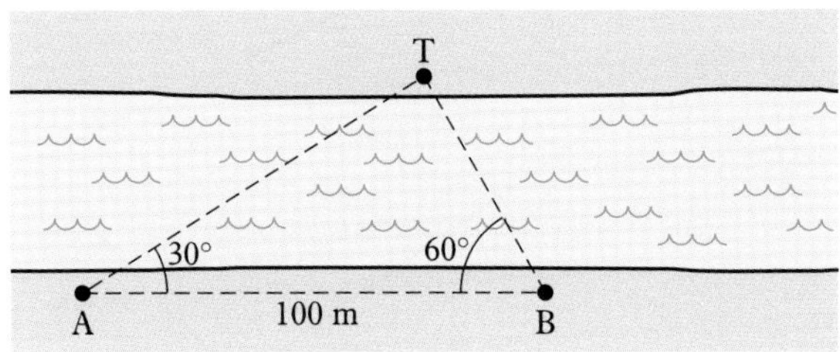

a Draw an accurate scale plan of this situation.

b Find the shortest distance from the tower to the bank of the river where Howard is standing.

4 An alien spaceship is able to shrink when under attack. When it shrinks all its angles stay the same. These are plan views of the ship before and after attack.

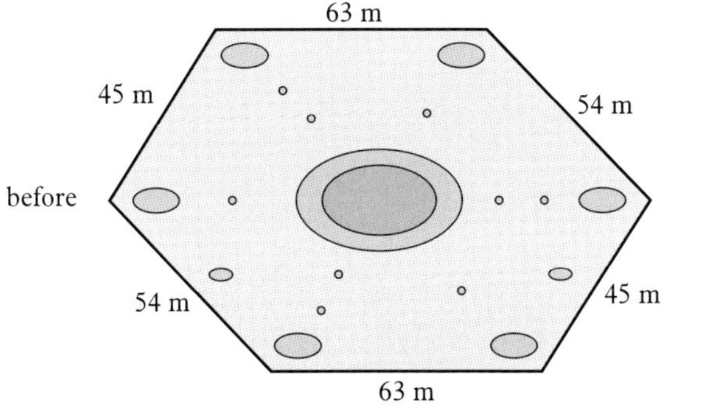

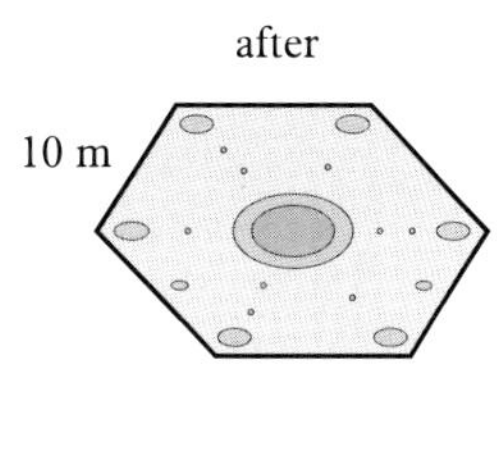

a Work out the scale factor of the enlargement.

b Find the lengths of the missing sides.

1 Copy these shapes onto squared paper. Enlarge each shape with the scale factor given. Use C as the centre of enlargement.

a **b**

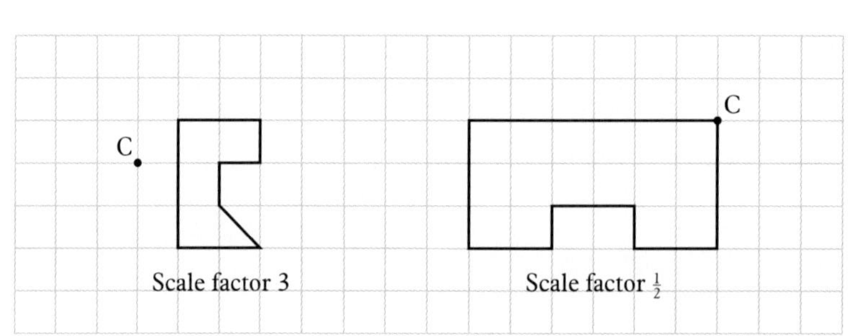

2 These two shapes are similar.
Find the missing lengths marked with letters.

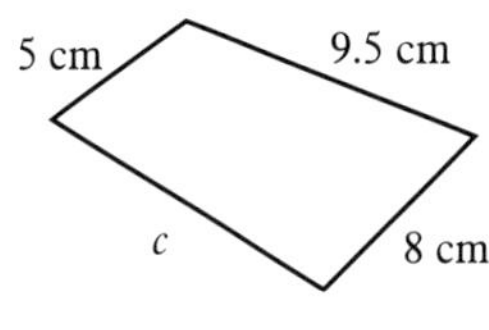

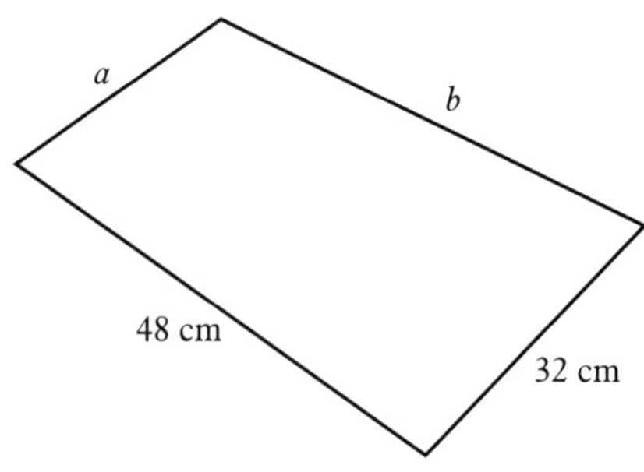

3 A triangle has a perimeter of 8.5 cm. The triangle is enlarged by a scale factor of 5. Write down the perimeter of the new triangle.

4 A map is drawn to the scale 1 : 30 000.
a How many kilometres are represented by 1 cm on the map?
b How many kilometres are represented by 7 cm on the map?

5 Construct these triangles.

a

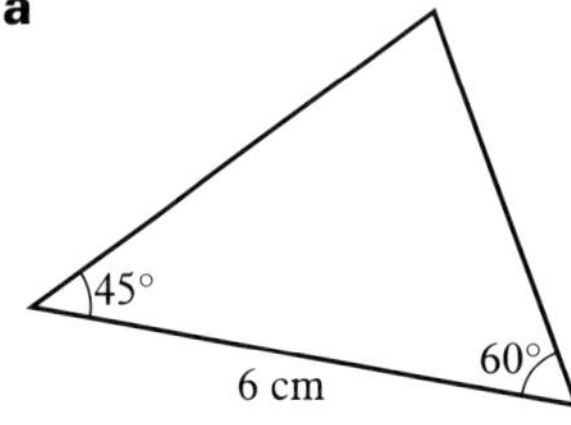

b

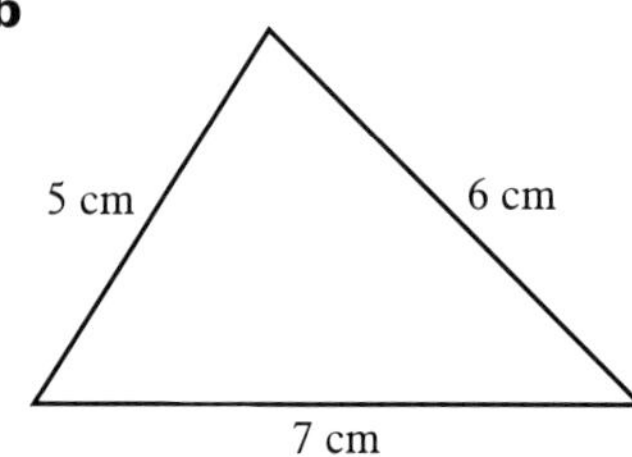

20 Graphs: moving on

CORE

1 Travel graphs
Measuring time
Using a calculator to work out times
Finding distances, speeds and times
Looking at compound units
Going on a journey

2 Line graphs
Deciding when to join points up
Going up in steps
Using graphs to change currencies

3 Graph sketching
Plotting points
Sketching graphs
Looking at slopes
Going round go-kart tracks
Designing water tanks

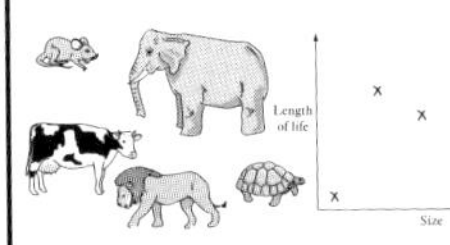

QUESTIONS

EXTENSION

TEST YOURSELF

1 Travel graphs

The scientists who did this learnt about this topic at school.
Look where it landed them!

Terry is a taxi driver.
He has to pick up Richard by 10.18 a.m.
He leaves at 9.32 a.m. The journey takes 45 minutes.
When does Terry reach Richard?

You can work this out using the clock.
From 9.32 a.m. it is 28 minutes to 10 a.m.
This uses 28 minutes of the 45 minutes.
So there are 45 − 28 = **17** minutes left.
These **17** minutes are after 10 a.m.
So Terry arrives at 10.17 a.m.

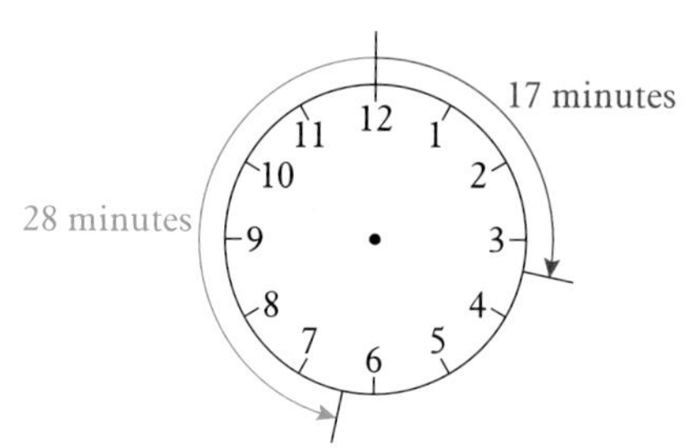

Exercise 20:1

1 Work out the time that Terry arrives to pick up these passengers.

a Terry sets off at 8.27 a.m. He takes 46 minutes to reach Fred.

b Terry sets off at 11.30 a.m. He takes 52 minutes to get to Ethel.

c Terry sets off at 2.26 p.m. He takes 48 minutes to reach Abigail.

d Terry sets off at 10.32 p.m. He takes 29 minutes to get to Nathan.

e Terry sets off at 9.35 a.m. He takes 2 hours 56 minutes to reach Amanda.

f Terry sets off at 14:12 He takes 30 minutes to get to Alan.

g Terry sets off at 06:32 He takes 4 hours 51 minutes to reach Chloe.

h Terry sets off at 22:48 He takes 2 hours 39 minutes to get to Mike.

There is another way of measuring time taken.

To find the length of time between time A and time B:

(1) **Find how long in minutes to the next hour from time A.**
(2) **Find how many whole hours are taken.**
(3) **Find how many minutes past the hour for time B.**
(4) Add all these times together.

So to find how long it is from 10.43 a.m. to 2.29 p.m.:

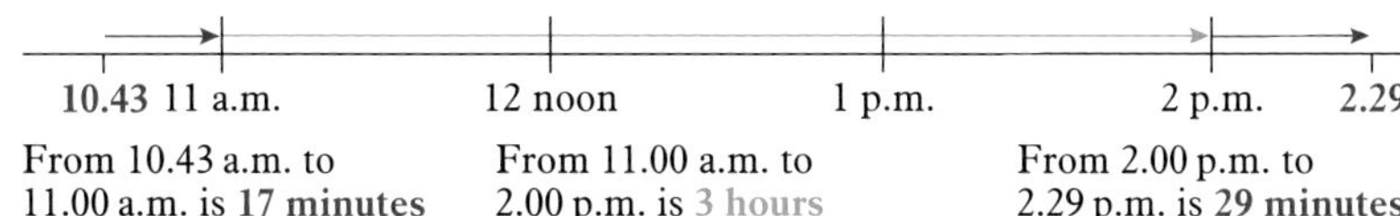

The total time is **17 minutes** + **3 hours** + **29 minutes** = **3 hours 46 minutes**

2 How long is it between these times?

a 2.20 p.m. and 3.40 p.m.
b 7.32 a.m. and 1.07 p.m.
c 21:35 and 23:42
d 22:49 and 06:38

Using a calculator to work out times

You can use these keys to work with times   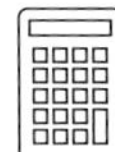 

The keys stand for degrees minutes and seconds. They are used for calculations with angles, but you can use them for time.

If you want to enter 2 h 45 min on the calculator:

Key in: 

your calculator shows 2°45
This means 2 h 45 min.

Key in: **2nd F** **DMS** to give 2.75
This is 2 h 45 min as a decimal.

Key in: 

your calculator shows 2° 45° 0
This means 2 h 45 min.

Key in: **Shift** **°’”** to give 2.75
This is 2 h 45 min as a decimal.

3 Copy this table. Enter each time into your calculator and fill in what your calculator shows.

Time	h min display	decimal display
2 h 30 min		
5 h 15 min		
01:40		
14:24		

You can use your calculator to work out lengths of times if you put the time in using the 24 hour clock.

If you want to find how long it is from 7.36 a.m. to 4.09 p.m.:
4.09 p.m. is 16:09 in 24 hour time and 7.36 a.m. is 07:36 in 24 hour time

Key in:  **1** **6** **DMS** **0** **9** **−** **0** **7** **DMS** **3** **6** **=**

or:  **1** **6** **° ’ ”** **0** **9** **° ’ ”** **−** **0** **7** **° ’ ”** **3** **6** **° ’ ”** **=**

This gives the answer of 8 h 33 min.

4 Use a calculator to find how long it is between these times.

a 7.40 a.m. to 8.20 a.m.
b 9.15 a.m. to 10.52 a.m.
c 3.41 a.m. to 11.09 a.m.
d 4.29 a.m. to noon
e 07:49 to 14:06
f 11.42 a.m. to 1.18 p.m.
g 9.37 a.m. to 7.04 p.m.
h 1.51 a.m. to midnight

Working with distances, speeds and times

Terry drives from Oxford to Southampton.

This is a distance of 100 km. It takes Terry 2 hours.

His average speed is $100 \div 2 = 50$ km per hour.

So $\text{average speed} = \dfrac{\text{total distance}}{\text{total time}}$

There is a triangle that can help you to remember how to use this formula.

You remember $S = \dfrac{D}{T}$ then write out this triangle.

Cover up the letter you want. Then what you see is the rule.

Example Terry drives 150 km in 2 hours 30 minutes.
Find his average speed.

You need the formula for speed:

If you cover S you see $\dfrac{D}{T}$ so $S = \dfrac{D}{T}$

$D = 150$ km, $T = 2$ h 30 min

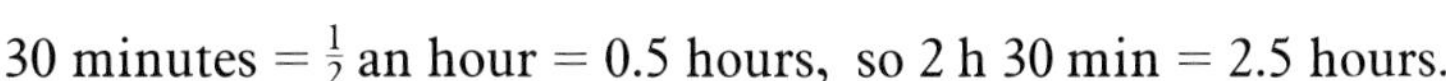

30 minutes = $\frac{1}{2}$ an hour = 0.5 hours, so 2 h 30 min = 2.5 hours.

Put these values in the formula. $S = \dfrac{150}{2.5}$ so $S = 60$ km/h.

If you have a **DMS** key, you can key in hours and minutes.

Key in:

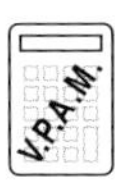

1 5 0 ÷ 2 ° ' " 3 0 ° ' " =

to get 60 km/h.

Exercise 20:2

1 Find the average speeds in km/h for each distance and time.

	distance	time		distance	time
a	120 km	2 h	**d**	189 km	2 h 15 min
b	270 km	6 h	**e**	270 km	15 min
c	330 km	5 h 30 min	• **f**	720 km	2 days

• **2** Robert drives a van for a removal company.
He sets off from the depot at 10.48 a.m.
He drives 12 km.
He arrives at Alice's old house at 10.58 a.m.
He completes the removals in 44 minutes.
Then Robert sets off for Alice's new house.
He drives 8 km. He arrives at 11.48 a.m.
Which journey does he drive at the greatest average speed?

Example Vanessa drives 243 km at an average speed of 54 km per hour. Find how long this journey takes.

You need the formula for time:

If you cover T you see $\frac{D}{S}$

so $T = \frac{D}{S}$

$D = 243$ km, $S = 54$ km/h

So put these values in the formula. $T = \frac{243}{50}$

Key in:  

 2 4 3 ÷ 5 4 = Shift °’”

to get 4 h 30 min.

3 Find the time for each of these journeys. Give your answer in hours.

	distance	average speed			distance	average speed
a	20 km	5 km/h		**d**	4 km	8 km/h
b	280 km	35 km/h		**e**	186 km	279 km/h
c	6000 km	800 km/h	•	**f**	4500 km	36 000 km/h

Example Franz skis for 2 hours 15 minutes at an average speed of 32 km/h. Find how far Franz skis.

You need the formula for distance:

If you cover D you see ST

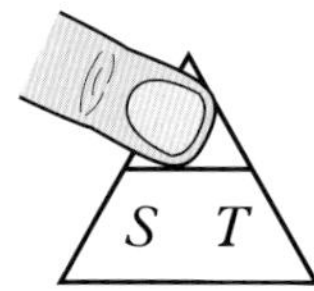

so $D = ST$

$S = 32$ km/h, $T = 2$ h 15 min

Key in:  2 DMS 1 5 2nd F DMS or  2 °’” 1 5 °’” = Shift °’”

to give 2 h 15 min = 2.25 h.

Then put these values in the formula: $D = 32 \times 2.25 = 72$ km

4 Find the distance for each of these journeys.

	time	average speed			time	average speed
a	2 h	15 km/h		**d**	2 h 12 min	12 miles/h
b	4 h	15 km/h		**e**	3 h 24 min	1870 km/h
c	19 seconds	11 m/s	•	**f**	202 days	36 000 km/h

Compound units You can measure speed in lots of different units, metres per second, miles per hour, kilometres per day …
Speed is an example of a quantity which has **compound units**.
This is because it is a combination of two separate measures: distance *and* time.

There are other quantities that have compound units.
A drill where the speed is measured in revolutions per minute, filling an oil tank where the rate of flow is measured in litres per second.
Measuring the rate a car uses petrol in miles per gallon.

Exercise 20:3

1 An antique turntable spins 312 times to play an old 4 minute record. How many revolutions per minute is this?

2 Reg is a runner bean picker. He picks 1008 pounds in 9 hours 20 minutes. Work out his rate of picking in pounds per hour.

3 A petrol pump fills a car with 32 litres of petrol in 2 minutes 8 seconds. Give this as a rate in:
a litres per second **b** litres per minute **c** litres per hour

4 A concert hall fills at an average rate of 142 people per minute. It takes 42 minutes to completely fill the hall. How many people does the hall hold?

5 Carolyn drives a thirsty car. She puts in 11 gallons of petrol and drives it 242 miles when it needs filling again. Work out its consumption in miles per gallon.

6 Dennis the farmer grows 14 kg of potatoes per square metre. He grows these in a field 80 m long by 120 metres wide. If he bags his potatoes in 50 kg bags, how many bags does he need?

7 In East Yorkshire, part of the coast is eroded at the rate of 40 centimetres per year. If this continues at this rate, how far inland will the coastline be in the year 4200? Give your answer in kilometres.

Travel graphs

Travel graphs are used to show distance and time.
They show you the distance that something has moved away from a starting point. Time always goes on the horizontal axis.
You can also work out speeds from travel graphs.

This graph shows Terry's journey from Oxford to Southampton.

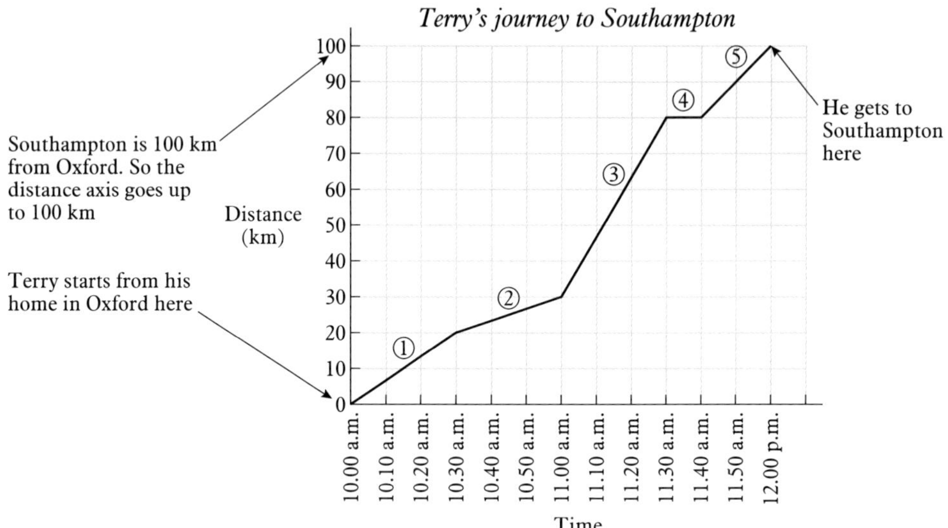

This is part ① of Terry's journey.
The graph is sloping upwards.
This means that Terry is driving away from his house.

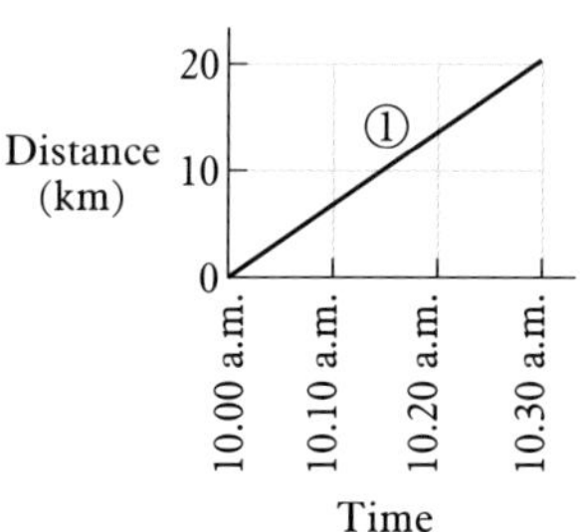

He drives 20 km in half an hour.
Speed = Distance ÷ Time
So his speed for this part is given by

$$S = \frac{20}{0.5} = 40 \text{ km/h}$$

In part ② of the graph, Terry is still travelling away from his house. He only moves 10 km in 30 minutes. He is probably stuck in slow moving traffic.
His speed here is

$$S = \frac{10}{0.5} = 20 \text{ km/h}$$

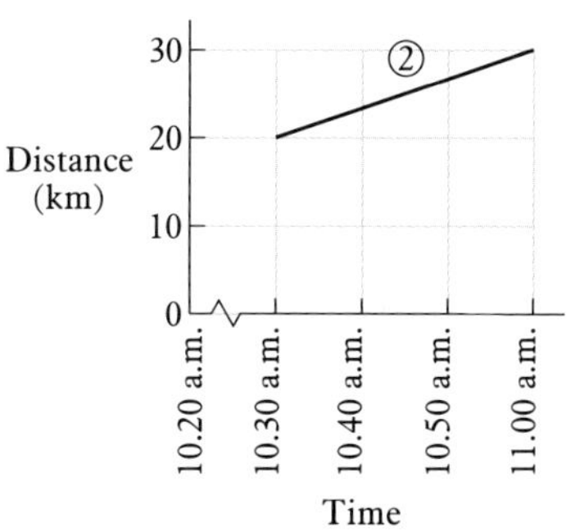

In part ③ of the graph, the graph has its steepest slope.
Terry travels 50 km in 30 minutes.
He is going much faster in this part.
His speed here is

$$S = \frac{50}{0.5} = 100 \text{ km/h}$$

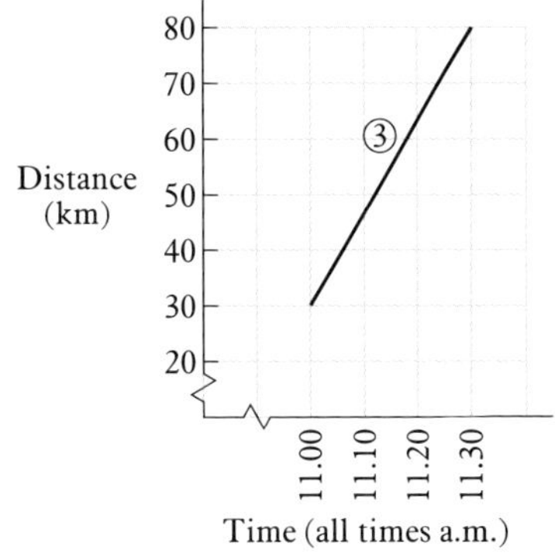

Part ④ of the graph looks like this.
The graph is horizontal.
This means that Terry is not moving.
He has stopped somewhere for 10 minutes.
His speed here is zero.

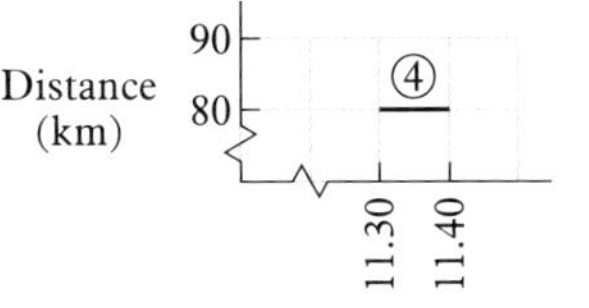

The last part of the graph looks like this.
The graph is sloping upwards again.
He travels 20 km in 20 minutes.
His speed here is

$$S = \frac{20}{0.\dot{3}} = 60 \text{ km/h}$$

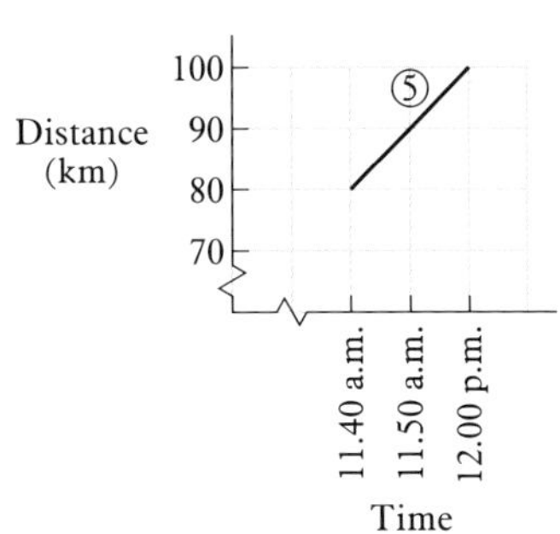

Look at the whole graph again.
The dotted red line covers the total distance. It also covers the total time.
You can use the red line to work out the average speed for the *whole* journey.

$$\text{Average speed} = \frac{\text{total distance}}{\text{total time}}$$

Terry travels 100 km in 2 hours.
So for this journey

$$\text{average speed} = \frac{100}{2} = 50 \text{ km/h}$$

Terry's journey to Southampton

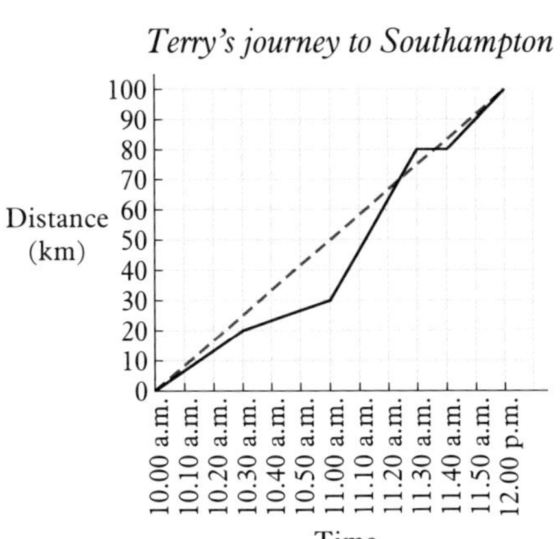

Exercise 20:4

1 This is a graph of John's trip to Wembley Stadium.
He is travelling to see Newcastle United in the F.A. Cup.

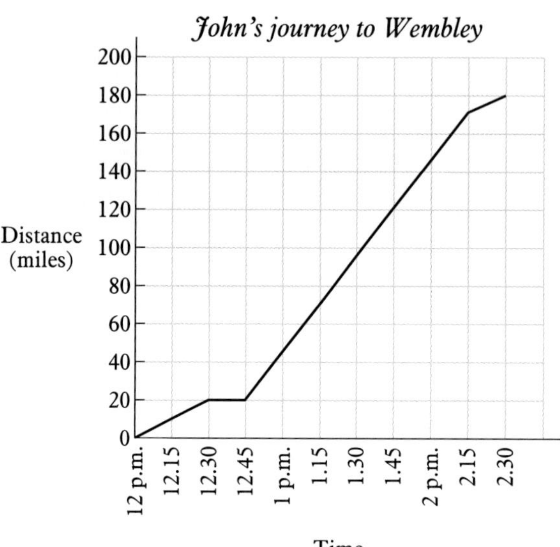

He starts by driving from his home in Sheffield to the station.

- **a** How long does this take?
- **b** How far is the station from his house?
- **c** Work out his speed in miles per hour for this part of the journey.
  John has to wait at the station for his train.
- **d** How long does he have to wait?
  John then catches a fast train to London.
- **e** How far does the train travel until John gets off at 2.15 p.m.?
- **f** Work out the speed of this train.
  John then catches an underground train. He doesn't have to wait.
  The underground train travels the last 10 miles in 15 minutes.
- **g** Work out the speed of this train.
- • **h** Work out John's average speed for the entire journey.

2 Sarah walks at 4 km/h for 30 minutes. Then she waits for a bus for 30 minutes. Then she travels for an hour on the bus at 40 km/h.

a Copy these axes on to squared paper.
b Show Sarah's journey on your graph.
c Work out Sarah's average speed for the whole journey.

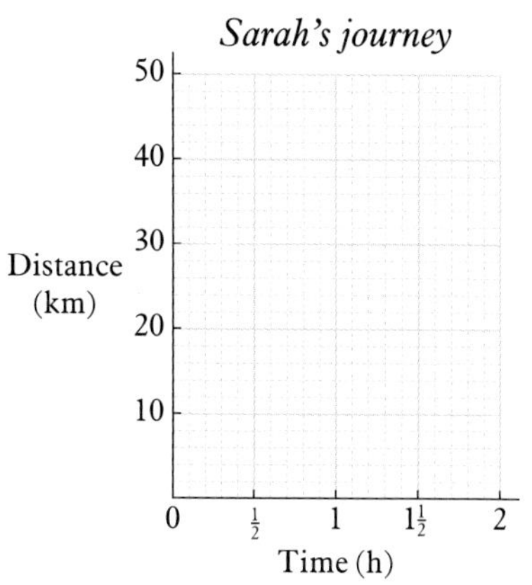

Some travel graphs show journeys that go back to where they started. You work out the average speed of the entire journey in a different way for these.

Mrs Shipley drives to Dover to catch a ferry. The ferry is cancelled because of storms. She has a cup of tea, then she drives back home to New Cross. The graph shows her journey.

Her speed on the outward journey is $\frac{100}{1} = 100$ km/h.

Her speed on the return journey is $\frac{100}{1.25} = 80$ km/h.

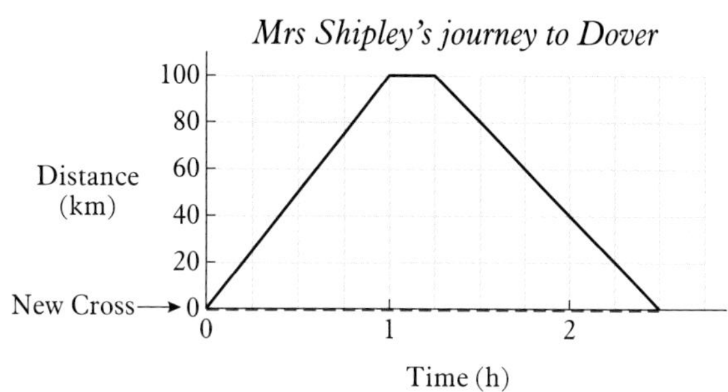

She has travelled a total distance of 200 km in a total time of $2\frac{1}{2}$ hours.

So her average speed for the entire journey is $\frac{200}{2.5} = 80$ km/h.

You use each distance from the graph and add them together to give the total distance. You do not use the red dotted line!

3 George walks to the local shop. The graph shows his journey. He buys a loaf and chats with the shopkeeper. Then he walks home. Work out his average speed:

a going to the shop
b going back home
c for the entire journey

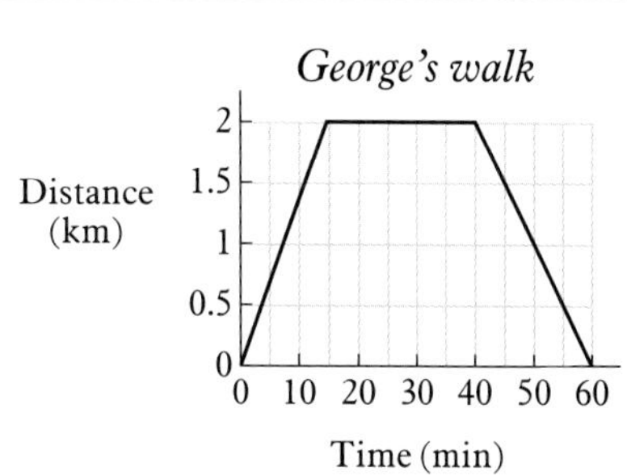

2 Line graphs

When you draw graphs you usually plot some points then join them with lines.

Sometimes you can't join the points. The lines in between the points may not have a meaning.

This happens a lot in statistics.
If you are plotting data about numbers of people, you can't join the points.
You can't have 2.8 people for example!

These two graphs show the number of people in a supermarket queue between 12:00 and 13:00.

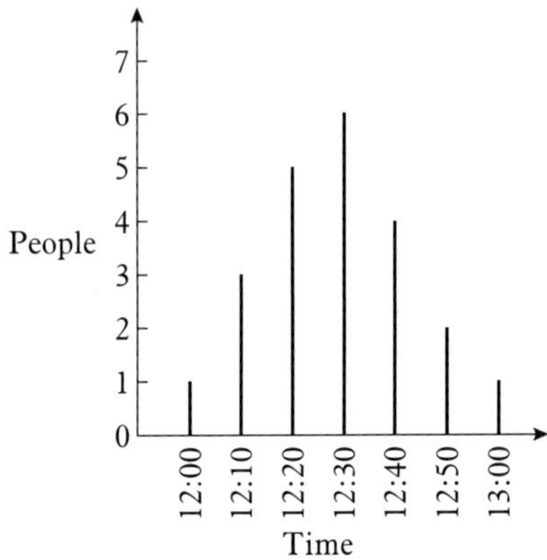

This is a **vertical line graph.**
It is like a bar chart with very thin bars!
This is the correct type of graph for this data.

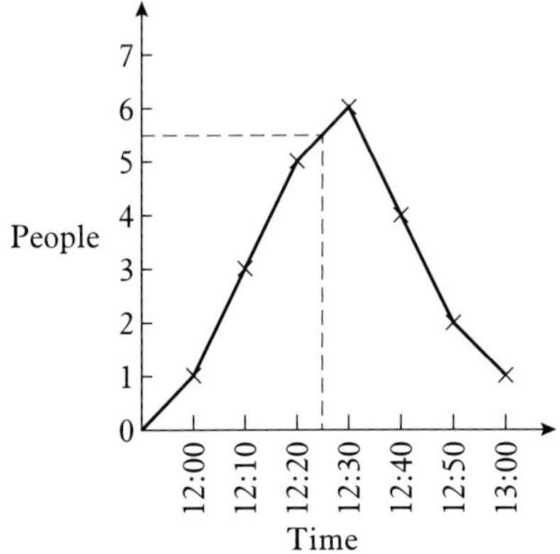

This is a **line graph**.
You can join the points together with straight lines.
This is the wrong type of graph for this data. It shows that there were 5.5 people in the queue at 12:25!

Exercise 20:5

1 Write down whether you would draw a line graph or a vertical line graph to show each of these:
a the number of bicycles sold each month by a shop
b the number of Smarties in 10 tubes
c the temperature of a cup of coffee as it cools down
d the number of people on a train during its journey
e the weight of a baby over a period of 8 weeks

2 Mr Jiwa has oil-fired central heating.
He records the amount of oil left in the tank every hour one afternoon.

Time	13:00	14:00	15:00	16:00	17:00
Oil left (litres)	155	148	140	132	125

a Draw a suitable graph of this data.
b Estimate the amount of oil left at 15:30.

3 The following data shows the number of people in a casualty waiting room every hour one afternoon.

Time	13:00	14:00	15:00	16:00	17:00
Number of people	16	21	23	19	31

Draw a suitable graph of this data.

Some graphs have their points joined up but also have gaps in them!
These graphs are called **step graphs**.

Example The current costs for first class mail are shown in this table.

Weight up to ...	60 g	100 g	150 g	200 g	250 g
Cost	27 p	41 p	57 p	72 p	84 p

Show this data on a graph.

All letters up to 60 g cost 27 p.
This produces the first horizontal line.
As soon as a letter goes over 60 g the cost jumps to 41 p.
This produces the second horizontal line.
The two lines are not joined together.
The graph continues in the same way and produces a series of steps.

The finished graph looks like this.

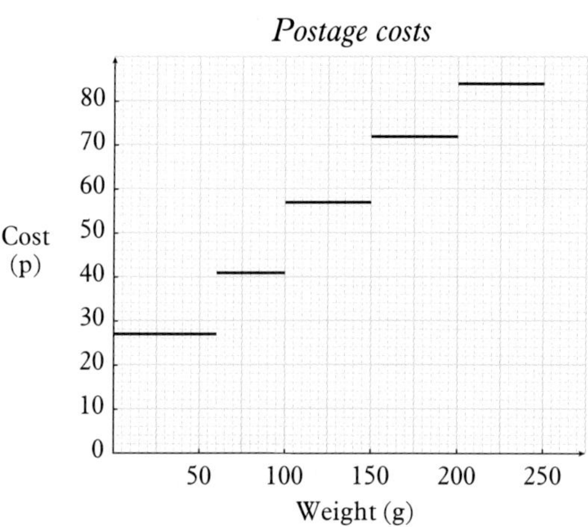

4 This table shows the costs for second class mail.

Weight up to ...	60 g	100 g	150 g	200 g	250 g
Cost	19 p	33 p	44 p	54 p	66 p

Draw a graph to show these costs.

5 The costs for special delivery are much higher.

Weight up to ...	100 g	500 g	1 kg	2 kg	10 kg
Cost	£3.50	£3.80	£4.95	£6.20	£17.80

Draw a graph to show these costs.

6 Radicomms is a new telephone company. Their prices for long distance calls are shown in the table.

RADICOMMS

Call time up to ...	1 min	3 min	5 min	10 min	20 min
Daytime cost	6 p	15 p	25 p	45 p	80 p
Evening cost	3 p	8 p	12 p	30 p	30 p

a Show both sets of data on the same graph.
Use different colours for each rate.

● **b** Radnet is Radicomms' main rival.
Their prices work differently. They charge 4.5 p per minute during the day and 2.5 p per minute in the evening. They charge by the second so their charges produce a straight line graph.
Draw Radnet's charges on your graph.

● **c** Radnet is cheaper than Radicomms in each charge rate at the start.
Write down the length of the call when Radicomms becomes cheaper than Radnet at each rate.

Conversion graphs

A conversion graph is a graph that you can use to change from one unit to another.
Conversion graphs are always straight lines.

Example

a Draw a conversion graph to change from miles to kilometres.
5 miles = 8 kilometres.

b Use your graph to convert 18 miles to kilometres.

c Use your graph to convert 32 km to miles.

a It does not matter which unit goes on which axis.
Plot the point (5 miles, 8 km) and the point (0 miles, 0 km).
Join the points with a straight line and extend the line upwards.

b Follow the blue line on the graph.
18 miles is 28.8 km.

c Follow the red line on the graph.
32 km is 20 miles.

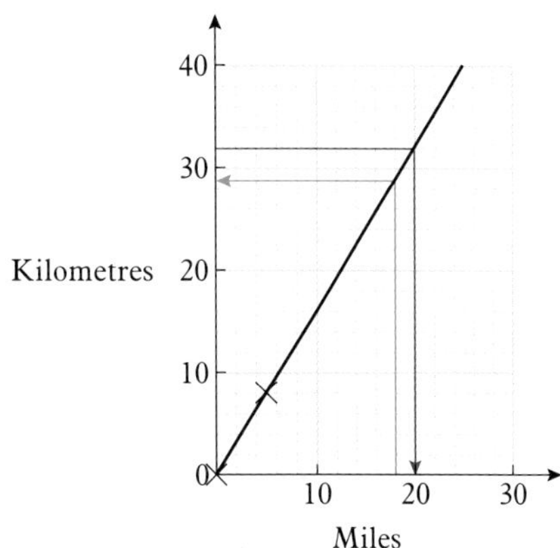

Exercise 20:6

1 Jaswinder is going on holiday to the USA. He needs to exchange his money into dollars ($).
£1 will buy $1.60
The bank has a graph to help customers.

a Draw axes from £0 to £50 and $0 to $80

b Mark the points (£0, $0) and (£50, $80).

c Join the points to make a conversion graph.

d Convert the following amounts into $.
(1) £20 (2) £35 (3) £42

e Convert the following amounts into £.
(1) $32 (2) $50 (3) $61

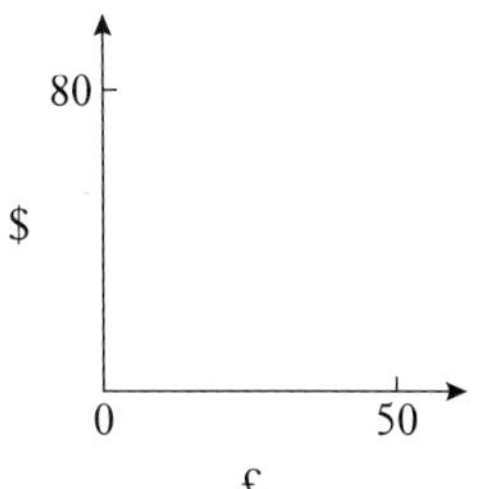

2 The graph to convert temperature from °C to °F is a straight line but it does not go through (0, 0).
This is because 0 °C = 32 °F.
The boiling point of water is 100 °C = 212 °F.
a Draw a conversion graph to convert temperature from °C to °F.
b Convert the following into °C (1) 41 °F (2) 59 °F (3) 140 °F
c Convert the following into °F (1) 30 °C (2) 75 °C (3) 81 °C

3 Banks actually buy and sell foreign currency at different rates.
If you sell foreign currency back to the bank when you return from your holidays, they will not give you such a good rate for your money.
Here are some examples of a bank's rates.

Currency	Bank sells at (for £1)	Bank buys at (for £1)
Euro	1.56	1.62
Hong Kong $	10.64	11.09
Norway krone	12.34	12.76

a For each currency draw a conversion graph showing both the buying and selling rates. Use different colours.
b Dave exchanges £40 into euro. How many euro does he get?
c Dave returns half his euro to the bank and exchanges them for £. How much does he get back?
● **d** What is his percentage loss?
e Anne returns from holiday with 600 Hong Kong $. How much will she get for them?
f If you exchanged £50 into krone and exchanged your krone straight back into £, how much would you lose?

4 Last year Lindsey went to Switzerland on a skiing holiday.
She converted her £ into Swiss Francs.
The rate was £1 = 2.18 Swiss Francs.
a Draw axes from £0 to £10 and 0 Francs to 240 Francs.
b Draw a conversion graph.
c Lindsey took £75. How many Swiss Francs did she get?
d This year, the rate is £1 = 2.29 Swiss Francs.
Put a new line on your graph to show this year's rate.
● **e** How many £ will Lindsey have to convert to get the same number of Swiss Francs as she did last year?

3 Graph sketching

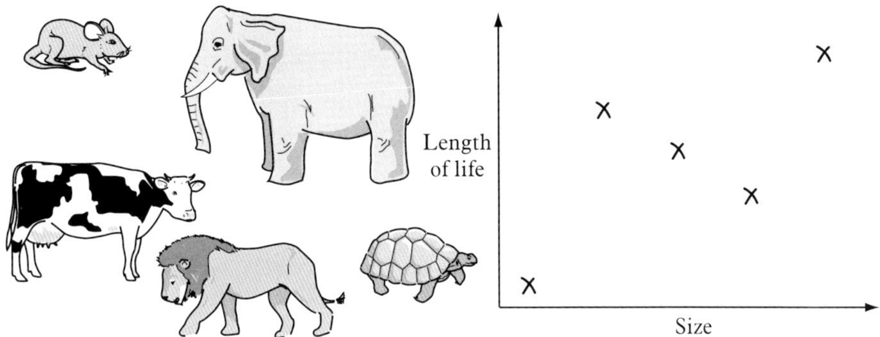

The graph shows the size and the length of life of the 5 animals in the picture. Can you decide which point represents each animal?

The graph does not have any scales on the axes. It is just a sketch graph. It is used to show a general pattern rather than to give accurate readings.

Exercise 20:7

1 Look at these pictures of cars.
Copy the axes shown and mark a point for each car.

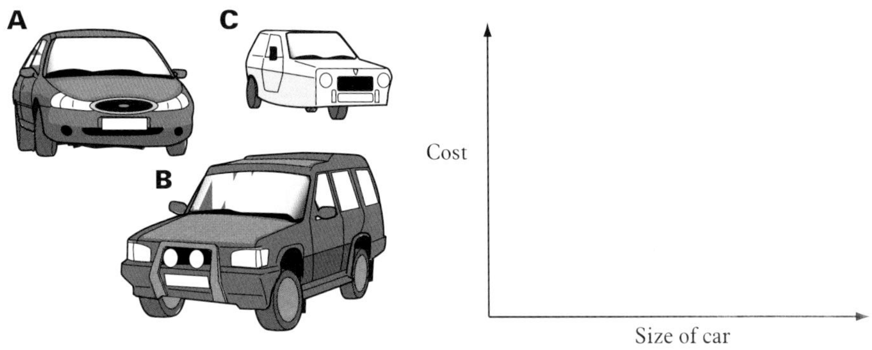

2 **a** Copy these axes.

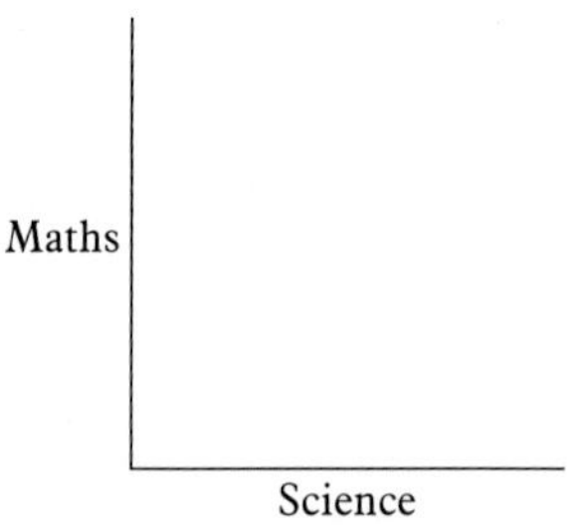

Six people took a Maths test and a Science test.
Here are some descriptions of how they did in their tests.
David: Did well in both Maths and Science.
Kirsty: Did well in Science but poorly in Maths.
Richard: Was ill when he took the tests. He did badly in both subjects.
Anisha: Did very well in Maths but only about average in Science.
Nathan: Got an average mark in both tests.
Catherine: Did well in Science but missed the Maths test and so scored 0.

b Mark a point on your graph to show each person's test results.

• **3** Look at this graph. It shows the cost of some boxes of chocolates and the number in each box.

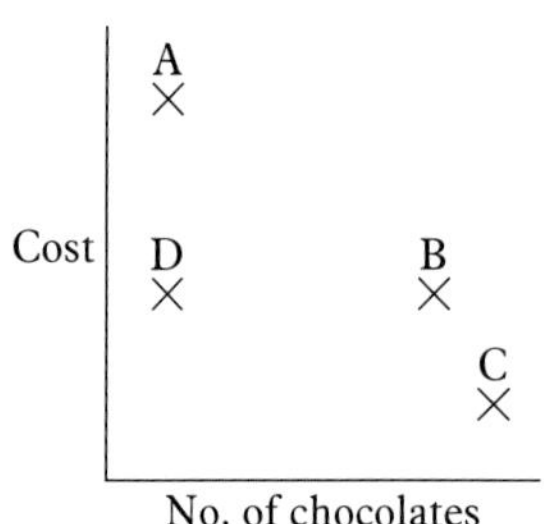

a Which box is the most expensive?
b Which box is the best value for money?
c Which boxes cost the same?
d Which boxes have the same number of chocolates in them?

Sketch graph A **sketch graph** can show a pattern or trend.

Example Paul cycles to school. After a while he goes uphill so he slows down. Later he goes downhill so he can speed up.

The graph shows the main features of the journey. It shows where Paul is speeding up or slowing down. It also shows if he is going faster at one point than another. You cannot tell his actual speed.
Between O and A Paul is speeding up.
From A to B he is going at a steady speed.
From B to C he is slowing down, he's going uphill.
From C to D he is speeding up, he's going downhill.

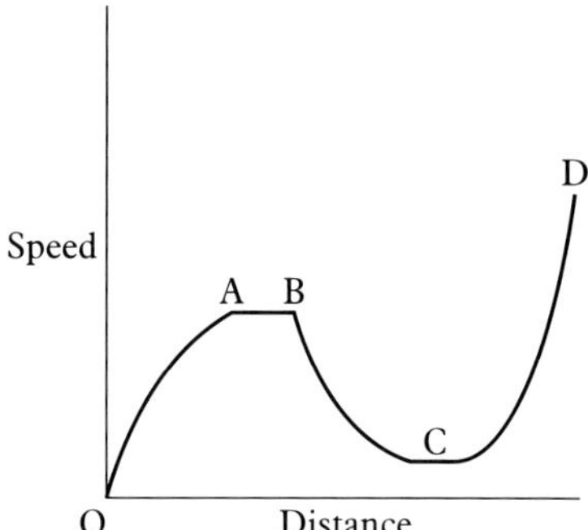

Gradient The **gradient** measures how steep a line or curve is.
The gradient of a straight line is the same all the way along.
The gradient of a curve changes.

Example A car accelerates rapidly to 30 mph. It continues to accelerate up to 60 mph but less rapidly. When it reaches 60 mph it travels at a steady speed.
Sketch a graph to show the car's acceleration.

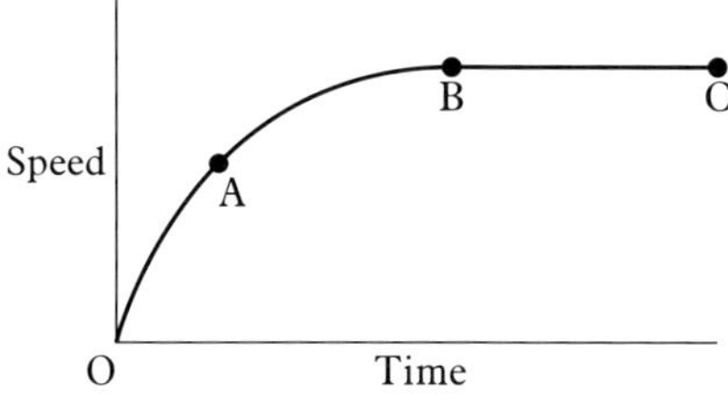

The gradient from O to A is steeper than from A to B as the car is accelerating more rapidly at first. The line from B to C is horizontal because the car is not accelerating. It is travelling at a steady speed. The gradient is 0.

Exercise 20:8

For each of these questions:

a Copy the axes.
b Draw a sketch of the graph from the description.
c Mark letters at important points and describe each section of the graph.

1 Howard cycles to school. The first part of his journey is along a level road. He then speeds up as he goes downhill. He slows down as he arrives at the school gate.

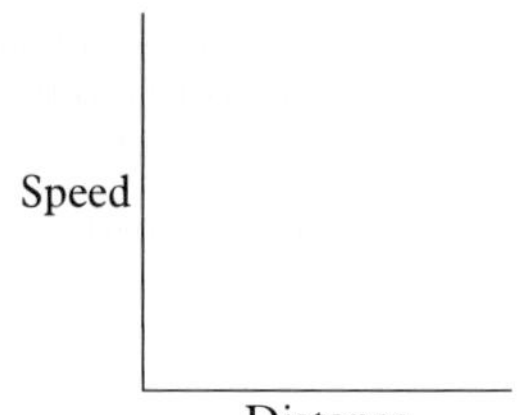

2 Lindsey jogs for the first part of her journey along a level road. The next part is uphill and she walks quite slowly.
She stops at the shops at the top of the hill.

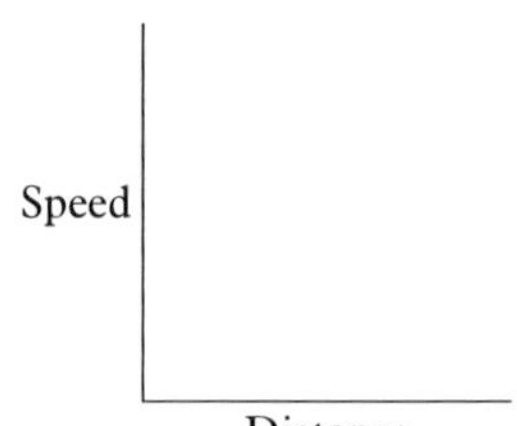

3 Kirsty made a jelly with boiling water. She put it in the fridge to cool. At first, it cooled very quickly, and then gradually settled down to a steady temperature.

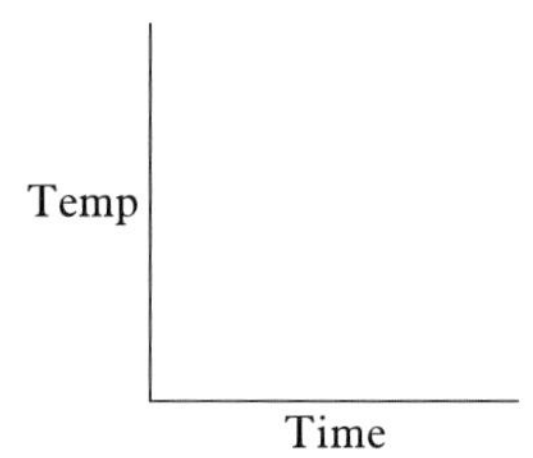

• **4** Andy is running a computer games stall at the school Christmas Fayre. He thinks that if the games are too cheap he will not make much money. If they are too expensive, very few people will want to pay.

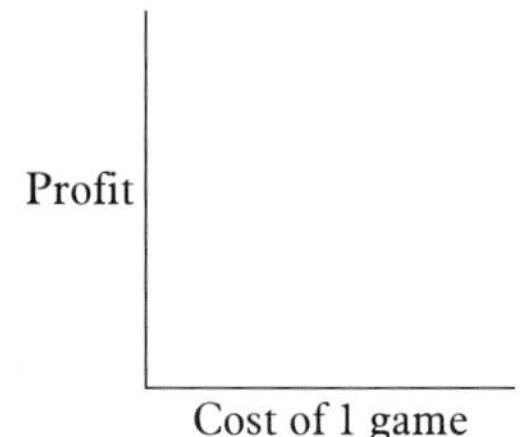

Anna is very keen on go-karting.
She likes to visit different tracks to practise.
It takes time to get used to a track and find out how quickly you can go on different parts of it.

Here is the diagram of Anna's home track.
She can go faster on the straights and slows down for the corners.
The graph shows Anna's speed as she goes around the track.

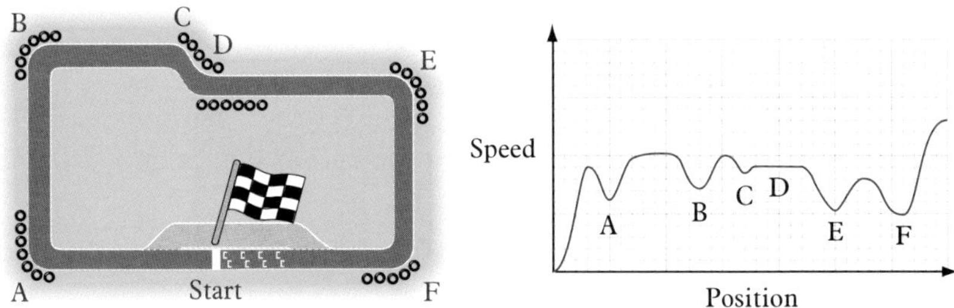

Look at the track and the graph together.
Read these notes that help to explain the graph.

From Start to A	Anna accelerates from the start. The graph goes up steeply.
A	Anna brakes into the corner and then accelerates out of it. The graph goes down and then back up again.
A to B	After Anna has accelerated out of the corner, she maintains a steady speed along the straight. The graph is horizontal.
B	Another corner like A.
B to E	This section is fairly straight so the graph is roughly horizontal. There are odd dips where Anna slows down for the gentle bends.
E to F	This section is almost the same as **A** to **B**.

Exercise 20:9

1 Look at this go-kart track.

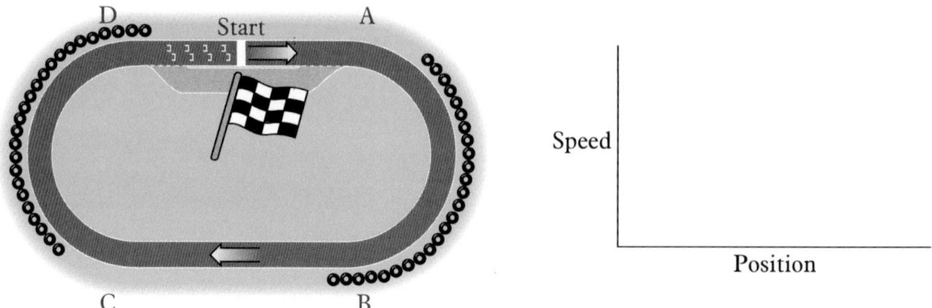

a What will happen to the speed of the kart between Start and A?
b What will happen to its speed as it goes around the corner from A to B?
c Where will the kart reach its highest speed?
d Copy the axes.
e Sketch a graph to show the speed of the kart as it goes once around the track.

2 Here is another go-kart track. The kart starts at S.
a Describe the speed of the kart once it has reached its full speed.
b Sketch a graph of the speed of the kart. Use the same axes as in question **1**.

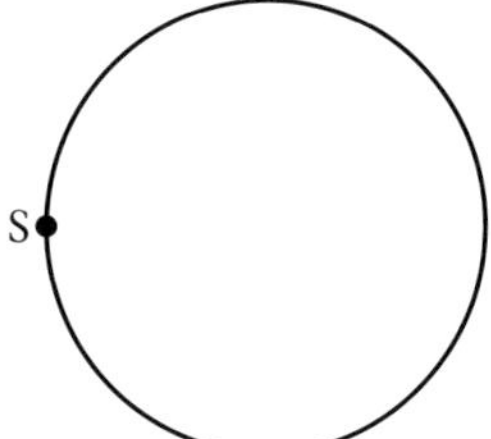

• **3** Look at this go-kart track.
Sketch a graph to show the speed of the kart as it goes around the track.

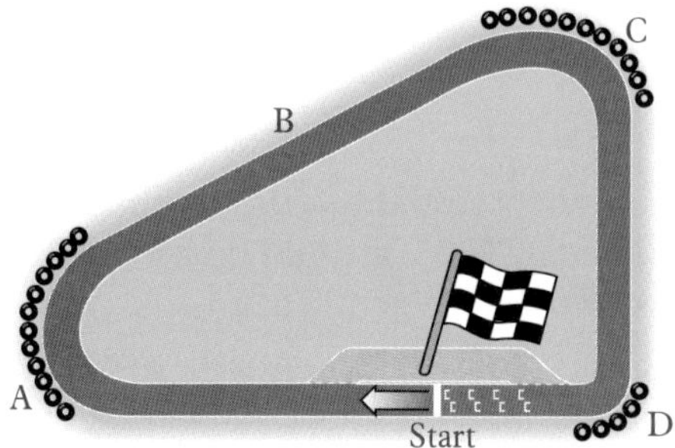

Exercise 20:10 – Designing a water tank

A water company are looking at new designs for water storage tanks.
The tanks need to hold 10 000 litres of water.
Here are some of the designs that have been suggested.

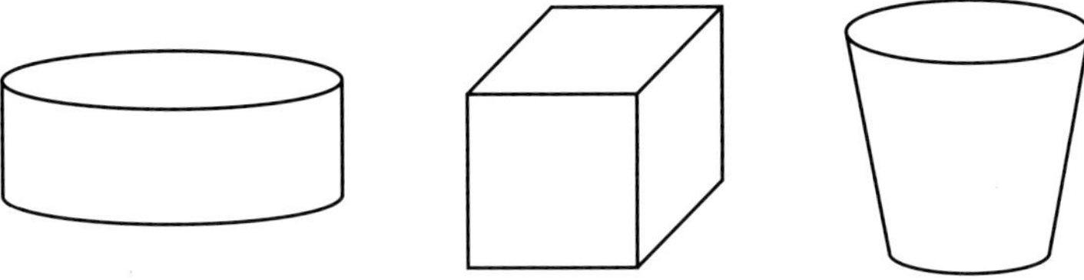

1 For each of the designs sketch a graph of the **height** of the water as they are filled up using a hose. Think about the **rate** at which the height would change.

2 Which of your graphs are straight lines and which are curves? Explain your answers.

• **3** Here is a graph for a fourth water tank.
Draw a sketch of the tank by looking at the graph.

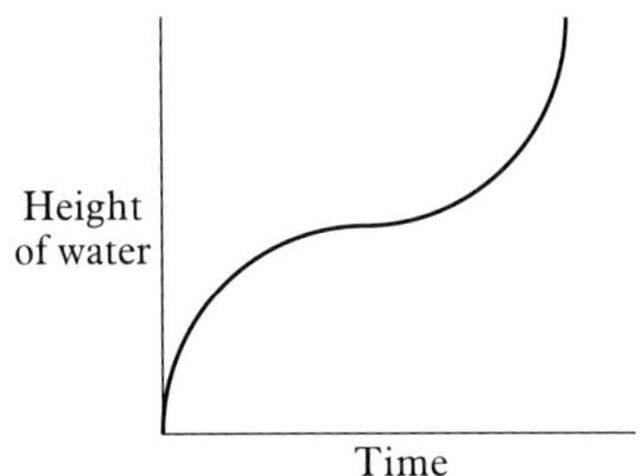

4 Design some water tanks of your own and sketch the graphs that go with them.

1 How long is it between these times?

a 7.20 a.m. and 8.52 p.m.

b 10.36 a.m. and 3.17 p.m.

c 14:35 and 23:42

d 21:46 and 17:18 the next day.

2 Geoff is a long distance lorrydriver. He travels from London to Scotland.

a On the way there he drives 560 km in 8 h. Work out his average speed.

b On the way back he drives 665.6 km in 12 h 48 min. Work out his average speed.

3 Adam enjoys cycle rides. He cycles around the Norfolk Broads.
He travels a distance of 72 km.
He rides at an average speed of 12 km/h. How long does it take him?

4 Gordon is a train driver. He drives for $2\frac{1}{2}$ h at an average speed of 74 km/h. How far does the train go?

5 An air pump fills a dinghy with 448 litres of air in 1 minute 52 seconds. Give this as a rate in:

a litres per second **b** litres per minute **c** litres per hour

6 This graph shows the journeys of two farm lorries from Rainham to Sandwich and back. Jon sets off at 10.00 a.m. and Andy sets off at 10.10 a.m.

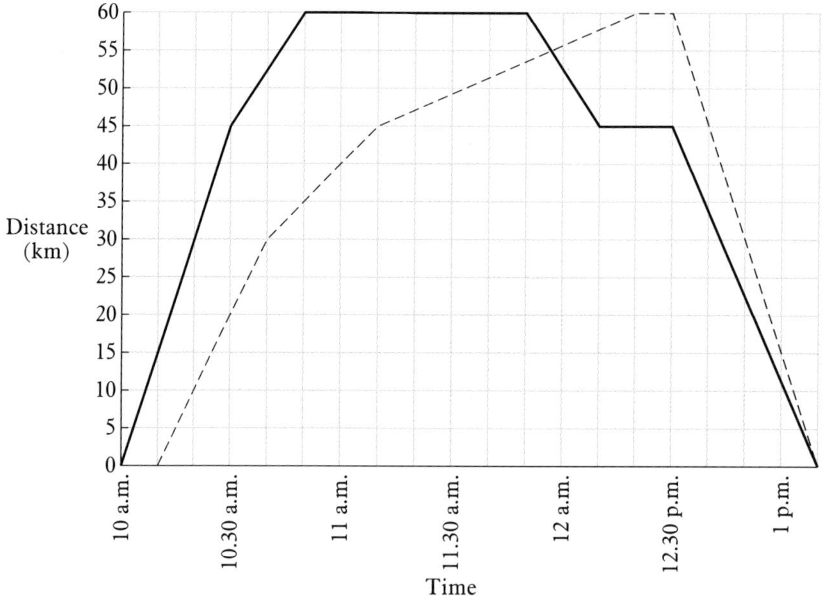

a How far had Jon's lorry travelled before Andy set off?

b Calculate Andy's slowest speed on the way to Sandwich. Give your answer in km/h.

c Andy passed Jon driving in the other direction. What time did this happen?

7 This table shows the costs of recorded delivery letters.

Weight up to …	60 g	100 g	150 g	200 g	250 g
Cost	90 p	104 p	120 p	135 p	147 p

Draw a graph to show these costs.

8 Last year Netty went to Belgium for a sightseeing trip.
She converted her £ into euro.
The rate was £1 = 1.55 euro.

a Draw axes from £0 to £100 and 0 euro to 180 euro.
b Draw a conversion graph.
c Netty took £60. How many Francs did she get?
d This year, the rate is £1 = 1.62 euro.
Put a new line on your graph to show this year's rate.

9 Ned is doing a parachute jump for charity.
As he jumps out of the plane, his speed increases rapidly.
He slows down suddenly as his parachute opens and then floats to the ground at a steady speed.

a Which of these three graphs shows Ned's jump?
Explain your answer.

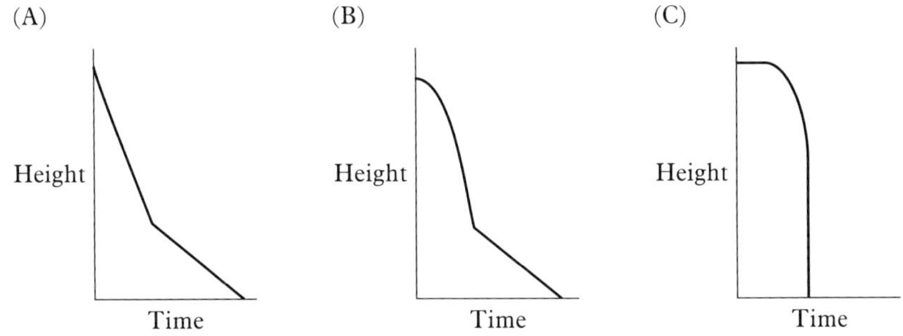

b Explain why the other two graphs are wrong.
c Sketch a graph of Ned's speed as he falls to the ground.

1 A spaceship sets off for Mars. It travels at 28 450 miles/h.
The route it takes is approximately 200 million miles.
How long does it take to get there:

a in hours **b** in days

2 A roller coaster goes along this track.

a Sketch a graph of the height of the roller coaster above the ground as it moves along the track. What do you notice?

b Sketch a graph of the **speed** of the roller coaster as it moves along the track.

c Explain the connection between your two graphs.

3 During the summer of 1995 the south west of England had swarms of ladybirds. This was because there were lots of greenfly around.
Ladybirds live on greenfly!
This graph shows the number of greenfly during the summer.

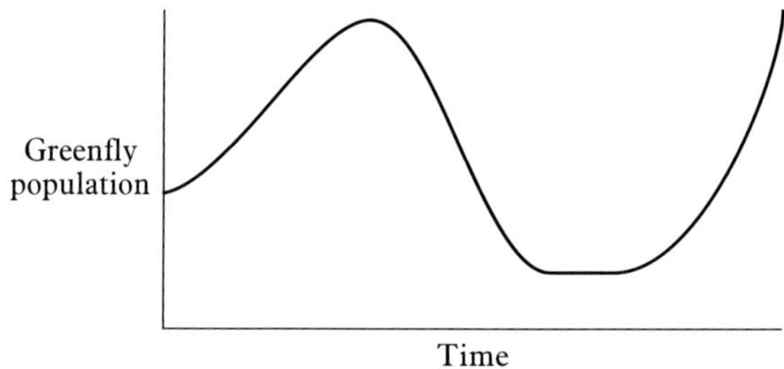

a Make a copy of this sketch graph. It does not have to be exact.

b Sketch the number of ladybirds on the same graph.
Think carefully about how long it will take for the ladybird population to increase.

1 This is an extract from a TV programme guide.

a How long does Eastenders last?

b Kevin records Songs of Praise and Sun Holiday. What is the total length of these two programmes?

c Kevin uses a 3 hour tape. How long will be left on the tape when he has recorded the two programmes?

BBC1 **pm**	
4:35	Eastenders
6:00	News
6:25	Songs of Praise
7:00	Wildlife on One
7:30	Fawlty Towers
8:00	Ground Force
8:40	Sun Holiday
9:20	As Time Goes By

2 A Japanese train travels with a speed of 200 km per hour.
How far does it travel in

a 4 hours **b** $\frac{1}{2}$ hour **c** 12 minutes?

3 **a** A bus travels 130 km in 2.5 hours.
Find the average speed of the bus.

b Martin travels 43 miles in 40 minutes.
Find his average speed in miles per hour.

4 Hattie can make 210 chocolates in half an hour.

a Give this as a rate in chocolates per hour.

b Give this as a rate in chocolates per minute.

c How long does Hattie take to make one chocolate?
Give your answer in seconds to 1 dp.

5 Mrs Rogers makes model animals.
The table shows the number of animals she made in one week.

Day	Mon	Tues	Wed	Thurs	Fri	Sat	Sun
Number of animals	8	12	19	9	4	7	14

Draw a vertical line graph to show this data.

6 Marty is going to pick up a new bike.
He walks to the shop then cycles back home.
The graph shows the journey.

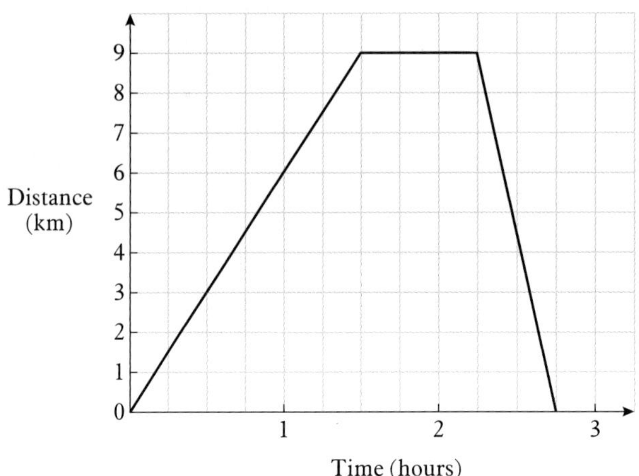

a How far is it from Marty's home to the shop?

b How long was he in the shop?

c How long did Marty take to cycle home?

d At what speed did Marty cycle home?

e What was Marty's average speed for the whole journey?
Give your answer to 1 dp.

7 The graph shows the delivery charge for a carpet warehouse. The charge depends on the mileage.

a Jan lives 18 miles away. How much does it cost her to have a carpet delivered?

b Peter's delivery charge was £6.
Copy this sentence. Fill in the missing numbers.
Peter lives between … and … miles from the warehouse.

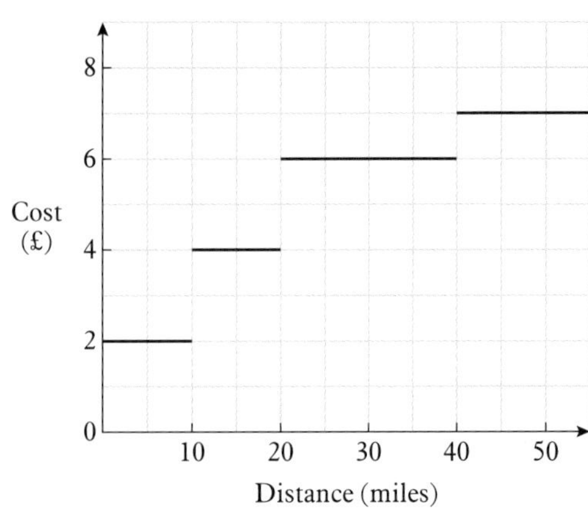

21 Trigonometry

1 Introduction
Measuring sides in right-angled triangles
Working out ratios of pairs of sides
Defining sin, cos and tan

CORE

2 Finding an angle
Using trigonometry to find angles
Solving real-life problems

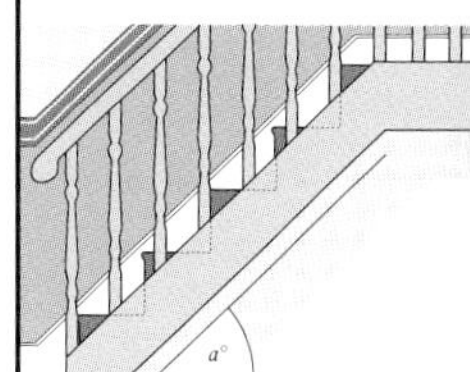

3 Finding a side
Using trigonometry to find lengths
Working in isosceles triangles
Solving real-life problems

QUESTIONS

EXTENSION

TEST YOURSELF

1 Introduction

Trigonometry is all about finding lengths and angles in triangles. It is used a lot in building and surveying.

Exercise 21:1

1 Look at this right-angled triangle.
It has a 30° angle at the base.

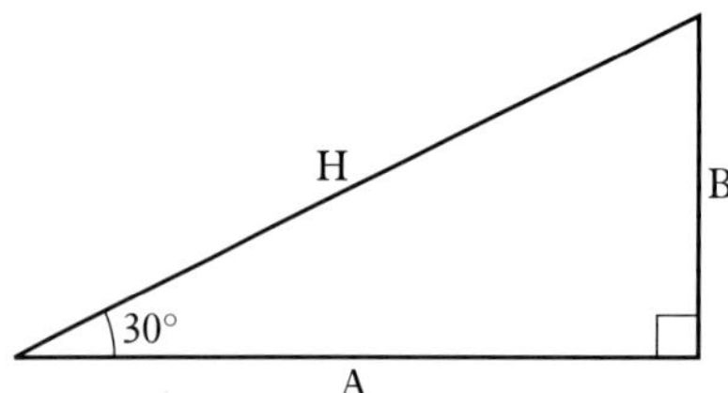

a Draw a right-angled triangle like this.
The angles must be the same as this.
It does not matter how long the sides are.

b Measure all three sides of the triangle to the nearest millimetre.
Be as accurate as you can.
Mark the lengths on your triangle.

c Draw two more triangles that have the same angles as before.
Make the lengths of the sides different.
Mark the lengths on each side. Number your triangles.

d Record your results in a table like this.
Leave the last three columns blank.

Diagram number	length A	length B	length H			

2 **a** For each of the triangles, calculate length **B** ÷ length **A**.
Fill in the answers in the fifth column of your table.
Round your answers to 3 dp where necessary.

Diagram number	length A	length B	length H	B ÷ A	A ÷ H	B ÷ H

b What do you notice about these numbers?
Now make sure that your calculator is working in degrees.

c 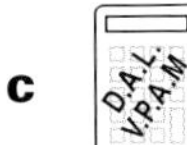 Key in: **tan** **3** **0**

You should get 0.577350269
Write down the answer.
Compare it with your answers to B ÷ A in your table.

3 **a** For each triangle, calculate length A ÷ length H.
Fill in the answers in your table.

b Fill in the answers to length B ÷ length H in your table.

c  Key in: **cos** **3** **0**

Write down your answer.

d  Key in: **sin** **3** **0**

Write down your answer.

e Compare the calculator answers with your table.
Which answer goes with which column?

---

tangent

The value of  **tan** **3** **0**
is called the **tangent of 30°**.
It is normally written tan 30° and said 'tan thirty'.

sine

The value of  **sin** **3** **0**
is called the **sine of 30°**.
It is normally written sin 30° and said 'sine thirty'.

cosine

The value of  **cos** **3** **0**
is called the **cosine of 30°**.
It is normally written cos 30° and said 'cos thirty'.

---

4 **a** Draw a right-angled triangle like this with a 50° angle.
b Measure the sides and record your results.
c Work out B ÷ A, A ÷ H and B ÷ H.
d Compare your answers to part **c** with tan 50°, cos 50° and sin 50°. Write down what you notice.

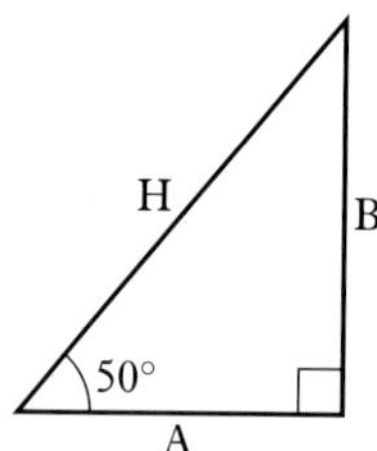

This sort of trigonometry only works in right-angled triangles.
The values stored in the calculator are very accurate and are much easier than taking measurements.

Sin, cos and tan always have the same value for right-angled triangles with the same angle. The size of the triangle does not matter. It is the angles in the triangle that are important.

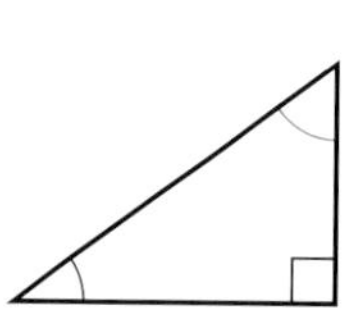

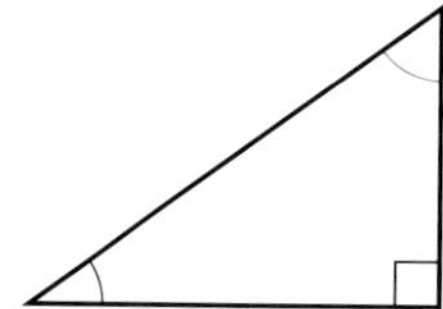

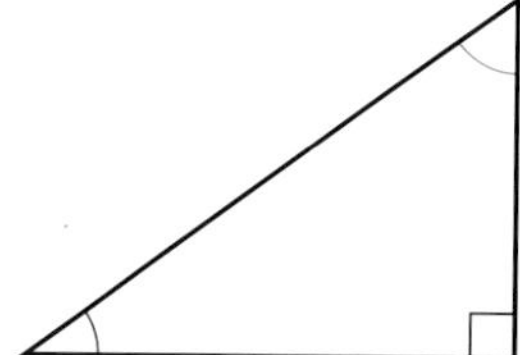

The sides of the triangle are given special names so that it is easy to write the formulas down.

Hypotenuse The **hypotenuse** is always the longest side. It never touches the right angle.

Opposite The **opposite** is the side *opposite* the angle you are working with. It is one of the two shorter sides.

Adjacent The **adjacent** is the side *next* to the angle you are working with. It touches that angle.

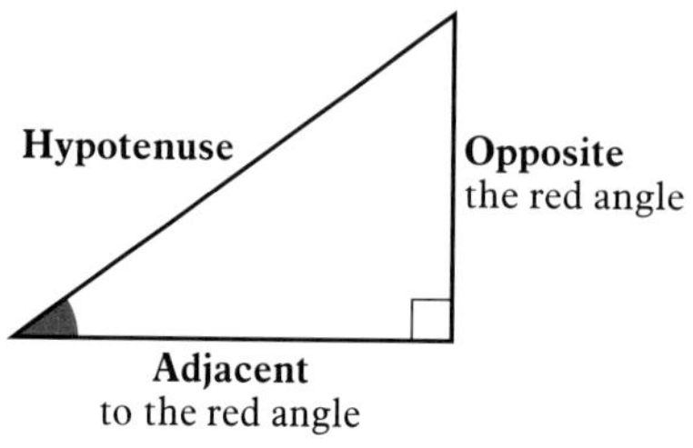

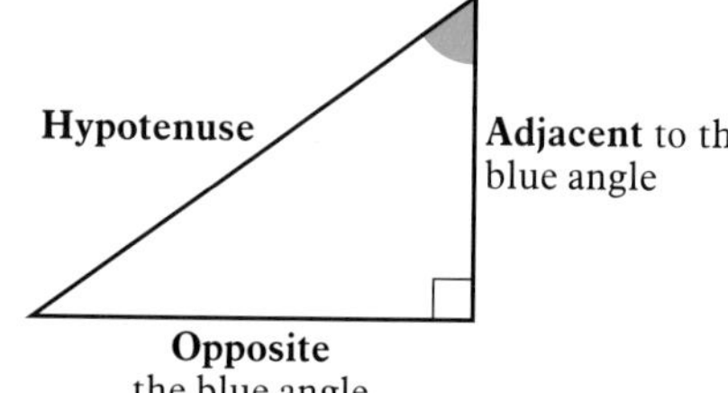

Exercise 21:2

1 Copy this table. Leave space for 10 triangles.

Triangle	Hypotenuse	Opposite the marked angle	Adjacent to the marked angle
a	C	D	E
b			

2 For each of these triangles, decide which sides are the **H**ypotenuse, the **O**pposite and the **A**djacent for the marked angle. Fill in the table. The first one is done for you.

a

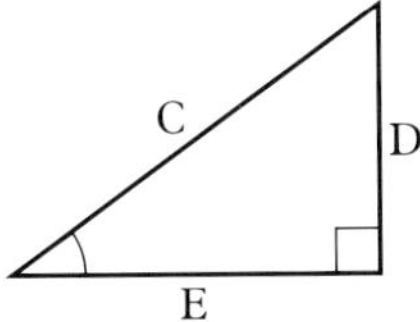

f

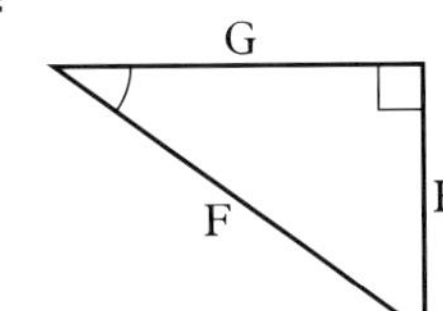

b

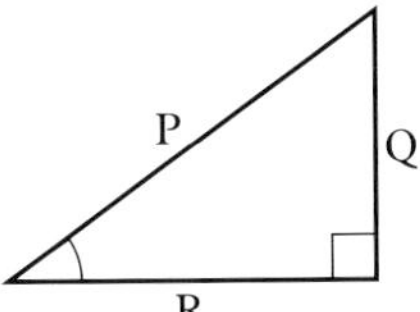

g

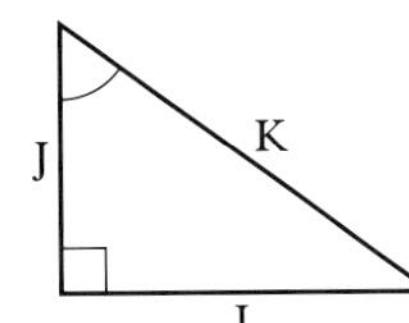

c

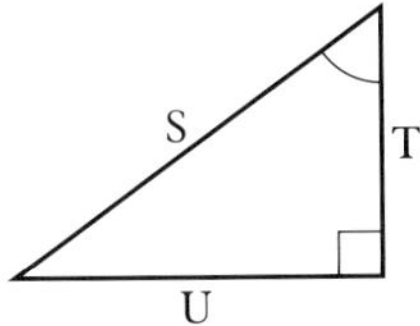

h

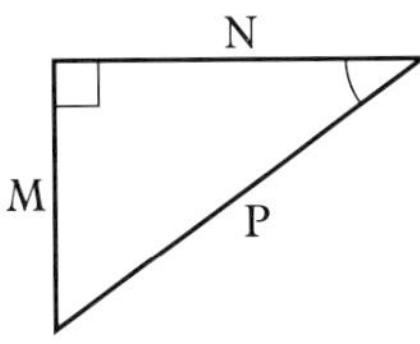

d

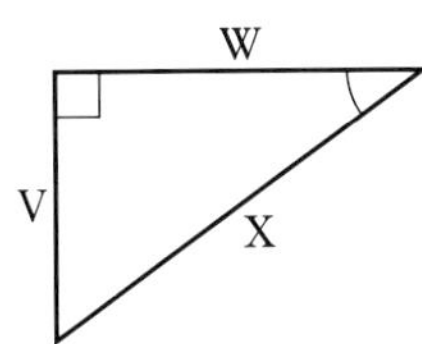

i

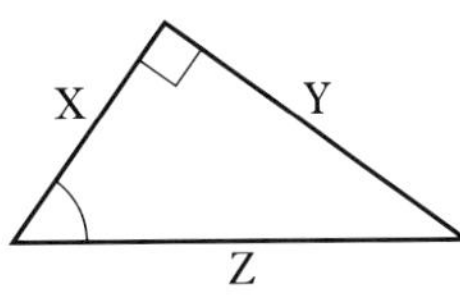

e

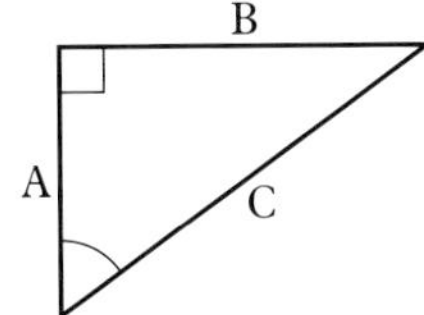

j

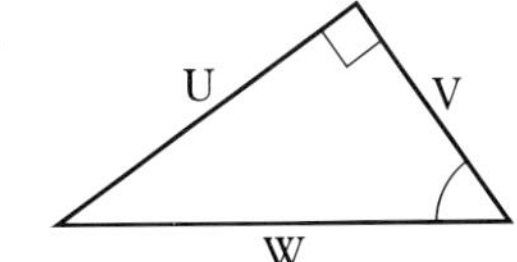

You can now write down formulas for sin, cos and tan using the names of the sides of the triangle.

Look at this triangle.
The sides are labelled for angle a

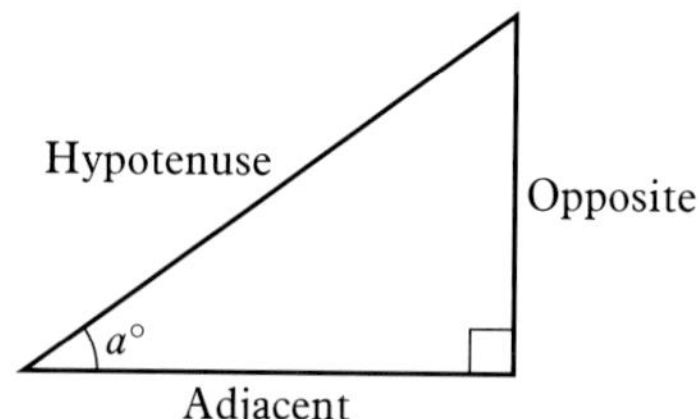

$$\sin a = \frac{\textbf{Opposite}}{\textbf{Hypotenuse}}$$

$$\cos a = \frac{\textbf{Adjacent}}{\textbf{Hypotenuse}}$$

$$\tan a = \frac{\textbf{Opposite}}{\textbf{Adjacent}}$$

Some people remember SOHCAHTOA which comes from the first letters of **S**in equals **O**pposite divided by **H**ypotenuse, **C**os equals **A**djacent …

These are often shortened to

$$\sin a = \frac{\text{Opp}}{\text{Hyp}} \qquad \cos a = \frac{\text{Adj}}{\text{Hyp}} \qquad \tan a = \frac{\text{Opp}}{\text{Adj}}$$

A useful rhyme to remember these is:

The	**C**at	**S**at
On	**A**n	**O**range
And	**H**owled	**H**orribly

Example Look at this triangle.
Work out sin 36°, cos 36° and tan 36°.

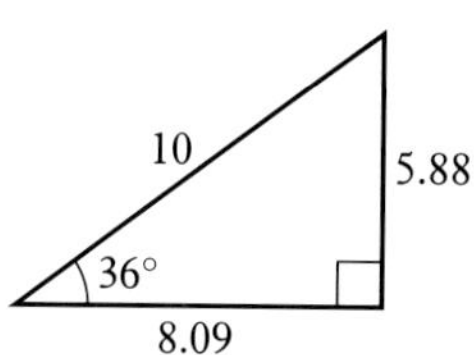

$$\sin 36° = \frac{\text{Opp}}{\text{Hyp}} = \frac{5.88}{10}$$

$= \mathbf{0.588}$ to 3 dp

$$\cos 36° = \frac{\text{Adj}}{\text{Hyp}} = \frac{8.09}{10}$$

$= \mathbf{0.809}$ to 3 dp

$$\tan 36° = \frac{\text{Opp}}{\text{Adj}} = \frac{5.88}{8.09}$$

$= \mathbf{0.727}$ to 3 dp

Exercise 21:3

Give all your answers to 3 dp.

1 Work out sin a, cos a and tan a.

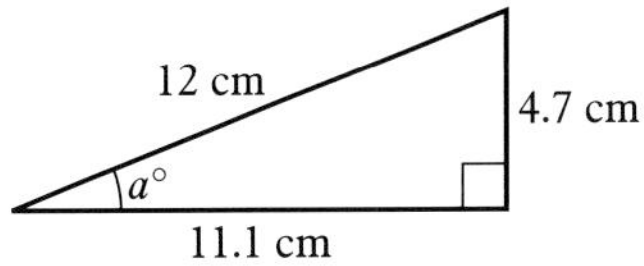

2 Work out sin b, cos b and tan b.

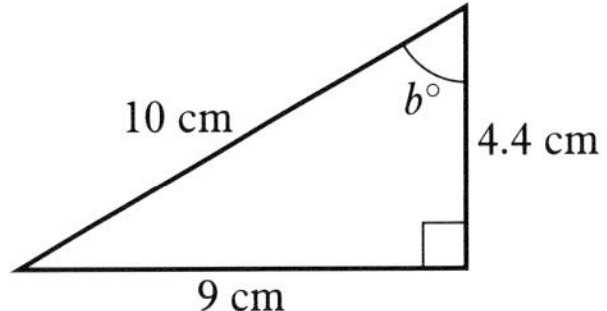

3 Work out sin c, cos c and tan c.

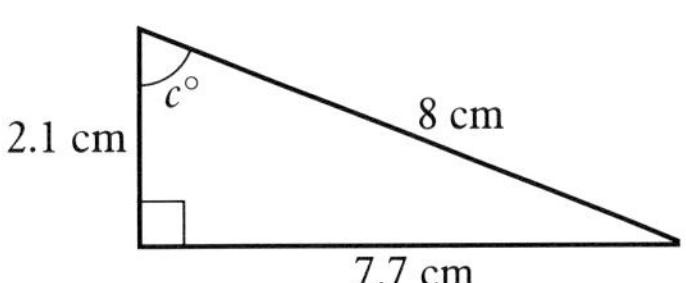

4 Work out sin d, cos d and tan d.

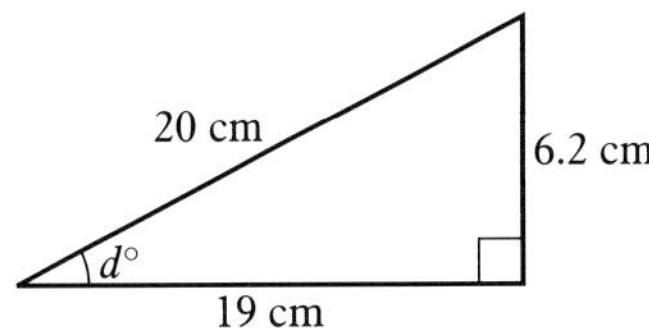

5 **a** Work out sin e, cos e and tan e.
b Work out sin f, cos f and tan f.

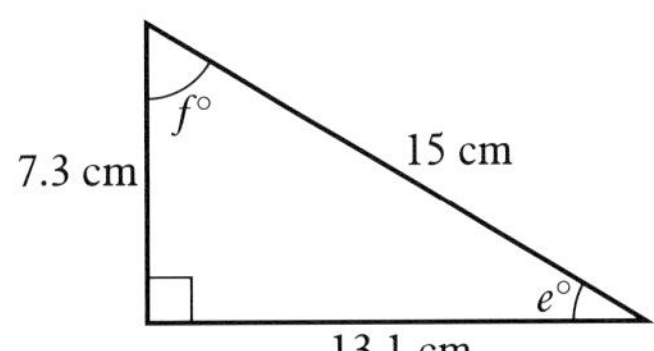

6 Here are the sizes of the angles used in questions **1–5**.

$a = 23°$ $b = 64°$ $c = 75°$ $d = 18°$ $e = 29°$ $f = 61°$

Use your calculator to check your answers for questions **1–5**.

2 Finding an angle

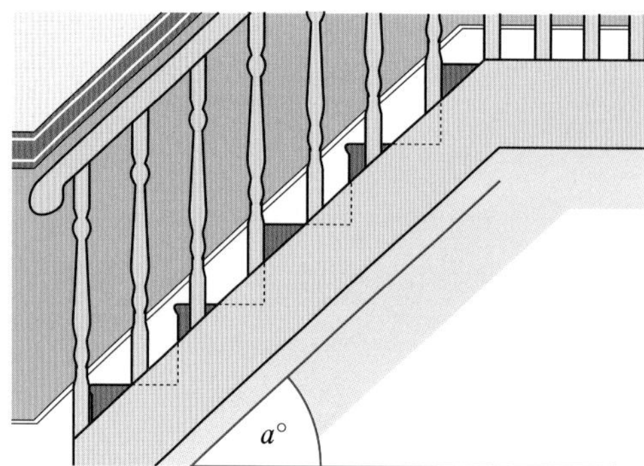

There is a legal limit on the value of angle a in houses. The maximum value is 42°.

Stairs cannot be steeper than this.

To find the angle marked a in this triangle:

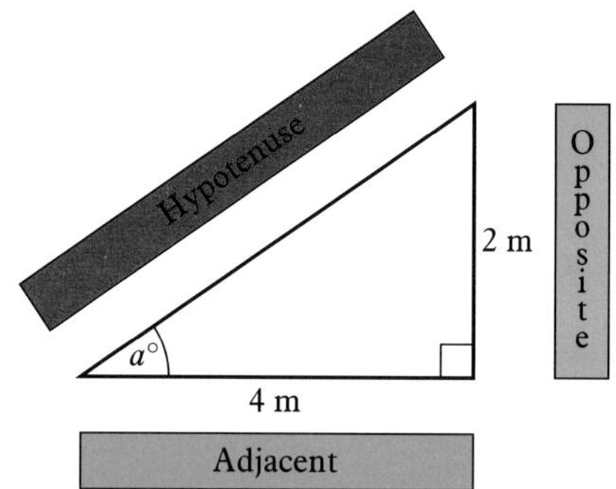

Which lengths do you know?

The 2 m side is opposite to a
The 4 m side is adjacent to a

Which formula do you need?

$\sin a = \dfrac{\text{Opp}}{\text{Hyp}}$ $\cos a = \dfrac{\text{Adj}}{\text{Hyp}}$ $\tan a = \dfrac{\text{Opp}}{\text{Adj}}$

Only the tan formula has opposite **and** adjacent in it.

Fill in the formula $\tan a = \dfrac{2}{4}$

Make sure that your calculator is working in degrees.

Key in: 

2nd F tan (2 ÷ 4) =

to get $a = 26.6°$ (1 dp).

You can use the other two formulas in the same way.

Exercise 21:4

For each question:

a Copy the triangle. Label the sides Hyp, Opp, Adj.

b Find the angle marked with a letter. Round your answer to 1 dp.

Check that your answers seem reasonable.

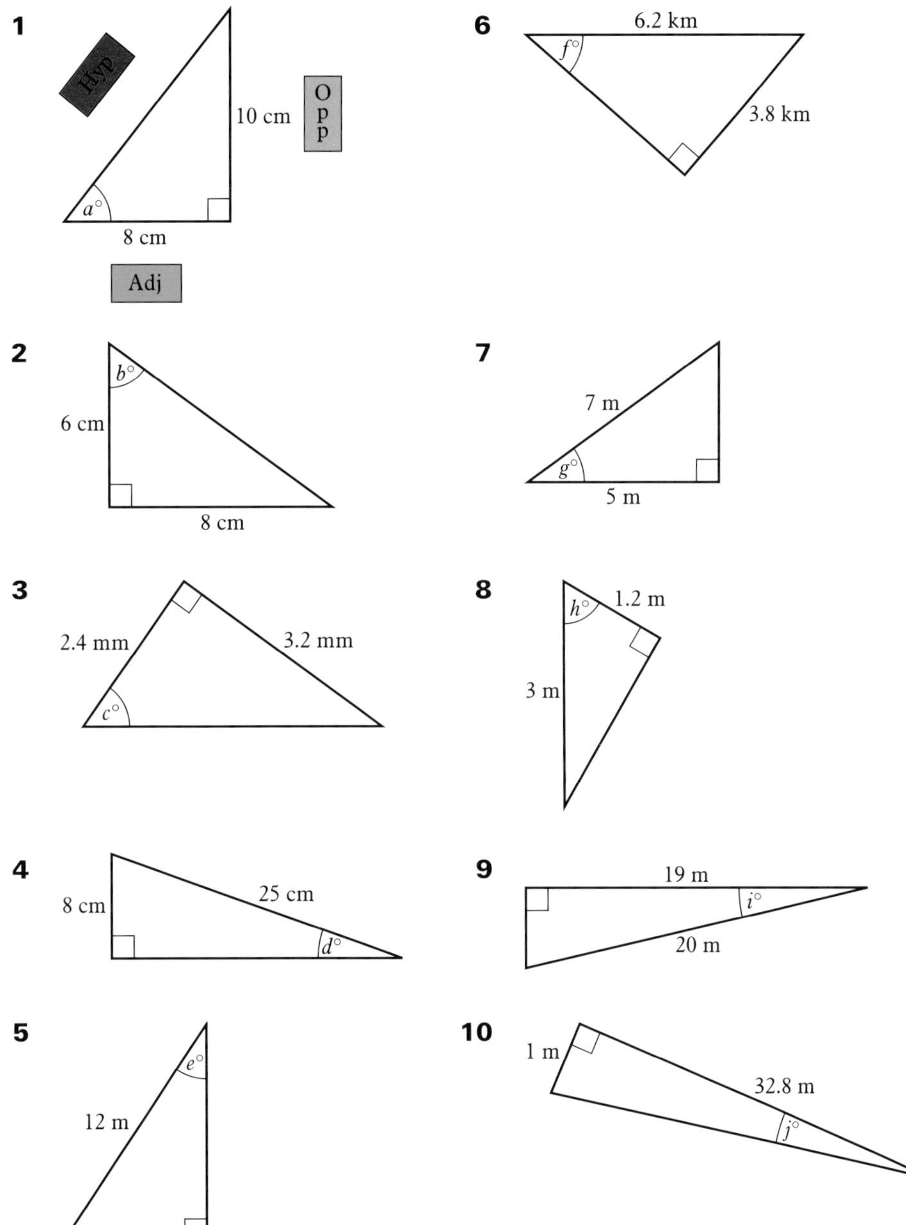

11

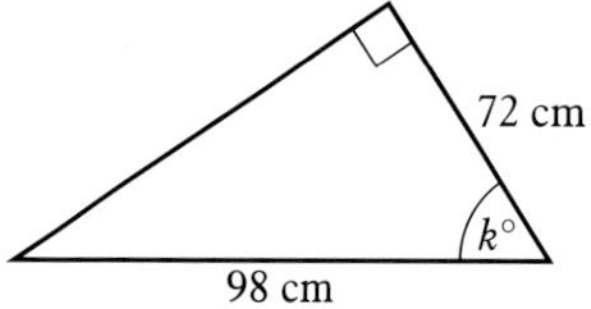

12

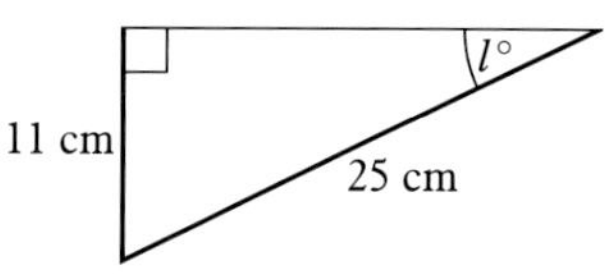

In some questions you have to find more than one angle.

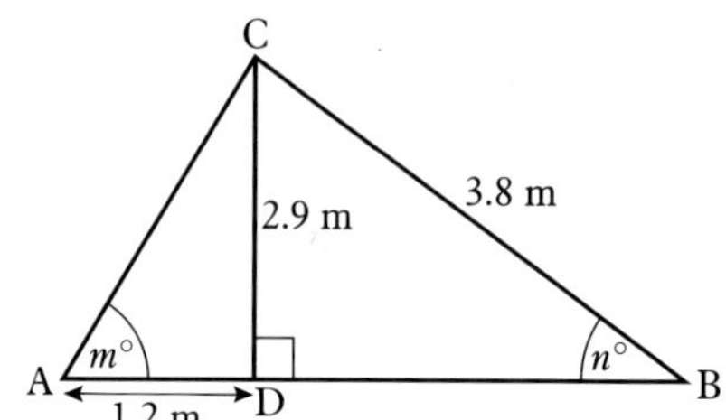

You draw a separate triangle for each angle that you need to find.
In this diagram you need to find angles $m°$ and $n°$.

To find $m°$ draw triangle ADC separately.
Then you work out $m°$ in the usual way.

Which formula do you need?
Only the tan formula has opposite **and** adjacent in it.

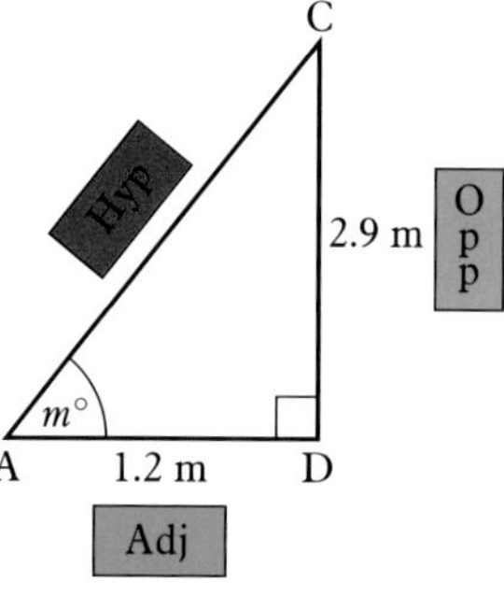

Fill in the formula $\tan m = \frac{2.9}{1.2}$

Key in:

SHIFT tan (2 . 9 ÷ 1 . 2) =

to get $m = 67.5°$ (1 dp).

You then work out $n°$ by drawing triangle BCD separately. This gives $n° = 49.7°$ (1 dp).

13

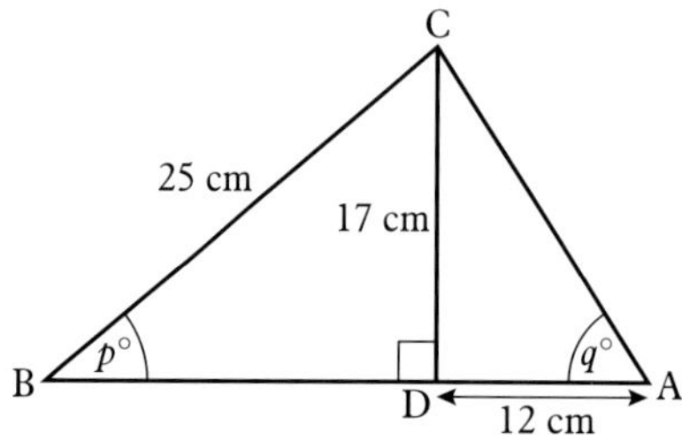

● **14** ABCD is a rectangle.

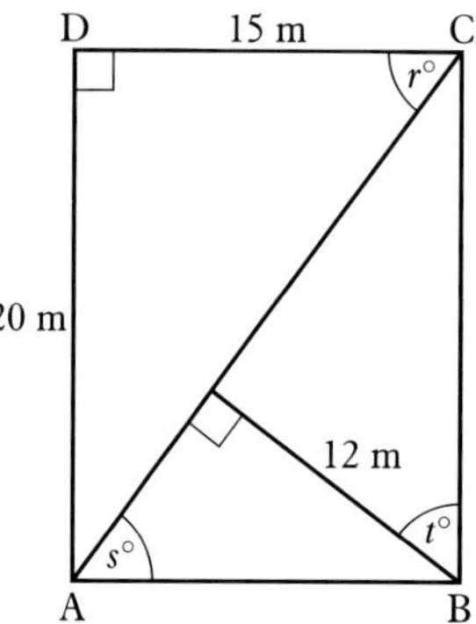

Exercise 21:5

In this exercise, round all your answers to 1 dp.

1 A flight of stairs rises 2.6 m. The horizontal distance under the stairs is 2.85 m.

a What is the angle that the stairs make with the ground?

The biggest angle allowed by law is 42°.

b Is this angle legal?

• **c** How could it appear to be legal in a report?

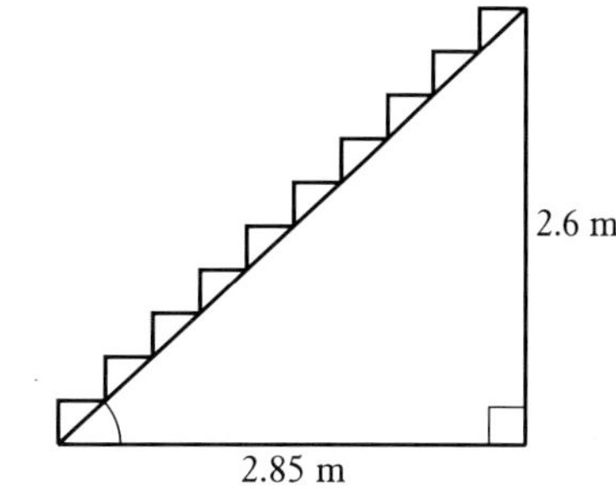

2 Evel Knievel is a world famous motorcycle stuntman.
What is his angle of take off if he uses this ramp?

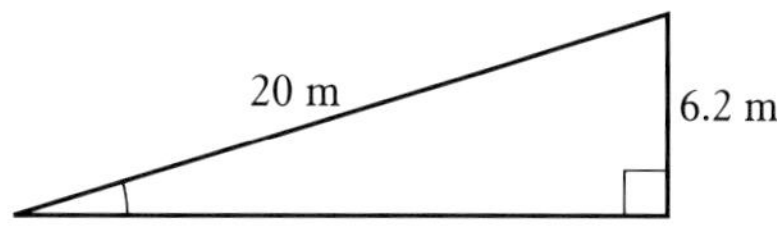

3 Claire Batin 'the human fly' is about to climb this overhang in the Pyrenees.
What angle does she need to climb out from the vertical?

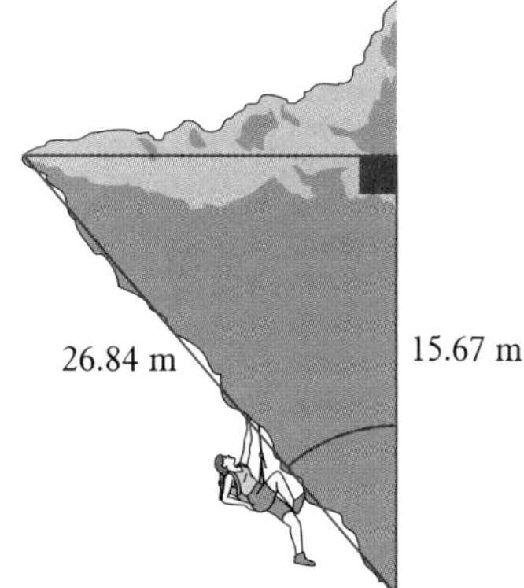

4 This is the descent slope of one of the world's tallest roller coasters.
What is the angle made with the ground?

3 Finding a side

How could you find the width of the Grand Canyon without crossing it?

To find the side marked a in this triangle:

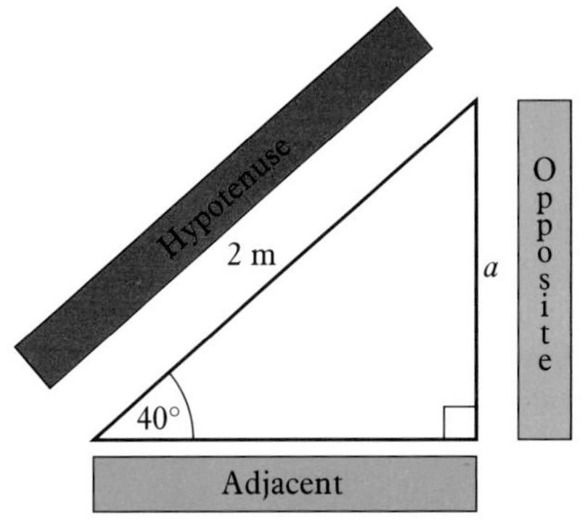

Which length do you know?
The length marked 2 m is the hypotenuse.

Which length do you need to find?
The length marked a is opposite the 40° angle.

Which formula do you need?

$\sin a = \frac{\text{Opp}}{\text{Hyp}}$ $\cos a = \frac{\text{Adj}}{\text{Hyp}}$ $\tan a = \frac{\text{Opp}}{\text{Adj}}$

Only the sin formula has opposite **and** hypotenuse in it.

Fill in the formula $\sin 40° = \frac{a}{2}$

Multiply both sides of the equation by 2 $2 \times \sin 40° = a$

Make sure that your calculator is working in degrees.

Key in:   2 sin 4 0 =

to get $a = 1.29$ m (3 sf).

You can use the other two formulas in the same way.

Exercise 21:6

For each question:

a Copy the triangle. Label the sides Hyp, Opp, Adj.

b Find the length of the side marked with a letter. Round your answer to 3 sf.

Check that your answers seem reasonable.

1

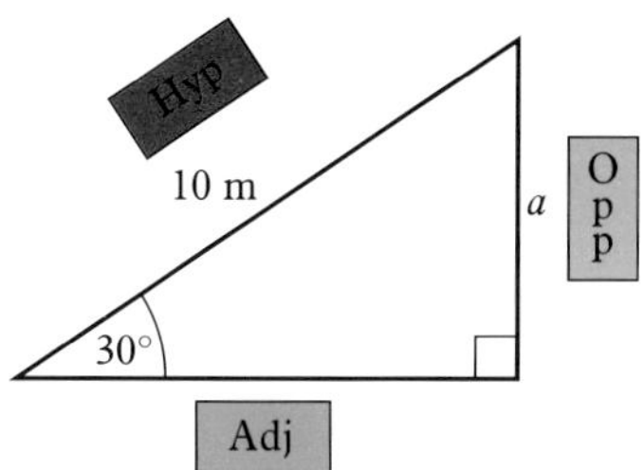

2

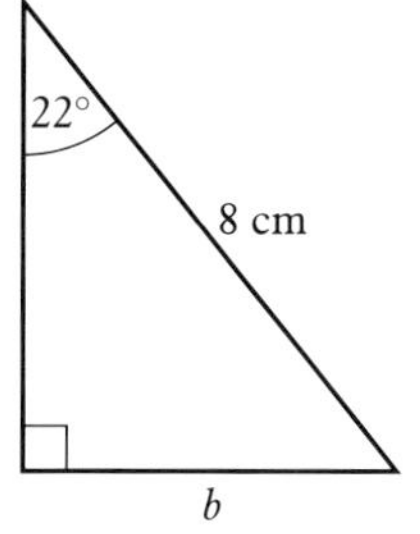

3

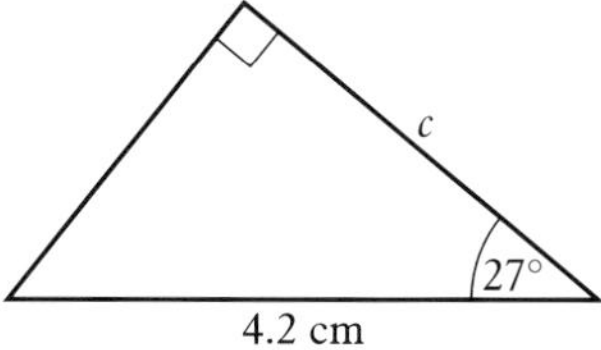

4

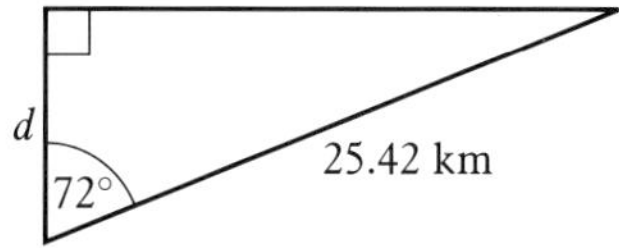

5

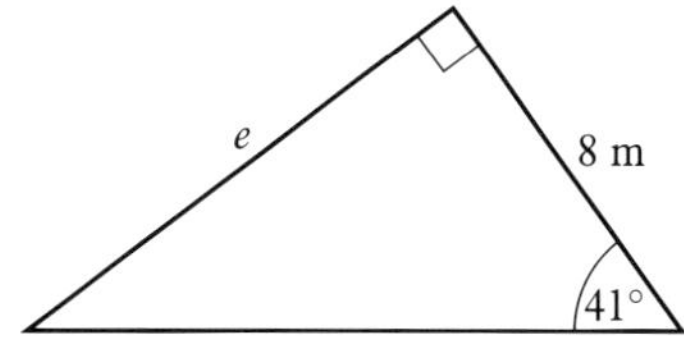

6

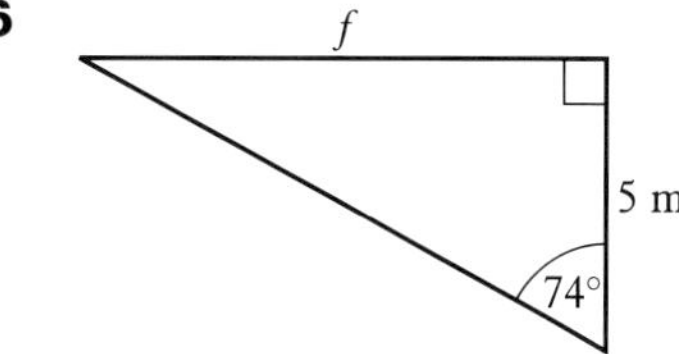

7

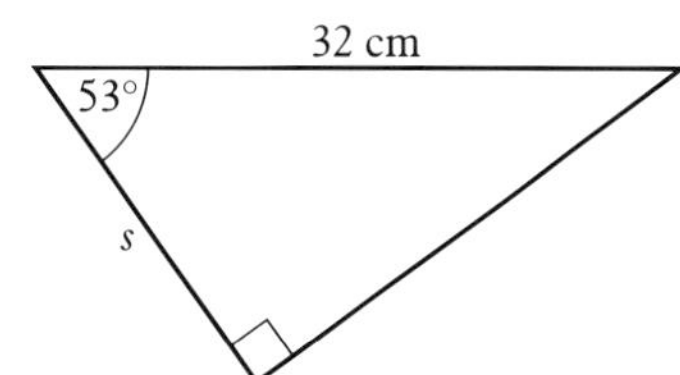

8

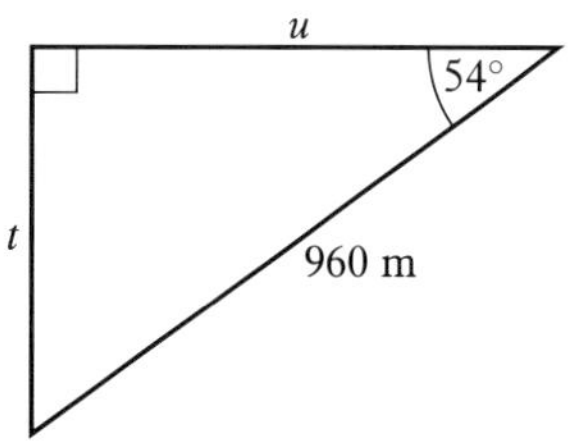

In some questions you have to work out more than one length. You draw a separate triangle for each length you need to find. In this diagram you need to find length a before you can find length b.

To find a draw triangle ADC separately. Then you work out a in the usual way.

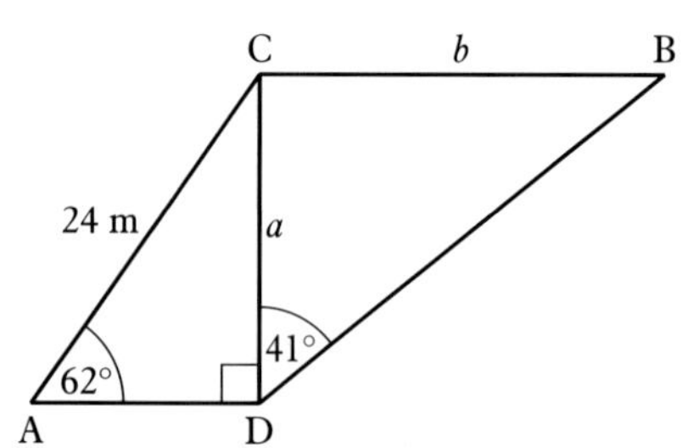

Which formula do you need?
Only the sin formula has opposite **and** hypotenuse in it.

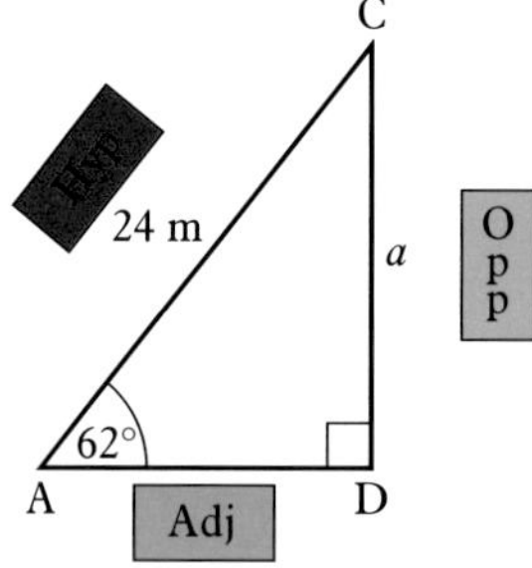

Fill in the formula $\sin 62^\circ = \frac{a}{24}$

Multiply both sides of the equation by 24 $24 \times \sin 62^\circ = a$

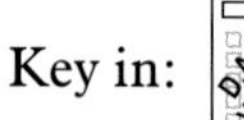  

to get $a = 21.2$ m (3 sf).

You will need this in the next part but you must not use this rounded answer.
Keep the **calculator** value of a on your calculator display.
Now work out b by drawing triangle BCD.

Which formula do you need?
Only the tan formula has opposite **and** adjacent in it.

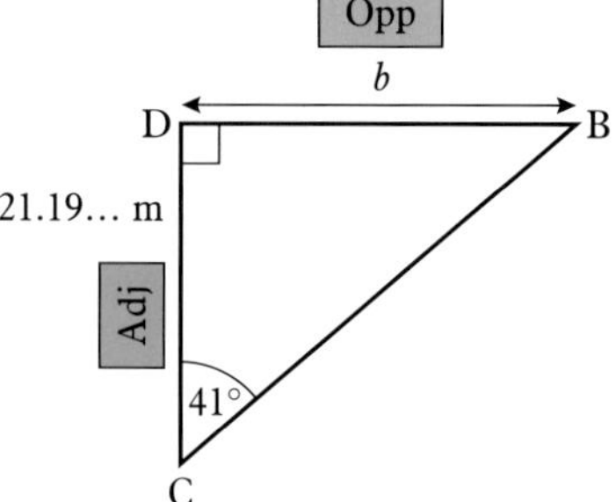

Fill in the formula $\tan 41^\circ = \frac{b}{21.19\ldots}$

Multiply both sides of the equation by 21.19… $21.19\ldots \times \tan 41^\circ = b$

a is still on your calculator display.

Key in: 

to get $b = 18.4$ m (3 sf).

9

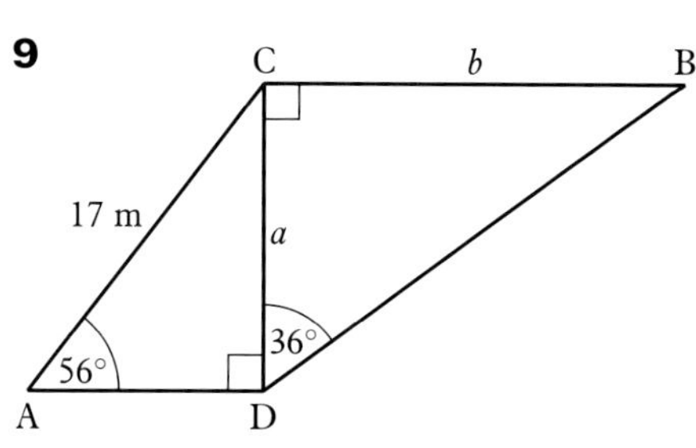

10

Working in isosceles triangles

You can split an isosceles triangle into 2 right-angled triangles.

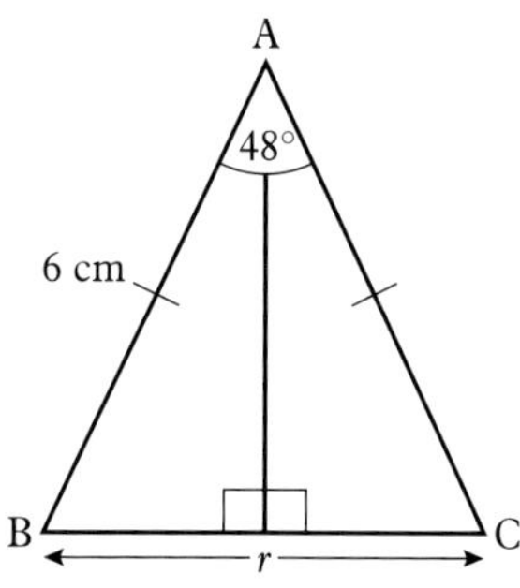

To find the base in this triangle split the triangle down the middle.
The angle in each half is $48 \div 2 = 24°$.

Now you have two right-angled triangles.
These triangles are exactly the same.
They are congruent.
Call the base of each triangle x.

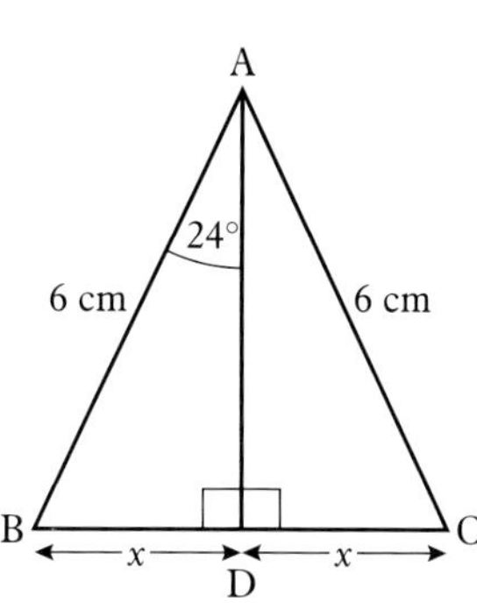

Look at triangle ABD $\qquad \sin 24° = \dfrac{x}{6}$

Multiply both sides by 6 $\qquad 6 \times \sin 24° = x$

$r = 2x$ so multiply both sides by 2 to get $\qquad 12 \times \sin 24° = r$

This gives $r = 4.88$ cm (3 sf).

11

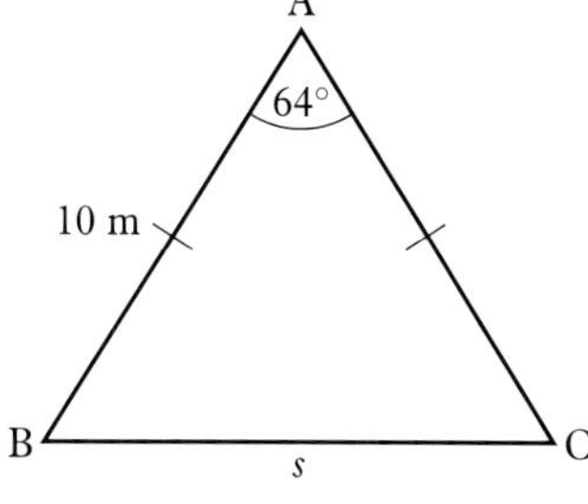

12

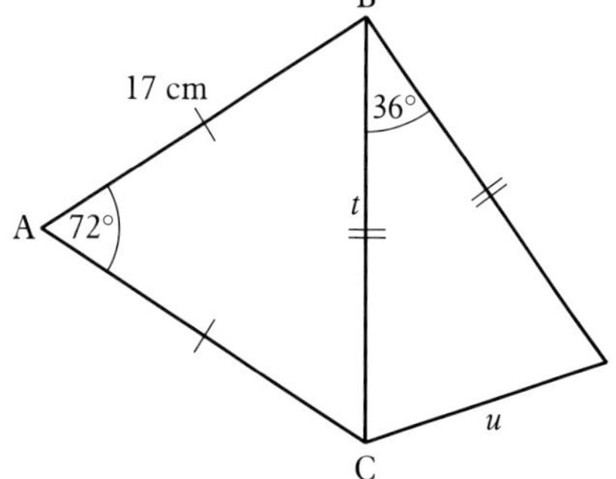

Exercise 21:7

In this exercise, round all your answers to 3 sf.

1 Billy is 27 metres from the base of a tree.
He measures the angle shown to the top of the tree. It is 42°. Find the height of the tree.

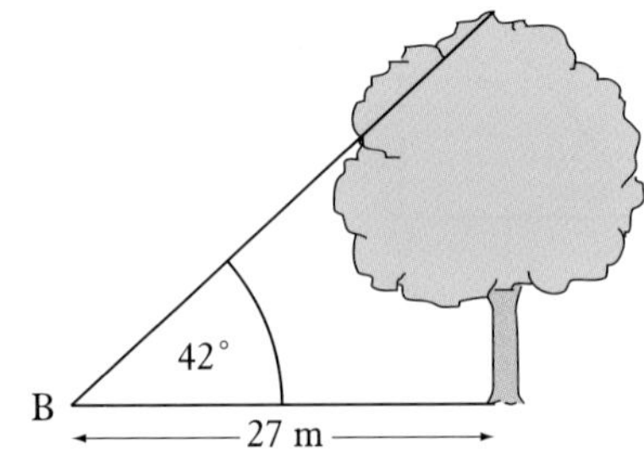

2 Sharon has climbed up the Impossible Pinnacle in the Cuillin hills. She sees her companion Jacqui further along on the ridge. Another friend takes this picture and measures the angle shown. Jacqui is 120 m from the base of the pinnacle. Find the height of the pinnacle.

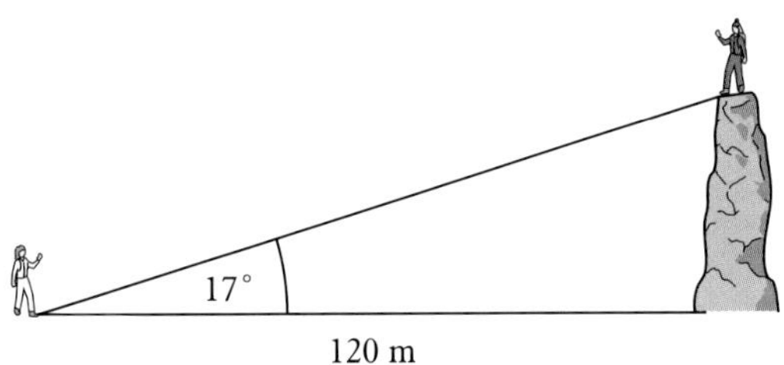

3 Rachel is running down the cliff path marked in red.

a How far has she descended vertically?

b How far to the left or right of point A is she when she reaches B?

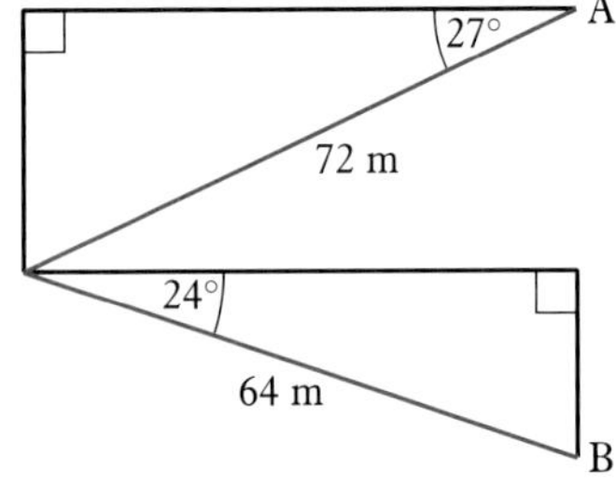

4 This is a section of the Grand Canyon.

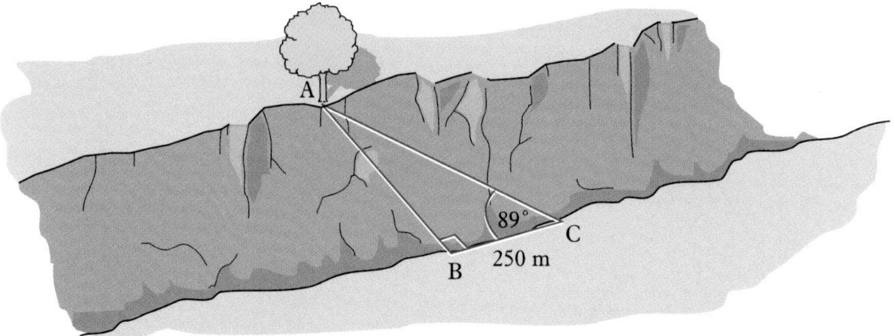

Sally stands at B. This is the point directly opposite the tree at A.
She then walks 250 m to C. Sally measures the angle BCA to be 89°.
Use Sally's measurements to find the distance AB across the Grand Canyon.

Exercise 21:8

In this exercise you will need to find angles and sides.
Find the angles and sides marked with letters.

1

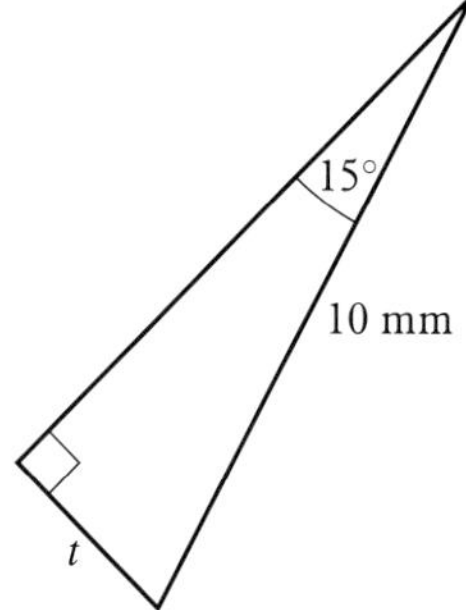

2

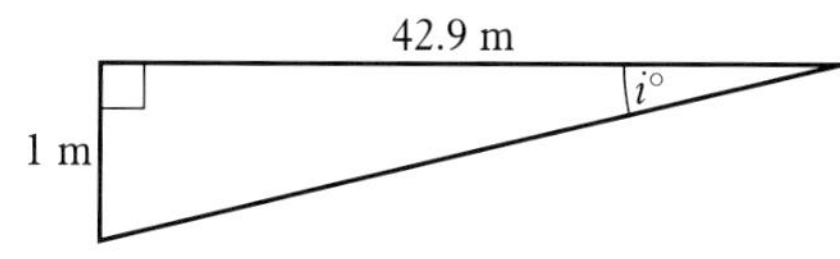

3

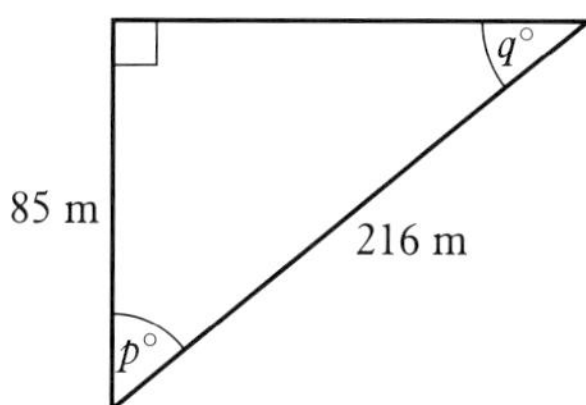

4

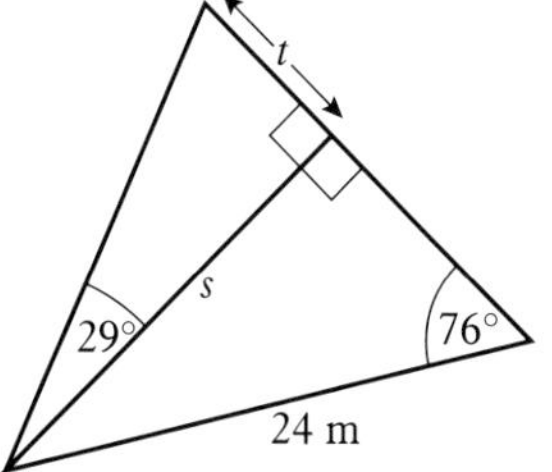

5

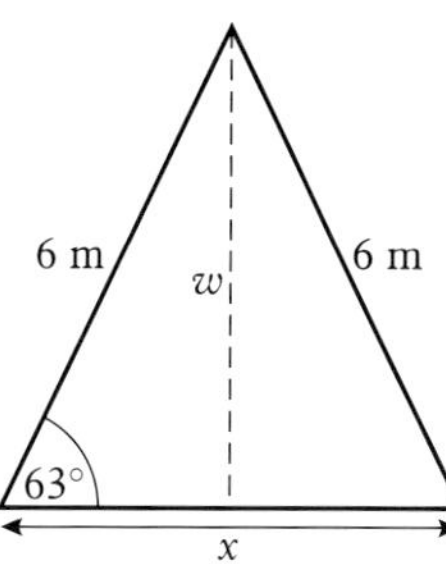

● **6**

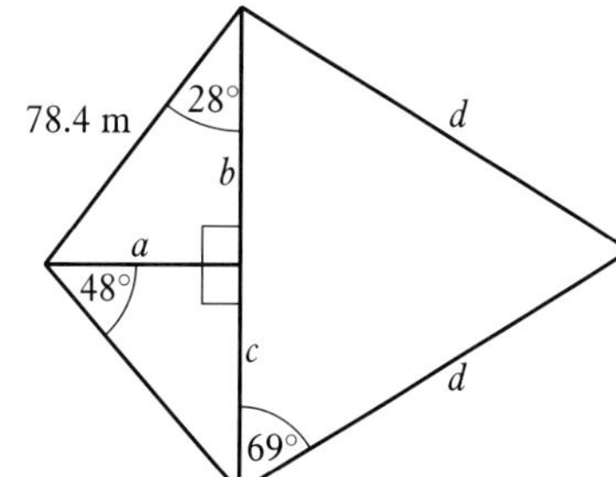

7 ABCD is a rectangle.

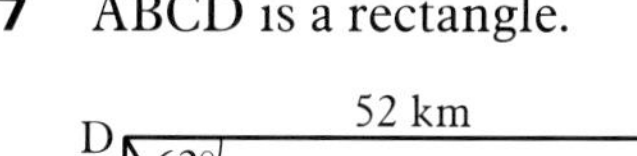

1 Asif has drawn a right-angled triangle RST.

a Write down the value of cos t for Asif's triangle.

b Write down the value of sin r.

c Write down what you notice about your answers to parts **a** and **b**.

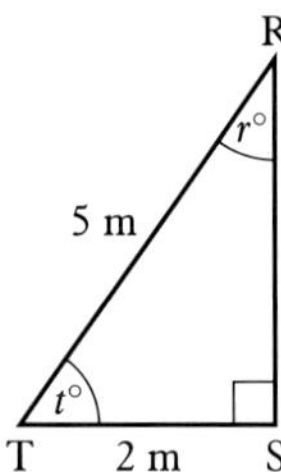

2 Round your answers to 1 dp in this question.

a Find the angle BAC.

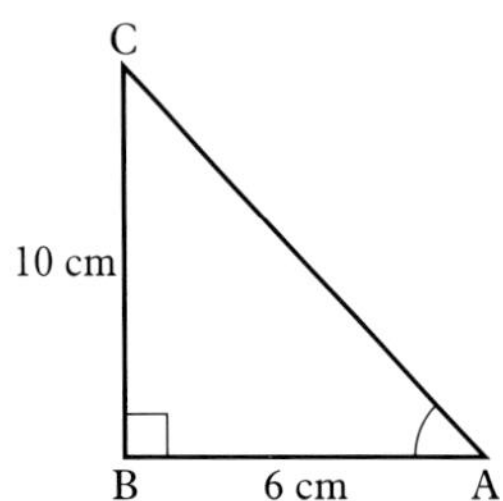

b Find the angle YXZ.

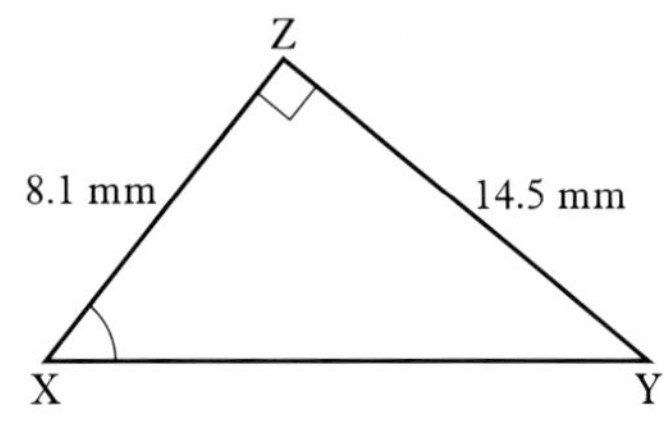

3 Round your answers to 3 sf in this question.

a Find the length JK.

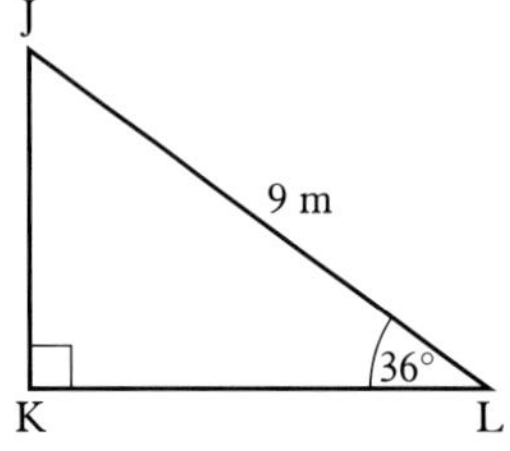

b Find the length RS.

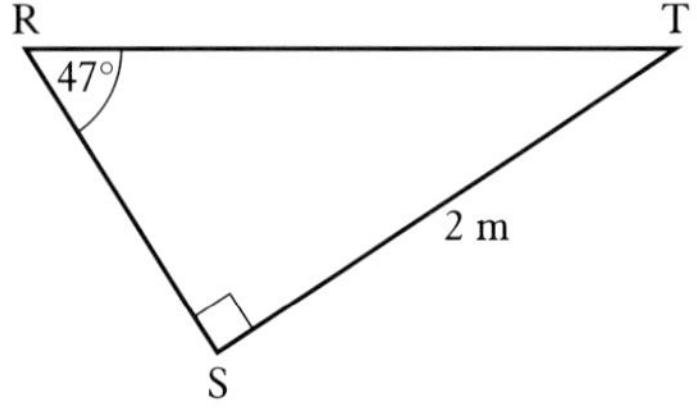

4 Susan wants to find the area of this parallelogram. She starts by working out the height.

a Find the height h.

b What is the area of the parallelogram? Round your answers to 3 sf.

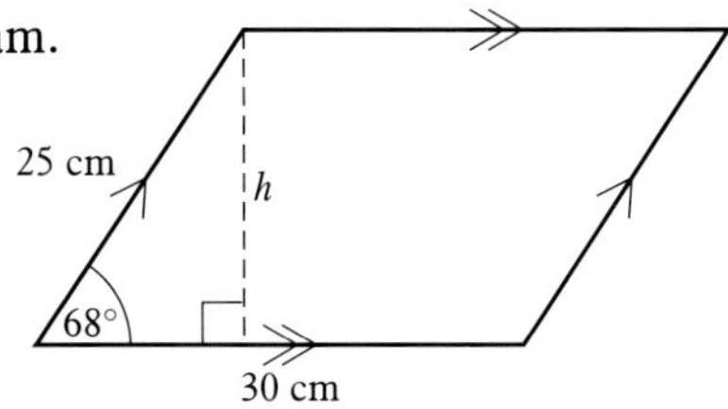

5 A UFO is 20 km from a mountain top. Its angle of descent is 22°. How high is it above the mountain?

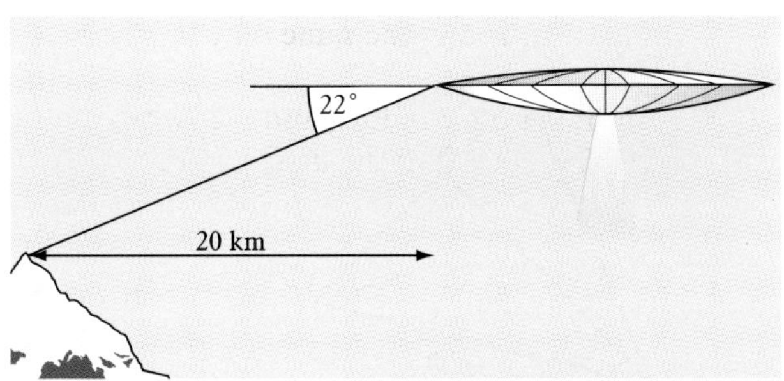

6 In each part of this question give the angles to a sensible degree of accuracy.

a Henry is making a support for a flagpole on the town hall. He uses two planks. One is 2.6 m and the other is 1.2 m long. Find the angle between the pole and the wall.

b Ten years later Neil comes to check the bolt at B with a ladder. B is 6 m above the pavement. The ladder is 8 m long. Calculate the angle that the ladder makes with the pavement.

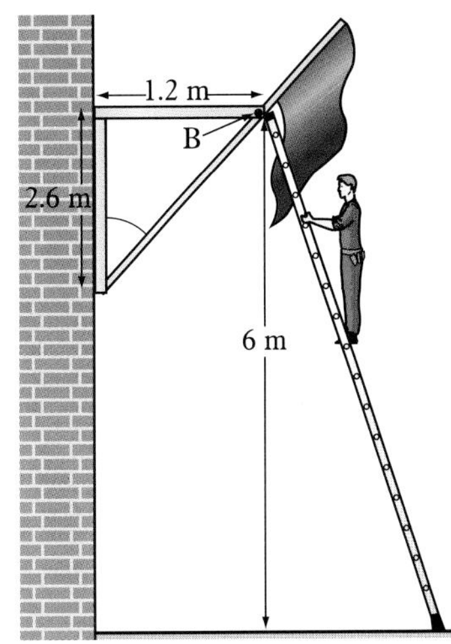

7 A stuntwoman makes a motorcycle jump from the top of one skyscraper to another. One building is 10 m higher than the other. The angle across from the roof of one building to the other is 72°. Calculate the horizontal distance that she must jump.

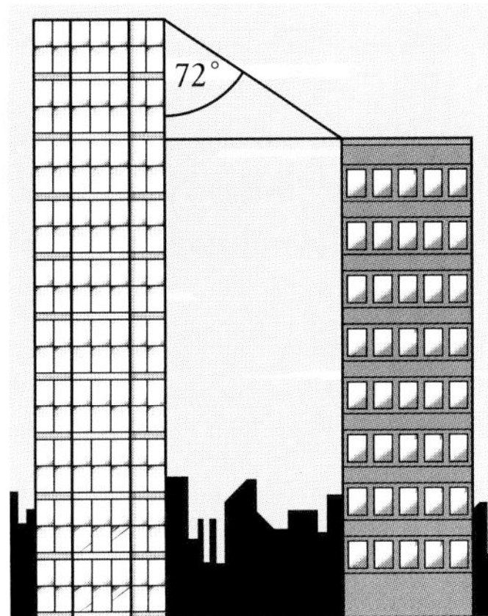

8 Ryan is crossing a mountain crevasse. He has to do it in two stages. He abseils down from A to D and then pushes off from D to the pinnacle at B. He then throws the same rope to Terry at C. If the rope is 7 m long and the angle ABC is 106°, find the distance AC.

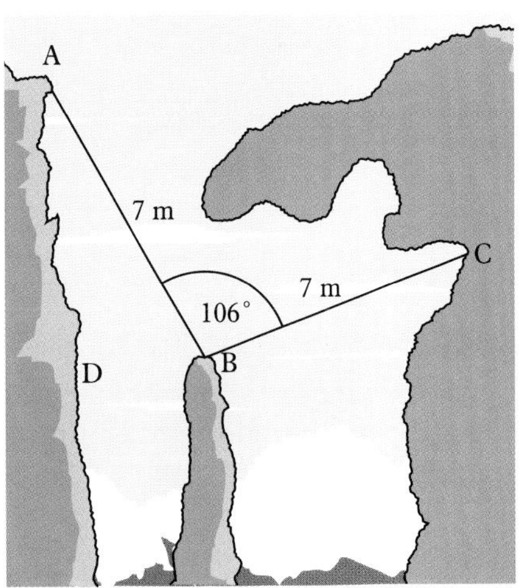

1 Find the angles marked with a letter. Give your answers to a sensible degree of accuracy.

$y°$
1 km
4.88 km
$x°$
2.78 km

2 Madison bridge has a roof. The roof is not symmetrical. Some special ironwork is needed over the ridge.

a Find angles p and q.

b Use these to work out angle r.

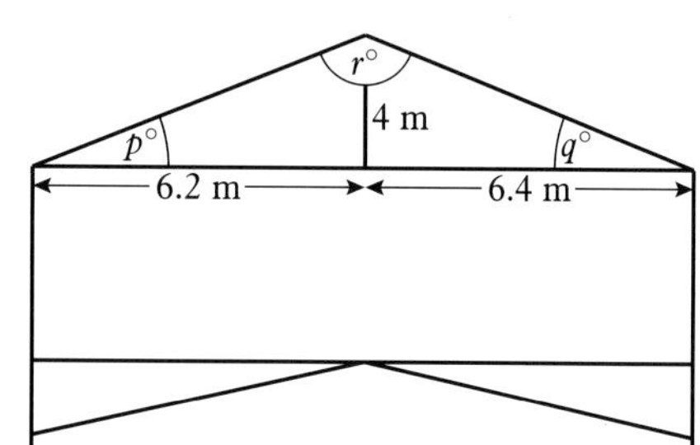

3 Steve has to drive his dumper up the track in a quarry. The track is a collection of slopes shown in red on the diagram. After a lot of excavation Steve's boss asked him to work out the depth of the quarry. This is Steve's diagram. He measured the angles shown with a clinometer.

a What is the depth of the quarry?

b What is the width of the quarry used for the tracks?

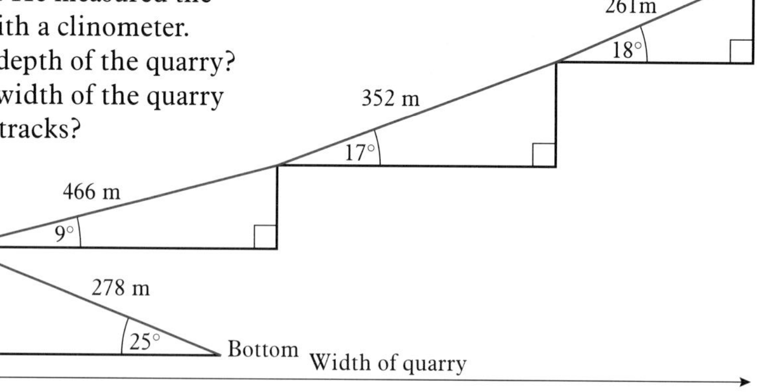

4 The picture shows the jib of a crane. Using the information given, work out the angle between the arms of the jib.

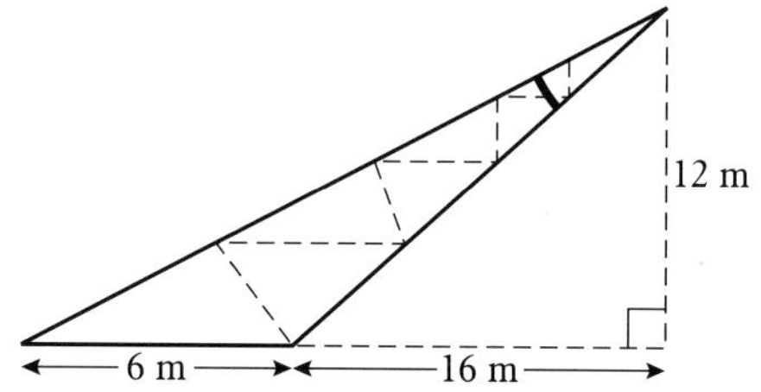

1 Find the angles marked with letters.
Give your answers to 1 dp.

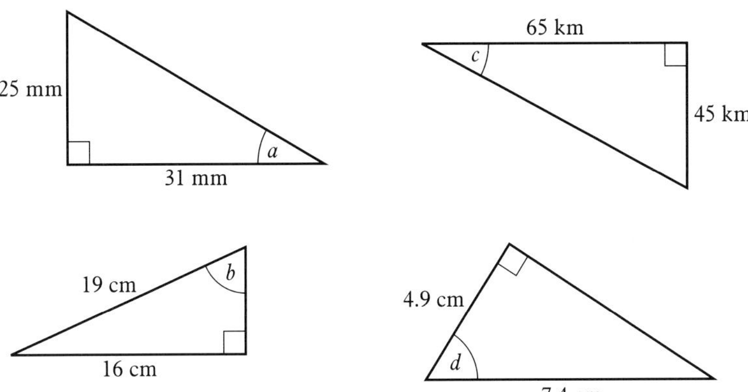

2 A railway climbs a cliff.
The track climbs steadily for 680 m.
The cliff is 147 m high.
Find the angle *x*.
Give your answer to 1 dp.

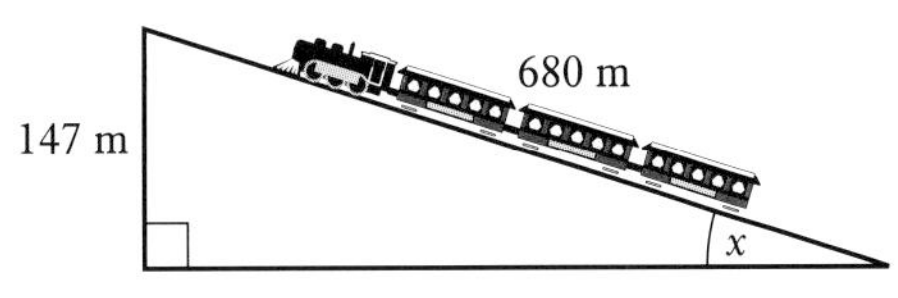

3 Find the sides marked with letters.
Give your answers to 3 sf.

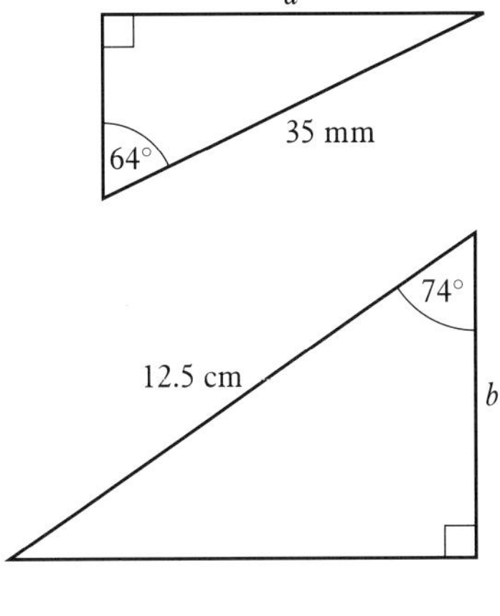

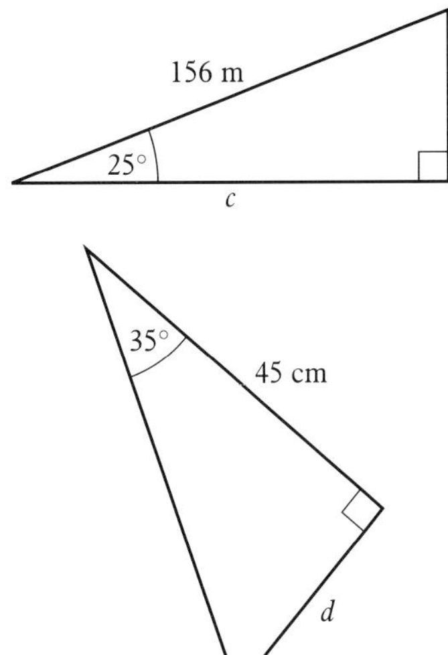

4 Find the angle x in this rectangle.
Give your answer to 1 dp.

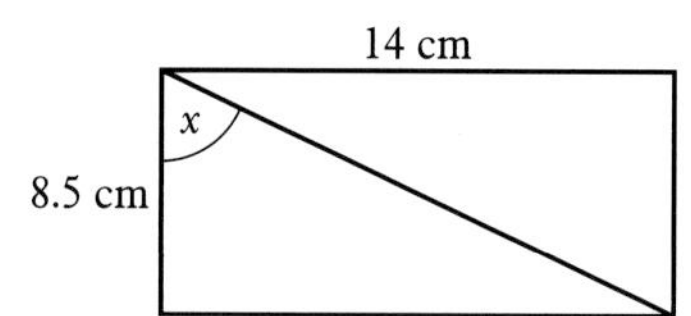

5 A boat leaves port and sails 21 nautical miles north and then 15 nautical miles east.
Find the bearing of its new position from the port.

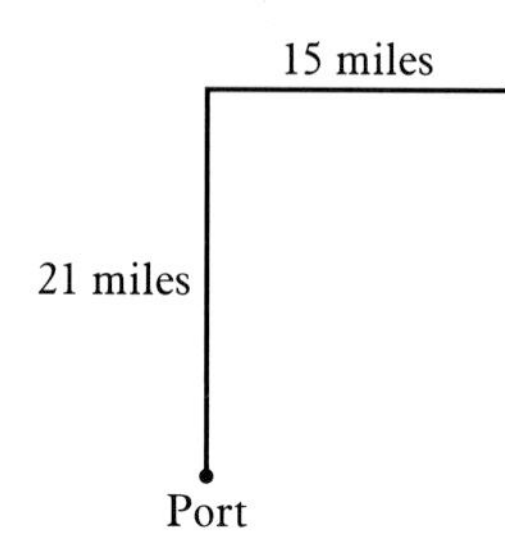

6 Find the length x in this equilateral triangle.
Give your answer to 3 sf.

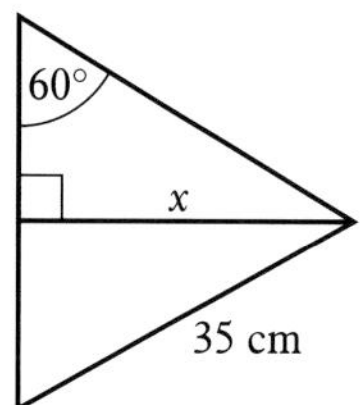

7 Matthew is using a ski-lift.
The lift travels 532 m at an angle of 43°.
How high does the lift climb?
Give your answer to 3 sf.

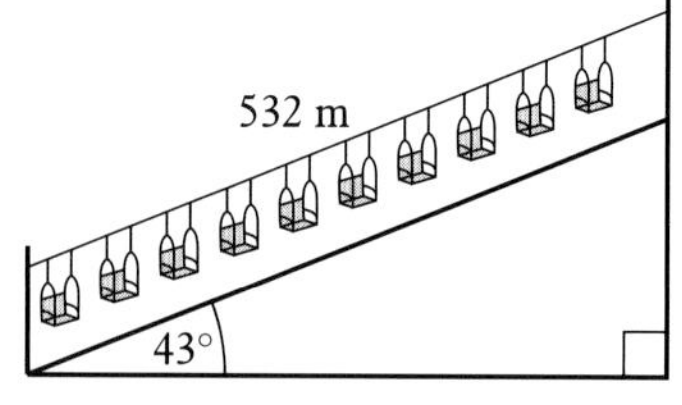

8 **a** The point P has co-ordinates (12, 28).
O is the origin (0, 0).
Find the angle x, to 1 dp.

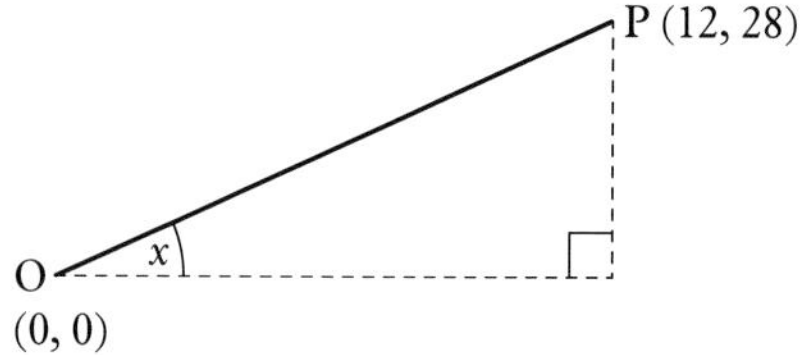

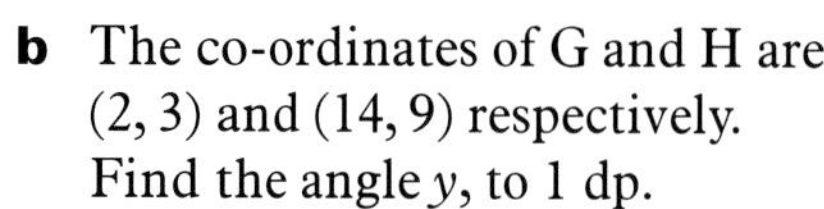

b The co-ordinates of G and H are (2, 3) and (14, 9) respectively.
Find the angle y, to 1 dp.

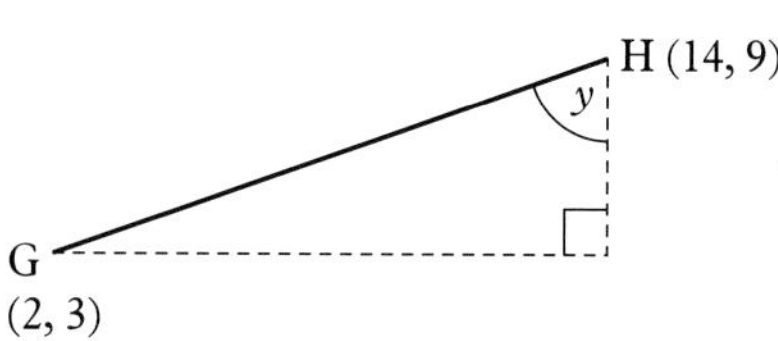

22 Algebra: changing form

CORE

1 Brackets
Collecting like terms
Multiplying out brackets
Multiplying out two brackets

2 Factorising
Looking for common factors
Cancelling algebraic fractions
Factorising quadratics

QUESTIONS

EXTENSION

TEST YOURSELF

1 Brackets

Let's face it, its about time you learnt how to multiply out brackets!

First, here is a recap of some of the skills you learnt in Chapter 8.

Collecting terms

Collecting terms means adding or subtracting terms in an equation or formula to make it simpler.
To collect terms together they must have exactly the same letters in them.

Example

Simplify these by collecting terms where possible.

a $t + t + t + t + t$ **c** $3ab^2 + 5ab^2 - 2ab^2$
b $3a + 6bc + 2a - 4bc$ **d** $3a^2b + 5ab^2$

a Adding 5 ts together gives 5 lots of t.
$t + t + t + t + t = 5 \times t = 5t$

b The terms involving a can be collected together.
So can the terms with bc in them.
You can't collect the as and the bcs together.
$3a + 6bc + 2a - 4bc = 5a + 2bc$

c The terms all involve ab^2 so these can be collected.
$3ab^2 + 5ab^2 - 2ab^2 = 6ab^2$

d Both terms involve a and b and 'squared' but the power 2 is on a different letter in each term.
These terms **cannot** be collected.

Exercise 22:1

1 Simplify these by collecting terms.

a $g + g + g + h + h$

b $k + k + k - s - s - s$

c $t + t - t + h - h + h$

d $k + k + k + r - r + r - r$

e $y + y + t - y + t + t$

f $a + a + a - a - a + b$

2 Simplify these by collecting terms.

a $3g + 3g + 7g + 2g$

b $5m + 7m - 5m + 3k + 5k$

c $3t + 7t + 5s - 6s + 9s$

d $3r - 6y + 5w - 9w$

e $7y - 6y + 2h - 4h + y$

f $5a - 12a + 3b - 5b + 8c$

3 Simplify these by collecting terms.

a $3ab + 9ab$

b $7mn - 5mn + 4mn$

c $6ts - 2st$

d $13pr - 8pr + 6kw - 10kw$

e $9xy - 11xy + 3xz - 4xz$

f $5ad - 9da + 6bc - 6cb$

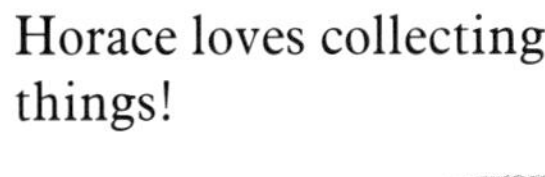

Horace loves collecting things!

4 Simplify these by collecting terms where possible.
When it is not possible to collect terms, give a reason.

a $3x^2 + 7x^2$

b $7x^2 - 8x^2$

c $5t^2 + 2t^3 + 2t^3$

d $9r^2s - 6rs^2$

e $5y^2 - 6y^2 - y^3$

f $5a^2 - 3a^2 + 6a^3$

5 Simplify these by collecting terms where possible.
When it is not possible to collect terms, give a reason.

a $7x^2 + 4x^2 + 8y^2 - 3y^2$

b $11x^2 - 15x^2 - 7z^2 - 2z^2$

c $5t^2y - 3h + 6ty^2 + 8h^2$

d $8a^2b - 3a^2b - 3a^2b$

e $3xy^2 + 9xy - 12x^2y$

f $3x^2yz + 3yx^2z - zyx^2$

You also learnt how to multiply out brackets.

Example Multiply out these brackets.

a $4(x + 7)$ **b** $-6(x^2 - 4)$ **c** $7(x^2 + 3x - 4)$

a To work out $4(x + 7)$ multiply the 4 and the x by the 7.

$$4(x + 7) = 4 \times x + 4 \times 7$$
$$= 4x + 28$$

b Notice that there is a minus sign outside the bracket.

$$-6(x^2 - 4) = -6 \times x^2 + (-6) \times (-4)$$
$$= -6x^2 + 24$$

c It doesn't matter how many terms there are in the bracket.

$$7(x^2 + 3x - 4) = 7 \times x^2 + 7 \times 3x + 7 \times (-4)$$
$$= 7x^2 + 21x - 28$$

Exercise 22:2

Multiply out these brackets.

1 $6(x + 3)$

2 $2(y - 5)$

3 $7(3x + 5)$

4 $5(7x - 3)$

5 $-3(x + 7)$

6 $4(2x - 1)$

7 $-6(5x + 5)$

8 $-5(y^2 - 3)$

9 $6(2y^2 - 4y)$

10 $5(x^2 - 3x - 7)$

11 $-4(x^2 + 5y - y^2)$

12 $-5(2xy - x^2z)$

You can also have letters outside the brackets.

Example Multiply out these brackets.

a $c(d + 4)$ **b** $f(5f - 7)$ **c** $y^2(2y - x)$

a To work out $c(d + 4)$, multiply the d and the 4 by c.

$$c(d + 4) = c \times d + c \times 4$$
$$= cd + 4c$$

b In this part, notice that $f \times f$ gives you f^2.

$$f(5f - 7) = f \times 5f - f \times 7$$
$$= 5f^2 - 7f$$

c Always make sure that letters are written in alphabetical order.

$$y^2(2y - x) = y^2 \times 2y - y^2 \times x$$
$$= 2y^3 - xy^2$$

Exercise 22:3

Multiply out these brackets.

1 $x(x + 3)$

2 $a(b - 7)$

3 $c(c + 9)$

4 $x(3x - 7)$

5 $x^2(2x + 4)$

6 $y(x^2 - 8)$

7 $y(y^3 - 5y^2)$

8 $4g(g^2 + 5g - 2)$

• **9** $xy^2(xy - xy^3)$

Multiplying out two brackets

Multiplying one bracket by another is just slightly more complicated. You have to remember to multiply *all* of the terms in the second bracket by *all* of the terms in the first bracket.

Here is a simple way of remembering how to do this.

Example Multiply out $(x + 4)(x - 2)$.

(1) Multiply the two **F**irst terms together: $(\mathbf{x} + 4)(\mathbf{x} - 2)$ $\mathbf{x^2}$

(2) Multiply the two **O**utside terms together: $(\mathbf{x} + 4)(x - \mathbf{2})$ $\mathbf{-2x}$

(3) Multiply the two **I**nside terms together: $(x + \mathbf{4})(\mathbf{x} - 2)$ $\mathbf{4x}$

(4) Multiply the two **L**ast terms together: $(x + \mathbf{4})(x - \mathbf{2})$ $\mathbf{-8}$

(5) Collect all the terms together: $x^2 - 2x + 4x - 8$
$= x^2 + 2x - 8$

You can remember this using the word **FOIL**.
If you draw lines between the terms as you multiply them, you get a face! This may also help you to remember to multiply all the terms.

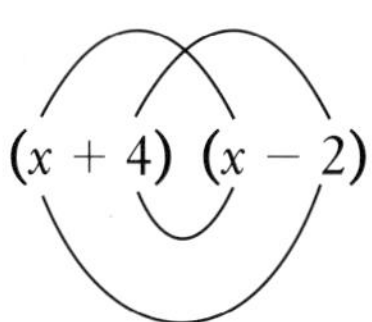

Exercise 22:4

1 Copy this diagram.
Use it to help you multiply out $(x + 3)(x + 2)$.

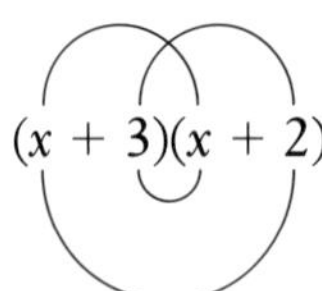

2 Copy this diagram.
Use it to help you multiply out $(x + 5)(x + 8)$.

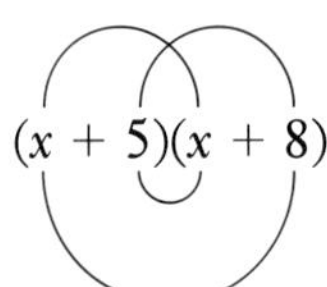

3 Multiply out each of these pairs of brackets.

a $(x + 3)(x + 7)$
b $(x + 4)(x - 7)$
c $(x + 3)(x - 9)$
d $(x - 4)(x + 5)$
e $(x + 5)(x - 3)$
f $(x - 4)(x + 2)$
g $(x - 10)(x - 5)$
h $(x - 4)(x - 8)$

4 Multiply out each of these pairs of brackets.

a $(2x + 3)(x + 2)$
b $(3x + 4)(x - 3)$
c $(4x + 3)(x - 1)$
d $(3x - 4)(x + 9)$
e $(2x + 5)(x - 6)$
f $(7x - 1)(2x + 2)$
g $(2x - 10)(3x + 6)$
h $(5x - 4)(5x - 6)$

2 Factorising

Terry and Louise are doing an investigation.

They have found different formulas for the same problem.

They want to know if they are the same.

Factorising is the opposite of multiplying out brackets.
When you factorise you put brackets in!

The first thing to look for is a common factor in the numbers.

Example

Factorise $6x + 10y$

The numbers 6 and 10 both have a factor of 2.
2 is the biggest number that divides exactly into 6 and 10.
You take the 2 outside a bracket as a factor.
$6x + 10y = 2(\qquad)$

Next, you work out what goes inside the bracket.
$2 \times 3x = 6x$ and $2 \times 5y = 10y$
So inside the bracket you are left with $3x + 5y$.

This means that $6x + 10y = 2(3x + 5y)$.

You can check that 2 is the largest factor you could have taken out by looking at what is left inside the bracket.
3 and 5 have no common factors so the 2 is correct.

Exercise 22:5

1 Factorise each of these.
Use the hints to help you in parts **a** to **g**.

a $6x + 14 \quad = 2(\qquad)$
b $3x - 9 \quad = 3(\qquad)$
c $8y - 12 \quad = 4(\qquad)$
d $5t + 15 \quad = 5(\qquad)$
e $14x - 7 \quad = 7(\qquad)$
f $16x - 12 \quad = 4(\qquad)$
g $24y - 36 \quad = 12(\qquad)$
h $9x - 15$
i $10x - 15$
j $18y - 12$
k $27t - 18$
l $15x - 10y + 20z$
m $6y - 6x - 6z$
n $12e + 4f - 24g$

You can also take letters outside brackets as common factors.

The expression $xy + xz$ has a common factor of x.
$xy + xz$ has an x in both terms.
So $xy + xz = x(y + z)$

The expression $y^2 + y$ has a common factor of y.
$y^2 + y$ has a y in both terms.
So $y^2 + y = y(y + 1)$

Notice the 1 at the end of the bracket. It is very important.
If you multiply the bracket out you must get back to where you started.

$$y(y + 1) = y \times y + y \times 1$$
$$= y^2 + y$$

If you missed the 1 out, you would not get the y term at the end.

---

2 Factorise each of these.
Use the hints to help you in parts **a** to **g**.

a $tx + ty \quad = t(\qquad)$
b $ab + ac \quad = a(\qquad)$
c $3x - xy \quad = x(\qquad)$
d $5x - 2xz = x(\qquad)$
e $y^2 + 5y \quad = y(\qquad)$
f $3x^2 + 5x = x(\qquad)$
g $2j + 4jk \quad = 2j(\qquad)$
h $pq - p^2$
i $t^3 + t$
j $x^3 + x^2 + x$
k $8xz - 3ax$
l $g^4 + g^2$
m $7x + 13x^3$
n $5y^2 + 3y + 4yz$

Sometimes you can take out numbers *and* letters as factors.

Example Factorise completely $15x^2 - 10x$.

15 and 10 have a common factor of 5.
So $15x^2 - 10x = 5(3x^2 - 2x)$

$3x^2$ and $2x$ have a common factor of x.
So $15x^2 - 10x = 5x(3x - 2)$

You could do this all at once by seeing that the common factor is $5x$.

Exercise 22:6

1 Factorise each of these.
Use the hints to help you.

a $6x^2 + 3x = 3x(\qquad)$
b $15y^2 - 5y = 5y(\qquad)$
c $4st + 8sr = 4s(\qquad)$
d $9t^2 - 3st = 3t(\qquad)$

2 Factorise each of these.

a $10x^2 + 5x$ **b** $12y^2 + 6y$ **c** $18st - 27sr$ **d** $40t^2 + 30st$

3 Factorise each of these.

a $6x^2 + 3xy - 12xz$
b $5t^2 - 5tr - 5ts$
c $4ab^2 + 8ab - 12a^2b$
d $36h^3 - 12h^2 + 18h$

4 Kelly factorises $24y^3 - 18y^2 + 30yz$.
She writes the answer as $3(8y^3 - 6y^2 + 10yz)$.

a Explain how you can tell that Kelly has not *fully* factorised the expression.
b Factorise the expression fully.

Cancelling fractions

Putting fractions into their simplest form is known as cancelling.

Example Write each of these fractions in their simplest form.

a $\frac{6}{9}$ **b** $\frac{10}{15}$

Look for the biggest number that divides exactly into both the numerator and denominator.

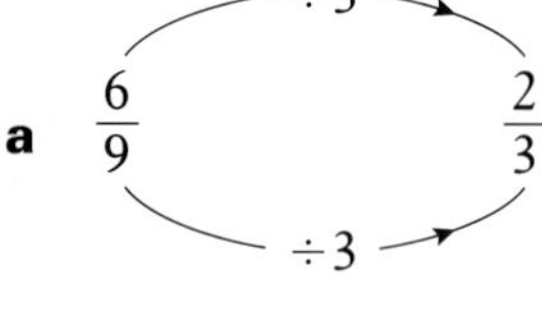

a $\frac{2}{3}$ is the simplest form of $\frac{6}{9}$

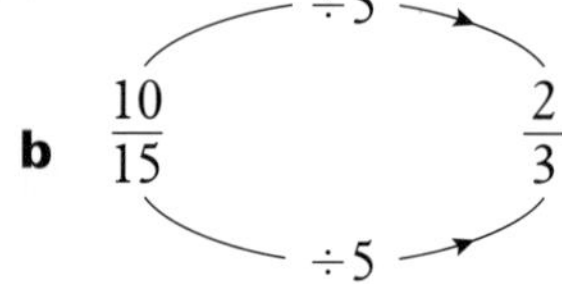

b $\frac{2}{3}$ is the simplest form of $\frac{10}{15}$

The fractions $\frac{2}{3}$, $\frac{6}{9}$ and $\frac{10}{15}$ are all equal.

They are called equivalent fractions.

Exercise 22:7

1 Write each of these fractions in their simplest form

a $\frac{12}{16}$ **b** $\frac{40}{100}$ **c** $\frac{16}{48}$ **d** $\frac{24}{60}$ **e** $\frac{14}{16}$ **f** $\frac{28}{42}$

2 Look at these fractions. $\frac{15}{20}$, $\frac{12}{32}$, $\frac{21}{28}$, $\frac{17}{34}$, $\frac{33}{88}$, $\frac{21}{42}$, $\frac{27}{36}$, $\frac{40}{80}$

Write down the fractions equivalent to

a $\frac{1}{2}$ **b** $\frac{3}{4}$ **c** $\frac{3}{8}$

Algebraic fractions work like normal fractions.
You can look at equivalent fractions.

Look at the fraction $\dfrac{5}{x}$

This is the same as the fraction $\dfrac{10}{2x}$

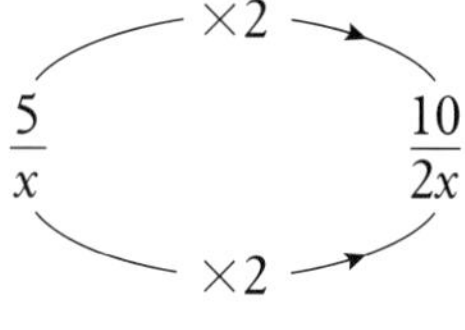

You can cancel fractions too.

The fraction $\dfrac{15}{3x}$ cancels down to give $\dfrac{5}{x}$.

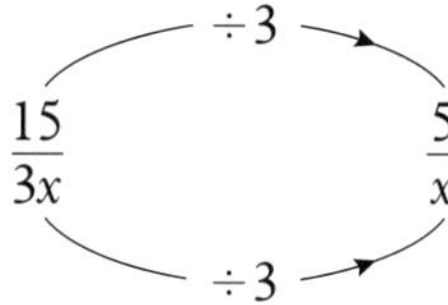

---

3 Copy these. Fill in the gaps.

a $\frac{5}{x} = \frac{\dots}{4x}$ **c** $\frac{7}{x} = \frac{\dots}{3x}$ **e** $\frac{9}{x} = \frac{9x}{\dots}$

b $\frac{4}{x} = \frac{8}{\dots}$ **d** $\frac{8}{x} = \frac{\dots}{5x}$ **f** $8 = \frac{\dots}{1} = \frac{\dots}{\mathrm{x}}$

4 Simplify these.

a $\frac{14}{7x}$ **c** $\frac{16x}{2}$ **e** $\frac{x^2}{x}$

b $\frac{3x}{5x}$ **d** $\frac{16x}{24x}$ **f** $\frac{6x^2}{3x}$

You can also cancel brackets

Example Write the fraction $\frac{4(x+1)}{3(x+1)}$ in its simplest form.

$$\frac{4(x+1)}{3(x+1)} \xrightarrow{\div(x+1)} \frac{4}{3}$$

$\frac{4}{3}$ is the simplest form of $\frac{4(x+1)}{3(x+1)}$

---

5 Simplify these.

a $\frac{8(x-2)}{9(x-2)}$ **c** $\frac{8(x^2-1)}{12(x^2-1)}$ **e** $\frac{4(x+1)(x-2)}{(x+1)(x-2)}$

b $\frac{4(2x+1)}{2(2x+1)}$ **d** $\frac{5(x+3)}{10(x+3)}$ **f** $\frac{18(x-5)}{9x(x-5)}$

6 **a** Factorise $x^2 + 5x$
b Use your answer to part **a** to simplify $\frac{x^2+5x}{2(x+5)}$

7 Factorise and simplify these fractions.

a $\frac{5x+15}{x+3}$ **c** $\frac{2x^2-x}{(2x-1)}$ **e** $\frac{8x-32}{4(x-4)}$

Factorising quadratics

Exercise 22:8

1 Multiply out each of these pairs of brackets:

a $(x + 3)(x + 7)$
b $(x + 4)(x - 7)$
c $(x + 3)(x - 9)$
d $(x - 4)(x + 5)$
e $(x + 5)(x - 3)$
f $(3x - 4)(2x + 2)$
g $(6x - 4)(2x - 5)$
h $(7x - 4)(2x - 8)$

2 Copy this table. Use your answers to question **1** parts **a** to **e** to fill it in. The first one is done for you.

	number at end of 1st bracket	number at end of 2nd bracket	coefficient of x	constant term
a	3	7	10	21
b	4	−7		
c	3	−9		
d	−4	5		
e	5	−3		

In question **2** you should have noticed that when you multiply out two brackets that both start with x:

The **coefficient of x** is found by *adding* the two numbers at the end of the brackets together.

The **constant term** is found by *multiplying* the two numbers at the end of the brackets together.

Example $(x + 4)(x - 7) = x^2 \quad -3x \quad -28$

$+4 + -7 = -3$ $\qquad$ $+4 \times -7 = -28$

Once you know these facts, you can use them to reverse the process. This means taking a quadratic expression and splitting it back into two brackets.
This process is known as **factorising a quadratic**.

Example Factorise $x^2 + 5x + 6$.

The brackets will be $(x + ?)(x + ?)$.

The two numbers at the end of the brackets
add together to give 5 and
multiply together to give 6.

The two numbers that do this are 2 and 3.
So $x^2 + 5x + 6 = (x + 2)(x + 3)$

3 Factorise these quadratic expressions.

a $x^2 + 7x + 10$
b $x^2 + 10x + 16$
c $x^2 + 12x + 27$
d $x^2 + 14x$
e $x^2 + 15x + 36$
f $x^2 - 3x - 18$
g $x^2 - 7x - 30$
h $x^2 + 4x - 32$
i $x^2 + 6x - 40$
j $x^2 - x$

You will also find it helpful to look at the signs in the equation you are factorising.

$x^2 + 5x + 6$
$= (x + ?)(x + ?)$

The number at the end is +6.
The numbers must be the same sign so that they multiply to give a +.
They must both be + because they add to give +5.

$x^2 - 7x + 10$
$= (x - ?)(x - ?)$

The number at the end is +10.
The numbers must be the same sign so that they multiply to give a +.
They must both be − because they add to give −7.

$x^2 + 3x - 10$
$= (x + ?)(x - ?)$

The number at the end is −10.
The numbers must have different signs so that they multiply to give a −.
The + number must be bigger because they add to give a + total.

4 Factorise these quadratic expressions.

a $x^2 + 5x - 14$
b $x^2 - 4x - 5$
c $x^2 - 12x + 32$
d $x^2 + 17x + 60$
e $x^2 + 8x - 20$
f $x^2 - x - 12$
g $x^2 + x - 12$
h $x^2 - 7x - 44$
● **i** $x^2 + x + 0.25$
● **j** $x^2 - 9$

Difference of two squares

A quadratic expression which is in the form $x^2 - a^2$ is known as the **difference of two squares**. Difference means subtract. The same rules still work when you are factorising it.

Example

Factorise $x^2 - 16$.
There is no x term so the numbers in the two brackets add to give 0 and multiply to give -16.
They are $+4$ and -4.
$x^2 - 16 = (x - 4)(x + 4)$

The general rule is $\boldsymbol{x^2 - a^2 = (x - a)(x + a)}$

Exercise 22:9

1 Factorise these quadratic expressions.

a $x^2 - 25$
b $x^2 - 36$
c $x^2 - 100$
d $x^2 - 1$
e $x^2 - 49$
● **f** $x^2 - b^2$
● **g** $x^2 - 0.25$
h $x^2 - 289$

2 You can use this method to speed up some calculations.

a Copy this and fill in the gaps.

$$36^2 - 34^2 = (36 + \ldots)(36 - \ldots)$$
$$= \ldots \times \ldots$$
$$=$$

b Use the same method to work out $49^2 - 48^2$.
c Work out $1001^2 - 999^2$.
d Work out $1\,000\,001^2 - 999\,999^2$.

Exercise 22:10

Sharon is still struggling with her algebra. She is still trying to cope without *Key Maths*!

Here is her factorising homework.

Decide which questions are correct and which are wrong.
For the questions you think are wrong, write out correct answers.

1 $3x + 6 = 3(x + 6)$

2 $xy + xz = x(y + z)$

3 $4y^2 + 5y = y^2(4 + 5)$

4 $sp^2 - sp = s(p^2 - p)$

5 $6ax + 4ay + 3az = 2a(3x + 2y + 1\frac{1}{2}z)$

6 $15x^2y + 5xy^2 = 5xy(3xy + y)$

7 $x^2 + 3x + 2 = (x + 3)(x + 1)$

8 $x^2 + 5x - 6 = (x - 2)(x - 3)$

9 $x^2 + 7x + 12 = (x + 3)(x + 4)$

10 $x^2 - 16 = (x - 4)(x - 4)$

11 $x^2 - 121 = (x - 11)(x + 11)$

12 $18^2 - 16^2 = (18 - 16)(18 + 16)$
$= 2 + 34$
$= 36$

1 Simplify these by collecting terms.

a $5f + 2f + 7f + 2f$

b $4n + 3n - 2n + 3j + 4j$

c $2v + 5v + 4h - 5h + 9h$

d $6ab + 5ab$

e $4mn - 3mn + 5mn$

f $5ba - 2ab$

g $5w - 4x + 2y - 3w$

h $7d - 5d + 3e - e + 4f$

i $6b - 12b + 3c - 4c + 6d$

j $11gh - 7gh + 8jk - 11jk$

k $6ab - 4ab + 7ac - 5ac$

l $3ac - 7ca + 9bc - 3cb$

2 Simplify these by collecting terms where possible.
When it is not possible to collect terms, give a reason.

a $5x^2 + 8x^2$

b $6y^2 - 7y^2$

c $4p^2 + 4t^3 + 4t^3$

d $9p^2 + p^2 + 4q^2 - 3q^2$

e $12a^2 - 14a^2 - 8c^2 - 2c^2$

f $6a^2b - 3c + 8ab^2 + 8c^2$

g $12x^2y - 6xy^2$

h $7y^3 - 6y^3 - y^3$

i $4a^2 - 3a^2 + a^3$

j $7a^2b - 4a^2b - 2a^2b$

k $7cd^2 + 10cd - 11c^2d$

l $2p^2qr + 4qp^2r - rqp^2$

3 Find the perimeter of each of these.
Simplify your answers.

a

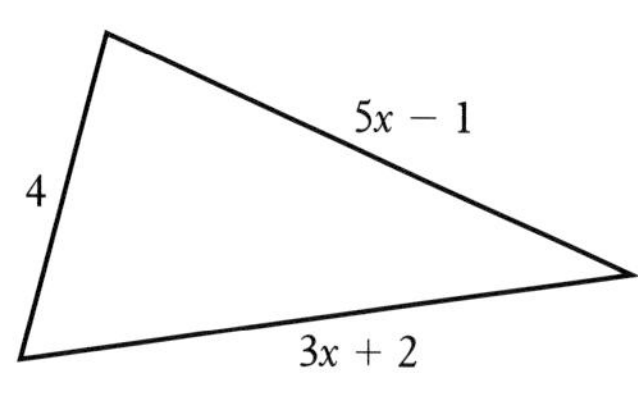

b

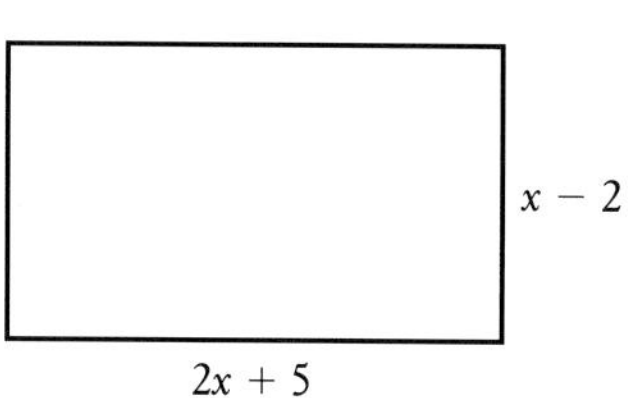

c

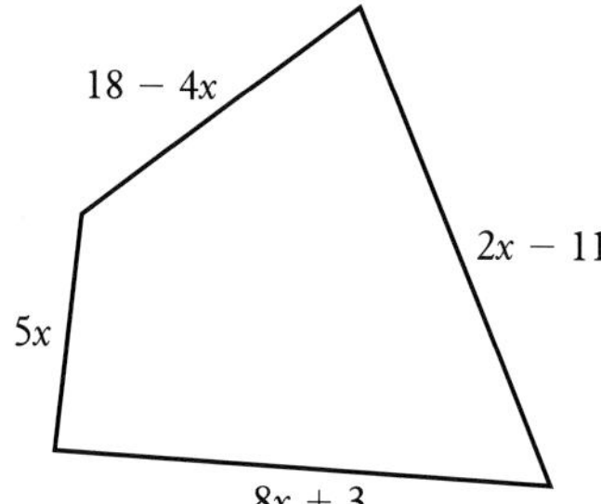

d

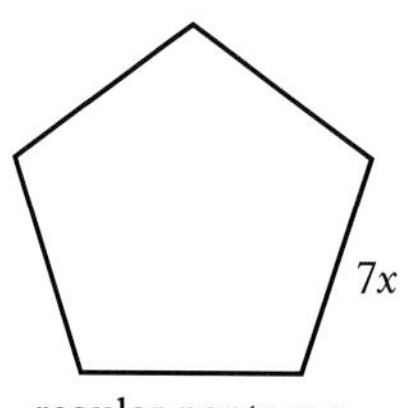

regular pentagon

4 Multiply out these brackets.

a $4(x+2)$
b $3(y-3)$
c $6(2x+3)$
d $5(5x-1)$
e $x(x+2)$
f $a(b-8)$
g $c(c+1)$
h $-2(x+3)$
i $3(3x-4)$
j $-3(4x+1)$
k $-4(y^2-4)$
l $x(4x-5)$
m $x^2(x+2)$
n $b(a^2-3)$
o $4(3y^2-7y)$
p $6(5x^2-2x-6)$
q $-5(2x^2+3y-y^2)$
r $-2(4xy-3x^2z)$
s $y(3y^2-3x^2)$
t $2k(k^2+3k-2)$
u $xy(x^2y-xy^2)$

5 Multiply out each of these pairs of brackets.

a $(x+2)(x+4)$
b $(x+4)(x-5)$
c $(x+5)(x-8)$
d $(x-3)(x+4)$
e $(2x+2)(x-2)$
f $(4x+1)(x-6)$
g $(3x-5)(x+7)$
h $(2x+5)(2x-4)$
i $(4x-3)(3x+1)$
j $(3x-8)(4x-4)$
k $(3x-10)(3x-5)$
l $(7x-4)(2x+2)$
m $(2x-10)(3x+2)$
n $(5x-3)(5x-5)$

6 Find the area of each of these rectangles.
Multiply out any brackets and simplify your answers.

a

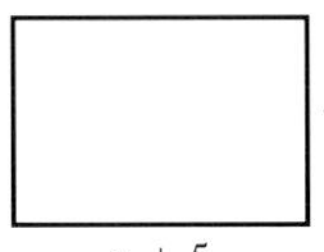

b

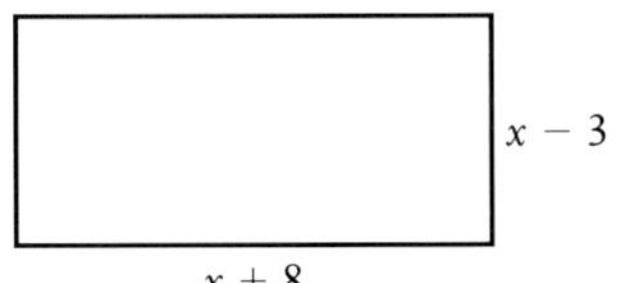

c

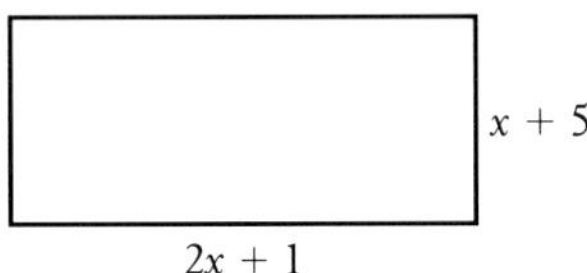

d

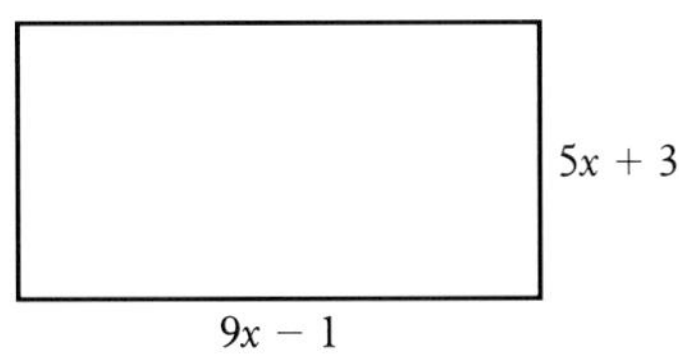

7 Factorise each of these.
Use the hints to help you in parts **a** to **g**.

a $6x + 12 = 6(\quad)$
b $4x - 12 = 4(\quad)$
c $9y - 15 = 3(\quad)$
d $6t + 18 = 6(\quad)$
e $16x - 8 = 8(\quad)$
f $12x - 8 = 4(\quad)$
g $20y - 30 = 10(\quad)$
h $4x - 8$
i $8x - 12$
j $24y - 12$
k $24t - 16$
l $20x - 15y + 20z$
m $3y - 3x - 3z$
n $12e + 4f - 24g$

8 Factorise each of these.
Use the hints to help you in parts **a** to **d**.

a $ta + tb = t(\quad)$
b $ax + ay = a(\quad)$
c $6x - xy = x(\quad)$
d $4x - 3xy = x(\quad)$
e $pr - p^2$
f $k^3 + k$
g $r^3 + r^2 + r$
h $6xy - 3ax$

9 Factorise each of these.
Use the hints to help you in parts **a** to **c**.

a $8y^2 + 4y = 4y(\quad)$
b $20t^2 - 5t = 5t(\quad)$
c $4r^2 + 8rs = 4r(\quad)$
d $12q^2 - 3pq$
e $12w^2 + 6w$
f $30f^2 + 20fg$

10 Simplify these.

a $\frac{15x}{30}$
b $\frac{7x^2}{14x}$
c $\frac{12(x + 2)}{8(x + 2)}$
d $\frac{12(x^2 + 5)}{20(x^2 + 5)}$
e $\frac{8x - 56}{16(x - 7)}$
f $\frac{4x + 24}{5x + 30}$

11 Factorise these quadratic expressions.

a $x^2 + 5x + 4$
b $x^2 + 9x + 14$
c $x^2 + 14x + 40$
d $x^2 + 16x$
e $x^2 + 13x + 36$
f $x^2 - 2x - 24$
g $x^2 - 8x - 20$
h $x^2 + 2x - 35$
i $x^2 + 7x - 30$
j $x^2 - 3x$

12 Factorise these quadratic expressions.

a $x^2 - 16$
b $x^2 - 49$
c $x^2 - 121$
d $x^2 - 4$
e $x^2 - 64$
f $x^2 - 0.64$
g $x^2 - y^2$
h $x^2 - 256$

1 A rectangle has a length of $(x + 5)$ cm and a width of $(x - 2)$ cm.
a If the perimeter of the rectangle is 24 cm find the value of x.
b If the area of the rectangle is 60 cm^2 show that $x^2 + 3x - 70 = 0$

2 When you square an expression you need to multiply it by itself.
If the expression is in a bracket this means that you must multiply the bracket by itself.
So $(x + 2)^2$ means $(x + 2)(x + 2)$
Work these out.

a $(x + 2)^2$	**c** $(x - 3)^2$	**e** $(2x + 3)^2$	**g** $(2x - 3)^2$
b $(x + 4)^2$	**d** $(x - 5)^2$	**f** $(3x + 8)^2$	**h** $(3x - 4)^2$

3 Not all quadratic expressions start with just x^2.
Many start with $2x^2$ or $3x^2$ etc.
If you want to factorise $2x^2 + 7x + 3$ you need to start by deciding what goes at the beginning of each bracket.
One of the brackets must begin with a $2x$.
This is the only way to get $2x^2$ as the first term.
So $2x^2 + 7x + 3 = (2x + ?)(x + ?)$
The two numbers at the end of the brackets must still multiply together to give the constant term.
So you need to try different pairs of values at the end of the brackets until you get the right answer.

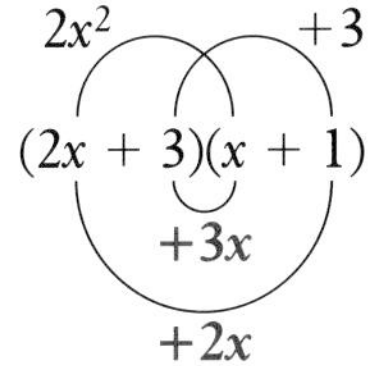

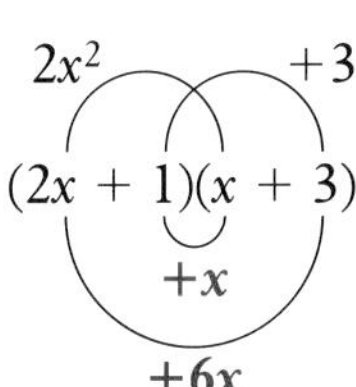

This is wrong because the $+3x$ and the $+2x$ give you $+5x$ and you need $+7x$.

This is right. The $+x$ and the $+6x$ give you $+7x$.

Factorise these quadratics.

a $2x^2 + 7x + 3$	**c** $2x^2 + 12x + 10$	**e** $5x^2 + 2x - 3$
b $3x^2 + 13x + 4$	**d** $7x^2 + 22x + 3$	**f** $2x^2 + 3x - 9$

1 Simplify these by collecting like terms.

a $5k - 2k + k + 7k - 4k$

b $10x - 3y + 2y - x + 4x$

c $2d + d^2 - 4 + 5d^2 - 8 + 3d$

d $6ab^2 + 3a^2b - 8ab^2$

2 Multiply out these brackets and simplify where possible.

a $4(y - 5)$

b $3(x^2 + 2x)$

c $2s(6s - 1)$

d $b^2(8b + 1)$

e $(x + 8)(2x - 1)$

f $(5x - 9)(4x - 1)$

3 **a** Find the perimeter of this quadrilateral. Simplify your answer.

b The perimeter is 38 cm. Write down an equation in x. Solve your equation.

c Use your answer to part **b** to find the lengths of the four sides.

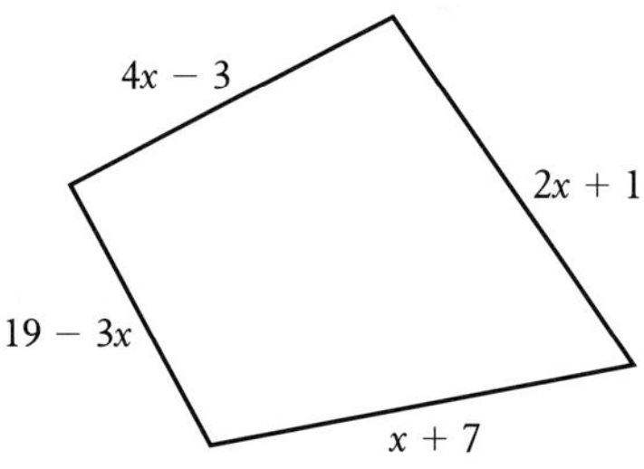

4 Write down the area of this rectangle. Multiply out the brackets and simplify the answer.

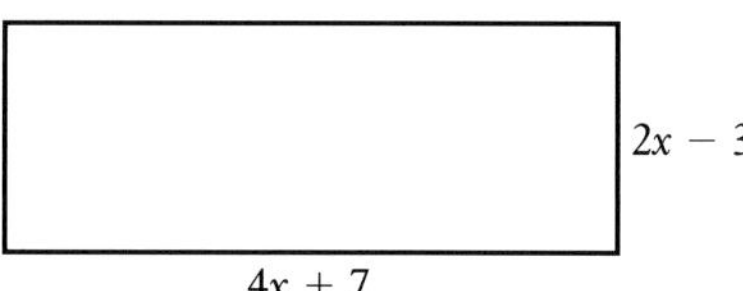

5 Factorise each of these.

a $6t - 4$

b $12y^2 + 4y$

c $24ab^2 + 10ab$

d $12x^2 - 6xy + 9xy^2$

6 Simplify these.

a $\dfrac{16x}{x}$

b $\dfrac{4a^2}{10a}$

c $\dfrac{7(x^2 - 1)}{14(x^2 - 1)}$

d $\dfrac{(x + 2)(x - 1)}{3(x - 1)}$

e $\dfrac{4x + 20}{3(x + 5)}$

f $\dfrac{4x - 2}{6x - 3}$

7 Factorise these quadratic expressions.

a $x^2 + x - 12$

b $a^2 + 8a + 7$

c $y^2 - 10y + 16$

d $x^2 - 81$

23 Round and round

CORE

1 Circumference and perimeter
Learning the names of parts of a circle
Learning about π
Finding the circumference
Finding the diameter and the radius, given the circumference
Finding the perimeter of polygons
Finding the perimeter of shapes involving parts of circles
Exact answers
Looking at dimensions

2 Units of length
Working with metric units of length
Working with imperial units of length
Converting between imperial and metric units of length
Estimating lengths

QUESTIONS

EXTENSION

TEST YOURSELF

1 Circumference and perimeter

The Earth moves in an orbit around the Sun. It takes the Earth 365 days, 5 hours, 48 minutes and 46 seconds to complete one orbit.

The Earth moves so that it is always between 91.4 and 94.6 million miles from the Sun.

If you take the orbit to be a circle of radius 93 million miles that takes 365 days to complete, then we are hurtling through space at more than 66 700 miles per hour!

Diameter

The distance across a circle is called the **diameter**.
A diameter must pass through the centre of the circle.

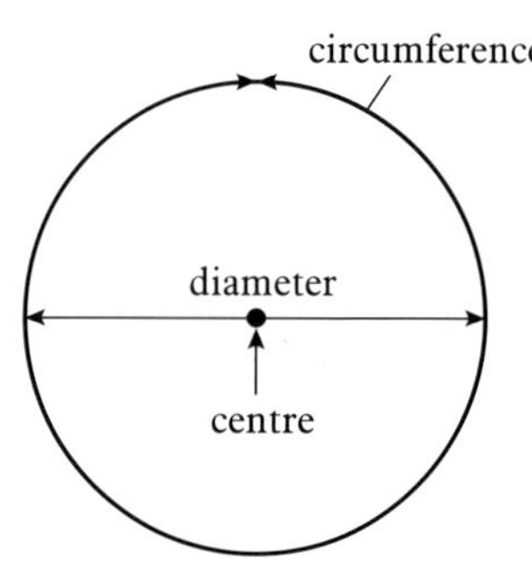

Circumference

The **circumference** of a circle is the distance around the edge of the circle.
The circumference depends on the diameter of the circle.

π

If you divide the circumference of any circle by its diameter you always get the same answer. This answer is a special number called pi. You say this as 'pie' and you write π.

For all circles
*C*ircumference = $\pi \times$ *d*iameter
This rule is often written $C = \pi d$

Key in π on your calculator.

You should get 3.1415927

You might get more digits than this.
It depends which calculator you have.

Example Find the circumference of this circle.

$C = \pi d$

$= \pi \times 8$

Key in: π × 8 =

25.132741

= 25.1 cm to 1 dp

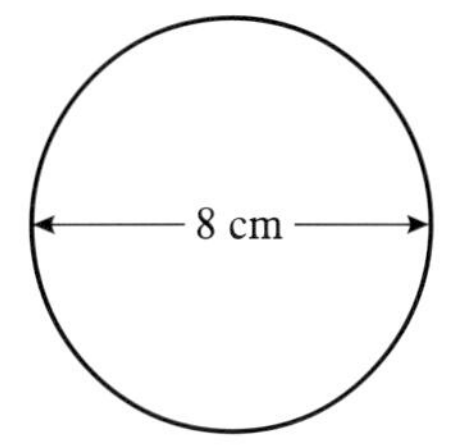

Exercise 23:1

1 Find the circumference of these circles. Give your answers to 1 dp.

a

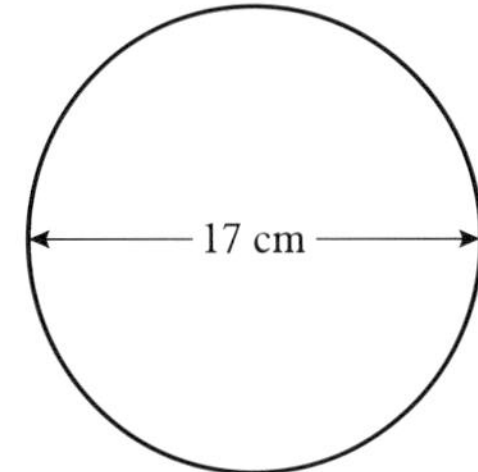

b

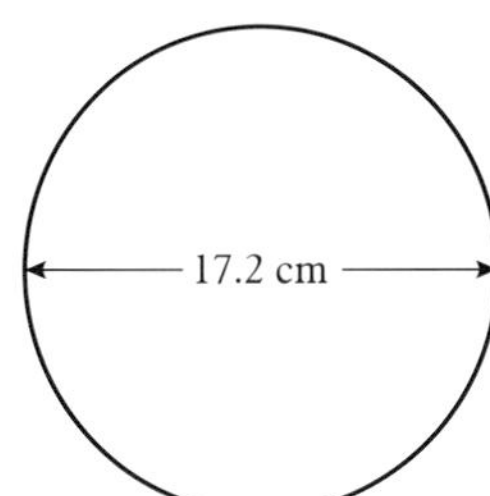

c

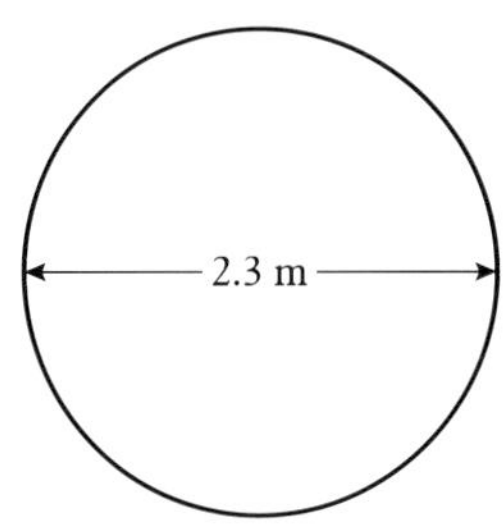

d

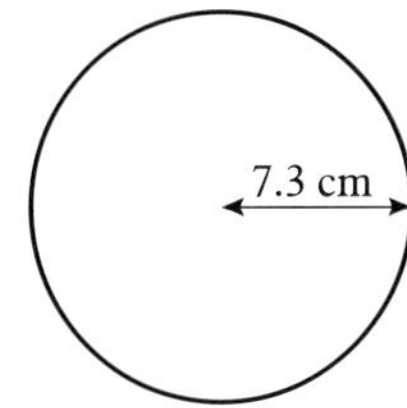

e

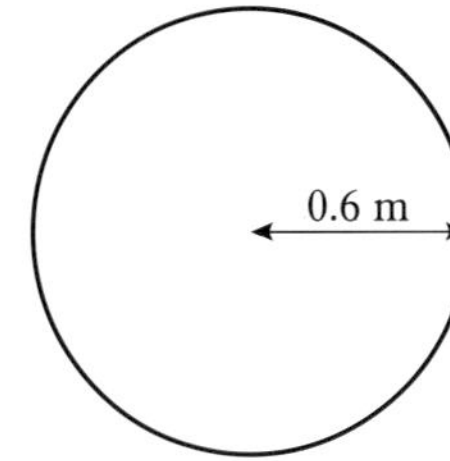

f

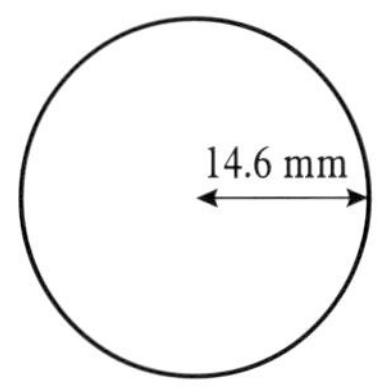

2 This is a photo of a motorway roundabout.
The diameter of the roundabout is 62 m.
Find the circumference of the roundabout.
Give your answer to the nearest metre.

3 Henry lives in a circular windmill. He is a bit eccentric. Every day he walks around the outside of his house 100 times. The windmill has a radius of 3.2 m.

a How far does Henry walk each time he goes round his house?

b How far does Henry walk each day? Give your answer to the nearest metre.

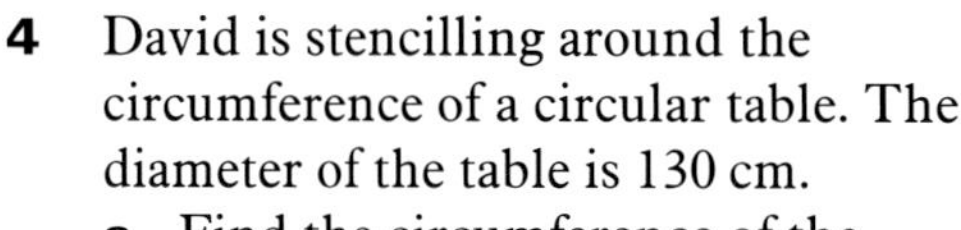

4 David is stencilling around the circumference of a circular table. The diameter of the table is 130 cm.

a Find the circumference of the table.

David is using a stencil that is 20 cm long.

b How many times can David repeat the pattern around the table?

● **c** The pattern must be evenly spaced. How much space should David leave between each pattern?

● **5** **a** Write down the formula for the circumference, C, of a circle with diameter d.

b Rearrange the formula to show that $d = \frac{C}{\pi}$.

This is the formula that you need to use to find the diameter if you are given the circumference.

c Find the diameter of a circle that has a circumference of 20 cm.

Radius The **radius** of a circle is the distance from the centre to the circumference. The radius is half the diameter.

Example The circumference of a circle is 38 cm.
Find **a** the diameter **b** the radius

a Use the formula $d = \frac{C}{\pi}$

$$d = \frac{38}{\pi}$$

Key in: 3 8 ÷ π =

$d = 12.1$ cm to 1 dp to get 12.095776

b The radius is half the diameter.
Don't use the rounded value for the diameter.

Keep the exact value from part **a** in your calculator display and halve that. 12.095776

Key in: ÷ 2 =

Then round your answer. to get 6.0478878

$r = 6.0$ cm to 1 dp

Exercise 23:2

1 Find
(1) the diameter
(2) the radius
of a circle with a circumference of:

a 80 cm **b** 25 cm **c** 120 cm **d** 47.3 cm

Give all your answers to 1 dp.

2 The circumference of a circle is 4 m.
Find **a** the diameter **b** the radius
Give your answers to 2 dp.

3 Find the radius of a circle that has a circumference of 124 cm.
Give your answer to 1 dp.

4 The world's largest Big Wheel is the *Cosmoclock 21* at Yokohama City in Japan. It has a circumference of 1031 feet. Find the radius of the wheel. Give your answer to the nearest foot.

Perimeter The **perimeter** of a shape is the distance around the edge of the shape.

To find the perimeter add up the lengths of all the sides.
The perimeter of this shape is
$4 + 6 + 10 + 14$
$= 34$ cm

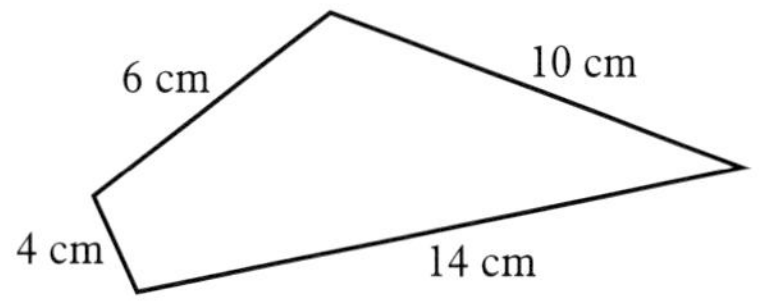

Exercise 23:3

1 Find the perimeter of each of these shapes.

a

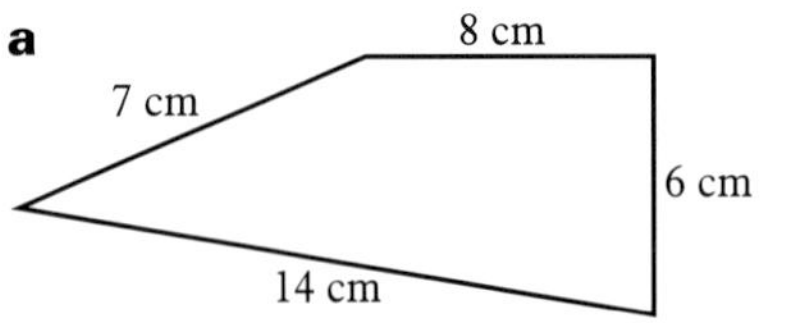

b

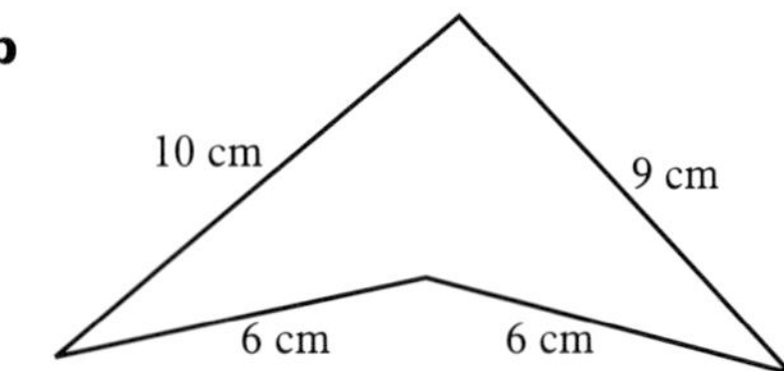

2 Find the perimeter of each of these shapes.
There is enough information to be able to do these questions!

a

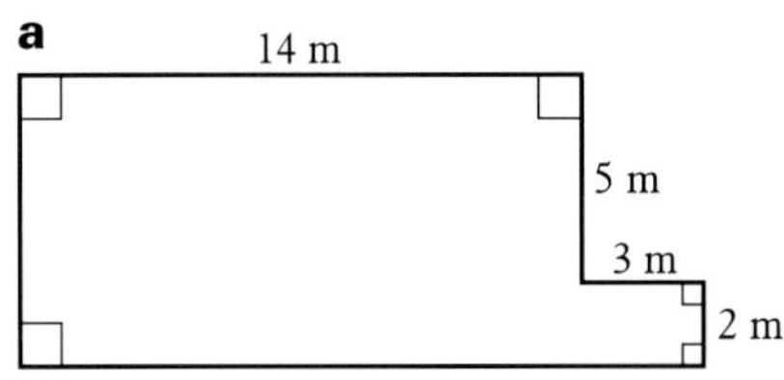

b

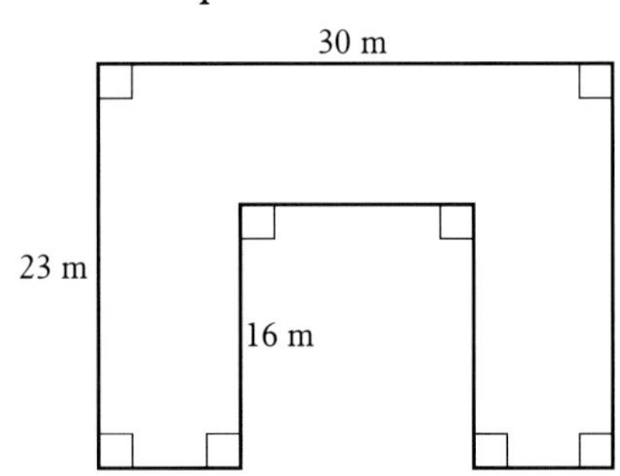

3 Find the perimeter of an equilateral triangle with sides of length 3.5 cm.

4 The Pentagon is the building that holds the offices of the US defence department.
It is the largest office building in the world.
It is a regular pentagon.
Each outside wall is 281 m long.
Find the perimeter of the building.

For a circle the perimeter is the circumference.

Example Find the perimeter of this shape.

The shape is a rectangle and a semi-circle.

Add up the lengths around the edge of the rectangle first.

Red perimeter $= 12 + 18 + 12$
$= 42$ cm

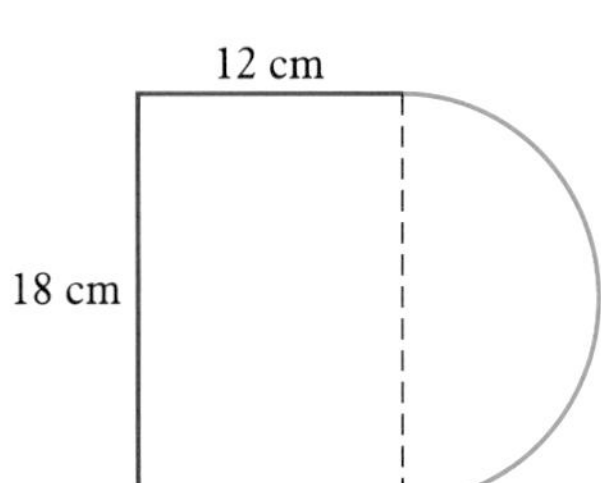

Now work out the blue part of the perimeter.
This is half of the circumference of a circle with diameter 18 cm.

Blue perimeter $= \frac{1}{2} \times \pi \times d$
$= \frac{1}{2} \times \pi \times 18$
$= 28.3$ cm to 1 dp

Key in:

Now add up the two parts of your answer.

Total perimeter $= 42 + 28.3$
$= 70.3$ cm

Exercise 23:4

Work out the perimeter of each of these shapes. Give all of your answers to 1 dp.

1

16 cm, 20 cm

2

4 cm, 4 cm

3

16 cm, 16 cm, 16 cm

4

5 cm

5

8 cm, 16 cm

6

6 cm, 6 cm

● **7**

3 cm, 4 cm, 4 cm, 4 cm, 4 cm

● **8**

3 cm, 18 cm, 3 cm, 5 cm, 5 cm

Sometimes a question will ask you to give an *exact* answer.

You have been working out circumferences using $\pi = 3.141592654$ on your calculator. Although this gives you 9 decimal places and is very accurate, it is not exact. This is because π is a decimal which goes on forever. You could never write the exact answer down as a decimal, however many digits your calculator had.

The only way to give an exact answer is to leave π in your answer.

Example Find the circumference of a circle with radius 12 cm. Leave your answer in terms of π.

$$\text{Circumference} = \pi \times \text{diameter}$$
$$C = \pi \times 24$$
$$= 24\pi$$

This is the exact answer.
Leave answers like this if you are asked for an exact answer or asked to leave your answer in terms of π.

Exercise 23:5

1 Find the circumference of each of these circles.
Leave your answers in terms of π.

a

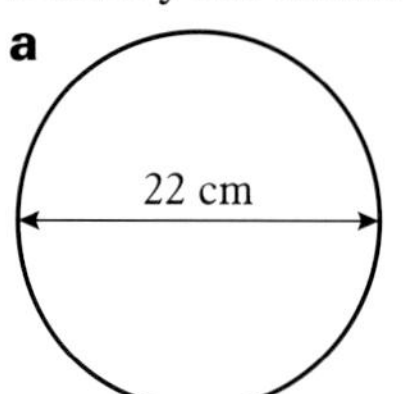

b

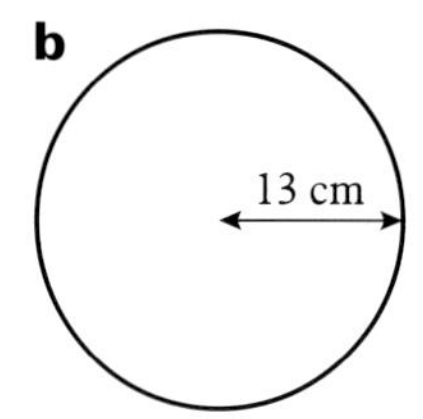

c

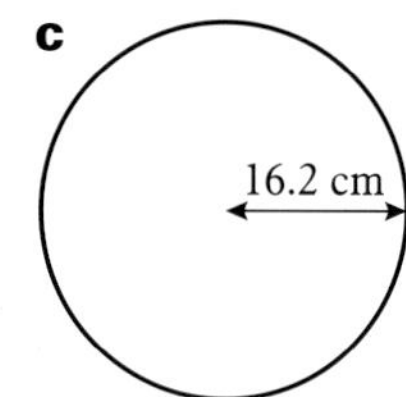

2 Find the exact perimeter of this shape.

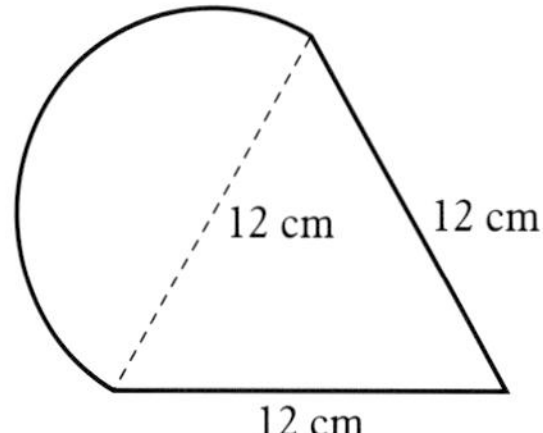

Using dimensions

You can use the dimension of a formula to help you decide what the formula is for. You will see more of this in Chapter 31.

Dimension

The **dimension** of a formula is the number of lengths that are multiplied together.

Length has **one** dimension.	$C = 2d$ is a length formula.
Any formula for length can only involve constants and **one** length.	2 is a constant. d is a length.

Constant

A **constant** has no dimension. It is just a number.
2, 3, 1.7, and π are all constants.

Area has **two** dimensions.	$A = \pi r^2$ is an area formula.
Any formula for area can only involve constants and **two** lengths that are multiplied together.	π is a constant. $r^2 = r \times r$ which is length $\times$ length.
Volume has **three** dimensions.	$V = \frac{4}{3}\pi r^2 h$ is a volume formula.
Any formula for volume can only involve constants and **three** lengths that are multiplied together.	$\frac{4}{3}$ and π are constants. $r^2 h = r \times r \times h$ which is length $\times$ length $\times$ length

---

Exercise 23:6

1 In this question p, q and r are lengths.
Write down the dimension of each of these expressions.

a p **c** $2rq$ **e** pqr **g** $3pq$
b $3p$ **d** $4pq$ **f** $5kr$ **h** $5p$

2 In this question l, b, h and r are lengths.
Which of these formulas could be for length?

a $3l$ **b** $2\pi l$ **c** $r(r + h)$ **d** $2\pi(r + b)$

3 In this question p, q, r, s and t are lengths.
Write down what each formula could represent.

a $p + s$ **c** $2rq + 4st$ **e** $5p + r$ **g** p^3
b $3q + 5t$ **d** $4pq + 2rp$ **f** $5\pi p + 3r$ **h** p^2q

2 Units of length

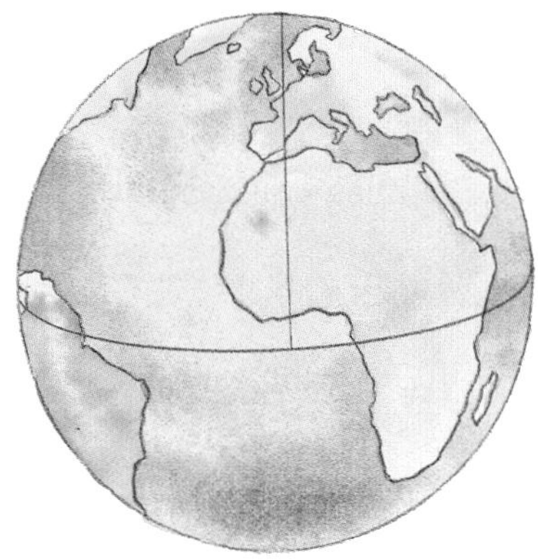

At the start of the 19th century French scientists invented a new unit of length. They worked out the distance from the North Pole to the Equator and divided it by 10 million. They called this distance 1 metre. The metric system of weights and measures is named after the metre.

Metric units of length

The **metric units of length** are millimetres (mm), centimetres (cm), metres (m) and kilometres (km).

1 cm = 10 mm
1 m = 100 cm
1 km = 1000 m

Example

Change each of these to the units given.

a 16 cm to mm **c** 0.98 km to m
b 3.7 m to cm **d** 2.3 m to mm

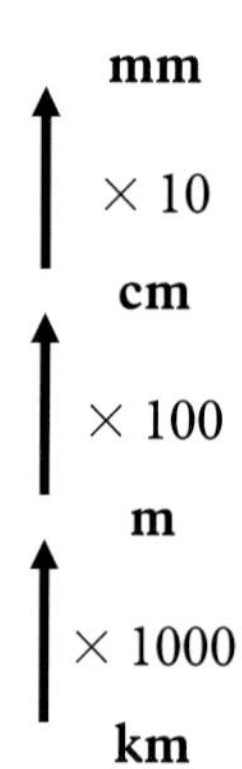

a There are 10 mm in every cm.
So 16 cm = 16 × 10 mm
= 160 mm

b There are 100 cm in every m.
So 3.7 m = 3.7 × 100 cm
= 370 cm

c There are 1000 m in every km.
So 0.98 km = 0.98 × 1000 m
= 980 m

d Do this question in two stages.
There are 100 cm in every m.
So 2.3 m = 2.3 × 100 cm
= 230 cm
There are 10 mm in every cm.
So 230 cm = 230 × 10 mm
= 2300 mm

Exercise 23:7

1 Change each of these lengths into mm.

a 7 cm	**d** 163 cm	**g** 0.6 cm	• **j** 2 m
b 32 cm	**e** 19.8 cm	**h** 23.5 cm	• **k** 5.2 m
c 125 cm	**f** 0.7 cm	**i** 10.4 cm	• **l** 67 m

2 Change each of these lengths into cm.

a 3 m	**d** 243 m	**g** 0.7 m	• **j** 3 km
b 24 m	**e** 24.1 m	**h** 12.6 m	• **k** 3.2 km
c 212 m	**f** 0.45 m	**i** 120.1 m	• **l** 56 km

3 Change each of these lengths into m.

a 4 km	**d** 159 km	**g** 0.74 km	**j** 0.342 km
b 82 km	**e** 32.8 km	**h** 23.51 km	**k** 5.122 km
c 121 km	**f** 0.5 km	**i** 10.42 km	**l** 67.341 km

4 Change each of these lengths into mm.

a 6 cm	**d** 113 m	**g** 0.8 m	**j** 4 cm
b 42 m	**e** 15.6 cm	**h** 23.1 cm	**k** 7.2 m
c 1.1 km	**f** 0.6 km	**i** 20.4 m	**l** 0.17 km

Example Change each of these to the units given.

a 230 mm to cm **c** 9780 m to km
b 135 cm to m **d** 1340 mm to m

a Every 10 mm make a cm.
Find how many lots of 10 mm are in 230 mm.
230 ÷ 10 = 23 so 230 mm = 23 cm

b Every 100 cm make a m.
Find how many lots of 100 cm there are in 135 cm.
135 ÷ 100 = 1.35 so 135 cm = 1.35 m

c Every 1000 m make a km.
Find how many lots of 1000 m there are in 9780 m.
9780 ÷ 1000 = 9.78 so 9780 m = 9.78 km

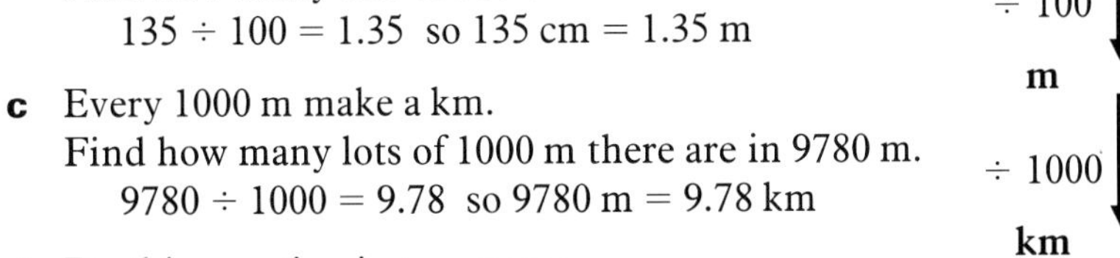

d Do this question in two stages.
Every 10 mm make a cm. So 1340 mm = 1340 ÷ 10 = 134 cm
Every 100 cm make a m. So 134 cm = 134 ÷ 100 = 1.34 m

Exercise 23:8

1 Change each of these lengths into cm.

a	70 mm	**d**	1630 mm	**g**	6 mm	**j**	9.3 mm
b	320 mm	**e**	198 mm	**h**	13.5 mm	**k**	5.2 mm
c	1250 mm	**f**	7 mm	**i**	10.4 mm	**l**	6.71 mm

2 Change each of these lengths into m.

a	400 cm	**d**	2430 cm	**g**	70 cm	**j**	3000 mm
b	2500 cm	**e**	241 cm	• **h**	6 cm	**k**	320 mm
c	2120 cm	**f**	45 cm	• **i**	8.1 cm	• **l**	56 mm

3 Change each of these lengths into km.

a	40 000 m	**d**	2100 m	**g**	7480 m	• **j**	3422 cm
b	8000 m	**e**	3200 m	**h**	2315 m	**k**	5 122 000 mm
c	3000 m	**f**	5210 m	**i**	104 200 cm	• **l**	67 341 mm

• **4** Change each of these lengths into km.

a	6000 m	**d**	1 213 000 mm	**g**	2800 cm	**j**	4 m
b	420 m	**e**	156 000 mm	**h**	1.2 m	**k**	720 cm
c	13 410 cm	**f**	232.6 m	**i**	70 000 mm	**l**	51 cm

5 Dave swims 40 lengths of the swimming pool each day.
The pool is 50 m long.
How many km does Dave swim each day?

6 The measurements of kitchen units are always given in mm.
Chris needs a unit to fit in a space that measures 150 cm × 58 cm × 87 cm.

He can buy units in three sizes.

Unit A 1600 mm × 500 mm × 870 mm
Unit B 1470 mm × 550 mm × 870 mm
Unit C 1500 mm × 600 mm × 870 mm

Which unit should he buy?
Explain your answer.

Imperial units of length

The **imperial units of length** are inches (in), feet (ft), yards (yd) and miles (m).
This system is mainly used in the UK and the USA.
Because m is used for metres as well as miles you have to be careful! In this section we will not use these abbreviations for the imperial units.

1 foot = 12 inches
1 yard = 3 feet
1 mile = 1760 yards

Example Change each of these to the units given.

a 3 feet to inches
b 4 yards to feet
c 6 feet 3 inches to inches
d $2\frac{1}{2}$ miles to yards

a There are 12 inches in every foot.
So 3 feet = 3×12 inches
= 36 inches

b There are 3 feet in every yard.
So 4 yards = 4×3 feet
= 12 feet

c 6 feet = 6×12 inches
= 72 inches
So 6 feet 3 inches = $72 + 3$ inches = 75 inches.

d There are 1760 yards in every mile.
So $2\frac{1}{2}$ miles = $2\frac{1}{2} \times 1760$ yards
= 4400 yards

inches
↑ × 12
feet
↑ × 3
yards
↑ × 1760
miles

Exercise 23:9

1 Change each of these lengths into inches.

a 7 feet
b 10 feet
c 12 feet
d 30 feet
e $2\frac{1}{2}$ feet
f $5\frac{1}{2}$ feet
g 6 feet 3 inches
h 15 feet 4 inches
i 10 feet 7 inches
j 9 feet 9 inches
k 5 feet 7 inches
l $7\frac{3}{4}$ feet

2 Change each of these lengths into feet.

a 4 yards
b 2 yards
c 12 yards
d 24 yards
e 40 yards
f 155 yards
g 1250 yards
h 6 yards 2 feet
i 8 yards 1 foot
j 300 yards 2 feet
k $3\frac{1}{2}$ yards
l $5\frac{1}{3}$ yards

3 Change each of these lengths into yards.

a	3 miles	**d**	21 miles	**g**	7 miles 123 yards	**j**	$3\frac{1}{2}$ miles
b	8 miles	**e**	30 miles	**h**	20 miles 345 yards	**k**	$5\frac{1}{2}$ miles
c	12 miles	**f**	50 miles	**i**	15 miles 129 yards	**l**	$6\frac{1}{4}$ miles

---

Example Change each of these to the units given.

a 108 inches to feet **c** 9680 yards to miles
b 12 feet to yards **d** 15 840 feet to miles

inches ↓ ÷ 12 **feet** ↓ ÷ 3 **yards** ↓ ÷ 1760 **miles**

a Every 12 inches makes a foot.
Find how many lots of 12 inches are in 108 inches.
$108 \div 12 = 9$ so 108 inches = 9 feet

b Every 3 feet make a yard.
Find how many lots of 3 feet are in 12 feet.
$12 \div 3 = 4$ so 12 feet = 4 yards

c Every 1760 yards make a mile.
Find how many lots of 1760 yards are in 9680 yards.
$9680 \div 1760 = 5.5$ so 9680 yards make 5.5 miles.
5.5 miles is the same as $5\frac{1}{2}$ miles.

d Do this question in two stages.
Every 3 feet make a yard. So 15 840 feet = $15\,840 \div 3$ = 5280 yards
Every 1760 yards make a mile. So 5280 yards = $5280 \div 1760$ = 3 miles

---

Exercise 23:10

1 Change each of these lengths into feet.

a 24 inches **b** 60 inches **c** 120 inches **d** 144 inches

2 Change each of these lengths into yards.

a 15 feet **b** 24 feet **c** 120 feet **d** 3540 feet

3 Change each of these lengths into miles.

a 3520 yards **b** 21 120 yards **c** 11 440 yards **d** 18 480 yards

4 Change each of these lengths into miles.

a	31 680 feet	**c**	32 736 feet	**e**	27 456 yards	**g**	126 720 inches
b	18 480 feet	**d**	11 264 yards	**f**	35 376 feet	**h**	221 760 inches

Example Change 6336 yards into miles and yards.

Every 1760 yards make a mile.
Find how many lots of 1760 yards are in 6336 yards
6336 yards = 6336 ÷ 1760 = 3.6 miles
3.6 miles is the same as 3 miles and 0.6 of a mile left over.
0.6 mile = 0.6 × 1760 = 1056 yards.
So 3.6 miles = 3 miles 1056 yards

5 Change each of these lengths into miles and yards.

a 5104 yards	**c** 25 344 yards	**e** 36 696 yards	● **g** 29 568 feet
b 18 480 yards	**d** 24 024 yards	● **f** 11 088 feet	● **h** 95 040 inches

6 Change each of these lengths into yards and feet.

a 13 feet	**c** 122 feet	**e** 12 233 feet	● **g** 396 inches
b 47 feet	**d** 3421 feet	● **f** 96 inches	● **h** 420 inches

7 Change each of these lengths into feet and inches.

a 78 inches	**b** 183 inches	**c** 561 inches	● **d** 380 inches

Converting between imperial and metric units

	Conversion number
1 inch is about 2.5 cm	**2.5**
1 foot is about 30 cm	**30**
1 yard is about 90 cm	**90**
1 yard is about 0.9 m	**0.9**
1 mile is about 1.6 km	**1.6**

If you want to convert from imperial to metric units you have to know these. It might help you to remember the conversion numbers.

To change from imperial to metric you **multiply** by the conversion number. To change from metric to imperial you **divide** by the conversion number.

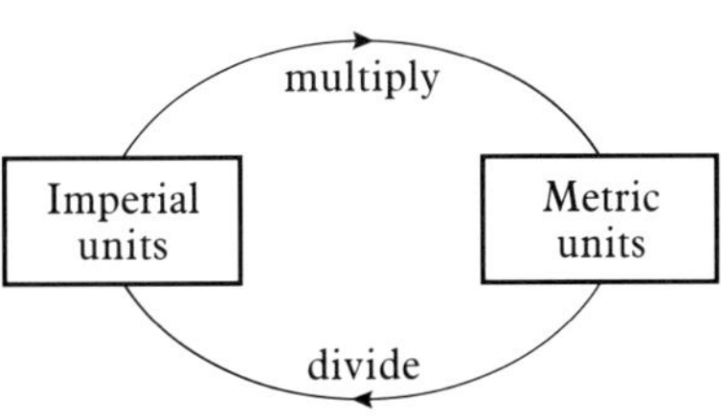

Example

a Convert 4 yards to cm.
b Convert 56 km to miles.

a Every yard is about 90 cm.
Multiply by the conversion number.
4 yards = $4 \times 90 = 360$ cm

b There are about 1.6 km in every mile.
Divide by the conversion number.
56 km = $56 \div 1.6 = 35$ miles

Exercise 23:11

Give your answers to 1 dp when you need to round.

1 Change each of these lengths into cm.

a 2 inches	**d** 120 inches	**g** 21 feet	**j** 12 yards
b 14 inches	**e** 3 feet	**h** 40 feet	**k** 25 yards
c 22 inches	**f** 5 feet	**i** 5 yards	**l** $6\frac{1}{2}$ yards

2 Change each of these lengths into m.

a 5 yards	**c** 50 yards	**e** 200 yards	● **g** 36 feet
b 20 yards	**d** 125 yards	**f** 500 yards	● **h** 354 feet

3 Change each of these lengths into km.

a 35 miles	**b** 110 miles	**c** 240 miles	**d** 500 miles

4 Change each of these lengths into inches.

a 25 cm	**c** 120 cm	**e** 21 cm	**g** 121 cm
b 40 cm	**d** 150 cm	**f** 47 cm	**h** 253 cm

5 Change each of these lengths into feet.

a 60 cm	**c** 45 cm	**e** 255 cm	● **g** 9 m
b 180 cm	**d** 135 cm	● **f** 50 cm	● **h** 180 m

6 Change each of these lengths into yards.

a 45 m	**c** 2 m	**e** 34 m	**g** 120 m
b 22.5 m	**d** 14 m	**f** 40 m	**h** 250 m

7 Change each of these lengths into miles.

a 8 km	**c** 120 km	**e** 15 000 km	**g** 100 km
b 40 km	**d** 5000 km	**f** 30 km	**h** 21 km

Exercise 23:12

1 Dave is 6 feet tall.
What is his height in cm?

2 Helen lives 3 km out of town.
How far from town does Helen live in miles?

3 A ruler is 12 inches long.
How many cm is this?

4 The distance from Sheffield to Leeds is about 60 km.
How far is this in miles?

5 A holiday brochure says that a hotel is 300 yards from the beach.
Convert this distance into
a metres **b** centimetres

● **6** Alice is going to a meeting in Paris.
She is travelling at 60 miles per hour.
She has just passed a road sign telling her that Paris is 140 km away.
She has to be there in $1\frac{1}{2}$ hours.
Will she get there in time if she travels at this speed?

You also need to be able to estimate lengths.
To do this you need to think about things that you know well.
Here are a few examples but you may think of others that help you more.

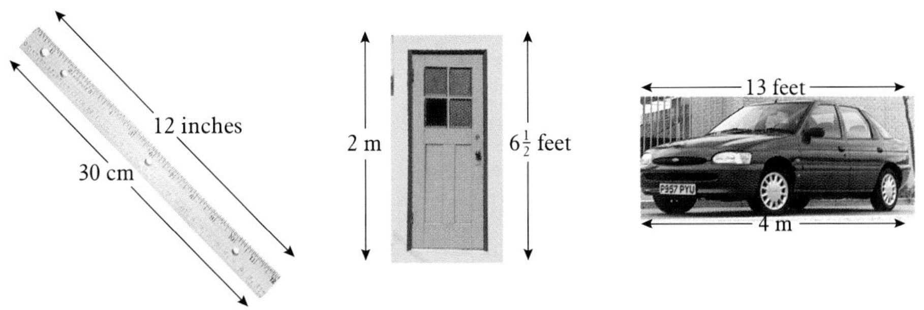

Exercise 23:13

Estimate the length of each of these.
Give your answers in both of the units shown.

1

a cm
b inches

2

a cm
b inches

3

a m
b feet

4

a cm
b inches

5

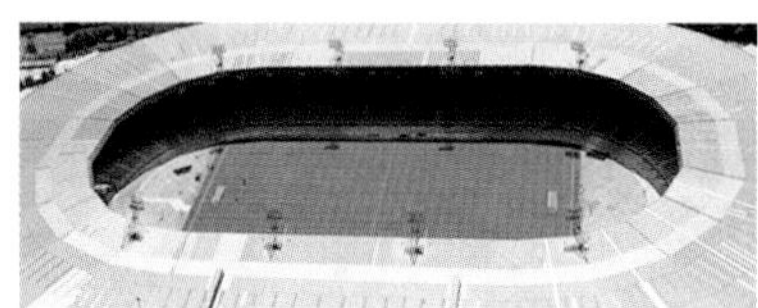

a m
b yards

6

a m
b feet

7

a m
b yards

8

a m
b yards

1 Find the circumference of these circles. Give your answers to 1 dp.

a

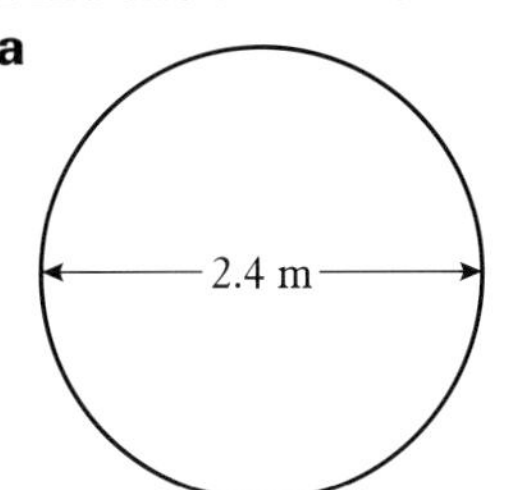

b

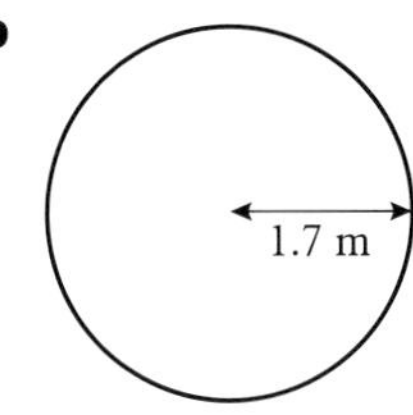

c

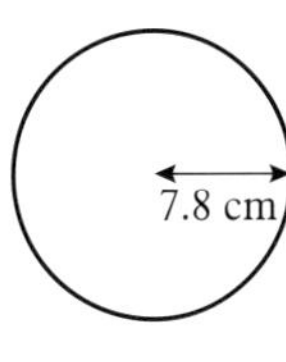

2 Find
(1) the diameter (2) the radius
of a circle with a circumference of:
a 70 cm **b** 45 cm **c** 320 cm **d** 47.1 cm
Give all your answers to 1 dp.

3 The circumference of a circle is 7 m.
Find **a** the diameter **b** the radius
Give your answers to 2 dp.

4 Find the perimeter of each of these shapes.

a

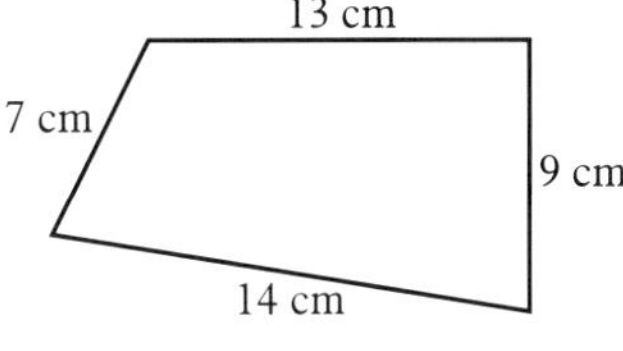

b

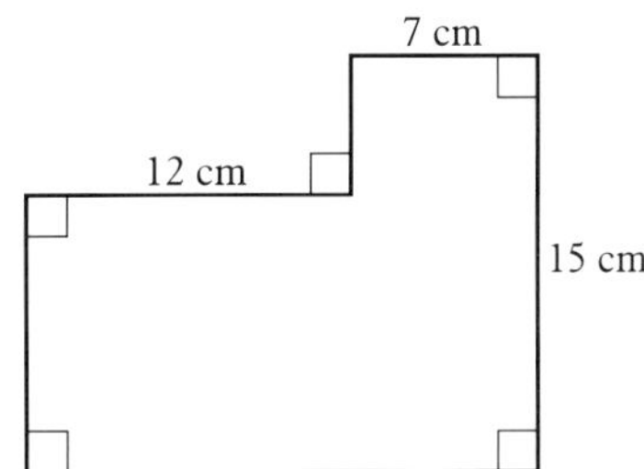

5 Find the perimeter of a regular pentagon with sides of length 4.5 cm.

6 Find the perimeter of this racetrack.
Both ends are semi-circles.
Leave your answer in terms of π.

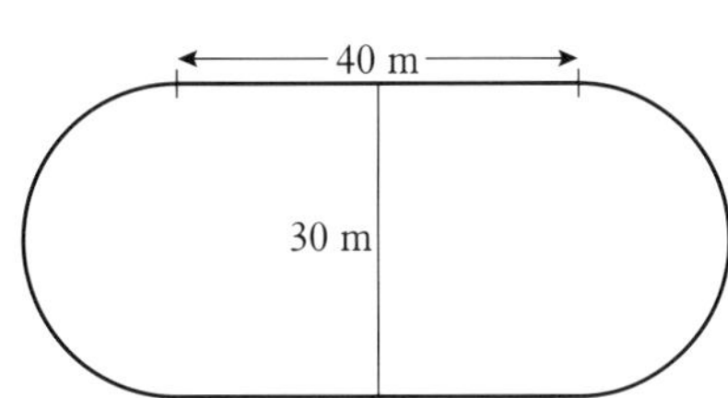

7 In this question r, s and t are lengths.
Write down the dimension of each of these expressions.
a s **c** $3rs$ **e** rst **g** $145s$
b $2t$ **d** $56st$ **f** $4t$ **h** $472rt$

8 **a** Change each of these lengths into mm.
(1) 6 cm (2) 143 cm (3) 0.7 cm (4) 3 m
b Change each of these lengths into cm.
(1) 4 m (2) 233 m (3) 0.8 m (4) 5 km
c Change each of these lengths into m.
(1) 7 km (2) 129 km (3) 0.74 km (4) 0.142 km

9 **a** Change each of these lengths into cm.
(1) 56 mm (2) 163 mm (3) 9 mm (4) 8 mm
b Change each of these lengths into m.
(1) 900 cm (2) 56 cm (3) 3000 mm (4) 600 mm
c Change each of these lengths into km.
(1) 4000 m (2) 6100 m (3) 8910 cm (4) 7593 mm

10 **a** Change each of these lengths into inches.
(1) 5 feet (2) 20 feet (3) 2 feet 3 inches (4) 7 feet 3 inches
b Change each of these lengths into feet.
(1) 5 yards (2) 14 yards (3) 125 yards (4) 20 yards 2 feet
c Change each of these lengths into yards.
(1) 4 miles (2) 25 miles (3) 3 miles 523 yards (4) $7\frac{1}{2}$ miles

11 **a** Change each of these lengths into feet.
(1) 48 inches (2) 72 inches (3) 240 inches (4) 144 inches
b Change each of these lengths into yards.
(1) 18 feet (2) 27 feet (3) 126 feet (4) 6510 feet
c Change each of these lengths into miles.
(1) 3520 yards (2) 21 120 yards (3) 11 440 yards (4) 18 480 yards
d Change each of these lengths into miles.
(1) 31 680 feet (2) 32 736 feet (3) 27 456 yards (4) 126 720 inches

12 Copy these. Fill them in.
a 1 metre is just over … feet.
b 1 yard is about … metre.
c 1 inch is about … cm.
d 1 foot is about … cm.
e 1 mile is about … km.
f 1 yard is about … cm.

13 **a** Change 20 inches into cm.
b Change 48 miles into km.
c Change 200 cm into inches.
d Change 16 km into miles.

1 Assume that the Earth travels in a circle of radius 93 million miles around the sun in 365 days.
How far does it travel in 1 day?

2 Each wheel of Andrea's bicycle has a radius of 35 cm.
How many complete turns of each wheel are needed for the bicycle to travel 50 metres?

3 A triangle has sides of length p cm, $(p + 4)$ cm and $(p - 5)$ cm.

a Write down and simplify an expression for the perimeter of the triangle.

The perimeter is 41 cm.

b Use your answer to part **a** to write down an equation for the perimeter.

c Solve the equation in part **b** and find the length of each side of the triangle.

4 Each side of the square is $2p$ cm long.
Each side of the equilateral triangle is $(3p - 1)$ cm long.

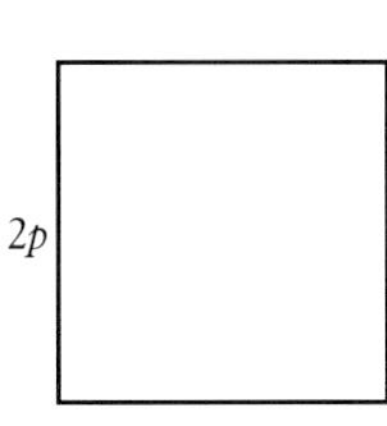

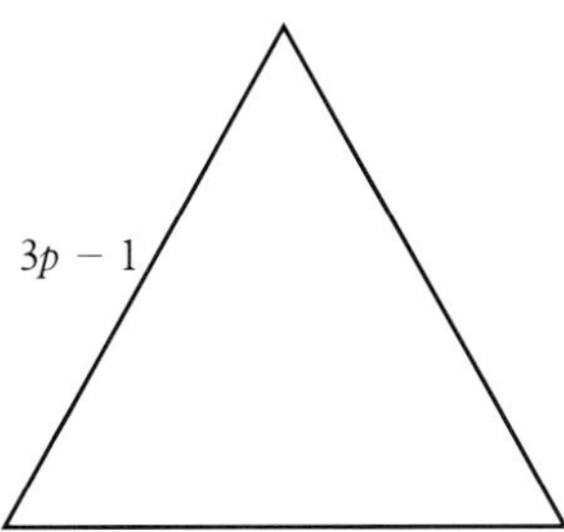

a Write down and simplify an expression for
(1) the perimeter of the square
(2) the perimeter of the triangle.

The two shapes have the same perimeter.

b Write down an equation that tells you that the two perimeters are equal.

c Solve the equation in part **b**.

d Work out the length of the side of
(1) the square (2) the triangle

5 The distance from Liverpool to Manchester is about 40 miles.
5 miles are about the same as 8 km.
Use this information to find the distance from Liverpool to Manchester in km.

1 The wheel of Mary's bicycle has a radius of 16 cm.

a Find the circumference of the wheel.

b Mary cycles 4 km.
How many complete revolutions does the wheel make?

2 Work out the perimeter of this shape.

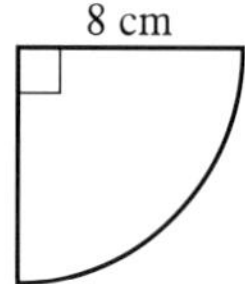

3 Find the exact perimeter of this shape.

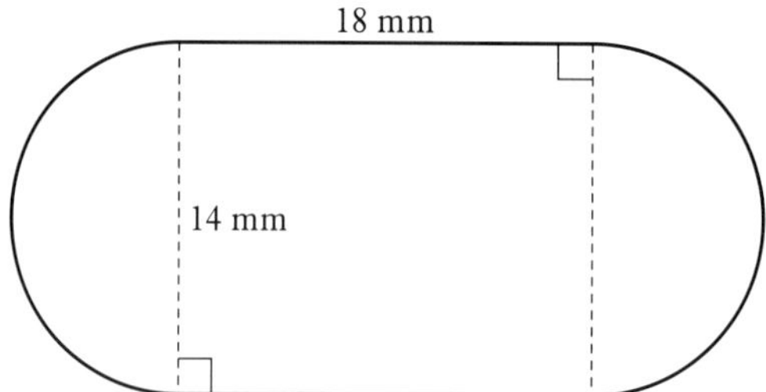

4 Change

a 47 mm to cm

b 7.2 m to cm

c 36 in to feet

d 4 yards to feet

e 7 miles to yards

f 6.5 yards to inches

5 There are 2.54 cm in 1 inch.
Change

a 1 foot into cm

b 2 yards into cm

c 20 yards into metres

d 3 metres into inches

24 Pythagoras' theorem

CORE

1 Finding areas
Using Pythagoras' theorem to find areas

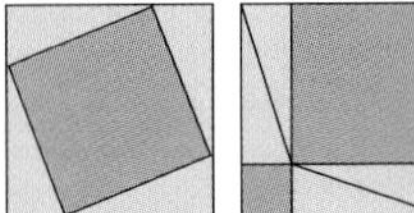

2 Finding lengths
Using Pythagoras' theorem to find the hypotenuse
Looking at Pythagorean triples
Using Pythagoras' theorem to find one of the shorter sides
Distance between two points
Angle in a semi-circle

QUESTIONS

EXTENSION

TEST YOURSELF

1 Finding areas

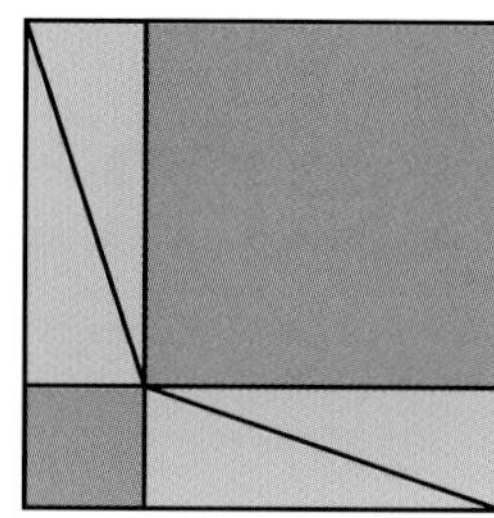

This picture shows you one of the many proofs of Pythagoras' theorem.

Can you see how it works?

Pythagoras' theorem

Pythagoras' theorem says that in any right-angled triangle, the area of the square on the hypotenuse is equal to the sum of the areas of the squares on the other two sides.

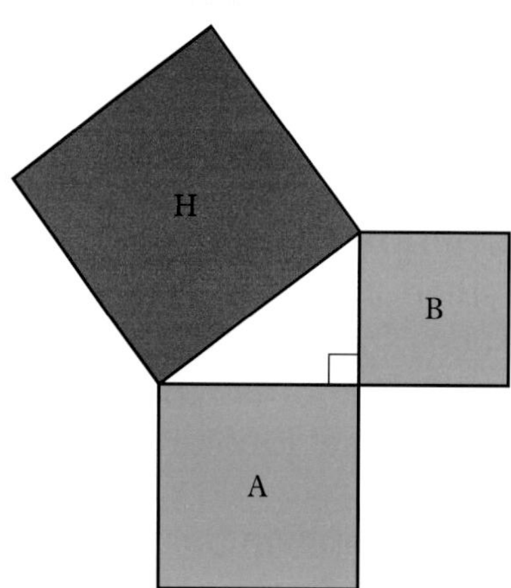

In this right-angled triangle, Pythagoras' theorem tells you that

area **H** = area **A** + area **B**

Example Find the red area in this diagram.

The red area is the sum of the blue areas.

Red area = 15 + 20
= 35 cm^2

When you are finding the area on the hypotenuse you add the areas of the other squares.

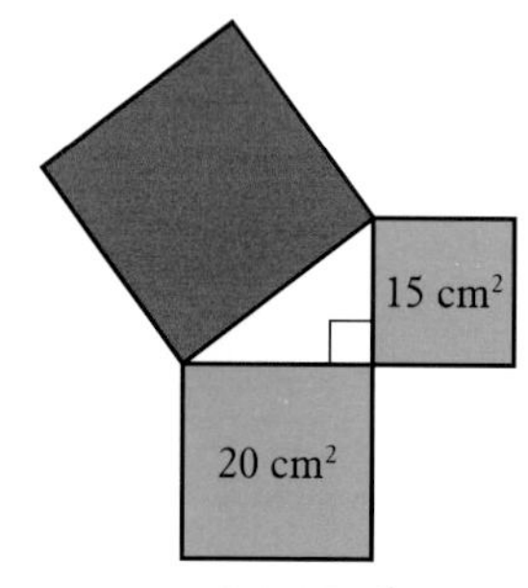

Exercise 24:1

1 Find the red area in each of these.

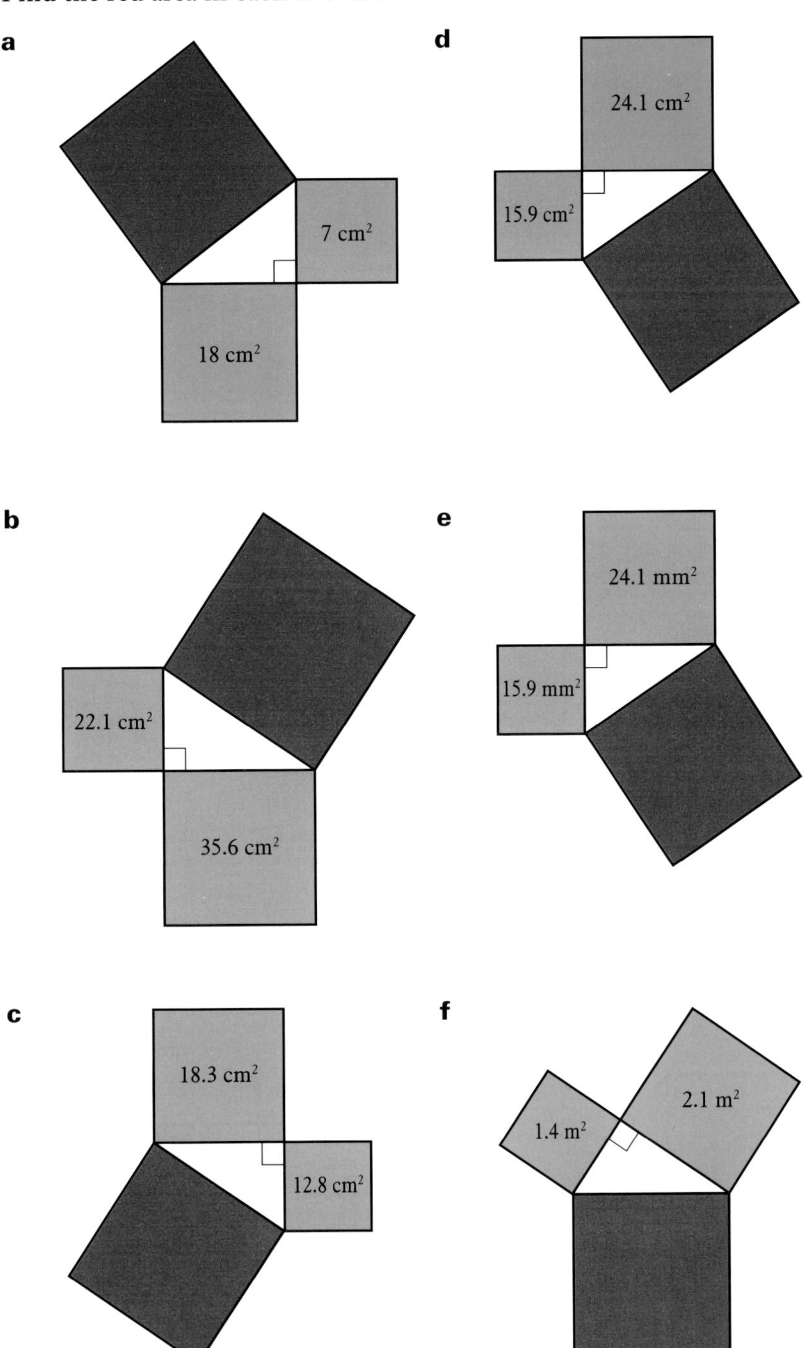

Example Find the missing blue area in this diagram.

The red area is the sum of the blue areas.

$$40 = 18 + \text{blue area}$$

So $\quad \text{blue area} = 40 - 18$

$= 22\text{ cm}^2$

When you are finding an area that is not on the hypotenuse you take the areas of the other two squares away.

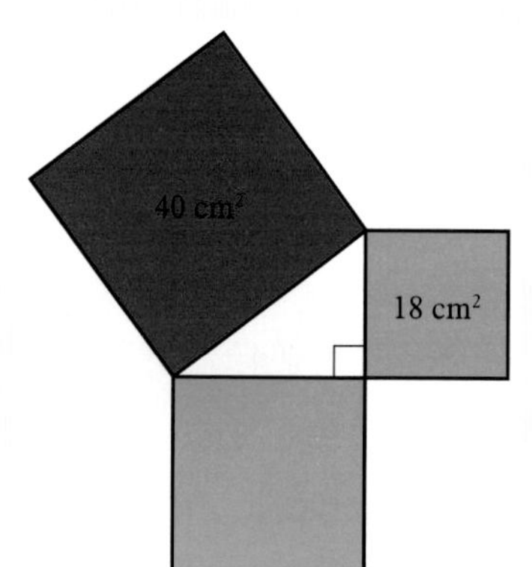

2 Find the blue area in each of these.

a

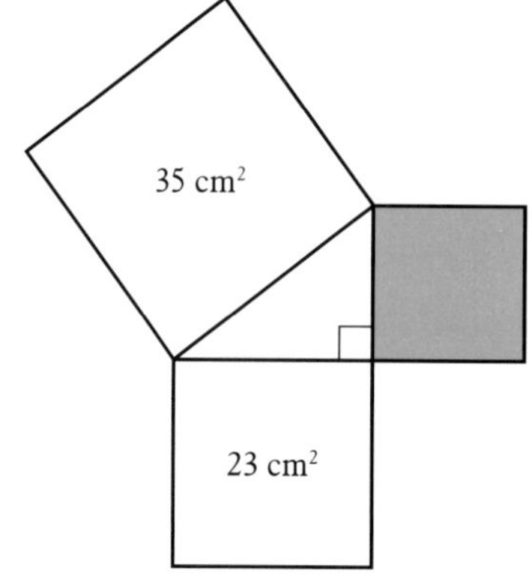

c

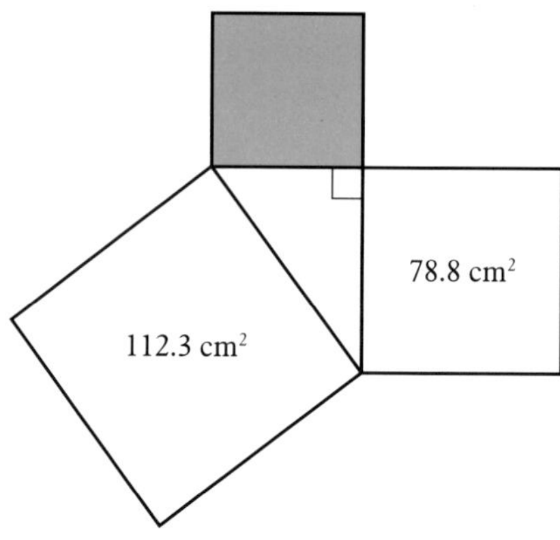

b

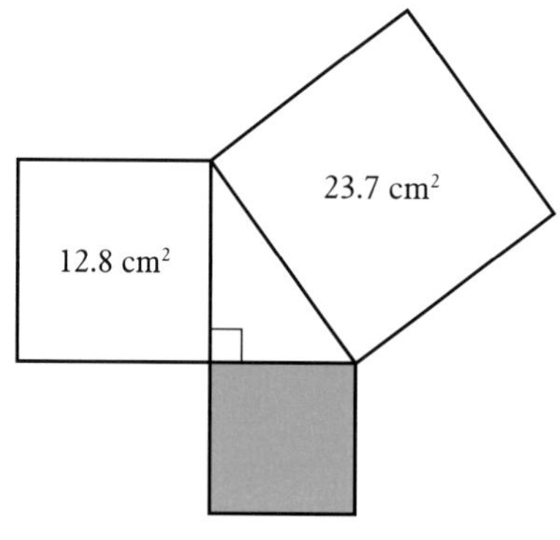

d

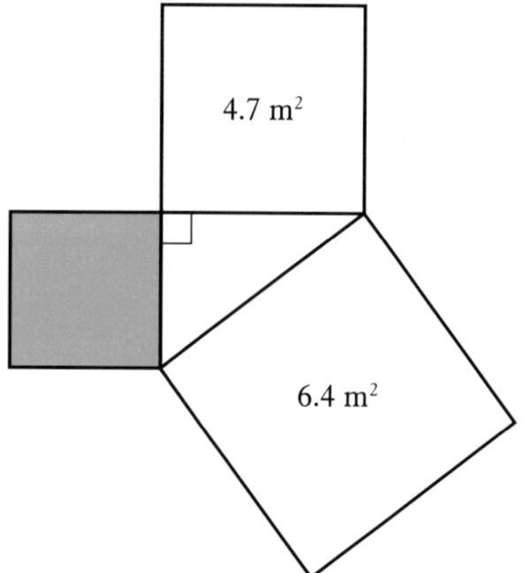

e

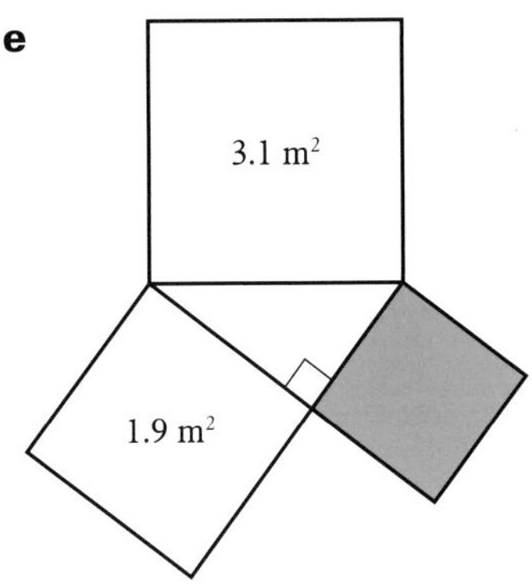

f

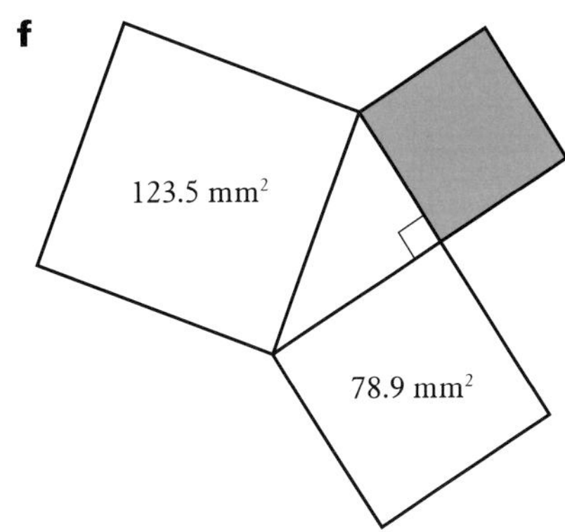

3 Helen is working out the area of the red square in this diagram.
She says that the area is 56 cm^2.
Explain how you know that she is wrong.

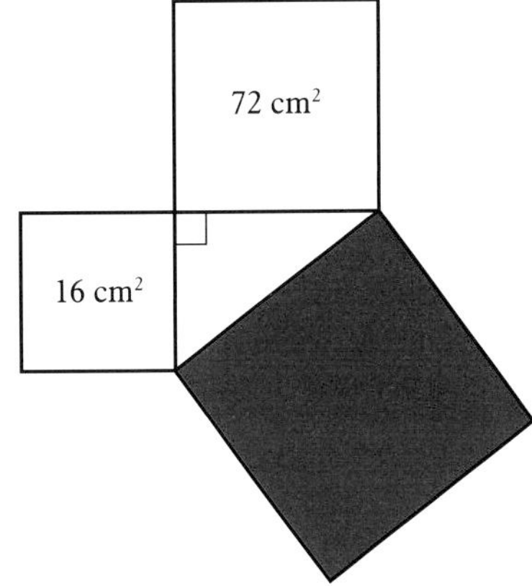

4 Jamie is working out the area of the blue square in this diagram.
He says that the area is 54 cm^2.

a Explain how you know that he is wrong.

b Explain how he got his answer.

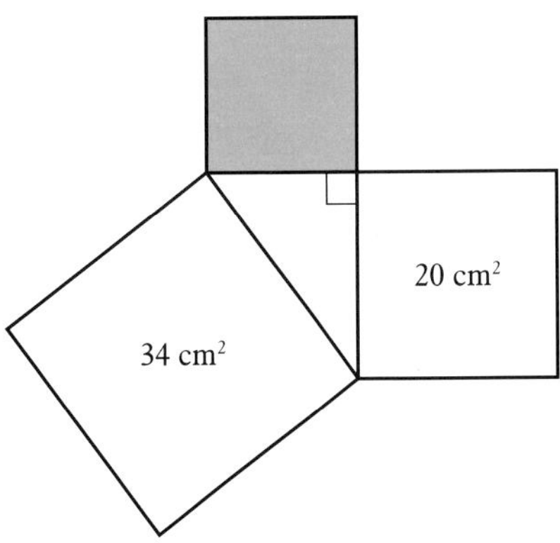

Pythagoras' theorem is usually written using the lengths of the sides of the triangle.

You need to remember that the area of a square with side $\boldsymbol{a}$ is $\boldsymbol{a}^2$.

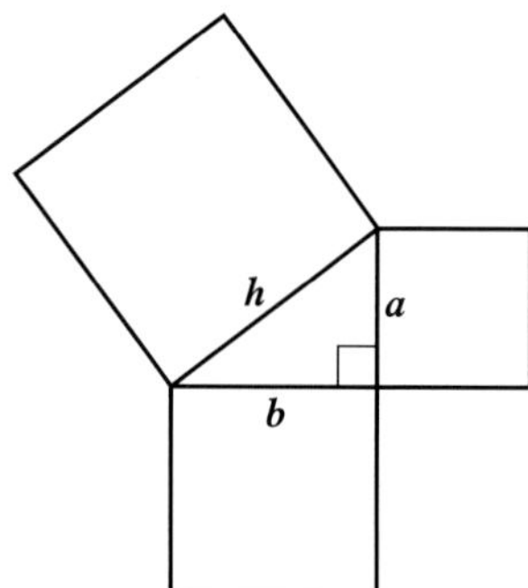

In this right-angled triangle, Pythagoras' theorem tells you that

$$h^2 = a^2 + b^2$$

The square of the hypotenuse is equal to the sum of the squares of the other two sides.

Example Find the area of each of the coloured squares.

The area of the red square is $10 \times 10 = 100\ \text{cm}^2$
The area of the blue square is $7 \times 7 = 49\ \text{cm}^2$

By Pythagoras' theorem
the area of the green square is
$100 - 49 = 51\ \text{cm}^2$

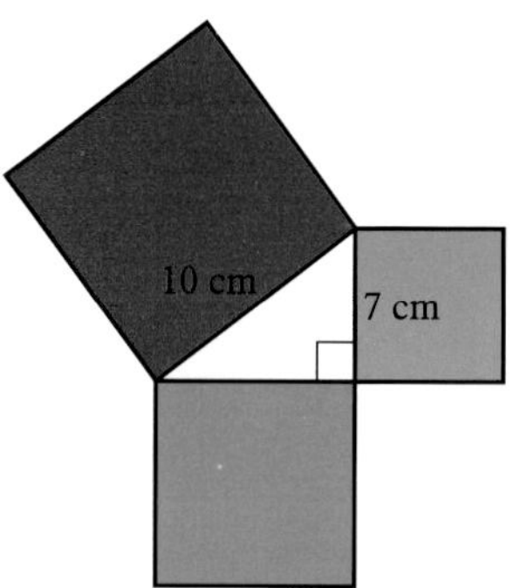

Exercise 24:2

1 Find the area of each of the coloured squares.

a

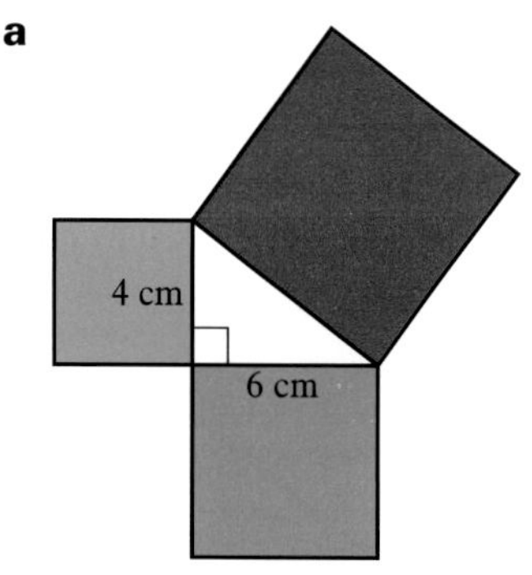

b

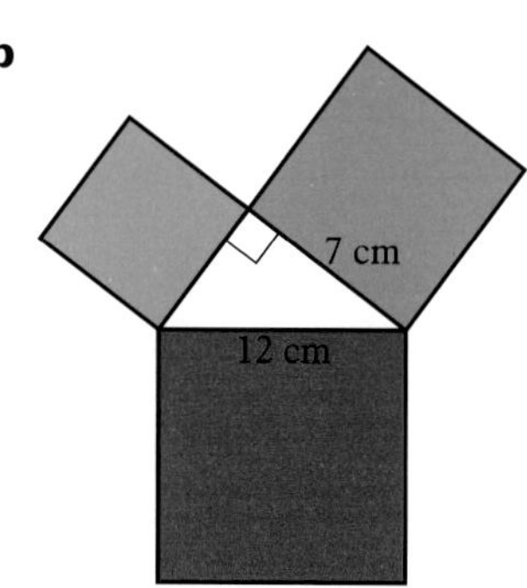

c

d

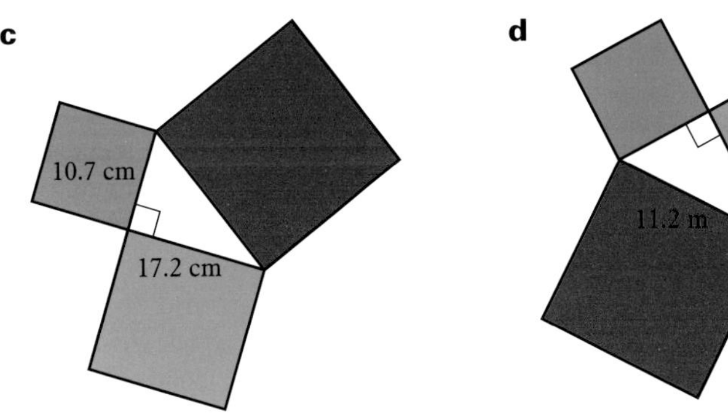

2 Find the area of the green square in each of these.

a

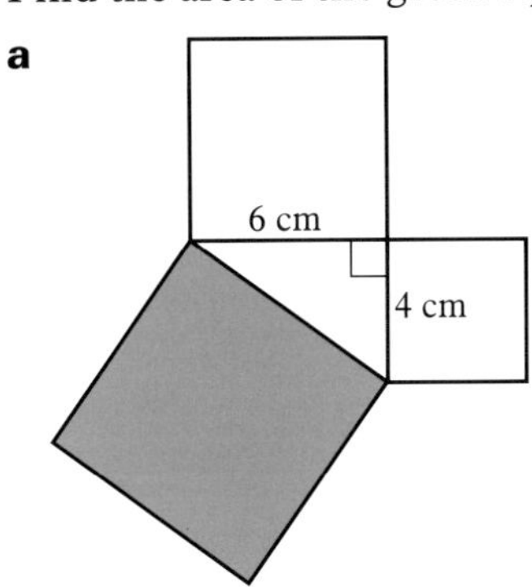

c

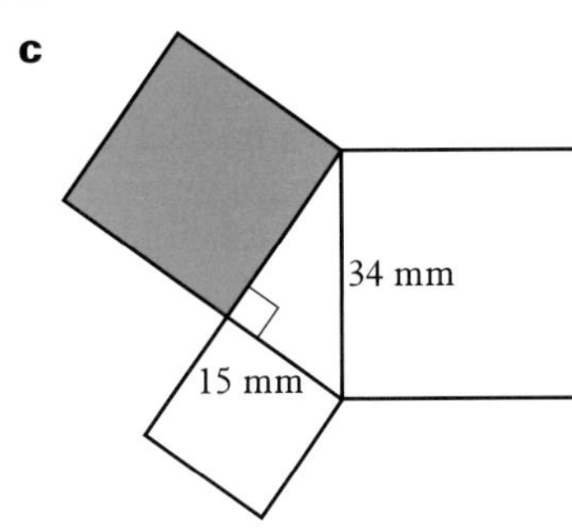

b

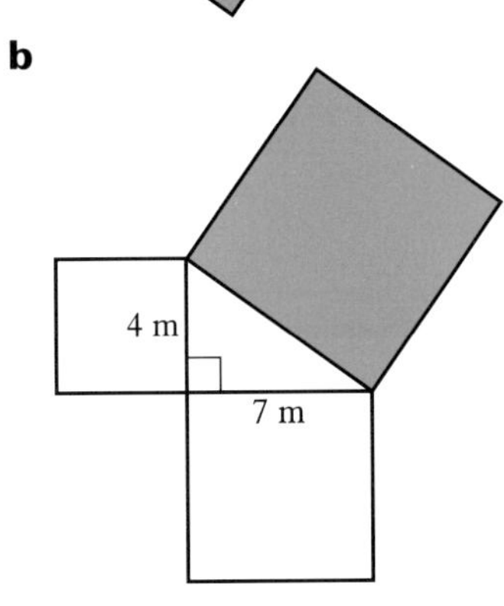

d

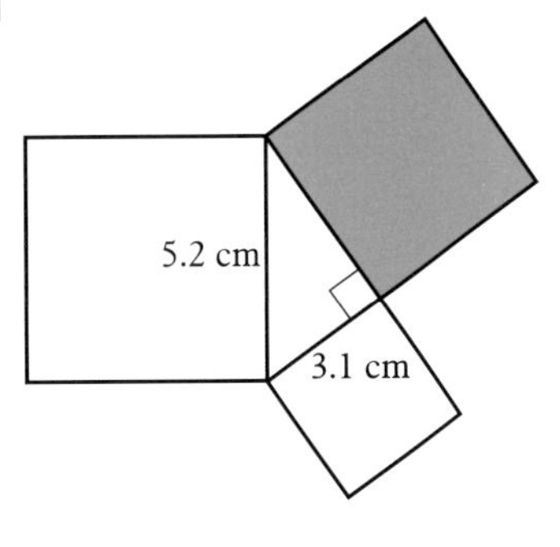

3 Eddie is trying to find the area of the green square.
He says that the area is 125 cm^2.
How do you know that he has to be wrong?

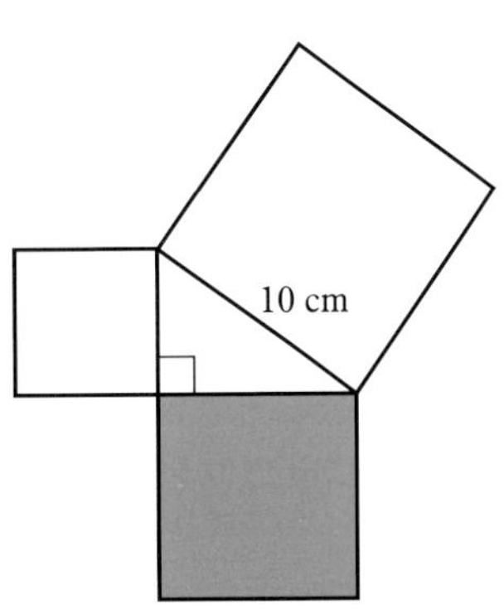

2 Finding lengths

Working in right-angled triangles has been important since the beginning of time. The oldest surviving Pyramid is the Djoser Step Pyramid at Saqqâra in Egypt, which was built around 2630 BC. Pythagoras 'discovered' his theorem in about 500 BC, over 2000 years after the ancient Egyptians had seen the importance of right angles!

Although Pythagoras' theorem talks about areas, it is usually used to find the length of a side in a right-angled triangle.
You can also use trigonometry to find the length of a side in a right-angled triangle.
When you want to use trigonometry you need to know an angle.
It is quicker to use Pythagoras' theorem when you don't know or want the angles.
You need to know two of the sides.
Then you can find the missing side.

Example Find the length of the hypotenuse of this triangle.

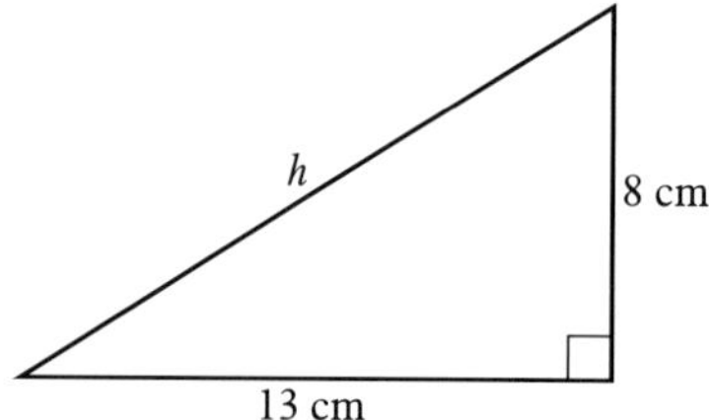

When you write out your answer to a question where you use Pythagoras' theorem, you must show your working.

Start by saying that you are using Pythagoras' theorem.	Using Pythagoras' theorem
Put the lengths into the formula.	$h^2 = 8^2 + 13^2$
Work out the squares.	$= 64 + 169$
Simplify your answer.	$= 233$
Now square root.	$h = \sqrt{233}$
Give your answer to a sensible accuracy.	$h = 15.3$ cm to 1 dp

Always check that the hypotenuse is the longest side in the triangle.
If the answer that you get for the hypotenuse is smaller than one of the other sides then you must have done something wrong!

Exercise 24:3

1 Find the length of the hypotenuse in each of these triangles.
Give your answers to 1 dp.

a

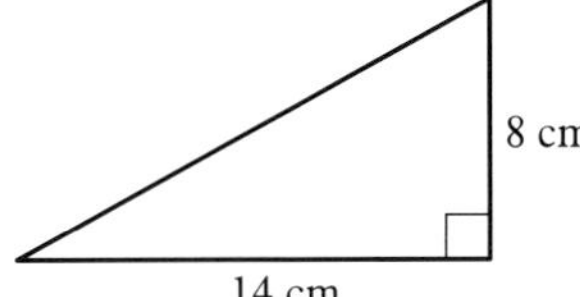

d

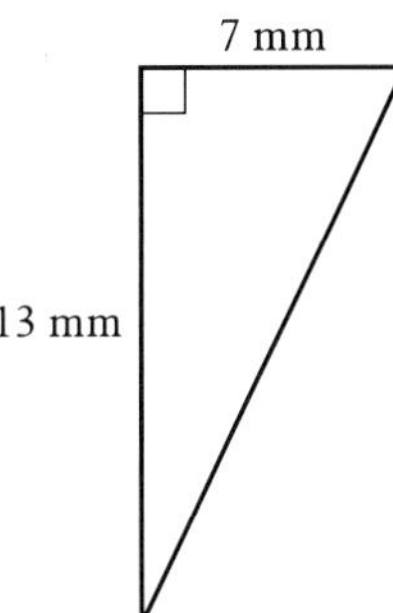

b

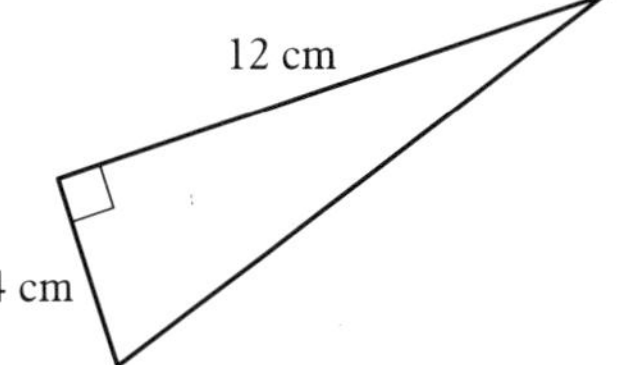

e

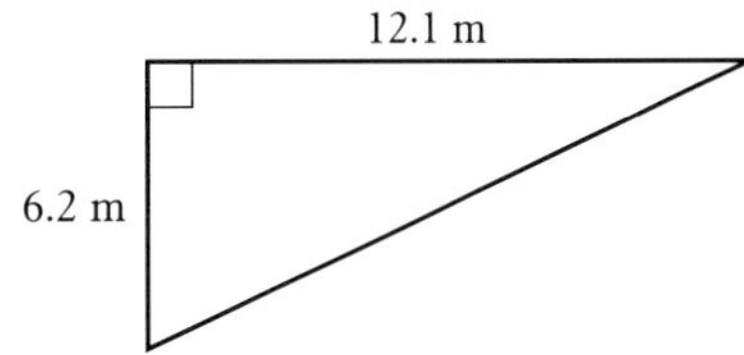

c

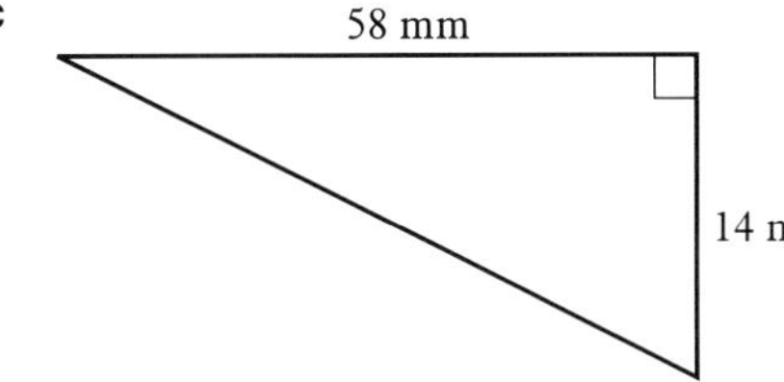

f

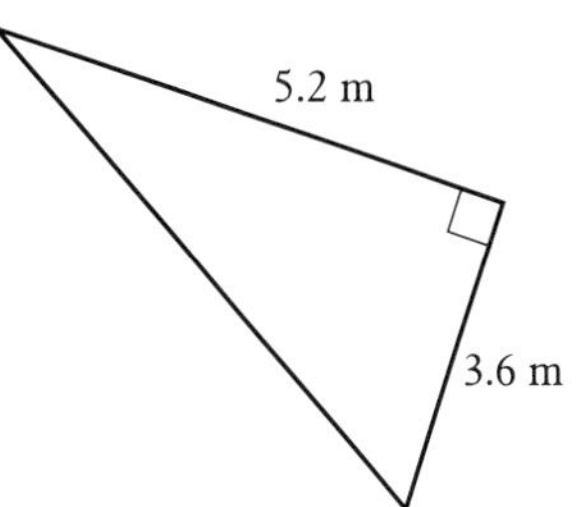

2 **a** Find the hypotenuse in each of these triangles.

(1)

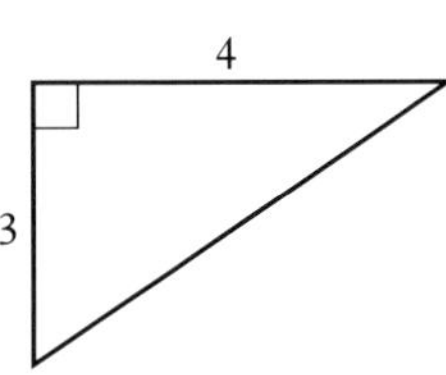

(3)

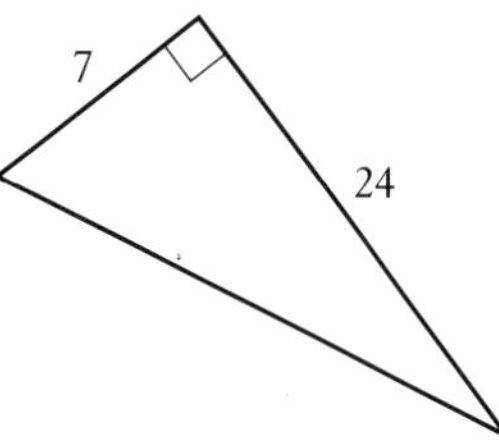

(2)

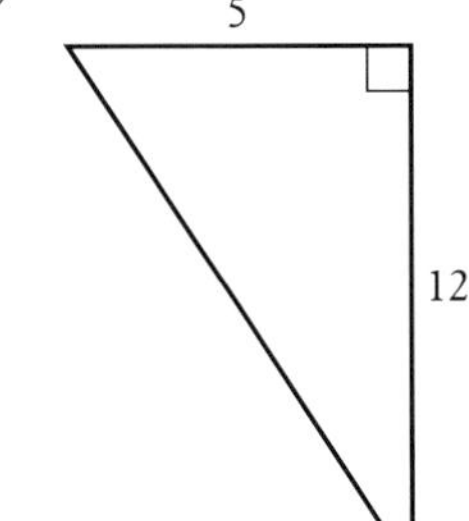

(4)

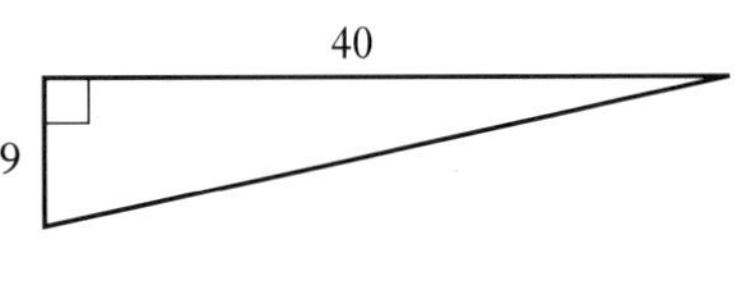

b Copy this table. Fill in the last column using your results from part **a**.

Triangle	Lengths of sides	
(1)	3	4
(2)	5	12
(3)	7	24
(4)	9	40

The sides in the triangles in question **2** are all whole numbers.

Pythagorean triple

When three whole numbers work in Pythagoras' theorem, the set of three numbers is called a **Pythagorean triple**.

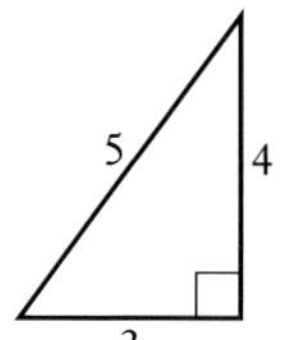

3 4 5 is a Pythagorean triple because $3^2 + 4^2 = 5^2$

3 **a** Find the hypotenuse in each of these triangles.

(1)

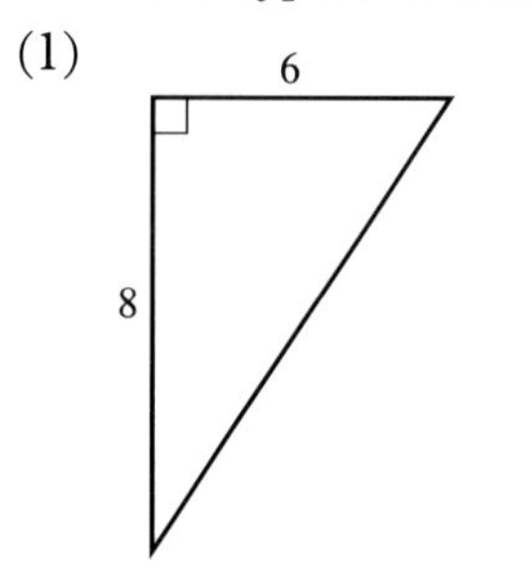

(3)

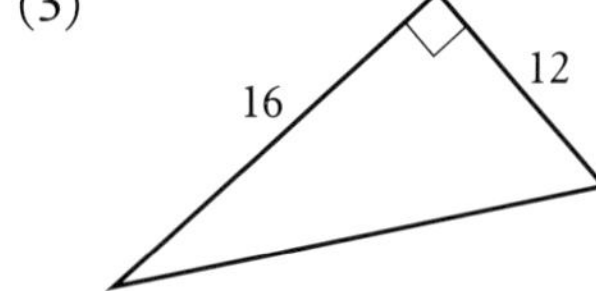

(2)

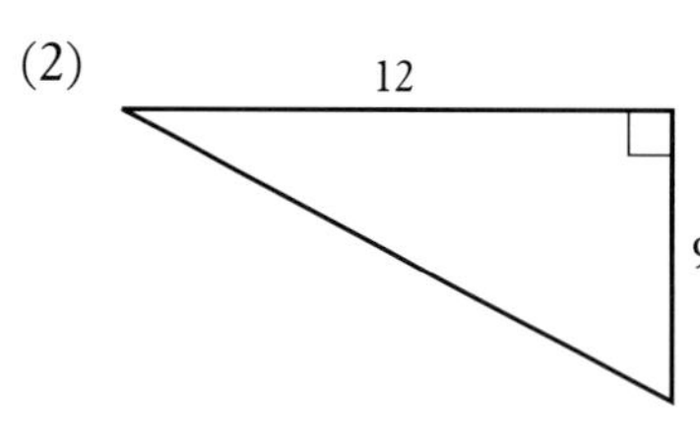

(4)

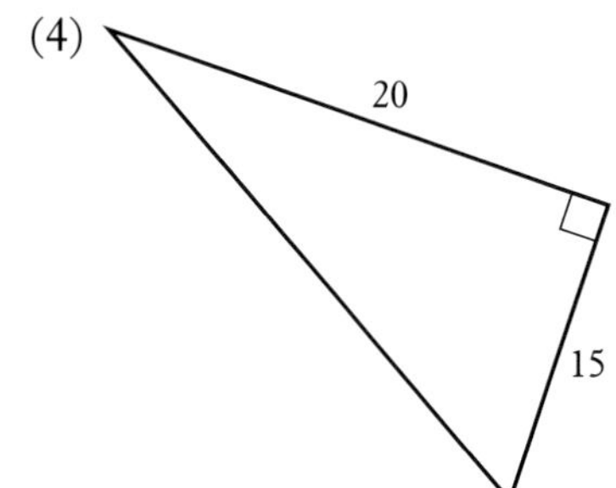

b All of the Pythagorean triples in part **a** are based on one Pythagorean triple. Explain how.

c Start with the Pythagorean triple 5 12 13.
Write down four more Pythagorean triples that are based on this one.

d Can you find a new Pythagorean triple that is not based on any you have seen so far. Try 8 for the smallest side.

4 Jill takes a short cut across this rectangular field to get home.
She walks along the diagonal of the field.
a How far does she walk?
● **b** Jill walks at 4 km per hour.
How much time does she save by taking this short cut?
Give your answer in seconds.

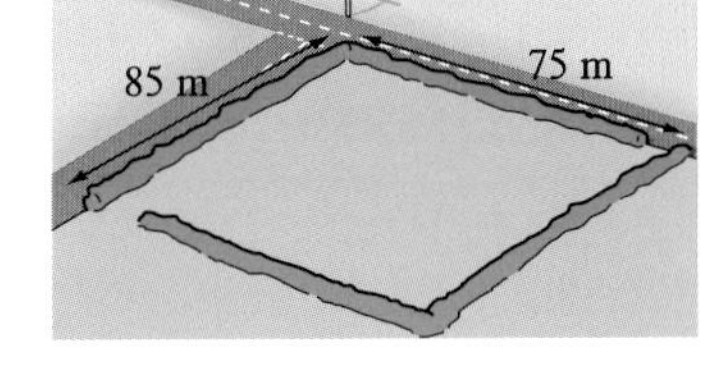

5 Farmer John is very proud of his square fields.
Every day he walks from his house along the diagonal of each field to get to his barn.
How far does he walk to get to his barn?

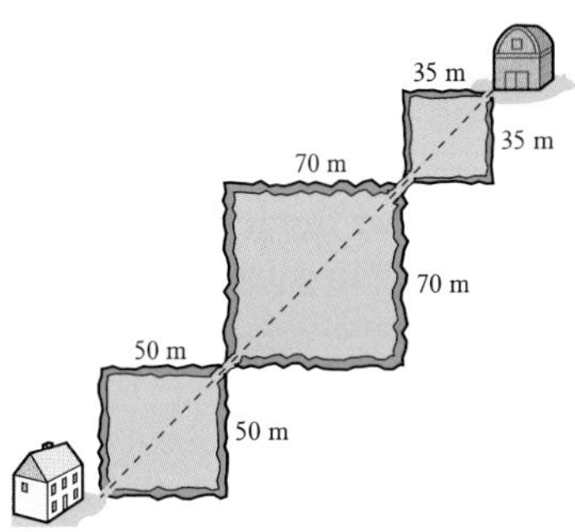

6 This transmitter is supported by 4 cables. Each cable is attached to a point on the mast that is 30 m above the ground. Each cable is attached to the ground 20 m from the base.
a How long is each cable?
b How much cable is used altogether?

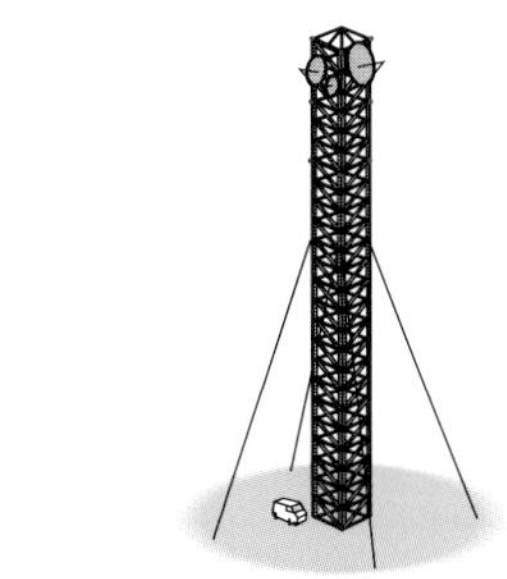

7 Ben is making a roof support.
He has joined two pieces of timber at right angles like this.
What length of wood does he need to finish the structure?

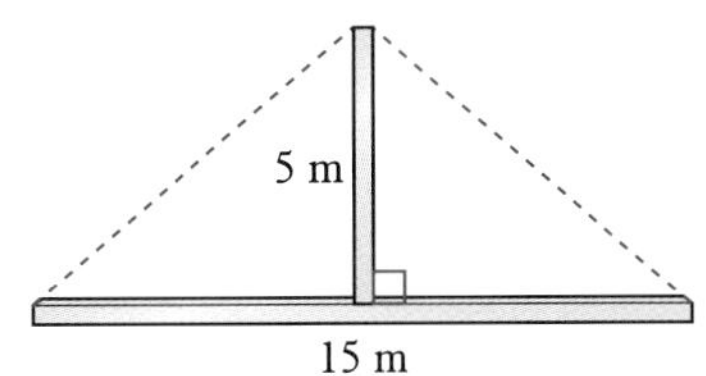

8 Diane is heading down a ski jump!
The height of the slope is 400 ft.
The horizontal distance across the bottom of the slope is 100 ft.
How far does Diane ski down the slope?

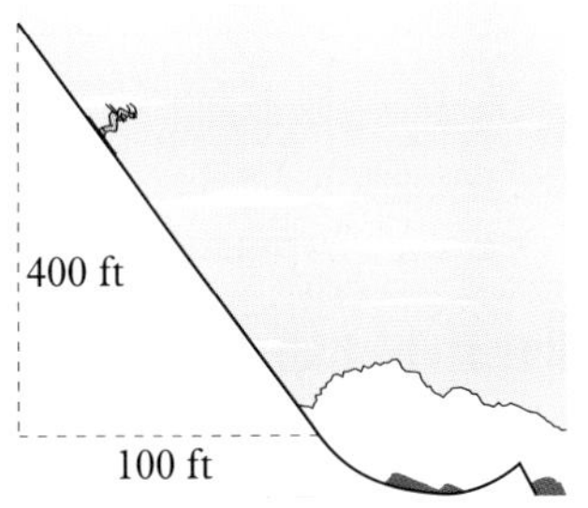

9 **a** Find the length of the sloping edge of the roof of this house.
b Find the area of the roof.

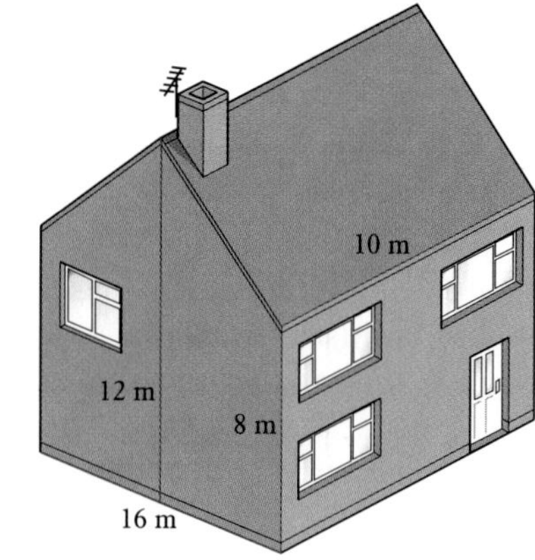

● **10** **a** Find the length of the hypotenuse in this triangle. Leave your answer as a square root.

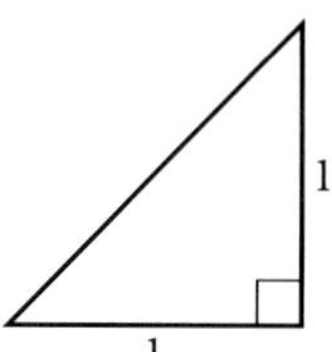

b Another triangle is added to the diagram like this. How long is the hypotenuse of the second triangle. Leave your answer as a square root.
c If you carried on adding triangles to your diagram, how long would the hypotenuse of the 50th triangle be?
d How long would the hypotenuse of the nth triangle be?

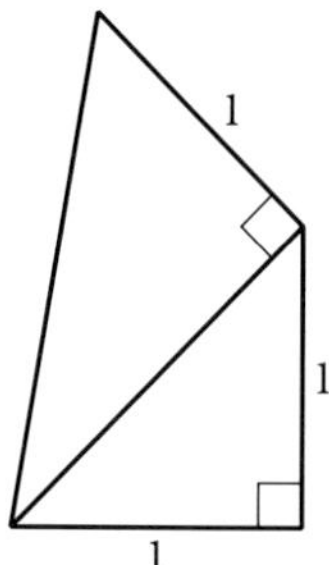

Finding one of the shorter sides

When you want to find one of the short sides, start by writing Pythagoras' theorem in the usual order starting with hypotenuse^2 = …

Then rearrange the equation to find the missing side.

Example Find the length of side a in this triangle.

Using Pythagoras' theorem:

$$23^2 = 18^2 + a^2$$
$$23^2 - 18^2 = a^2$$
$$529 - 324 = a^2$$

So $a^2 = 205$

Now square root:

$$a = \sqrt{205}$$
$$a = 14.3 \text{ cm to 1 dp}$$

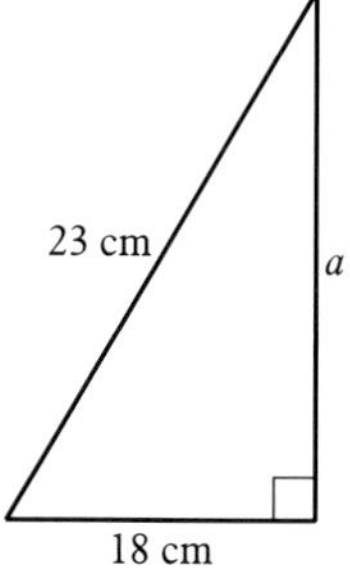

Check that the hypotenuse is the longest side. If the answer that you get for a short side is bigger than the hypotenuse you must have done something wrong!

Exercise 24:4

1 Find the length of the missing side in each of these triangles.
Give your answers to 1 dp.

a

18 cm
25 cm

b

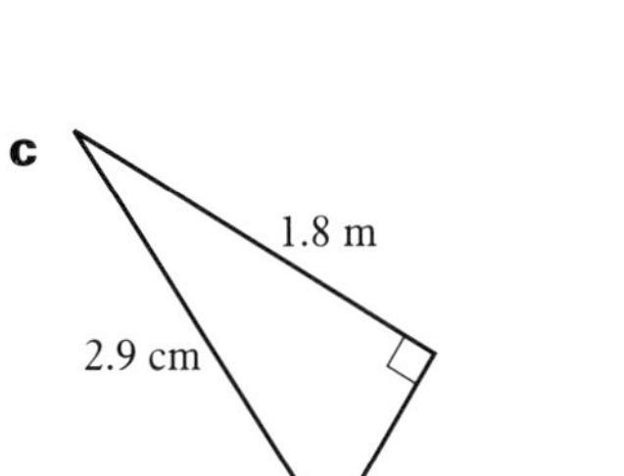

c

1.8 m
2.9 cm

d

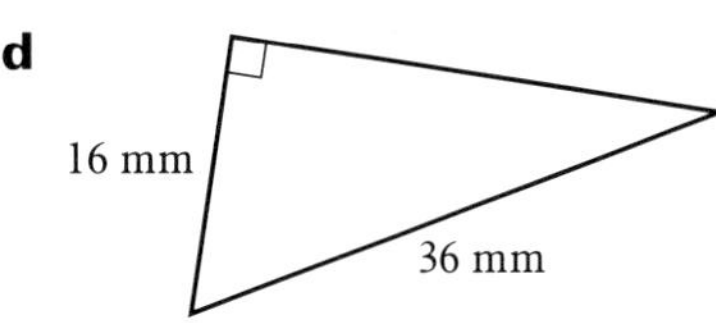

e

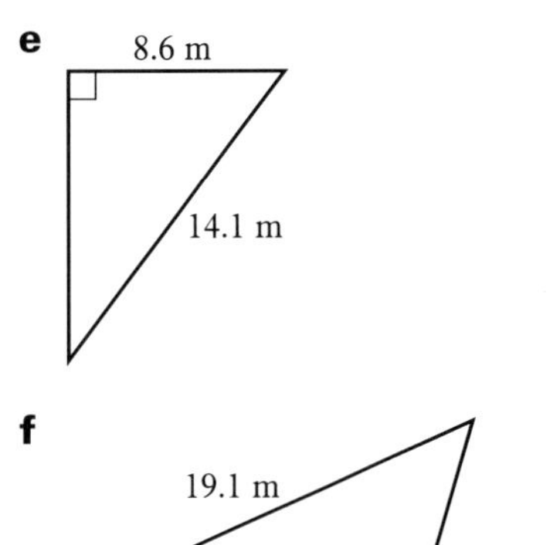

f

19.1 m
12 m

2 A mast is held in position by two wires.
Both wires are 20 m long.
The first is attached to the ground 14 m from the base of the mast.
The second is attached to the ground 16 m from the base of the mast.
How far is it between the two points where the wires join the mast?

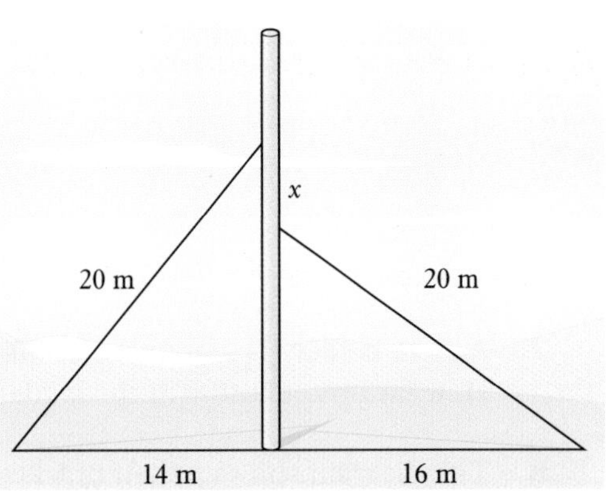

3 This is a cross section through the Great Pyramid.
Each sloping side is about 180 m long.
The base of the pyramid is about 230 m.
How high is the pyramid?

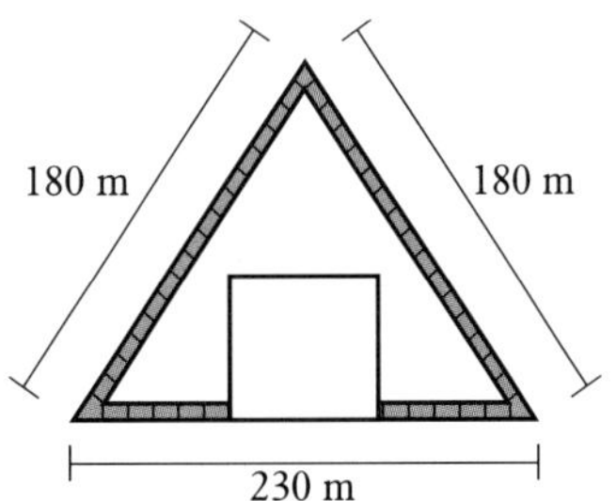

4 This is Katie's kite.
The wooden supports have cracked.
What length of wood does she need to get to fix it?

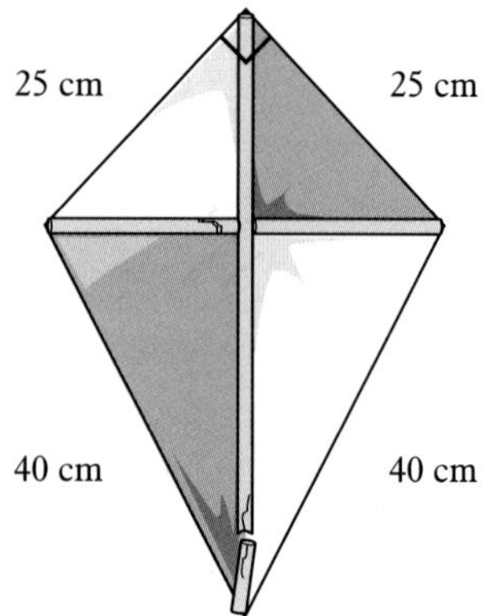

5 A stirring rod sticks out from the top of a beaker.
The beaker is 10 cm across the base.
The beaker is 15 cm tall.
The stirring rod is 25 cm long.
How much of the stirring rod is outside the beaker?

6 This is a diagram showing a road up a hill.
How far does the road rise vertically up the hill?

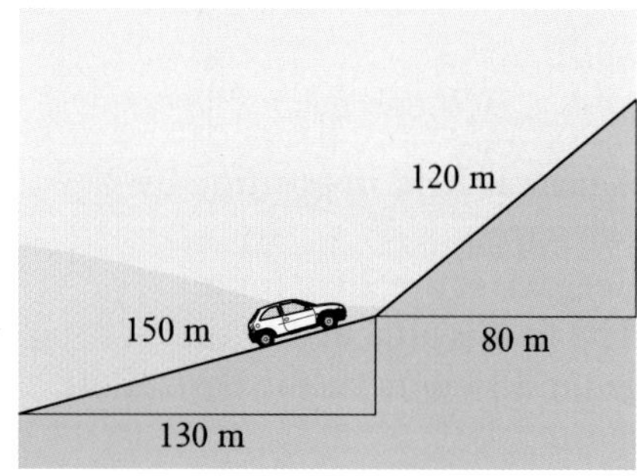

7 A 25 m ladder is placed so that the base is 12 m from a vertical wall.
How far up the wall will the ladder reach?

8 The diagram shows a shelf bracket.

The shelf must be horizontal and must not overlap the bracket.
What is the greatest width of shelf that this bracket can support?

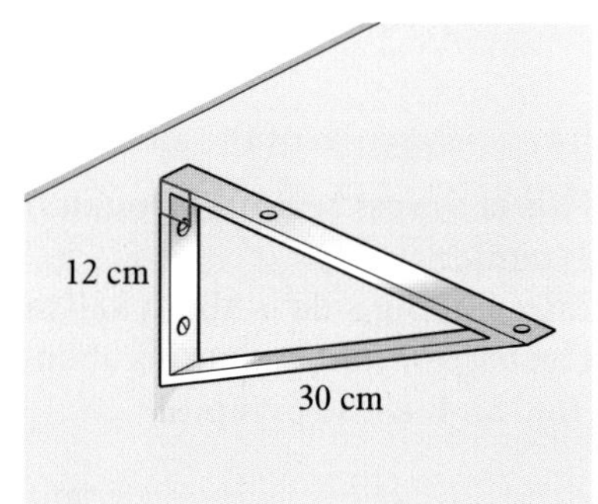

9 This is a picture of a child's slide.
What is the length of the ladder?

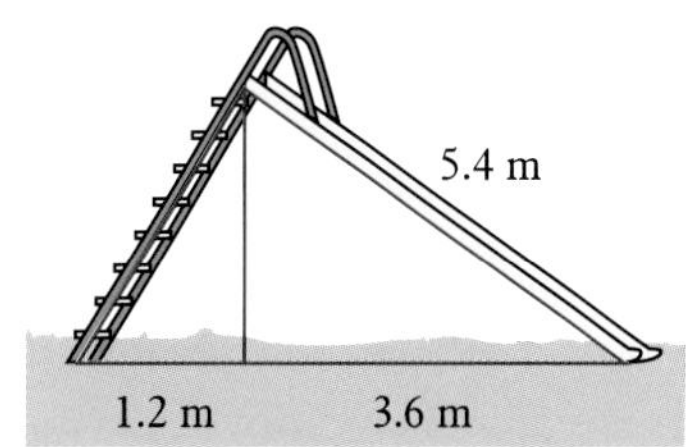

● **10** The diagram shows the positions of two lighthouses.
A ship is due south of lighthouse A.
The ship is 50 km from lighthouse B.
How far is the ship from lighthouse A?

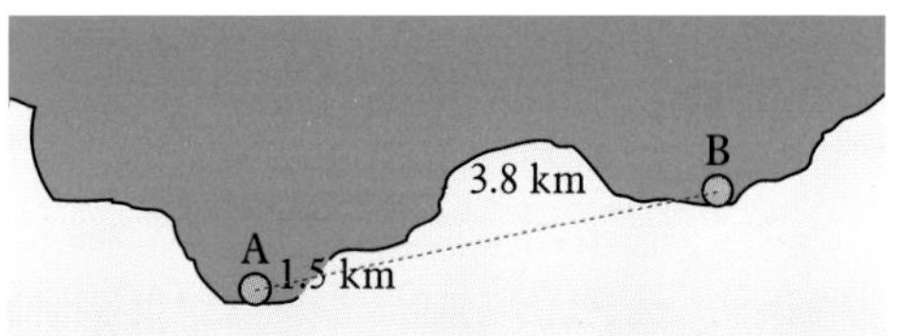

One or more of the lengths might be given as a square root of a number.
This is because it is more exact than a rounded decimal.

In fact this makes it very easy to square.
Remember that when you square the square root of a number you get back to the original number!
This is because squaring and square rooting are inverses of each other.
So $\sqrt{8} \times \sqrt{8} = 8$.

Example Find the length of the hypotenuse of this triangle.

$$x^2 = (\sqrt{8})^2 + (\sqrt{6})^2$$
$$= 8 + 6$$
$$= 14$$
So $x = \sqrt{14}$ cm

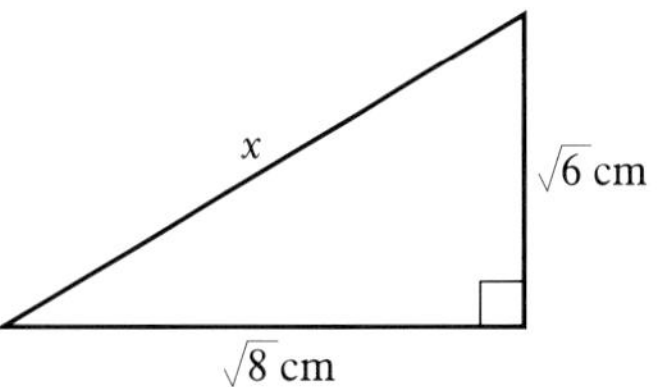

Leave your answer as a square root if you are asked for an exact answer.

---

11 Find the lengths of the sides marked with letters.
Give exact answers.

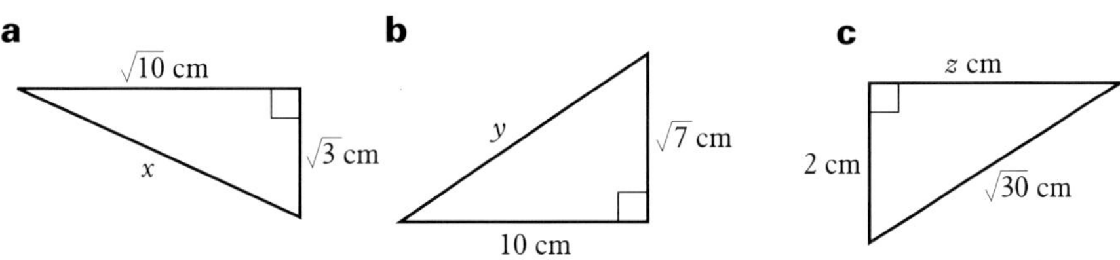

You can use Pythagoras' theorem to find the distance between two points.

Points A(**1**, 2) and B(**6**, 5) are marked on this diagram.
B is **6** − **1** = 5 cm to the right of A.
B is 5 − 2 = 3 cm above A.

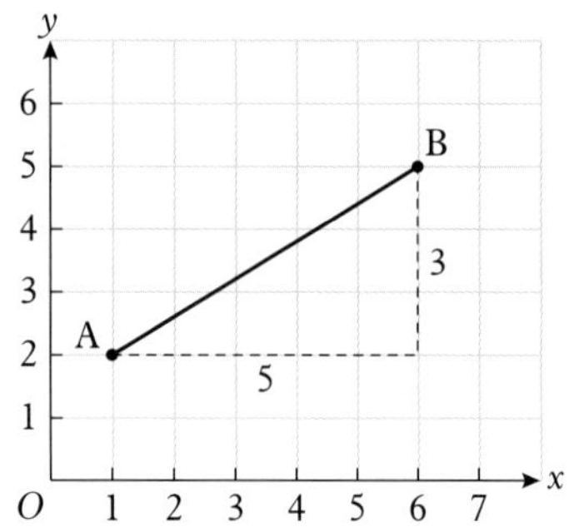

You can use Pythagoras' theorem to find the distance AB.

$$(AB)^2 = 5^2 + 3^2$$
$$= 25 + 9$$
$$= 34$$
$$AB = \sqrt{34} = 5.83 \text{ cm (2 dp)}$$

So the distance between A and B is $\sqrt{34}$ cm or 5.83 cm (2 dp).

Exercise 24:5

1 Find the distance between the following pairs of points.
Give your answers to 2 dp.
- **a** A and B
- **b** C and D
- **c** E and F
- **d** A and F

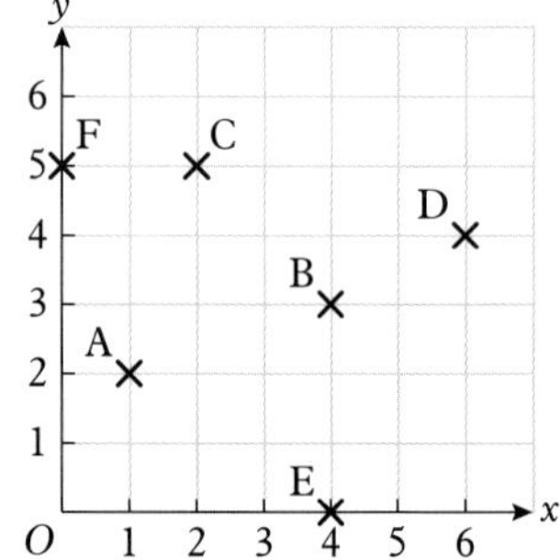

2 Find the distance between the points A(2, 3) and B(6, 6).

3 A boat sails 4 nautical miles due east and then 7 km due south.
How far is the boat from its starting point?

4 Point B is 6 cm to the right of point A.
It is $\sqrt{61}$ cm in a straight line from A.

How far is point B above point A?

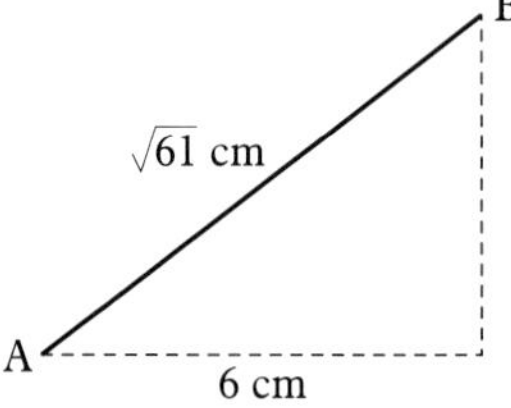

5 Three points are A(0, 1), B(3, 5) and C(6, 8).
- **a** Find the distances AB and BC.
- **b** Find the distance AC.

Exercise 24:6

1 **a** Draw a circle with radius 5 cm.
b Draw a diameter AB in your circle.
c Join A and B to any point on the circumference of the circle. Call this point P.
d Measure the angle APB. This is called the angle in a semi-circle.

Angle in a semi-circle

The **angle in a semi-circle** is the angle made by joining both ends of a diameter of a circle to a point on the circumference. The **angle in a semi-circle** is 90°.

AB is a diameter of the circle centre O.

The angle APB is 90°.

This means that you can now use Pythagoras' theorem in semi-circles.

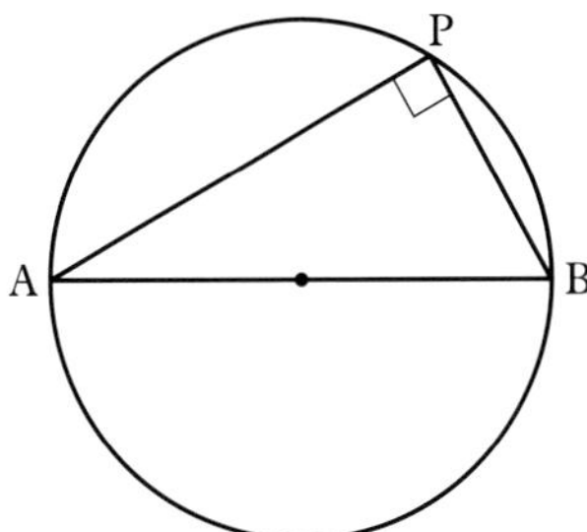

---

2 Find the length marked with a letter in each of these.

a

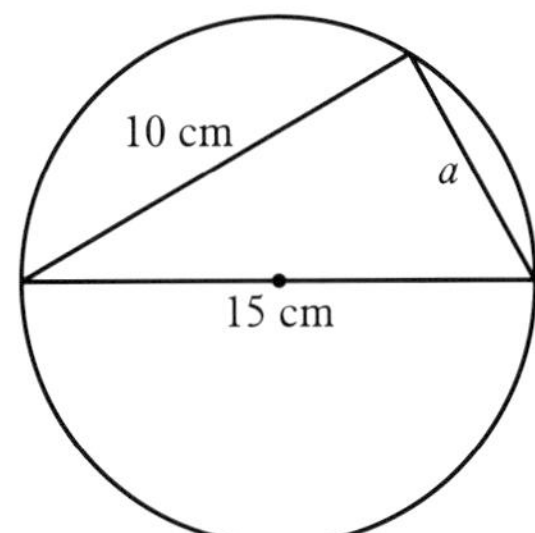

b

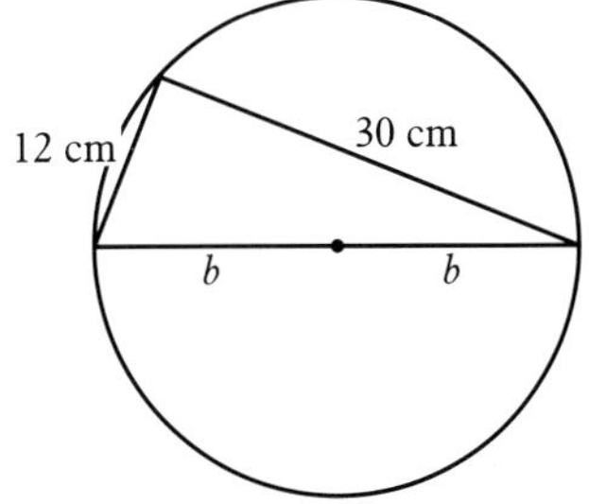

c

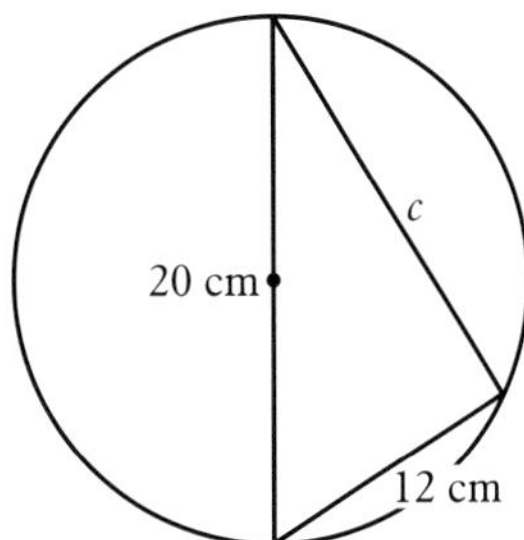

● **d**

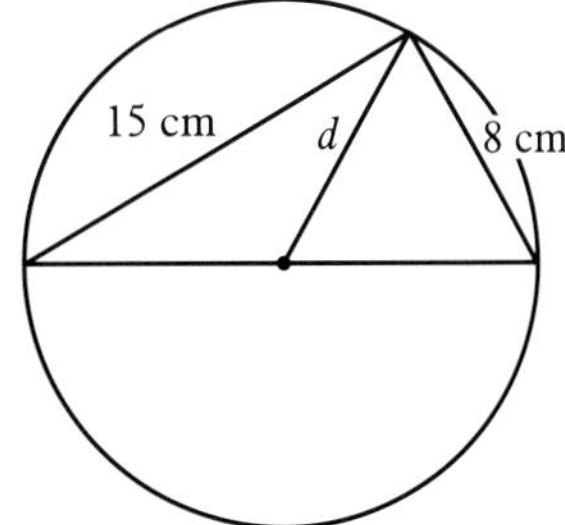

1 Find the red area in each of these.

a

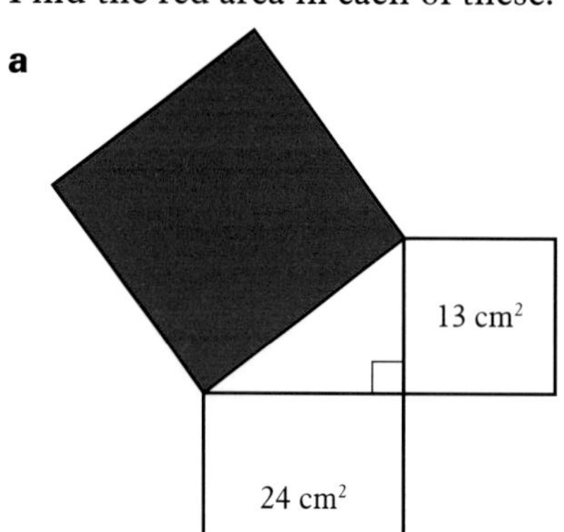

b

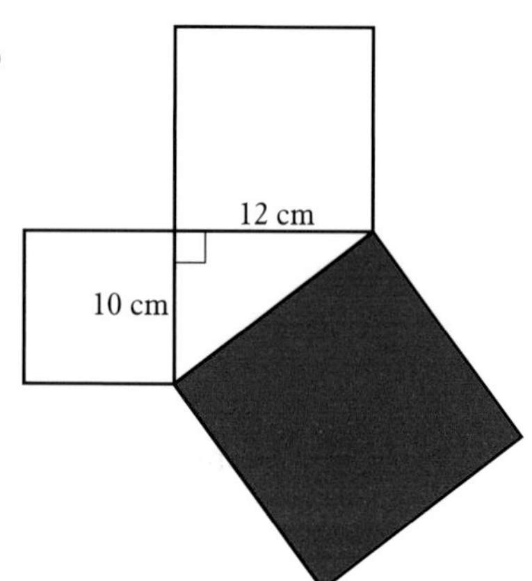

2 Find the blue area in each of these.

a

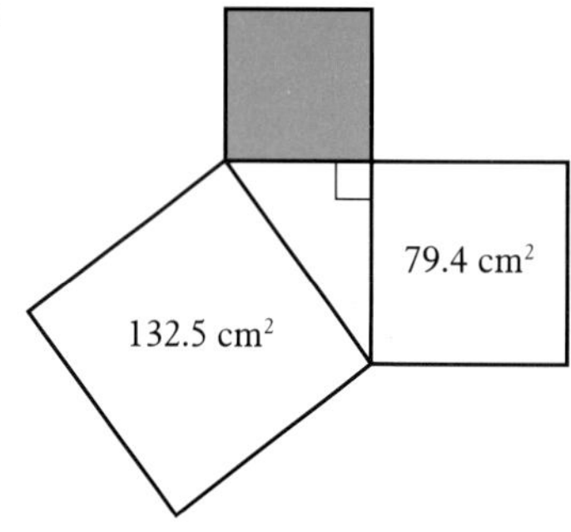

b

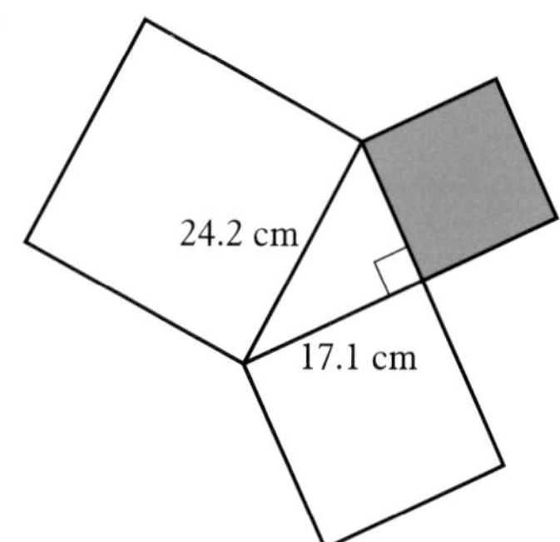

3 Find the length of the hypotenuse in each of these triangles.
Give your answers to 1 dp.

a

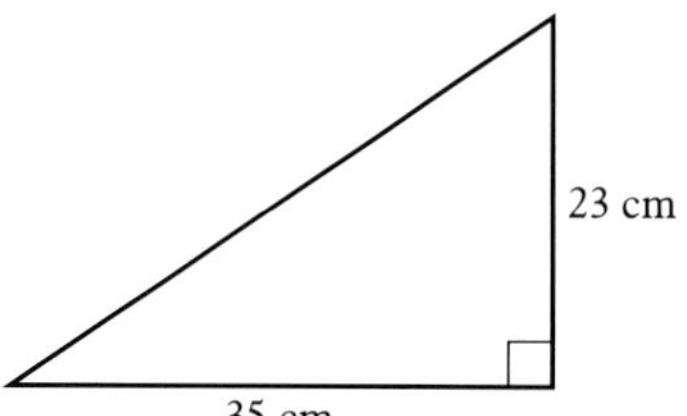

b

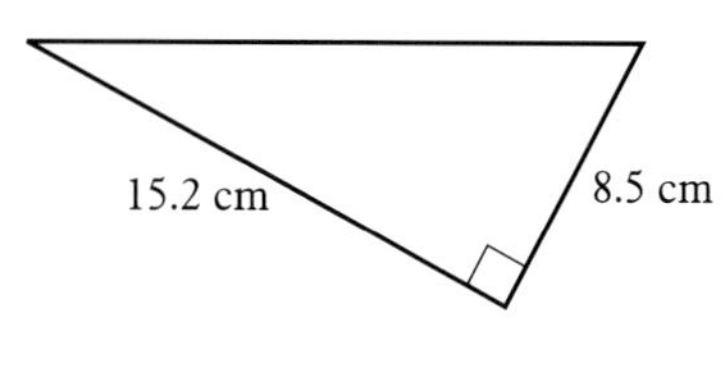

4 Find the length of the missing side in each of these triangles.
Give your answers to 1 dp.

a

23 cm
12 cm

b

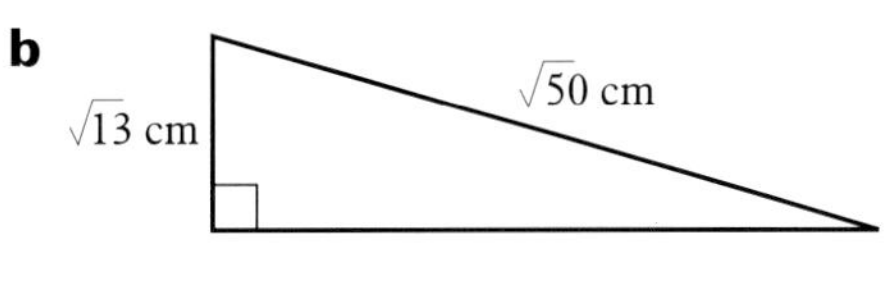

5 Find the missing lengths in each of these triangles.
Give your answers to 1 dp.

a

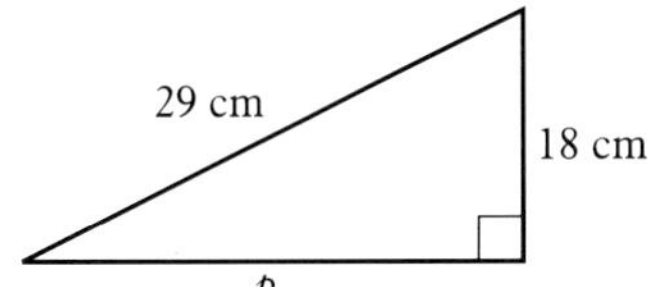

c

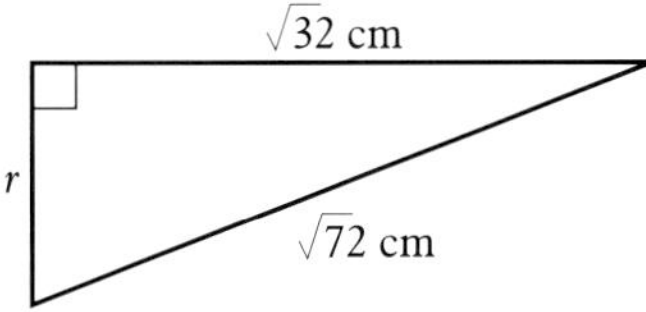

b

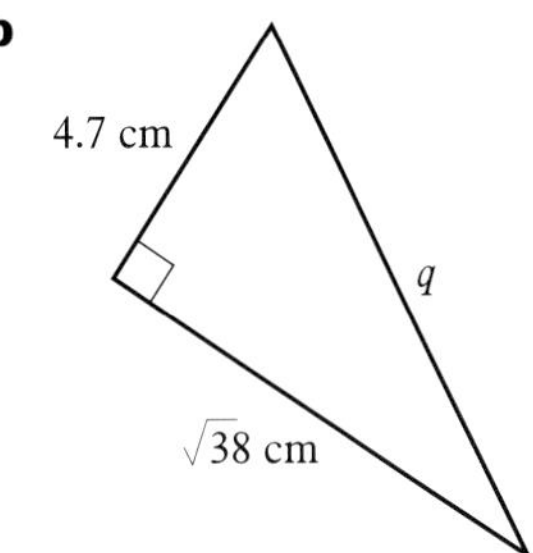

d

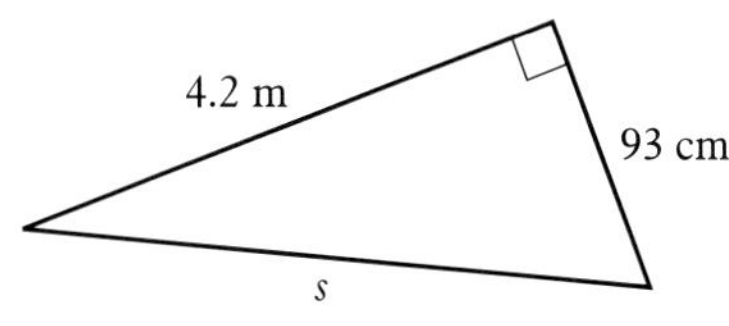

6 Find the distance between

a E and F

b O and G

c G and H

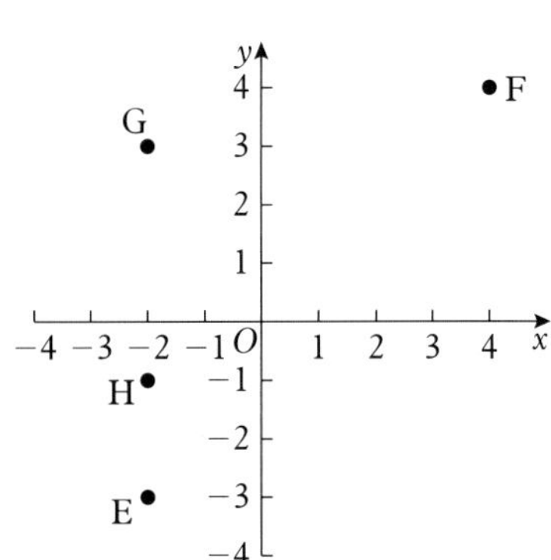

7 This diagram shows the position of three ports.
Two of the ports are on one side of the river and the other port is on the opposite side.
The distance from A to B is 75 km.
The distance from B to C is 65 km.
Find the distance between ports A and C.

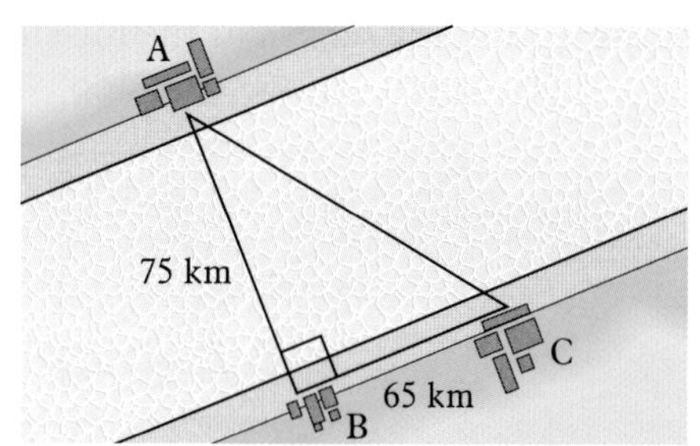

8 Find the value of x in this right-angled triangle.

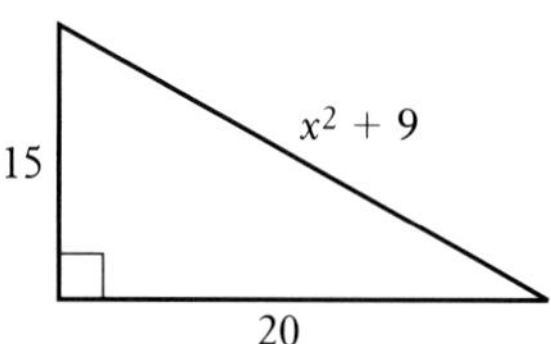

9 Here is a table for showing some Pythagorean triples.

a	b	h
3	4	
	12	13
7		
		41

a Copy the table. Fill it in.

b Add an extra 5 rows to your table.
There is a pattern in each column.
Fill in the next 5 entries in each column.

c Check that your five extra rows are all Pythagorean triples.

d There are other Pythagorean triples that are not part of this pattern.
Write down one of them. Use 8 as the smallest number.
Can you find any more? You cannot use any multiples of the ones in the pattern or of your answer to this part!

10 The diagram shows a chord of a circle.

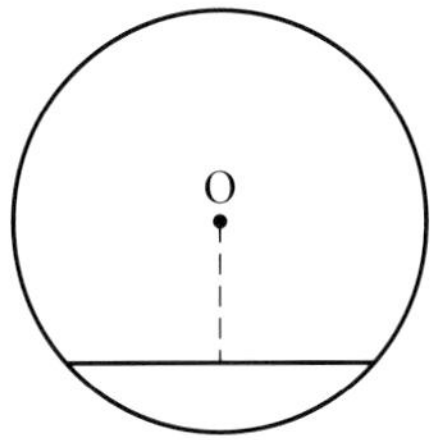

The circle has radius 8 cm.
The chord is 13 cm long.
Find the distance from the centre of the circle, O, to the chord.

11 Gerald is taking a stroll around the grounds of Holkom Hall.
He walks along the red route.
The paths are shown in blue.

a How far has Gerald walked altogether?
b How far north has Gerald moved?
c How far west has Gerald moved?
d How far is Gerald from his starting point?
e Gerald returns home along the paths.
He walks at 1 m/s. How much quicker is his return journey?

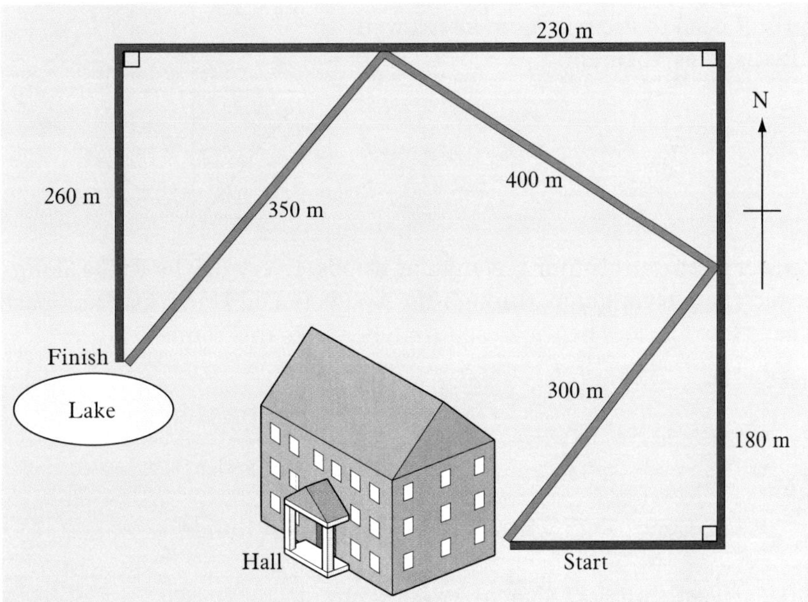

1 The diagram shows an equilateral triangle of side 12 cm.

a Copy the diagram. Split the triangle into two right-angled triangles.

b Use Pythagoras' theorem to find the height of the triangle.

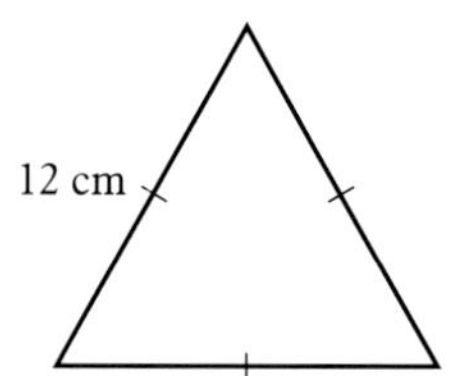

2 **a** Write down an expression for the square of the hypotenuse in this triangle. Simplify your answer.

b Write down the square of each of the other two sides.

c Write down Pythagoras' theorem for the triangle.

d Solve the equation to find the value of x.

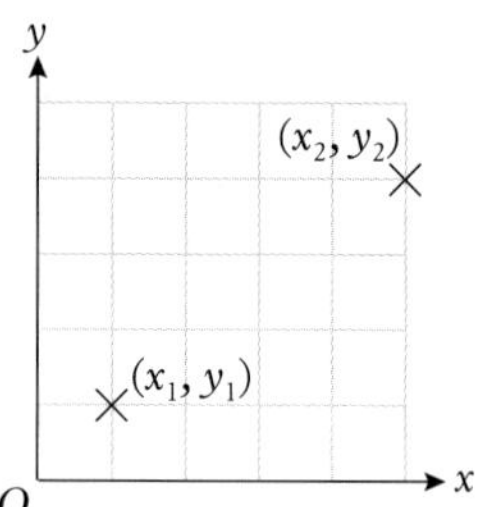

3 Show that the distance between the two points (x_1, y_1) and (x_2, y_2) is $\sqrt{(x_2 - x_1)^2 + (y_2 - y_1)^2}$

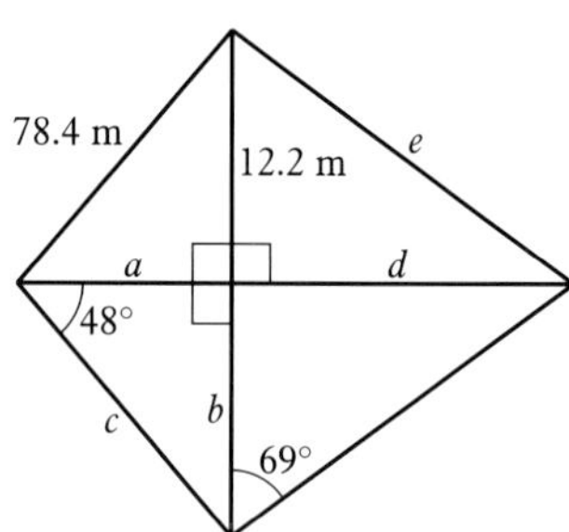

4 Find the lengths labelled with letters in this diagram. You will need to use trigonometry as well as Pythagoras' theorem.

5 Forester Fred patrols four rectangular woods. Every day he walks along the red route from home, through the woods to Old Harry Oak and back home. How far does he walk each time he walks this route?

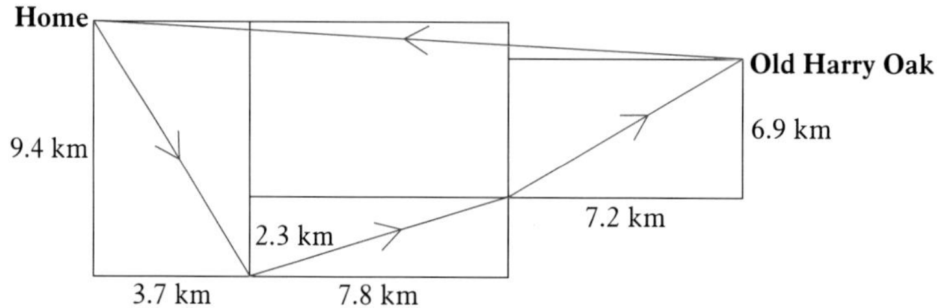

1 Find the coloured area in each of these:

a

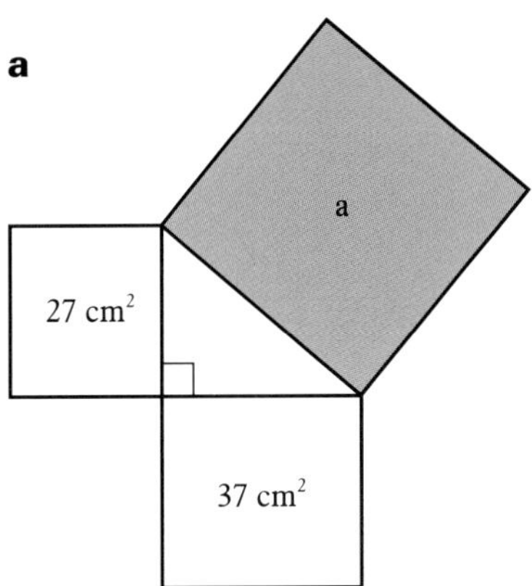

b

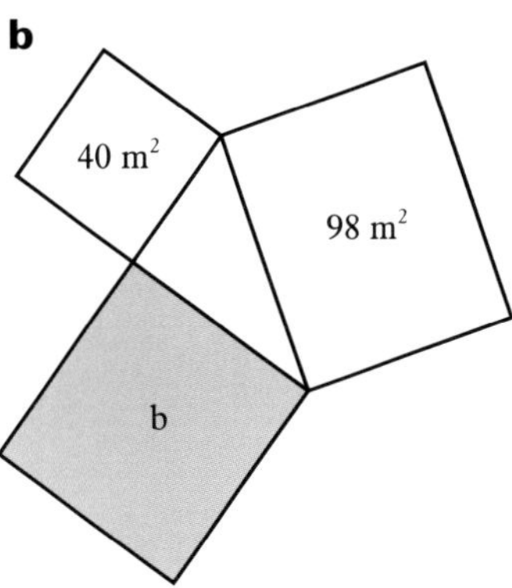

2 Find the lengths marked with letters.

a

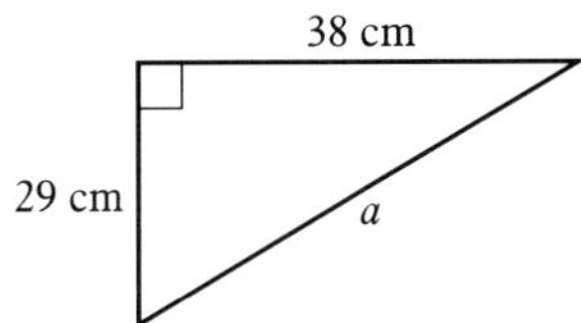

c

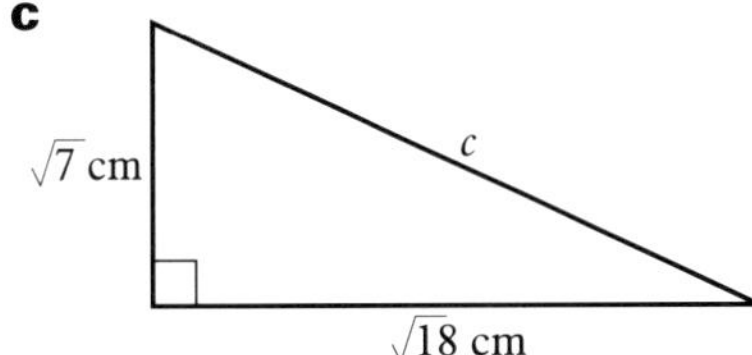

b

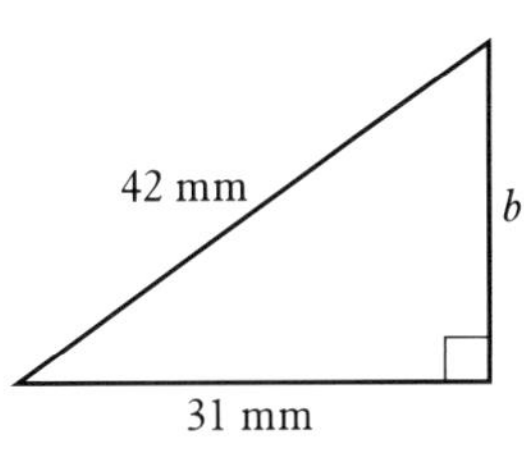

d

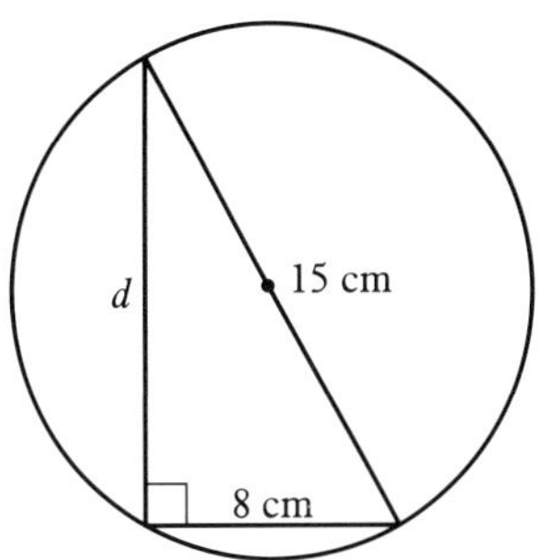

3 Write down the missing number in each of these Pythagorean triples.

a 3 4 … **b** 7 … 25 **c** … 12 13 **d** 8 … 17

4 Find the length OR.

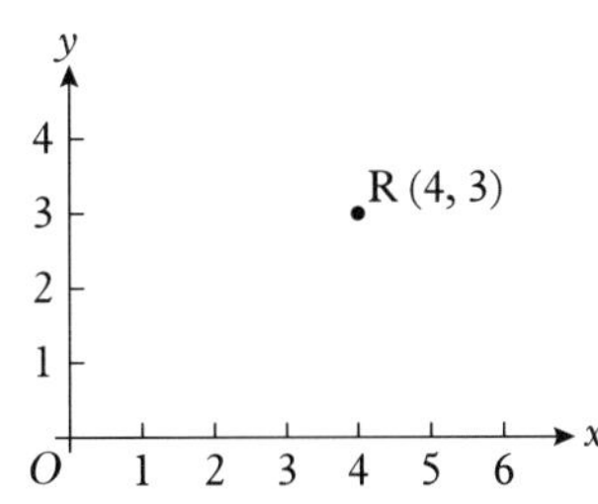

5 Find the distance between P and Q where P is the point (2, 5) and Q is the point (7, 15).

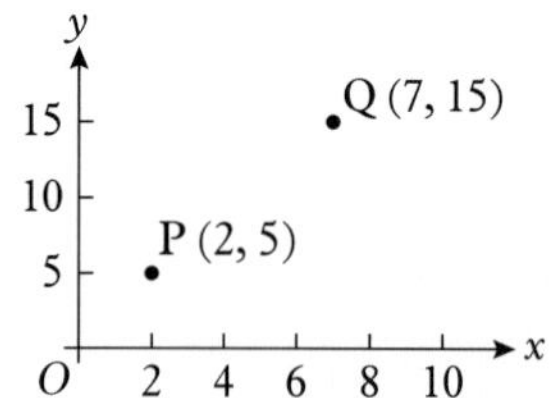

6 Find the missing length in this trapezium.

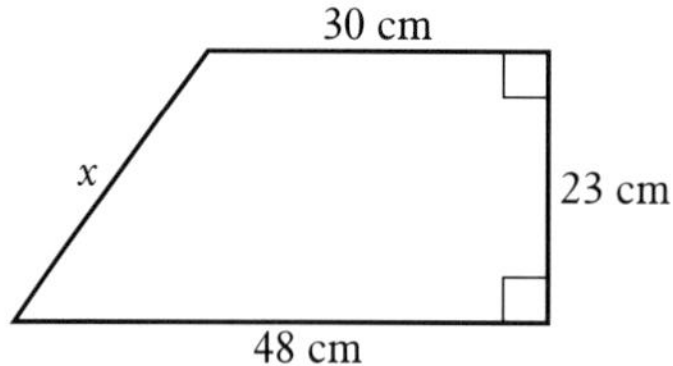

7 A ship sails from a port to an oil rig. The oil rig is 47 nautical miles north and 62 nautical miles east of the port. Find the distance between the port and the oil rig.

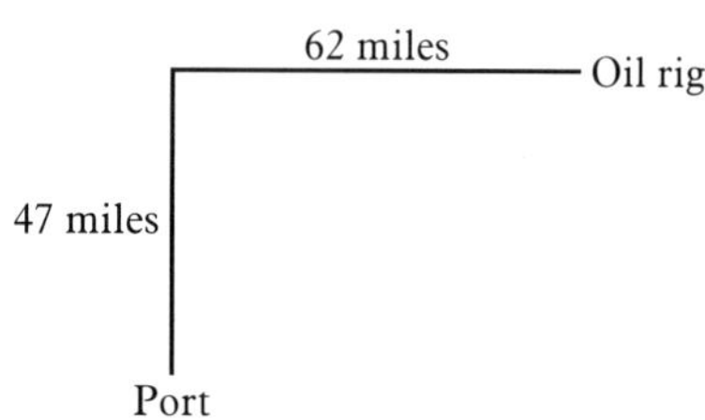

8 An aircraft travels 2800 m while rising 1500 m and then 5000 m while rising 1000 m. How much horizontal distance has it covered in this time?

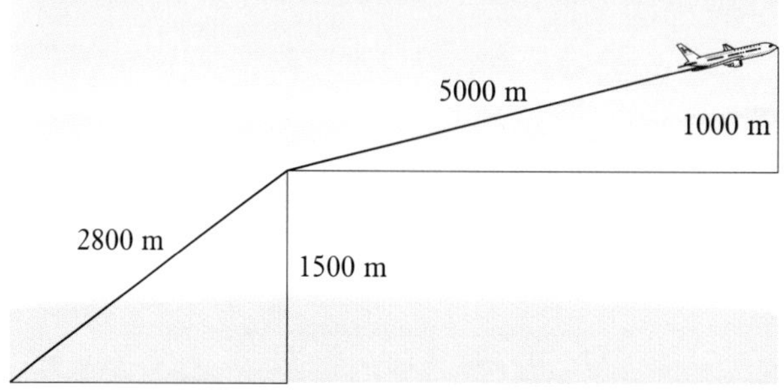

25 The power of graphs

1 Lines and curves
Drawing straight line graphs
Drawing quadratic graphs
Function notation

CORE

2 More curved graphs!
Drawing cubic graphs
Looking at the symmetry of cubic graphs
Drawing graphs involving $\frac{1}{x}$

QUESTIONS

EXTENSION

TEST YOURSELF

1 Lines and curves

Each of the searchlights has a special mirror inside it. It is in the shape of a parabola. It focuses the light in to a beam.

A parabola is the shape of the graph produced by a quadratic equation.

In this section you will learn how to draw this type of graph.

The equation of a straight line is $y = mx + c$.
m is the gradient of the line.
c is called the intercept.
It is the point where the graph crosses the y axis.

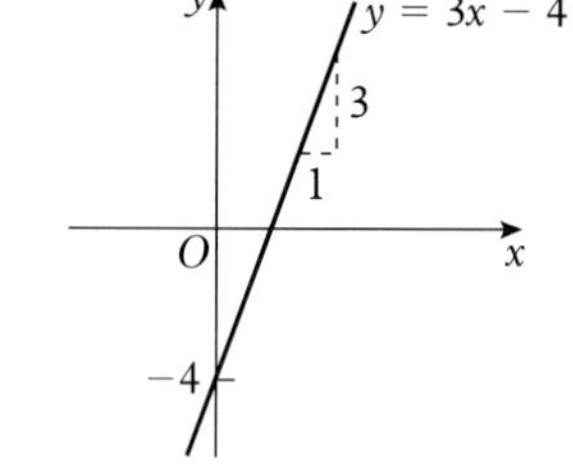

The equation of this straight line is $y = 3x - 4$.
The gradient of the line is 3.
The graph crosses the y axis at −4.

To draw the graph of a straight line you can fill in a table.

Example Draw the graph of $y = 3x - 4$. Use x values from −4 to +4.

(1) Draw a table. Put the x values along the top.

(2) Use a separate row for each part of the equation.
In this case there is one row for the $3x$ and one row for the −4
Fill in these two rows.

(3) Add the two rows together to get the y values.

x	−4	−3	−2	−1	0	1	2	3	4
$3x$	−12	−9	−6	−3	0	3	6	9	12
−4	−4	−4	−4	−4	−4	−4	−4	−4	−4
y	−16	−13	−10	−7	−4	−1	2	5	8

(4) Use the x and y values as co-ordinates to plot your graph.

(5) Make sure that you label your graph.

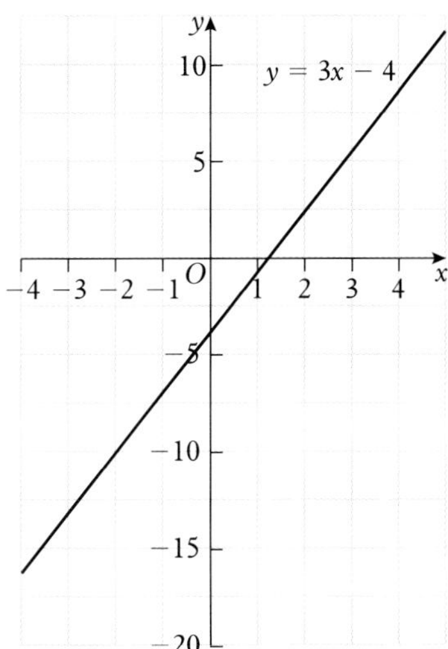

Exercise 25:1

1 **a** Copy this table for $y = 2x + 3$.

x	**−4**	**−3**	**−2**	**−1**	**0**	**1**	**2**	**3**	**4**
$2x$	−8	−6			0	2			
+3	3	3			3	3			
y	**−5**	**−3**			**3**	**5**			

b Fill in the missing values.
c Draw axes with x from −4 to 4 and y from −6 to 12.
d Draw the graph of $y = 2x + 3$.
Don't forget to label it.

2 **a** Copy this table for $y = 3x - 1$.

x	**−4**	**−3**	**−2**	**−1**	**0**	**1**	**2**	**3**	**4**
$3x$		−9			0		6		
−1		−1			−1		−1		
y		**−10**			**−1**		5		

b Fill in the missing values.
c Draw axes with x from −4 to 4 and y from −15 to 15.
d Draw the graph of $y = 3x - 1$.
Don't forget to label it.

3 For each of these equations:

(1) Draw a table.

(2) Fill in the values.

(3) Draw a set of axes. They need to fit the values in your table.

(4) Draw the graph of the equation.

a $y = 2x - 6$

b $y = 4x - 2$

c $y = \frac{1}{2}x + 3$

d $y = 0.2x - 2$

If the number in front of the x term of the equation is negative, the line slopes downwards.
You have to be a little more careful when you fill in the table.

Example Draw the graph of $y = 5 - 2x$. Use x values from -4 to $+4$.

The table looks like this:

x	**−4**	**−3**	**−2**	**−1**	**0**	**1**	**2**	**3**	**4**
5	5	5	5	5	5	5	5	5	5
$-2x$	8	6	4	2	0	−2	−4	−6	−8
y	**13**	**11**	**9**	**7**	**5**	**3**	**1**	**−1**	**−3**

Notice that when $x = -4$, $-2x = 8$.
This is because $-2 \times -4 = 8$.

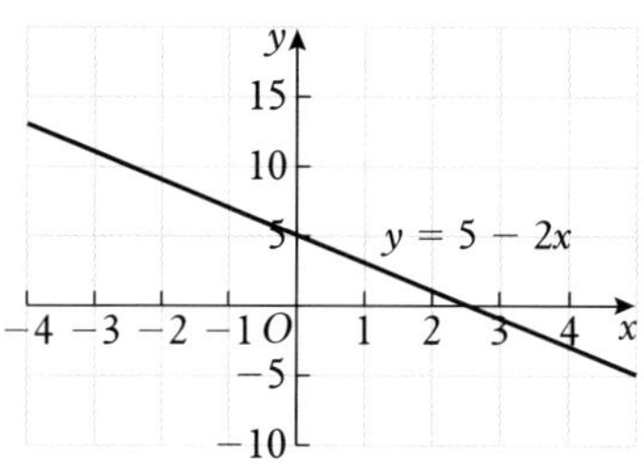

This is the graph of $y = 5 - 2x$.

---

4 For each of these equations:

(1) Draw a table.

(2) Fill in the values.

(3) Draw a set of axes that fits the values in your table.

(4) Draw the graph of the equation.

a $y = 3 - 2x$

b $y = 6 - x$

c $y = 0.5 - 4x$

d $y = 3 - \frac{1}{2}x$

Quadratic graphs

Quadratic

A **quadratic** equation or formula is one which has an x^2 in it.

It must not have any other powers of x such as x^3 or $\frac{1}{x}$.
It can have xs and numbers in it.

These are all quadratic equations:
$y = x^2 + 3$
$y = 3x^2 + 5x - 3$
$y = 8x - x^2$

Graphs of quadratic equations are curves not straight lines.

Exercise 25:2

1 **a** Copy this table. Fill it in.
Remember x^2 means $x \times x$.

x	−5	−4	−3	−2	−1	0	1	2	3	4	5
$y = x^2$	25	16	9			0	1				

b Draw an x axis from −5 to +5 and a y axis from 0 to 25.

c Plot the points from your table.

d Join the points with a **smooth** curve.
Label your curve $y = x^2$.
This type of curve is called a **parabola**.
All quadratic graphs are parabolas.

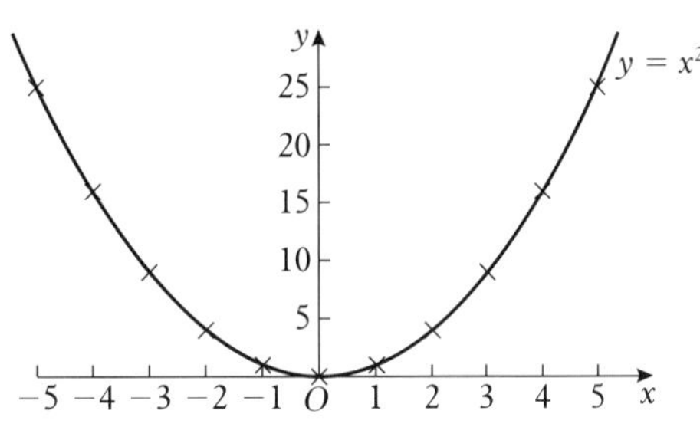

2 **a** Copy this table for $y = x^2 + 5$.

x	**−4**	**−3**	**−2**	**−1**	**0**	**1**	**2**	**3**	**4**
x^2	16	9			0		4		
+5	5	5			5		5		
y	**21**	**14**			**5**		**9**		

b Fill in the missing values.

c Draw axes with x from -4 to $+4$ and y from 0 to 25.
d Draw the graph of $y = x^2 + 5$
Make the curve as smooth as you can.

3 **a** Copy this table for $y = x^2 - 3$.

x	-4	-3	-2	-1	0	1	2	3	4
x^2	16	9			0			9	
-3	-3	-3			-3			-3	
y	**13**	**6**			**−3**			**6**	

b Fill in the missing values.
c Draw axes with x from -4 to $+4$ and y from -5 to 15.
d Draw the graph of $y = x^2 - 3$

4 Look at the graphs you have drawn for questions **1** to **3**.
a All the graphs are symmetrical.
Write down the equation of the line of symmetry.
b Look at graph **2**.
What effect has the $+5$ in the equation had on the graph?
c Look at graph **3**.
What effect has the -3 in the equation had on the graph?
• **d** What would the graph of $y = x^2 + 10$ look like?
Sketch the graph.

Quadratic formulas can have multiples of x^2 in them.
It is important to remember that $3x^2$ means find x^2 *then* multiply by 3.

5 **a** Copy this table for $y = 3x^2 + 4$

x	-4	-3	-2	-1	0	1	2	3	4
$3x^2$	48	27				3	12		
$+4$	4	4				4	4		
y	**52**	**31**				**7**	**16**		

b Fill in the missing values.
c Draw axes with x from -4 to $+4$ and y from 0 to 60.
d Draw the graph of $y = 3x^2 + 4$

Quadratic formulas can have three terms in them.

They can have an x^2 term, an x term and a number term.

The number term is sometimes called the constant term.

To draw a graph of these formulas, you will need three rows of working in your table.

Example Draw the curve of $y = x^2 + 3x + 1$
Use x values from -5 to $+3$

(1) Complete a table showing each part of the formula $y = x^2 + 3x + 1$ separately.

x	-5	-4	-3	-2	-1	0	1	2	3
x^2	25	16	9	4	1	0	1	4	9
$+3x$	-15	-12	-9	-6	-3	0	3	6	9
$+1$	1	1	1	1	1	1	1	1	1
y	11	5	1	-1	-1	1	5	11	19

(2) Draw an x axis from -5 to $+3$ and a y axis from -2 to 20.

(3) Plot the points from your table.

(4) Join the points with a **smooth** curve.
Your finished curve should look like this:

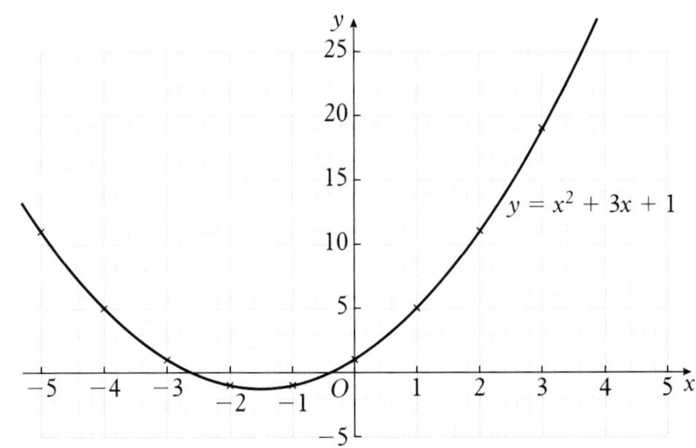

Exercise 25:3

1 **a** Copy and complete this table for $y = x^2 + 2x + 3$

x	−5	−4	−3	−2	−1	0	1	2	3
x^2	25	16				0			9
$+2x$	−10	−8				0			6
$+3$	3	3				3			3
y	**18**	**11**				**3**			**18**

b Draw an x axis from −5 to +3 and a y axis from 0 to 20.
c Plot the points from your table.
d Join the points with a **smooth** curve.

2 **a** Copy and complete this table for $y = x^2 + 3x - 5$

x	−5	−4	−3	−2	−1	0	1	2	3
x^2	25	16				0			
$+3x$	−15	−12				0			
-5	−5	−5				−5			
y	**5**	**−1**				**−5**			

b Draw an x axis from −5 to +3 and a y axis from −10 to 15.
c Plot the graph of $y = x^2 + 3x - 5$ from your table.
d Draw the line of symmetry on your graph.
• **e** Write down the equation of the line of symmetry.

3 **a** Complete this table for $y = x^2 - x - 3$
Notice how both the minus signs in the formula are included in the table.
Remember that if $x = -5$ then $-x = 5$

x	−5	−4	−3	−2	−1	0	1	2	3
x^2	25	16							
$-x$	5	4					−1	−2	
-3	−3	−3							
y	**27**	**17**							

b Draw an x axis from −5 to +3 and a y axis from −5 to 30.
c Plot the points from your table.
d Join the points with a **smooth** curve.

4 For each part of this question:

(1) Draw a table using the x values given.
(2) Draw axes to fit the values in the table.
(3) Draw a graph from your table.

a $y = 2x^2 + 2x - 5$ x from -4 to $+4$
b $y = x^2 - x - 3$ x from -4 to $+4$
c $y = 3x^2 + x$ x from -4 to $+4$
d $y = x^2 - 3x$ x from -4 to $+4$

If the x^2 term in a quadratic formula is negative, the graph is turned upside down.

It is important to remember that $-x^2$ means find x^2 and *then* make the answer minus. Because x^2 is always a positive number, $-x^2$ will always be negative.

Example Work out $-3x^2$ when **a** $x = 4$ **b** $x = -5$

a $x = 4$

$$-3x^2 = -3 \times 4^2 = -3 \times 16 = -48$$

b $x = -5$

$$-3x^2 = -3 \times (-5)^2 = -3 \times 25 = -75$$

Exercise 25:4

1 **a** Copy and complete this table for $y = -x^2 + 2x$.

x	-5	-4	-3	-2	-1	0	1	2	3
$-x^2$	-25	-16				0		-4	-9
$+2x$	-10	-8				0			6
y	-35	-24				0			-3

b Draw an axis from -5 to $+3$ and a y axis from -35 to 5.
c Plot the points from your table.
d Join the points with a **smooth** curve. The curve should look like this.

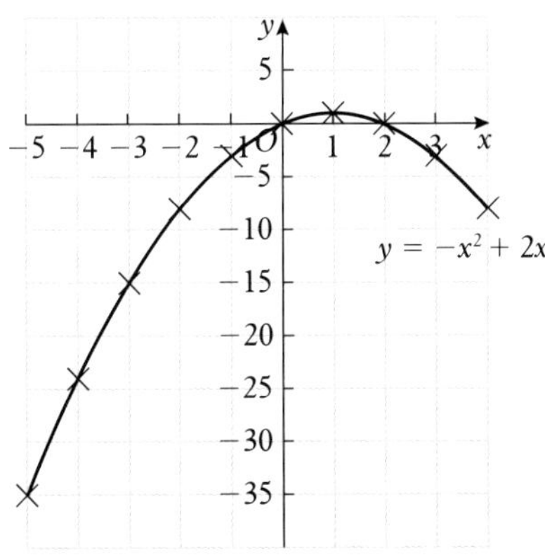

2 **a** Copy and complete this table for $y = -x^2 - 2x + 10$

x	−4	−3	−2	−1	0	1	2	3	4
$-x^2$	−16			−1		0		−9	
$-2x$	8		4			0			−8
$+10$	10	10				10			
y	2					10			

b Draw an axis with x from −4 to +4 and a y axis from −15 to 15.
c Draw the graph of $y = -x^2 - 2x + 10$
d Write down the equation of the line of symmetry of the curve.

3 Look carefully at this table for the graph of $y = (x + 1)^2$

x	−4	−3	−2	−1	0	1	2	3	4
$x + 1$	−3	−2	−1	0	1				
y	9	4	1	0	1				

a Copy and complete the table.
b Draw a graph of $y = (x + 1)^2$

• **4** For each part of this question:
(1) Draw a table using the x values given.
(2) Draw axes to fit the values in the table.
(3) Draw a graph from your table.

a $y = -2x^2 + 2x + 12$ x from −4 to +4
b $y = (x - 3)^2$ x from −4 to +4
c $y = -(x + 4)^2$ x from −4 to +4
d $y = -\frac{1}{2}x^2 + 2x - 3$ x from −4 to +4

Exercise 25:5

1 A ball is thrown in the air at a speed of 20 m/s. The height of the ball during its journey is calculated using the formula $h = 20t - 5t^2$. t is the number of seconds the ball has been in the air.

a Copy this table. Fill in the missing values.

t	0	0.5	1	1.5	2	2.5	3	3.5	4
$20t$	0			30					80
$-5t^2$	0			−11.25					−80
h	0			18.75					0

b Draw axes with t on the horizontal scale and h on the vertical scale.
c Draw the path of the ball as it travels through the air.
d What is the maximum height that the ball reaches?

• **2** The formula that the police use to calculate car stopping distances is

$$d = \frac{s^2 + 20s}{60}$$

d is the stopping distance in metres and s is the speed of the car in miles per hour.

a Copy this table and fill it in. It shows stopping distances for speeds from 10 mph to 70 mph.

s	10	20	30	40	50	60	70
s^2							
$20s$							
$d = \frac{s^2 + 20s}{60}$							

b Draw a graph to show the stopping distances of cars.
c Use your graph to estimate the stopping distance of a car travelling at 55 mph.

Function notation

It is sometimes easier to write the equations of graphs in **function notation.**
You replace y with $f(x)$ so you write $y = x^2$ as $f(x) = x^2$.
You read $f(x)$ as 'f of x'. It is short for 'function of x'.
You can think of this as a formula written in terms of x.

To show that you want the value of $f(x)$ when $x = 3$, you write $f(3)$.

Example

$f(x) = x^2 + 3x - 2$
Work out: **a** $f(3)$ **b** $f(5)$ **c** $f(-2)$

a $f(3)$ means replace x by 3 in $f(x)$
$f(x) = x^2 + 3x - 2$
$f(3) = 3^2 + 3 \times 3 - 2 = 16$
b $f(5) = 5^2 + 3 \times 5 - 2 = 38$
c $f(-2) = (-2)^2 + 3 \times (-2) - 2 = -4$

Exercise 25:6

1 $f(x) = 4x + 5$
Work out **a** $f(2)$ **b** $f(6)$ **c** $f(8)$

2 $f(x) = 7x - 3$
Work out **a** $f(4)$ **b** $f(-1)$ **c** $f(-5)$

3 $f(x) = x^2 + 6$
Work out **a** $f(2)$ **b** $f(5)$ **c** $f(-3)$

4 $f(x) = 2x^2 + x$
Work out **a** $f(3)$ **b** $f(-1)$ **c** $f(0)$

5 $f(x) = 3x^2 - 2x + 3$
Work out **a** $f(2)$ **b** $f(-3)$ **c** $f(0)$

6 **a** Copy this table for $f(x) = 2x - 3$.

x	−1	0	1	2	3	4
$2x$						
−3						
$f(x)$						

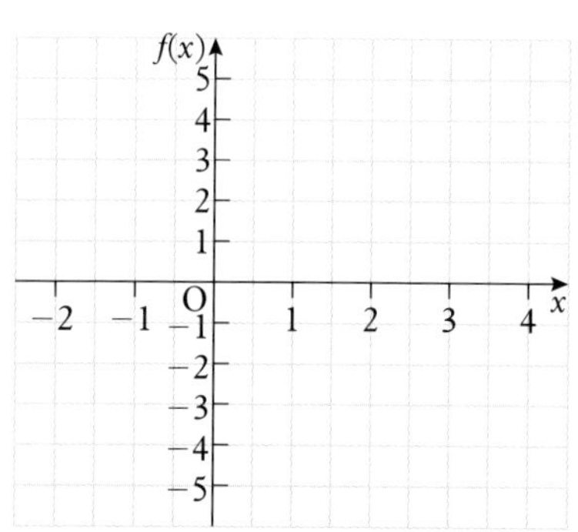

b Copy the axes.
c Draw the graph of $f(x) = 2x - 3$.

2 More curved graphs!

There are lots of ways to choose an equation that will make a curve.

Cubic

A **cubic** equation or formula is one which has an x^3 in it.

It must not have any higher powers of x or terms like $\frac{1}{x}, \frac{1}{x^2}$, etc.

It can have x^2 and x terms and numbers.

$y = 5x^3 - 2x$ and $y = \frac{x^3}{2} + x^2 - 5$ are cubic equations.

$y = 5x^3 - \frac{2}{x}$ and $y = 2x^4 + x^3 + 1$ are not cubic equations.

The graph of a cubic equation is a curve. It is different from a quadratic curve.

Exercise 25:7

1 Write down the letters of the cubic equations.

A $y = x^2 - 3x + 2$	D $y = 2x^3$	G $y = x - 0.5x^3$
B $y = x^3$	E $y = x^3 + x^4$	H $y = x^3 - 2x^2 - 3$
C $y = x^3 + 2x - 1$	F $y = x^3 - \frac{1}{x}$	I $y = \frac{1}{x^3}$

Sometimes a cubic is written in factorised form.

• **2** Write down the letters of the cubic equations.

A $y = x^2(x + 2)$	C $y = x(x + 1)^2$	E $y = x(x + 1)(x - 2)$
B $y = x^3(x - 5)$	D $y = (x - 2)^3$	F $y = x^3(x^3 + 2)$

3 **a** Copy these axes on to graph paper.

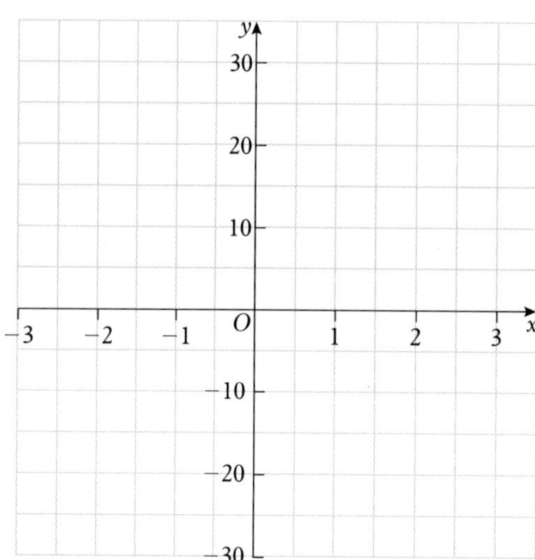

b Copy the table. Fill in the missing values.
You can work out x^3 as $x \times x \times x$ or you can use the x^y key on your calculator.

x	−3	−2	−1	0	1	2	3
$y = x^3$	−27					8	

c Plot the points from your table.
Join them with a smooth curve.
Label your graph $y = x^3$.

d The curve has rotational symmetry.
(1) Write down the order.
(2) Give the co-ordinates of the centre of rotation.

4 **a** Copy the table for $y = x^3 + 3$. Fill in the missing values.

x	**−3**	**−2**	**−1**	**0**	**1**	**2**	**3**
x^3	−27					8	
+3	3					3	
y	**−24**					**11**	

b Plot the points from your table on the same diagram as question **3**.
Join them with a smooth curve.
Label the curve $y = x^3 + 3$.

c Describe the symmetry of the curve.

5 **a** Copy the table for $y = x^3 - 3$. Fill in the missing values.

x	−3	−2	−1	0	1	2	3
x^3	−27					8	
−3	−3					−3	
y	−30					5	

b Plot the points from your table on the same diagram as question **3**.
Join them with a smooth curve.
Label the curve $y = x^3 - 3$

c Describe the symmetry of the curve.

● **6** **a** Draw the graph of $y = x^3 + 2$ on the same diagram.
Don't use a table of values.

b Explain how you were able to draw the graph in **a**.

c Draw the graph of $y = x^3 - 2$ on the same diagram.

All of the cubic graphs drawn so far have flattened in the middle and then turned upwards again. Some cubic graphs dip in the middle before turning upwards.

Example Draw the graph of $y = x^3 - 8x + 5$
Use x values from −4 to 4.

(1) Complete a table showing each part of the equation separately.

x	−4	−3	−2	−1	0	1	2	3	4
x^3	−64	−27	−8	−1	0	1	8	27	64
$-8x$	32	24	16	8	0	−8	−16	−24	−32
+5	5	5	5	5	5	5	5	5	5
y	−27	2	13	12	5	−2	−3	8	37

(2) Draw an x axis from −4 to 4 and a y axis from −30 to 40.
Remember that you can use a different scale for the y axis.

(3) Plot the points from your table.

(4) Join the points with a smooth curve.

Your finished curve should look like this.

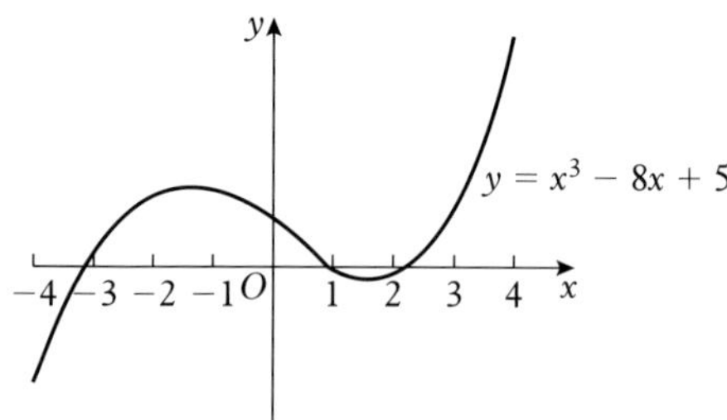

Exercise 25:8

1 **a** Copy this table for $y = x^3 - 5x + 10$

x	**−4**	**−3**	**−2**	**−1**	**0**	**1**	**2**	**3**	**4**
x^3	−64			−1				27	
$-5x$	20			5				−15	
$+10$	10			10				10	
y	**−34**			**14**				**22**	

b Fill in the missing values.
c Draw axes with x from −4 to 4 and y from −35 to 55.
d Draw the graph of $y = x^3 - 5x + 10$

2 **a** Copy this table for $y = x^3 - 6x - 5$

x	**−4**	**−3**	**−2**	**−1**	**0**	**1**	**2**	**3**	**4**
x^3	−64			−1				27	
$-6x$	24			6				−18	
-5	−5			−5				−5	
y	**−45**			**0**				**4**	

b Fill in the missing values.
c Draw axes with x from −4 to 4 and y from −45 to 35.
d Draw the graph of $y = x^3 - 6x - 5$

3 **a** Copy this table for $y = x^3 + 6x - 5$

x	**−3**	**−2**	**−1**	**0**	**1**	**2**	**3**
x^3			−1				27
$+6x$			−6				18
-5			−5				−5
y			**−12**				**40**

b Fill in the missing values.
c Draw axes with x from −3 to 3 and y from −50 to 40.
d Draw the graph of $y = x^3 + 6x - 5$
e Describe how this curve is different to the ones that you have drawn before.

So far, you have found three types of graph for cubic equations.

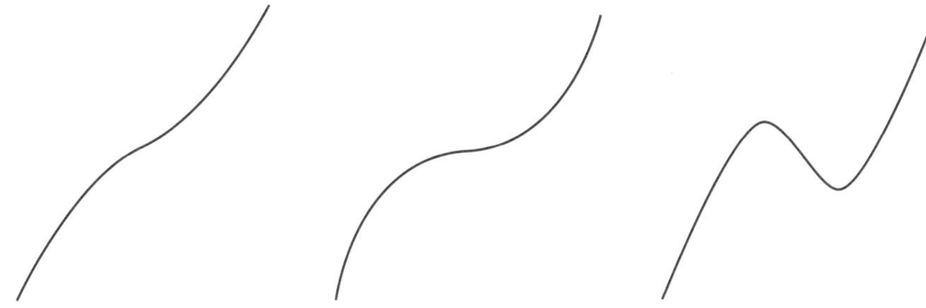

One thing that these graphs have in common is that, apart from the bit in the middle, they all slope upwards from left to right. But, if the x^3 term is negative then the opposite happens.

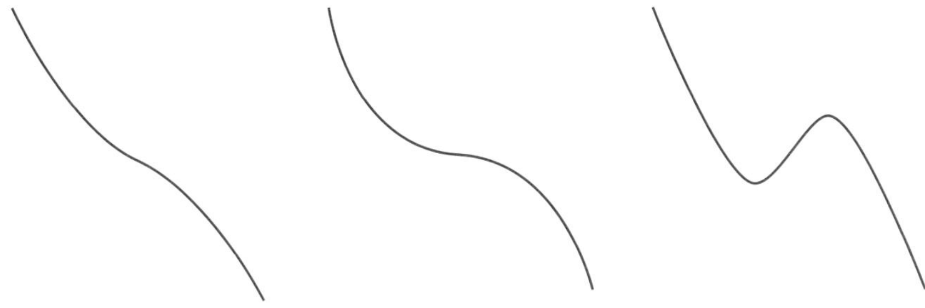

Exercise 25:9

1 **a** Copy this table for $y = -x^3 - 4x + 10$

x	**−3**	**−2**	**−1**	**0**	**1**	**2**	**3**
$-x^3$			1				−27
$-4x$			4				−12
$+10$			10				10
y			**15**				**−29**

b Fill in the missing values.
c Draw axes with x from −3 to 3 and y from −30 to 50.
d Draw the graph of $y = -x^3 - 4x + 10$
e Describe the shape of the curve.

2 **a** Copy this table for $y = -x^3 + 10x$

x	**−4**	**−3**	**−2**	**−1**	**0**	**1**	**2**	**3**	**4**
$-x^3$	64			1				−27	
$+10x$	−40			−10				30	
y	**24**			**−9**				**3**	

b Fill in the missing values.
c Draw axes with x from −4 to 4 and y from −25 to 25.
d Draw the graph of $y = -x^3 + 10x$
e Describe the shape of the curve.

3 **a** Copy this table for $y = -x^3 + 3x^2 - 3x$

x	**−2**	**−1**	**0**	**1**	**2**	**3**	**4**
$-x^3$	8				−8		
$+3x^2$	12				12		
$-3x$	6				−6		
y	**26**				**−2**		

b Fill in the missing values.
c Draw axes with x from −2 to 4 and y from −30 to 30.
d Draw the graph of $y = -x^3 + 3x^2 - 3x$
e Describe the shape of the curve.

Twist and turn

You will need tracing paper for this investigation.
It will be helpful if you have a graph plotter that will print the graphs.

1 You have already drawn the graphs of some cubic equations. Trace each of these curves and then rotate the tracing paper through 180°. Does the traced curve always match the original when it is upside down?

2 Draw the graphs of some new cubic equations. Use a graph plotter if you have one. Do all of these curves have rotational symmetry?

3 The centre of rotational symmetry for many of the curves that you have drawn lies on the y axis. Try to find a rule for when this happens.

4 Find the x co-ordinate of the centre of rotational symmetry for each of these.

a $y = x^3 + 3x^2$
b $y = x^3 - 3x^2$
c $y = x^3 + 6x^2$
d $y = x^3 - 6x^2$
e $y = x^3 + 9x^2$
f $y = x^3 - 9x^2$
g $y = 2x^3 + 12x^2$
h $y = 5x^3 - 15x^2$

5 Look at your answers to question **4**. Try to find a rule when the equation takes the form

a $y = x^3 + bx$
b $y = ax^3 + bx$

6 Find the x co-ordinate of the centre of rotational symmetry for each of these. Compare your results with question **4**.

a $y = x^3 + 3x^2 + 4$
b $y = x^3 - 3x^2 - 3$
c $y = x^3 + 6x^2 + x$
d $y = x^3 - 6x^2 - 2x$
e $y = x^3 + 9x^2 + 3x$
f $y = x^3 - 9x^2 - 2$
g $y = 2x^3 + 12x^2 + x - 5$
h $y = 5x^3 - 15x^2 - 2x + 6$

7 Use your results from question **6** to find a rule when the equation takes the form $y = ax^3 + bx^2 + cx + d$.

Another type of equation that has a curved graph is one where the x appears on the bottom line of a fraction.

Example Draw the graph of $y = \frac{5}{x}$. Use values of x from 1 to 5.

(1) Complete a table of values. Remember that $\frac{5}{x}$ means $5 \div x$.

x	1	2	3	4	5
y	5	2.5	1.7	1.25	1

(2) Draw x and y axes from 1 to 5.
(3) Plot the points from your table.
(4) Join the points with a smooth curve.

Your finished curve should look like this.

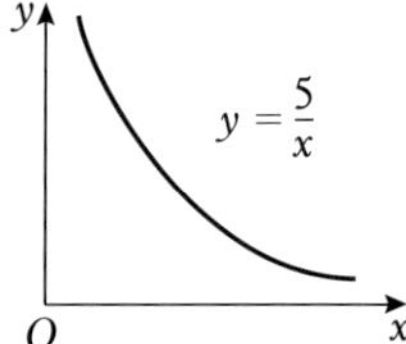

Exercise 25:10

1 **a** Draw x and y axes from -5 to 5.
b Copy the table. Fill it in.
Give the y values to 2 dp when you need to round.

x	0.2	0.3	0.4	0.5	1	2	3	4	5
$y = \frac{1}{x}$									

c Plot the points from the table. Join them with a smooth curve.

2 **a** Copy the table. Fill it in.
Round the y values to 2 dp when necessary.

x	-5	-4	-3	-2	-1	-0.5	-0.4	-0.3	-0.2
$y = \frac{1}{x}$									

b Plot the points on the same diagram as question **1**.
Join the points with a smooth curve.

Your diagram should now look like this.

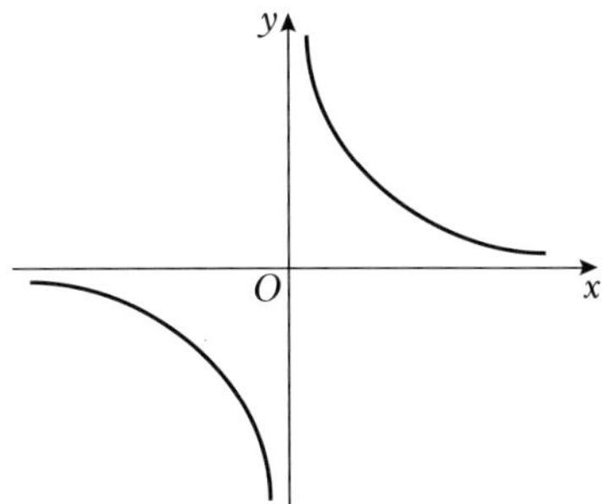

The graph of $y = \frac{1}{x}$ is in two halves. The two halves don't meet because it is impossible to find a value for y when $x = 0$.

3 **a** How many lines of symmetry does the graph of $y = \frac{1}{x}$ have?

b Draw the lines of symmetry on your diagram.

c Label each line of symmetry with its equation.

d Describe the rotational symmetry of the graph.

4 **a** Draw the graph of $y = \frac{1}{x}$ again on a new set of axes from -5 to 5.

b Draw the graph of $y = \frac{1}{x} + 1$ on the same diagram. Label your graph.

c Draw the graph of $y = \frac{1}{x} - 1$ on the same diagram. Label your graph.

5 **a** Draw x and y axes from -6 to 6.

b Copy the table. Complete it for $y = x + \frac{1}{x}$

Give the y values to 2 dp when you need to round.

x	0.2	0.3	0.4	0.5	1	2	3	4	5
$\frac{1}{x}$	5					0.5			
y	5.2					2.5			

c Plot the points from the table. Join them with a smooth curve.

6 **a** Copy the table. Complete it for $y = x + \frac{1}{x}$

Give the y values to 2 dp when you need to round.

x	-5	-4	-3	-2	-1	-0.5	-0.4	-0.3	-0.2
$\frac{1}{x}$	-0.2					-2			
y	-5.2					-2.5			

b Plot the points from your table on the same diagram as question **5**.
c Join the points with a smooth curve.
d Describe the symmetry of the complete graph of $y = x + \frac{1}{x}$

7 **a** Copy the table. Fill it in.
Give the y values to 2 dp when you need to round.

x	-3	-2	-1	-0.5	0.5	1	2	3
$y = \frac{1}{x^2}$		0.25						0.11

b Draw an x axis from -3 to 3 and a y axis from 0 to 5.
c Plot the points from your table.
d Join the points using two smooth curves.

Your diagram should look like this.

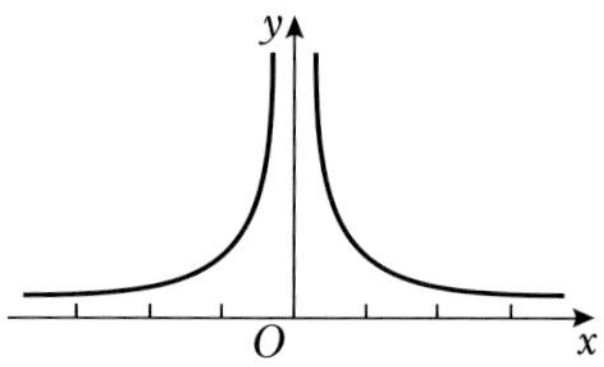

1 **a** Copy this table for $y = 2x - 7$

x	-4	-3	-2	-1	0	1	2	3	4
$2x$		-6			0		4		
-7		-7			-7		-7		
y		-13			-7		-3		

b Fill in the missing values.
c Draw axes with x from -4 to 4 and y from -15 to $+5$.
d Draw the graph of $y = 2x - 7$
Don't forget to label it.

2 For each of these equations:
(1) Draw a table.
(2) Fill in the values.
(3) Draw a set of axes. They need to fit the values in your table.
(4) Draw the graph of the equation.

a $y = 4x - 3$ **b** $y = 6 - 2x$ **c** $y = \frac{1}{2}x - 2$ **d** $y = 0.8x + 3$

3 **a** Copy this table for $y = 2x^2 + 8$

x	-4	-3	-2	-1	0	1	2	3	4
$2x^2$	32		8			2			
$+8$	8		8			8			
y	40		16			10			

b Fill in the missing values.
c Draw axes with x from -4 to $+4$ and y from 0 to 50.
d Draw the graph of $y = 2x^2 + 8$
Make the curve as smooth as you can.

4 **a** Copy and complete this table for $y = -2x^2 + x - 2$

x	-5	-4	-3	-2	-1	0	1	2	3
$-2x^2$			-18				-2		
$+x$			-3				1		
-2			-2				-2		
y			-23				-3		

b Draw an x axis from -5 to $+3$ and a y axis from -60 to 30.
c Plot the points from your table.
d Draw the line of symmetry on your graph.
e Write down the equation of the line of symmetry.

5 A stone is dropped from the top of a cliff.
The distance the stone has travelled is worked out using the formula
$d = 4.9t^2$
d is the distance in metres and t is the time in seconds.

a Copy this table. Fill in the values of d.

t	1	2	3	4	5	6	7	8
d								

b Draw a graph to show the distance that the stone has fallen.
Put t on the horizontal axis and d on the vertical axis.

c Another cliff is 280 m high.
Use your graph to estimate the time it would take for a stone to fall from this height.

6 **a** Copy the table. Complete it for $y = \frac{1}{x^2} + 1$
Give the y values to 2 dp when you need to round.

x	-3	-2	-1	-0.5	0.5	1	2	3
$\frac{1}{x^2}$		0.25						0.11
$+1$		1						1
y		**1.25**						**1.11**

b Draw an x axis from -3 to 3 and a y axis from 0 to 5.

c Plot the points from your table.

d Join the points using two smooth curves.

7 **a** Copy the table. Complete it for $y = x^2 + \frac{1}{x}$
Round the y values to 2 dp where necessary.

x	-3	-2	-1	-0.5	-0.2	0.2	0.5	1	2	3
x^2		4								9
$+\frac{1}{x}$		-0.5								0.33
y		**3.5**								**9.33**

b Draw an x axis from -3 to 3 and a y axis from -5 to 10.

c Plot the points from your table.

d Join the points using two smooth curves.

8 $f(x) = 2x + 6$
Work out **a** $f(1)$ **b** $f(0)$ **c** $f(-3)$

9 $f(x) = 5x - 2$
Work out **a** $f(4)$ **b** $f(0)$ **c** $f(-7)$

10 $f(x) = x^2 + 2$
Work out **a** $f(0)$ **b** $f(3)$ **c** $f(-3)$

11 $f(x) = 3x^2 - 2x$
Work out **a** $f(3)$ **b** $f(-1)$ **c** $f(0)$

12 $f(x) = 2x^2 - 5x + 4$
Work out **a** $f(1)$ **b** $f(-1)$ **c** $f(-2)$

13 $f(x) = x^3$
Work out **a** $f(2)$ **b** $f(-2)$ **c** $f(-3)$

14 **a** Copy this table for $f(x) = 6 - 2x$.

x	−1	0	1	2	3	4
6						
$-2x$						
$f(x)$						

b Copy the axes.
c Draw the graph of $f(x) = 6 - 2x$.

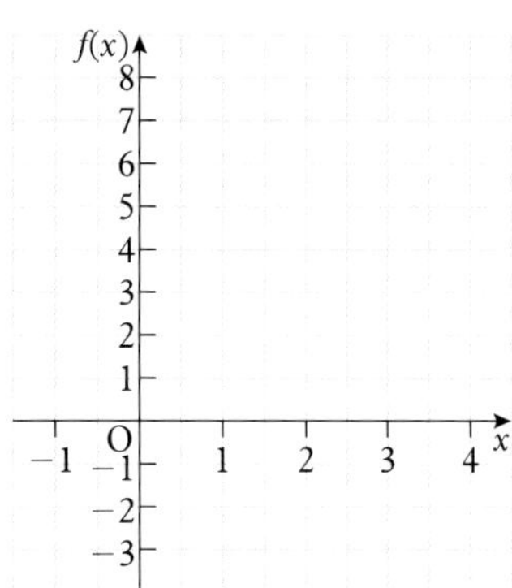

15 **a** Copy this table for $f(x) = x^2 + x - 6$.

x	−4	−3	−2	−1	0	1	2	3
x^2								
x								
−6								
$f(x)$								

b Copy the axes.
c Draw the graph of $f(x) = x^2 + x - 6$.

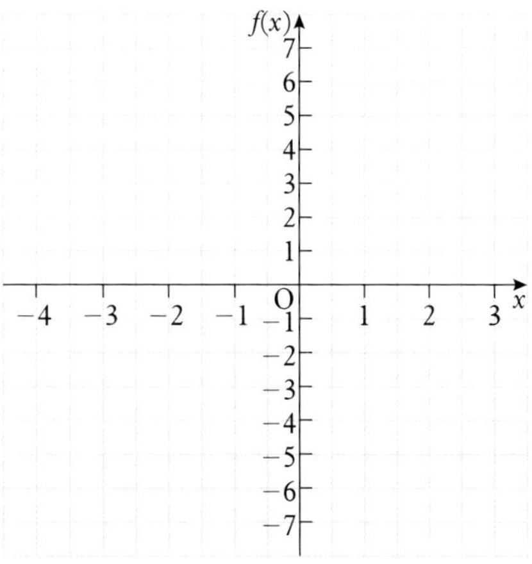

25 EXTENSION

1 These are the sketches of the graphs $y = x^2$ and $y = -x^2$.
Use these to help you sketch each of these graphs.

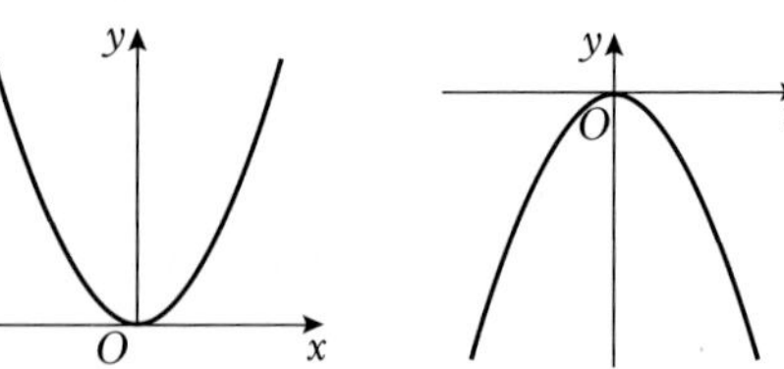

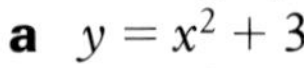

a $y = x^2 + 3$
b $y = x^2 + 7$
c $y = x^2 - 2$
d $y = x^2 - 5$
e $y = -x^2$
f $y = -x^2 + 2$
g $y = -x^2 - 5$
h $y = -x^2 + 3.2$

2 **a** Draw an x axis from -5 to $+5$ and a y axis from 0 to 30.
b Draw the graph of $y = x^2$ on your axes.
c Copy and complete this table for $y = (x - 3)^2$

x	-2	-1	0	1	2	3	4	5
y	25	16	9					

d Plot the graph of $y = (x - 3)^2$ from your table.
e Copy and complete this table for $y = (x + 2)^2$

x	-4	-3	-2	-1	0	1	2	3
y	4	1					16	

f Plot the graph of $y = (x + 2)^2$ from your table.

Compare your three graphs.
g Describe how $y = x^2$ has moved to get the graph of $y = (x - 3)^2$
h Describe how $y = x^2$ has moved to get the graph of $y = (x + 2)^2$

3 Match each of these equations with its graph.
a $y = 5x + 3$
b $y = 4 - x^2$
c $y = x^2 - 3x + 2$
d $y = \frac{1}{x} + 3$
e $y = x^3 - 2x$
f $y = 4x - x^3$

Write down pairs of letters and numbers.

(1)
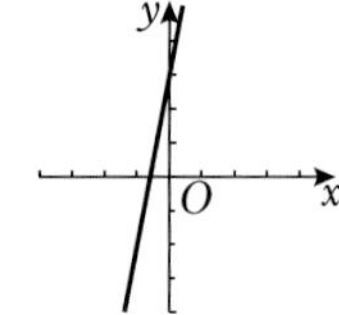

(3)
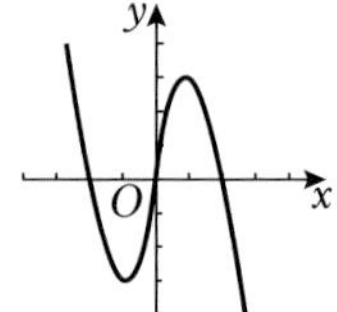

(5)
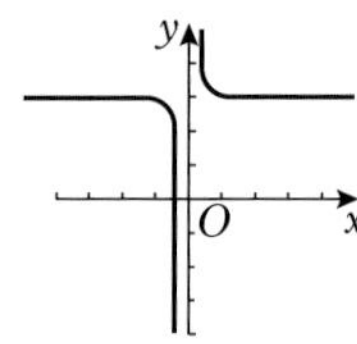

(2)
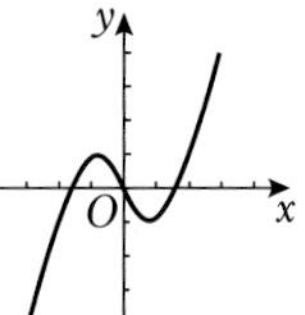

(4)
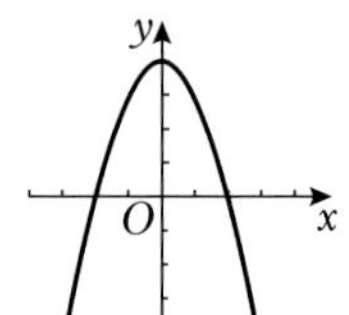

(6)
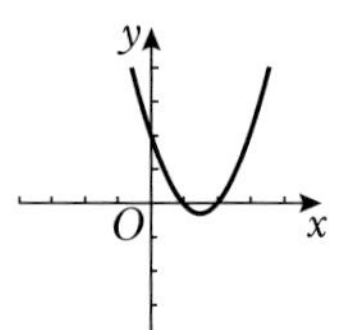

1 **a** Draw and fill in a table of values for $y = 2x - 3$
b Copy these axes.
c Draw the graph of $y = 2x - 3$
d Draw and fill in a table of values for $y = 6 - x$
e Draw the graph of $y = 6 - x$ on the same set of axes.
f Write down the co-ordinates of the point where the two lines cross.

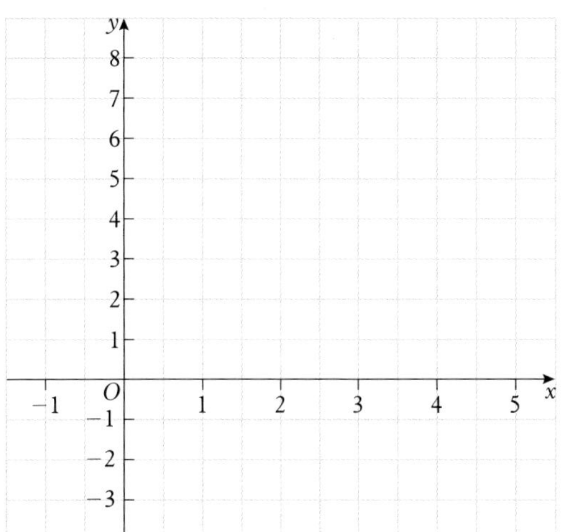

2 Look at these equations.

A $y = 7 - x^2$ **B** $y = 3 - 2x$ **C** $y = 5x^2 + x^3 - 1$

Write down the special name for each equation.
Choose from linear, quadratic and cubic.

3 Copy this table for $y = x^2 - 4x + 3$

x	-2	-1	0	1	2	3	4	5	6
x^2	4						16		
$-4x$	8						-16		
$+3$	$+3$						$+3$		
y	15						3		

a Fill in the missing values in the table.
b Draw axes with x from -3 to 7 and y from -2 to 16.
c Draw the graph of $y = x^2 - 4x + 3$
d Draw the line of symmetry on your graph.
e Write down the equation of the line of symmetry.
f What is the value of y when $x = 2.5$?
g What are the values of x when $y = 10$?
h What value of x gives $x^2 - 4x + 3$ its lowest value?

4 Copy this table for $y = x^3 - x^2 - 6x$

x	**−3**	**−2**	**−1**	**0**	**1**	**2**	**3**	**4**
x^3	−27							64
$-x^2$	−9							−16
$-6x$	+18							−24
y	**−18**							**24**

a Fill in the missing values in the table.
b Draw axes with x from −3 to 4 and y from −20 to 25.
c Draw the graph of $y = x^3 - x^2 - 6x$
d What is the value of y when $x = -1.5$?
e What are the values of x when $y = 1$?
f On the same set of axes draw the line AB where A is the point (−3, −10) and B is the point (4, 10).
g Find the gradient of the line AB to 1 dp.
h Write down the co-ordinates of the points where the line AB cuts the curve.

5 Match each of these equations with its graph.

A $y = 7 - 2x$ **C** $y = \frac{1}{x} - 2$ **E** $y = 10x - x^3$

B $y = x^2 + 1$ **D** $y = -x^3$ **F** $y = 1 - x^2$

(1)
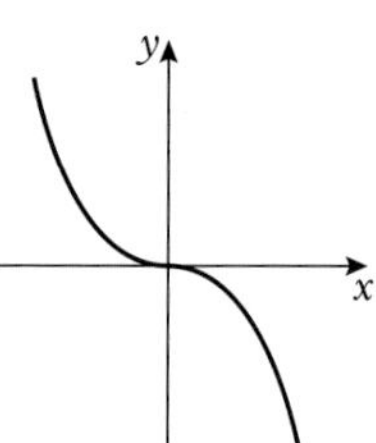

(3)
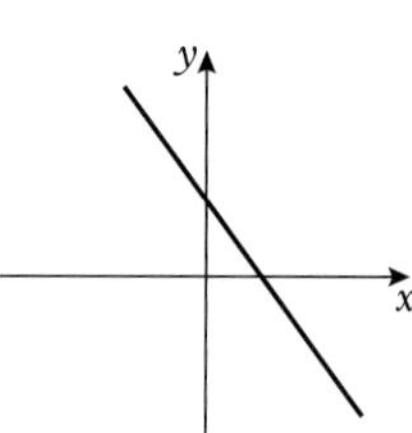

(5)
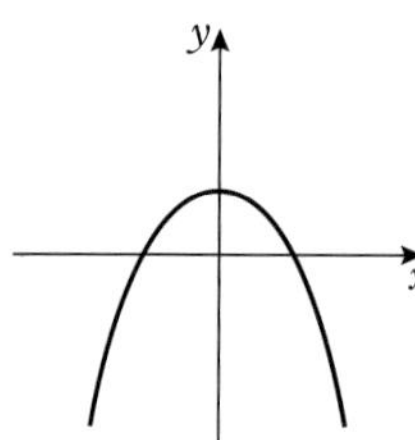

(2)
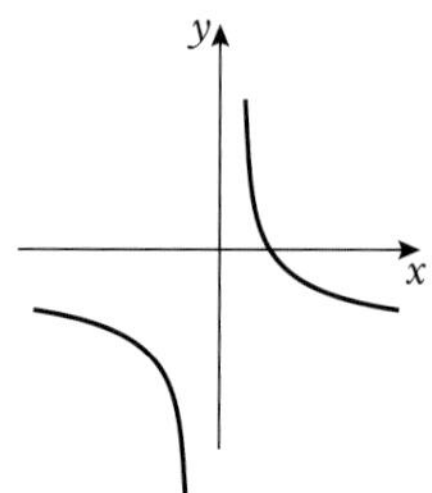

(4)
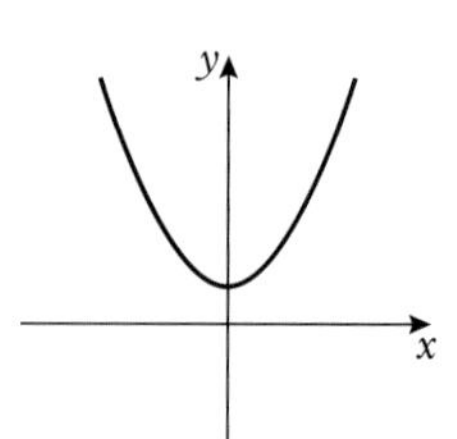

(6)
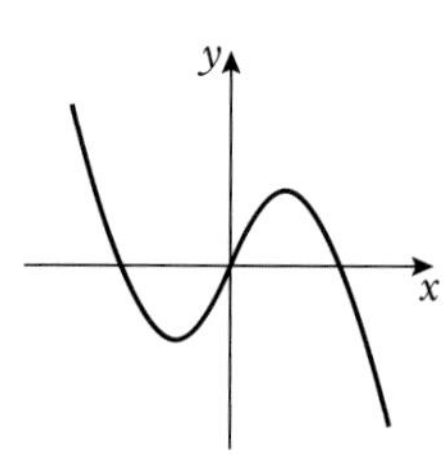

26 Simultaneous equations

1 Using graphs
Playing a game – Match Point
Using graphs to solve simultaneous equations

2 Using algebra
Solving simultaneous equations using algebra
- subtracting the two equations
- adding the two equations
- multiplying one equation before adding or subtracting
- multiplying both equations before adding or subtracting

Setting up simultaneous equations before solving them

CORE

3 Changing the subject
Rearranging formulas involving $+$, $-$, $\times$ and $\div$
Rearranging formulas involving squares and square roots
Solving simultaneous equations by substitution

QUESTIONS

EXTENSION

TEST YOURSELF

1 Using graphs

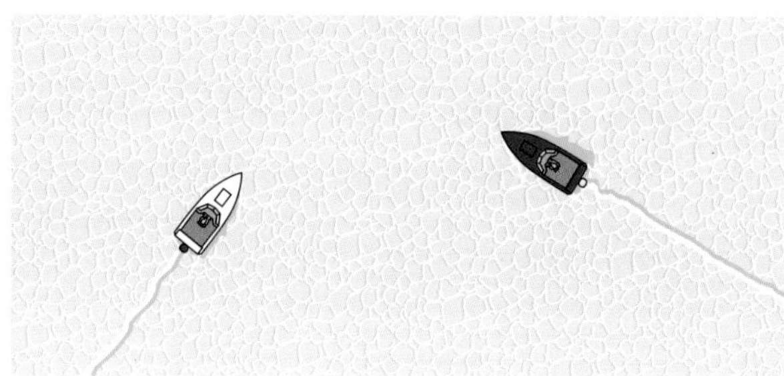

Points of intersection are sometimes of interest.

Game: Match Point

This is a game for two players.
One player needs Worksheet 26:1(A).
The other needs Worksheet 26:1(B).

Game (1)
Look at the equation for Game (1) on your worksheet. Keep it to yourself.
The equation for Player A is different from the one for Player B.
Decide who will start the game.

On your turn …
Find a pair of values x and y, that make your equation work. They will always be between 0 and 20.
Write your values as co-ordinates on your game sheet.
Tell your partner the values that you have found.

On your partner's turn …
Write your partner's values as co-ordinates on your game sheet.
Check to see if this pair of values makes your equation work.
If they work then your partner wins the game. Underline the winning values.
If not it is your turn again.

Play the other games on the sheet in the same way.
When you have played all six games you will need Worksheet 26:2.

(1) Plot all of the points found for each game on the matching grid.
(2) What pattern should your points make on each grid?
(3) What pattern should your partner's points make on each grid?
(4) What is special about the position of the winning point on each grid?
(5) What is special about the x and y values at each winning point?

Simultaneous equations

When you solve two equations at the same time you are solving **simultaneous equations**.

Example

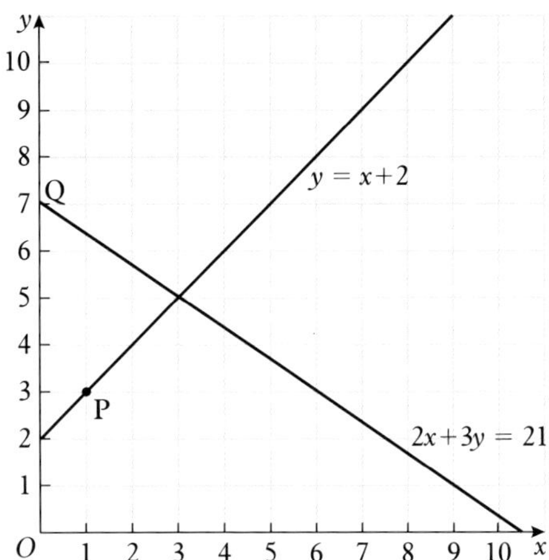

a Check that the (x, y) co-ordinates at P work in the equation $y = x + 2$.

b Check that the (x, y) co-ordinates at Q work in the equation $2x + 3y = 21$.

c Use the diagram to solve the simultaneous equations:

(1) $y = x + 2$
(2) $2x + 3y = 21$

d Check that the solution works in both equations.

a P has co-ordinates (1, 3).
So at P: $x = 1$ and $y = 3$.
$3 = 1 + 2$ so $y = x + 2$ ✓

b Q has co-ordinates (0, 7).
So at Q: $x = 0$ and $y = 7$.
$2x + 3y = 2 \times 0 + 3 \times 7 = 21$ ✓

c The lines intersect at (3, 5) so the solution is $x = 3$ and $y = 5$.

d $5 = 3 + 2$ so $y = x + 2$ ✓
$2x + 3y = 2 \times 3 + 3 \times 5 = 21$ ✓

Exercise 26:1

1 **a** Check that the (x, y) co-ordinates at P work in the equation $y = x - 1$.
b Check that the (x, y) co-ordinates at Q work in the equation $x + 3y = 9$.
c Use the diagram to solve the simultaneous equations:
(1) $y = x - 1$
(2) $x + 3y = 9$
d Check that the solution works in both equations.

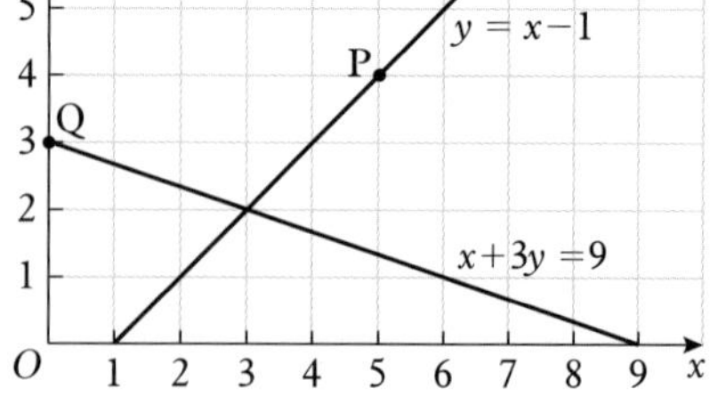

2 **a** Check that the (x, y) co-ordinates at P work in the equation $y = x + 5$.
b Check that the (x, y) co-ordinates at Q work in the equation $x + 2y = 4$.
c Use the diagram to solve the simultaneous equations:
(1) $y = x + 5$
(2) $x + 2y = 4$
d Check that the solution works in both equations.

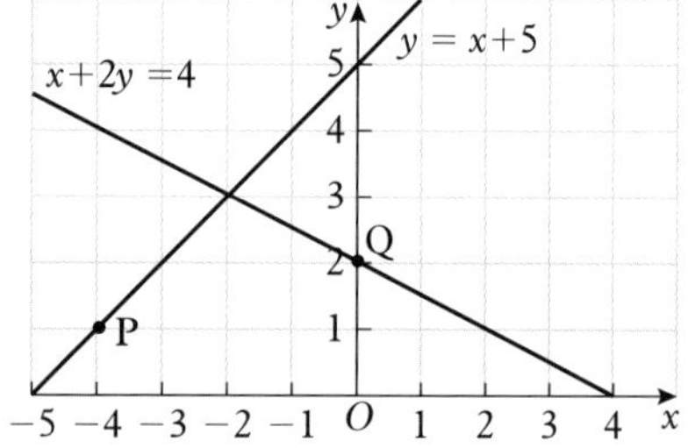

3

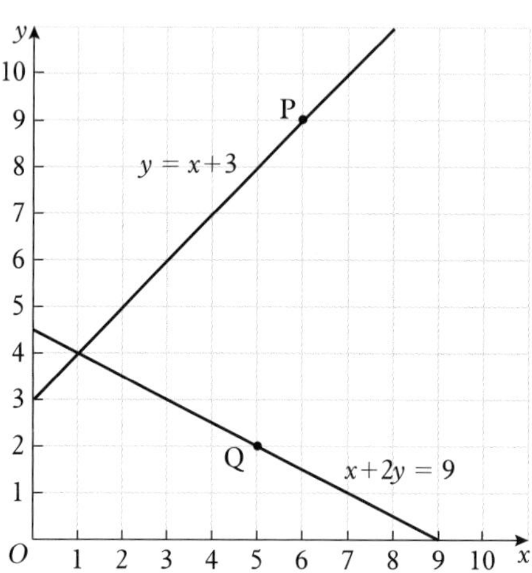

a Check that the (x, y) co-ordinates at P work in the equation $y = x + 3$.
b Check that the (x, y) co-ordinates at Q work in the equation $x + 2y = 9$.
c Use the diagram to solve the simultaneous equations:
(1) $y = x + 3$
(2) $x + 2y = 9$
d Check that the solution works in both equations.

Answer questions **4–6** using this diagram.

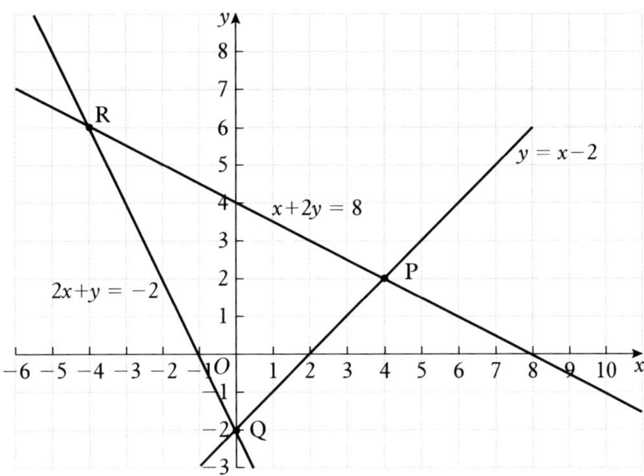

4 **a** Write down a pair of simultaneous equations that work at P.
b Solve the equations.
c Check that the solution works in both equations.

5 **a** Write down a pair of simultaneous equations that work at Q.
b Solve the equations.
c Check that the solution works in both equations.

6 **a** Write down a pair of simultaneous equations that work at R.
b Solve the equations.
c Check that the solution works in both equations.

7 **a** Draw a set of axes on squared paper.
Use values of x from 0 to 7 and values of y from -5 to 5.
b Plot some points for the equation $2x + 3y = 12$.
c Draw the graph of $2x + 3y = 12$.
d Plot some points for the equation $y = 2x - 4$.
e Draw the graph of $y = 2x - 4$.
f Solve the simultaneous equations $2x + 3y = 12$ and $y = 2x - 4$.
g Check that your solution works in both equations.

2 Using algebra

Sometimes you have to get rid of things to make progress.

You can solve simultaneous equations using algebra.

Example Solve this pair of simultaneous equations

$$5x + y = 20$$
$$2x + y = 11$$

Number the equations

(1) $5x + y = 20$
(2) $2x + y = 11$

Subtract to get rid of y
This finds x

Subtracting $3x \quad = 9$
$x = 3$

Use equation (1) to find y

Put $x = 3$ in equation (1)
$5 \times 3 + y = 20$
$15 + y = 20$
$y = 5$
The answer is $x = 3, y = 5$

Use equation (2) to check your answer $2x + y = 6 + 5 = 11$ ✓

Exercise 26:2

Solve these pairs of simultaneous equations.
Start by subtracting the equations each time.

1 $3x + y = 17$
$x + y = 9$

2 $3x + 2y = 16$
$x + 2y = 12$

3 $5x + y = 28$
$2x + y = 13$

4 $3x + 2y = 23$
$2x + 2y = 20$

5 $5x + 3y = 26$
$2x + 3y = 14$

6 $4x + y = 26$
$x + y = 11$

• **7** $6x + y = -18$
$2x + y = 10$

• **8** $9x + y = -37$
$3x + y = -13$

• **9** $2x + 3y = 18$
$2x + y = 10$

• **10** $5x + 4y = 40$
$5x + y = 25$

Example Solve this pair of simultaneous equations

$$3x + y = 19$$
$$x - y = 1$$

Number the equations

$$(1)\quad 3x + y = 19$$
$$(2)\quad x - y = 1$$

Add to get rid of y
This finds x

Adding $4x = 20$
$x = 5$

Use equation (1) to find y

Put $x = 5$ in equation (1)

$$3 \times 5 + y = 19$$
$$15 + y = 19$$
$$y = 4$$

The answer is $x = 5, y = 4$

Use equation (2) to check your answer $x - y = 5 - 4 = 1$ ✓

Exercise 26:3

Solve these pairs of simultaneous equations.
Start by adding the equations each time.

1 $2x + y = 14$
$3x - y = 11$

2 $5x + y = 26$
$2x - y = 2$

3 $4x + 2y = 30$
$2x - 2y = 6$

4 $x + 5y = 15$
$3x - 5y = 25$

• **5** $4x + y = 16$
$3x - y = -2$

• **6** $7x + 5y = -85$
$3x - 5y = -15$

If the terms have the same number in front of them and the signs are the same, you get rid of them by subtracting the equations.

If the terms have the same number in front of them but the signs are different, you get rid of them by adding the equations.

Example Use each pair of equations to make a new equation just in terms of x.

a $7x + 3y = 25$
$3x - 3y = 15$

b $11x - 19y = 36$
$8x - 19y = 21$

a The y terms both have a 3 in front of them but the signs are different.
Adding the equations gives $10x = 40$.
You can check that the solution is $x = 4, y = -1$.

b The y terms are identical.
Subtracting the equations gives $3x = 15$.
You can check that the solution is $x = 5, y = 1$.

Exercise 26:4

Solve these pairs of simultaneous equations.
You need to decide whether to add or subtract the equations.

1 $x + y = 15$
$5x - y = 9$

2 $4x + 2y = 28$
$x - 2y = 2$

3 $5x + 3y = 19$
$2x + 3y = 13$

4 $3x - y = 11$
$2x - y = 5$

5 $3x + 2y = 16$
$x + 2y = 12$

• **6** $4x - 5y = 15$
$3x - 5y = -5$

7 $4x + 2y = 38$
$3x - 2y = 11$

8 $5x + 3y = 27$
$4x - 3y = 0$

• **9** $3x + 4y = 7$
$3x + 3y = -3$

• **10** $5x - 9y = -23$
$2x - 9y = 7$

You sometimes have to multiply one of the equations by a number before adding or subtracting.

Example Solve this pair of simultaneous equations

$$2x + 3y = 13$$
$$4x - y = 5$$

Number the equations

(1) $2x + 3y = 13$
(2) $4x - y = 5$

To get rid of the *y*s you need to multiply (2) by 3 so that you have $3y$ in each equation.

(1) $2x + 3y = 13$
(2) × 3 $12x - 3y = 15$

Add to get rid of *y*
This finds *x*

Adding $14x = 28$
$x = 2$

Use equation (1) to find *y*

Put $x = 2$ in equation (1)
$2 \times 2 + 3y = 13$
$4 + 3y = 13$
$3y = 9$
$y = 3$
The answer is $x = 2, y = 3$

Use equation (2) to check your answer

$4x - y = 8 - 3 = 5$ ✓

Exercise 26:5

Solve these pairs of simultaneous equations.
You need to multiply one equation by a number.

1 $2x + 3y = 19$
$x + y = 8$

2 $5x - 3y = 16$
$x + y = 16$

3 $3a + 2b = 8$
$2a - b = 3$

4 $5p - 2q = 7$
$3p + q = 13$

● **5** $7c - 3d = 26$
$c - d = 10$

● **6** $j + 3k = 17$
$2j - 5k = 23$

You sometimes have to multiply both equations by a number before adding or subtracting.

Example Solve this pair of simultaneous equations

$$3x + 5y = 30$$
$$2x + 3y = 19$$

Number the equations

(1) $3x + 5y = 30$
(2) $2x + 3y = 19$

Multiply (1) by 2
Multiply (2) by 3

$(1) \times 2 \quad 6x + 10y = 60$
$(2) \times 3 \quad 6x + 9y = 57$

Now subtract to get rid of x

$$y = 3$$

Use equation (1) to find y

Put $y = 3$ in equation (1)

$$3x + 15 = 30$$
$$3x = 15$$
$$x = 5$$

The answer is $x = 5, y = 3$

Use equation (2) to check your answer

$2x + 3y = 2 \times 5 + 3 \times 3 = 10 + 9 = 19$ ✓

Exercise 26:6

Solve these pairs of simultaneous equations.
You will need to multiply one or both of the equations by a number.

1 $3x + 2y = 18$
$x + y = 7$

2 $7x - 3y = 48$
$2x + y = 10$

3 $3a + 4b = 41$
$4a - 5b = 3$

● **4** $4p - 2q = 7$
$3p + q = 11\frac{1}{2}$

● **5** $5m + 3n = 17$
$2m + 5n = 12\frac{1}{2}$

● **6** $g + 4h = -9$
$5g - 2h = -1$

You can use simultaneous equations to solve problems.

Example In a sale, all compact discs are one price.
All tapes are also one price.
Jenny buys two **c**ompact discs and one **t**ape for £10.
Peter buys one **c**ompact disc and two **t**apes for £8.
Find the cost of a **c**ompact disc and the cost of a **t**ape.

You need to use letters to stand for the unknown amounts.
You can then write equations to represent the information in the question.

Using £c for the cost of a compact disc and £t for the cost of a tape:

Jenny's equation is $2c + t = 10$
Peter's equation is $c + 2t = 8$

You solve these in the usual way to find that $c = 4$, $t = 2$.

This means that the cost of a compact disc is £4 and the cost of a tape is £2.

Exercise 26:7

1 Paul and Petra took part in a school quiz.
They had to choose a **s**tandard or a **h**ard question on each turn.
Paul answered 3 **s**tandard and 2 **h**ard questions correctly and scored 7 points.
Petra answered 1 **s**tandard and 4 **h**ard questions correctly and scored 9 points.
Find the points awarded for a **s**tandard question and for a **h**ard question.

2 A school sells two types of calculator.
One is a **b**asic model and the other is a **s**cientific.
The cost of one **b**asic and one **s**cientific is £10.
The cost of 3 **b**asic and 2 **s**cientific is £24.
Find the cost of a **b**asic model and the cost of a **s**cientific model.

• **3** Hannah buys 4 choc ices and 3 cornets for £11.25
Terri buys 3 choc ices and 2 cornets for £8
Find the cost of 1 choc ice and the cost of 1 cornet.

3 Changing the subject

Liz's Mum is asking what she's doing today.
Liz doesn't want to talk about it.
She is trying to change the subject.

You need to be able to change the subject in Maths too.
This doesn't mean getting your teacher to talk about something else!

The subject of a formula is the letter that appears on its own on the left-hand side.
v is the subject in the formula $v = u + at$.
Changing the subject of a formula uses the same skills as solving an equation.
But instead of getting a number as an answer, you are now trying to get a different letter on its own.

Examples **1** Make u the subject of the formula $v = u + at$

You need to remove the *at* term from the right-hand side.
This will leave the u by itself.
The *at* is *added* to the RHS (Right Hand Side) at the moment.
So *subtract at* from each side.

$$v - at = u + at - at$$
$$v - at = u$$

Write the new formula the other way round with the subject on the LHS (Left Hand Side).

$$u = v - at$$

2 Make g the subject of the formula $v = 6g$
Write the formula the other way round. This gets the $6g$ on the LHS.

$$6g = v$$

The g is *multiplied by* 6 at the moment.
So *divide by* 6 on each side.

$$\frac{6g}{6} = \frac{v}{6}$$
$$g = \frac{v}{6}$$

g is now the subject of the formula.

3 Make y the subject of the formula $x = 4y - 2z$
First, you need to remove the $2z$ term from the RHS
This will leave the $4y$ by itself.
The $2z$ is *subtracted* at the moment.
So *add* $2z$ to each side.

$$x + 2z = 4y - 2z + 2z$$
$$x + 2z = 4y$$

Now write the formula the other way round

$$4y = x + 2z$$

The y is *multiplied by* 4 at the moment.
So *divide by* 4 on each side to leave the y on its own.

$$y = \frac{x + 2z}{4}$$

y is now the subject of the formula.

Exercise 26:8

Make the red letter the subject in each of these formulas.

1 $y = b + n$

2 $u = f - 7$

3 $e = s - 4u$

4 $p = 6a$

5 $h = 5g$

6 $v = 3t + u$

7 $k = 5r - 3z$

8 $r = wx + yt$

9 $5v = u + at$

● **10** $k = 5t - 3z$

Example Make u the subject of the formula $v = \frac{u}{5}$

Write the formula the other way round. This gets the u term on the LHS.

$$\frac{u}{5} = v$$

The u is *divided by* 5 at the moment.
So *multiply by* 5 on each side.

$$5 \times \frac{u}{5} = 5 \times v$$
$$u = 5v$$

u is now the subject of the formula.

Exercise 26:9

Make the red letter the subject in each of these formulas.

1 $y = \dfrac{e}{5}$

2 $u = \dfrac{p}{15}$

3 $e = \dfrac{m}{3}$

4 $p = \dfrac{w}{4}$

5 $h = \dfrac{x}{7}$

6 $v = \dfrac{a}{5} - 5$

7 $k = \dfrac{y}{5} + 4$

8 $3r = \dfrac{5w}{8}$

• **9** $v = \dfrac{5x}{7} - 1$

• **10** $4k = 5t - \dfrac{k}{6}$

Some equations have lots of terms.
You need to remember **BODMAS** to help you to change the subject of these equations.

Example Make $\boldsymbol{t}$ the subject of the formula $c = \dfrac{zt + yb}{2}$

Look at the letter $\boldsymbol{t}$ on the RHS of the formula.
Using **BODMAS** the $\boldsymbol{t}$ has

been	**multiplied** by z
then had	yb **added** to it
and then been	**divided** by **2**

Undo these operations in the reverse order by using their inverses.

First	**multiply** by **2**	$2c = zt + yb$
then	**subtract** yb	$2c - yb = zt$
and then	**divide** by z	$\dfrac{2c - yb}{z} = t$
So		$t = \dfrac{2c - yb}{z}$

$\boldsymbol{t}$ is now the subject of the formula.

Exercise 26:10

Make the red letter the subject in each of these formulas.

1 $t = \dfrac{z + g}{7}$

2 $r = \dfrac{4h + 6j}{6}$

3 $3t = \frac{4\boldsymbol{f} + 7r}{2}$

4 $at = \frac{\boldsymbol{p}z + 5t}{y}$

5 $yk = \frac{u\boldsymbol{r} + gj}{8}$

6 $\frac{r}{4} = \frac{\boldsymbol{h} + 8e}{3}$

7 $3d = \frac{4h + 6\boldsymbol{j}}{5}$

● **8** $5u = \frac{4h - 3\boldsymbol{d}}{t}$

Some formulas have squares and square roots in them.
These two operations are the inverses of each other.
To remove a square, square root each side.
To remove a square root, square each side.

Examples **1** Make t the subject of the formula $s = \sqrt{t + r}$

To remove the square root, square each side

$$s^2 = t + r$$

Now subtract r

$$s^2 - r = t$$

So $t = s^2 - r$

2 Make g the subject of the formula $r = 3g^2$

First divide by the 3

$$\frac{r}{3} = g^2$$

To remove the square, square root both sides:

$$g = \sqrt{\frac{r}{3}}$$

Exercise 26:11

Make the **bold** letter the subject in each of these formulas.

1 $w = \sqrt{2\boldsymbol{t} - s}$

2 $d = \sqrt{5t + 6\boldsymbol{p}}$

3 $y = \sqrt{\frac{6\boldsymbol{x}}{5}}$

4 $A = \pi\boldsymbol{r}^2$

5 $e^2 = \boldsymbol{t}^2 - 6f$

6 $k - 5 = gh - 2\boldsymbol{p}^2$

You can use substitution to solve simultaneous equations.

Example 1 Solve this pair of simultaneous equations

(1) $2x + y = 8$
(2) $y = 3x - 7$

Use equation (2) to substitute for y in equation (1) $\quad 2x + (3x - 7) = 8$
Simplify the equation $\quad 5x - 7 = 8$
Add 7 to both sides $\quad 5x = 15$
Divide both sides by 5 $\quad x = 3$

Put this in equation (2) to find y $\quad y = 3 \times 3 - 7$
$y = 2$

The solution is $x = 3, y = 2$ Check in (1) $2 \times 3 + 2 = 8$ ✓

Example 2 Solve this pair of simultaneous equations

(1) $3x - 2y = 9$
(2) $y + 2x = 13$

Make y the subject of equation (2)
Take $2x$ from both sides $\quad y = 13 - 2x$
Substitute for y in equation (1)
Remember to use brackets. $\quad 3x - 2(13 - 2x) = 9$
Simplify the equation $\quad 3x - 26 + 4x = 9$
$7x - 26 = 9$
Add 26 to both sides $\quad 7x = 35$
Divide both sides by 7 $\quad x = 5$

Put this in equation (2) to find y $\quad y + 2 \times 5 = 13$
$y = 3$

The solution is $x = 5, y = 3$ Check in (1) $3 \times 5 - 2 \times 3 = 9$ ✓

Exercise 26:12

Solve these pairs of simultaneous equations using substitution.

1 $2x + y = 16$
$y = x + 7$

2 $3x + y = 17$
$y = 2x - 8$

3 $2x + 3y = 26$
$y = x + 2$

4 $3x - 2y = 14$
$y = x - 3$

5 $2x + 5y = 69$
$y - x = 4$

6 $4x + 3y = -18$
$y - 2x = 4$

1 Sue and Kim are trying to solve the simultaneous equations $y = 2x - 1$ and $2x + y = 11$. Sue thinks that the solution is $x = 5, y = 9$.
Kim thinks that the solution is $x = 3, y = 5$.
Who is right? Explain your answer.

2 **a** Draw a set of axes on squared paper.
Use values of x from -3 and $+3$ and values of y from -4 to $+7$.

b Plot some points for the equation $y = 4x - 3$

c Draw the graph of $y = 4x - 3$

d Plot some points for the equation $2x - 3y = -6$

e Draw the graph of $2x - 3y = -6$

f Solve the simultaneous equations $y = 4x - 3$ and $2x - 3y = -6$

g Check that your solution works in both equations.

3 **a** Draw a set of x and y axes on graph paper from $x = -4$ to $x = 4$ and from $y = -4$ to $y = 4$. Use 2 cm per unit for both axes.

b Draw the graph of $y = \frac{4}{x}$

c On the same set of axes draw the graph of $y = x$.

d Solve the simultaneous equations $y = \frac{4}{x}$ and $y = x$.

4 Solve these pairs of simultaneous equations.
Start by subtracting the equations each time.

a $5x + 3y = 28$
$4x + 3y = 23$

b $11x + 2y = 43$
$6x + 2y = 28$

c $5x - 4y = 14$
$4x - 4y = 8$

d $3p - 4q = -11$
$p - 4q = -17$

5 Solve these pairs of simultaneous equations.
Start by adding the equations each time.

a $3x + 2y = 26$
$2x - 2y = 4$

b $3x - 8y = 11$
$2x + 8y = 18$

c $3m + 5n = 31$
$10m - 5n = -5$

d $7i - 3j = 19$
$6i + 3j = 33$

6 Solve these pairs of simultaneous equations.
You need to decide whether to add or subtract the equations.

a $2x + y = 13$
$3x - y = 12$

b $4x + 2y = 6$
$x - 2y = 9$

c $3x + 2y = 12$
$x + 2y = 2$

d $6x + 3y = 21$
$2x + 3y = 11$

7 Make the red letter the subject in each of these formulas.

a $p - 5 = q$

b $3m + 4 = n$

c $pq - r = s$

d $u(v + w) = x$

e $u(v + w) = x$

f $g = k - fh$

8 Make the red letter the subject in each of these formulas.

a $r = \frac{p}{q}$

b $h = \frac{j + m}{n}$

c $t = \frac{u}{r} + v$

d $w = \frac{x}{y}$

e $y = \sqrt{x - 3w}$

f $g = \sqrt{ax + b}$

9 Larry is using this formula $h = \frac{4a - 3b^2}{2}$

a Use the formula to find the value of h when $a = 12$ and $b = 2$.
b Rearrange the formula to make a the subject.
c Find the value of a when $h = 14$ and $b = 6$.

10 Solve these pairs of simultaneous equations using substitution.

a $y = 2x - 3$
$3y + 4x = 31$

b $x = 2y - 7$
$3y = 3 - x$

c $x = 12 - y$
$2y = 31 - 3x$

d $y = 7 - 5x$
$21 = 3y + 4x$

1 Solve the simultaneous equations shown by the lines in these diagrams.

a

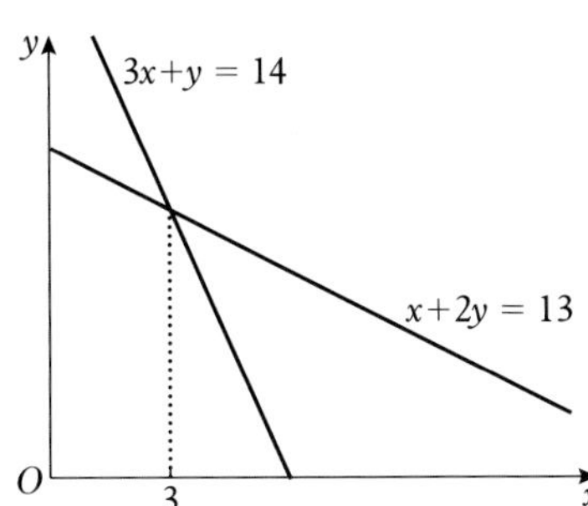

c

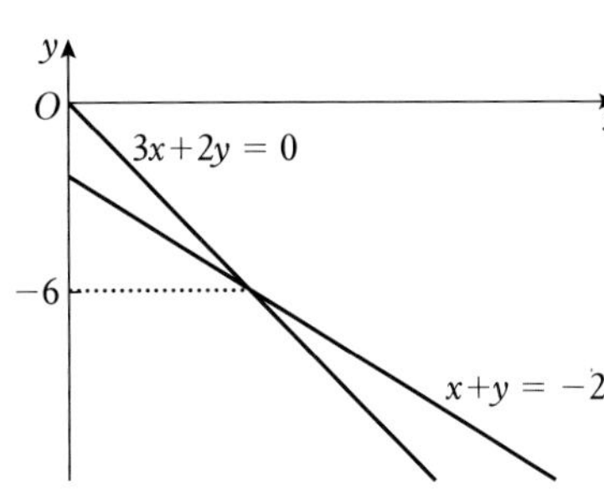

b

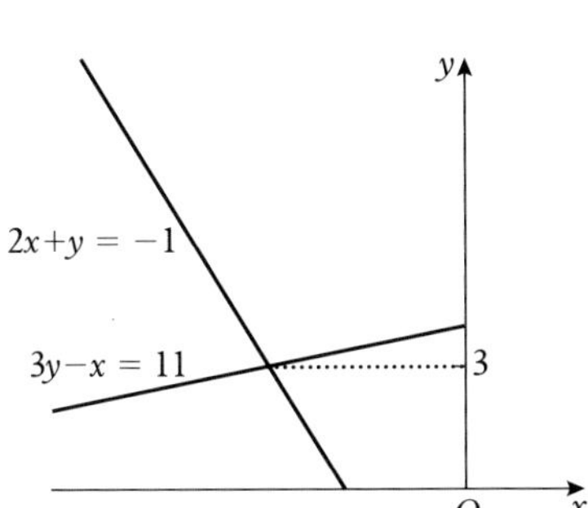

d

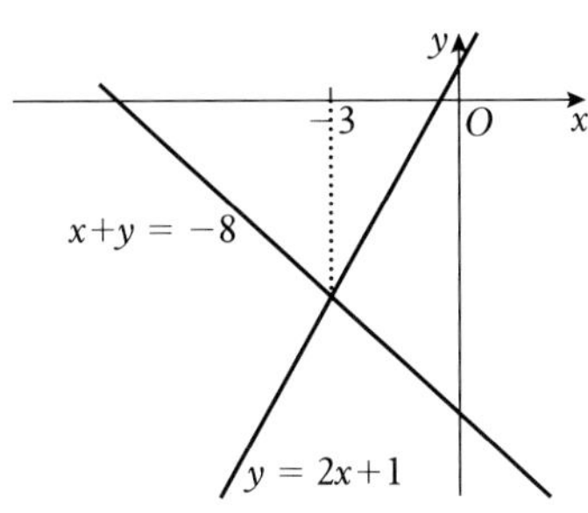

2 Solve these pairs of simultaneous equations.

a $3x + 5y = 36$
$x + y = 10$

b $4x - 9y = 8$
$x + y = 15$

c $2p - 3q = -23$
$3p - 2q = -22$

d $4m - 5n = 1$
$3m - 2n = -8$

e $3x + 2y = 7$
$y = 2x + 14$

f $5x + 4y = -29$
$2y = 10 + x$

3 Three bags of chips cost £2 more than one portion of fish.
Three portions of fish and one bag of chips cost £7.

a How much is a bag of chips?

b How much is a portion of fish?

1 **a** Draw a set of axes on squared paper.
Use values of x from -1 to 4 and values of y from -4 to 8.
b Plot some points for the equation $y = 3x - 1$
c Draw the graph of $y = 3x - 1$
d Plot some points for the equation $2x + y = 4$
e Draw the graph of $2x + y = 4$
f Solve the simultaneous equations $y = 3x - 1$ and $2x + y = 4$
g Check that your solution works in both equations.

2 Solve these pairs of simultaneous equations.

a $3x - 2y = 7$
$x + 2y = 5$

b $5x - 2y = 10$
$3x - 2y = 2$

c $3x - y = 13$
$2x + 3y = 5$

d $7x + 2y = 28$
$2x + 3y = 25$

3 Make the red letter the subject in each of these formulas.

a $g = 4h - 7$

b $w = \frac{t}{5} + 2$

c $y = \frac{3x}{4} - 6$

d $s = 10 + 3t^2$

4 Sally is using this formula: $A = \frac{\sqrt{w^2 + 3xy}}{10}$

a Use the formula to find the value of A when $w = -1$, $x = 8$ and $y = 2$.
b Rearrange the formula to make w the subject.
c Find the value of w when $A = 1$, $x = 4$ and $y = 7$.

5 Solve these pairs of simultaneous equations using substitution.

a $y = 5 - 2x$
$3y + x = 10$

b $x = 4y - 6$
$14 = 8y - 3x$

27 Area

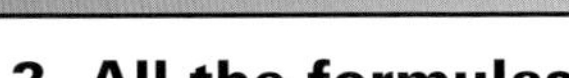

1 Counting and estimating
Finding areas by counting squares
Estimating areas of irregular shapes

2 All the formulas
Finding the area of
- a rectangle
- a square
- a triangle
- a trapezium
- a parallelogram
- a kite
- a rhombus
- a circle

Finding the area of more complicated shapes

3 Nets and surface areas
Drawing nets
Identifying nets
Finding the surface area of solid shapes
Converting square units

CORE

QUESTIONS

EXTENSION

TEST YOURSELF

1 Counting and estimating

The Amazon is in South America.
It is one of the world's largest forests.
It covers an area of 2 million square miles.
Every year a large part of the forest is destroyed.

Area

The **area** of a shape is the amount of space it covers.
Area is measured using squares.

This square has sides of 1 cm.
The area of the square is 1 square centimetre.
You write this as 1 cm^2.

This rectangle covers 8 squares.
The area of the rectangle = 8 cm^2

Exercise 27:1

For each of the rectangles in questions **1–4**, write down:

a the number of squares it covers

b the area of the rectangle in cm^2

1

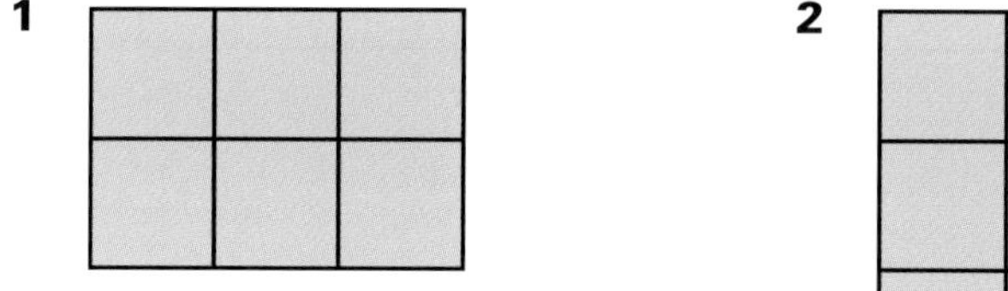

2

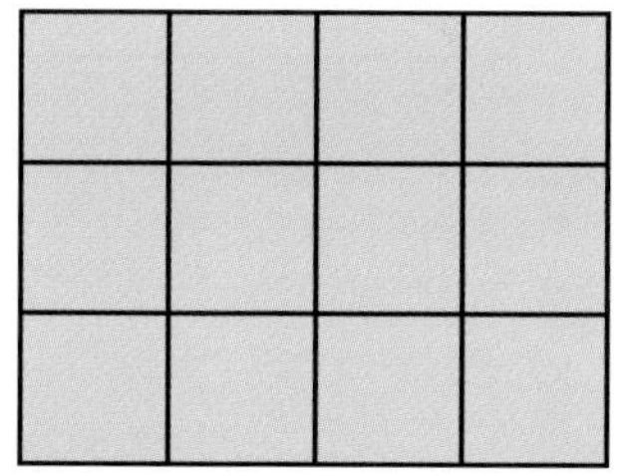

3

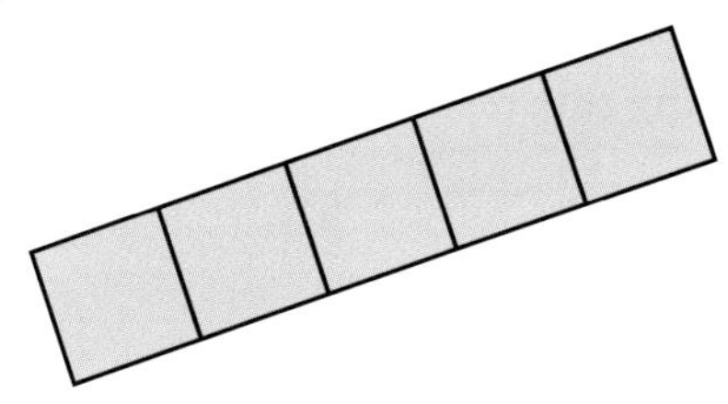

4

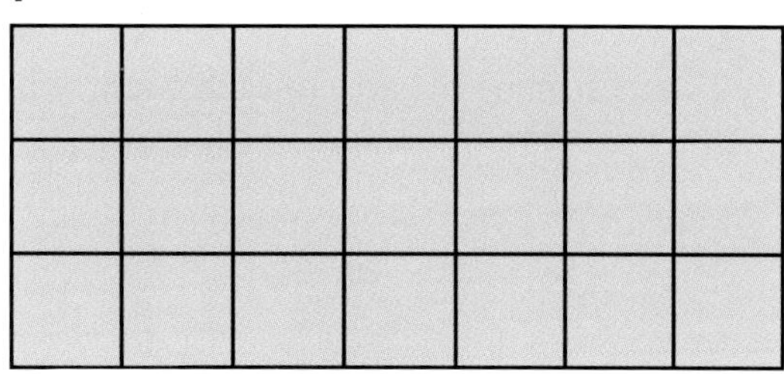

Write down the area of each of the shapes in questions **5–8**.

5

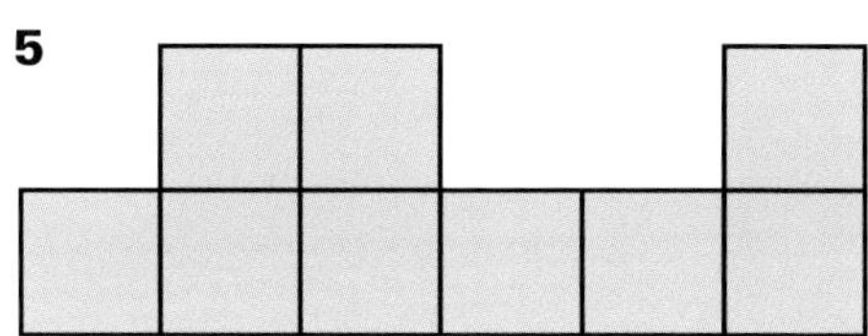

7

6

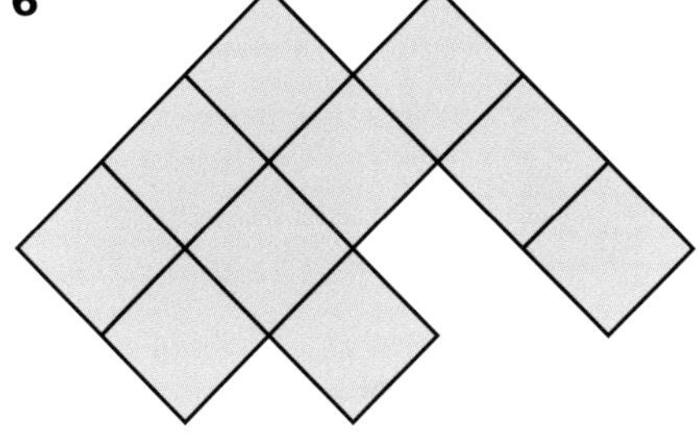

8

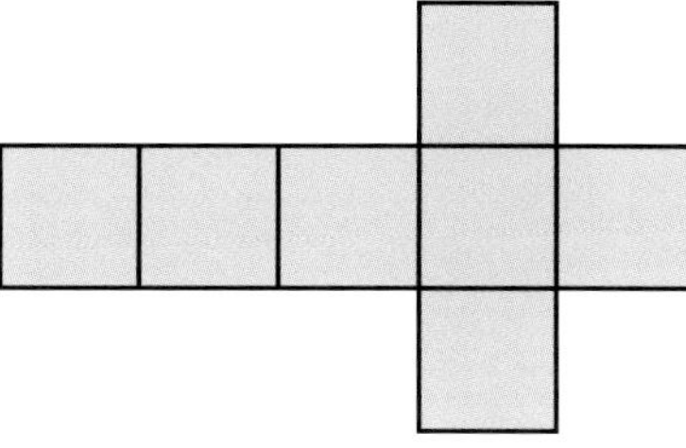

Some areas are more difficult to work out.
This is a drawing of the county of Cheshire.
You can only estimate the area of the drawing.
To estimate the area:

(1) Count whole squares.
There are 5 of these.

(2) Count squares which lie more than half inside the outline.
There are 4 of these.

(3) Add the two numbers together.
$5 + 4 = 9$

An estimate of the area is 9 squares.

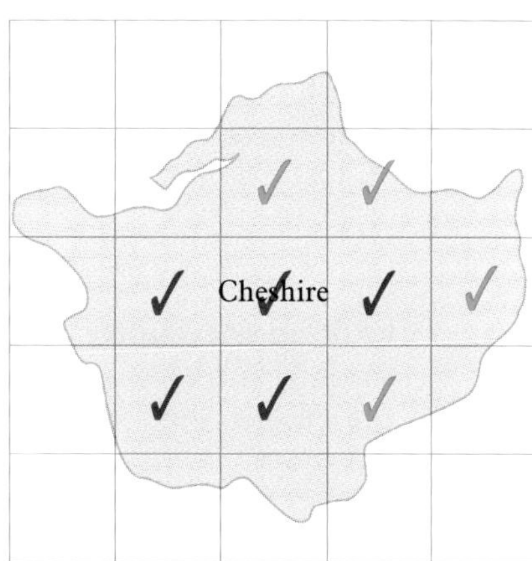

Exercise 27:2

Estimate the area of each country by counting squares.
Give your answers in squares.

1

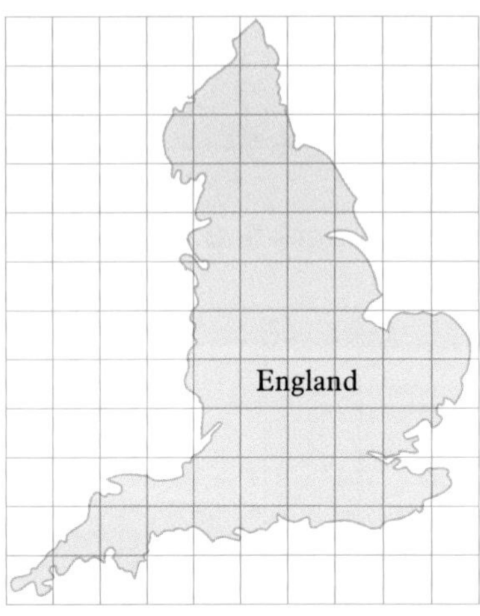

3

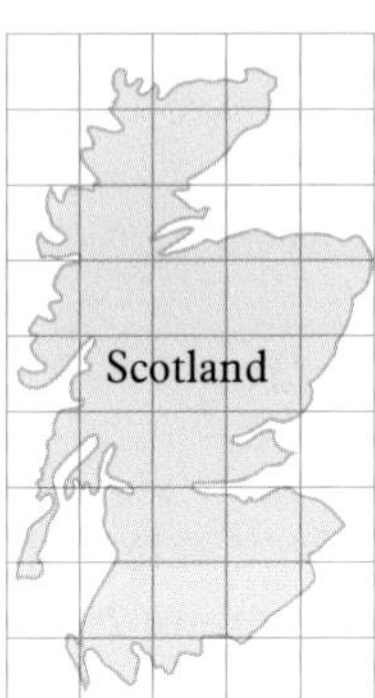

2

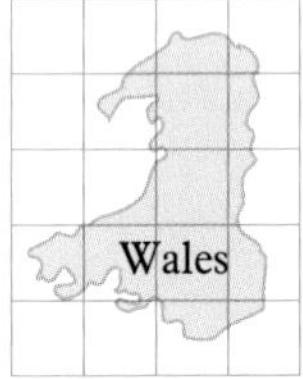

4

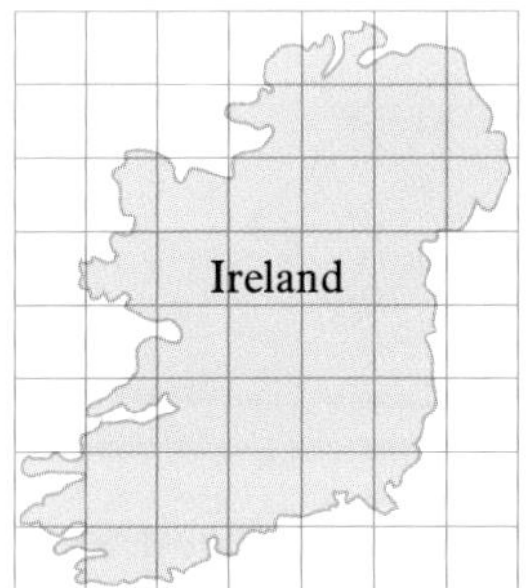

5 Write down the country in the British Isles with:

a the largest area

b the smallest area.

Squaring the circle

You will need 0.5 cm^2 paper for this activity.
Draw a circle with a 1 cm radius.
Put the centre on a point where the lines cross.
Estimate the area of the circle in cm^2.
Calculate the area of a square 1 cm by 1 cm.
Divide the area of the circle by the area of the square.

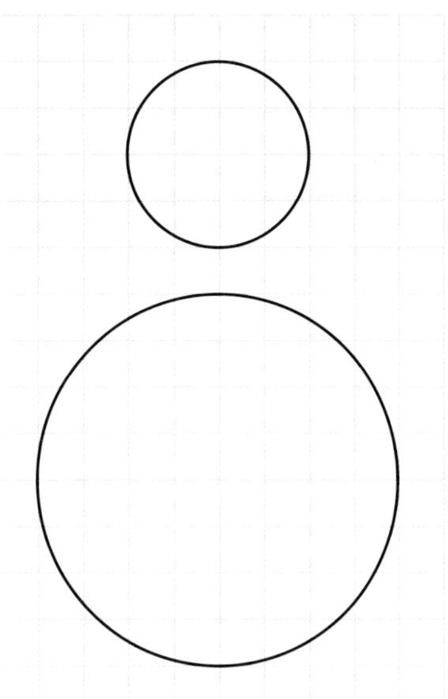

Now draw a circle with a 2 cm radius.
Put the centre on a point where the lines cross.
Estimate the area of the circle in cm^2.
Calculate the area of a square 2 cm by 2 cm.
Divide the area of the circle by the area of the square.
Record your results in the best way you can.

Repeat this for circles with radii of 3 cm, 4 cm, etc.
Can you see a pattern in your results?
What do you think would happen to your results if you kept going?

Look at the red shape.
Each small square shows 1 cm^2.

It covers 6 whole squares and 4 half squares.
The 4 halves make 2 whole ones.
The area of the shape is $6 + 2 = 8$ cm^2

Look at the blue shape.
This shape covers 10 whole squares and 5 half squares.
The 5 halves make $2\frac{1}{2}$ whole ones.
The area of the shape is $10 + 2\frac{1}{2} = 12\frac{1}{2}$ cm^2

Exercise 27:3

1 Work out the area of each of these coloured shapes in square centimetres. They are drawn on 1 cm^2 paper.

a

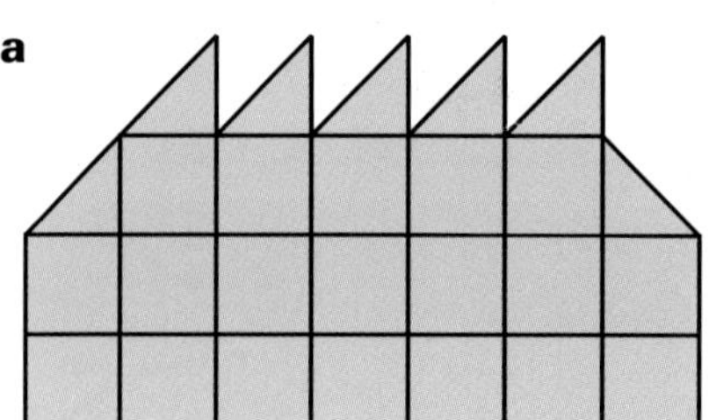

c

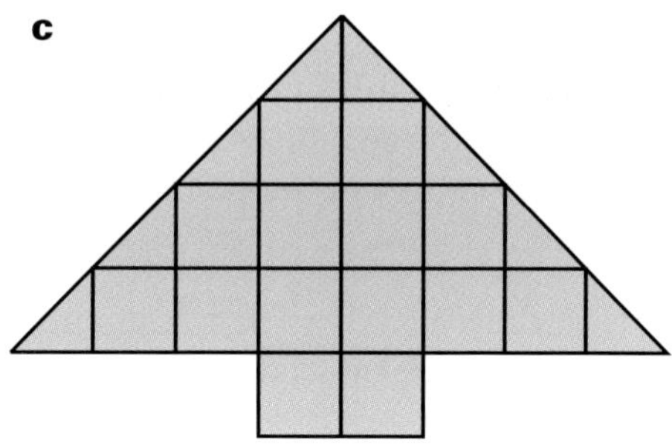

b

d

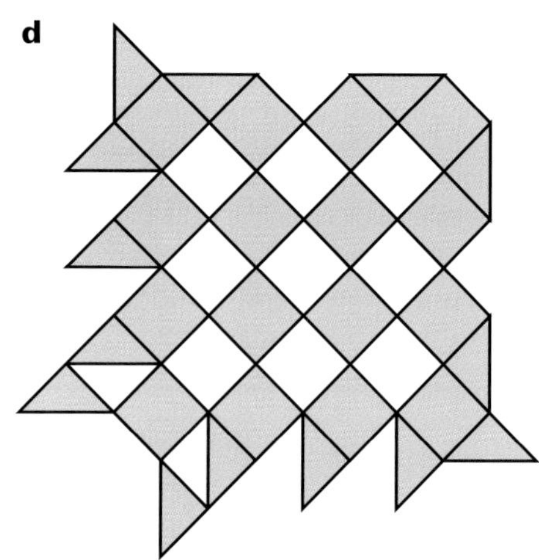

2 Samuel has drawn a plan of his wall on squared paper.
Each square shows an area of 100 cm^2.
Find the area, in square centimetres, of:

a the poster
b the no smoking sign
c the flag.

Estimate the area, in square centimetres, of:

d the dartboard
e the mirror.

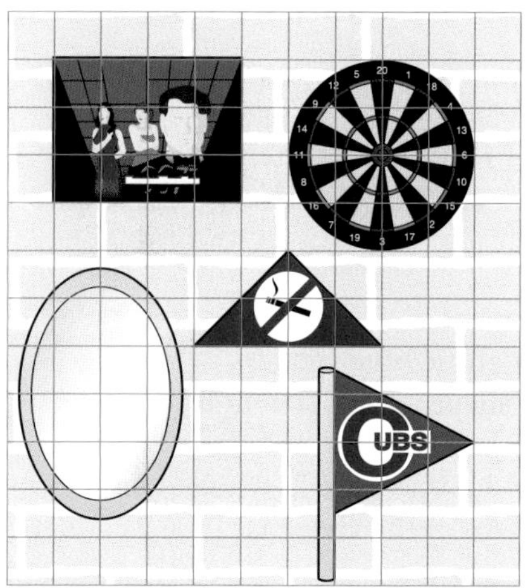

2 All the formulas

This is the Pentagon in Arlington, USA. It is the office building with the largest ground floor area in the world.

29 000 people work in the Pentagon.

There are 7748 windows to be cleaned. Can you estimate the total area of windows to be cleaned?

Area of a rectangle

Area of a rectangle = length × width

This calculates the number of 1 cm squares in this rectangle.

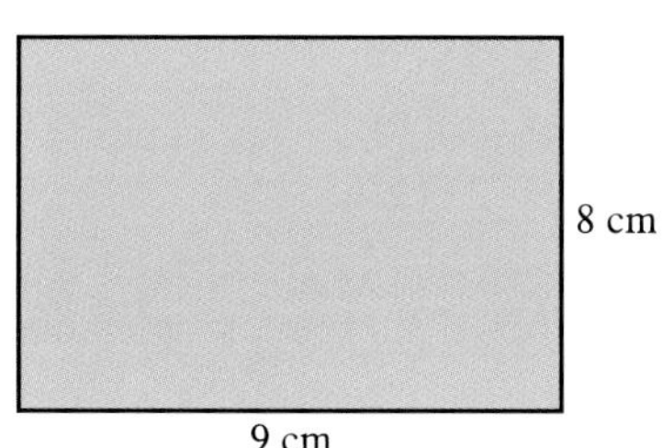

The area of this rectangle $= 9 \times 8\ \text{cm}^2$
$= 72\ \text{cm}^2$

Exercise 27:4

1 Find the area of these rectangles.
Make sure that you use the correct units.

a

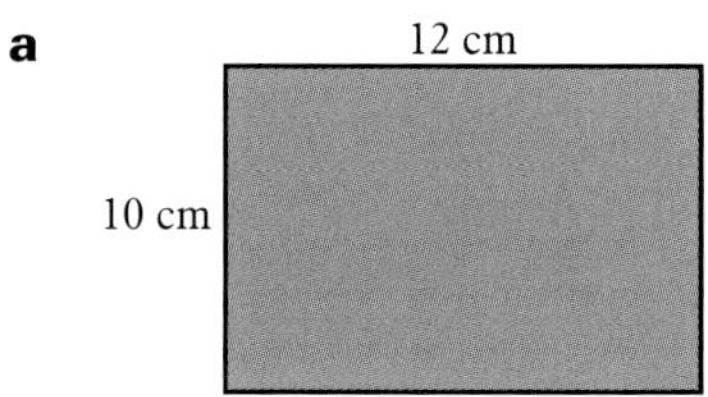

b

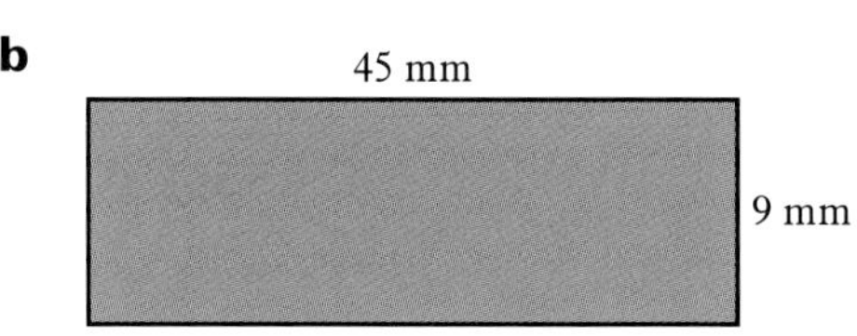

c

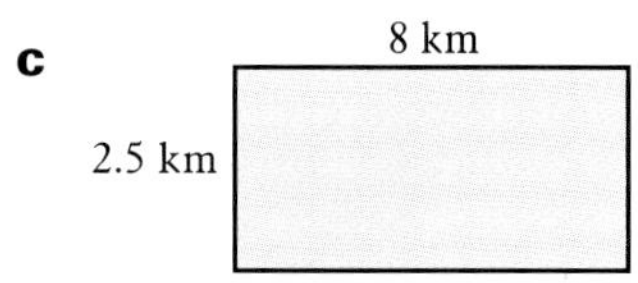

d

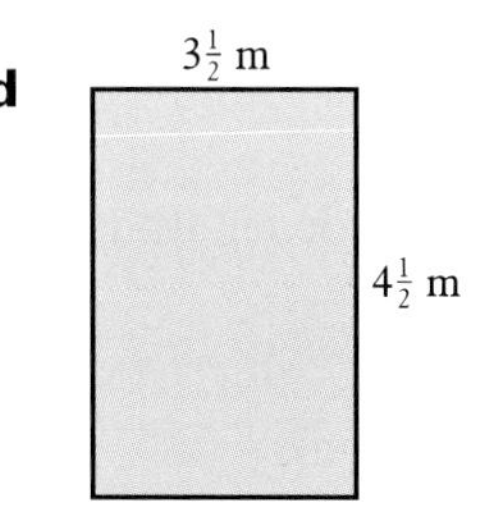

2 Find the area of a rectangle with these measurements:

a length = 14 cm width = 6 cm
b length = 4.2 km width = 1.8 km
c length = 6.32 m width = 14.95 m

3 Find the areas of these squares.

a

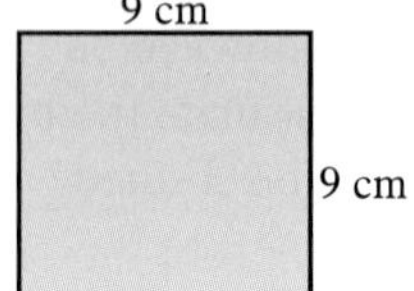

b

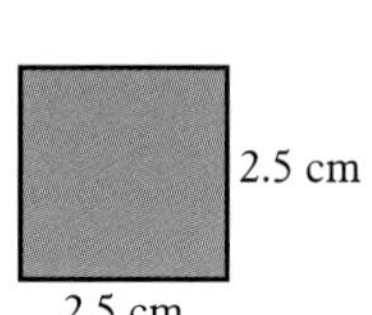

c

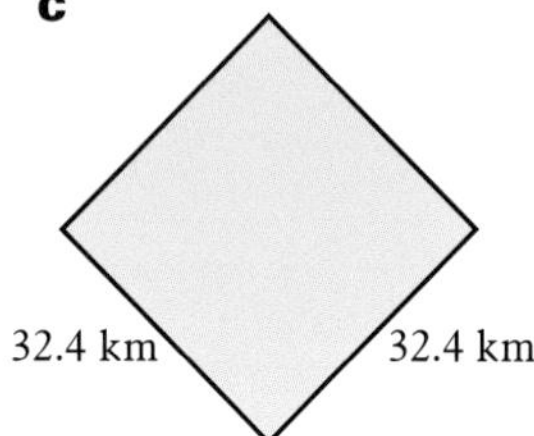

4 Find the area of a square with side:

a 15 cm
b 1.2 m
● **c** $12\frac{1}{4}$ km

5 All of these rectangles have an area of 306 cm^2.

a Find the width of this rectangle.

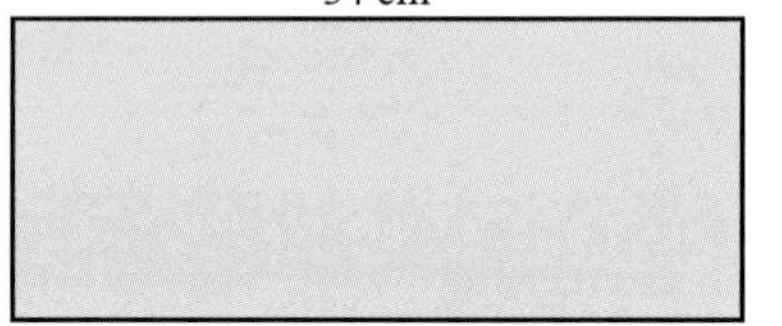

c Find the width of this rectangle.

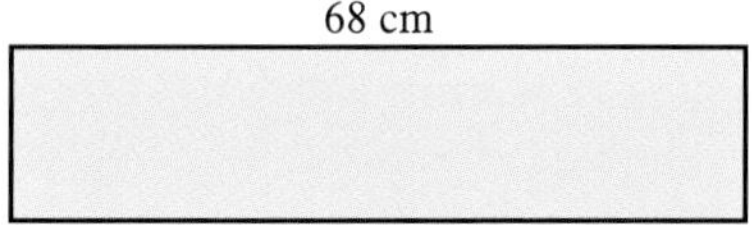

b Find the length of this rectangle.

● **d** Find the length of this rectangle.

● **6** Find the side length of a square with an area of:

a 4 cm^2
b 64 cm^2
c 289 cm^2
d 729 cm^2

Finding the area of a triangle

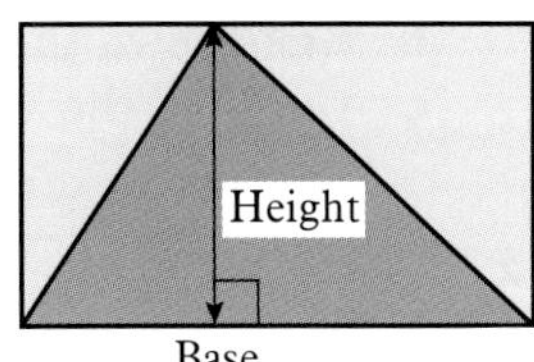

Look at this triangle.
You can draw a rectangle around it.

The **length** of the rectangle is the **base** of the triangle.
The **width** of the rectangle is the **height** of the triangle.
The area of the rectangle = length × width
= base × height

The triangle is half the area of the rectangle.
The area of the triangle = area of the rectangle ÷ 2
= (base × height) ÷ 2

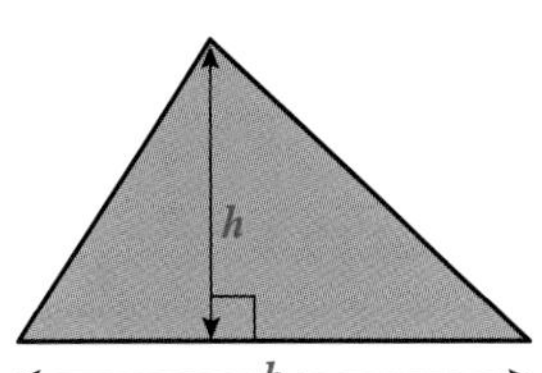

If you call the **h**eight h
and you call the **b**ase b
Then the area of a triangle is $(b \times h) \div 2$

You can write this as $\frac{b \times h}{2}$ or $\frac{1}{2}bh$

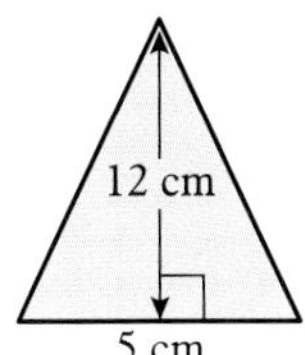

The area of this triangle = $(5 \times 12) \div 2$
$= 60 \div 2$
$= 30\ \text{cm}^2$

The height of this triangle is outside the triangle.
The area of this triangle = $(8 \times 7) \div 2$
$= 56 \div 2$
$= 28\ \text{cm}^2$

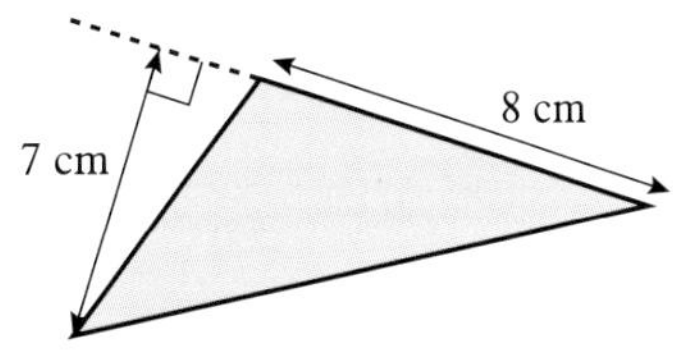

Exercise 27:5

1 Find the area of each of these triangles:

a

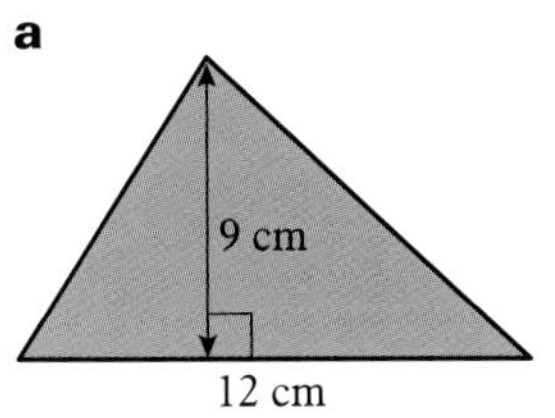

b

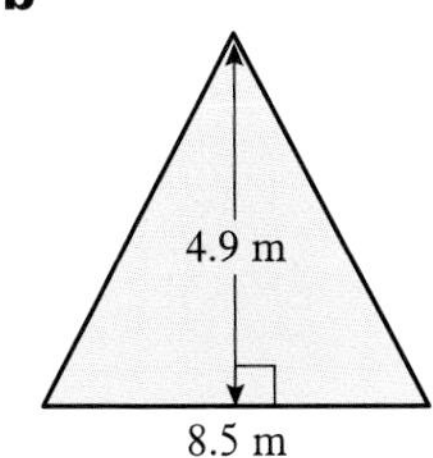

c

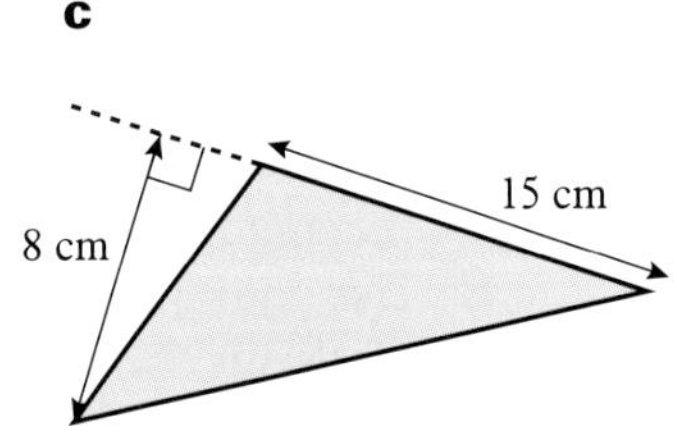

The triangles in questions **2** to **5** are drawn on 1 cm squared paper.
For each triangle:

a write down the base
b write down the height
c work out the area.

2

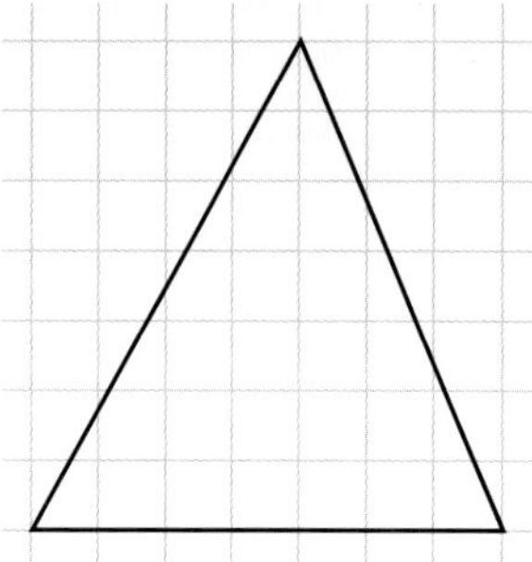

4

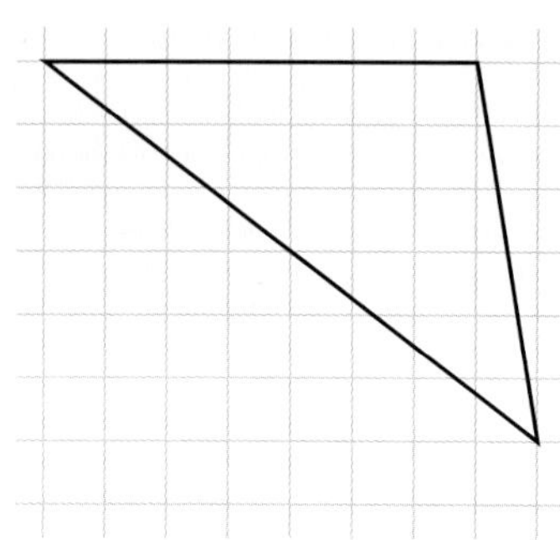

3

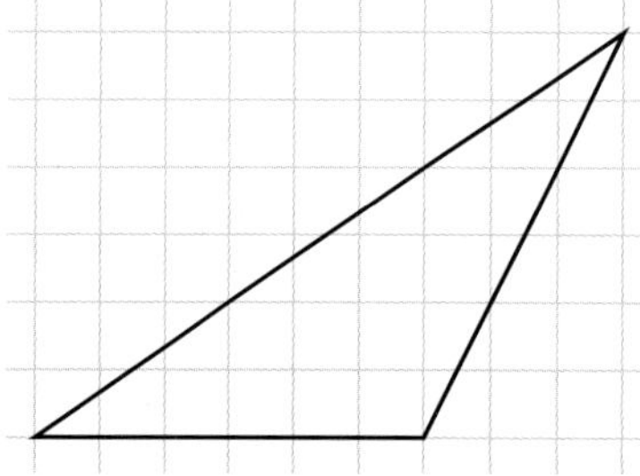

5

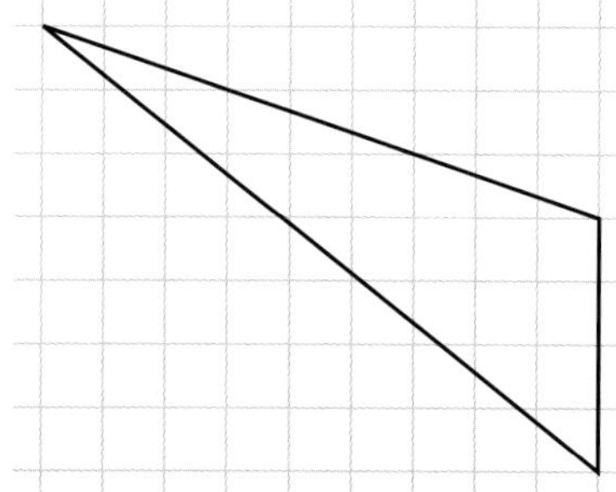

6 Natasha has designed this flag.

a Find the area of the red triangle.
b Find the area of the blue triangle.
c Find the total area of the two triangles.
d Find the total area of the rectangular flag.
e Use your answers to **c** and **d** to work out the area of the green section.

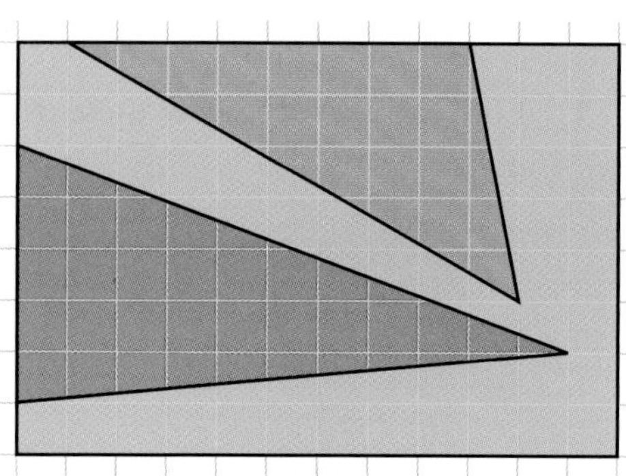

Area of a trapezium

You can split a trapezium into a rectangle and a triangle.

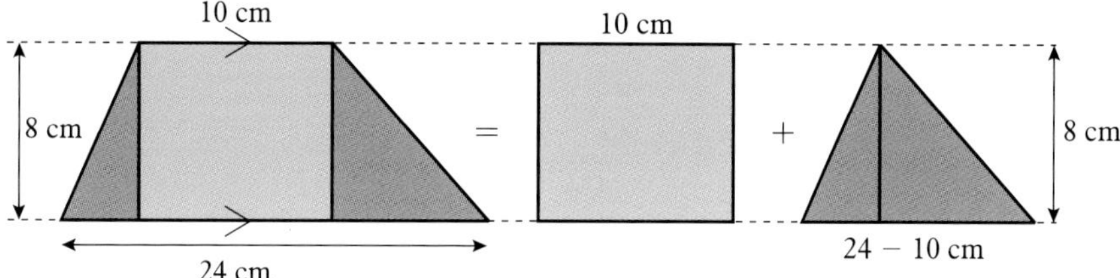

Area of rectangle	$= 10 \times 8$	$= 80\ \text{cm}^2$
Area of triangle	$= \frac{1}{2} \times 14 \times 8$	$= 56\ \text{cm}^2$
So the area of the trapezium is		$136\ \text{cm}^2$

Exercise 27:6

Find the area of each of these trapeziums:

1

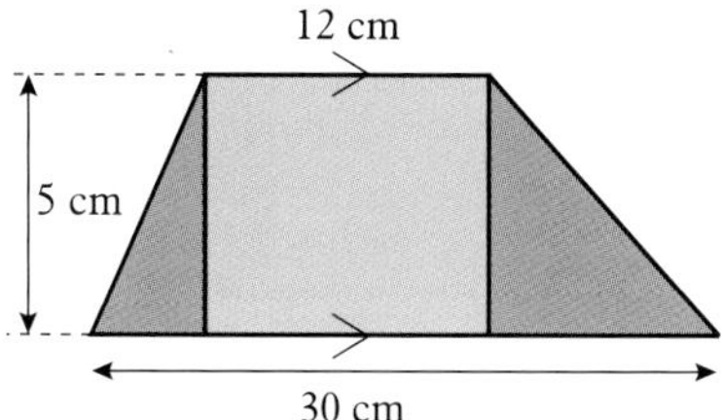

3

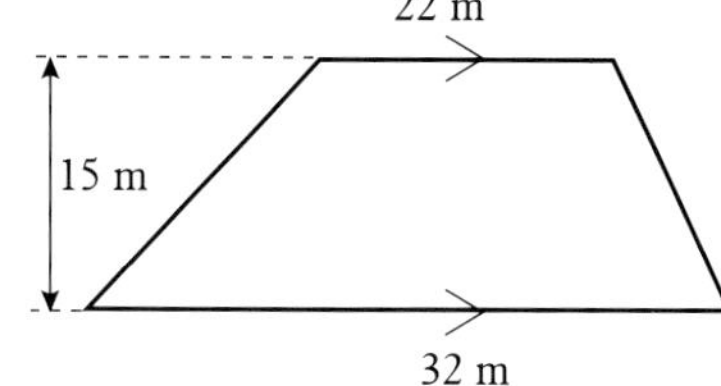

2

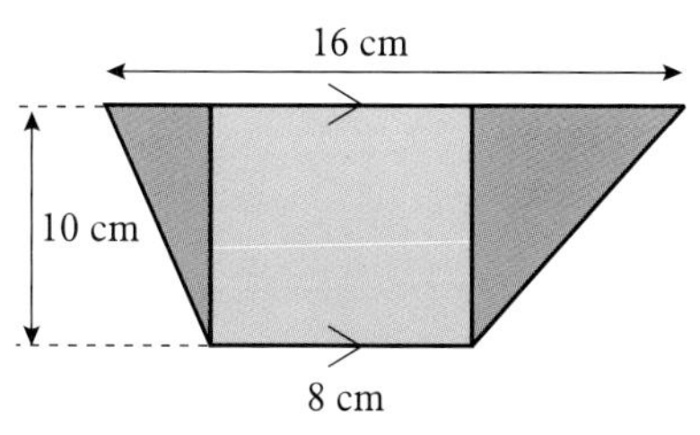

4

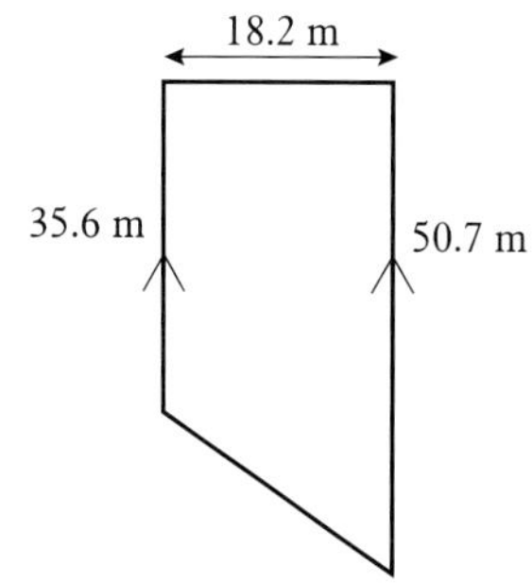

There is another way to find the area of a trapezium.
You can split it into two triangles.

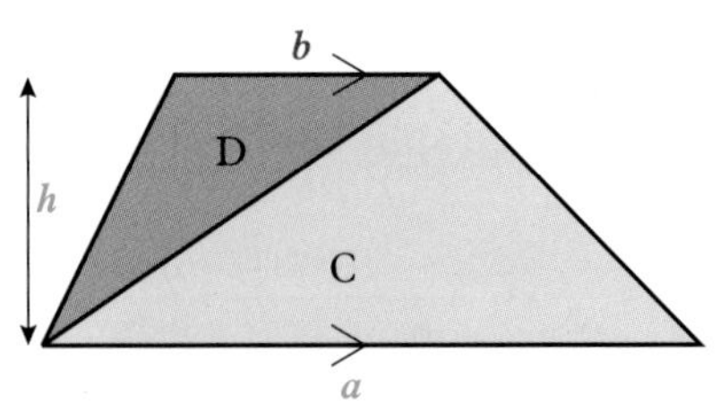

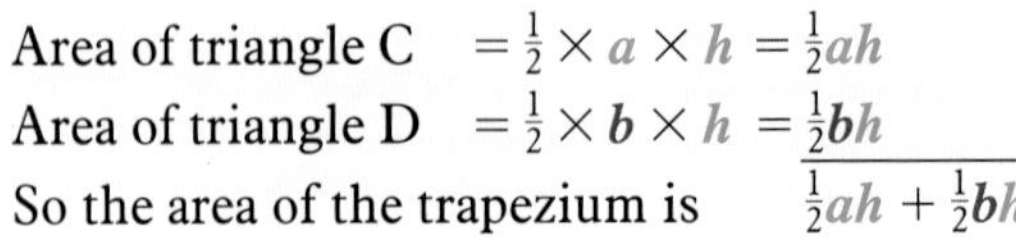

Area of triangle C $= \frac{1}{2} \times a \times h = \frac{1}{2}ah$
Area of triangle D $= \frac{1}{2} \times b \times h = \frac{1}{2}bh$
So the area of the trapezium is $\frac{1}{2}ah + \frac{1}{2}bh$

The expression $\frac{1}{2}ah + \frac{1}{2}bh$ has a common factor of $\frac{1}{2}h$.

So $\frac{1}{2}ah + \frac{1}{2}bh = \frac{1}{2}h(a + b)$

This can be written as $\dfrac{(a + b)}{2} \times h$

which is the mean of the parallel sides times the height.

5 Find the area of this trapezium.

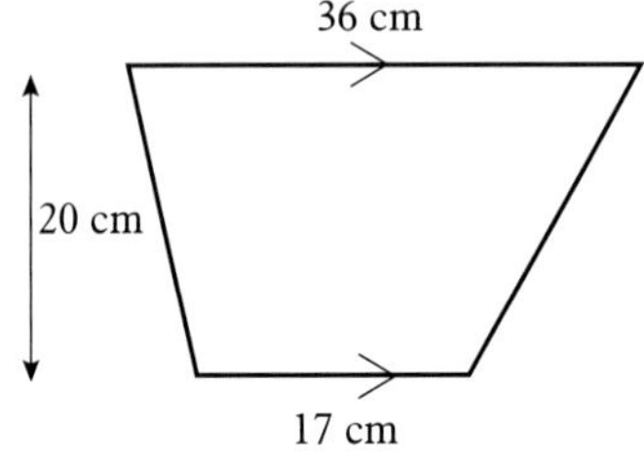

6 Find the area of this trapezium.

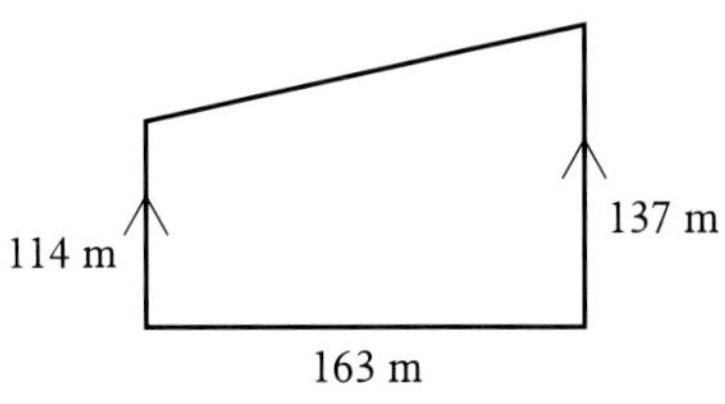

7 This is a field of wheat.
Find the area.

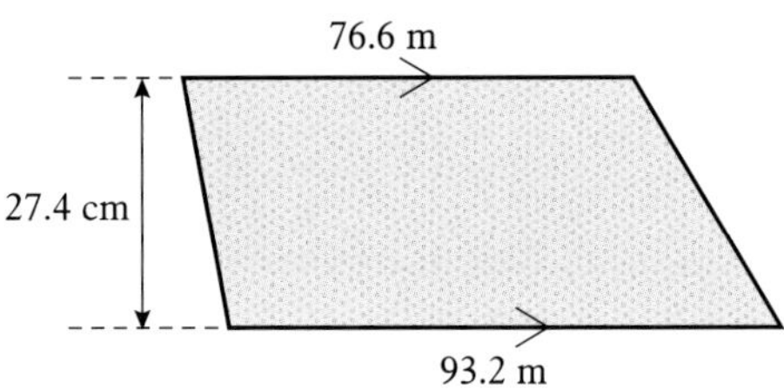

● **8** This is a cross section through a swimming pool. Find the area.

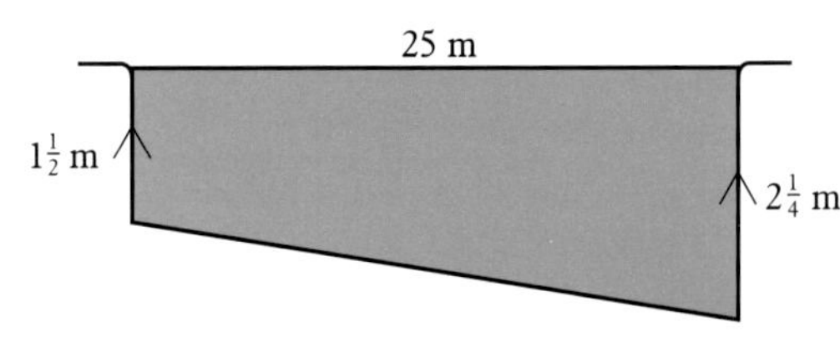

Area of a parallelogram

You can split a parallelogram into two triangles.

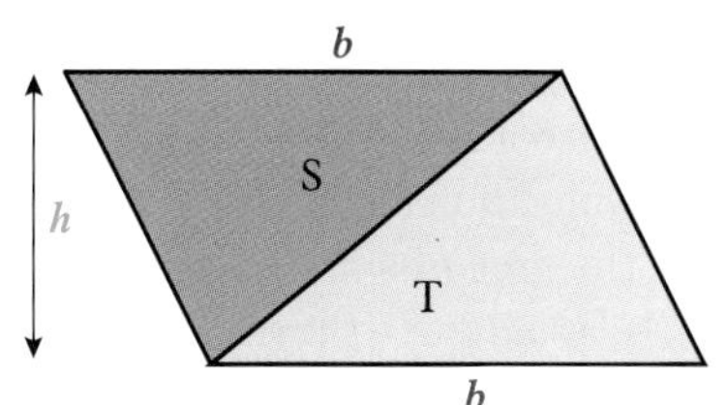

Area of triangle S $= \frac{1}{2} \times b \times h = \frac{1}{2}bh$

Area of triangle T $= \frac{1}{2} \times b \times h = \frac{1}{2}bh$

So the area of a parallelogram is bh

You can write Area = **base** × height or A = bh

9 Find the area of these parallelograms.

a

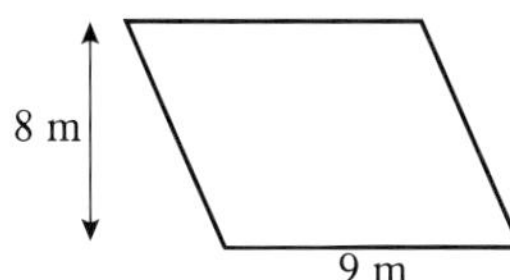

b

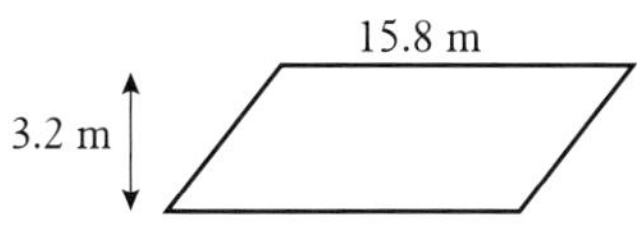

c

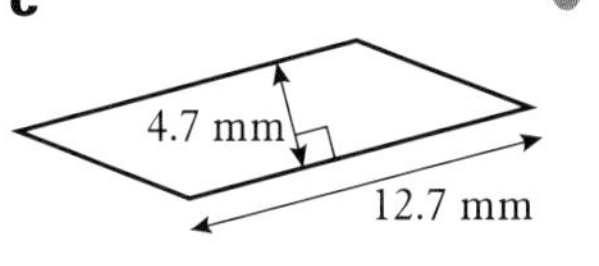

d

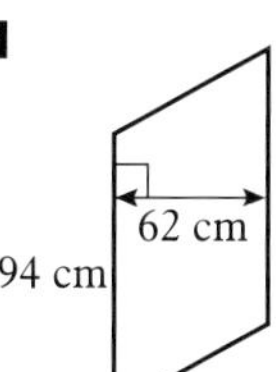

● **e**

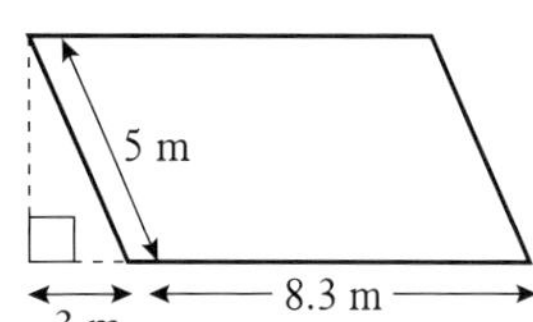

Hint: Use Pythagoras to work out the height

Area of a kite

You can split a kite into two equal triangles.

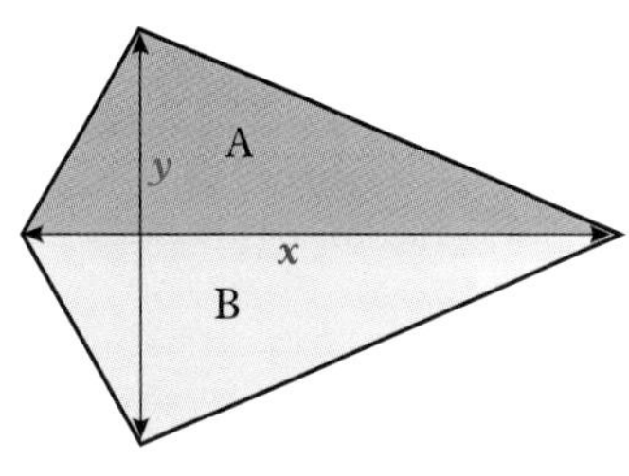

Area of triangle $= \frac{1}{2}$ base × height

Area of triangle A $= \frac{1}{2} \times x \times \frac{1}{2}y = \frac{1}{4}xy$

Area of triangle B $= \frac{1}{2} \times x \times \frac{1}{2}y = \frac{1}{4}xy$

So the area of a kite is $\frac{1}{2}xy$

You can write Area = $\frac{1}{2}$ of the diagonals multiplied together or $A = \frac{1}{2}xy$

10 Find the area of these kites.

a

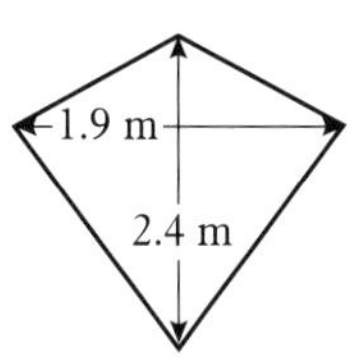

b

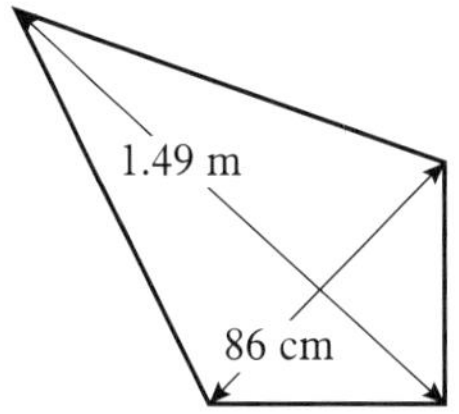

c

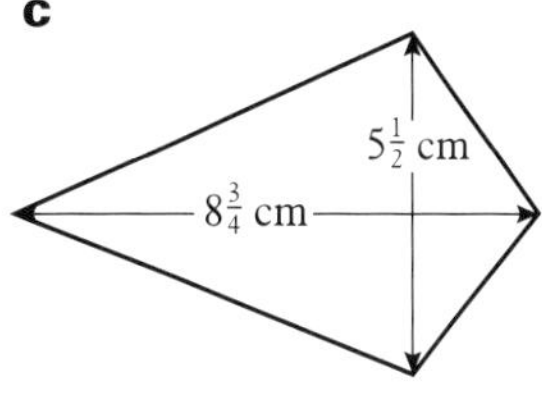

Area of a rhombus

A rhombus is a special sort of parallelogram.
It is also a special sort of kite.
So you can use either of these formulas for the area of a rhombus.
$A = bh$ and $A = \frac{1}{2}xy$

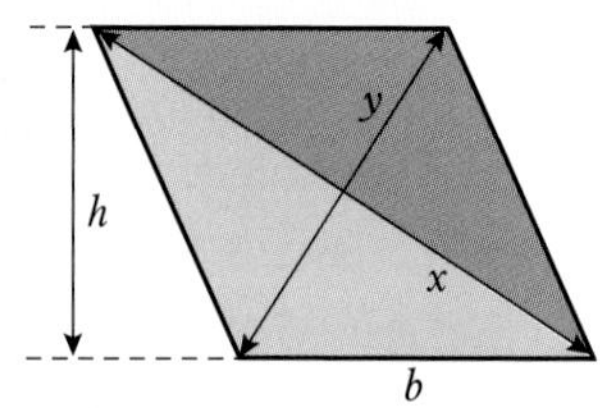

Find the area of each rhombus.

11 **a**

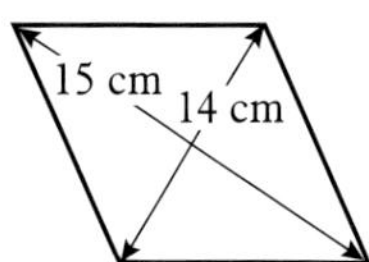

c

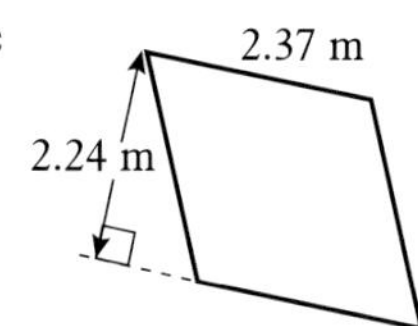

e

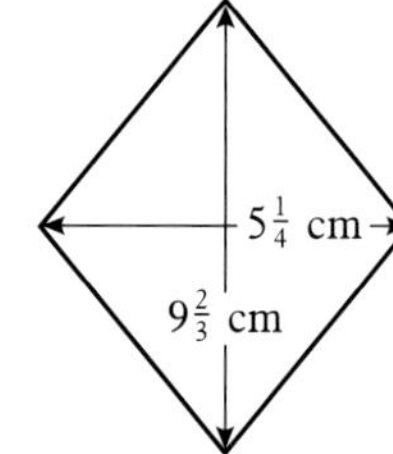

b

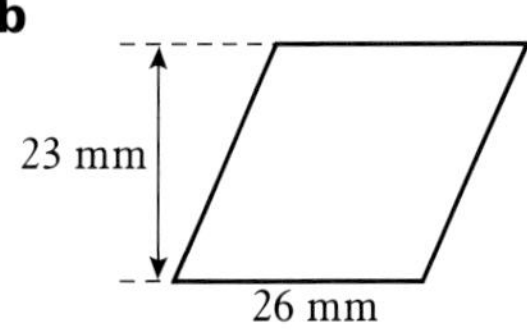

d

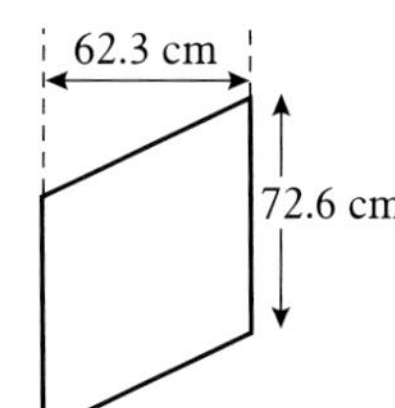

● **f**

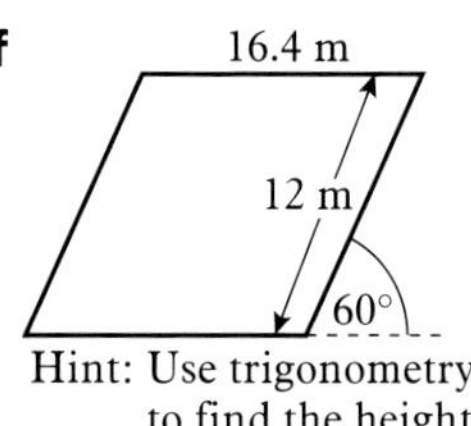

Hint: Use trigonometry to find the height

Area of a circle

The **area of a circle** depends on the radius of the circle.
The formula is
Area of circle = $\pi \times$ radius $\times$ radius.
This rule is often written $A = \pi \times r \times r$
or $A = \pi r^2$ $(r^2 = r \times r)$

Example Find the area of this circle.

$A = \pi r^2$
$= \pi \times 4^2$
$= \pi \times 4 \times 4$
$= \pi \times 16$
$= 50.3$ cm^2 to 1 dp

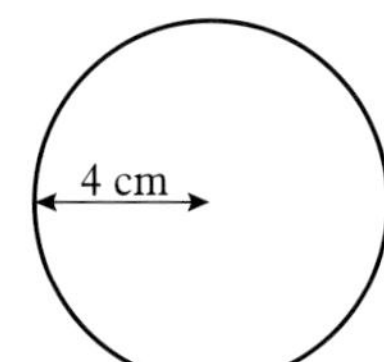

Exercise 27:7

Give your answers in this exercise correct to 1 dp where appropriate.

1 Find the area of these circles:

a

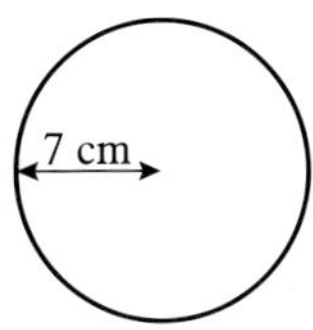

c

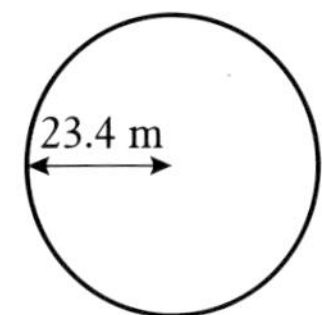

e

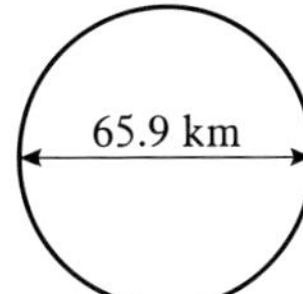

b

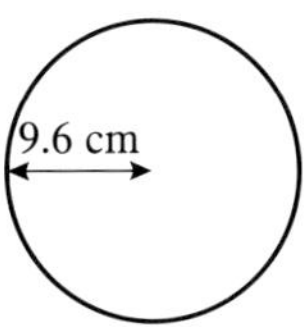

d

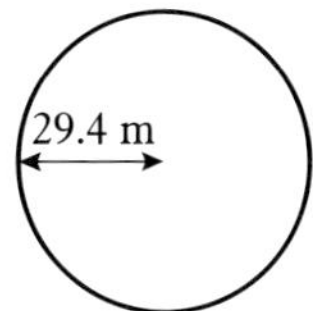

f

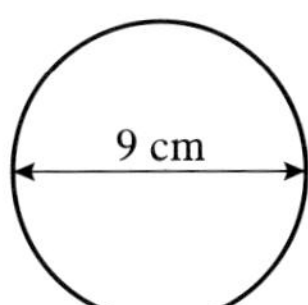

Example Find the exact area of this circle.

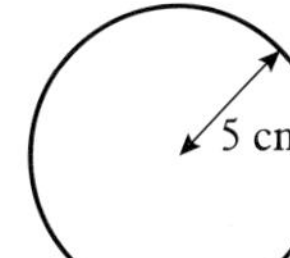

$$A = \pi r^2 = \pi \times 25$$
$$= 25\pi$$

The answer must be exact so you cannot round the calculator answer.
The anwer must be left as 25π cm^2.

---

2 Find the exact area of these circles.

a

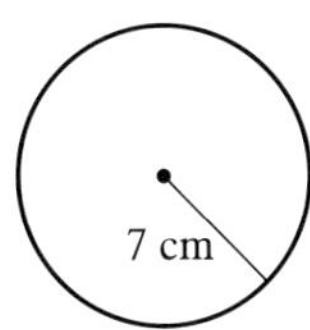

b

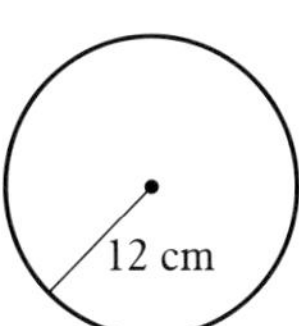

c

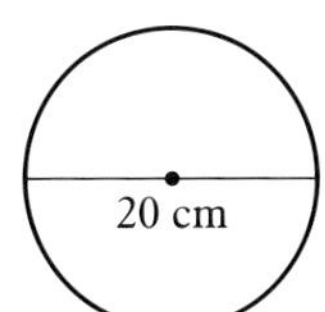

3 Find the area of these shapes.

a

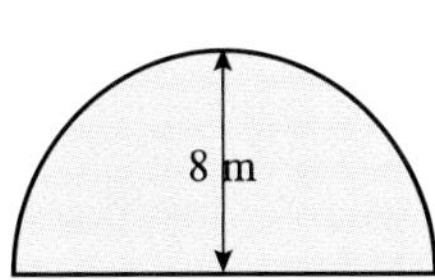

b

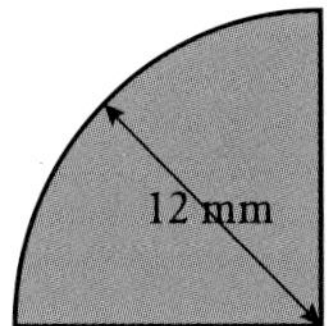

4 Use $\pi = 3$ to *estimate* the areas of the circles in question **1**.

5 The diameter of a £2 coin is 28.5 mm.
Find the area of one face of the coin.

6 Find the area of this circular helicopter landing pad.
Use $\pi = 3\frac{1}{7} = \frac{22}{7}$

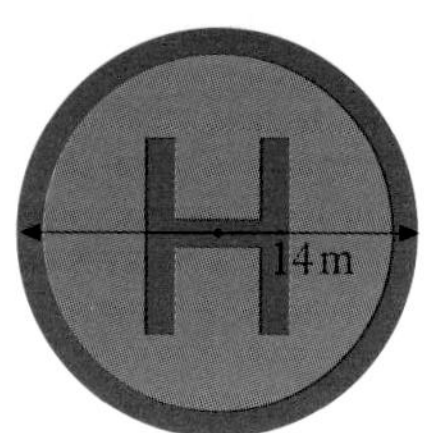

7 Find the area of each of these portholes.
Use $\pi = 3\frac{1}{7} = \frac{22}{7}$

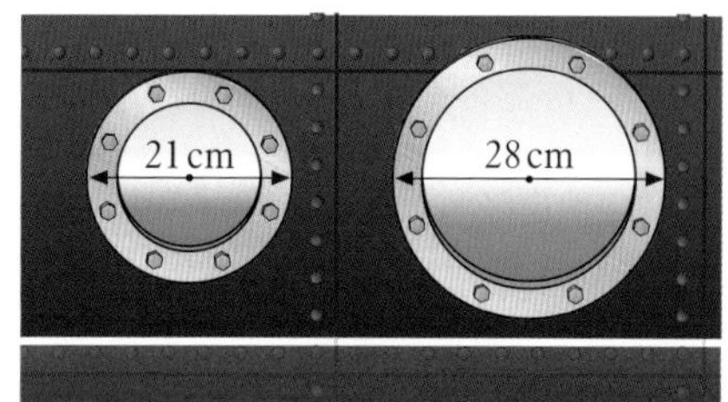

● **8** A tarmac path runs around a circular park.
The path is 5 m wide.
The outer radius of the path is 70 m and the radius of the park is 65 m.

a Find the area of the park.
b Find the area of the park and the path.
c Use your answers to **a** and **b** to find the area of the path.

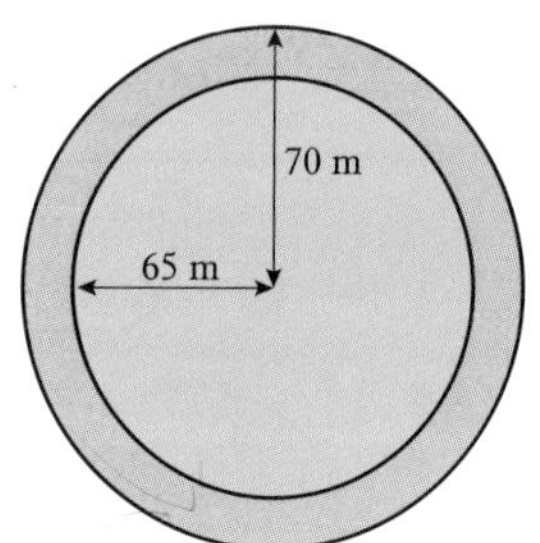

● **9** The diagram shows a circular go-kart track.
The area of the grass in the centre is 2500 m^2.

a Rearrange the formula $A = \pi r^2$ to make r the subject of the formula.
b Use your new formula to find the radius of the grass area.

The area of the track is 1400 m^2.

c Work out the area of the grass and track.
d Find the radius of the outer edge of the track.
e How wide is the go-kart track?

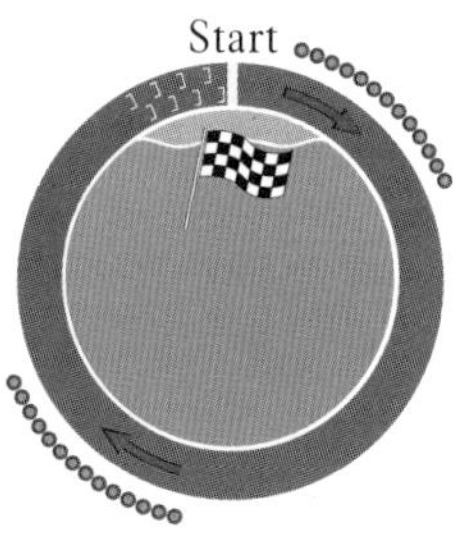

Finding the areas of more complicated shapes

To find these areas you need to:

(1) Decide how to split the shape into parts.
(2) Give each part a letter.
(3) Find any missing lengths.
(4) Work out the area of each part.
(5) Add all these areas to get the total area.

Look at this shape.
The shape is made from a rectangle and a triangle.

Area of rectangle A is $12.5 \times 8.4 = 105\text{ cm}^2$

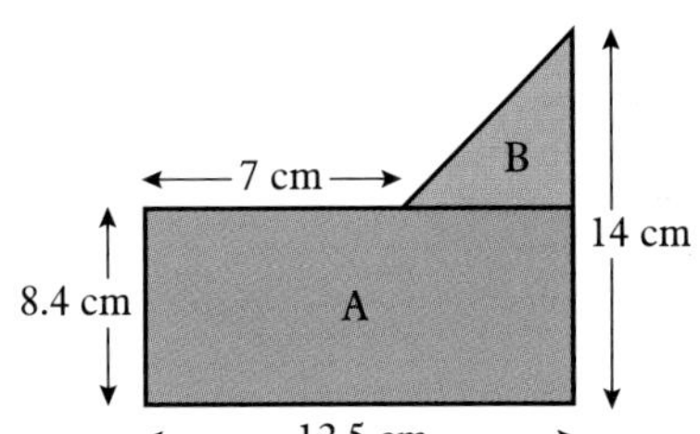

For triangle B you need to find the base and height.
The base of triangle B is $12.5 - 7 = 5.5$ cm
The height of triangle B is $14 - 8.4 = 5.6$ cm

Area of triangle B is $(5.5 \times 5.6) \div 2 = 15.4\text{ cm}^2$

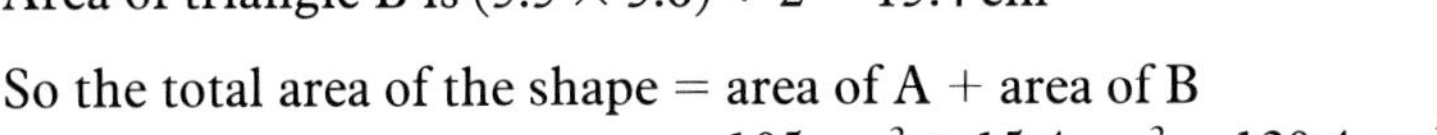

So the total area of the shape $=$ area of A $+$ area of B
$= 105\text{ cm}^2 + 15.4\text{ cm}^2 = 120.4\text{ cm}^2$

Exercise 27:8

1 Two rectangles have been joined to make this shape.

a Find the area of C.
b Find the area of D.
c Find the total area of the shape.

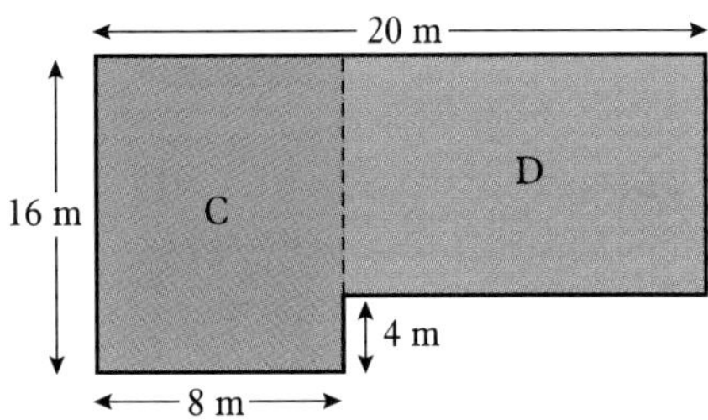

2 Find the total area of each of these shapes:

a

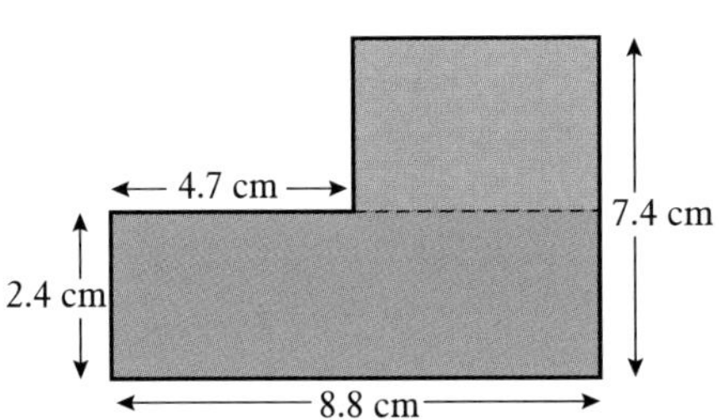

b

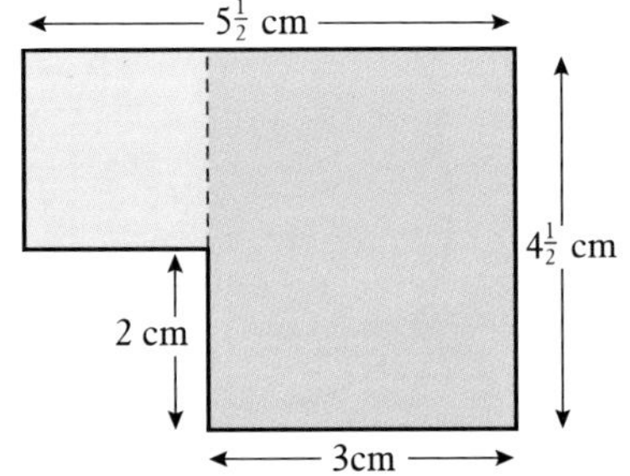

3 Find the areas of these shapes:

a

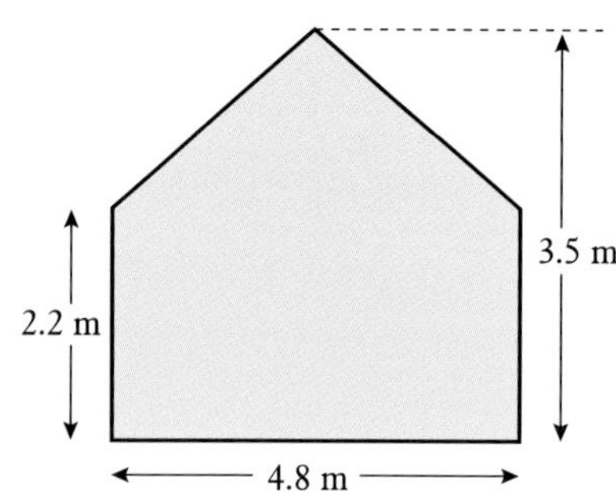

c

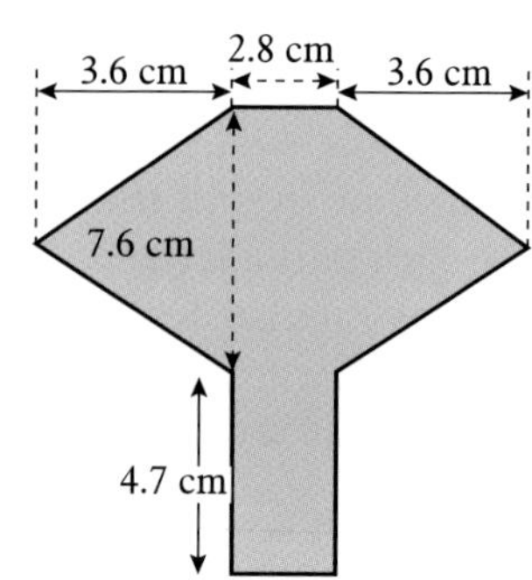

b

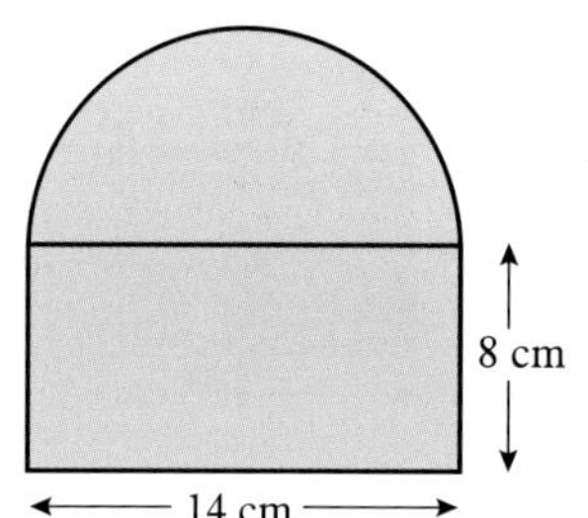

d

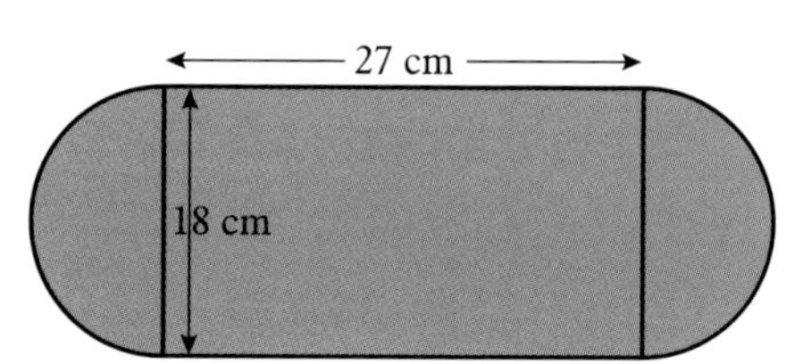

4 Find the areas of these shapes:

a

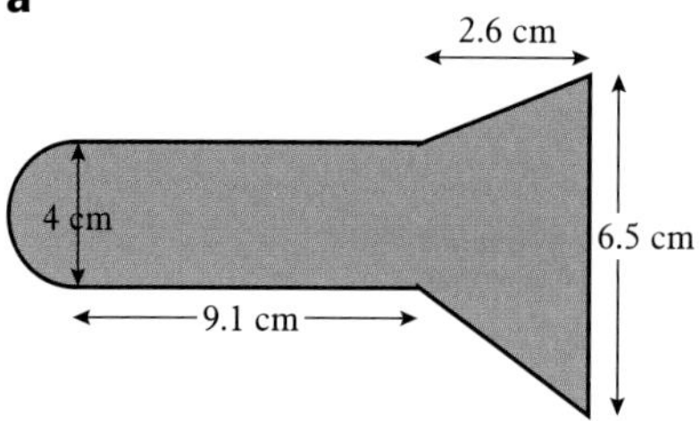

● **c**

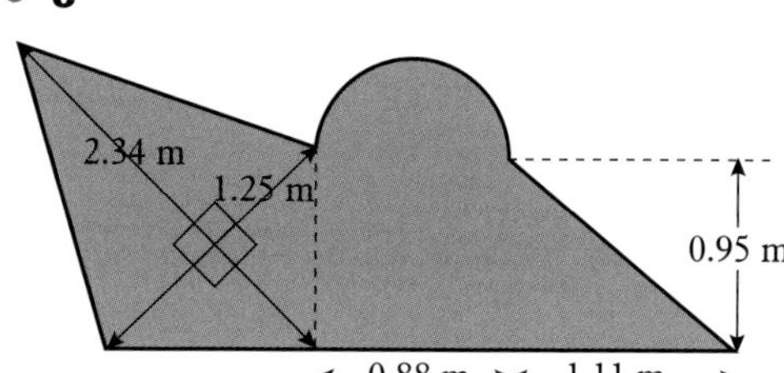

b

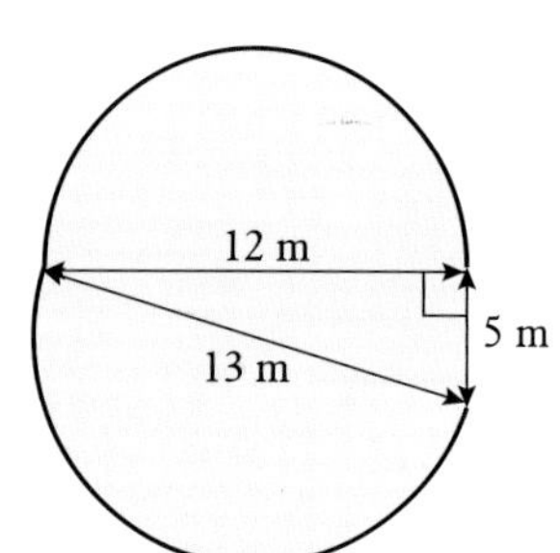

● **d**

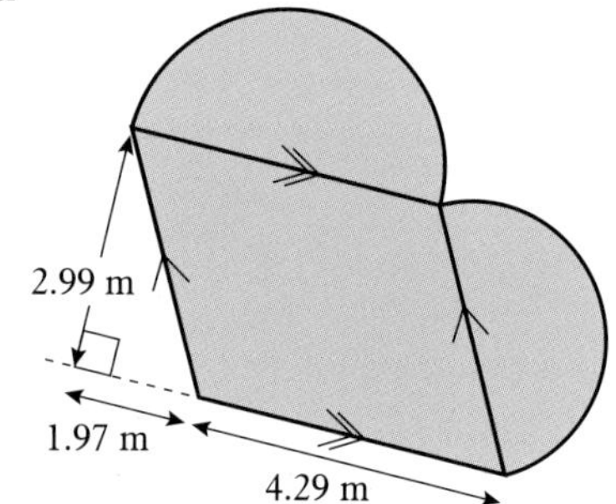

5 The customer area of a restaurant has a floorplan like this.

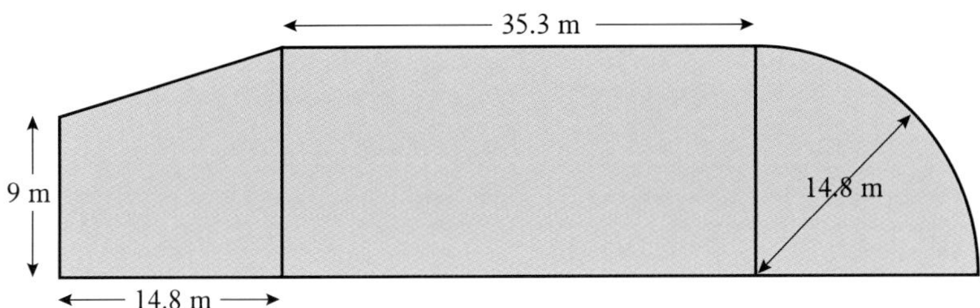

Work out the area available for seating.

● **6** This door has five glass panels.

a Find the total area of the glass panels.

b Find the area of the whole door.

c Use your answers to **a** and **b** to find the area of wood in the door.

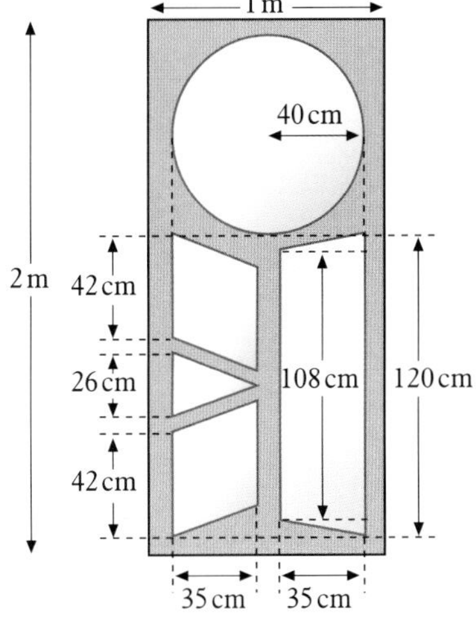

● **7** A castle has a plan like this.
The dark line round the outside shows the castle wall.
The castle grounds are shown in green.
The castle keep is shown with a blue line.

a Find the floor area of the keep.

b Find the area of the castle grounds.

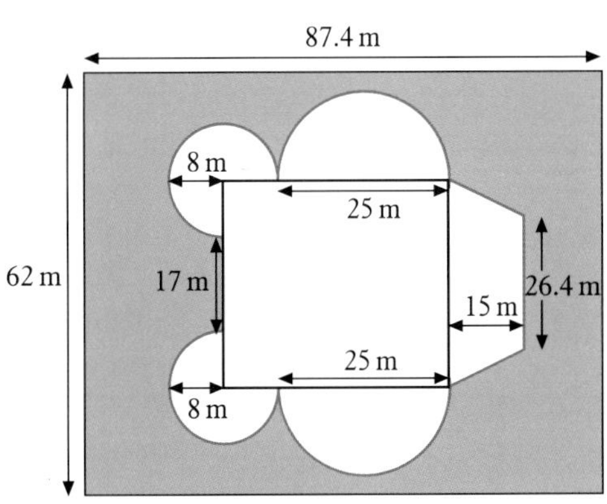

3 Nets and surface areas

Maltesers come in boxes of different shapes and sizes. Each of them has to be made from a single piece of card. Think about how they do it.

Net

When a solid is opened out and laid flat, the shape that you get is called a **net** of the solid.

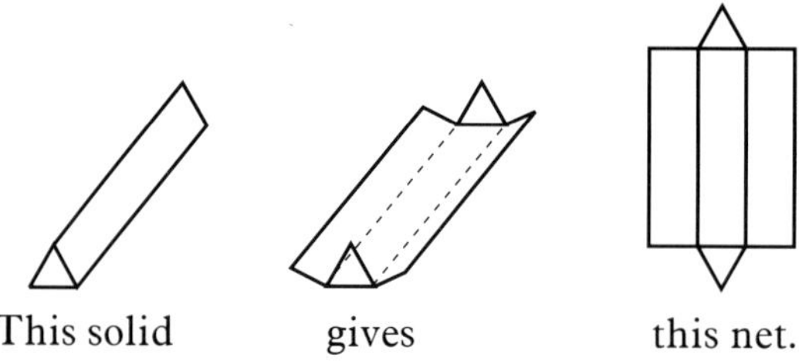

This solid gives this net.

You can have more than one net for a solid. This is also a net of the same solid.

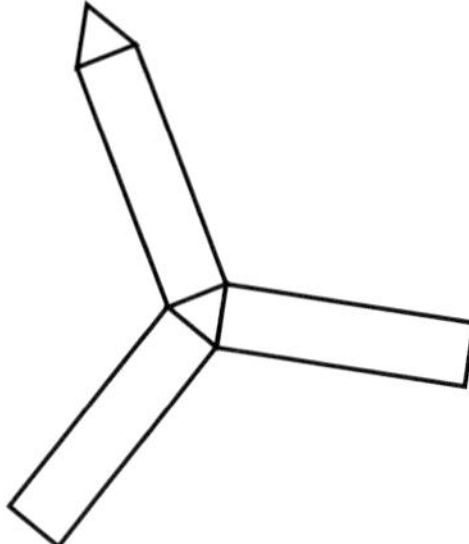

Exercise 27:9

1 Here are some patterns of shapes. Some of them are nets of cubes.
- **a** Draw the patterns on to squared paper.
- **b** Cut them out.
- **c** Fold them up to see if they make a cube.
- **d** Write down the letters of the ones that make cubes.

P 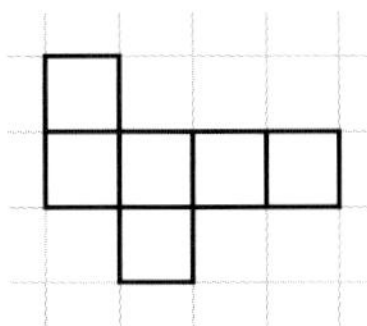

R 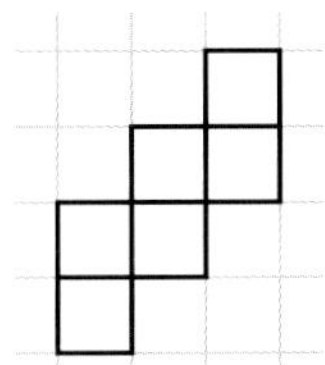

T 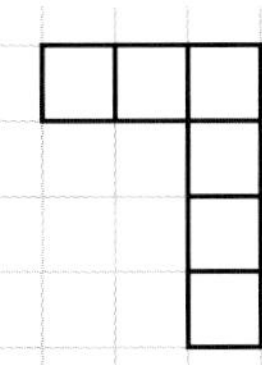

Q 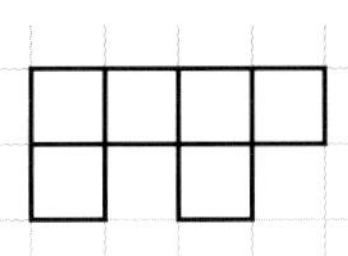

S 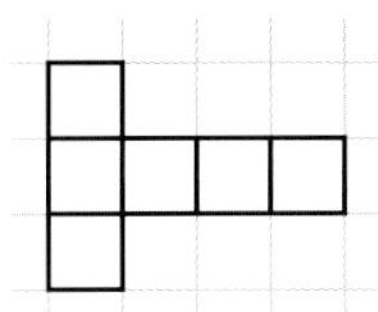

U 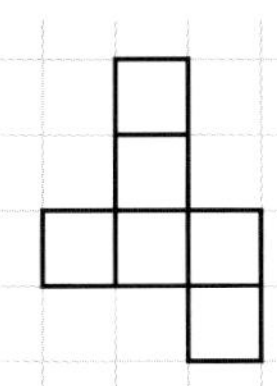

2 **a** Copy this net on to 1 cm squared paper.

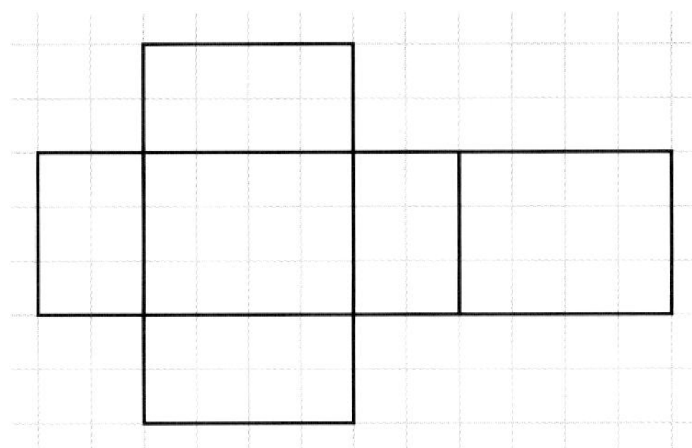

b Cut out the net. Fold it to make a solid.
c Write down the name of the solid.
d The length of the solid is 4 cm.
Write down the width and the height of the solid.

3 **a** Copy this net.
Cut it out.
b Fold it along the lines.
c Write down the name of the solid that it makes.

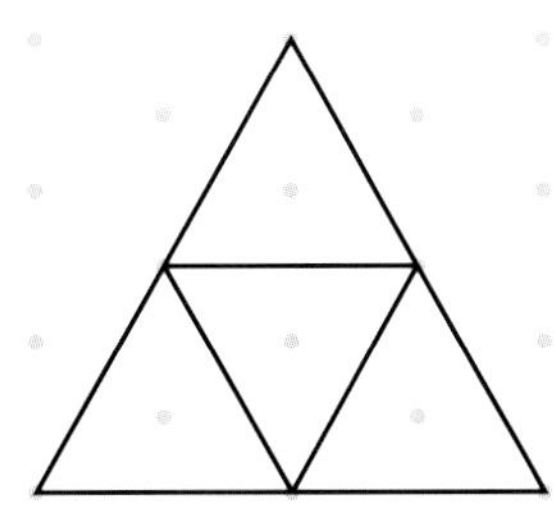

4 Sketch the net of this square-based pyramid.

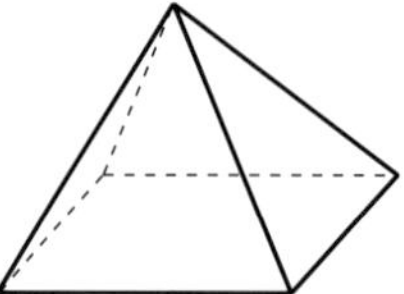

5 Match each solid with its net.

a

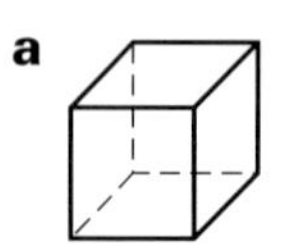
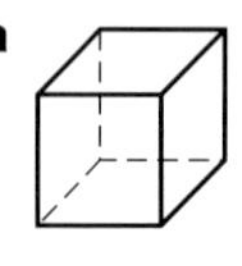

P

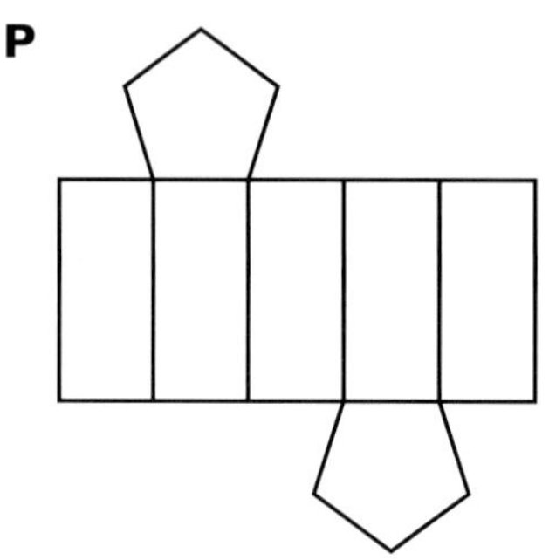

S

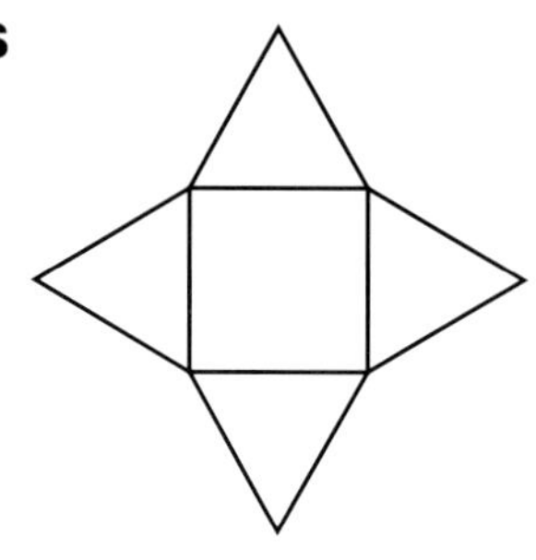

b

c

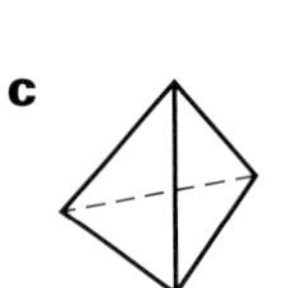

Q

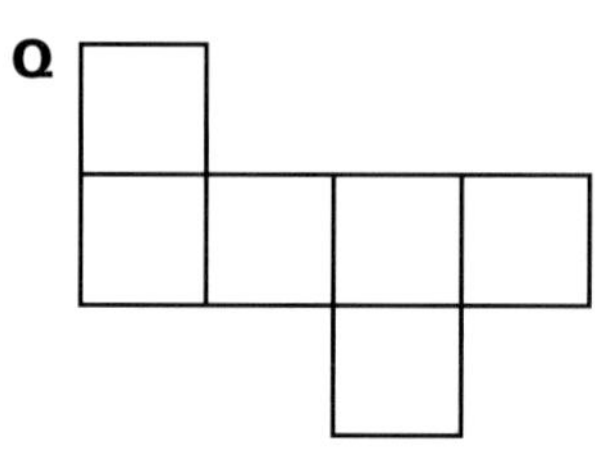

U

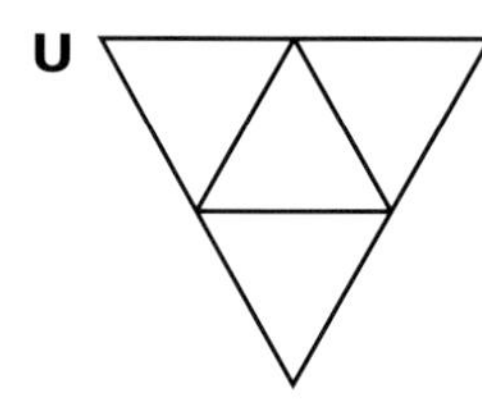

d

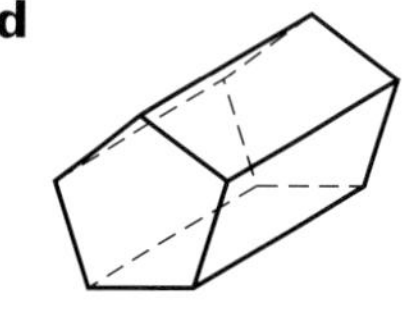

e

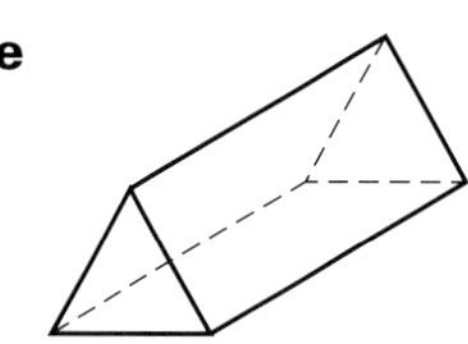

T

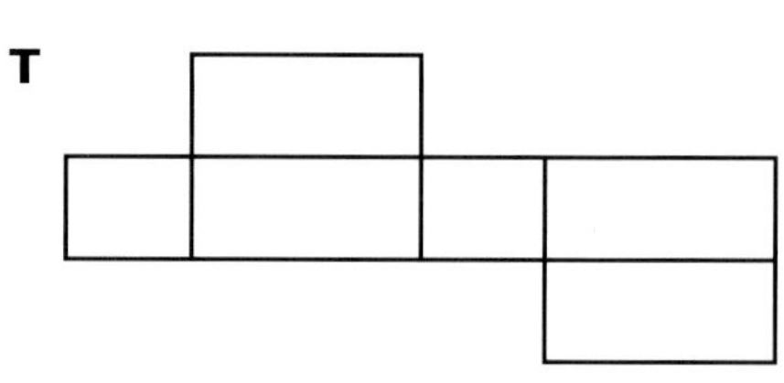

f

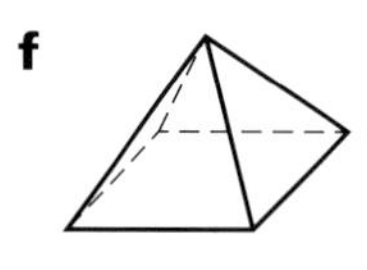

g

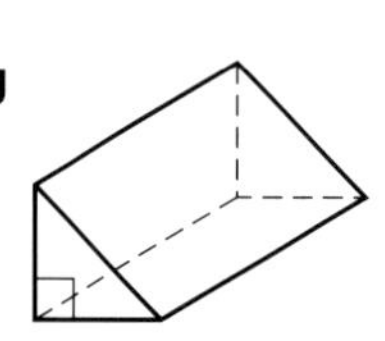

R

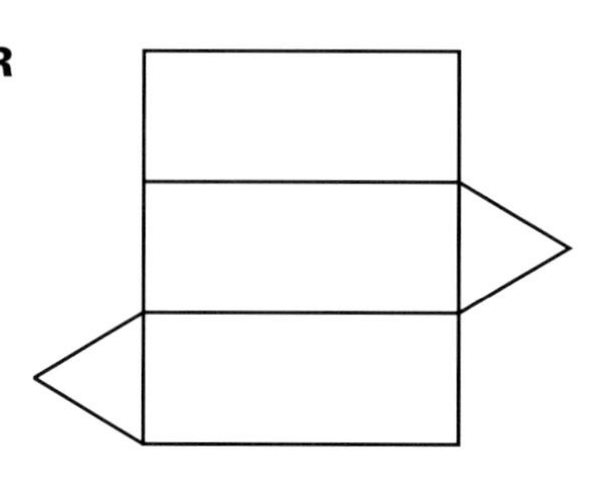

V

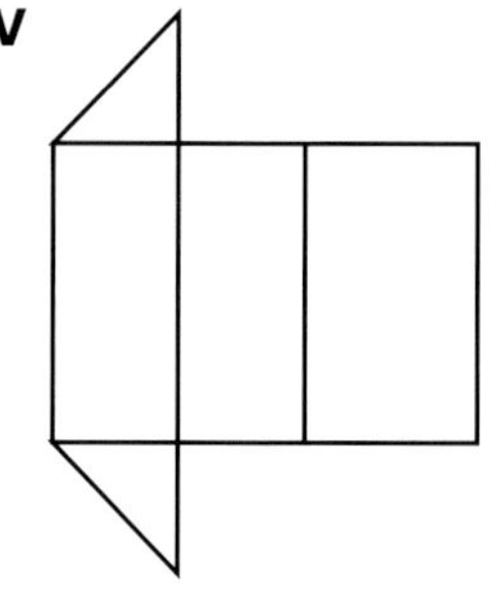

Finding the surface area of a solid

A simple way to do this is to sketch the net.
Then you will not miss any faces.

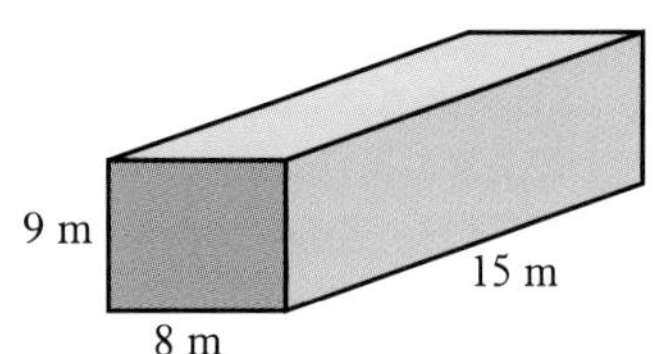

To find the surface area of a solid:
(1) Sketch the net
(2) Work out the areas of the different faces
(3) Find the total of all the areas.

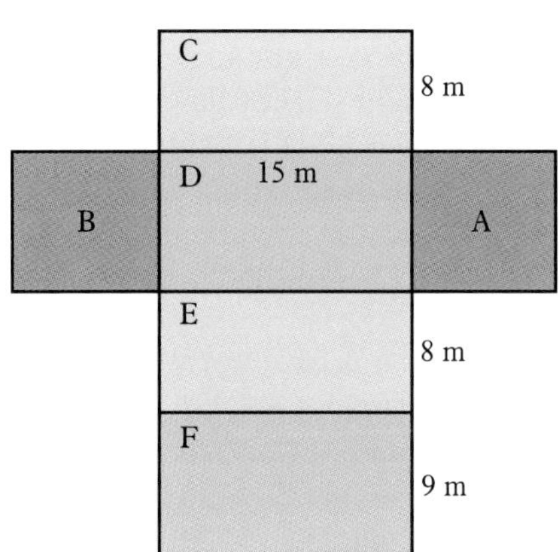

In this cuboid, there are 3 pairs of faces the same size.
They are **A** and **B**, **C** and **E** and **D** and **F**.

Area of rectangles **A** and **B**	$= 2 \times 8 \times 9$	$= 144\ \text{m}^2$
Area of rectangles **C** and **E**	$= 2 \times 15 \times 8$	$= 240\ \text{m}^2$
Area of rectangles **D** and **F**	$= 2 \times 15 \times 9$	$= 270\ \text{m}^2$
Total surface area		$= 654\ \text{m}^2$

Exercise 27:10

Work out the surface areas of the solids in questions **1–3**.

1

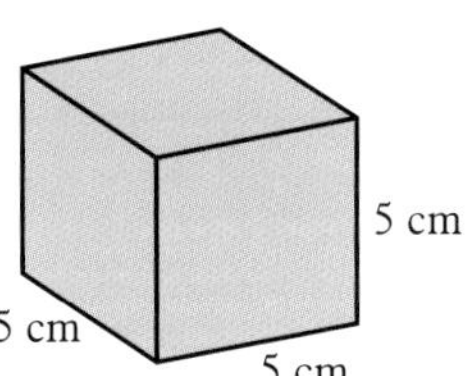

2

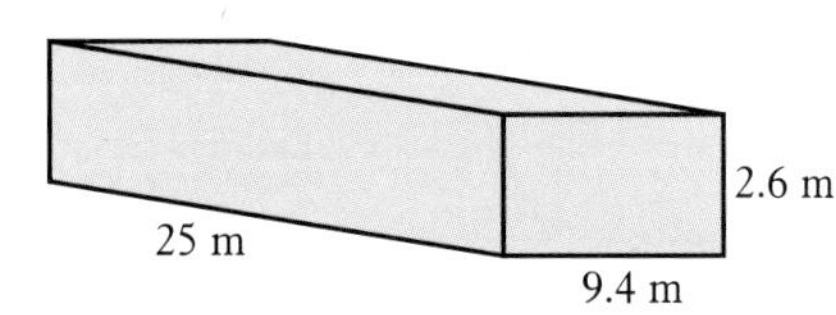

3 This is a square-based pyramid. All the triangular sides are the same size.

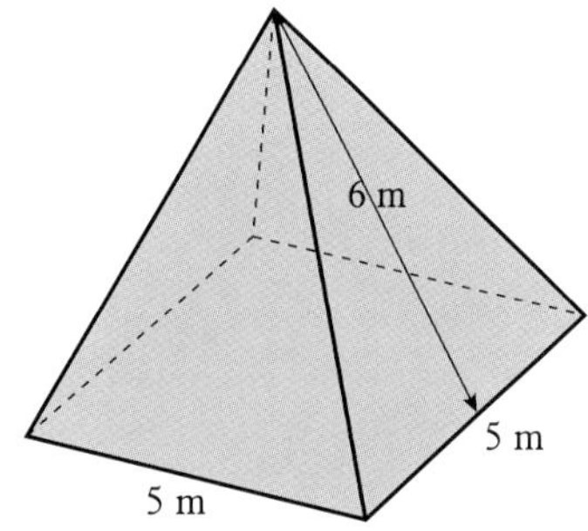

Finding the surface areas of prisms

To find the surface area of a prism:
(1) Sketch the net,
(2) Work out the areas of the different faces,
(3) Find the total of all the areas.

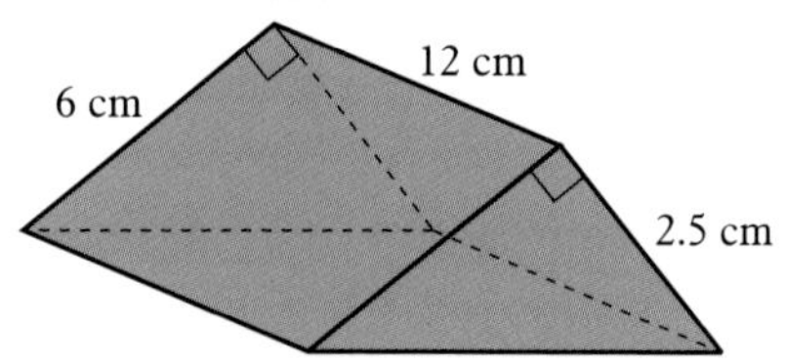

For this prism, right angled triangles A and B are congruent so they have the same area.
The hypotenuse of triangle A is the width of rectangle C.
The hypotenuse is worked out by Pythagoras:
$h^2 = 6^2 + (2.5)^2$ so that $h = 6.5$ cm

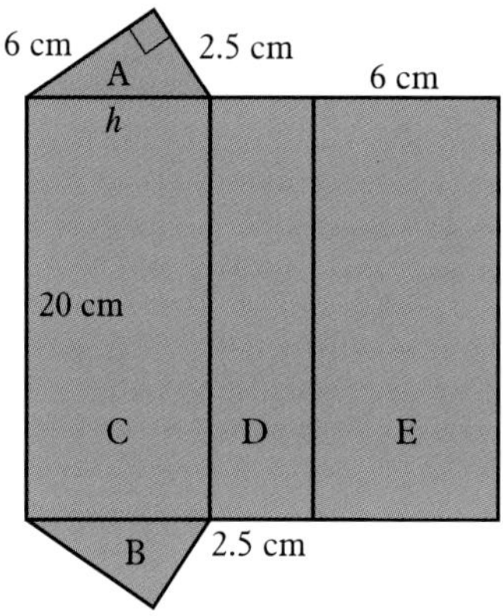

Area of triangle A	$= \frac{1}{2} \times 6 \times 2.5$	$= 7.5$ cm²
Area of triangle B	$= \frac{1}{2} \times 6 \times 2.5$	$= 7.5$ cm²
Area of rectangle C	$= 20 \times 6.5$	$= 130$ cm²
Area of rectangle D	$= 20 \times 2.5$	$= 50$ cm²
Area of rectangle E	$= 20 \times 6$	$= 120$ cm²
Total surface area		$= 315$ cm²

4 Work out the surface area of these prisms. You will need to use Pythagoras.

a

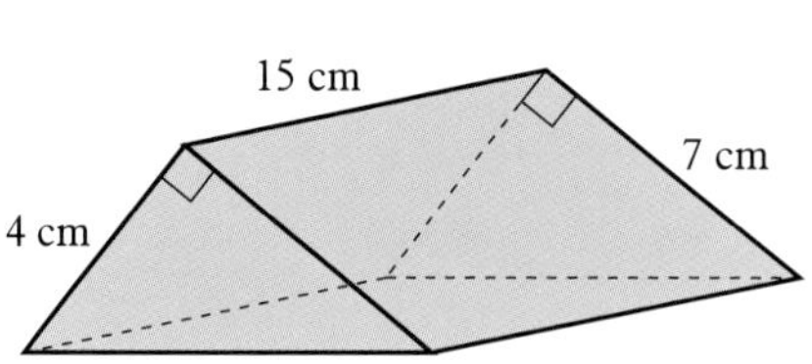

● **c**

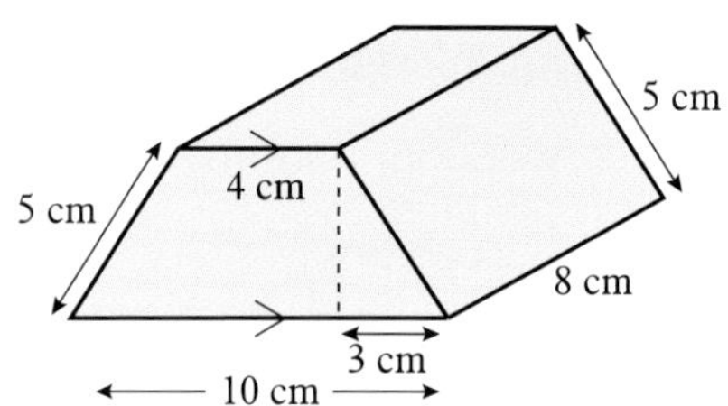

b

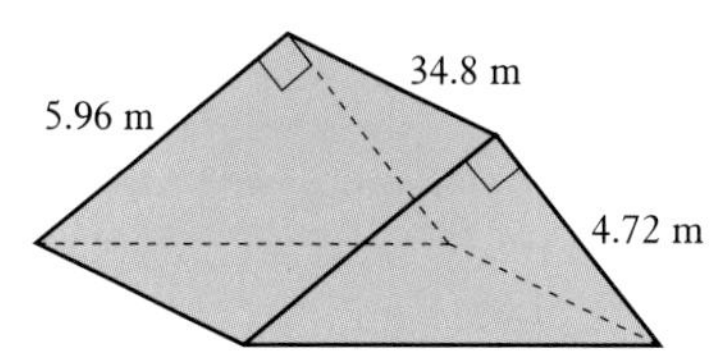

● **d**

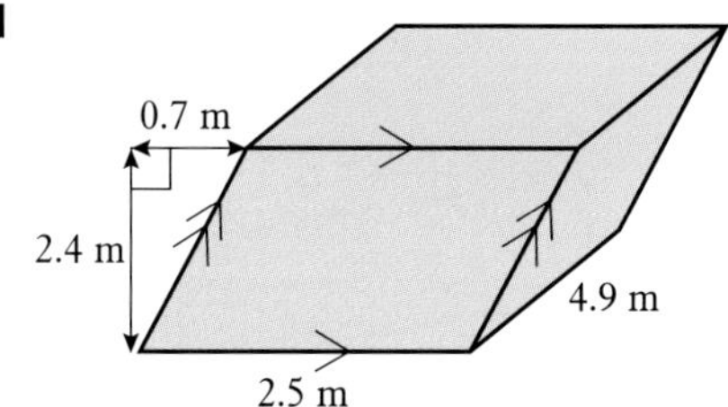

This is a square millimetre.

1 mm
1 mm

This is a square centimetre.

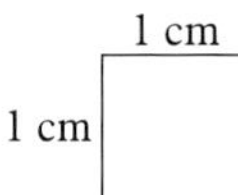

There are 10 mm in every 1 cm.
So the square centimetre
is 10 mm across
and 10 mm down.
So there are $10 \times 10 = 100$ mm^2 in 1 cm^2.

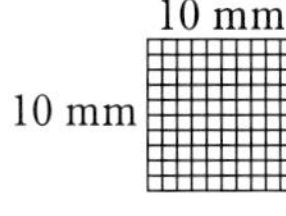

A square metre is too big to draw here!
This is a diagram of one.
There are 100 cm in every 1 m.
So the square metre
is 100 cm across
and 100 cm down.
So there are $100 \times 100 = 10\,000$ cm^2 in 1 m^2.

100 cm
100 cm

There are 1000 m in every 1km.
So there are $1000 \times 1000 = 1\,000\,000$ m^2 in 1 km^2.

This diagram shows you how to convert square units.

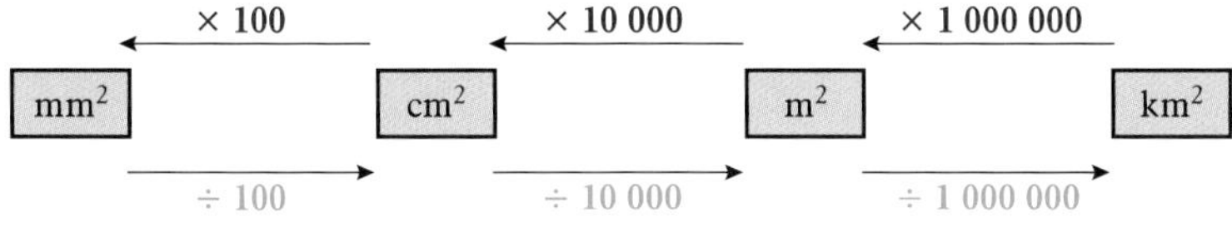

Exercise 27:11

1 Draw a square 2 cm by 2 cm. Find the area in square millimetres.

2 Change each of these areas into square centimetres.

a 2 m^2 **c** 12 m^2 **e** 0.43 m^2 **g** 128 mm^2 **i** 2050 mm^2
b 8 m^2 **d** 0.9 m^2 **f** 400 mm^2 **h** 672 mm^2 **j** 25 mm^2

3 Change each of these areas into square metres.

a 40 000 cm^2 **b** 7900 cm^2 **c** 0.4 km^2 **d** 8.95 km^2

4 Change each of these areas into square kilometres.

a 10 000 m^2 **b** 7 500 000 m^2 ● **c** 10^9 m^2 ● **d** 2.3×10^7 m^2

1 Write down the area of each of these shapes.
They are drawn on 1 cm squared paper.

a **b** **c**

2 Estimate the area of each of these shapes.
They are drawn on 1 cm squared paper.

a **b** **c**

3 Find the area of each of these shapes:

a

5.4 m 5.4 m

b

22.3 cm
14.9 cm

c

28 cm
46 cm

d

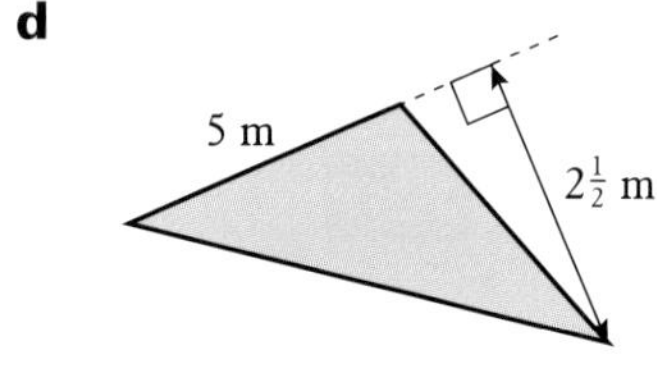

e

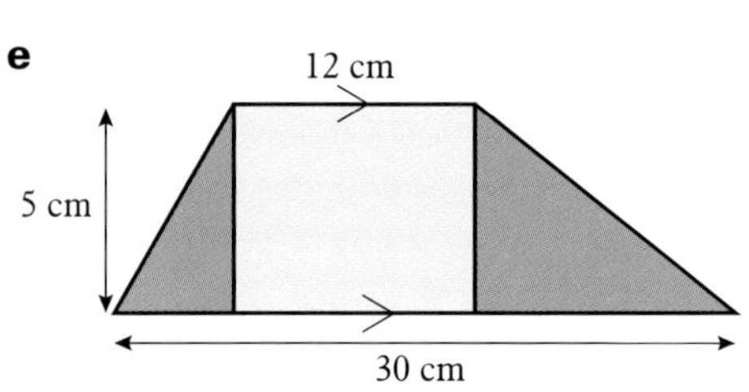

f

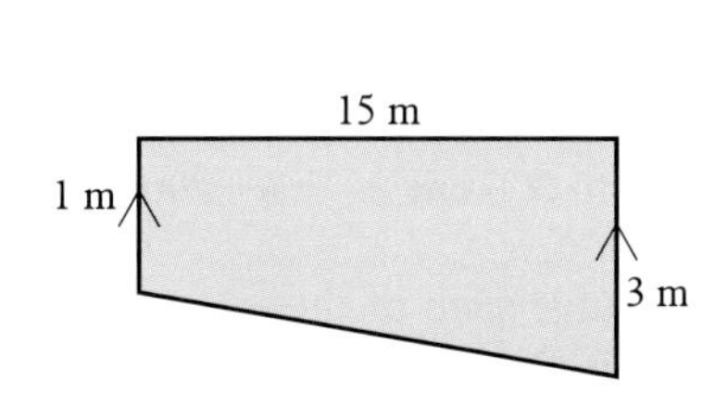

4 Find the area of each of these shapes:

a

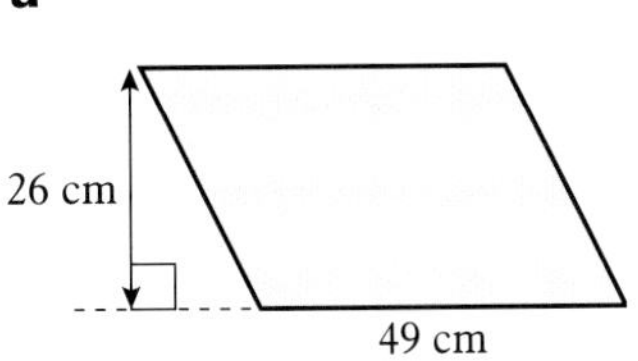

b

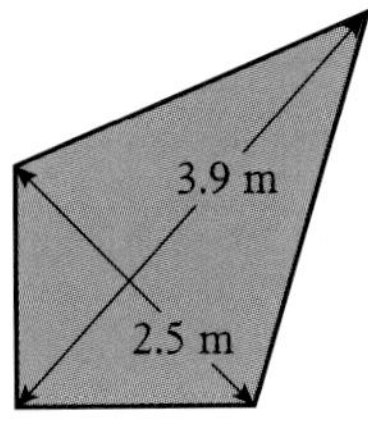

c

86.7 cm
56.7 cm

5 Find the area of each of these shapes:

a

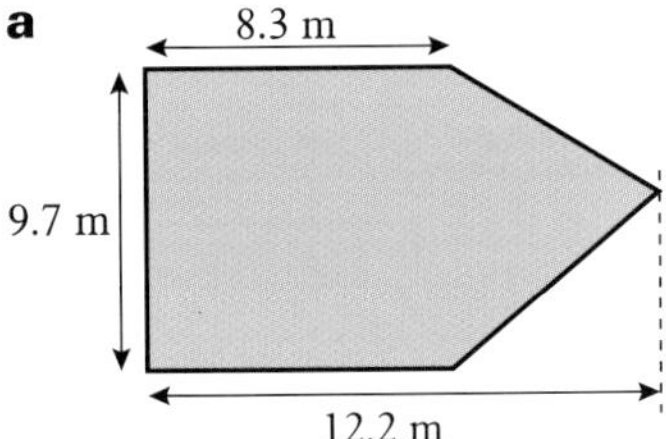

b

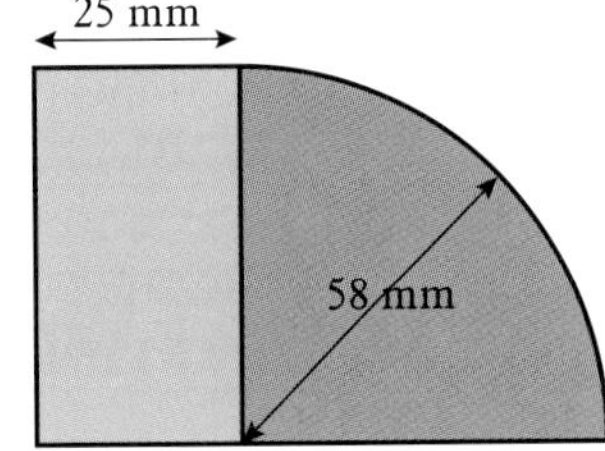

6 This is a rectangular-based pyramid.

a Draw the net.

b Work out the surface area.

10.8 m
11.7 m
12 m
8 m

7 Farmer Smith has 5 fields in a piece of land called Flowerdown. Each field is a trapezium. He grows vegetables in each field.

a Work out the area of each field.

b Work out the area of Flowerdown.

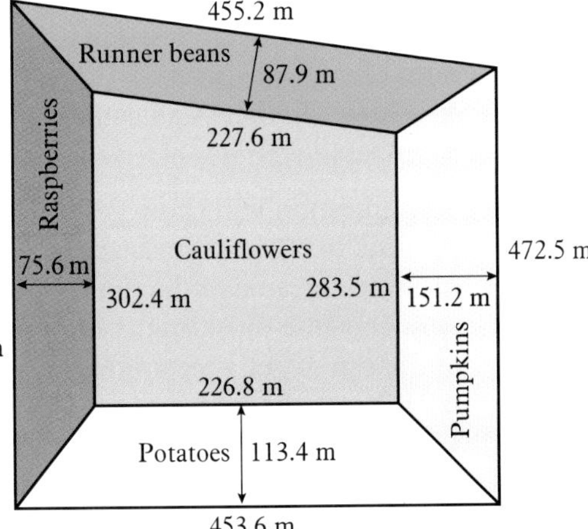

1 Look at this rectangle.
The area is the same as the perimeter.
Find another two rectangles like this.
You will need to use trial and improvement.

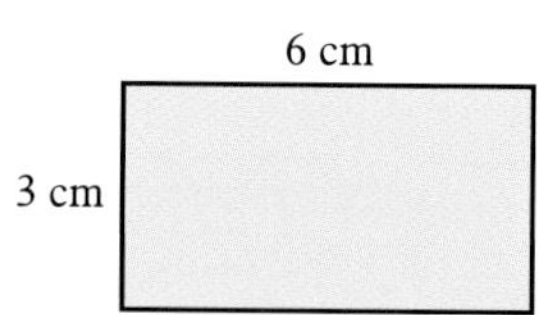

2 The points A, B, C, D and E have co-ordinates:
A (1, 2), B (5, 1), C (6, 4), D (6, 6) and E (2, 5).

a Copy these axes. Plot the points A, B, C, D and E. Join them up to get a pentagon.

b Plot the points S (1, 0), T (2, 0), U (5, 0) and V (6, 0).

c Find the area of the trapeziums:
(1) ABUS (2) BCVU (3) SAET (4) TEDV

d Use your answer to **c** to work out the area of the pentagon ABCDE.

e Write down another way you could work out this area.

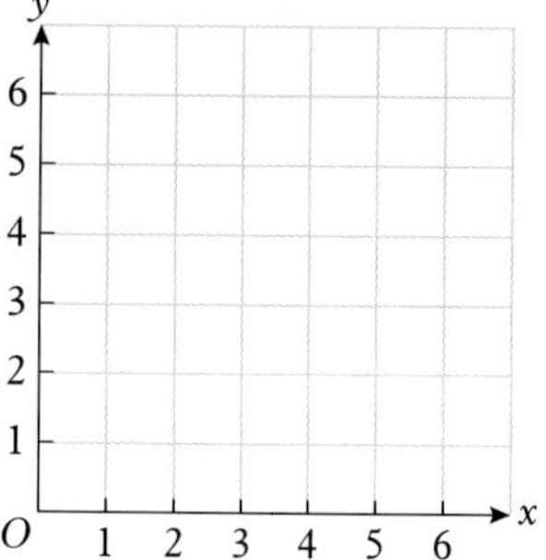

3 Alan's school has just got a new tartan track!
The diagram shows the 400 m track.
There are 8 lanes.
Each lane is 1.5 m wide.
Alan wants to work out some distances and areas. He calls you in to help.

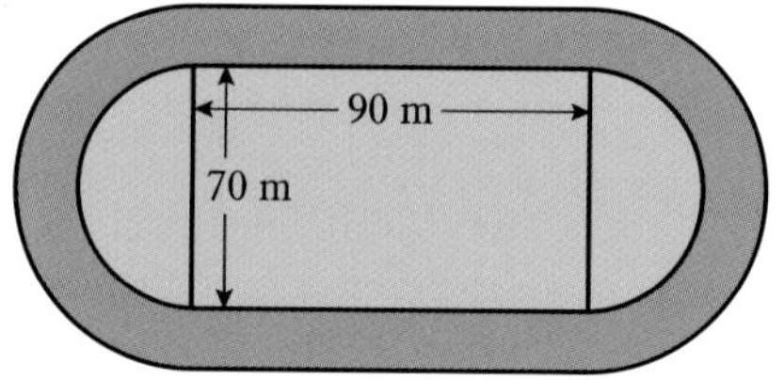

a Work out the distance round the inside of each lane.

b Work out the maximum length across the grass area.

c Work out the area of the grass inside the tartan track.

d Work out the area of the tartan track.

At a presentation ceremony Alan wants to fit the whole school into one of the grass semicircles. There are 880 pupils and 47 staff. Each person needs 1.2 m^2 of space.

e Show whether Alan can do this or not.

4 This question will show you how to find a formula to find the surface area of a cylinder.

a Find the area of the top and bottom.

Now imagine unrolling the side of the can to get a rectangle.

b What is the length of the rectangle?

c Find the total surface area of the can.

Use r for the radius and h for the height.

d Work out a formula for the surface area.

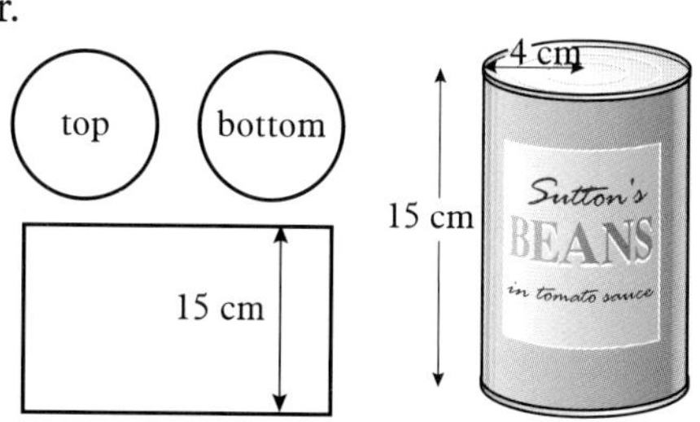

1 These shapes are drawn on 1 cm squared paper.

a Write down the area of this shape.

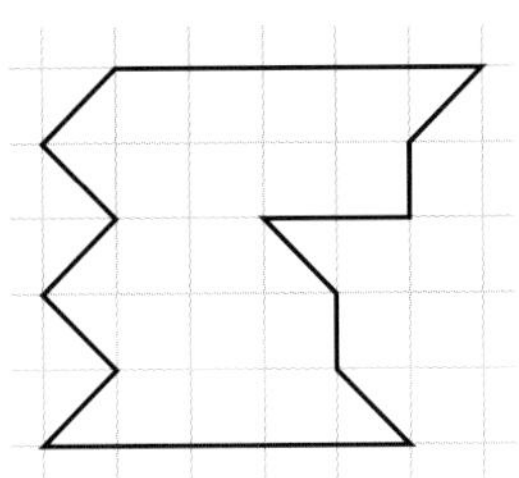

b Estimate the area of this shape.

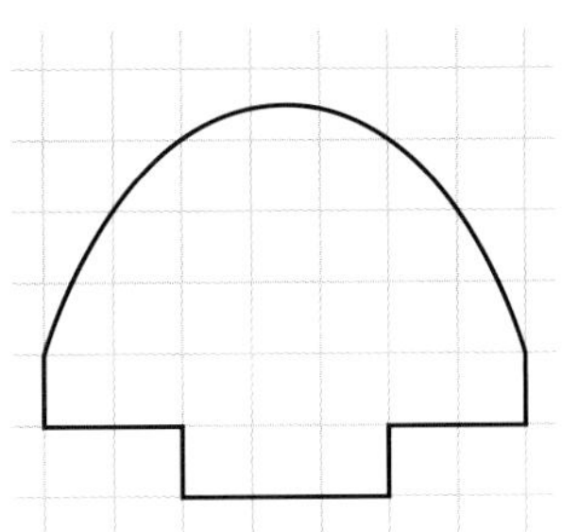

2 Find the area of each of these shapes.

a

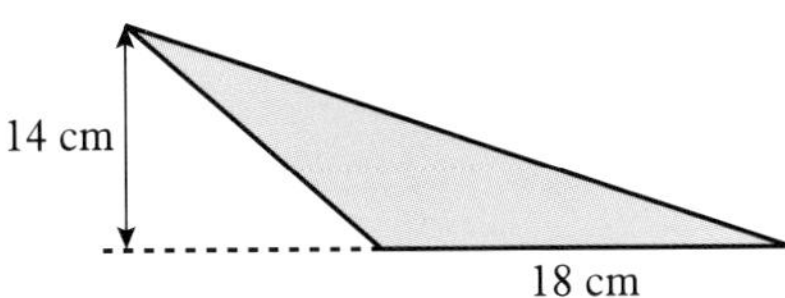

b

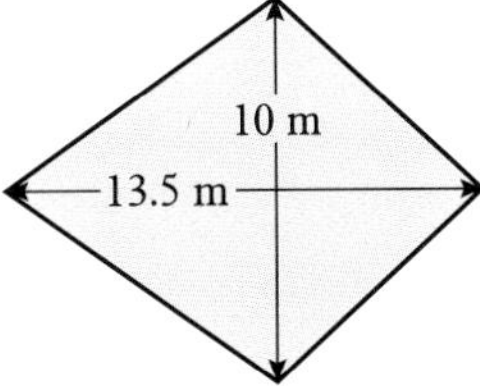

c

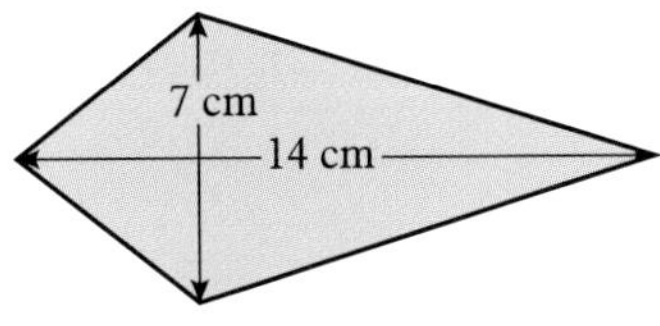

d

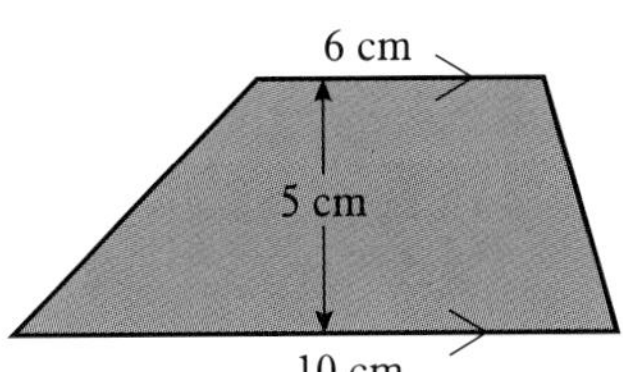

e

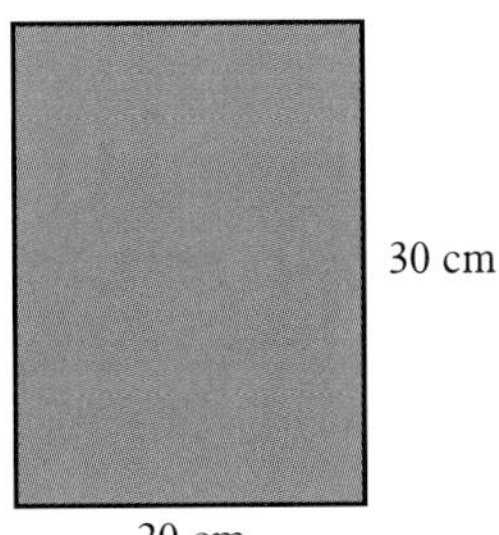

f

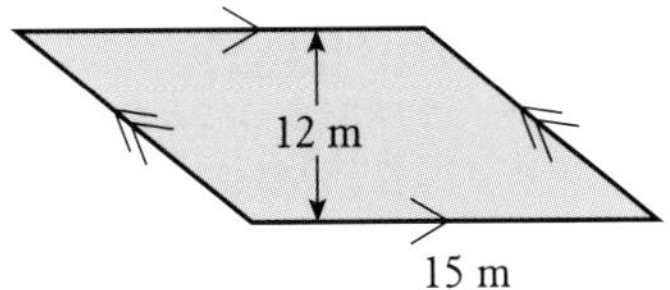

3 Find the area of each of these shapes.

a

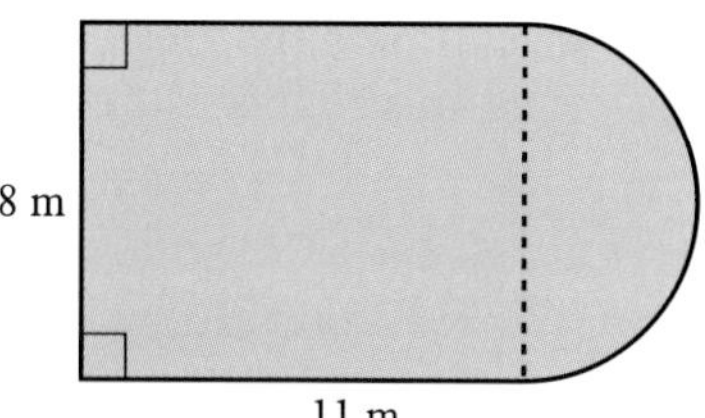

c

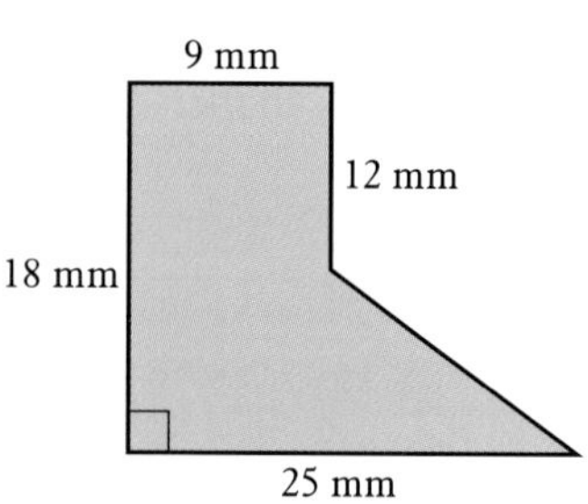

b

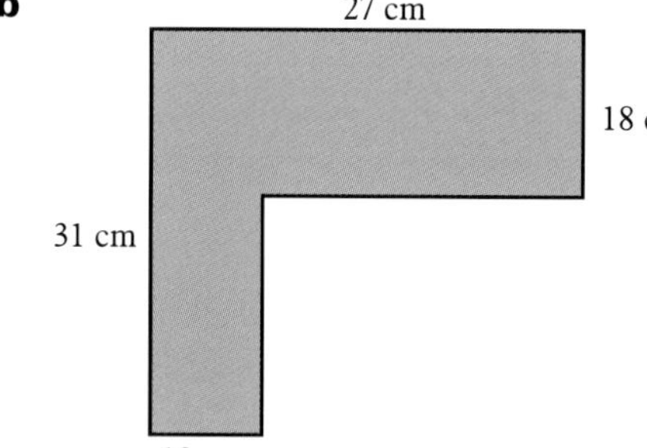

d

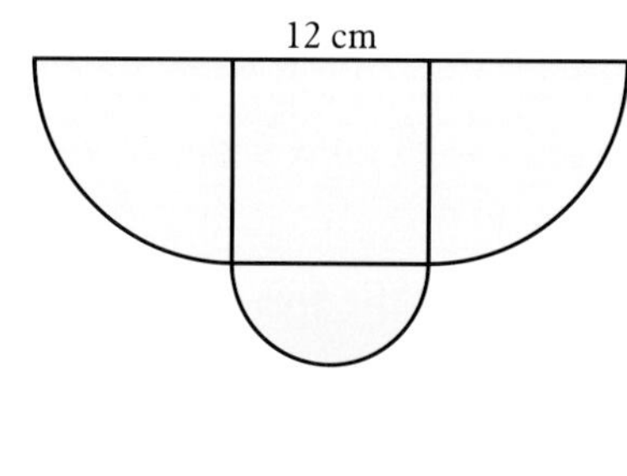

4 For each of these solids (1) Sketch the net.
(2) Work out the surface area.

a

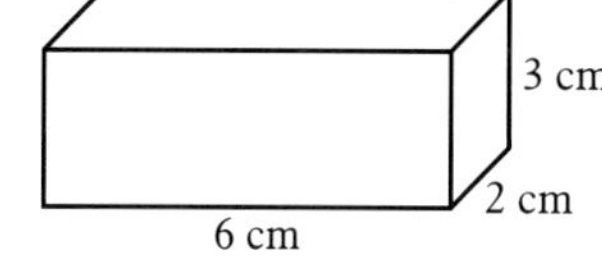

b

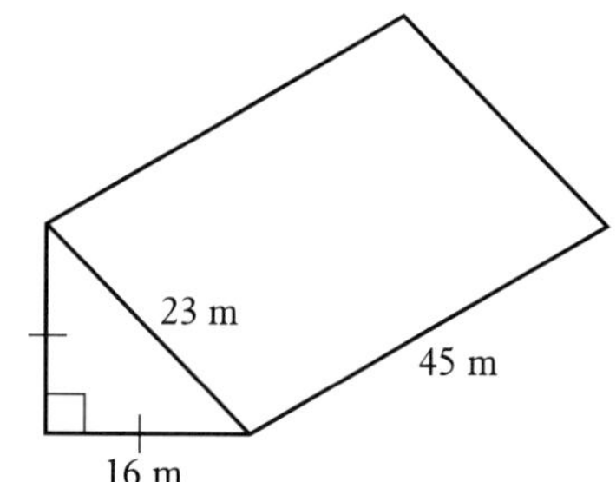

5 Change

a 3 cm^2 into mm^2

b 4 m^2 into cm^2

c 750 000 mm^2 into cm^2

d 5×10^{12} m^2 into km^2

28 Pattern power

CORE

1 Time for a change
Changing old money
Working with weird and wonderful units!

2 Sequences
Looking at number sequences
Finding missing terms
Using the formula for a sequence
Finding the formula when differences between terms are the same
Finding the formula when the second differences are the same

QUESTIONS

EXTENSION

TEST YOURSELF

1 Time for a change

This was the currency in the UK until 1971. It was much more difficult to change between units than it is today.

These are the conversion factors for old money.

4 farthings	= 1 penny	12 pence	= 1 shilling
2 halfpennies	= 1 penny	20 shillings	= 1 pound
1 halfcrown	= 2 shillings and six pence	1 sixpence	= 6 pence
1 florin	= 2 shillings	1 threepennybit	= 3 pence

Example Change each of these to the units given.

a £1 to shillings **b** 1 shilling to farthings

a There are 20 shillings in every pound.

So £1 = 20 shillings

This diagram shows how to convert from £ to shillings.

£ —— ×20 ——→ shillings

b There are 12 pence in every shilling.

So 1 shilling = 12 pence

There are 4 farthings in every penny.

So 1 shilling = 12 × 4 farthings
= 48 farthings

This diagram shows how to convert shillings to pence and pence to farthings.

shillings —— ×12 ——→ pence —— ×4 ——→ farthings

Exercise 28:1

1 **a** Copy this diagram.
Fill in the missing number.

pence —— × ...... ——→ farthings

b Change 1 penny to farthings.
c Change each of these into farthings:
(1) 3 pence (2) 7 pence (3) 11 pence

2 **a** Copy this diagram.
Fill in the missing numbers.

shilling —— × ...... ——→ pence —— × ...... ——→ farthings

b Change 1 shilling to farthings.
c Change each of these into farthings:
(1) 4 shillings (2) 8 shillings (3) 10 shillings

3 **a** Copy this diagram.
Fill in the missing numbers.

£ —— × ...... ——→ shillings —— × ...... ——→ pence

b Change £1 to pence.
c Change each of these into pence:
(1) £2
(2) £5
(3) £10

4 Change each of these to pence:
a 1 florin **c** 7 florins **e** 2 halfcrowns
b 3 florins **d** 1 halfcrown **f** 5 halfcrowns

5 Change each of these to farthings:
a 10 shillings **c** 1 florin **e** 1 halfcrown
b £1 **d** 6 florins **f** 4 halfcrowns

6 About 50 years ago the coins used in India were pies, annas and rupees.
There were 12 pies to an anna and 16 annas to a rupee.

a Copy this diagram.
Fill it in. anna —— × …… ⟶ pies

Draw diagrams to show how to convert:

b rupees to annas
c rupees to pies.

Convert each of these:

d 1 anna to pies	**f** 7 rupees to annas	**h** 4 rupees to pies
e 3 annas to pies	**g** 1 rupee to pies	**i** 48 annas to rupees

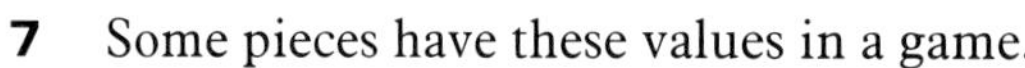

7 Some pieces have these values in a game.
1 castle = 5 cannons
1 cannon = 4 foot soldiers
1 horse = 2 foot soldiers

a Copy this diagram.
Fill it in.
castles —— …… ⟶ cannons —— …… ⟶ foot soldiers

b Change each of these to foot soldiers.

(1) 1 castle	(3) 1 cannon	(3) 1 horse
(2) 12 castles	(4) 7 cannons	(6) 3 horses

c How many horses is 1 castle worth?

8 In a far off land the units of currency are plars, sags, mors and gats.
1 plar = 9 sags, 1 sag = 10 mors and 2 plars = 3 gats.
Convert each of these:

a 5 plars to sags	**c** 3 plars to mors	**e** 6 gats to sags
b 4 plars to gats	**d** 50 mors to sags	● **f** 360 mors to gats

9 The village of Bartwell operates a barter system.
These are the values of some items.
1 hour of manual work = 2 sacks of potatoes
1 hour of babysitting = $\frac{1}{2}$ a sack of potatoes
1 hour of skilled work = 2 hours of manual work
1 week's supply of vegetables = 3 hours of manual work.
What is the value of:

a 2 hours of manual work in hours of babysitting
b 3 hours of skilled work in sacks of potatoes
c 4 weeks supply of vegetables in hours of skilled work?

2 Sequences

Fibonacci was an Italian mathematician.
He knew how important and useful patterns in numbers can be.
He is famous for discovering a special sequence called the Fibonacci numbers.
The Fibonacci numbers are

1, 1, 2, 3, 5, 8, 13, 21, 34, 55, 89, …

Each number is obtained by adding the previous two.
The amazing thing about the Fibonacci numbers is how many times they appear in nature.
Look for Fibonacci numbers in the pictures.

Number sequence A **number sequence** is a list of numbers that follow a rule.

Term Each number in a sequence is called a **term**.
The rule tells you how to get from one term to the next.

Example

a Write down the rule for this sequence
40, 35, 30, 25, 20, …

b Write down the next two terms.

a

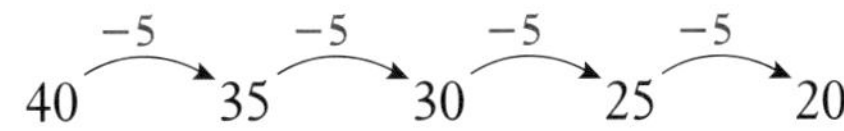

Each new term is 5 less than the previous term.
The rule is **subtract** 5.

b The next two terms are 15 and 10.

Exercise 28:2

For each of questions **1** to **4** write down:

a the rule for the sequence **b** the missing terms.

1 5, 11, …, 23, …, 35

2 7, 3, …, −5, −9, …

3 2, 6, 18, …, …, 486

4 …, 800, 400, 200, 100, …

5 Look at this sequence of numbers: 8, 9, 12, 21
The rule that has been used to get the sequence is
'subtract 5 and then multiply by 3'.
Write down the next two numbers in the sequence.

6 The number of dots in these patterns form a sequence.

a Write down the number of dots in each of these patterns.
b Write down the rule for the sequence.
c Write down the next two terms in the sequence.

7 The first term of a sequence is 8.
The rule is 'subtract 3 and multiply by 2'.
Write down the first four terms of the sequence.

8 The formula for this sequence is $4n$: 4, 8, 12, 16, 20, …
Write down the first 5 terms of the sequence with the formula $6n$.

9 Write down the formula for each of these sequences:
a 2, 4, 6, 8, 10, …
b 5, 10, 15, 20, 25, …
c 12, 24, 36, 48, 60, …
d 20, 40, 60, 80, 100, …

10 The formula for a sequence is $5n - 1$.
a Copy this table to find the first three terms. Fill it in.

1st term	$5 \times 1 - 1 \;= 5 - 1 \;= 4$
2nd term	$5 \times 2 - 1 \;= \ldots - 1 = \ldots$
3rd term	$5 \times \ldots - 1 = \ldots - 1 = \ldots$

b Use the formula to find the 10th term.

11 The formula for a sequence is $2n + 4$.
The first three terms are 6, 8, 10.
Find the next two terms.

12 A sequence has the formula $6n - 3$.
Write down:
a the first three terms **b** the 8th term **c** the 20th term.

Finding formulas that contain n

Look at this sequence. Find a formula for the nth term.

6 $\xrightarrow{+7}$ 13 $\xrightarrow{+7}$ 20 $\xrightarrow{+7}$ 27 $\xrightarrow{+7}$ 34

You can draw a sequence diagram to find the formula for the sequence.
The rule for this sequence is **add 7** so it must be related to $7n$.
Write the sequence $7n$ underneath. Compare the two sequences.

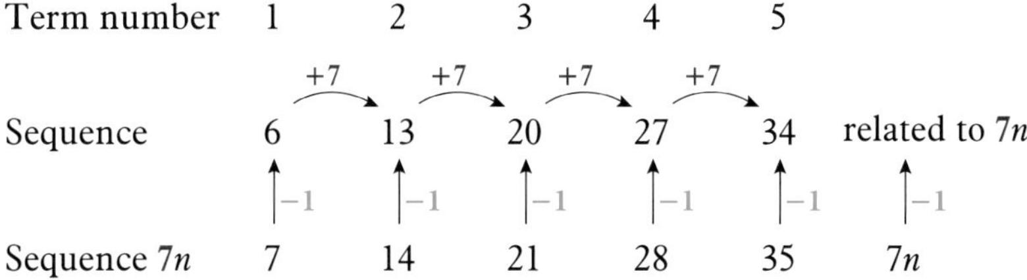

You need to subtract 1 from every term in $7n$ to make the sequence.
So the formula for the nth term of the sequence is $7n - 1$.

Exercise 28:3

1 **a** Copy the sequence diagram for the sequence 4, 7, 10, 13, 16, …
Fill in the missing numbers.

Term number	1	2	3	4	5	
	…	…	…	…		
Sequence	4	7	10	13	16	related to …n
	↑…	↑…	↑…	↑…	↑…	↑…
Sequence …n	3	6	…	…	…	…n

b Copy this. Fill in the spaces.

You need to ………………… every term in ……… to make the sequence.

So the formula for the nth term of the sequence is ………………

2 **a** Copy the sequence diagram for the sequence 3, 8, 13, 18, 23, …
Fill in the missing numbers.

Term number	1	2	3	4	5	
	… →	… →	… →	… →		
Sequence	3	8	13	18	23	related to …n
	↑ …	↑ …	↑ …	↑ …	↑ …	↑ …
Sequence …n	…	…	…	…	…	…n

b Copy this. Fill in the spaces.

You need to ………………… every term in ……… to make the sequence.

So the formula for the nth term of the sequence is ………………

For each of the sequences in questions **3–8**:
a draw a sequence diagram **b** find the formula for the nth term.

3 6, 8, 10, 12, 14, …

4 3, 7, 11, 15, 19, …

5 2, 9, 16, 23, 30, …

6 11, 19, 27, 35, 43, …

7 4, 14, 24, 34, 44, …

8 14, 23, 32, 41, 50, …

9 **a** Write this shape sequence as a number sequence.

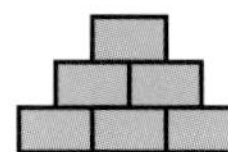 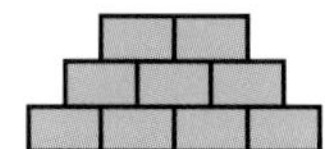 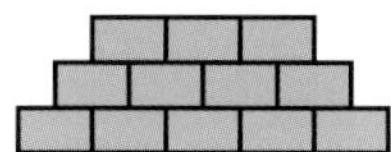 

b Use a sequence diagram to work out the formula for the nth term.

10 **a** Write the number of sticks in these patterns as a number sequence.

 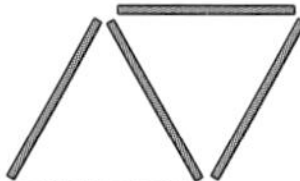  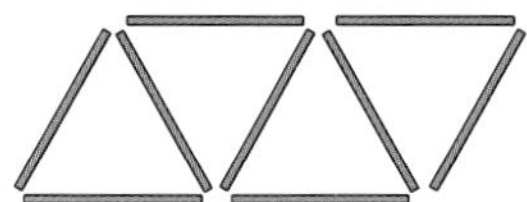

b Write down the next two terms in the sequence.
c Use a sequence diagram to work out the formula for the nth term.

Finding formulas that contain n^2

Example Find a formula for the nth term of the number sequence
5, 19, 41, 71, 109, ...

Look at the differences between the terms:
These differences are not the same.
Look at the differences between these numbers:
These are called the **second differences**.

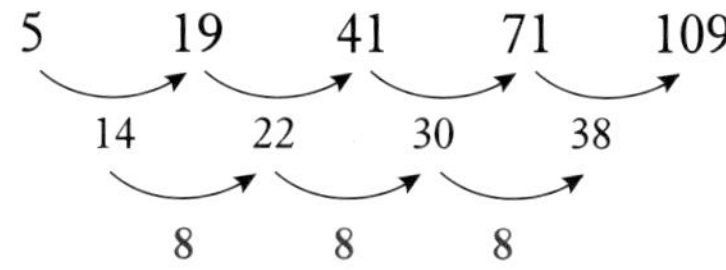

If the **second differences are the same**, the formula for the ***n*th term contains n^2**.
The number in front of n^2 is **half** the constant difference.

In the example the constant difference is 8.
The number in front of n^2 is half of 8, which is 4.
The first part of the formula is $4n^2$.

Make a table to help you find the rest of the formula.
Fill in the value of $4n^2$ for each term.

Term number	1	2	3	4	5
Sequence	5	19	41	71	109
	↑+1	↑+3	↑+5	↑+7	↑+9
Value of $4n^2$	4	16	36	64	100
Now look for what you need to add to get the sequence.	1	3	5	7	9

You now find the formula for this part of the sequence as before

Term number	1	2	3	4	5
Sequence	1	3	5	7	9
The differences are all +2	+2	+2	+2	+2	↑−1
Value of $2n$	2	4	6	8	10

The formula for the second part is $2n - 1$.

You now put the two parts of the formula together.
The formula for the nth term of the sequence is $4n^2 + 2n - 1$.
Check the formula by finding term number 5.
$n = 5$, $4n^2 + 2n - 1 = 100 + 10 - 1 = 109$ ✓

Exercise 28:4

1 **a** Copy the sequence diagram for the sequence 8, 18, 34, 56, 84, …
Fill in the missing numbers.

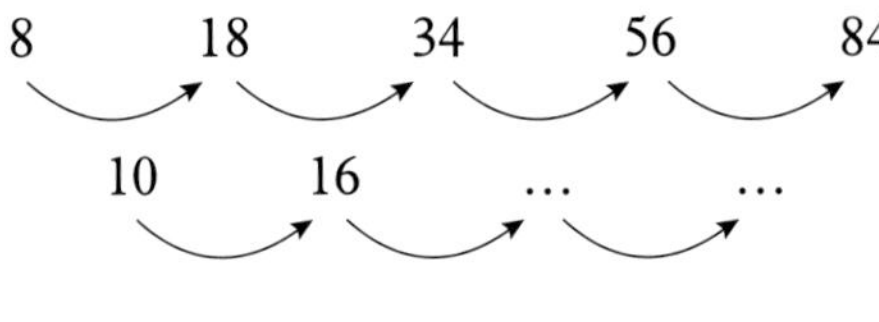

The second differences are the same.

b Copy this. Fill in the missing numbers.
The constant difference is …
The number in front of n^2 is half of …, which is …
The first part of the formula is …n^2.

c Copy this to find the rest of the formula.
Fill in the missing numbers.

Term number	1	2	3	4	5
Sequence	8	18	34	56	84
Value of …n^2	…	…	…	…	…
Now look for what you need to add to get the sequence.	…	…	…	…	…

To find the formula for this part of the sequence

Term number	1	2	3	4	5
Sequence	…	…	…	…	…

The differences are all …

Value of …n	…	…	…	…	…

The formula for the second part is ………………

The formula for the nth term of the sequence is ………………

Check the formula by finding term number 5

$n = 5$, …………… = …………… = ………

2 **a** Copy the sequence diagram for the sequence 0, 9, 22, 39, 60, …
Fill in the missing numbers.

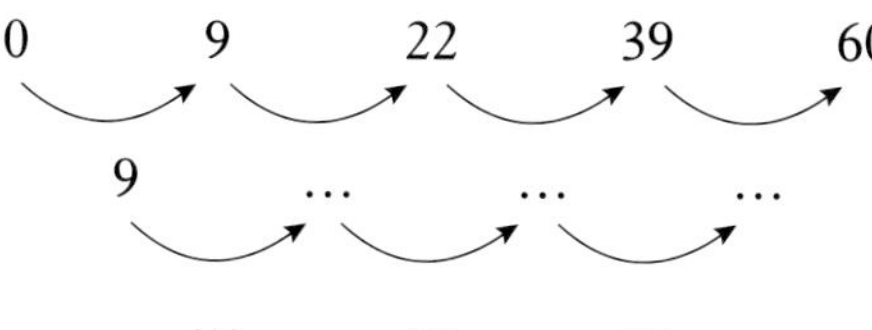

The second differences are the same.

b Copy this. Fill in the missing numbers.
The constant difference is …
The number in front of n^2 is half of …, which is …
The first part of the formula is …n^2.

c Copy this to find the rest of the formula.
Fill in the missing numbers.

Term number	1	2	3	4	5
Sequence	0	9	22	39	60
Value of …n^2	…	…	…	…	…
Now look for what you need to add to get the sequence.	…	…	…	…	…

To find the formula for this part of the sequence

Term number	1	2	3	4	5
Sequence	…	…	…	…	…

The differences are all …

Value of …n	…	…	…	…	…

The formula for the second part is ………………

The formula for the nth term of the sequence is ………………

Check the formula by finding term number 5

$n = 5$, …………… = …………… = ………

For the number sequences in questions **3** to **10**:

a Find the formula for the nth term.

b Find the 5th term using your formula.
Check to see that it is correct.

3 15, 22, 31, 42, 55, …

4 4, 13, 26, 43, 64, …

5 3, 7, 13, 21, 31, …

6 5, 12, 21, 32, 45, …

7 3, 14, 31, 54, 83 …

8 6, 23, 48, 81, 122, …

9 8, 19, 34, 53, 76, …

● **10** 2, 10, 24, 44, 70, …

11 The formula for a sequence is $5n^2 - 2n + 1$.
a Copy this table to find the first four terms.
Fill it in.

1st term	$5 \times 1 - 2 + 1$	$= 5 - 2 + 1$	$= \ldots$
2nd term	$5 \times 4 - 4 + 1$	$= 20 - 4 + 1$	$= \ldots$
3rd term	$5 \times \ldots - \ldots + 1$	$= \ldots - \ldots + \ldots$	$= \ldots$
4th term	$5 \times \ldots - \ldots + \ldots$	$= \ldots - \ldots + \ldots$	$= \ldots$

b Find the 6th term.
c Find the 10th term.

12 The formula for a sequence is $3n^2 + n - 3$.
a Copy this table to find the first four terms.
Fill it in.

1st term	$3 \times 1 + 1 - 3$	$= 3 + 1 - 3$	$= 1$
2nd term	$3 \times 4 + 2 - 3$	$= 12 + 2 - 3$	$= \ldots$
3rd term	$3 \times \ldots + \ldots - 3$	$= \ldots + \ldots - \ldots$	$= \ldots$
4th term	$3 \times \ldots + \ldots - \ldots$	$= \ldots + \ldots - \ldots$	$= \ldots$

b Find the 10th term.
c Find the 11th term.
d Is the number 349 a term in the sequence? Explain your answer.

13 The formula for a sequence is $5n^2 + 4n - 6$.

a Find the first 4 terms.

b Find the 10th term.

14 The formula for a sequence is $2n^2 + n - 7$.

a Find the first 4 terms.

b Find the 10th term.

c Use trial and improvement to find which term has the value 734.

15 The formula for a sequence is $5n^2 + 4n - 6$.

a Find the first 4 terms.

b Find the 10th term.

c Use trial and improvement to find which term has the value 5571.

16 Which of these numbers belong to the sequence with the formula $4n^2 + 5n - 12$?

a 624 **b** 1698 **c** 1229

17 The numbers of planes in these patterns form a sequence.

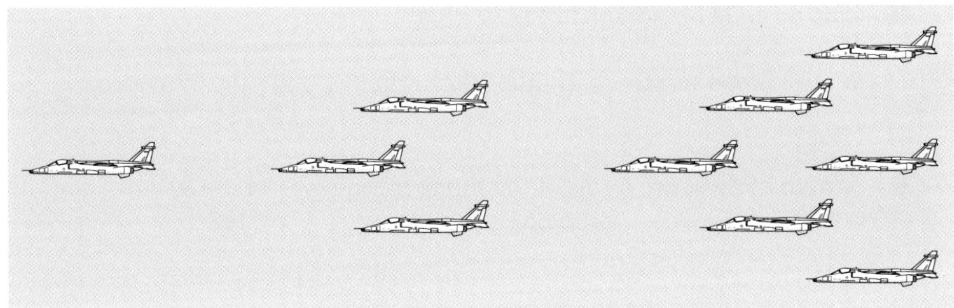

a Write down the number of planes in each of these patterns.

b Write down the special name for this sequence.

c Write down the first five terms of this sequence.

d Use a sequence diagram to find the formula for the nth term.

e Find the 4th term using your formula to check that it is correct.

1 A player can be awarded units of credit in a game.
The units of credit are yings, mangs, rungs and tongs.

1 ying = 8 mangs
1 mang = 5 rungs
1 rung = 3 tongs

Work out the value of:

a 4 yings in mangs
b 5 yings in rungs
c 9 tongs in rungs
d 15 rungs in mangs
e 30 tongs in mangs
f 3 yings in tongs.

2 The first term of a sequence is 256.
The rule is 'divide by 2'.
Write down the first 6 terms of the sequence.

3 The first term of a sequence is 7.
The rule is 'subtract 4 and multiply by 2'.
Write down the first 6 terms of the sequence.

4 The formula for a sequence is $12n - 9$.
Write down:

a the first 4 terms **b** the 10th term **c** the 20th term.

5 The formula for a sequence is $20 - 2n$.
Write down:

a the first 4 terms **b** the 10th term **c** the 25th term.

6 Which of these are terms of the number sequence $11n + 8$?

a 33 **b** 63 **c** 118

7 A sequence has the formula $3n - 6$.
Use trial and improvement to find which term has a value of 123.

8 A sequence has the formula $15 - 4n$.

a Find the first 5 terms.
b Find the 30th term.
c Use trial and improvement to find which term has a value of -189.

9 **a** Copy the sequence diagram for the sequence 9, 15, 21, 27, 33, …
Fill in the missing numbers.

Term number	1	2	3	4	5	
Sequence	9	15	21	27	33	related to …n
Sequence …n	…	…	…	…	…	…

b Copy this. Fill in the spaces.

You need to ………………… every term in ……… to make the sequence.

So the formula for the nth term of the sequence is ………………

10 For each of these sequences:
a draw a sequence diagram
b find the formula for the nth term.

(1) 7, 11, 15, 19, 23, …
(2) 1, 7, 13, 19, 25, …
(3) 9, 14, 19, 24, 29, …
(4) −1, 1, 3, 5, 9, …

11 The formula for a sequence is $6n^2 - 5n + 4$.
a Find the first 4 terms.
b Find the 10th term.
c Use trial and improvement to find which term has a value of 10 883.

For the number sequences in questions **12** to **17**:
a Find the formula for the nth term.
b Find the 5th term using your formula.
Check to see that it is correct.

12 3, 11, 21, 33, 47, …

13 7, 17, 31, 49, 71, …

14 1, 11, 27, 49, 77, …

15 4, 22, 50, 88, 136, …

16 0, 11, 26, 45, 68, …

17 −3, 10, 31, 60, 97, …

1 2 bings = 5 bongs　　1 bong = 6 bangs
3 bungs = 4 bongs　　3 bengs = 10 bings

Find the value of:

a 8 bings in bongs
b 30 bings in bengs
c 8 bings in bangs
d 96 bangs in bungs
e 75 bongs in bengs
f 15 bungs in bings
g 48 bangs in bungs
h 15 bengs in bangs

2 Find a formula for the nth term of each of these number sequences:

a $-1, 7, 15, 23, 31, \ldots$　　**b** $-7, -3, 1, 5, 9, \ldots$

3 The formula for the nth term of a sequence is $2n^3 - 3n^2$.
Which term has the value:

a 27　　**b** 175　　**c** 3887

4 The formula for the nth term of a sequence is $3n^2 + n - 5$.

a Find the first four terms.
b Find the 15th term.
c Use trial and improvement to find which term has the value 2049.

5 Find a formula for the nth term of the sequence

$$-2, -1, 2, 7, 14, \ldots$$

For the number sequences in questions **6** to **9**:

a Find the formula for the nth term.
b Find the 5th term using your formula.
Check to see that it is correct.

6 3, 3, 5, 9, 15, …

7 2, 6, 16, 32, 54, …

8 7, 12, 21, 34, 51, …

9 0, 12, 34, 66, 108, …

1 Gary has made a new board game based on the Civil Wars. Different pieces are used in the game and have different values.

The pieces are: cannon, horse, gun, archer, foot soldier, arrow.

1 cannon = 5 horses   1 horse = 2 guns   1 gun = 20 arrows

1 horse = 3 archers   2 archers = 5 foot soldiers

Find the value of

a 5 horses in guns

b 2 cannons in arrows

c 15 archers in horses

d 4 horses in foot soldiers

2 The first term of a sequence is 10 and the rule is 'multiply by 2 and subtract 12'.
Find the first 5 terms of the sequence.

3 The formula for a sequence is $7n + 3$.
Write down:

a the first 4 terms

b the 10th term

4 A sequence has the formula $250 + 27n$

a Find the 50th term.

b Use trial and improvement to find which term has the value 709.

5 **a** Write down the first 5 terms of the sequence with the formula
(1) $3n$ (2) $4n$ (3) $5n$

b Write down the formula for each of these sequences
(1) 7, 14, 21, 28, 35, …
(2) 11, 22, 33, 44, 55, …
(3) 15, 30, 45, 60, 75, …

6 These sequences are all related to the sequence $4n$.
Write down the formula for the nth term of each sequence.

a 5, 9, 13, 17, 21, …

b 13, 17, 21, 25, 29, …

c 1, 5, 9, 13, 17, …

7 Copy the sequence diagram for the sequence 2, 8, 14, 20, 26, …
Fill in the missing numbers.

Term number	1	2	3	4	5	
Sequence	2	8	14	20	26	related to …n
Sequence …n	…	…	…	…	…	…

You need to ……………… every term in ……… to make the sequence.
So the formula for the nth term of the sequence is ………..

8 Look at the sequence 4, 15, 32, 55, 84, …

a Draw a sequence diagram.

b Find a formula for the nth term.

9 A sequence has the formula $n^2 - 5n + 10$

a Find the first 5 terms.

b Find the 20th term.

c Use trial and improvement to find the term which has the value 1486.

10 The nth term of a sequence is $\frac{16 - 2n}{n + 1}$

a Write down the first three terms of this sequence.

b Which term of the sequence has the value 1?

29 Angles and bearings

CORE

1 Angles
Measuring and drawing angles
Calculating angles – on a straight line
– around a point
Calculating opposite angles
Calculating angles in triangles and quadrilaterals
Looking at angles on parallel lines
Calculating angles in circles
Discovering the circle theorems

2 Get your bearings
Calculating bearings
Solving bearings problems
Drawing to scale

QUESTIONS

EXTENSION

TEST YOURSELF

1 Angles

The angles in this bike frame are very important to its strength.

Designing all sorts of structures involves calculating angles. Look at the entrance to the Louvre in Paris on the cover of this book!

Here are some angle rules that you might remember.

Full turn There are 360° in a **full turn**.

Half turn There are 180° in a **half turn**.

Quarter turn A **quarter turn** is 90°.
This is known as a **right angle**.

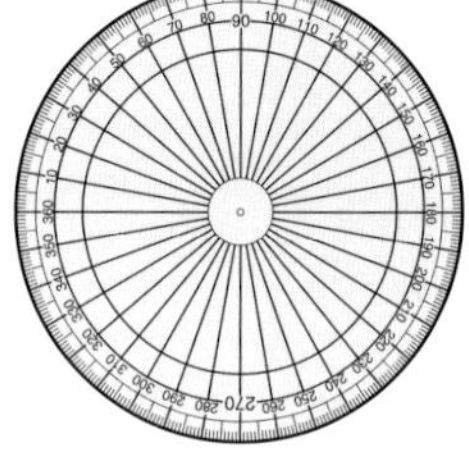

Acute angle An **acute angle** is an angle less than 90°.

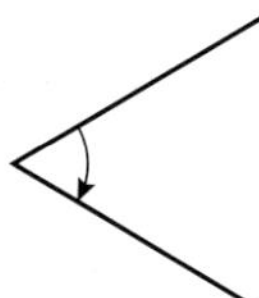

Obtuse angle An **obtuse angle** is between 90° and 180°.

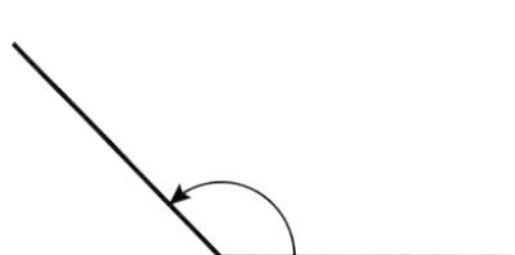

Reflex angle A **reflex angle** is bigger than 180°.

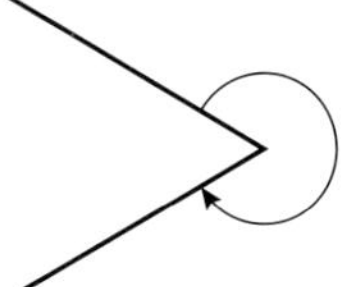

Exercise 29:1

1 Look at each of these angles.
Write down whether they are acute, right, obtuse or reflex angles.

a

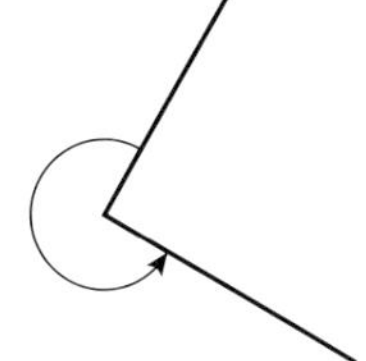

c

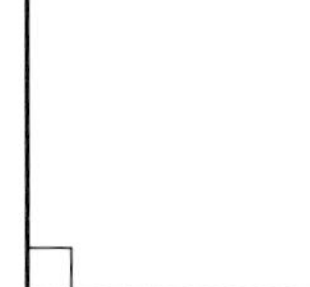

e

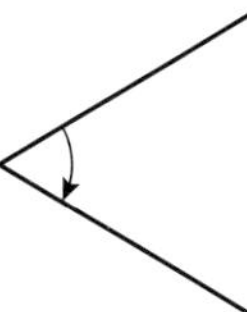

b

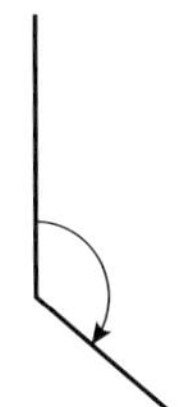

d

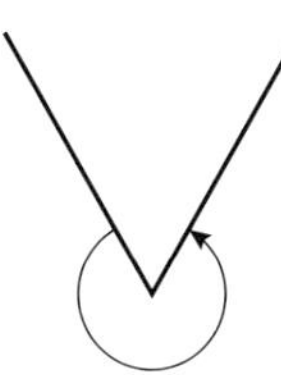

f

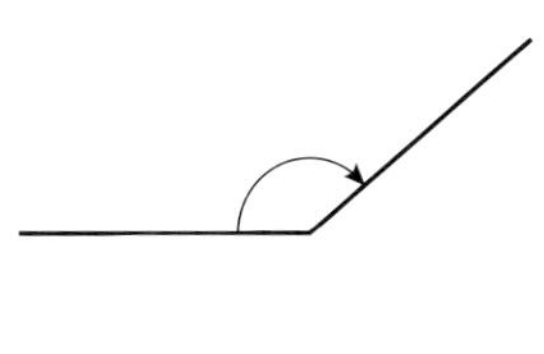

2 Use an angle measurer or protractor to draw each of these angles.
Write under each one whether it is an acute, right, obtuse or reflex angle.
a 30° **b** 135° **c** 210° **d** 342° **e** 193°

3 Use an angle measurer or protractor to measure each of these angles.

a

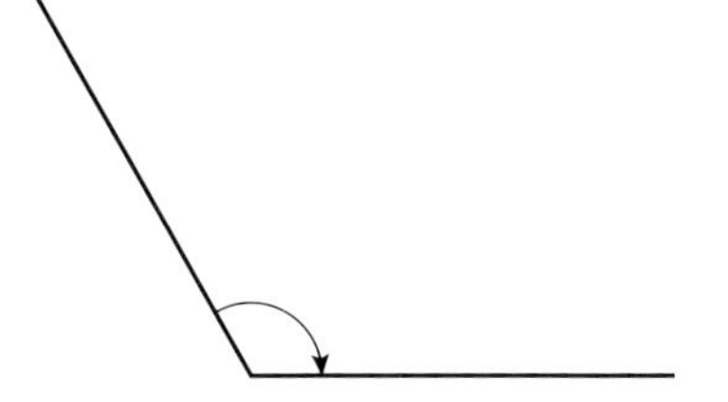

c

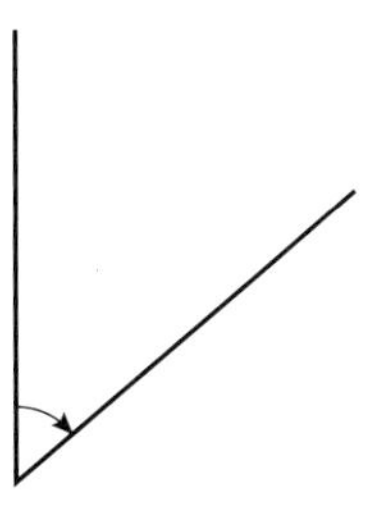

b

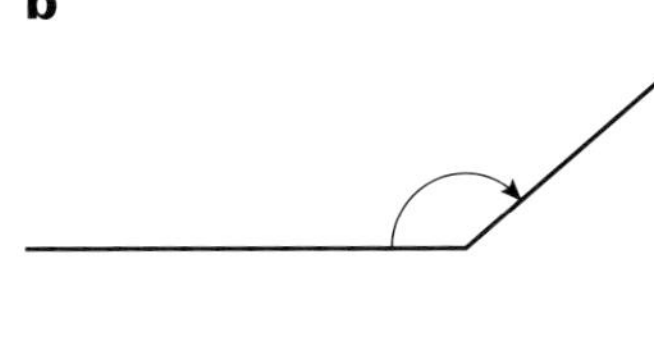

d

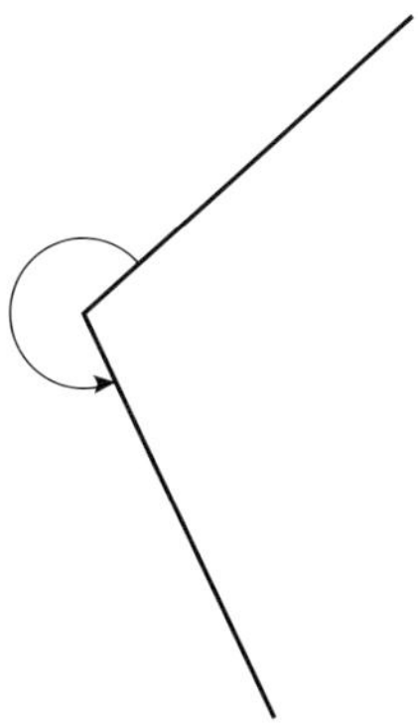

4 Estimate the size of each of these angles.
Measure them afterwards to check your answers.

a

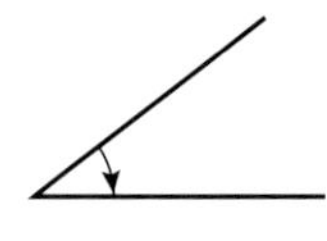

b

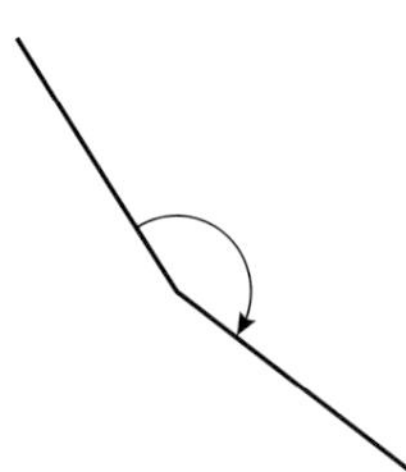

c

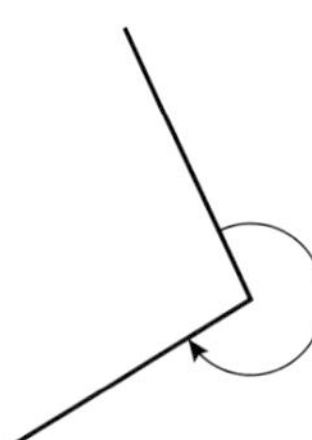

Angles on a straight line add up to 180°. This is because a half turn makes a straight line.

You can use this rule to calculate angles.

Example Work out the angle marked $a°$.

The angles add up to 180°.
So $a° = 180° - 70°$
$= 110°$

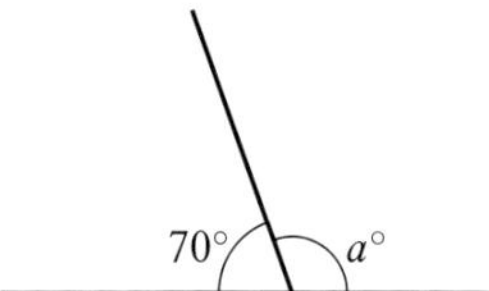

Exercise 29:2

Calculate the angles marked with letters.

1

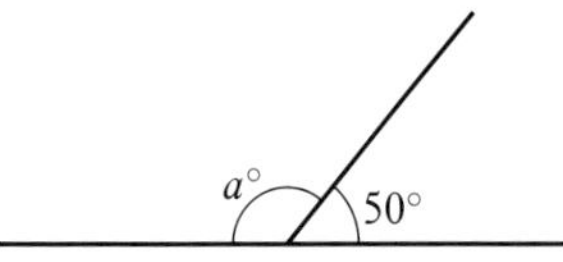

4

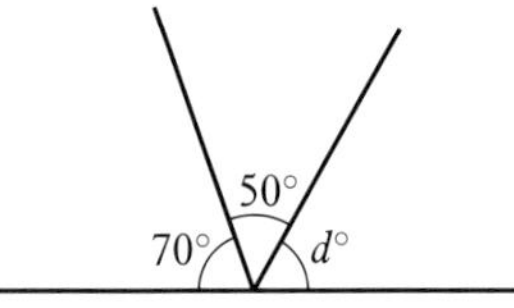

2

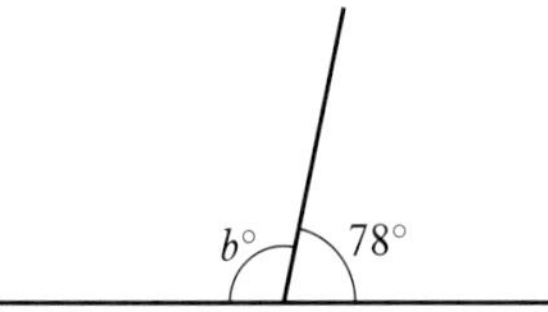

5

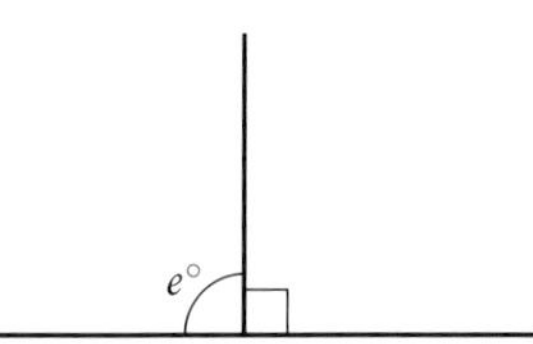

3

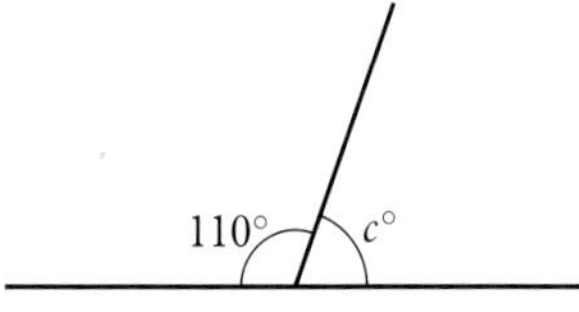

● **6**

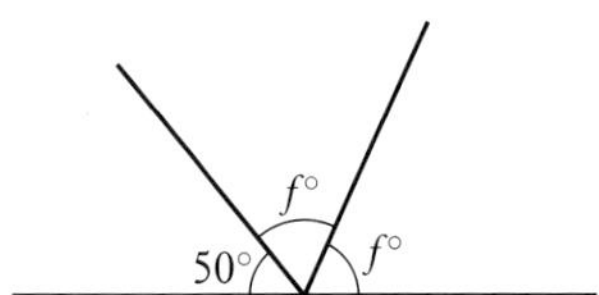

Angles around a point add up to 360°.
This is because they make up a full turn.

Example Work out the angle marked $b°$.

The angles add up to 360°.

So $b° = 360° - 70° - 120°$
$= 170°$

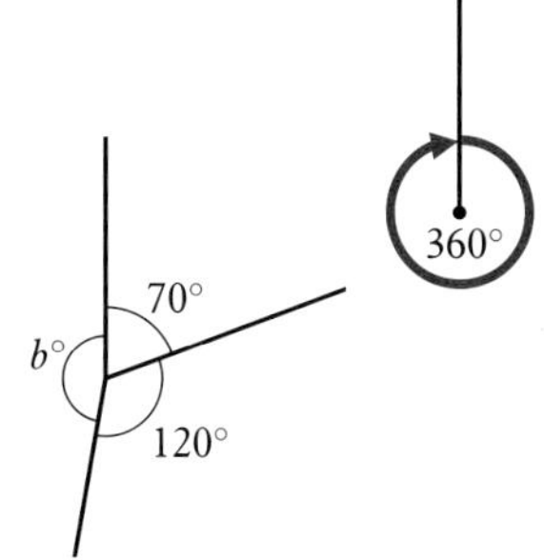

Calculate the angles marked with letters.

7

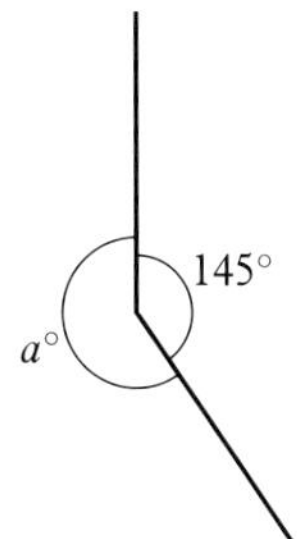

8

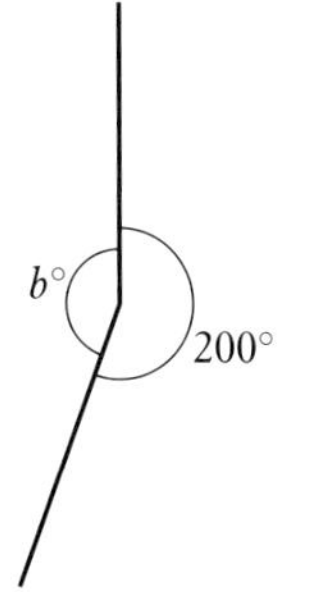

9

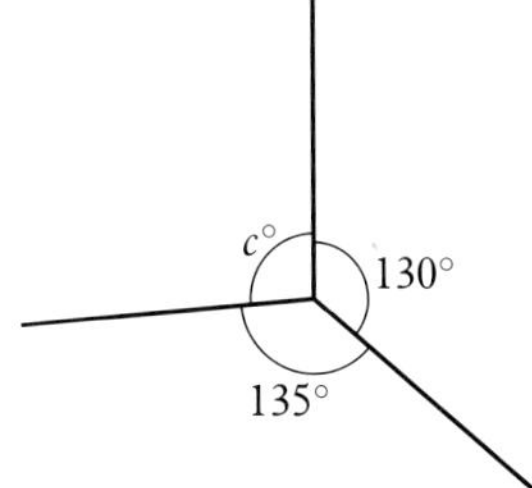

10

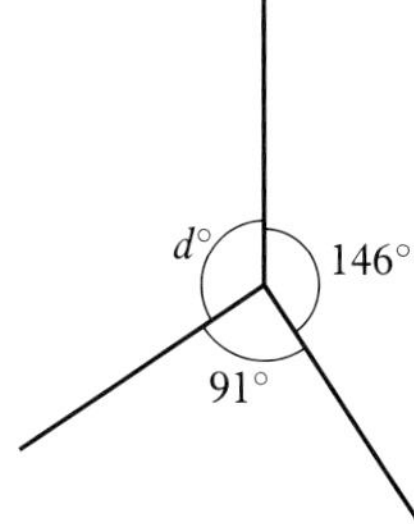

11

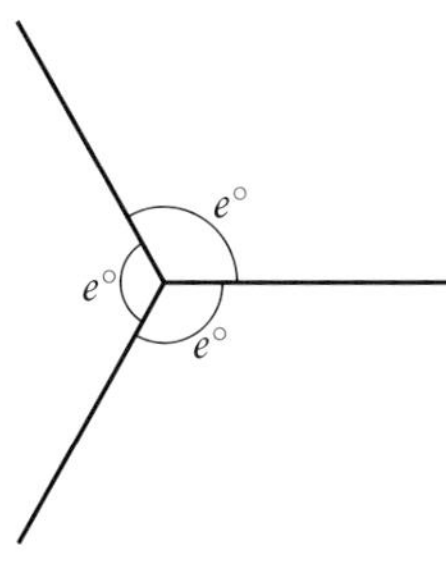

12

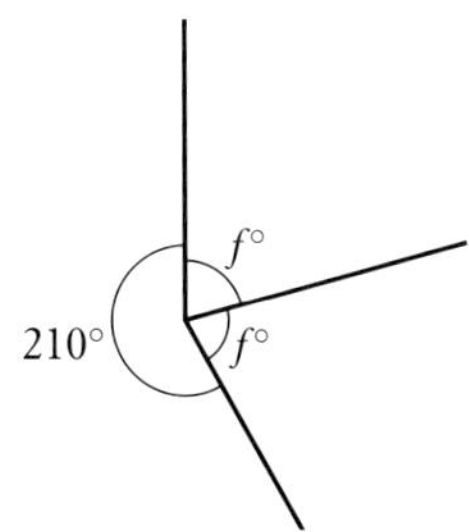

Opposite angles Angles that are opposite each other in a cross are equal.
They are known as **opposite angles**!

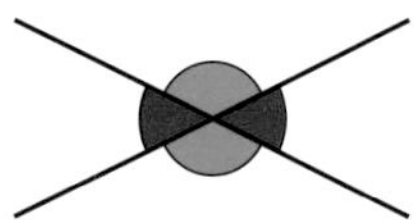

Example Find the angles marked with letters.

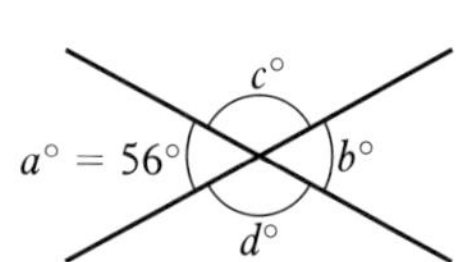

$b°$ is opposite $a°$ and so it is the same angle:
$b° = 56$

$c°$ makes a straight line with $a°$.
This means that $a° + c° = 180°$.
$c° = 180° - 56° = 124°$

$d°$ is opposite $c°$ and so it is the same angle:
$d° = 124°$

Exercise 29:3

Calculate the angles marked with letters.

1

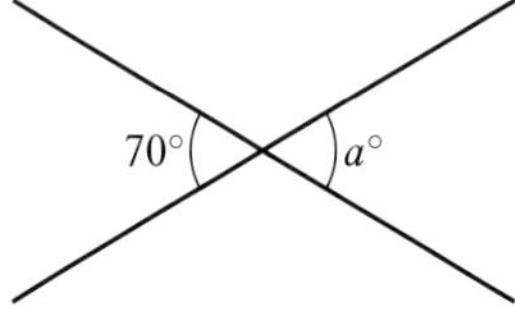

4

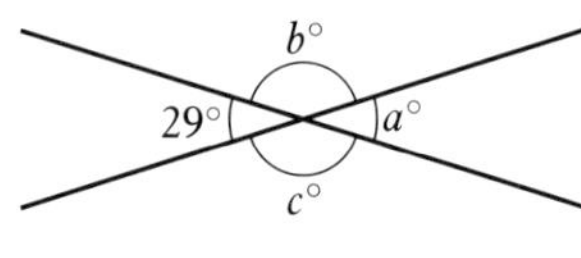

2

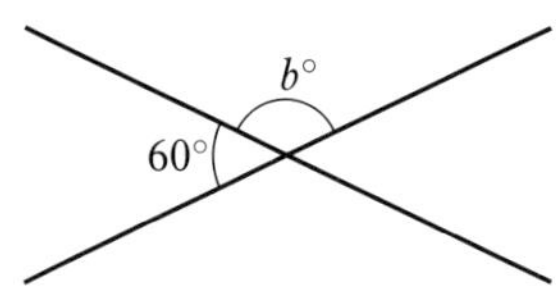

5

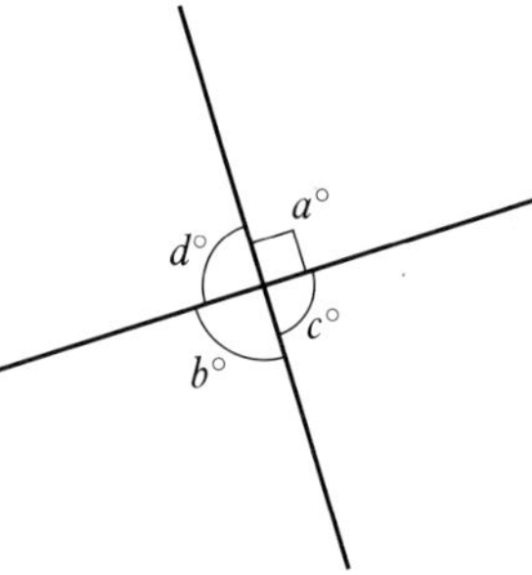

3

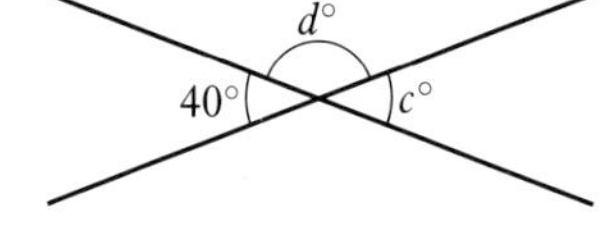

6

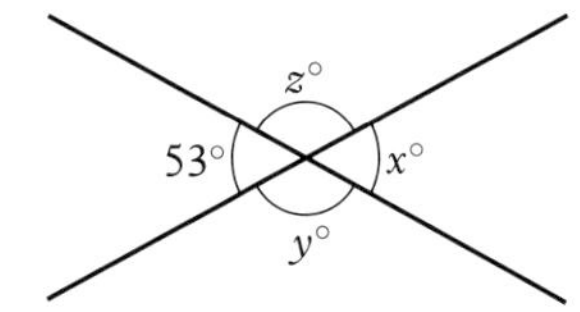

Angles in a triangle

Angles in a triangle add up to 180°.

Example

Find the angle marked $x°$.

The angles add up to 180°.
So $x° = 180° - 73° - 46°$
$x° = 61°$

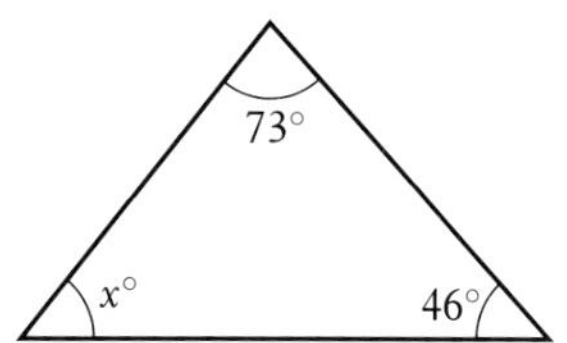

Exercise 29:4

Calculate the angles marked with letters.

1

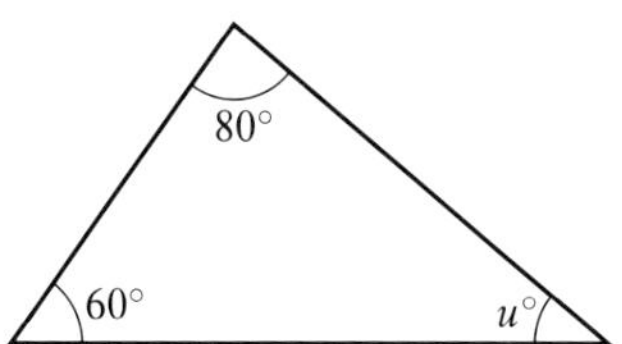

4

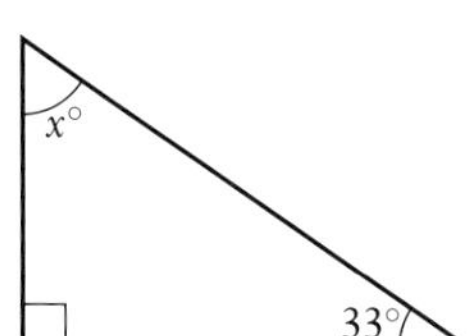

2

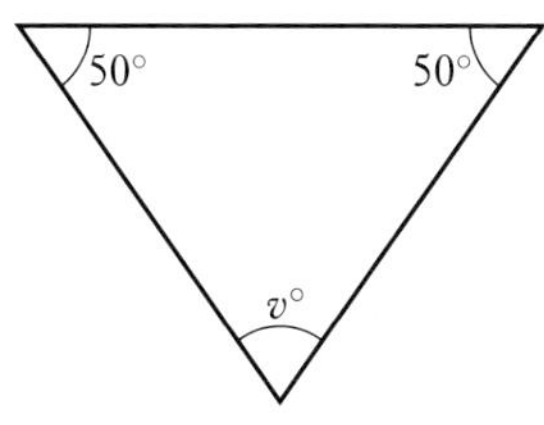

5

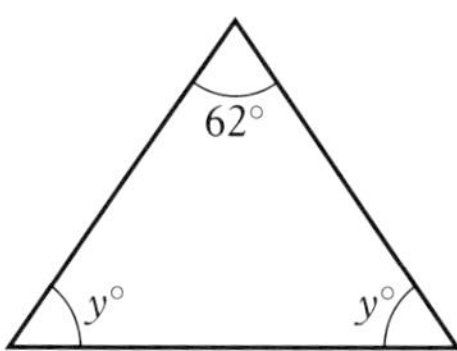

3

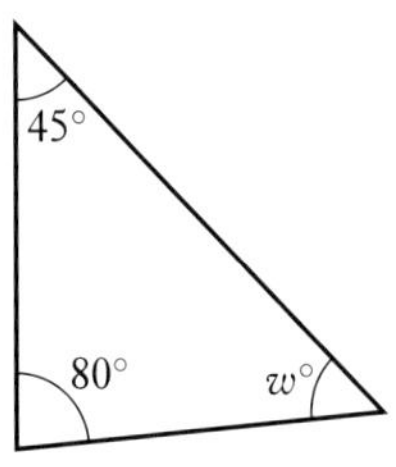

6

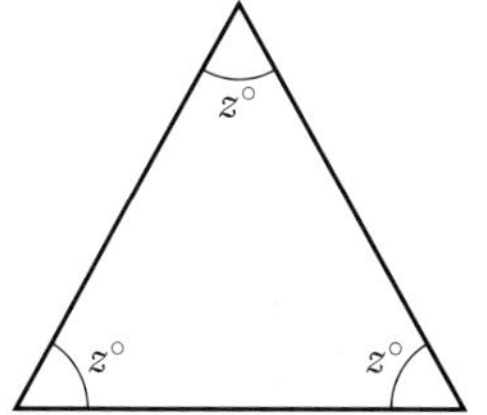

All quadrilaterals are made up of two triangles.

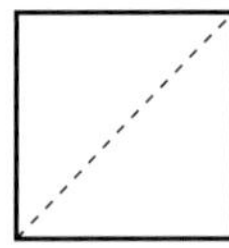

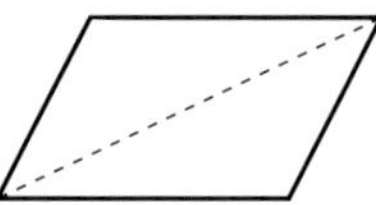

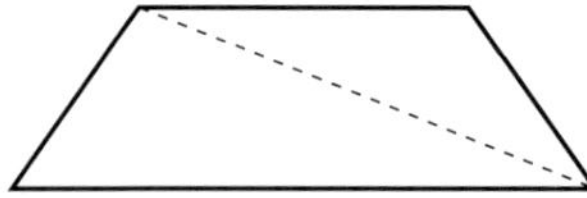

Because the angles in a triangle add up to 180°, the angles in a quadrilateral add up to $2 \times 180° = 360°$.

Example Find the angle marked $x°$.

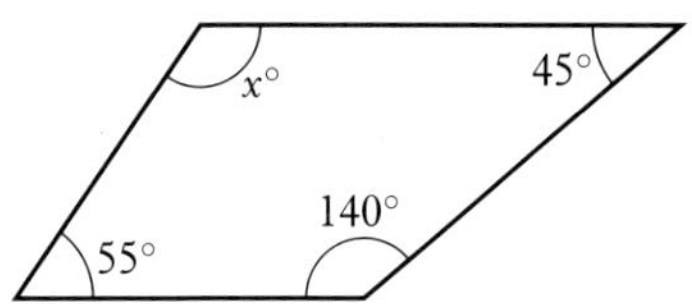

$x° = 360° - 140° - 45° - 55°$
$x° = 120°$

Exercise 29:5

Calculate the angles marked with letters.

1

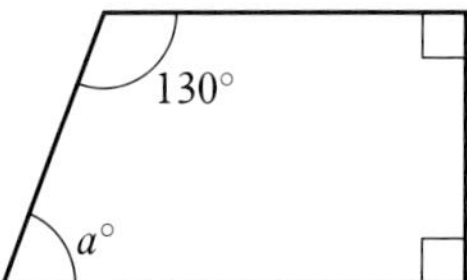

4

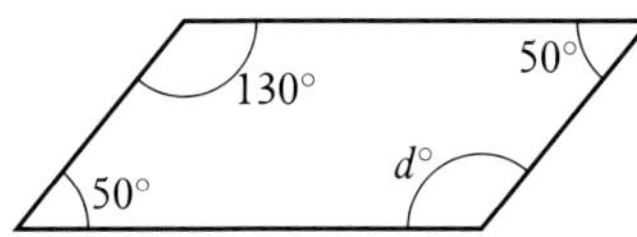

2

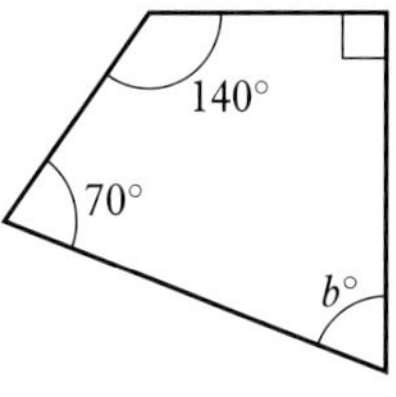

● **5**

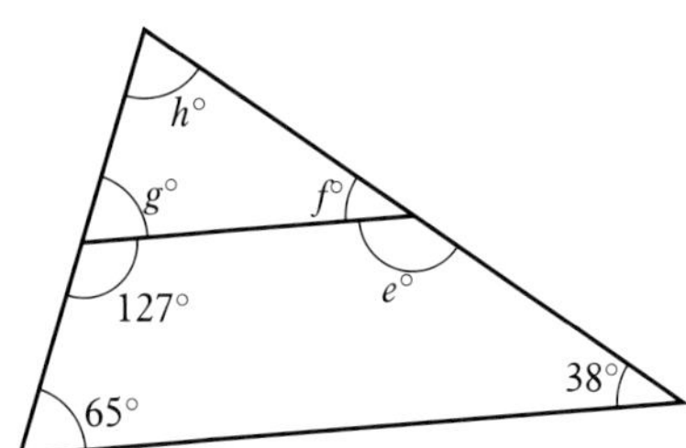

3

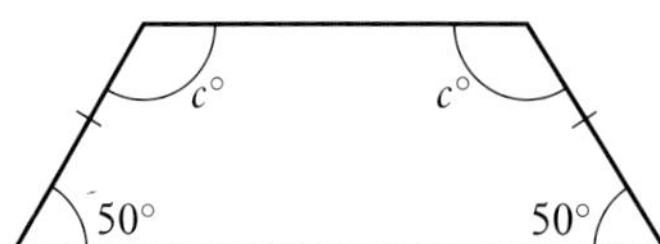

● **6**

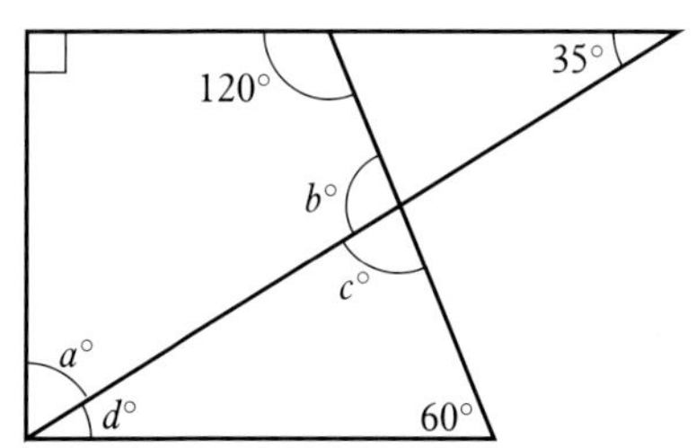

You can use the opposite angles rules to work out **angles on parallel lines**.

$a°$ and $b°$ are equal because they are opposite angles.

The sloping line crosses the bottom line at the same angle that it crosses the top line. This means that $p°$ and $q°$ are the same as $a°$ and $b°$.

Angles $c°$, $d°$, $r°$ and $s°$ are all equal in the same way.

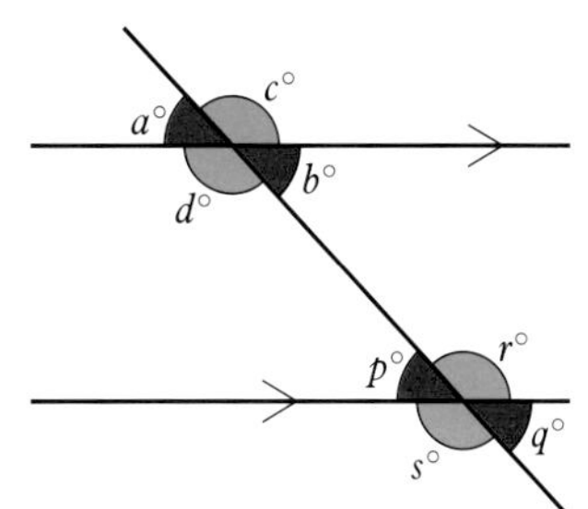

Exercise 29:6

1 **a** Copy this diagram. The angles do not need to be exact.

b Colour all the angles **red** that are equal to $a°$.

c Colour all the angles blue that are equal to $b°$.

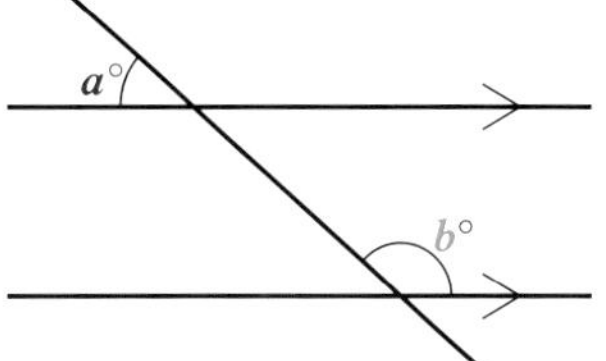

2 **a** Write down the letters of all the angles that are 70°.

b Write down the letters of all the angles that are 110°.

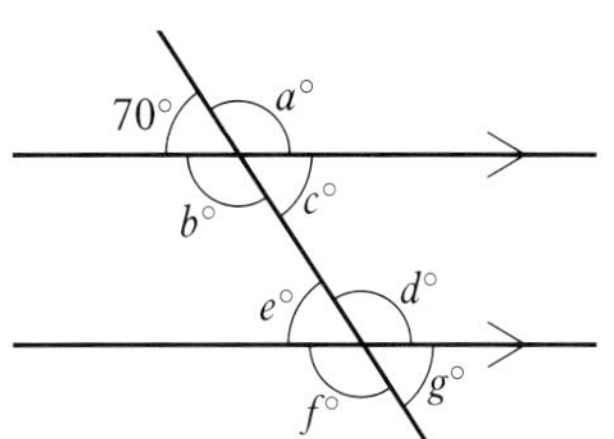

3 Calculate the angles marked with letters.

a

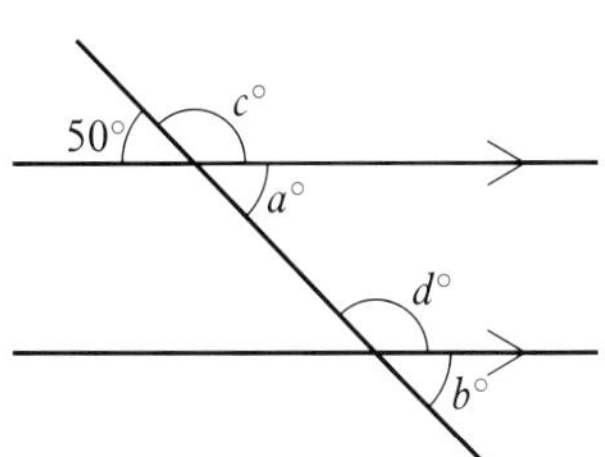

c

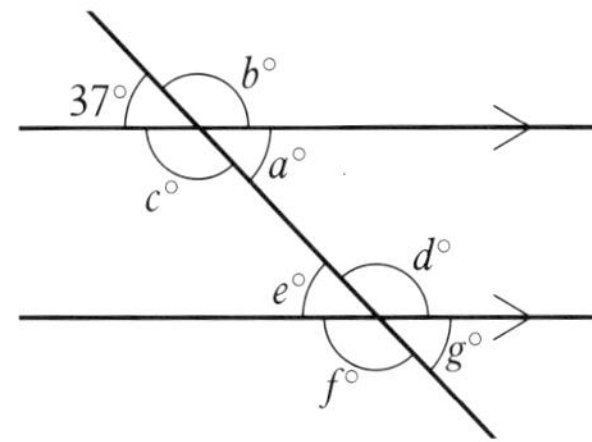

b

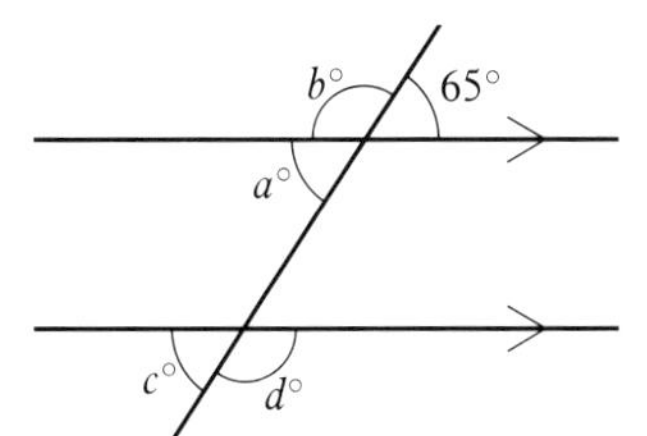

d

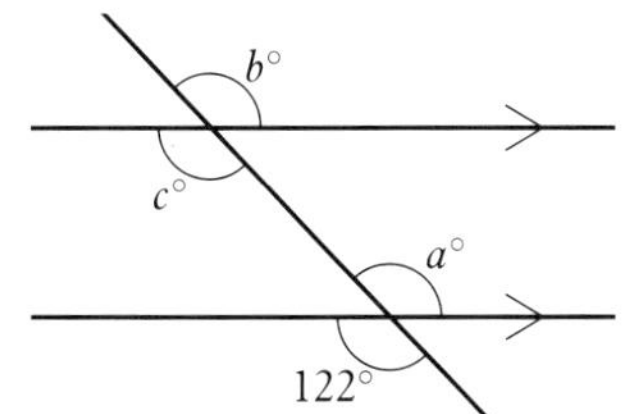

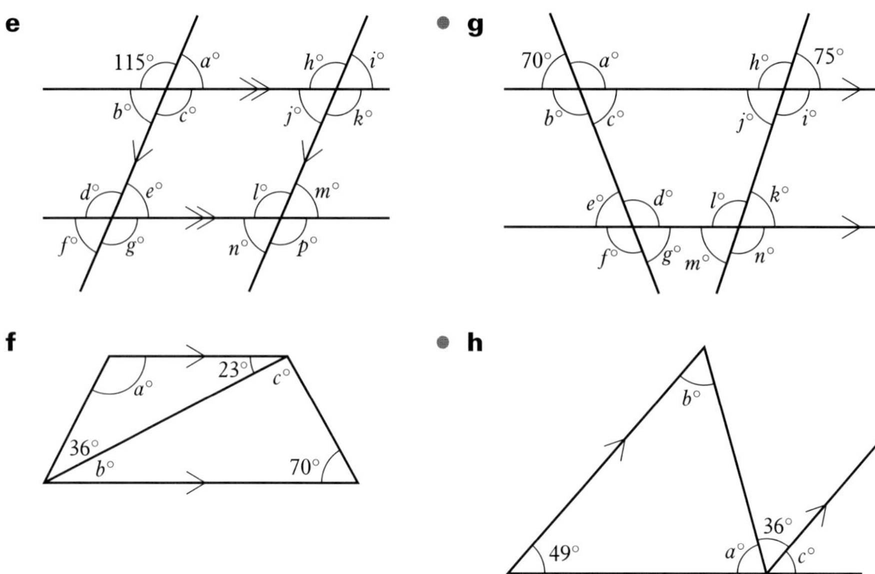

Angles in circles

There are some special angle rules for circles. Before you learn these, you need to make sure that you know the names of parts of the circle.

You should already know these:
radius, diameter, circumference.

Also an **arc** is part of the circumference.

Now you need to know these:

Chord

A **chord** is a straight line going from one point on the circumference to another and *not* going through the centre.

Tangent

A **tangent** is a straight line that just touches the circle.

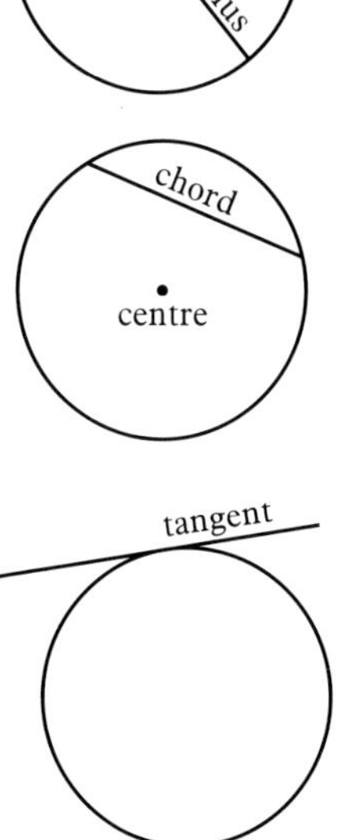

Here are the rules you need to know.

Angle in a semi-circle

The **angle in a semi-circle** is the angle made by joining both ends of a diameter of a circle to a point on the circumference.
The **angle in a semi-circle** is 90°.
In this diagram, angle APB is 90°.

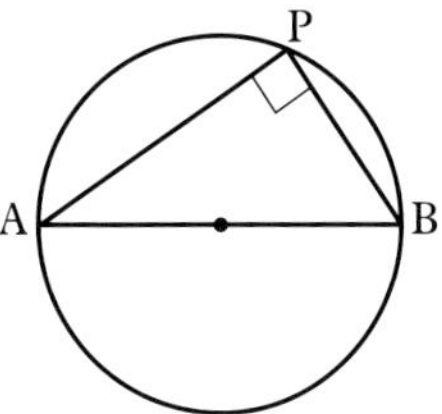

Tangent and radius

A **radius** drawn to the point where a **tangent** touches the circle is at right angles to that tangent.

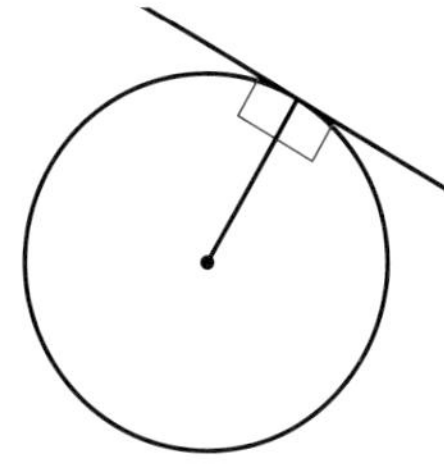

Midpoint of a chord

A line drawn from the centre of a circle to the **midpoint of a chord** is always at right angles to the chord.

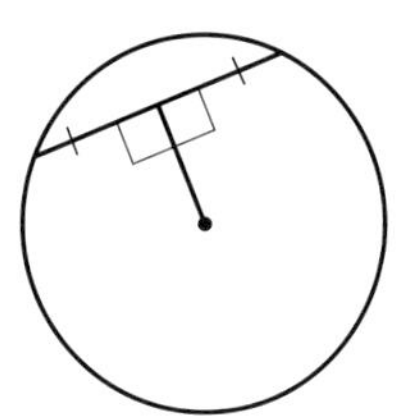

Example Find the angles marked with letters.
Write down the rules that you use.

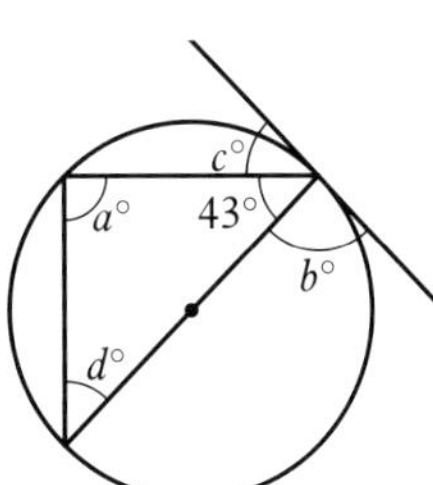

$a° = 90°$ because it is an angle in a semi-circle.
$b° = 90°$ because it is formed by a radius joining a tangent.

$c° = 180° - 43° - b°$
$= 180° - 43° - 90°$
$= 47°$

because angles on a straight line add up to 180°.

$d° = 180° - 43° - a°$
$= 180° - 43° - 90°$
$= 47°$

because angles in a triangle add up to 180°.

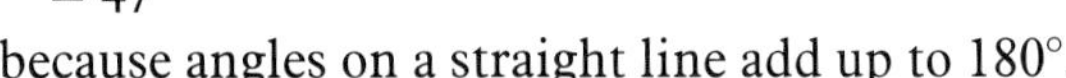

Exercise 29:7

Calculate the angles marked with letters.

1

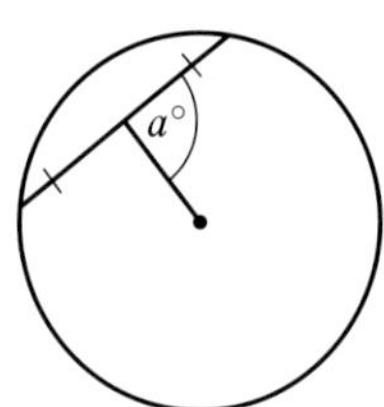

6

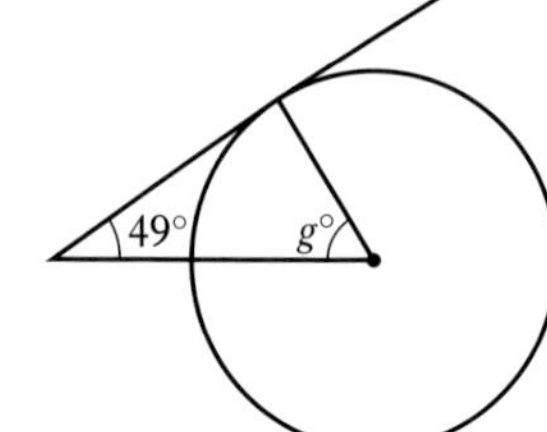

2

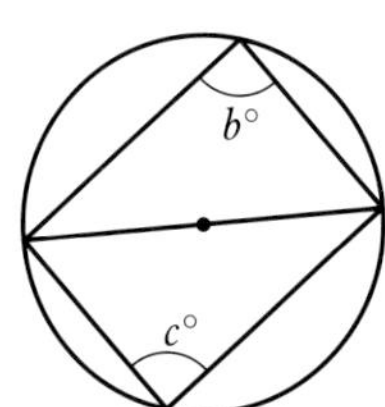

● **7**

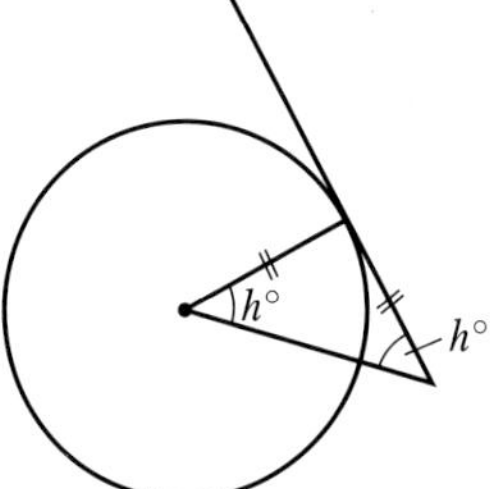

3

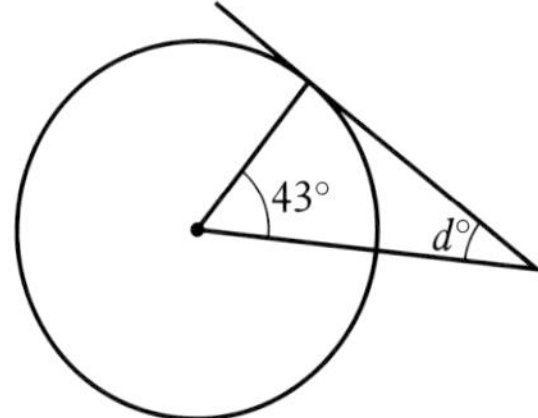

8

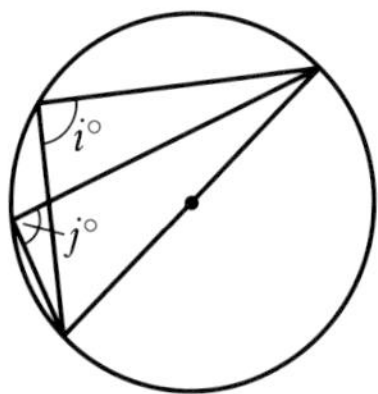

4

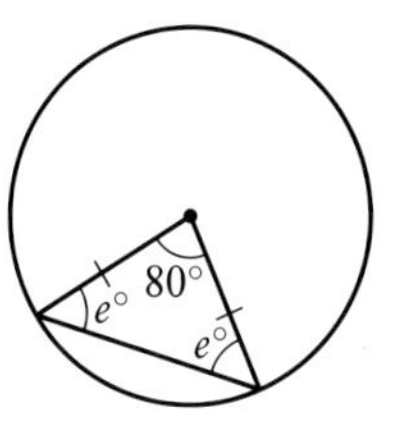

9

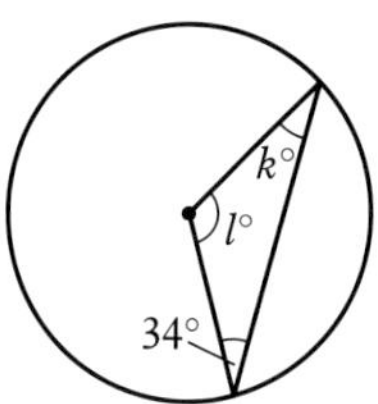

5

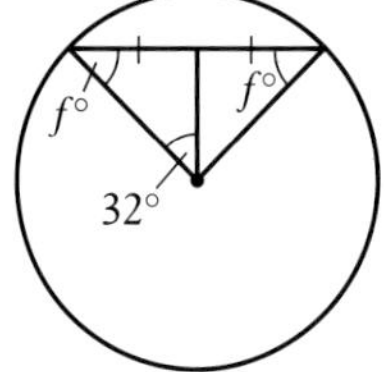

10

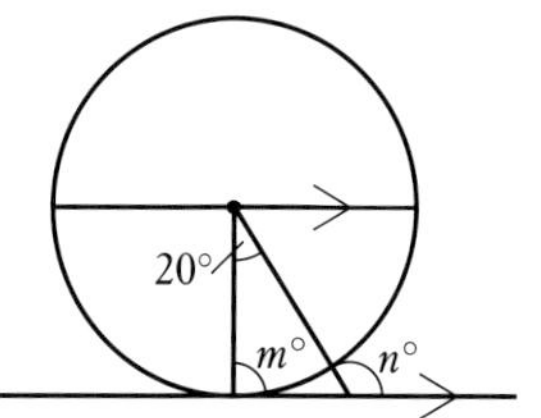

You can draw two tangents to a circle from any point outside the circle.

There are two tangents from the point P to this circle.

They touch the circle at the points A and B.
PA and PB are the two tangents from P to the circle.
The two tangents are equal.

So PA = PB.

This is an important result to remember.
This means that triangle ABP is an isosceles triangle.

So the angles $P\hat{A}B$ and $P\hat{B}A$ are equal.

The centre of the circle is O.
OA is a radius of the circle. OB is also a radius.

So OA = OB.

This means that triangle AOB is also an isosceles triangle.

So the angles $O\hat{A}B$ and $O\hat{B}A$ are equal.

Exercise 29:8

1 Find the angles marked with letters in each part.
You might need to draw extra lines to help you solve the problem.

a

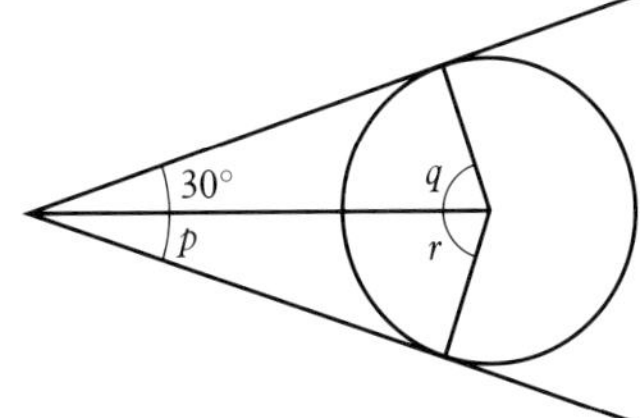

c

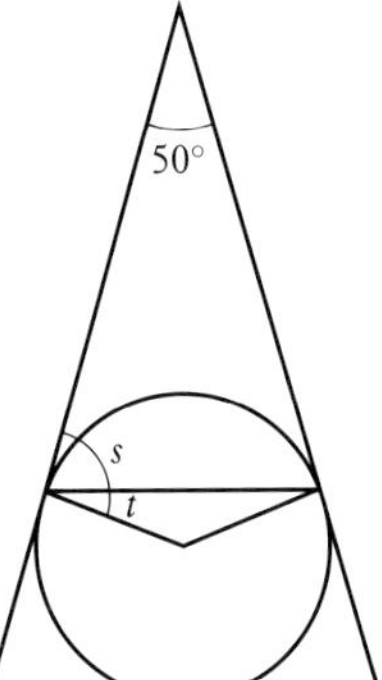

b

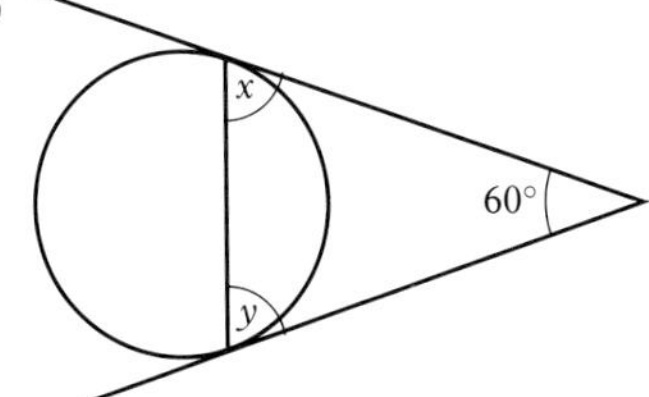

d

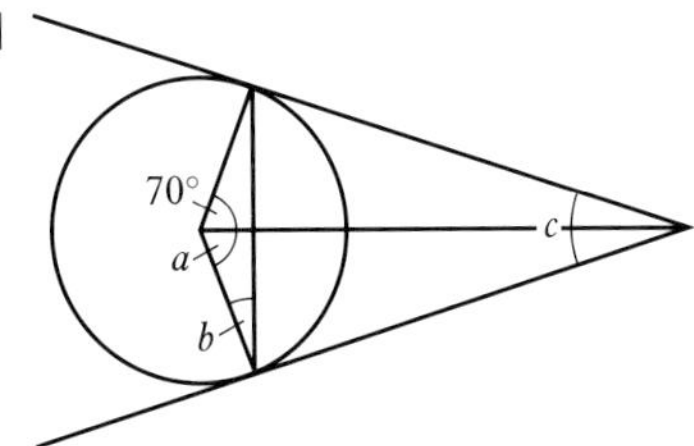

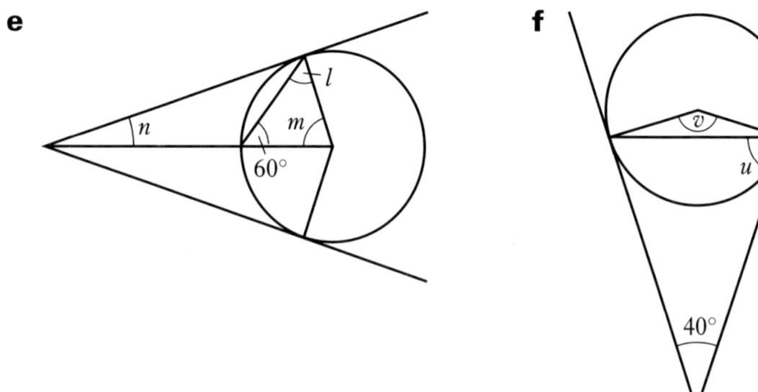

Cyclic quadrilateral

If you draw 4 points on a circle and join them together like this you get a **cyclic quadrilateral**.
ABCD is a cyclic quadrilateral.

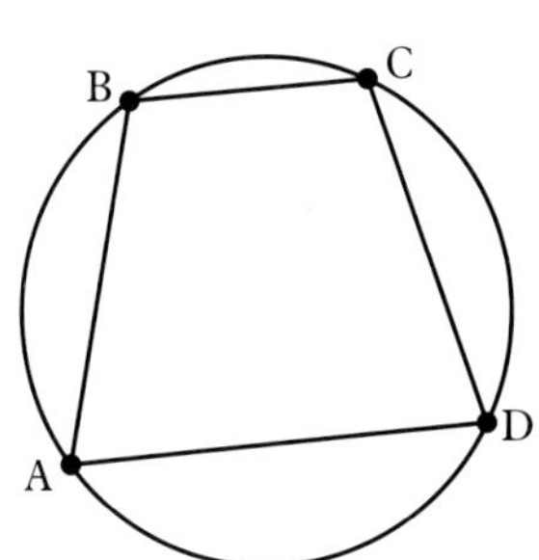

2 **a** Draw a circle with radius 5 cm.

b Draw any cyclic quadrilateral ABCD using your circle.
You need to label the vertices so that A is opposite C and B is opposite D.

c Copy this table.

A	C	B	D

Measure the angles inside the cyclic quadrilateral at A, B, C and D.
Fill in your results in the first row of the table.

d Draw two more cyclic quadrilaterals. Label them ABCD.
Measure the angles. Fill in the other two rows of the table.

e Look at your angles.
Find a rule that connects the angles A and C, and the angles B and D.
Write down the rule.
You need to know the rule before you can do the next question.

3 Find the angles marked with letters in each part.

a

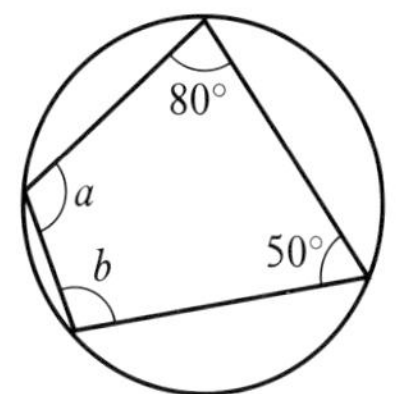

b

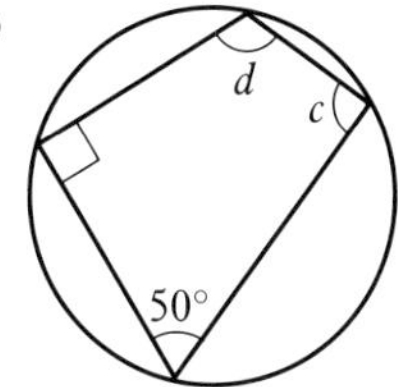

c

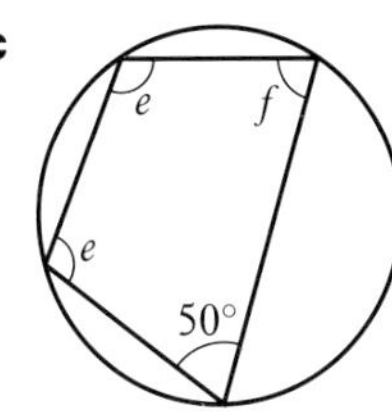

If you draw a chord in a circle you split the circle into two segments.

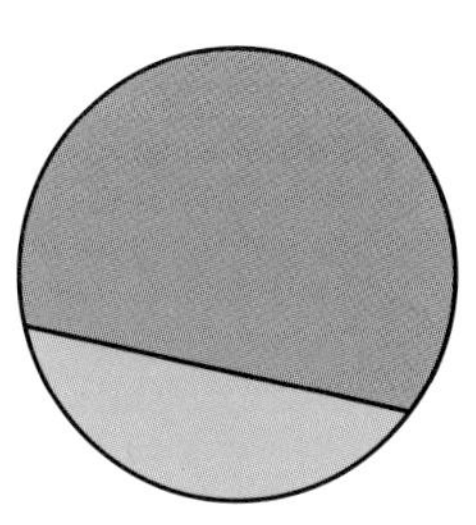

The red segment is bigger than the blue segment.

The red segment is called the **major segment**.

The blue segment is called the **minor segment**.

You can draw angles in a segment by joining both ends of the chord to a point on the circumference.

This is an angle drawn in the major segment.

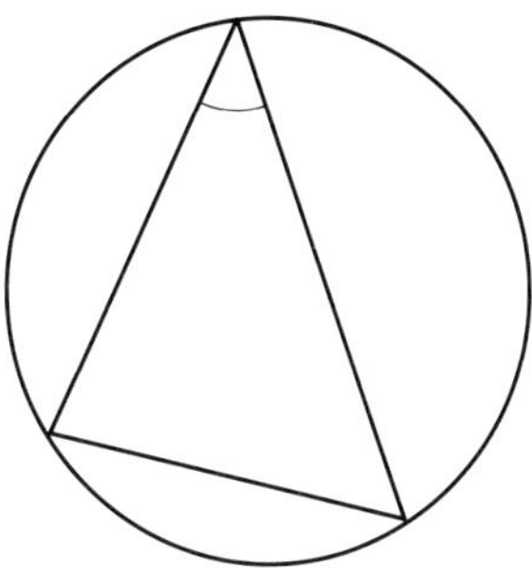

This is an angle drawn in the minor segment.

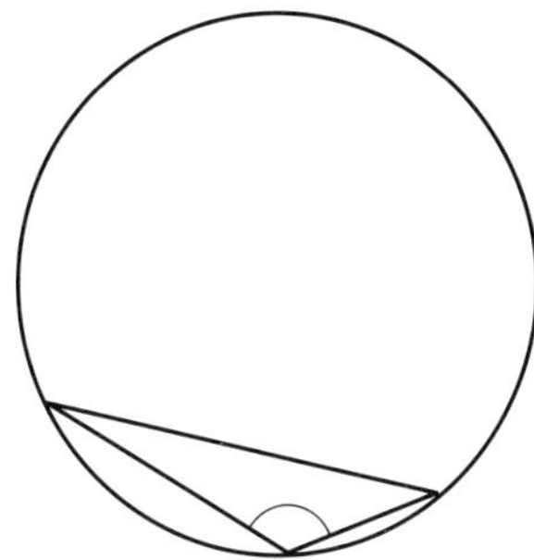

Exercise 29:9

1 **a** Draw a circle with radius 5 cm.
b Draw a chord AB in your circle.
c Draw three angles in the *major* segment in your diagram.
d Measure each of the angles you have drawn.
e Copy this. Fill it in.

The angles in the major segment are ....

2 **a** Draw a circle with radius 5 cm.
b Draw a chord AB in your circle.
c Draw three angles in the *minor* segment in your diagram.
d Measure each of the angles you have drawn.
e Copy this. Fill it in.

The angles in the minor segment are ....

f Write one sentence that summarises the results in the last two questions. Check that you have the right answer before you do the next question.

3 Find the angles marked with letters in each part.

a

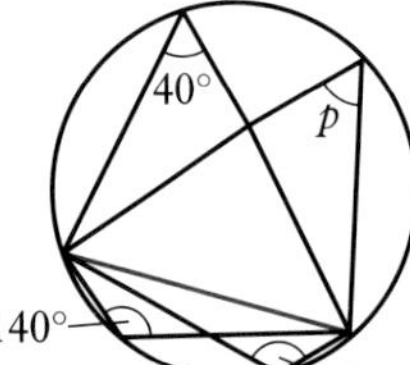

b

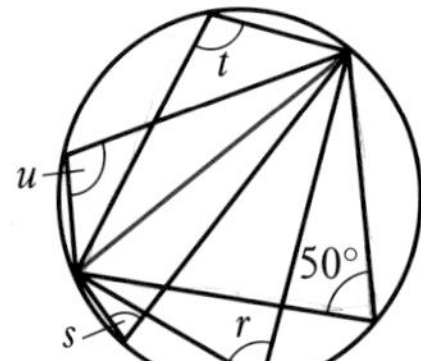

● **c**

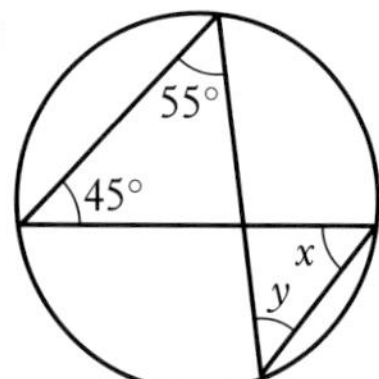

An angle in a segment is sometimes called an **angle at the circumference**.

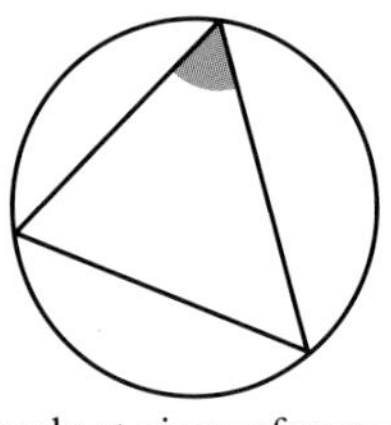

angle at circumference in major segment

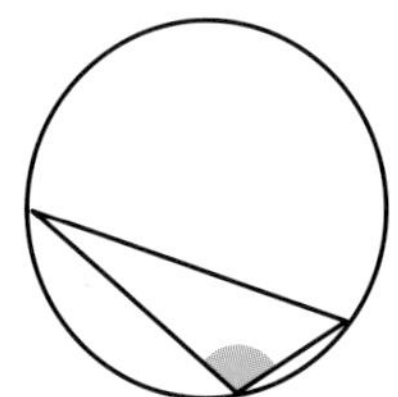

angle at circumference in minor segment

You can join the ends of the chord to the centre of the circle.

This gives you two **angles at the centre**.

There is a connection between the angle at the circumference and one of the angles at the centre.

The one that you use depends on which segment you're looking at.

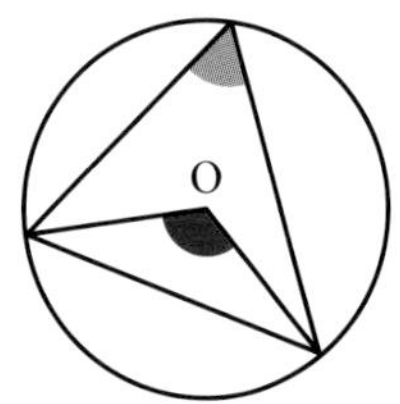

angle at the centre for angle at circumference in major segment

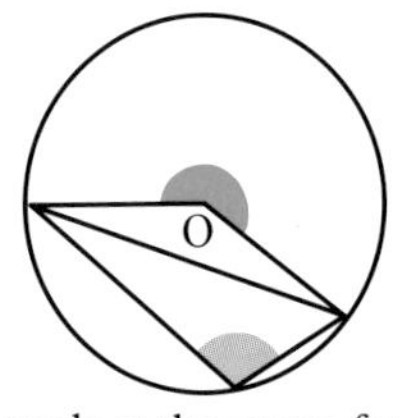

angle at the centre for angle at circumference in minor segment

4 **a** Draw a circle with radius 5 cm.
b Draw a chord AB in your circle.
c Draw an angle in the *major* segment in your diagram.
d Draw the angle at the centre for the angle in the segment you have drawn.
e Measure the angle at the centre and the angle at the circumference. Copy this. Fill it in.
The angle at the centre is equal to .... the angle at the circumference.

5 **a** Draw a circle with radius 5 cm.
b Draw a chord AB in your circle.
c Draw an angle in the *minor* segment in your diagram.
d Draw the angle at the centre for the angle in the segment you have drawn.
e Measure the angle at the centre and the angle at the circumference. Copy this. Fill it in.
The angle at the centre is equal to .... the angle at the circumference.

● **6** You already know that the angle in a semi-circle is 90°. Explain why this is true using your answers to questions **4** and **5**.

You have now seen all the results that you need to learn about circles!

The angle in a semi-circle is 90°.

A radius drawn to the point where a tangent touches a circle is at right angles to that tangent.

A line drawn from the centre of a circle to the midpoint of a chord is at right angles to the chord.

The two tangents to a circle from a point outside a circle are equal in length.

The opposite angles in a cyclic quadrilateral add up to 180°.

Angles in the same segment are equal.

The angle at the centre is twice the angle at the circumference.

Now you need to be able to use all the results that you've discovered.

Exercise 29:10

Write down the angles marked with letters.

1

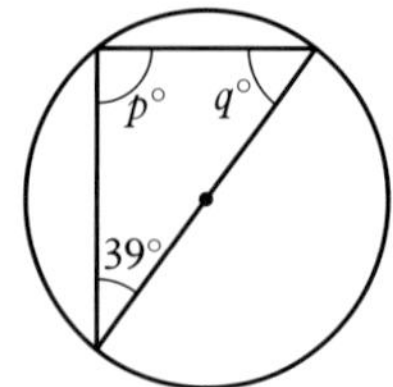

2

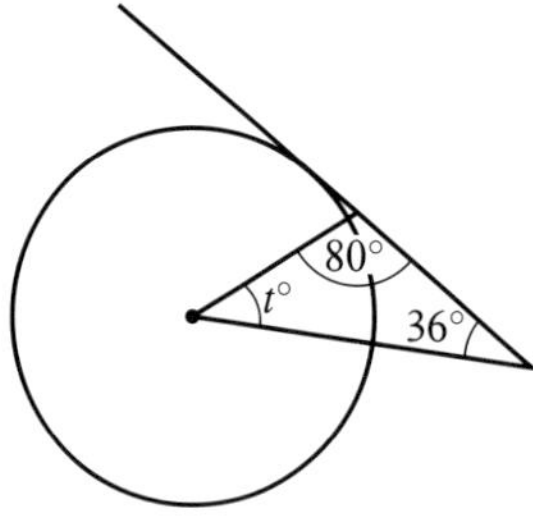

3

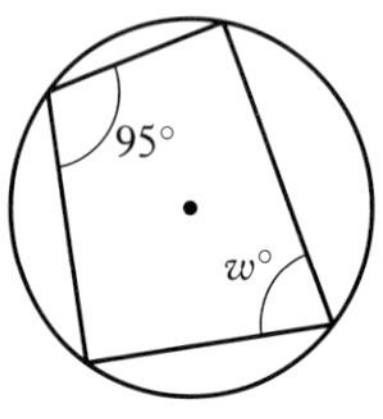

4

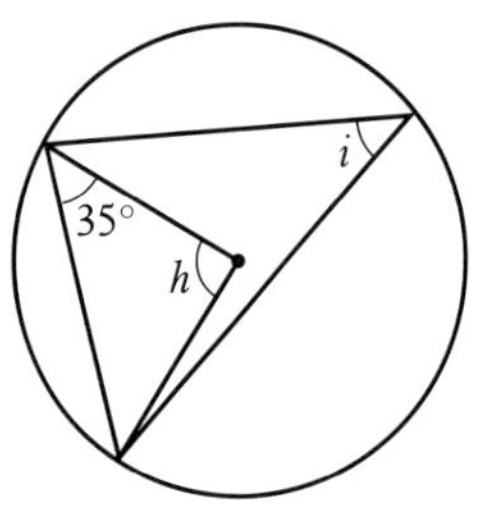

5

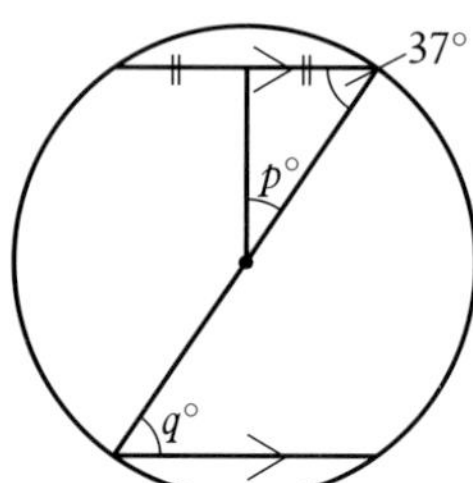

6

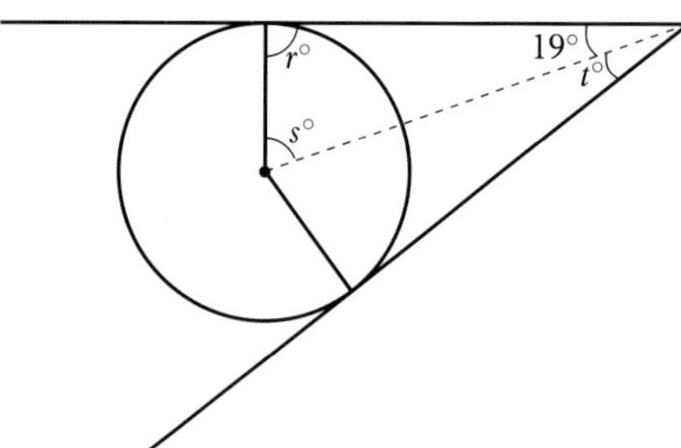

● **7**

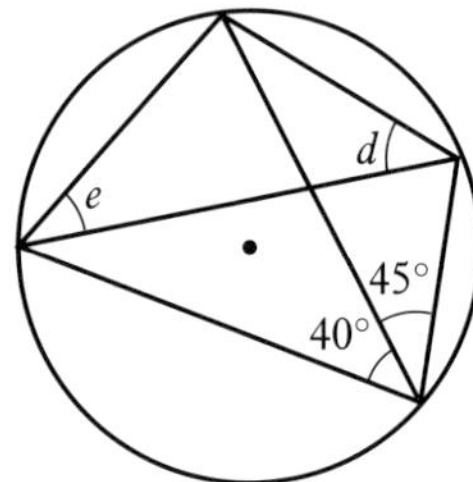

● **8**

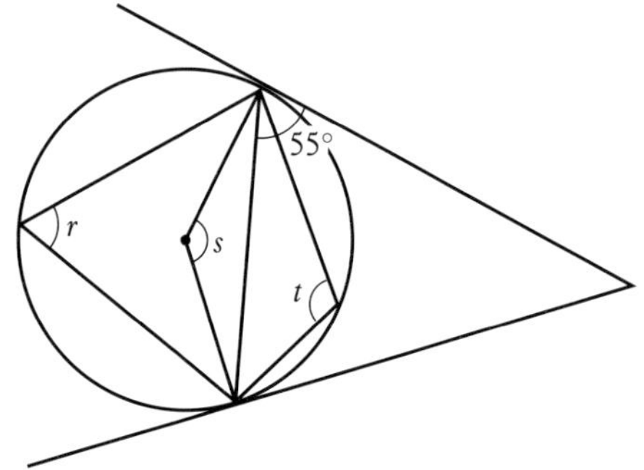

2 Get your bearings

The rescue services need to be able to pinpoint accurately the location of someone in trouble.

They use bearings to help them.

A bearing is an angle.

It is always measured in the same way so that no-one is confused about what the angle means.

Bearing

A **bearing** is an angle.
Bearings are *always* measured clockwise starting from north.
A bearing must always have 3 figures.
If the angle is less than 100° put a zero as the first digit.
030° is the bearing for an angle of 30° clockwise from north.

Bearing of B from A

The **bearing of B from A** means that you are at A.

The **bearing of B from A** is the angle in red.
You start at A.
You face north.
You turn clockwise until you are facing B.

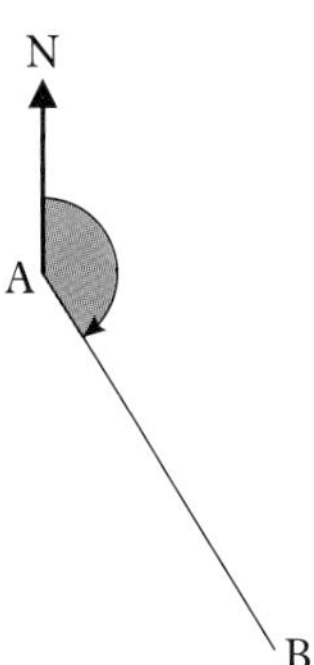

Bearing of A from B

The **bearing of A from B** means that you are at B.

The **bearing of A from B** is the angle in blue.
You start at B.
You face north.
You turn clockwise until you are facing A.

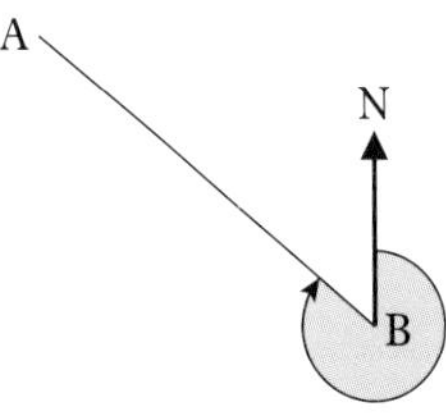

Example Work out:
a the bearing of B from A
b the bearing of A from B.

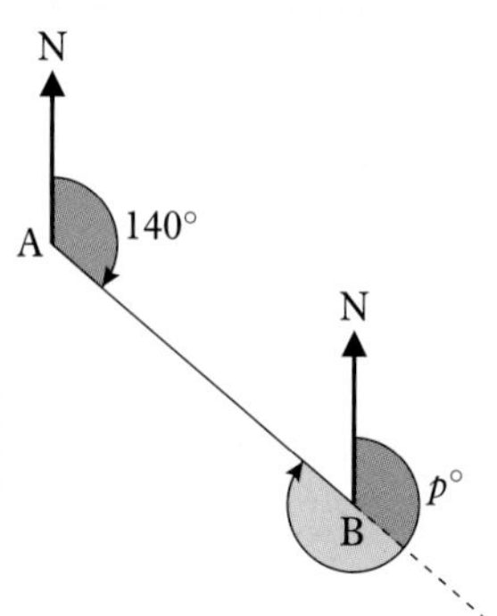

a Draw a north line at A.
Join A to B with a straight line.
Measure clockwise from North to the line joining A to B.
The bearing is 140°.

b Draw a north line at B.
You must measure the bearing clockwise from this North line.
You want angle $p°$.
Angle $p°$ is 320°.
It is made up of two angles **140°** and **180°**
The red angle is 140° because the two north lines are parallel.
The blue angle is 180° because it is on a straight line.
The bearing of A from B is 320°.

Exercise 29:11

1 In each of these find the **bearing of A from B**.

a
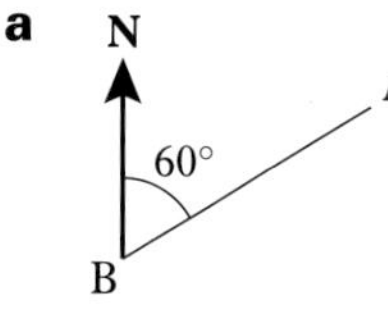

c
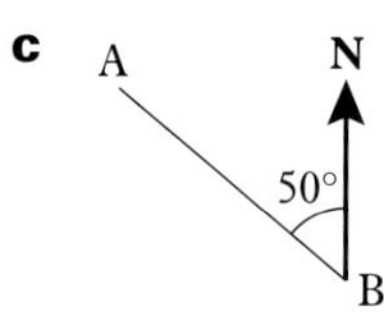

e
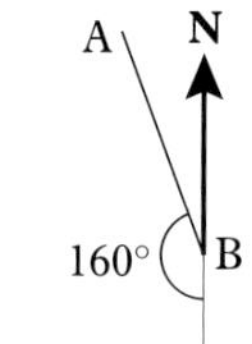

b
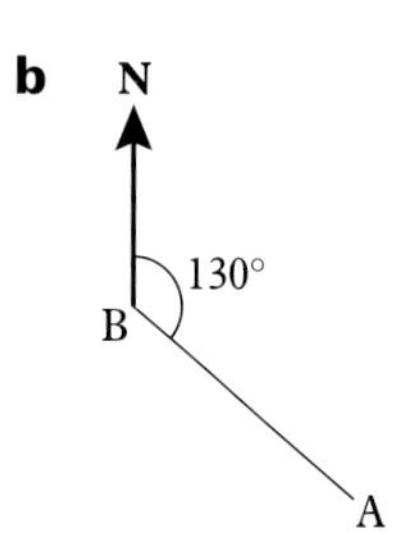

d
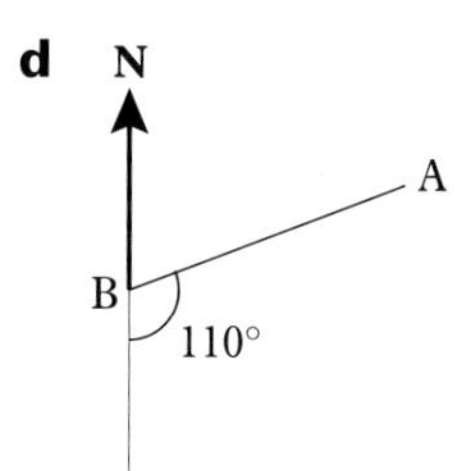

f
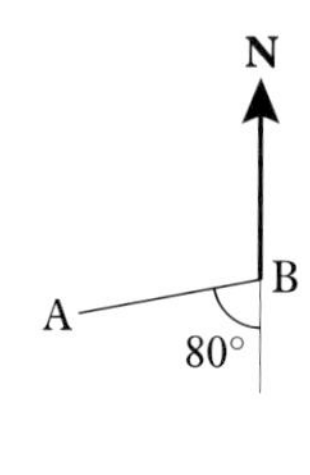

2 For each part of question **1**:

a Copy the diagram.

b Draw in a north line at A.

c Use the angle facts that you know to find the **bearing of B from A**.

3 Asif is in charge of a lifeboat.
These are some of his journeys to rescues.
The lifeboat starts at A. The rescue is at B.
The diagrams show you the bearing that he uses to get to the rescue.

For each part:
(1) Write down the bearing of his journey to the rescue point B.
(2) Work out the bearing for his return journey from B to A.

a N 72° B A

b N 106° A B

c

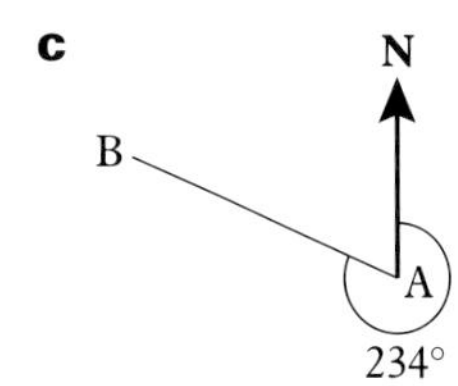

4 Nathan is orienteering.
This diagram shows the route that he takes.

a Write down the bearing for the first part of his journey from A to B.

b Work out the bearing for the second part of his journey from B to C.

c When Nathan gets to point C, he realises that he has left his sandwiches at B! Work out the bearing he should use to return from C to B.

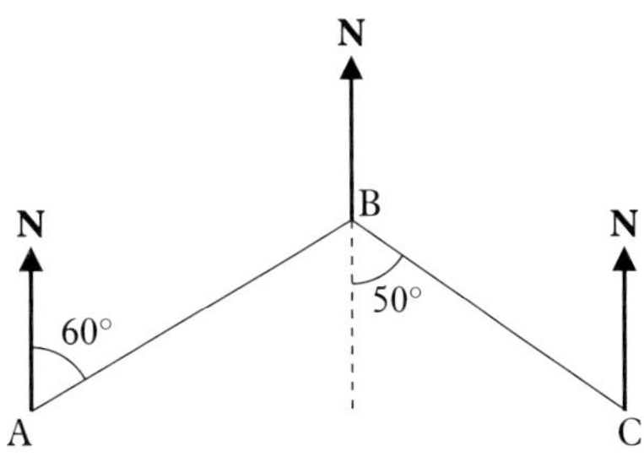

● **5** This diagram shows the flight path of an aeroplane.
Find the bearing of R from Q.

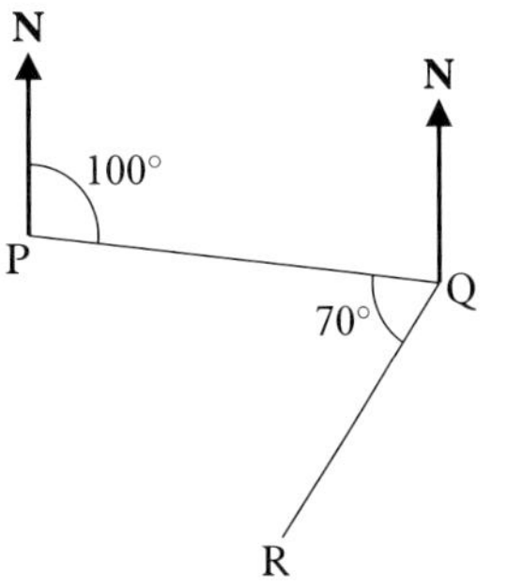

It is often useful to do a scale drawing to solve bearing problems.
An accurate drawing allows you to measure both distances and bearings.

Remember that diagrams should always be drawn in pencil and as accurately as possible.

Example Charlotte is planning an orienteering course.
Checkpoint A is 500 m from the start on a bearing of 070°.
Checkpoint B is 700 m from B on a bearing of 170°.

a Make a scale drawing showing the positions of A and B.
Use a scale of 1 cm = 100 m.

b Find the bearing of the Start from Checkpoint B.

a It is sensible to make a sketch first.
This helps you to plan your sketch on the page.

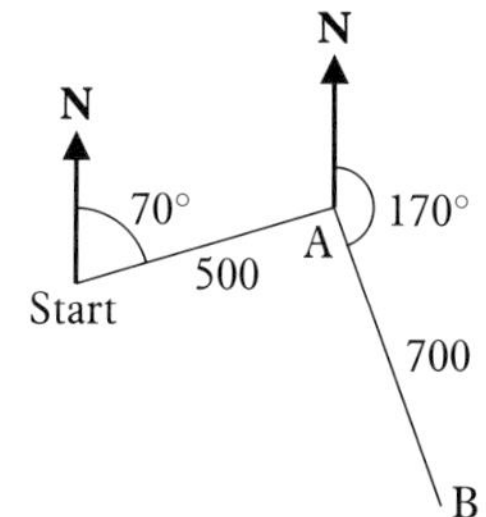

Now make an accurate scale drawing.
Remember that all bearings are measured **clockwise** from **north**.
Make sure that the 0° on your angle measurer is on the north line.

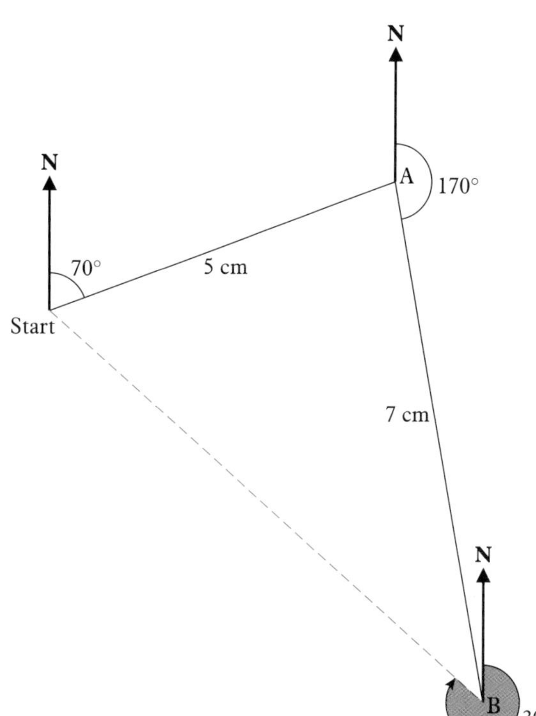

b The bearing of the Start from B is measured clockwise from the North line at B.
The bearing is 308°.

Exercise 29:12

1 A plane flies 50 km on a bearing of 050° from Anston to Bridgehope. It then flies 60 km on a bearing of 140° to Crudgington.

a Make a scale drawing showing the positions of the three towns. Use a scale of 1 cm = 10 km.

b Use your diagram to find the bearing of Anston from Crudgington.

2 A coastguard is trying to pinpoint a yacht in trouble off the coast. He measures the bearing from two points A and B. Point B is due east of A.

The bearing of the yacht from point A is 035°.
The bearing of the yacht from point B is 330°.
Points A and B are 1200 m apart.

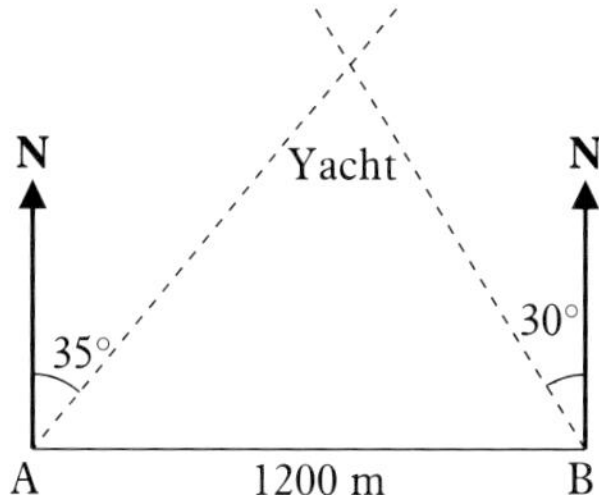

a Make a scale drawing showing the positions of A, B and the yacht. Use a scale of 1 cm = 200 m.

b Use your diagram to find the distance of the yacht from point A.

3 A ship sails 7 km on a bearing of 150°. It then sails a further 9 km on a bearing of 230°.

a Make a scale drawing showing the path the ship takes. Use a scale of 1 cm = 1 km.

b Use your diagram to find the bearing the ship should sail on to return to its starting point.

4 Fiona lives in Manchester. Her sister lives in Doncaster which is 70 km from Manchester on a bearing of 080°. Her brother lives in Derby which is also 70 km from Manchester but on a bearing of 140°.

a Draw an accurate scale drawing, showing Manchester, Doncaster and Derby.

b Use your diagram to find the distance from Doncaster to Derby.

c Find the bearing of Derby from Doncaster.

1 Calculate the angles marked with letters.

a

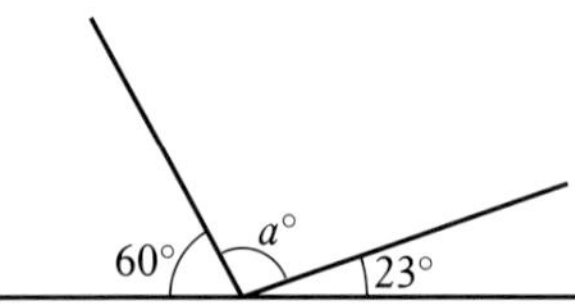

d

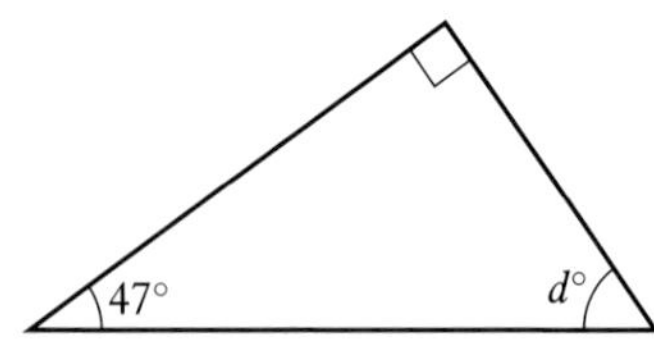

b

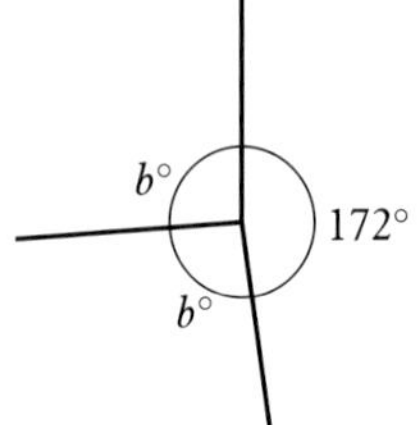

e

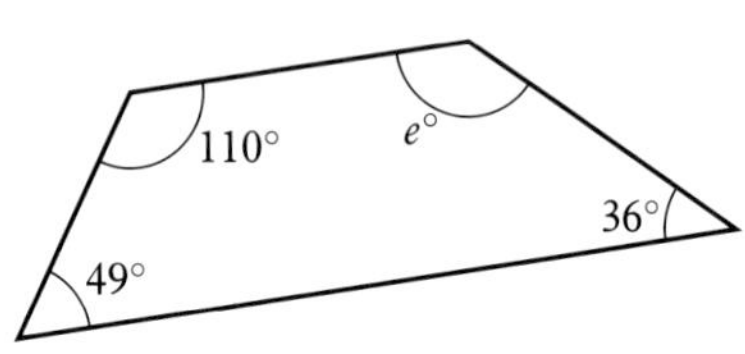

c

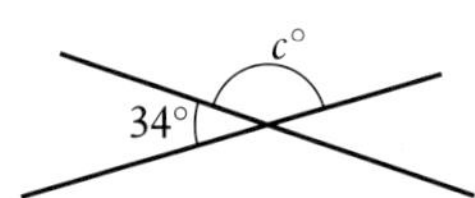

f

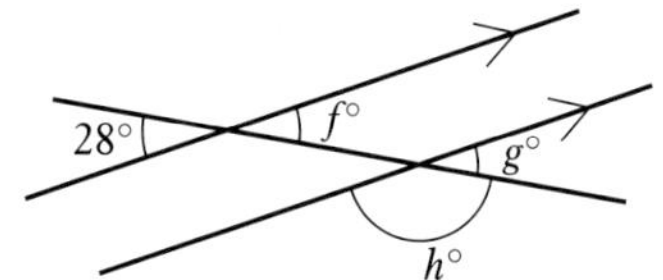

2 Calculate the angles marked with letters.

a

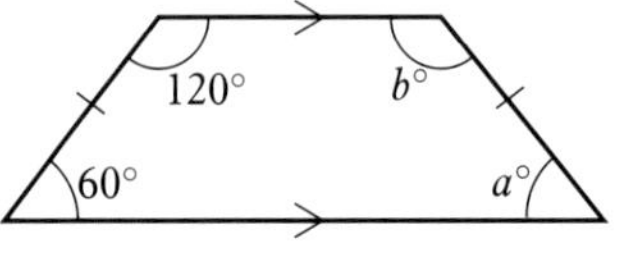

d

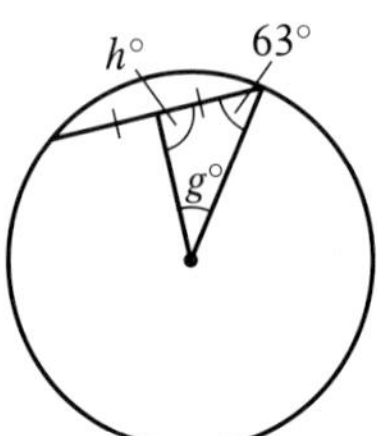

b

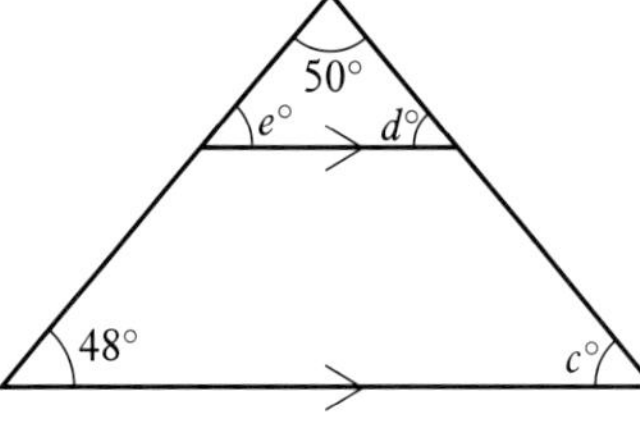

e

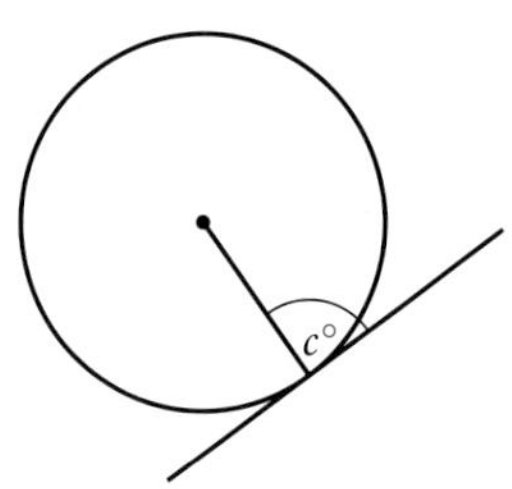

c

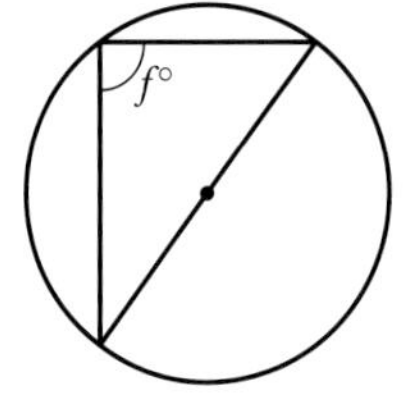

f

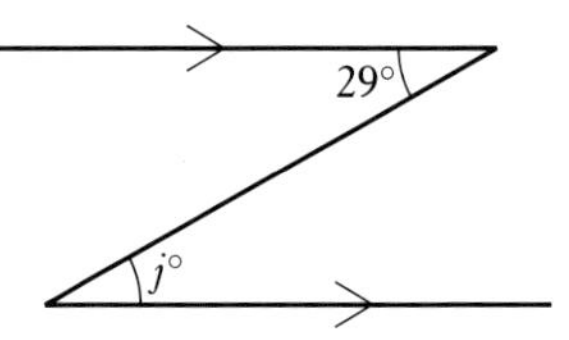

3 A ship sails 5 km on a bearing of 130°. It then sails a further 7 km on a bearing of 215°.

a Make a scale drawing showing the path the ship takes.
Use a scale of 1 cm = 1 km.

b Use your diagram to find the bearing the ship should sail on to return to its starting point.

4 A jet flies 220 km due east. It then turns and flies 300 km due south.

a Draw a sketch of the jet's journey.

b Make a scale drawing of the jet's journey.
Use a scale of 1 cm = 40 km.

c Use your diagram to find out how far the jet now is from its starting point.

d Measure the bearing that the jet should travel on to return to its starting point.

5 This scale drawing shows the position of three islands.
The scale is 1 cm = 10 km.

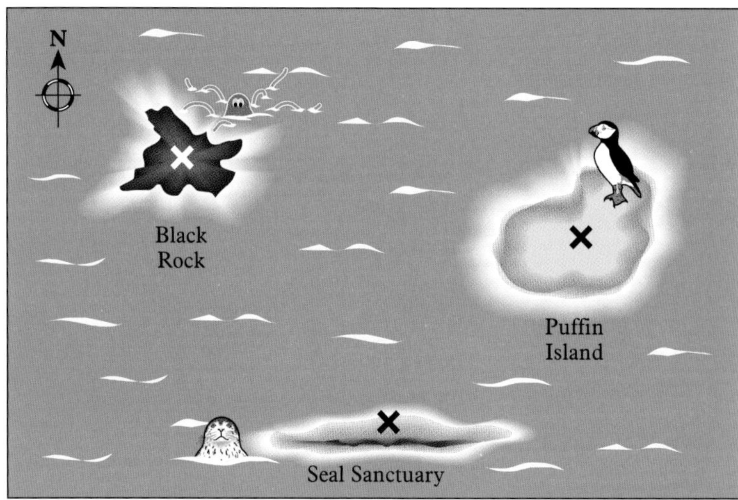

a Measure the distance from Black Rock to Puffin Island.

b Measure the bearing of Black Rock from Puffin Island.

c Measure the distance from Black Rock to Seal Sanctuary.

d Measure the bearing of Black Rock from Seal Sanctuary.

1 Calculate the angles marked with letters.

a

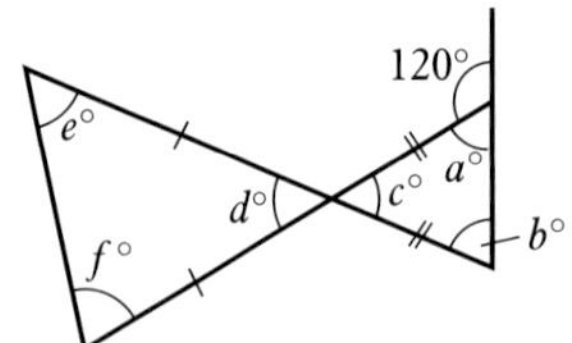

d

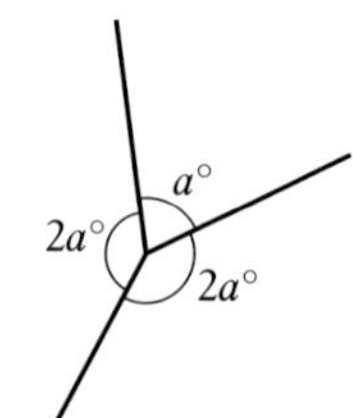

b

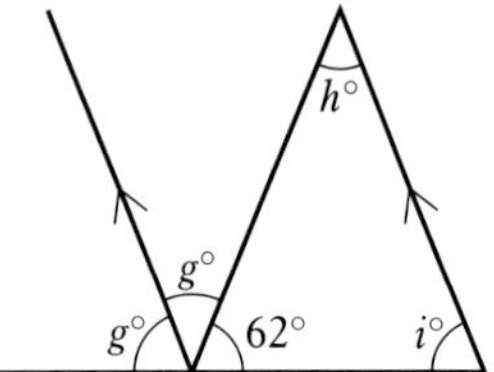

e

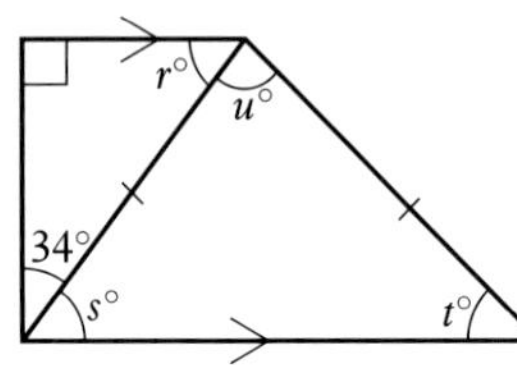

c

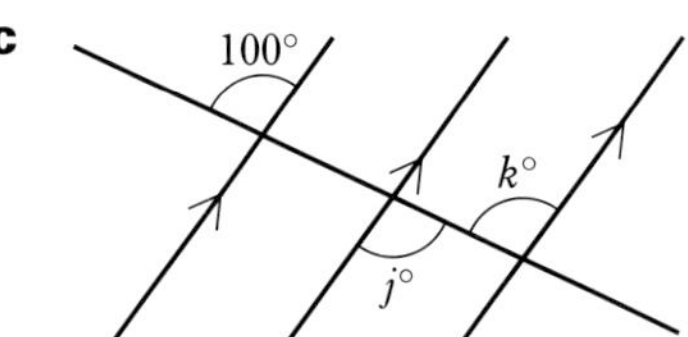

f

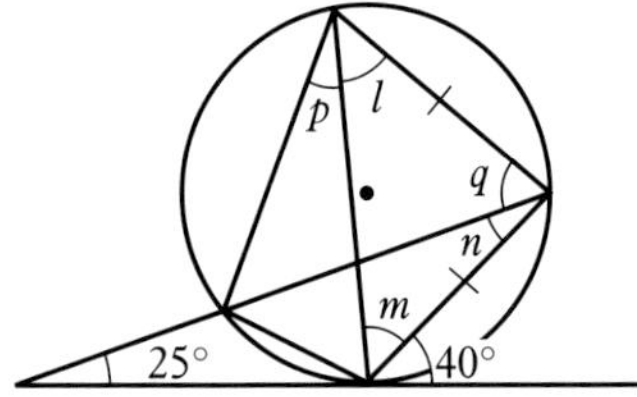

2 Look at this plan of an orienteering course.

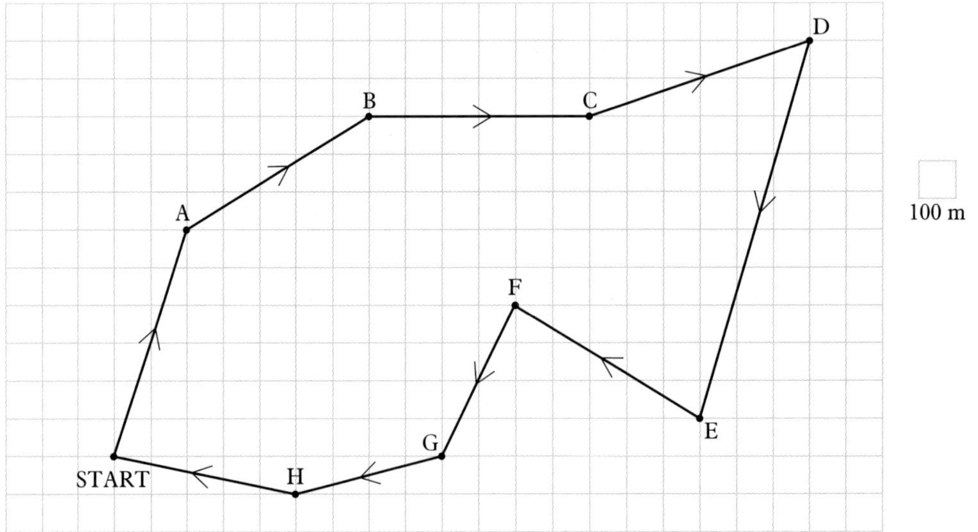

a Make an accurate copy of the plan.

b Write a list of instructions that could be used to get around the course.
You need to include distances and bearings.
You can measure the lengths or calculate them using Pythagoras' theorem.

1 Find the angles marked with letters. Give a reason for each answer.

a

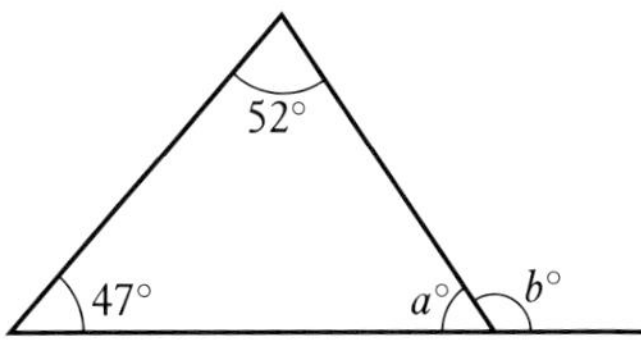

d

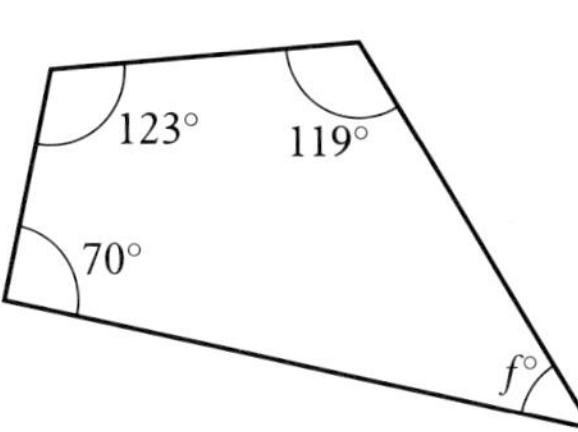

b

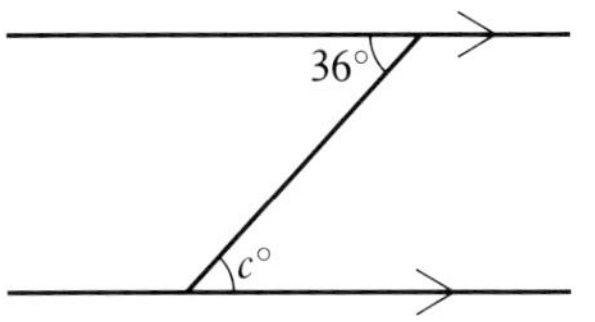

e

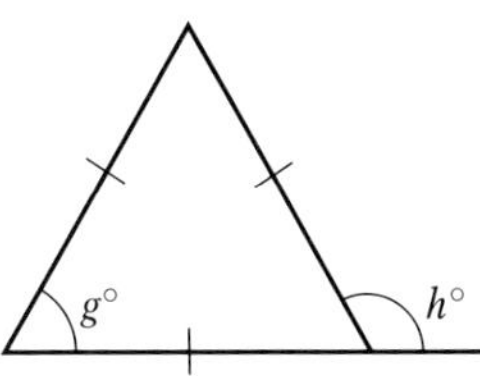

c

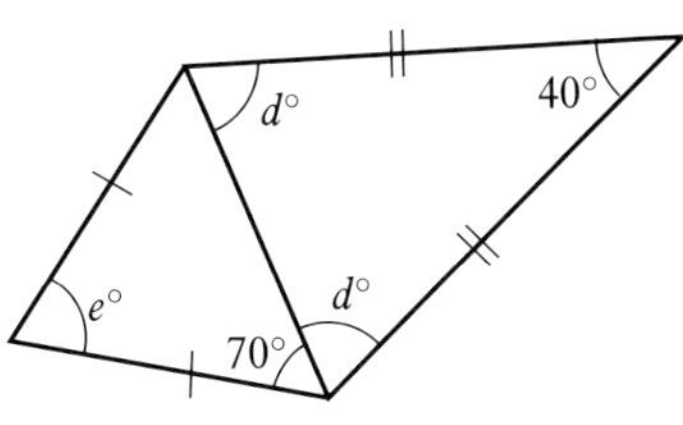

f

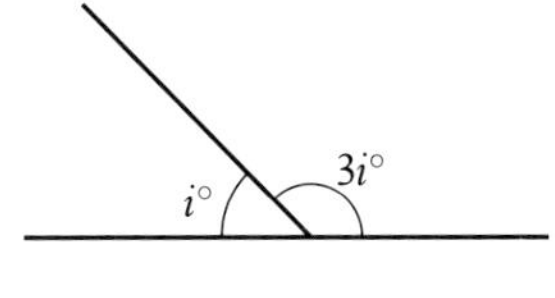

2 For each part, write down the angles marked with letters. Give a reason for each answer.

a

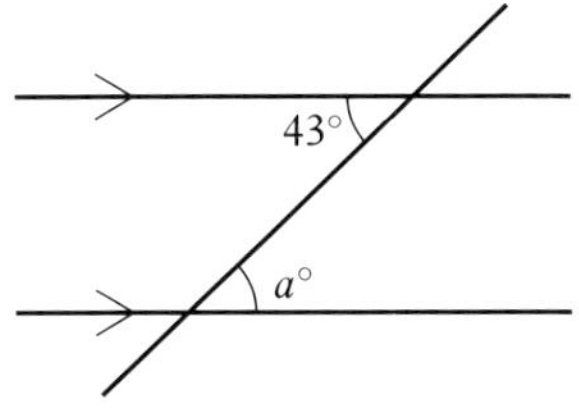

c

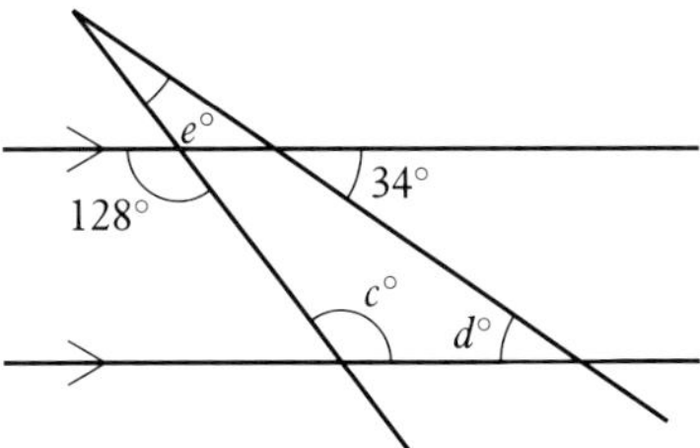

b

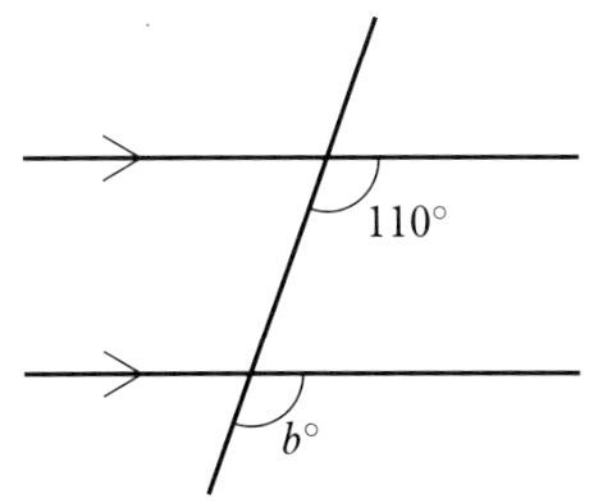

d

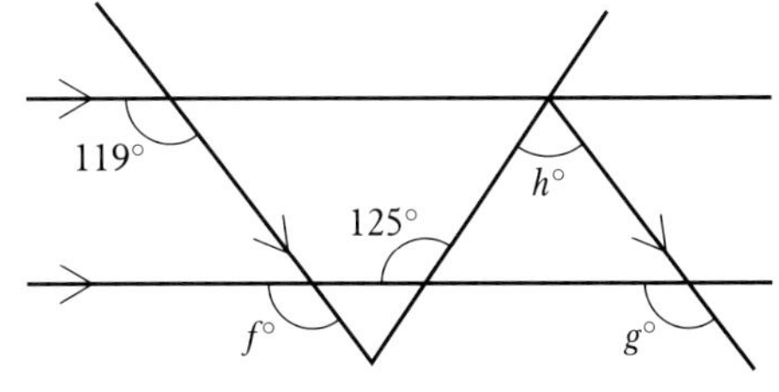

3 For each part, write down the angles marked with letters.
Give a reason for each answer.

a

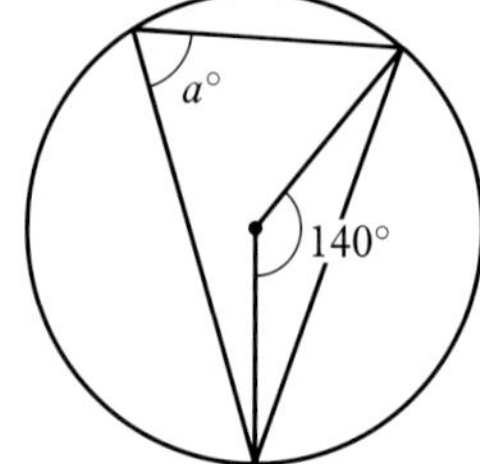

c

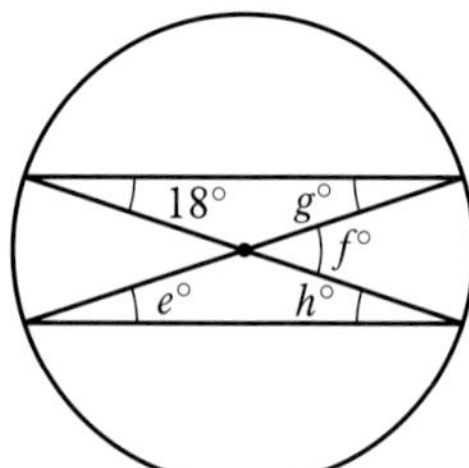

b

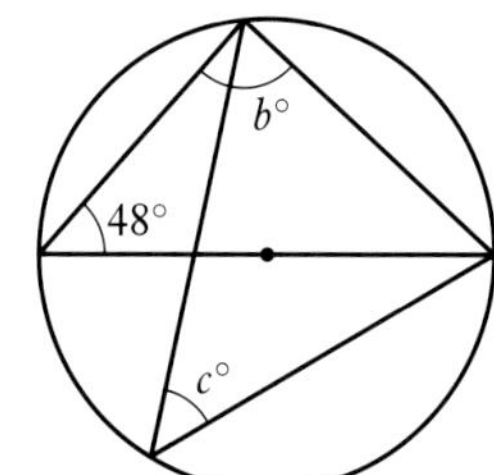

d

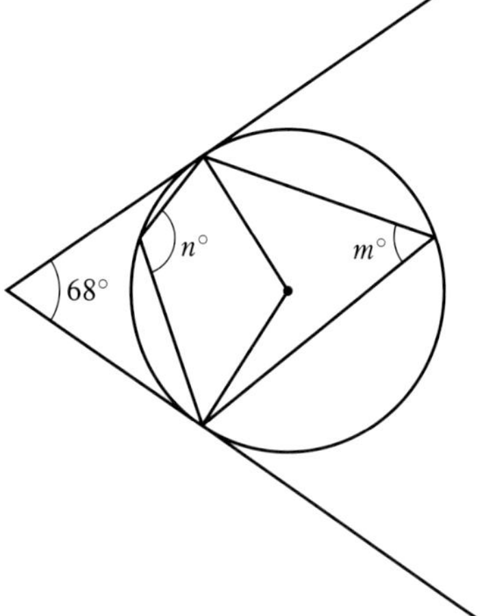

4 For each part, find
(1) the bearing of A from B
(2) the bearing of B from A

a

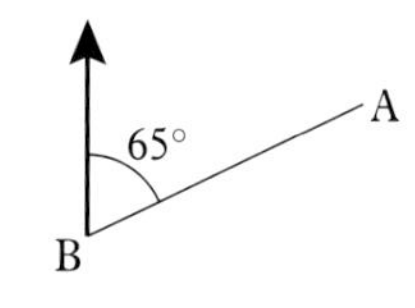

b

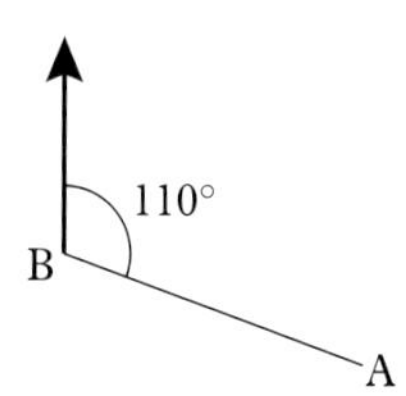

c

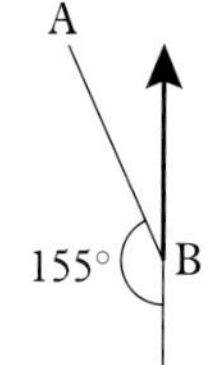

5 A plane flies 20 km from Ampton to Boxford on a bearing of 044°.
It then flies 15 km on a bearing of 102° to Canborough.
a Draw an accurate scale drawing to show this information.
b Use your diagram to find the distance of Canborough from Ampton.
c Use your diagram to find the bearing of Canborough from Ampton.

30 Mainly quadratics

CORE

1 Brackets and factorising
Multiplying out brackets
Looking for common factors
Multiplying out two brackets
Changing the subject

2 Factorising and solving quadratics
Factorising quadratics
Factorising the difference of two squares
Solving quadratic equations
Sketching the graphs of quadratic equations

QUESTIONS

EXTENSION

TEST YOURSELF

1 Brackets and factorising

Alan sometimes took removing brackets too far!

First, a quick recap on how to multiply a bracket by a number.

Example

Multiply out these brackets.

a $3(2x + 7)$ **b** $-6(5y - 2)$ **c** $7(3x^2 + 9x - 8)$

a To work out $3(2x + 7)$ multiply both the $2x$ and the 7 by the 3.

$$3(2x + 7) = 3 \times 2x + 3 \times 7 = 6x + 21$$

b Notice that there is a minus sign outside the bracket.

$$-6(5y - 2) = -6 \times 5y + (-6) \times (-2) = -30y + 12$$

c It doesn't matter how many terms there are in the bracket.

$$7(3x^2 + 9x - 8) = 7 \times 3x^2 + 7 \times 9x + 7 \times (-8) = 21x^2 + 63x - 56$$

Exercise 30:1

Multiply out these brackets.

1 $4(x + 6)$

2 $6(2s - 7)$

3 $5(4t + 12)$

4 $9(5x - 5)$

5 $-3(2x + 9)$

6 $7(3x - 1)$

7 $-6(7y - 8)$

8 $5(2c^2 - c - 3)$

9 $6(5y^3 - 60y)$

10 $5(3x^2 - 2x - 7)$

11 $-(2x^2 + 2y - z^2)$

12 $-7(3y - 5r + 2w)$

You can also have letters outside the bracket.

Example

Multiply out these brackets.

a $c(2c + 6)$ **b** $f(3f^2 - 5f + 10)$

a To work out $c(2c + 6)$ multiply both the $2c$ and the 6 by the c.

$$c(2c + 6) = c \times 2c + c \times 6$$
$$= 2c^2 + 6c$$

b In this part, remember that $f \times f^2$ gives you f^3.

$$f(3f^2 - 5f + 10) = f \times 3f^2 - f \times 5f + f \times 10$$
$$= 3f^3 - 5f^2 + 10f$$

Exercise 30:2

Multiply out these brackets.

1 $x(2x + 7)$

2 $a(a - 9)$

3 $c(d + 9)$

4 $x(4x - 8)$

5 $x^2(3x + 2)$

6 $y(x^2 - 4x - 3)$

7 $b^2(b^2 - 5b + 7)$

8 $4g(3g^2 + g - 9)$

● **9** $xy(x^2y - xy^3)$

Factorising

Factorising is the opposite of multiplying out brackets.
The first thing to look for is a common factor in the numbers:

Example

Factorise $6x + 10y$

The numbers 6 and 10 both have a factor of 2.
2 is the biggest number that divides exactly into 6 and 10.
You take the 2 outside a bracket as a factor.
$6x + 10y = 2(\quad)$

Next, you work out what goes inside the bracket.
$2 \times 3 = 6$ and $2 \times 5 = 10$
So inside the bracket you are left with $3x + 5y$

This means that $6x + 10y = 2(3x + 5y)$.

You can check that 2 is the largest factor you could have taken out by looking at what is left inside the bracket.
3 and 5 have no common factor so the 2 was correct.

Exercise 30:3

Factorise each of these.
Use the hints to help you in questions **1–4**.

1 $4x + 18 = 2(\quad)$

2 $3x - 27 = 3(\quad)$

3 $12y - 16 = 4(\quad)$

4 $35x - 25 = 5(\quad)$

5 $6x - 36$

6 $8x^2 - 16y$

7 $30t - 40s - 50r$

8 $21y - 49z$

You can also take letters outside brackets as common factors.

The expression $xy + xz$ has a common factor of x.
$xy + xz$ has an x in both terms.
So $xy + xz = x(y + z)$.

The expression $y^2 + y$ has a common factor of y.
$y^2 + y$ has a y in both terms.
So $y^2 + y = y(y + 1)$

Notice the 1 at the end of the bracket. It is very important.
If you multiply the bracket out you must get back to where you started.

$$\begin{aligned} y(y + 1) &= y \times y + y \times 1 \\ &= y^2 + y \end{aligned}$$

If you missed the 1 out, you would not get the y term at the end.

Exercise 30:4

Factorise each of these. Use the hints to help you in questions **1–4**.

1 $ax + bx = x(\quad)$

2 $5xy - 6xz = x(\quad)$

3 $5bc - 8bd = b(\quad)$

4 $7x - 9xy = x(\quad)$

5 $6x^2 - 11x$

● **6** $t^3 + t^2$

7 $3x^3 + 5x^2 + 7x$

● **8** $12xy^2 - 13x^2y$

Sometimes you can take out numbers and letters as factors.

Example Factorise completely $15x^2 - 10x$

15 and 10 have a common factor of 5.
So $15x^2 - 10x = 5(3x^2 - 2x)$

$3x^2$ and $2x$ have a common factor of x.
So $15x^2 - 10x = 5x(3x - 2)$
You could do this all at once by seeing that the common factor is $5x$.

Exercise 30:5

Factorise each of these.

1 $3x^2 + 6x$

2 $15xy - 20xz$

3 $18x^2 - 9x$

4 $45ax - 35bx + 25cx$

5 $16m^2 + 8mn$

6 $14abc - 21acd$

7 $18x^2y + 36xy^2$

8 $9x + 18x^2 - 27x^3$

Now that you can factorise you can use this skill to cancel factors in fractions.

Fractions will cancel when the top line and the bottom line have a common factor.

The 2s cancel because 2 is a factor of the top and bottom lines. $\frac{6}{8} = \frac{2 \times 3}{2 \times 4} = \frac{3}{4}$

An x cancels because x is a factor. $\frac{4x^3}{7x} = \frac{4x^2}{7}$

This leaves an x^2 on the top because $x^3 = x^2 \times x$

The $(x + 1)$s cancel here once you factorise. $\frac{2x + 2}{5x + 5} = \frac{2(x + 1)}{5(x + 1)} = \frac{2}{5}$

You can also cancel an $(x + 2)$ here. $\frac{2(x + 2)^2}{x(x + 2)} = \frac{2(x + 2)}{x}$

This leaves an $(x + 2)$ on the top because $(x + 2)^2 = (x + 2) \times (x + 2)$. You cannot cancel the xs at the end as the x on the top is not a factor of the top line.

Exercise 30:6

Simplify these expressions by cancelling common factors

1 $\dfrac{12}{18}$

2 $\dfrac{3x}{5x}$

3 $\dfrac{2x^2}{3x}$

4 $\dfrac{4(x+6)}{7(x+6)}$

5 $\dfrac{3(x-3)^2}{5(x-3)}$

6 $\dfrac{4(x+4)^2}{x(x+4)}$

7 $\dfrac{2x+6}{3x+9}$

8 $\dfrac{x^2+x}{5x+5}$

● 9 $\dfrac{3y^2+6y}{6y+12}$

● 10 $\dfrac{x^2y-xy^2}{4xy}$

Multiplying out two brackets

You also need to be able to multiply out two brackets.
You have to remember to multiply *all* the terms in the second bracket by *all* the terms in the first bracket.

Here is a simple way of remembering how to do this.

Example Multiply out $(x+4)(x-2)$.

1 Multiply the two **F**irst terms together: $(x+4)(x-2)$ x^2

2 Multiply the two **O**utside terms together: $(x+4)(x-2)$ $-2x$

3 Multiply the two **I**nside terms together: $(x+4)(x-2)$ $+4x$

4 Multiply the two **L**ast terms together: $(x+4)(x-2)$ -8

5 Collect all the terms together: $x^2-2x+4x-8$
$=x^2+2x-8$

You can remember this using the word **FOIL**.
If you draw lines between the terms as you multiply them, you get a face! This may also help you to remember to multiply all the terms.

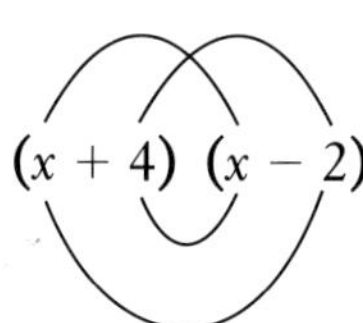

Exercise 30:7

1 **a** Copy this diagram. Use it to help you multiply out $(x + 5)(x + 3)$

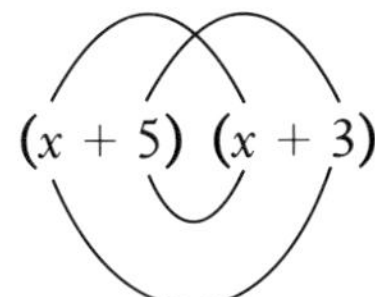

b Copy this diagram. Use it to help you multiply out $(x + 9)(x + 10)$

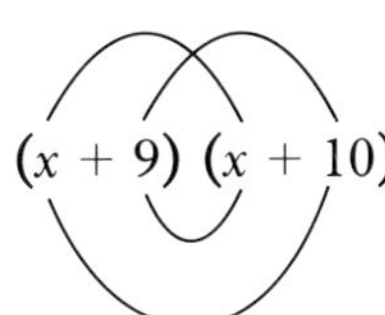

2 Multiply out each of these pairs of brackets.

a $(x + 8)(x + 6)$

b $(x + 7)(x - 8)$

c $(x + 1)(x - 5)$

d $(x - 4)(x + 9)$

e $(x + 8)(x - 1)$

f $(x - 2)(x + 2)$

g $(x - 11)(x - 11)$

h $(x - 5)(x - 15)$

3 Multiply out each of these pairs of brackets.

a $(3x + 1)(x + 2)$

b $(3x + 2)(2x - 7)$

c $(6x - 1)(x + 9)$

d $(x + 5)(\frac{1}{2}x - 6)$

e $(5x + 4)(2x - 7)$

f $(5x - 1)(6x + 1)$

g $(4x - 12)(2x + 7)$

h $(5x - 4)(5x + 4)$

i $(8x - 1)(\frac{1}{2}x + 2)$

j $(7x - 12)(8x + 7)$

k $(10x - 4)(10x + 4)$

l $(10x - 4)(10x - 4)$

4 Multiply these out.

a $(x + 3)^2$

b $(x + 7)^2$

c $(x - 4)^2$

d $(x - 2)^2$

e $(x + 6)^2$

f $(x - 10)^2$

g $(2x - 3)^2$

h $(3x - 8)^2$

i $(2x + 1)^2$

j $(3x - 2)^2$

k $(4x + 1)^2$

l $(7x + 6)^2$

5 Simplify these expressions.

a $(x + 6)^2 + (x + 1)^2$

b $(x + 4)^2 + (2x + 1)^2$

c $(2x + 3)^2 - (x + 1)^2$

d $(4x + 1)^2 - (x + 4)^2$

e $(3x - 1)^2 - (x - 1)^2$

f $(4x - 1)^2 - (x - 2)^2$

Changing the subject

You will need the skills of factorising and multiplying out brackets to solve some changing the subject problems.

You need to re-arrange some formulas in which the new subject appears twice. To do this you need to collect the terms with the new subject in together and then factorise.

Examples **1** Make t the subject of the formula $8tx = 3ty + s$

First get any terms involving the new subject onto one side and get any terms not involving the new subject onto the other side. $8tx - 3ty = s$

Now factorise out the new subject. $t(8x - 3y) = s$

Finally, divide by the bracket to leave t as the subject. $t = \dfrac{s}{8x - 3y}$

2 Make r the subject of the formula $s = \dfrac{r + 4}{r}$

First multiply both sides by r to remove the fraction. $rs = r + 4$

Then move all the r terms to the LHS. $rs - r = 4$

Now factorise out the r. $r(s - 1) = 4$

Finally divide by the bracket. $r = \dfrac{4}{s - 1}$

Exercise 30:8

Make the **red** letter the subject of each of these formulas.

1 $3xa = 5xb + c$

2 $5yz = 3yx + z$

3 $s = \dfrac{r - 3}{r}$

4 $t = \dfrac{s - p}{2s}$

5 $q = \dfrac{3 + q}{t}$

6 $q + p = 3qt - s$

7 $f = \sqrt{\dfrac{g + 7}{g}}$

8 $y = \sqrt{\dfrac{x - 5}{x}}$

● **9** $f = \sqrt{\dfrac{g^2 + 7}{g^2}}$

● **10** $s = \dfrac{t^2 - 7}{3t^2}$

2 Factorising and solving quadratics

The path of a stone thrown in the air is worked out using quadratic equations.

Ben is doing his Maths homework!

Coefficient The number in front of a letter is called a **coefficient**. In $x^2 + 2x - 8$, 2 is called the coefficient of x.

Constant term The number on the end of the equation is known as the **constant term**. In $x^2 + 2x - 8$, -8 is the constant term.

Exercise 30:9

1 Multiply out each of these pairs of brackets:

a $(x + 2)(x + 6)$

b $(x + 8)(x - 7)$

c $(x + 4)(x - 7)$

d $(x + 9)(x - 10)$

e $(x - 6)(x + 2)$

f $(x - 10)(x + 10)$

2 Copy this table. Use your answers to question **1** to fill it in. The first one is done for you.

	Number at end of 1st bracket	Number at end of 2nd bracket	Coefficient of x	Constant term
a	2	6	8	12
b	8	−7		
c	4	−7		
d	9	−10		
e	−6	2		
f	−10	10		

In question **2** you should have noticed that when you multiply out two brackets that both start with x:

> The **coefficient of** x is found by *adding* the two numbers at the end of the brackets together.
> The **constant term** is found by *multiplying* the two numbers at the end of the brackets together.

Example $(x + 4)(x - 7) = x^2 \quad -3x \quad -28$

$+4 + -7 = -3 \qquad +4 \times -7 = -28$

Once you know these facts, you can use them to reverse the process. This means taking a quadratic expression and splitting it back into two brackets.
This process is known as **factorising a quadratic**.

Example Factorise $x^2 + 5x + 6$

The brackets will be $(x + ?)(x + ?)$

The two numbers at the end of the brackets
add together to give 5 and
multiply together to give 6.

The two numbers that do this are 2 and 3.
So $x^2 + 5x + 6 = (x + 2)(x + 3)$
You can write these brackets either way round.

You may also find it helpful to look at the signs in the equation you are factorising.

$x^2 + 5x + 6$	The number at the end is $+6$.
$= (x + ?)(x + ?)$	The numbers must be the same sign so that they multiply to give a $+$. They must both be $+$ because they add to give $+5$.
$x^2 - 7x + 10$	The number at the end is $+10$.
$= (x - ?)(x - ?)$	The numbers must be the same sign so that they multiply to give a $+$. They must both be $-$ because they add to give -7.
$x^2 + 3x - 10$	The number at the end is -10.
$= (x + ?)(x - ?)$	The numbers must have different signs so that they multiply to give a $-$. The $+$ number must be bigger because they add to give a $+$ total of $+3$.

---

3 Factorise these quadratic expressions.

a $x^2 + 4x + 3$

b $x^2 + 9x + 20$

c $x^2 + 9x + 18$

d $x^2 + 14x + 49$

e $x^2 + 11x + 30$

f $x^2 - 5x + 4$

g $x^2 - 29x - 30$

h $x^2 + 4x - 60$

i $x^2 + 6x + 9$

j $x^2 - x - 2$

k $x^2 - 8x + 15$

l $x^2 - 8x - 33$

m $x^2 + 10x - 24$

n $x^2 + 13x - 30$

o $x^2 + 4x$

p $x^2 - 9$

● **q** $x^2 + 100x + 2100$

● **r** $x^2 + 98x + 2392$

● **s** $x^2 - x - 306$

● **t** $x^2 + x - 600$

Difference of two squares

A quadratic expression which is in the form $x^2 - a^2$ is known as the **difference of two squares**. Difference means subtract. The same rules still work when you are factorising it.

Example

Factorise $x^2 - 16$.
You can think of this as $x^2 + 0x - 16$
The numbers in the two brackets add to give 0 and multiply to give -16.
They are $+4$ and -4
$x^2 - 16 = (x - 4)(x + 4)$

The general rule is $\mathbf{x^2 - a^2 = (x - a)(x + a)}$

Exercise 30:10

Factorise these quadratic expressions.

1 $x^2 - 9$

2 $x^2 - 64$

3 $x^2 - 4$

4 $x^2 - 1$

5 $x^2 - 144$

● **6** $x^2 - y^2$

● **7** $x^2 - \frac{1}{4}$

8 $x^2 - 324$

Quadratic equations

Once you can factorise a quadratic expression, you can solve a quadratic equation.

When you have solved a quadratic equation, you can sketch the graph of the quadratic.

Solving the quadratic equation tells you where the graph crosses the x axis.

Example Solve $x^2 + 5x + 6 = 0$

1 Factorise the quadratic.

$(x + 2)(x + 3) = 0$

You now have two brackets *multiplied* together to give 0.
The only way two things can multiply together to give 0 is if one of them is 0.
It is very important that the quadratic **is always equal to 0.**

2 Put the two brackets equal to 0.

This means that either $x + 2 = 0$ or $x + 3 = 0$

3 Solve these simple equations.

$x + 2 = 0$ $\quad$ $x + 3 = 0$
$x = -2$ $\quad$ $x = -3$

These are both solutions of $x^2 + 5x + 6 = 0$
Quadratic equations always have two solutions.

4 You can check your answers by putting them back into the original equation.

Put $x = -2$ into $x^2 + 5x + 6$: $= (-2)^2 + 5 \times (-2) + 6$
$= 4 - 10 + 6$
$= 0$

Put $x = -3$ into $x^2 + 5x + 6$: $= (-3)^2 + 5 \times (-3) + 6$
$= 9 - 15 + 6$
$= 0$

This shows that both answers are correct.

Exercise 30:11

1 Follow these steps to solve $x^2 - 3x - 18 = 0$

a Factorise $x^2 - 3x - 18$

b Put each bracket equal to zero.

c Solve the equations you wrote down in part **b**.

d Check your answers by putting them back into the original equation. They should both give 0.

2 Follow these steps to solve $x^2 + 8x + 15 = 0$

a Factorise $x^2 + 8x + 15$

b Put each bracket equal to zero.

c Solve the equations you wrote down in part **b**.

d Check your answers by putting them back into the original equation. They should both give 0.

3 Solve these quadratic equations.

a $x^2 + 4x + 3 = 0$

b $x^2 + 13x + 42 = 0$

c $x^2 + x - 6 = 0$

d $x^2 - 7x + 12 = 0$

e $x^2 + 6x = 0$

f $x^2 - 11x - 26 = 0$

g $x^2 + 7x - 30 = 0$

h $x^2 - 11x + 30 = 0$

i $x^2 + 5x + 4 = 0$

j $x^2 + 12x + 35 = 0$

• **k** $x^2 + x = 6$

• **l** $x^2 + 10x = -24$

4 Solve these quadratic equations.

a $x^2 - 9 = 0$

b $x^2 - 25 = 0$

c $x^2 - 100 = 0$

d $x^2 + 5x = 0$

e $x^2 - 11x = 0$

f $x^2 + 10x = 0$

g $x^2 = 16$

h $x^2 = 36$

i $x^2 = 121$

• **j** $x^2 = 19$

• **k** $x^2 = 24$

• **l** $x^2 = 50$

• **5** Solve these quadratic equations.

a $36 - x^2 = 0$

b $49 - x^2 = 0$

c $121 - x^2 = 0$

d $0.25 - x^2 = 0$

In Chapter 19 you saw how to draw graphs of quadratic equations. Factorising a quadratic equation allows you to draw a sketch of the graph. A sketch graph shows the shape of the graph and the points where it crosses the axes. You can't read off exact values from a sketch graph.

Example

Sketch $y = x^2 - x - 12$.
Show all the points where the graph crosses the axes.

1 Find the points where the graph crosses the x axis.
These are the points where $y = 0$.
To do this, solve the quadratic equal to 0.

$x^2 - x - 12 = 0$
$(x + 3)(x - 4) = 0$
Either $x + 3 = 0$ or $x - 4 = 0$
So $\boldsymbol{x = -3}$ or $\boldsymbol{x = 4}$
The graph crosses the x axis at $x = -3$ and at $x = 4$.

2 Find the point where the graph crosses the y axis.
To do this, put $x = 0$.

$y = x^2 - x - 12$
$= 0^2 - 0 - 12$
$= -12$

3 Draw the axes and mark the crossing points.

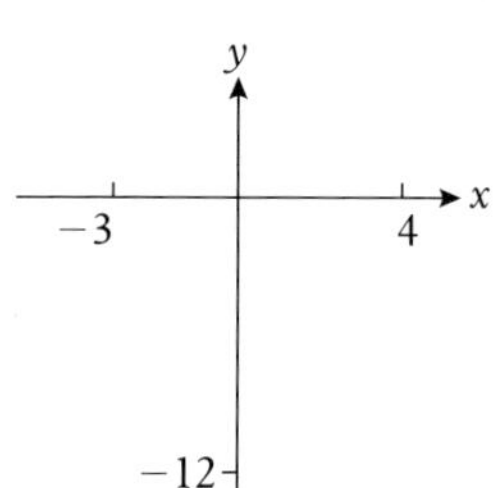

4 Sketch the graph.
Quadratic graphs are always symmetrical.
The bottom of this curve must be halfway between the points where the curve crosses the x axis.

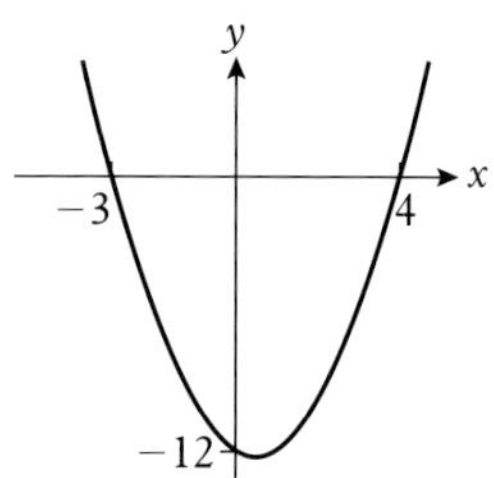

Exercise 30:12

1 Follow these steps to sketch the graph of $y = x^2 - 3x - 10$.

a Find the points where the graph crosses the x axis.
To do this, solve the quadratic equal to 0.

$x^2 - 3x - 10 = 0$
$(x \qquad)(x \qquad) = 0$

Either x........... $= 0$ or x........... $= 0$
So $\mathbf{x = \ldots}$ or $\mathbf{x = \ldots}$

The graph crosses the x axis at $x = \ldots$ and at $x = \ldots$

b Find the point where the graph crosses the y axis.
To do this, put $x = 0$.

$y = x^2 - 3x - 10$
$= \ldots$
$= \ldots$

c Draw the axes and mark the crossing points.

d Sketch the graph.

2 Follow these steps to sketch the graph of $y = x^2 + x - 12$.

a Find the points where the graph crosses the x axis.
To do this, solve the quadratic equal to 0.

$x^2 + x - 12 = 0$
…
…

The graph crosses the x axis at $x = \ldots$ and at $x = \ldots$

b Find the point where the graph crosses the y axis.
To do this, put $x = 0$.

$y = x^2 + x - 12$
$= \ldots$
$= \ldots$

c Draw the axes and mark the crossing points.

d Sketch the graph.

3 Sketch the graph of each of the following quadratic equations.

a $y = x^2 + 4x + 3$

b $y = x^2 + 2x - 15$

c $y = x^2 + 4x - 12$

d $y = x^2 - 4x - 5$

e $y = x^2 + 3x$

f $y = x^2 - 11x - 26$

g $y = x^2 - 16$

h $y = x^2 - 25$

● **4** Sketch the graph of each of the following quadratic equations.

a $y = x^2 + 6x + 9$

b $y = x^2 - 4x + 4$

c $y = x^2 - 6x + 9$

d $y = x^2 + 10x + 25$

This is a sketch graph of $y = -x^2$.

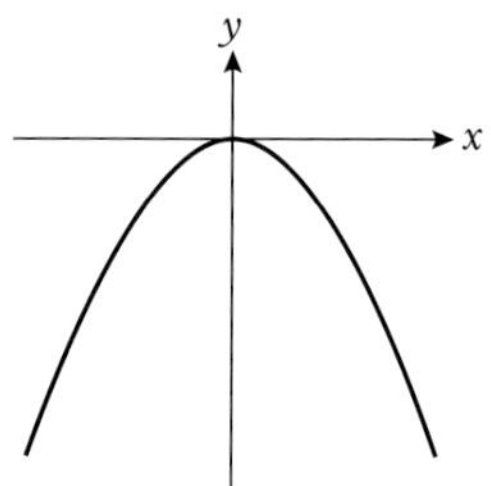

When the x^2 term is negative, a quadratic graph is turned upside down.

● **5** Sketch the graph of each of the following quadratic equations.

a $y = 9 - x^2$

b $y = 6 + x - x^2$

c $y = -x^2 + 7x - 10$

● **6** The height of a ball as it travels through the air is worked out using the equation $h = 20t - 5t^2$.
h is the height in metres and t is the time in seconds.

a Sketch a graph of this equation.

b How many seconds is the ball in the air?

1 Multiply out these brackets.

a $4(x + 2)$
b $3(y - 3)$
c $6(2x + 3)$
d $5(5x - 1)$
e $-2(x + 3)$
f $-4(3x - 4)$
g $-3(4x + 1)$
h $-6(y^2 - 4)$
i $y(3y^2 - 7y)$
j $x(5x^2 - 2x - 6)$
k $2x(2x^2 + 3y - y^2)$
l $3y(4xy - 3x^2z)$

2 Factorise each of these.
Use the hints to help you in parts **a–f**.

a $18y - 12 \quad = 6(\qquad)$
b $15x - 45 \quad = 5(\qquad)$
c $4x^2 + 8x \quad = 4x(\qquad)$
d $12pq - 20pr \quad = 4p(\qquad)$
e $27x^2 - 36x \quad = 9x(\qquad)$
f $12px + 24qx + 48rx = 12x(\qquad)$
g $5r - 15s - 50t$
h $21y - 49z$
i $7m^2 + 8mn$
j $4abc - 6acd$
k $24x^2y + 36xy^2$
l $9y + 18y^2 - 27y^3$

3 Multiply out each of these pairs of brackets.

a $(x + 3)(x + 6)$
b $(2x + 5)(x + 3)$
c $(3x + 2)(x + 2)$
d $(x + 3)(x + 6)$
e $(2x - 7)(x + 3)$
f $(3x + 2)(x - 2)$
g $(2x - 8)(x + 3)$
h $(3x + 4)(x - 2)$
i $(2x - 2)(2x + 3)$
j $(5x - 6)(6x - 4)$
k $(3x - 8)(2x - 7)$
l $(2x - 1)(2x - 3)$
m $(5x + 4)(6x - 4)$
n $(3x + 1)(2x + 7)$
o $(5x + 2)(6x - 4)$
p $(3x + 3)(2x - 7)$

4 Factorise these quadratic expressions.

a $x^2 + 3x + 2$
b $x^2 + 6x + 5$
c $x^2 + 11x + 24$
d $x^2 - 9x + 18$
e $x^2 - 14x + 49$
f $x^2 + 12x + 36$
g $x^2 - 4x + 5$
h $x^2 - 29x - 30$
i $x^2 - 6x - 7$
j $x^2 + 14x - 32$
k $x^2 + 8x - 48$
l $x^2 + 6x$
m $x^2 + 7x$
n $x^2 - 16$
o $x^2 - 0.64$
p $x^2 + 8x + 16$
q $x^2 + 16x + 64$
r $x^2 - 6.25$

5 Solve these quadratic equations.

a $x^2 - 3x + 2 = 0$

b $x^2 - 4x + 3 = 0$

c $x^2 + 5x + 4 = 0$

d $x^2 - x - 6 = 0$

e $x^2 + 7x + 12 = 0$

f $x^2 - 4x = 0$

g $x^2 + 12x = 0$

h $x^2 - 5x - 6 = 0$

i $x^2 + 5x - 24 = 0$

j $x^2 - 8x + 20 = 0$

k $x^2 + 15x + 14 = 0$

l $x^2 - 15x + 56 = 0$

m $x^2 + 2x = 3$

n $x^2 - 4x = 5$

6 Follow these steps to sketch the graph of $y = x^2 - 7x + 12$.

a Find the points where the graph crosses the x axis.
To do this, solve the quadratic equal to 0.

$x^2 - 7x + 12 = 0$
$(x \qquad)(x \qquad) = 0$

Either x........... $= 0$ or x........... $= 0$
So **$x = \ldots$** or **$x = \ldots$**

The graph crosses the x axis at $x = \ldots$ and at $x = \ldots$

b Find the point where the graph crosses the y axis.
To do this, put $x = 0$.

$y = x^2 - 7x + 12$
$= \ldots$
$= \ldots$

c Draw the axes and mark the crossing points.

d Sketch the graph.

7 Sketch graphs of these quadratic equations.

a $y = x^2 + 5x + 4$

b $y = x^2 + 5x - 6$

c $y = x^2 + x - 6$

d $y = x^2 - 5x - 6$

e $y = x^2 + 3x$

f $y = x^2 - 11x$

g $y = x^2 - 4x + 3$

h $y = x^2 + 4x - 12$

i $y = x^2 + 9x$

j $y = 9 - x^2$

k $y = x - x^2$

l $y = -x^2 + 4$

1 Look at this rectangle.

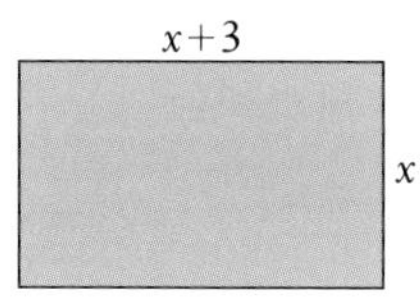

a Write down and simplify an expression for the area of the rectangle.

The area of the rectangle is 10 cm^2.

b Write down an equation using your answer to **a**.

c Solve the equation to find two values of x.

d Explain why only one of the values in **c** is the answer to this problem.

2 p and q are consecutive whole numbers where $p > q$.

a Write down the value of $p - q$.

b Factorise $p^2 - q^2$

c Use your answers to **a** and **b** to prove that $p^2 - q^2 = p + q$.

3 Not all quadratic equations start with just x^2.
Many start with $2x^2$ or $3x^2$ etc.
If you want to solve $2x^2 - 7x + 3 = 0$ you need to start by factorising.
One of the brackets must begin with a $2x$.
This is the only way to get $2x^2$ as the first term.
So $2x^2 - 7x + 3 = (2x - ?)(x - ?)$
The two numbers at the end of the brackets must still multiply together to give the constant term.
So you need to try different pairs of values at the end of the bracket until you get the right answer.

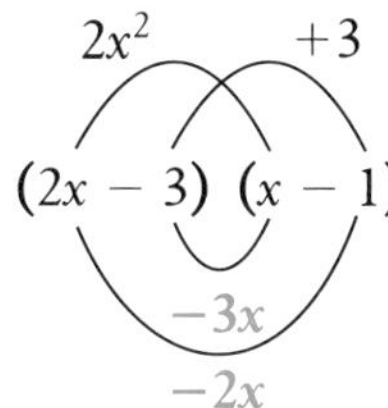

This is wrong because the $-3x$ and the $-2x$ give you $-5x$ and you need $-7x$.

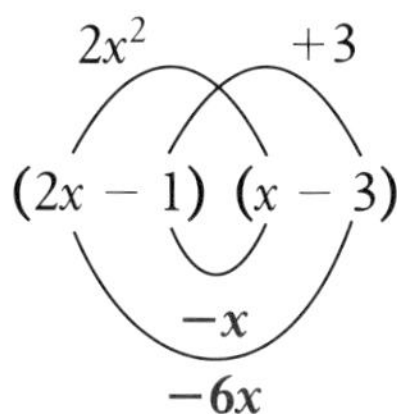

This is right. The $-x$ and the $-6x$ give you $-7x$.

Now you need to solve $(2x - 1)(x - 3) = 0$

Either $2x - 1 = 0$ or $x - 3 = 0$

So $x = \frac{1}{2}$ or $x = 3$

Solve these quadratic equations.

a $2x^2 - 5x + 2 = 0$

b $2x^2 - 7x + 5 = 0$

c $2x^2 + 5x + 3 = 0$

d $5x^2 + 26x + 5 = 0$

e $5x^2 - 9x - 2 = 0$

f $2x^2 + 3x - 9 = 0$

1 Multiply out each of these brackets.

a $3(x + 4)$ **c** $-5(3x - 3)$

b $x(x - 7)$ **d** $x(6x^2 + 2x)$

2 Multiply out each of these pairs of brackets.

a $(x + 3)(x + 4)$ **c** $(2x - 5)(3x - 3)$

b $(x + 2)(x - 7)$ **d** $(7x - 4)(6x + 2)$

3 Factorise each of these expressions.

a $3x + 6y$ **c** $3tx - 9ty$

b $x^2 + 3x$ **d** $15xyz - 6xz$

4 Factorise these quadratic expressions.

a $x^2 + 5x + 6$ **c** $x^2 - 3x - 28$

b $x^2 + 10x + 21$ **d** $x^2 + 7x - 30$

5 Solve these quadratic equations.

a $x^2 + 8x + 15 = 0$ **c** $x^2 + 2x - 3 = 0$

b $x^2 - 8x + 12 = 0$ **d** $x^2 - 4x - 12 = 0$

6 Sketch graphs of these quadratic equations.

a $y = x^2 - 2x - 15$

b $y = x^2 + 5x - 14$

7 Make the **red** letter the subject of each of these formulas.

a $6r = 3rt + 4$ **c** $t = \frac{r + 4}{r}$

b $7x + 3y = 3xt$ **d** $3z = \frac{4y - 3}{y}$

31 Solid shapes

1 Drawing shapes
Drawing shapes based on cubes on isometric paper
Completing part drawn cuboids on isometric paper
Drawing missing pieces of cuboids
Plans and elevations

2 Units of mass and capacity
Converting metric units of mass
Converting metric units of capacity
Converting imperial units of mass
Converting imperial units of capacity
Converting between metric and imperial units of mass and capacity
Estimating masses and capacities

CORE

3 Volume
Introducing volume and capacity
Finding volumes of blocks of 1 cm^3 cubes
Volume of a cuboid = length × width × height
Volume of a prism
Volume of a cylinder
Volume of compound shapes

4 Density
Defining density
Using the density formula to find mass and volume

5 Dimensions
Using dimensions to analyse formulas for length, area and volume

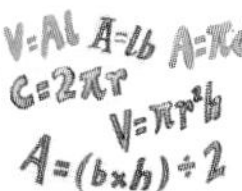

QUESTIONS

EXTENSION

TEST YOURSELF

1 Drawing shapes

Look at this picture carefully.

Can you see what is wrong with it?

You can use isometric paper to help you draw some 3D shapes.
But you must remember to use it the right way up. It must show vertical lines.

Example Copy the cube on to the grid.

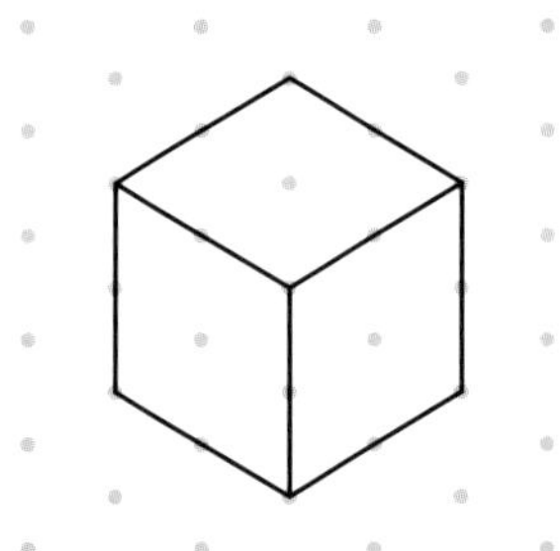

Start at a corner.

Use the grid this way up.

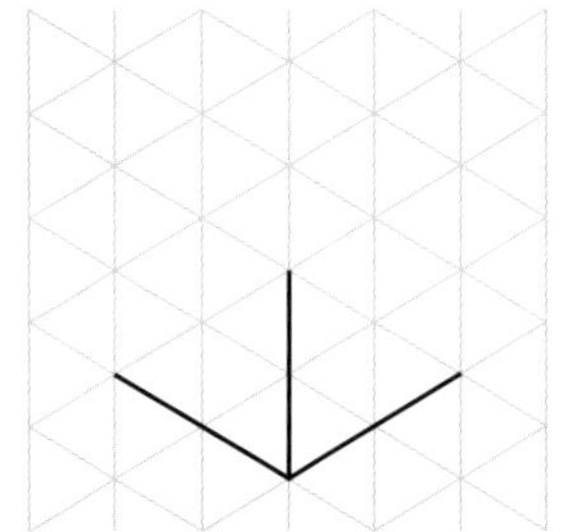

Every line on the grid is in one of these directions.

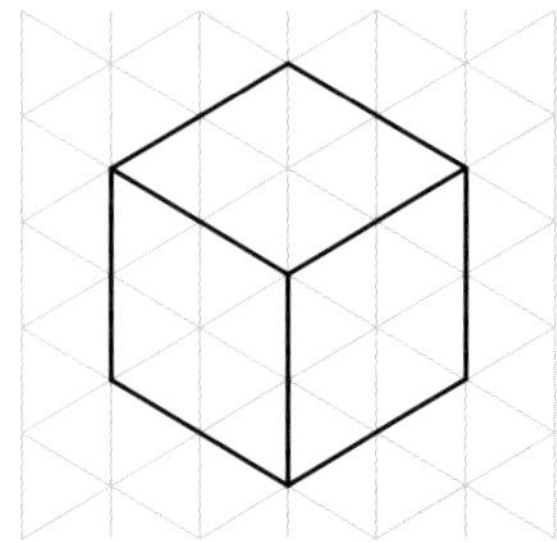

Follow the grid lines to complete the drawing.

Exercise 31:1

1 Copy these objects on to isometric paper.

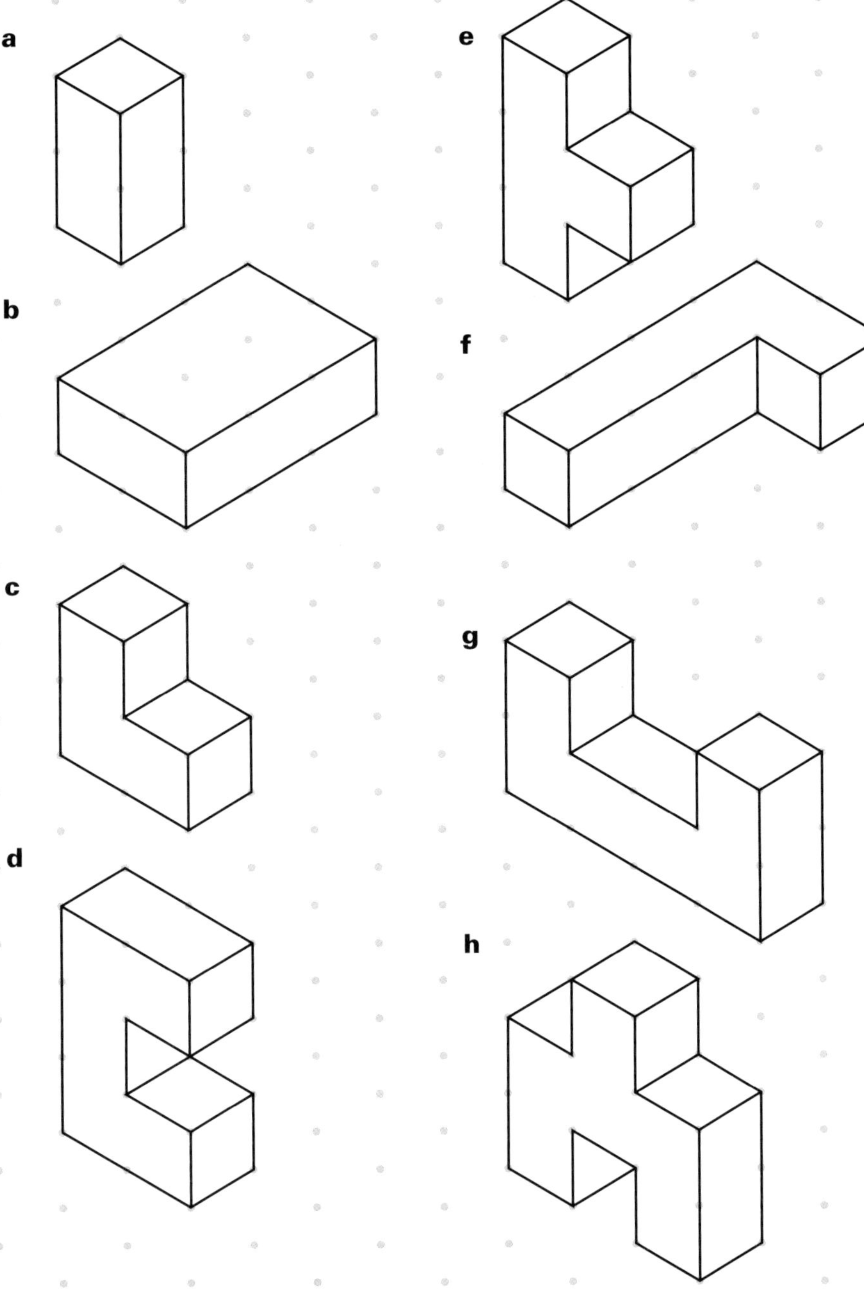

2 Copy and complete each diagram so that it shows a cuboid.

a

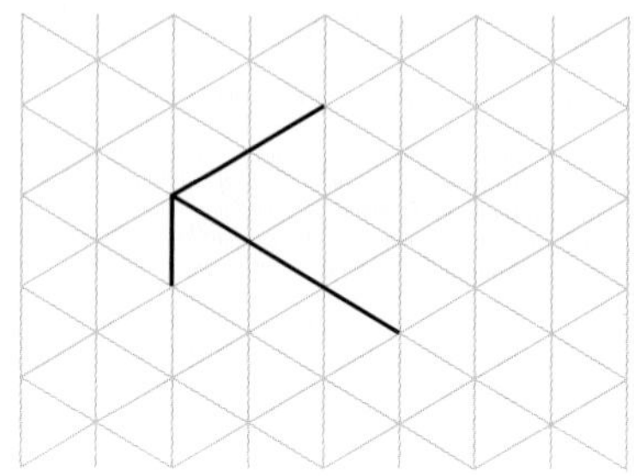

d

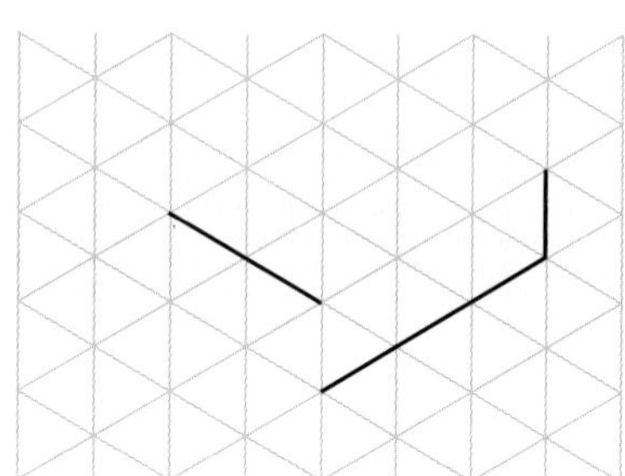

b

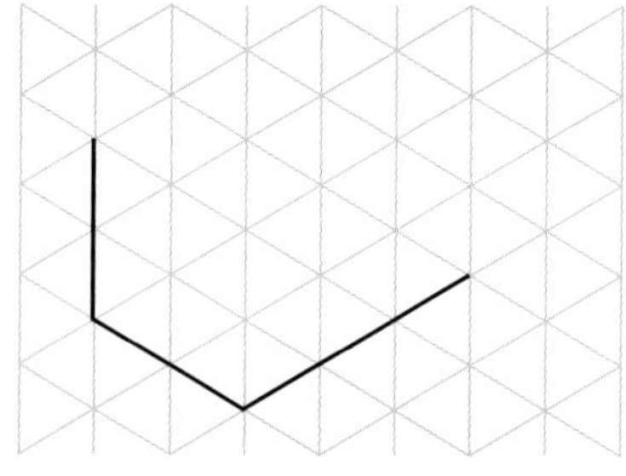

e

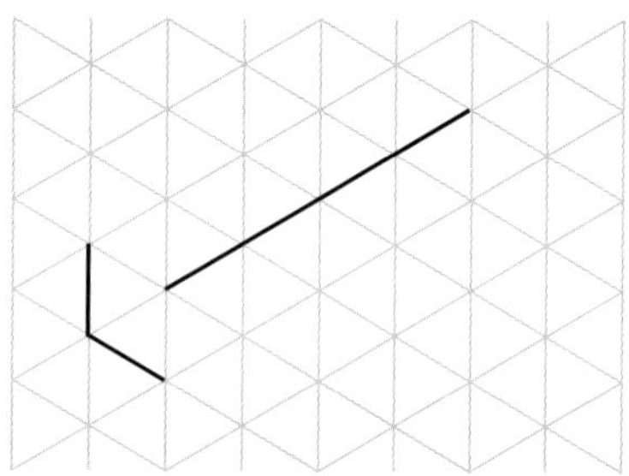

c

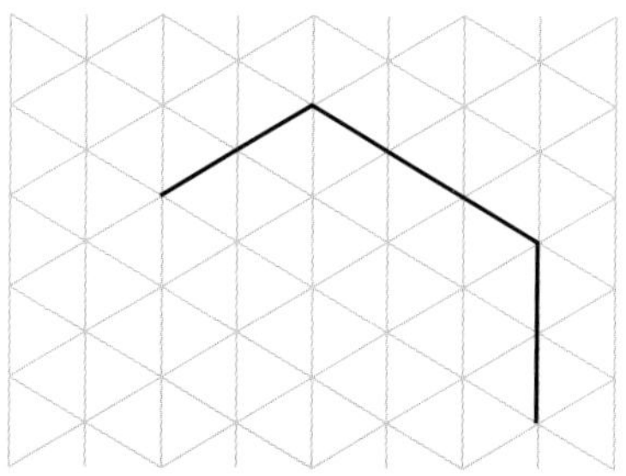

f

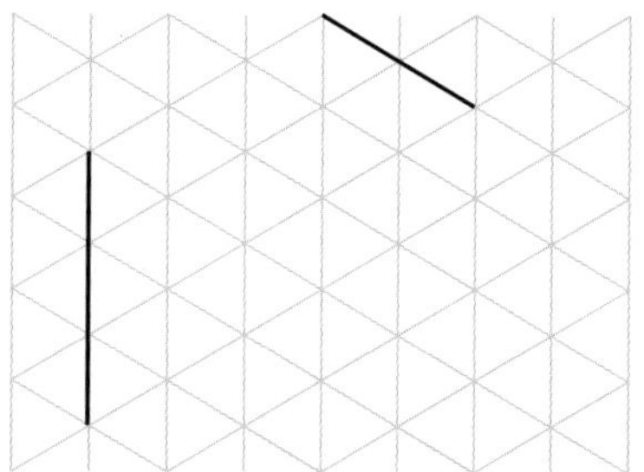

3 Each diagram shows a cuboid with a piece missing.
Draw the missing piece.

a

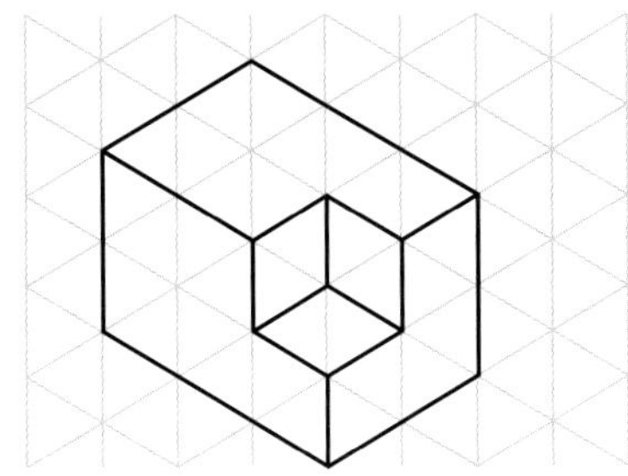

d

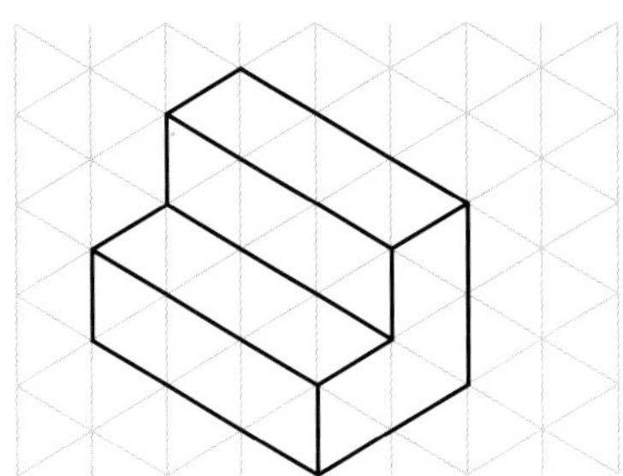

b

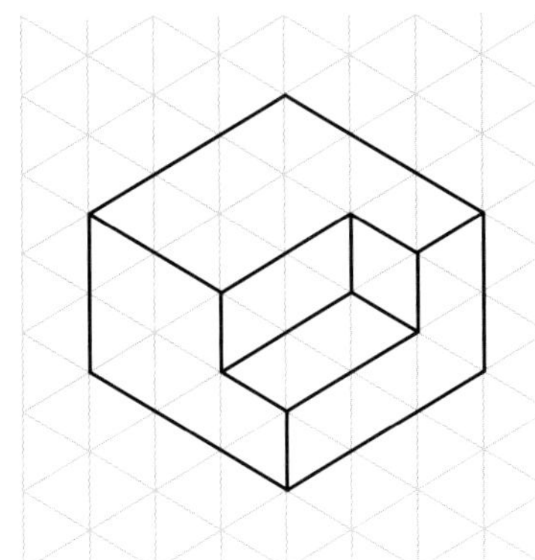

e

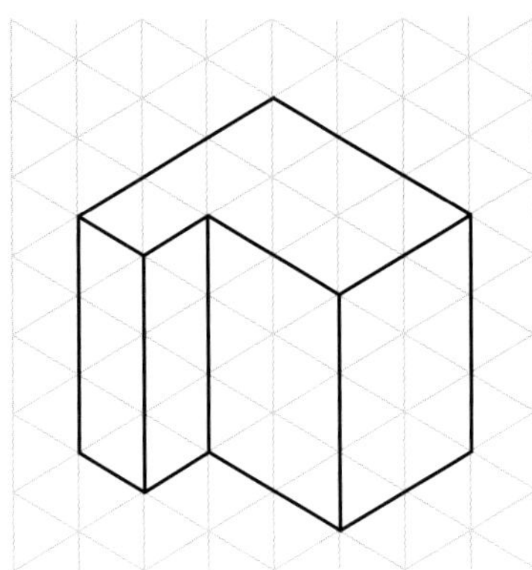

c

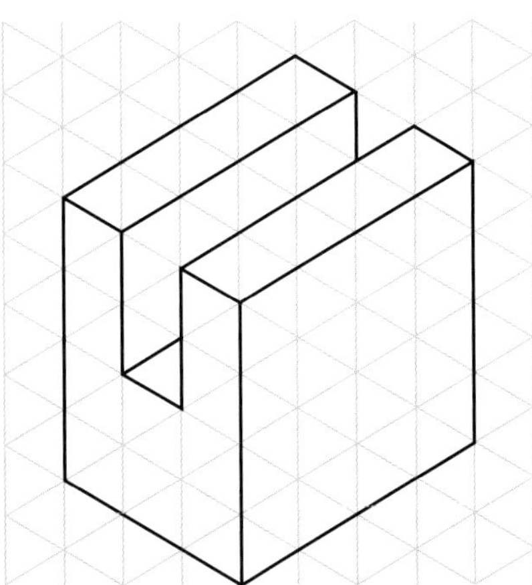

f

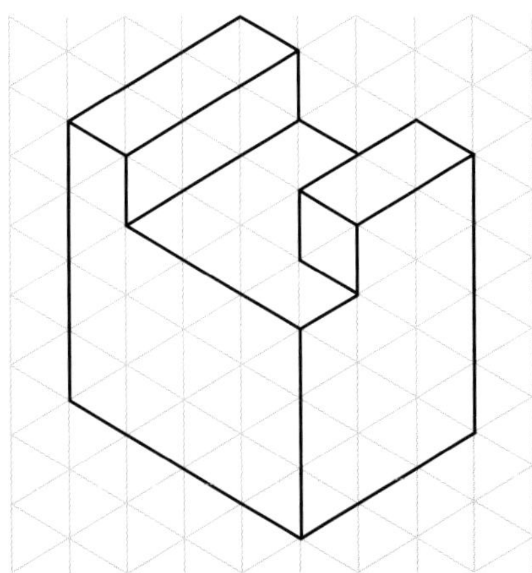

Here is an object made up of cubes.

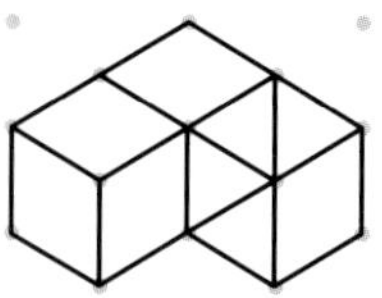

Katie is looking at the object from directly above.
This is what she sees.

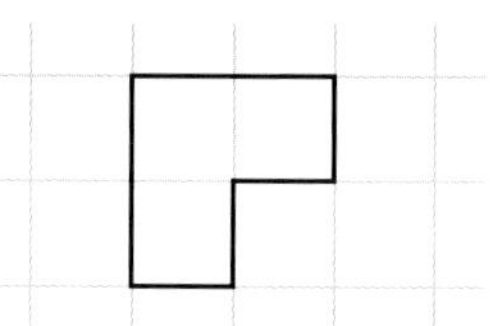

This is called the plan view of the object.

Exercise 31:2

1 Draw the plan view of each of these objects.

a

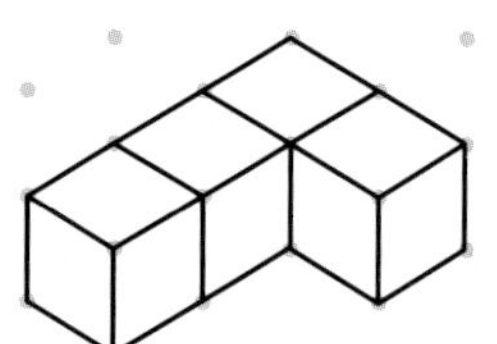

c

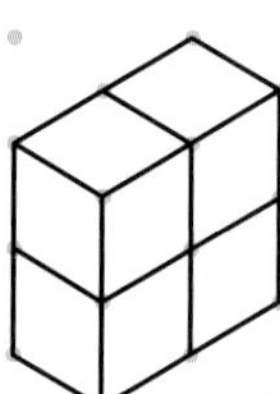

b

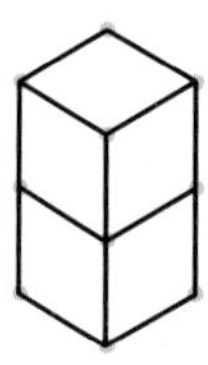

d

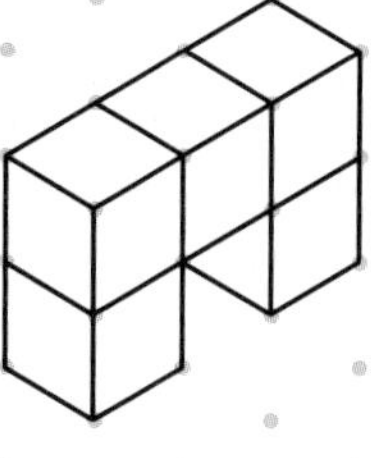

Here is another object.

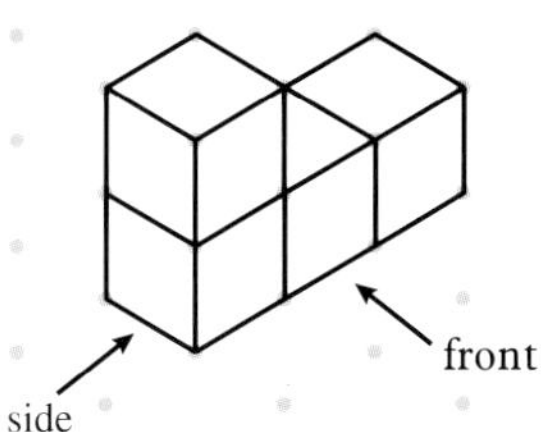

Leah is looking at the object from the front.
This is what she sees.

Danielle is looking at the object from the side.
This is what she sees.

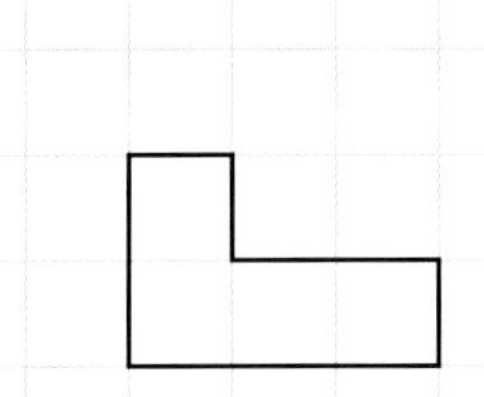

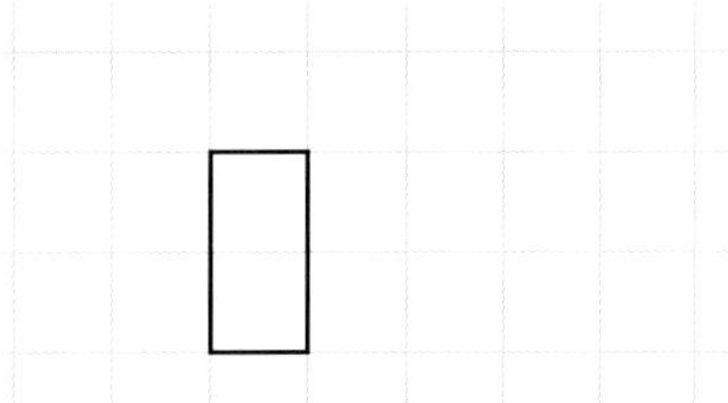

This is called the front elevation of the object.

This is called the side elevation of the object.

2 Draw the front elevation of each of these objects.

a

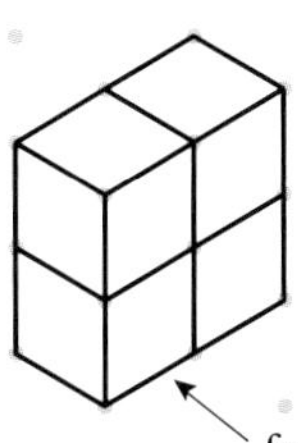

b

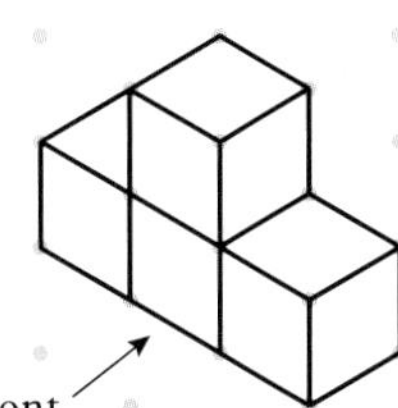

● **3** Draw the front and side elevations of each of these objects.

a

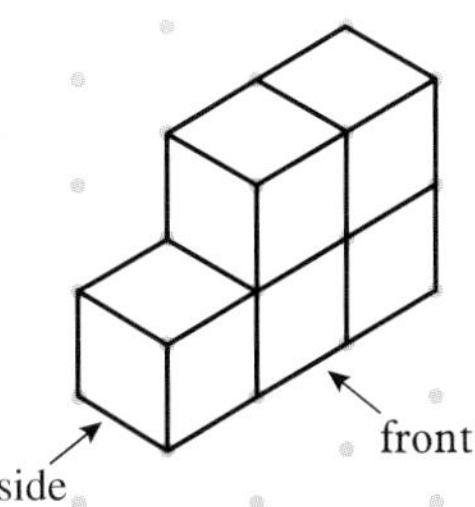

b

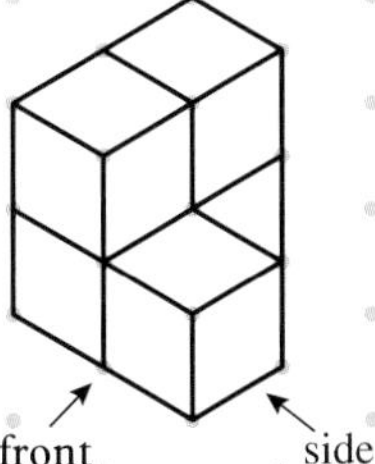

This is what Lee drew for the side elevation in question 3a.

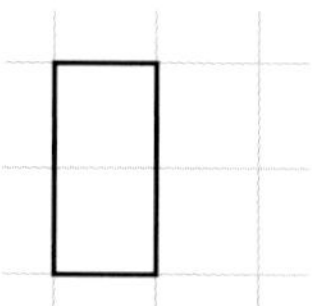

This does not show that the bottom cube isn't directly below the top one.

There is a better way of drawing plans and elevations when the various parts aren't in line with each other.

You use a dashed line to separate the parts that aren't lined up.

The correct elevation for question 3a is

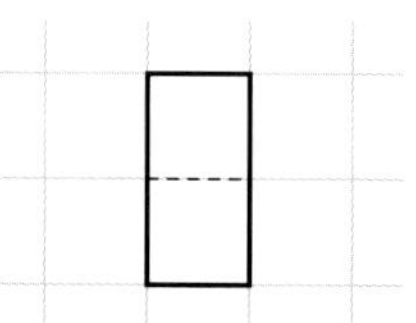

4 Draw the front elevation of each of these objects.

a

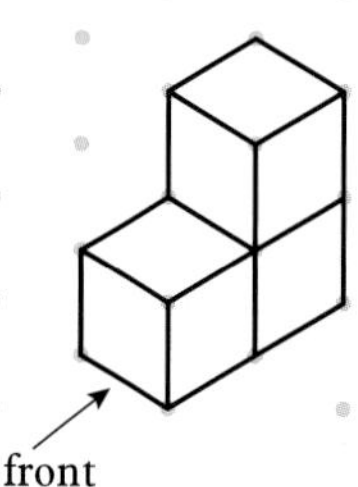

b

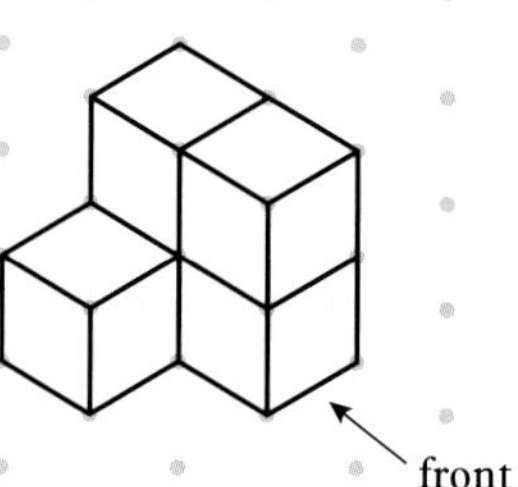

● **5** Draw the front and side elevations of each of these objects.

a

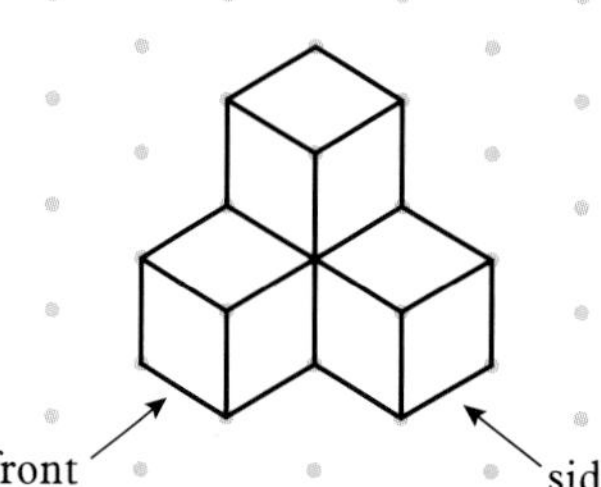

b

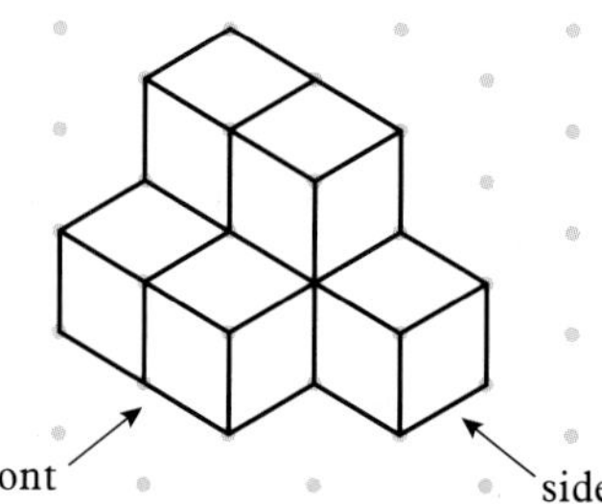

2 Units of mass and capacity

The weight of an object depends on where it is!
The mass of an object is always the same.
People often talk about the weight of something and most of the time they really mean the mass.

Metric units of mass

The **metric units of mass** are milligrams (mg), grams (g), kilograms (kg) or tonnes (t).

1000 mg = 1 g
1000 g = 1 kg
1000 kg = 1 t

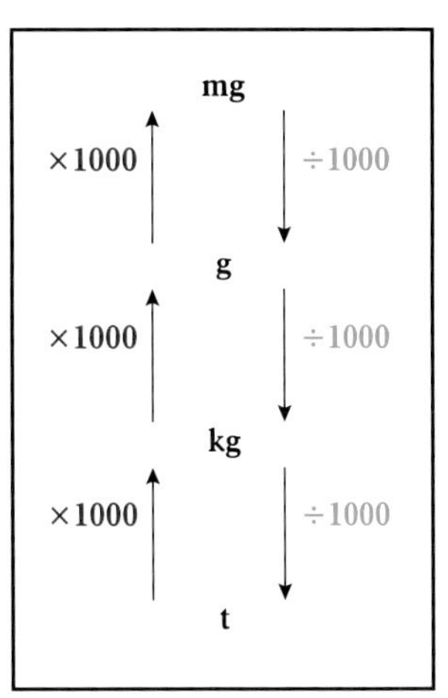

Example Change each of these to the units shown.

a 0.37 t to kilograms
b 2400 mg to grams

a There are 1000 kg in every tonne
So 0.37 t = 0.37 × 1000 kg
= 370 kg

b Every 1000 mg make 1 g.
Find how many lots of 1000 mg there are in 2400 mg.
2400 ÷ 1000 = 2.4 so 2400 mg = 2.4 g

Exercise 31:3

1 Change each of these masses into kilograms.

a 3 t **b** 7.12 t **c** 0.5 t **d** 0.046 t

2 Change each of these masses into grams.

a 2 kg **c** 10.5 kg **e** 0.31 kg **g** 5.246 kg
b 3.2 kg **d** 0.4 kg **f** 0.302 kg **h** 2.046 kg

3 Change each of these masses into kilograms.

a 7000 g **c** 8450 g **e** 10 000 g **g** 960 g

b 3600 g **d** 4030 g **f** 750 g **h** 45 g

4 Change each of these into the units shown.

a 25 g to milligrams **c** 8400 kg to tonnes ● **e** 10 000 000 g to tonnes

b 1200 mg to grams **d** 720 kg to tonnes ● **f** 7.35 kg to milligrams

5 The largest fish ever caught on a rod and line was a great white shark.
The shark's mass was 1537 kg.
Write this mass in tonnes.

6 A gudgeon is a small freshwater fish.
The largest gudgeon ever caught had a mass of 141 g.
Write this weight in kilograms.

Metric units of capacity

The **metric units of capacity** are millilitres (ml), centilitres (cl) and litres (l)

10 ml = 1 cl
1000 ml = 1 l
100 cl = 1 l

Example Change each of these into the units shown.

a 2.5 l to ml **b** 750 cl to l

a There are 1000 ml in every l so

$2.5l = 2.5 \times 1000$ ml
$= 2500$ ml

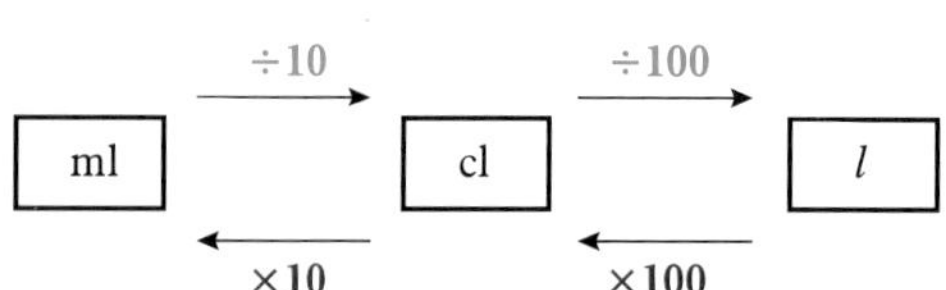

b Every 100 cl make 1 l.
Find how many lots of 100 cl there are in 750 cl.

$750 \div 100 = 7.5$ so 750 cl = 7.5 l

Exercise 31:4

1 Change each of these units into centilitres.

a 12 *l*	**c** 7.5 *l*	**e** 40 ml	**g** 600 ml
b 230 *l*	**d** 0.45 *l*	**f** 67 ml	**h** 964 ml

2 Change each of these units into litres.

a 500 cl	**d** 850 cl	**g** 2800 ml	**j** 400 ml
b 7000 cl	**e** 4350 cl	**h** 250 ml	**k** 50 ml
c 20 000 cl	**f** 17 cl	**i** 750 ml	**l** 8 ml

3 Change each of these units into millilitres.

a 40 cl	**d** 2.4 cl	**g** 7.4 *l*	**j** 0.06 *l*
b 5 cl	**e** 12.5 cl	**h** 3.124 *l*	**k** 0.075 *l*
c 9.4 cl	**f** 4.08 cl	**i** 0.8 *l*	**l** 0.0304 *l*

4 Change each of these into the units shown.

a 200 cl to litres	**c** 2.5 *l* to centilitres	**e** 850 ml to centilitres
b 550 cl to litres	**d** 0.75 *l* to centilitres	**f** 45 cl to millilitres

5 A 2 litre bottle of Ribena makes 66 servings.
Find the number of ml in each serving.
Give your answer to the nearest whole number.

6 A bottle of milk holds 568 ml.
Len has 50 crates of milk on his milk-float.
Every crate holds 20 bottles.
How many litres of milk are there
on Len's milk-float?

Imperial units of mass

The **imperial units of mass** are ounces (oz), pounds (lb) and stones (st).
16 oz = 1 lb   14 lb = 1 st

Example

Change each of these into the units shown.
a 8 st to pounds   **b** 72 oz to pounds

a There are 14 pounds in every stone.
So 8 stones = $8 \times 14 = 112$ pounds

b Every 16 ounces make 1 pound.
Find how many lots of 16 ounces there are in 72 ounces.
$72 \div 16 = 4.5$ so 72 ounces = $4\frac{1}{2}$ pounds

Exercise 31:5

1 Change each of these to ounces.
a 3 pounds **b** 7 pounds **c** $4\frac{1}{2}$ pounds ● **d** 6 pounds 3 ounces

2 Change each of these to pounds.
a 3 stones **b** 8 stones **c** $9\frac{1}{2}$ stones ● **d** 8 stone 12 pounds

3 Change each of these to stones.
a 98 pounds **b** 168 pounds **c** 115.5 pounds **d** 127.75 pounds

4 Kathryn weighs 10 stone 4 pounds.
What is her weight in pounds?

5 Alan's grandmother sends him to the shops for $\frac{1}{2}$ stone of potatoes.
How many pounds of potatoes should he buy?

6 Americans always give their weight in pounds.
Zak weighs 178 pounds.
What is his weight in stones and pounds?

Imperial units of capacity

The **imperial units of capacity** are pints (pt), quarts (qt) and gallons (gal).
2 pt = 1 qt   8 pt = 4 qt = 1 gal

Example

A milk churn holds 20 gallons. How many pints is this?
There are 8 pints in every gallon.

$$\begin{aligned} 20 \text{ gal} &= 20 \times 8 \text{ pt} \\ &= 160 \text{ pt} \end{aligned}$$

Exercise 31:6

1 Marion buys 1 gallon of milk.
How many pints is this?

2 An elephant drinks about 25 gal of water each day.
How many pints of water does an elephant drink each day?

3 An average person uses 160 pt of water each day.
How many gallons is this?

• **4** Carsington reservoir in Derbyshire holds 7800 million gallons of water.
How many 1 pt bottles could you fill from the reservoir?

Converting between metric and imperial units

It might help you to use conversion numbers.
You saw this in Chapter 23 where you converted lengths.

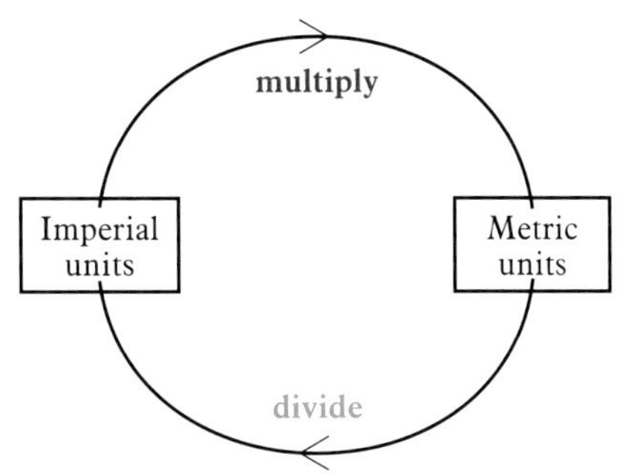

To change from imperial to metric you **multiply** by the conversion number.
To change from metric to imperial you divide by the conversion number.

		Conversion number
Mass	1 oz is about 30 g	30
	1 lb is about 450 g	450
	1 lb is about 0.45 kg	0.45
	1 st is about 6.5 kg	6.5
Capacity	1 pt is about 600 ml	600
	1 pt is about 0.6 *l*	0.6
	1 gal is about 4.5 *l*	4.5

You need to remember how to do these conversions.
Your exam paper will not tell you the conversion numbers!

Exercise 31:7

1 Change each of these masses into the units given.

a 2 oz into grams **c** 2.3 st into kilograms **e** 1170 g into ounces
b 14 lb into kilograms **d** 3 lb into grams **f** 2925 kg to pounds

2 Change each of these capacities into the units given.

a 4 pt into millilitres **c** 5.7 gal into litres **e** 30.6 *l* into gallons
b 7.3 pt into litres **d** 4.8 *l* into pints **f** 6600 ml into pints

3 An average person should drink 4 pt of liquid each day.
How many litres is this?

• **4** A recipe asks for 4 kg of sugar. How many pounds is this?

• **5** Janet's fuel tank has a capacity of 55 *l*. How many gallons is this?

Estimating

You also need to be able to estimate masses and capacities.
To do this you need to think about things that you know well.
Here are some examples but you may think of others that help you more.

Mass

30 g or 1 ounce

1 kg or 2.2 pounds

70 kg or 11 stones

Capacity

250 ml or $\frac{1}{2}$ pint

2 litres or $3\frac{1}{2}$ pints

90 litres or 20 gallons

Exercise 31:8

1 Estimate the mass of each of these in the units shown.

a

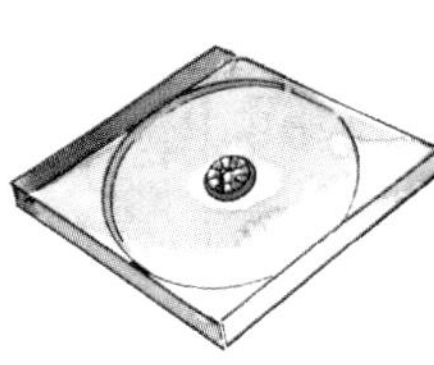

(1) grams
(2) ounces

b

(1) grams
(2) ounces

c

(1) kilograms
(2) pounds

d

(1) kilograms
(2) pounds

2 Estimate the capacity of each of these in the units shown.

a

(1) millilitres
(2) pints

b

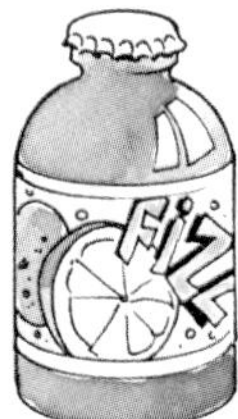

(1) millilitres
(2) pints

c

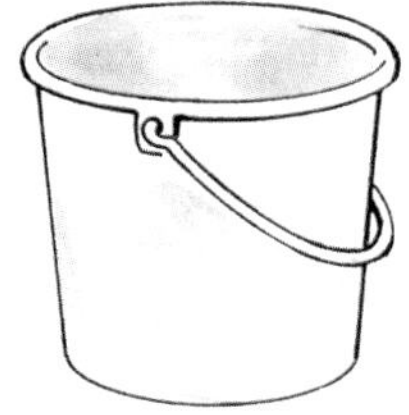

(1) litres
(2) gallons

d

(1) litres
(2) gallons

3 Volume

Jim is building a garage.
He needs to make a solid base to put the garage on.
This is called the 'footings' for the garage.
He digs out a cuboid shape and fills it with concrete.
He needs to know how much concrete to order.
He needs to be able to work out the volume of the footings.

Volume

The amount of space that an object takes up is called its **volume**.

Volume is measured in cubic units.
These can be millimetres cubed (**mm³**), centimetres cubed (**cm³**) or metres cubed (**m³**).

1 cm³

1 cm³ is the space taken up by a cube with all its edges 1 cm long.

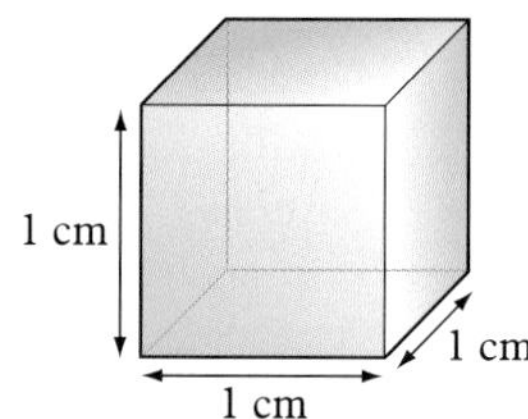

Capacity

The **capacity** of a hollow object is the volume of space inside it.

1 ml

This cube has been filled with water.
The volume of liquid inside is **1 millilitre**.
This is written **1 ml**.

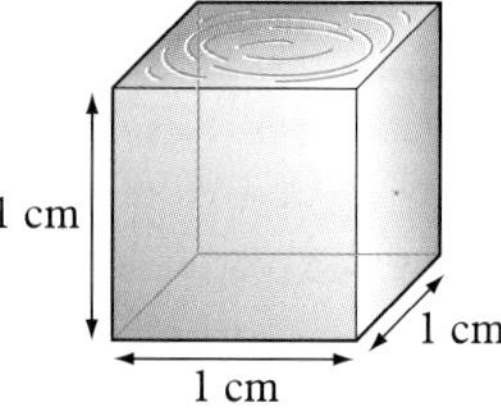

1 litre

Large volumes are measured in **litres**.
1 litre = 1000 ml   1 litre is written **1 *l***.

A capacity of **1 ml** is the same as a volume of **1 cm³**.
1000 **ml** is the same as 1 litre.

Exercise 31:9

1 Draw a diagram of a cube that has a volume of:
a 1 cm³   **b** 1 mm³   **c** 1 m³   • **d** 8 cm³

2 The capacity of a normal can of Pepsi is 330 ml.
Estimate the capacity in millilitres of each of these:

a  **b**  **c**  **d** 

3 The capacity of this bottle of lemonade is $2\,l$.
Estimate the capacity in litres of each of these.

a 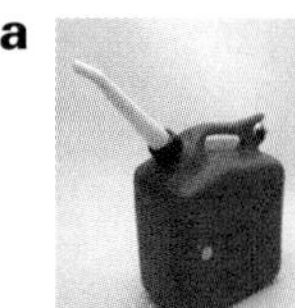 **b**  **c** 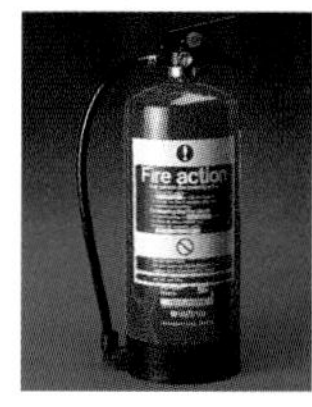

d 

● **4** **a** Write down the volume of each drink in centimetres cubed.
b Calculate the volume of Coca-Cola that you get for 1 p for each container.
Give your answers to 2 dp.
c Which container gives the best value for money?

---

1 cm³ A cube that has sides of 1 cm is called a 1 cm cube.
It has a volume of 1 cm cubed.
This is written as **1 cm³**.

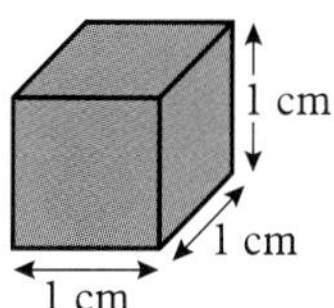

This cuboid has 12 cubes in each layer.
Each cube has a volume of 1 cm³
It has 2 layers.
The volume of the cuboid is
$12 \times 2 = 24$ cm³

Exercise 31:10

For each of these cuboids, write down:

a the number of cubes in one layer
b the number of layers
c the volume of the cuboid.

• **11** Look at this solid.
The yellow cubes go right through the shape.
a Find the volume of the red cubes.
b Find the volume of the yellow cubes.
c Find the total volume of the shape.

Volume of a cuboid

There is a faster way to find the volume of a block of cubes.
(1) Multiply the length by the width.
This tells you how many cubes there are in one layer.
(2) Multiply your answer by the height.
This tells you how many cubes there are altogether.

Volume of a cuboid

You can do this all at once:
Volume of a cuboid = length × width × height

Example

Work out the volume of this block of cubes.

Volume = length × width × height
= 6 × 3 × 4
= 72 cm^3

Exercise 31:11

In questions **1–8**, find the volume of each of the blocks. Write your answers in cm^3.

1

2

3

4

5

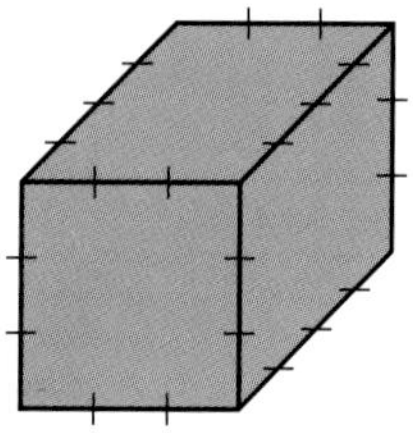

6

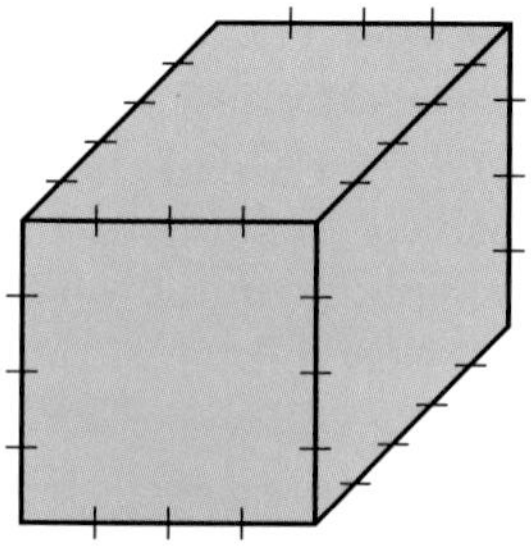

7

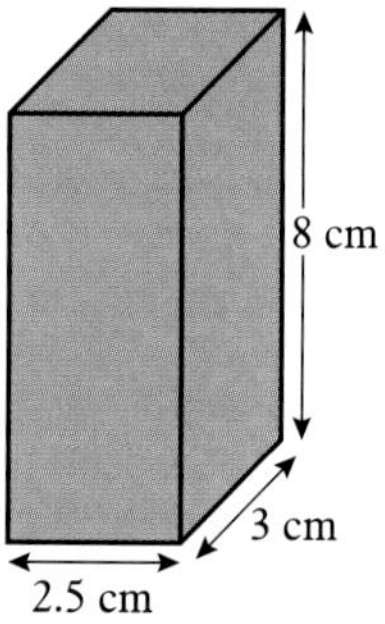

8 cm

3 cm

2.5 cm

● **8**

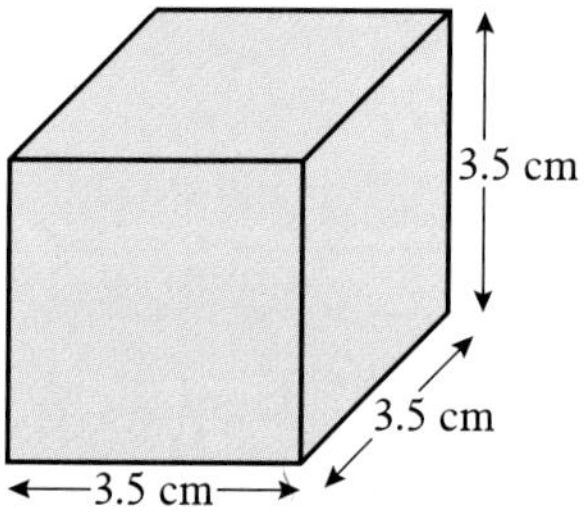

3.5 cm

3.5 cm

3.5 cm

9 A 750 g cereal box has sides of length 7 cm, 19 cm and 29 cm. Find the volume of the box.

10 A 1 litre carton of orange juice is in the shape of a cuboid. It measures 5.9 cm by 9 cm by 19.5 cm.

a Find the volume of the box.

● **b** How much space is there in the box if it contains exactly 1 *l* of orange juice?

In this exercise you need to use the correct units in your answers.
So far you have only used cm^3 for volume.
In this exercise you will need to use m^3 and mm^3 too.
Look carefully at the units in the question to help you give the right units in your answer.

Exercise 31:12

1 Work out the volume of this boxroom.
It is a cube of side 3 m.

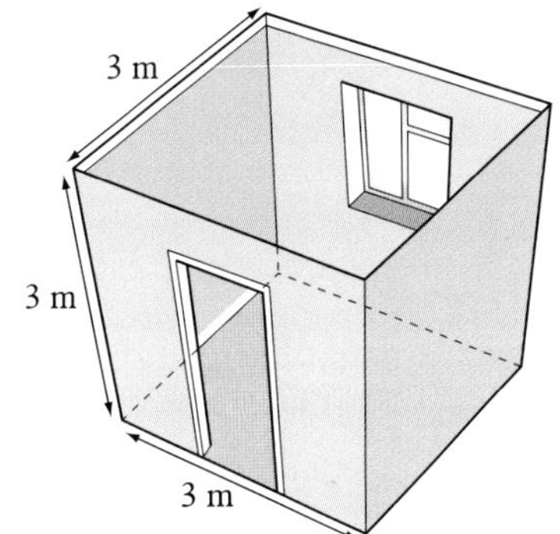

2 **a** Jim dug a hole for his garage footings.
The hole was 5 m long, 3 m wide and 0.5 m deep.
Find the volume of earth that he removed.

b He had to buy the concrete in litres.

$1\ m^3 = 1000\ l$

How many litres of concrete did Jim have to buy?

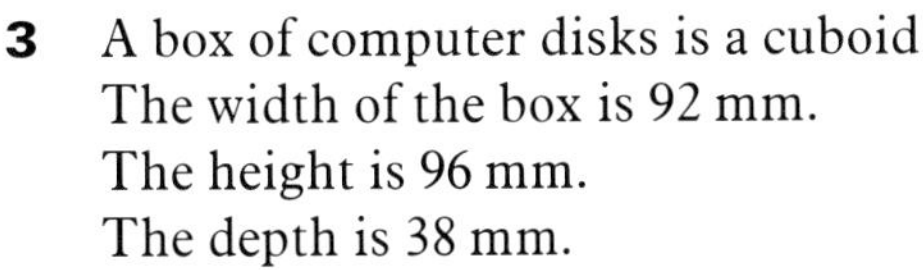

3 A box of computer disks is a cuboid.
The width of the box is 92 mm.
The height is 96 mm.
The depth is 38 mm.
Find the volume of the box.

4 **a** Measure the length, the width and the depth of your *Key Maths GCSE* book in millimetres to the nearest millimetre.
Write down your answers.

b Work out the volume of paper in the book.

● **5** This cuboid has length x cm, width y cm and height z cm.
Write down the volume of the cuboid in terms of x, y and z.

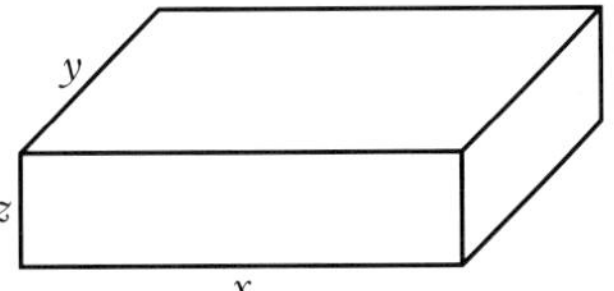

Prism

A **prism** is a solid which is exactly the same shape and size all the way through.

When you cut a slice through the solid it is the same size and shape.

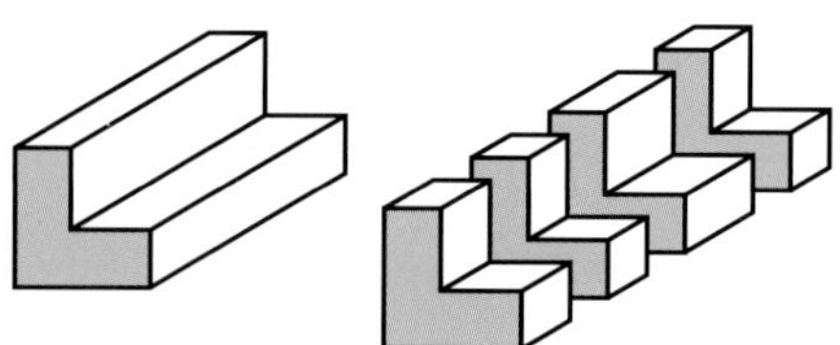

Cross section

The shape of this slice is called the **cross section** of the solid.

The shape of the cross section is often used to name the prism.

This is a triangular prism

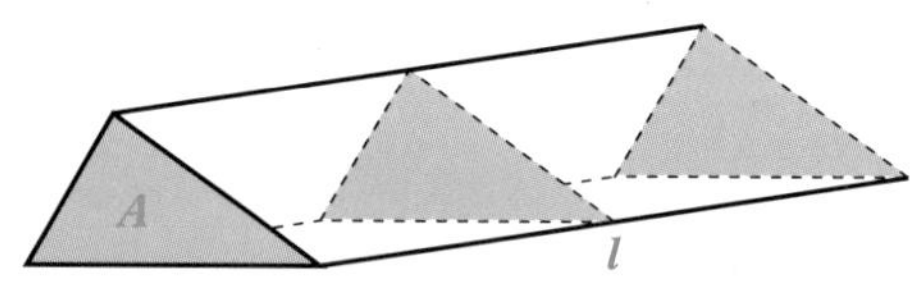

*V*olume of a prism = *A*rea of cross section × *l*ength
You can write this as $V = Al$

Example

Find the volume of this prism.

The cross section is a triangle.
The area of this triangle
$= (5 \times 12) \div 2$
$= 60 \div 2$
$= 30\ \text{cm}^2$

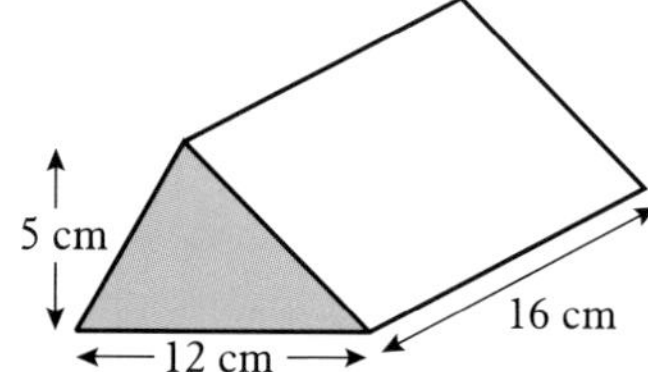

So volume $= 30 \times 16 = 480\ \text{cm}^3$

Exercise 31:13

Work out the volumes of the stage blocks in questions **1–4**.
All the blocks are prisms.
Give your answers to 3 sf when you need to round.

1

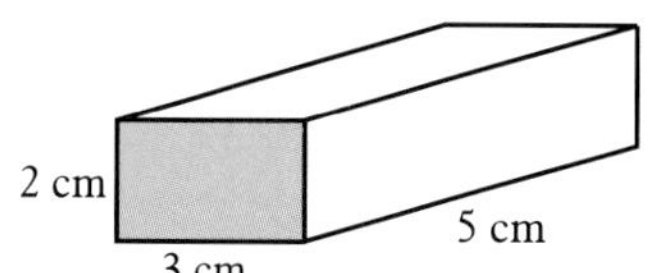

2

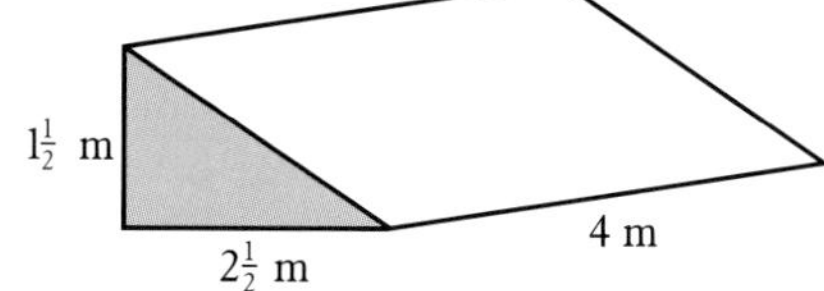

3

1.4 m
2.6 m
2.7 m

4

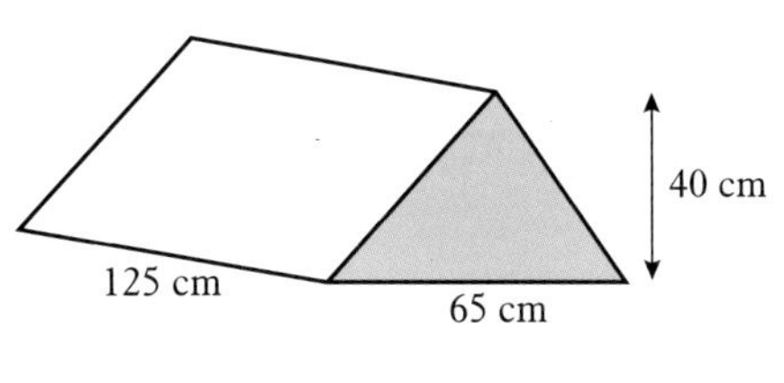

Work out the volumes of these prisms.
Give your answers to 3 sf when you need to round.

5

3.2 m
4.5 m
3.6 m

6

28 mm
84 mm
39 mm

7

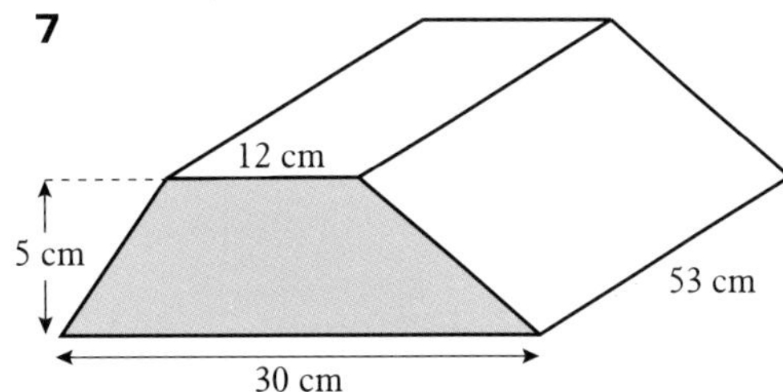

● **8**

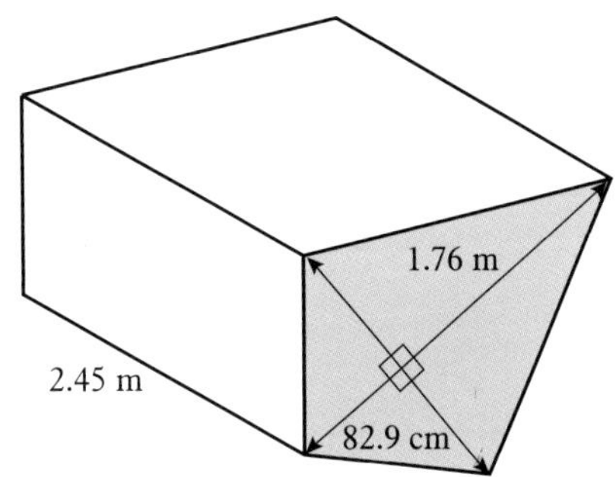

9 Find the volume of this swimming pool.

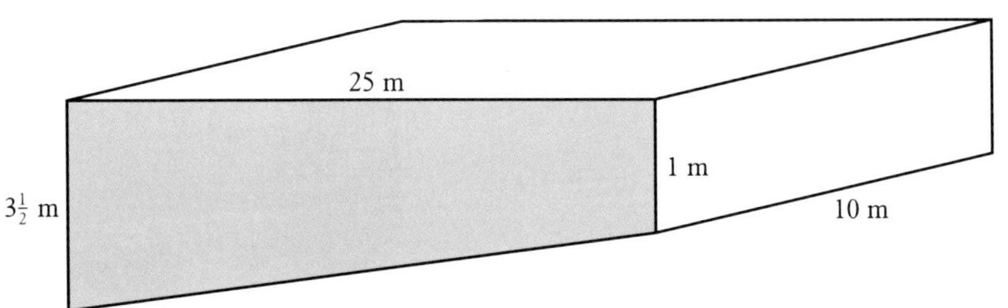

Cylinders

A cylinder is like a prism but it has a circle as its cross section.
The area of the cross section is πr^2 where r is the radius of the circle.
The volume of a cylinder is $V = \pi r^2 h$ where r is the radius and h is the height.

Example Find the volume of this cylinder.

Here $r = 12$ so $A = \pi \times 12^2$
So Volume $= \pi \times 12^2 \times 20$
$= 9047.78 \ldots$
$= 9050 \text{ cm}^3$ to 3 sf

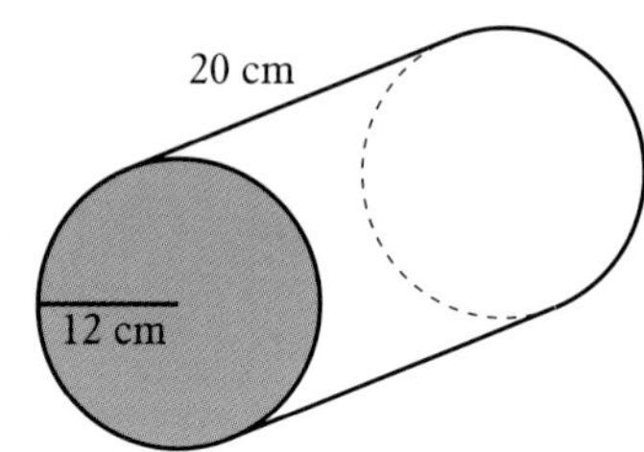

Exercise 31:14

Work out the volumes of the storage tanks in questions **1–4**.
All the tanks are cylinders. Round your answers to 3 sf

1

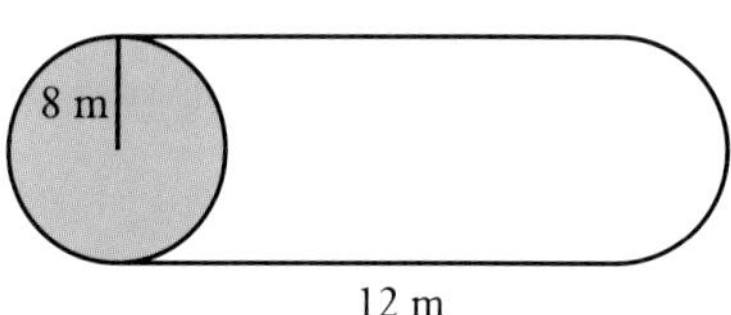

3

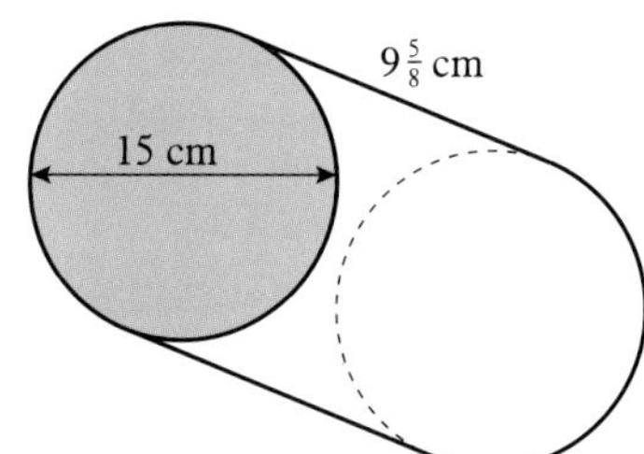

2

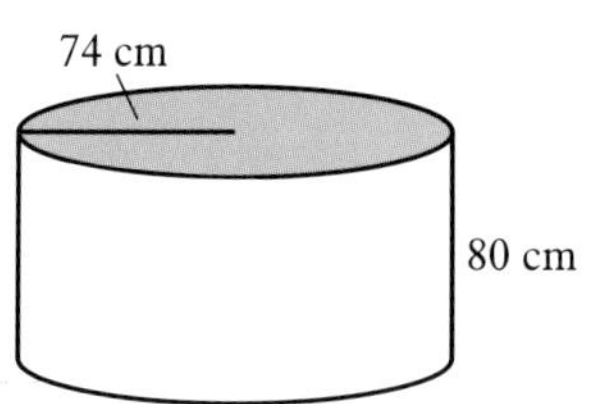

● **4**

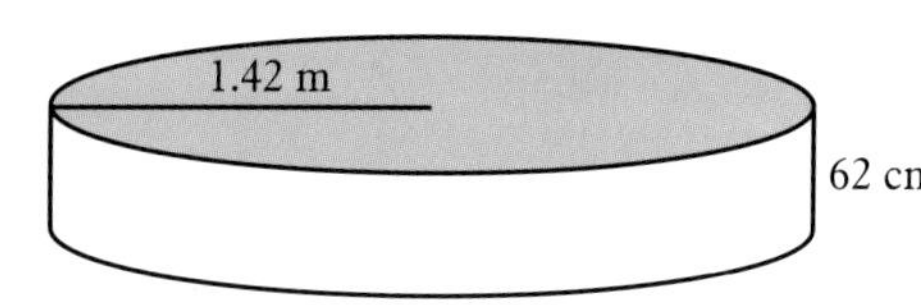

5 The trailer of a wine lorry carries a cylinder.
The cylinder is 10 m long.
The radius of the cross section is 1.2 m.
How many litres of wine does it carry?
$1000\, l = 1 \text{ m}^3$

If you know the volume and length of a prism, you can work out the cross sectional area.

You need to make Area the subject of

$$\textbf{Volume} = \text{Area of cross section} \times \text{length}$$

You can write this as $V = Al$

Dividing both sides by l gives $\frac{V}{l} = A$

so $\text{Area} = \frac{\text{Volume}}{\text{length}}$

The volume of this prism is 6912 cm³.

$$\text{Area of cross section} = \frac{6912}{24}$$

So the blue area is 288 cm².

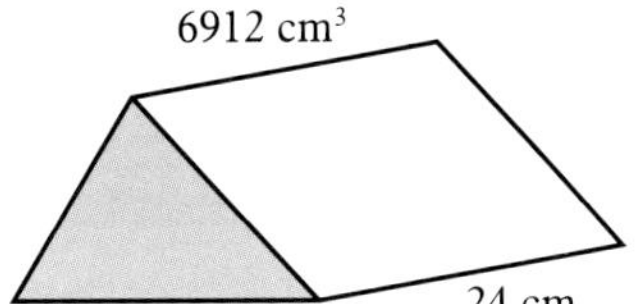

You can also make length the subject of

$$\text{Volume} = \text{Area of cross section} \times \text{length}$$

Start with $V = Al$

Dividing both sides by A gives $\frac{V}{A} = l$

so $\text{length} = \frac{\text{Volume}}{\text{Area}}$

The volume of this prism is 1080 m³.

$$\text{length} = \frac{1080}{40}$$

So the green length is 27 m

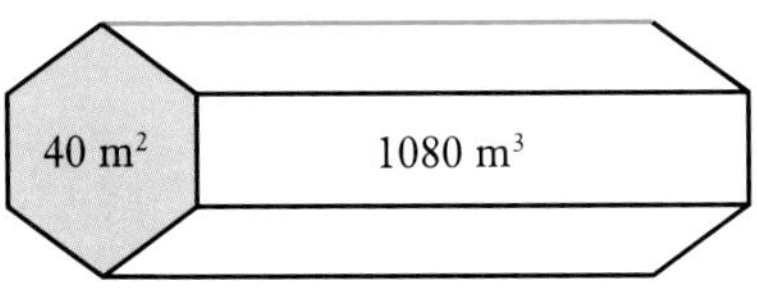

Exercise 31:15

1 Find the cross sectional areas of the prisms.
Make sure you use sensible units for your answers.

a

8 m

20 m^3

c

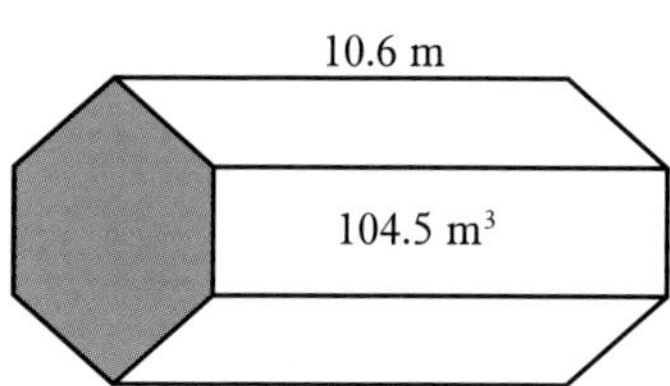

b

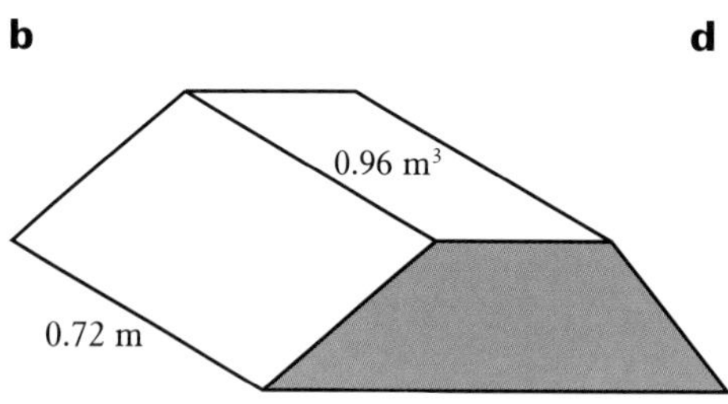

d

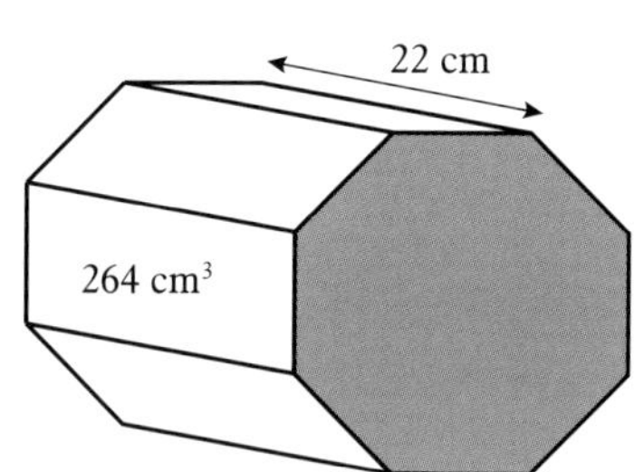

2 Find the lengths of these prisms.
Give your answers to 3 sf.

a

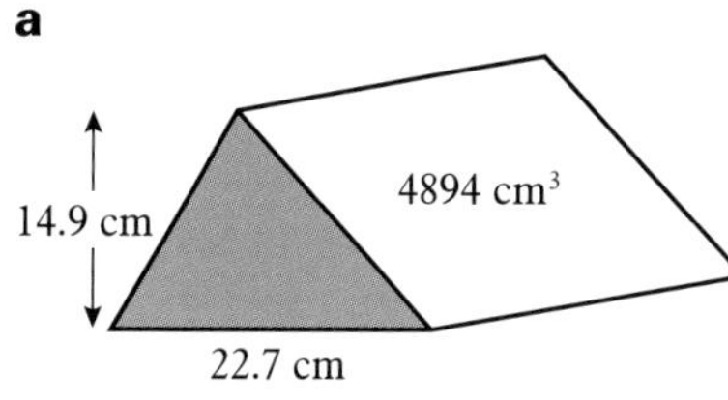

b

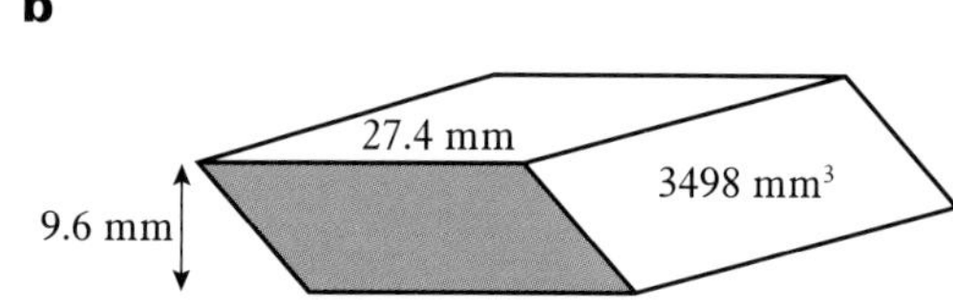

• **3** Tony drives a grain lorry.
The lorry has a trailer in the shape of an open cuboid.
The width of the trailer is 2.1 m.

The trailer is filled with 18 400 litres of grain.
The grain is filled to a depth of 1.45 m.
You can assume the surface of the grain is horizontal and level with the top of the trailer.
Work out the length of the lorry to 3 sf.
1000 litres = 1 m^3

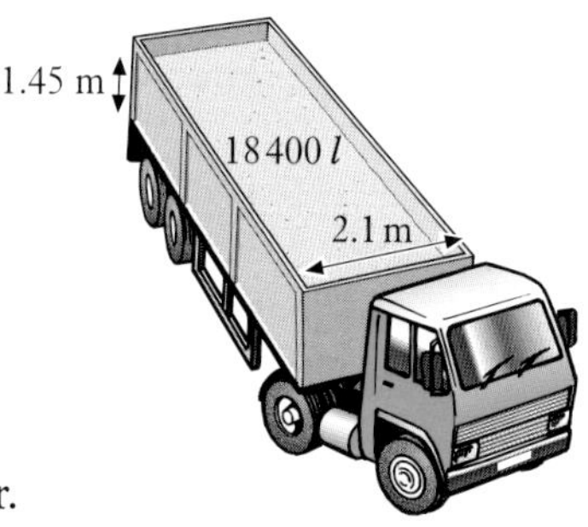

If you know the volume and height of a cylinder, you can work out the radius.
You need to make r the subject of $V = \pi r^2 h$

Start with $V = \pi r^2 h$

Dividing both sides by π gives $\frac{V}{\pi} = r^2 h$

Dividing both sides by h gives $\frac{V}{\pi h} = r^2$

Taking the square root of both sides gives $r = \sqrt{\frac{V}{\pi h}}$

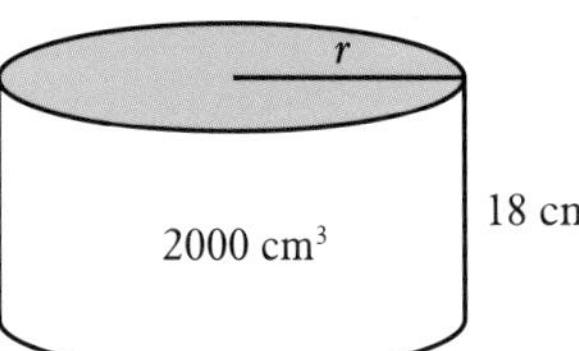

The volume of this cylinder is 2000 cm^3
The height is 18 cm

Substituting these values into the formula for r gives:

$$r = \sqrt{\frac{2000}{3.141\ldots \times 18}}$$

so $r = 5.95$ cm (3 sf)

If you know the radius and volume of a cylinder, you can work out the height.
You need to make h the subject of $V = \pi r^2 h$

Start with $V = \pi r^2 h$

Dividing both sides by π gives $\frac{V}{\pi} = r^2 h$

Dividing both sides by r^2 gives $\frac{V}{\pi r^2} = h$

So for this cylinder $h = \frac{660}{3.141\ldots \times 5^2}$

So $h = 8.4$ cm

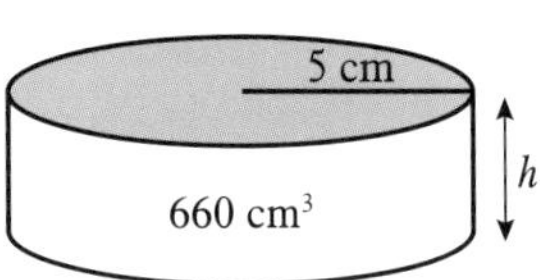

4 Find the heights of these cylinders.
Give your answers to 3 sf.

a

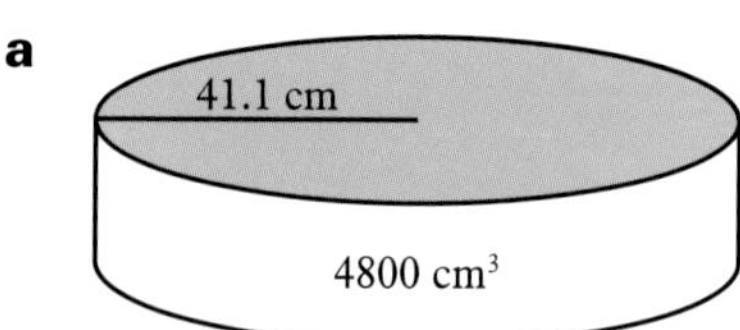

c

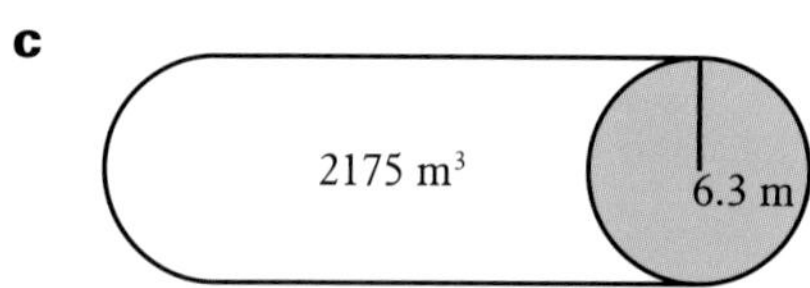

b

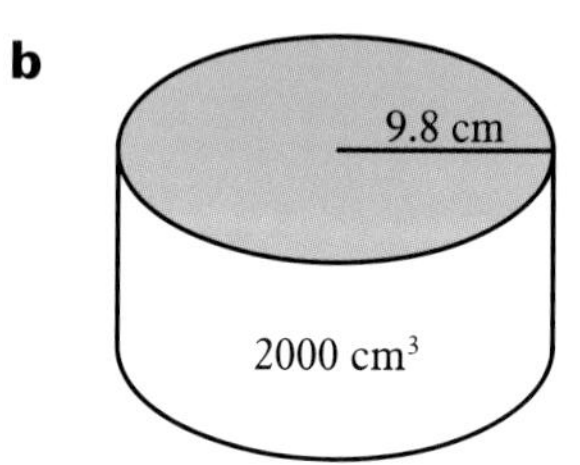

d

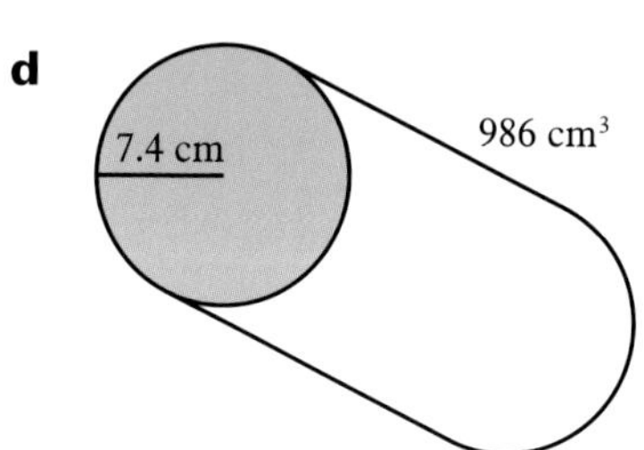

5 Find the radius of each of these cylinders. Give your answers to 3 sf.

a

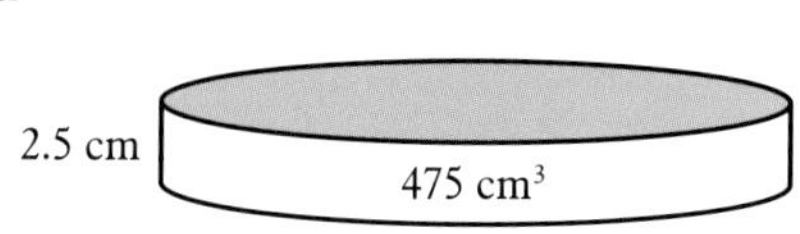

c

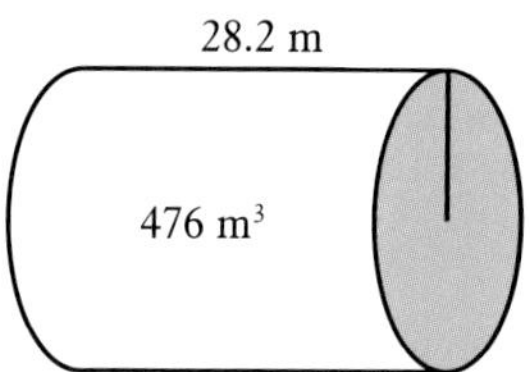

b

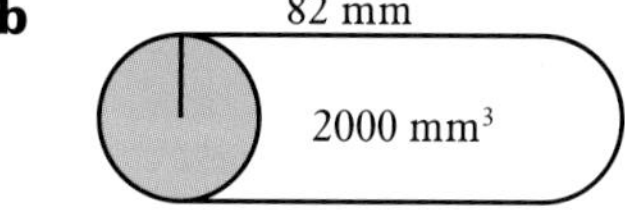

d

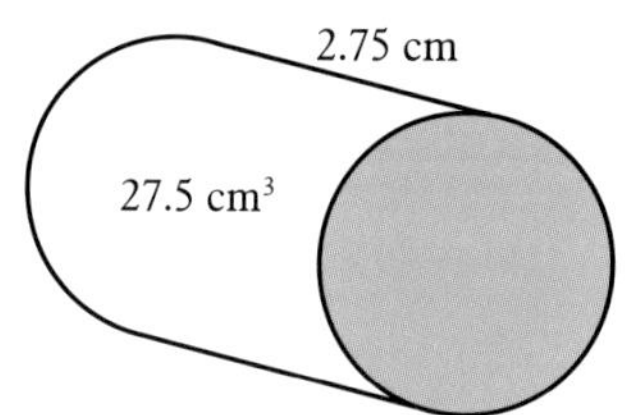

6 An oil drum has a capacity of 900 litres
There are 750 litres of oil in it.
The radius of the drum is 48 cm.

a Work out the height of the oil drum.

b Work out the depth of the oil in the drum.

Finding the volumes of more complicated shapes with constant cross sections

To find these volumes you need to:

(1) decide how to split the cross-sectional area into parts
(2) label each part with a letter
(3) find any missing lengths
(4) work out the area of each part
(5) add all these areas to get the total cross-sectional area
(6) multiply the cross-sectional area by the length.

Look at this cross-sectional area.
The shape is made from a semicircle and a trapezium.

Area of semicircle A $= 0.5 \times \pi \times (6.5)^2$
$= 66.36\ldots \text{ cm}^2$

For trapezium B you need to find the missing lengths.
The top parallel side of trapezium B is
$2 \times 6.5 = 13 \text{ cm}$
The height of trapezium B is $14.5 - 6.5 = 8 \text{ cm}$

Area of trapezium B is $0.5 \times (7 + 13) \times 8 = 80 \text{ cm}^2$

So the cross-sectional area of the shape is area of A + area of B

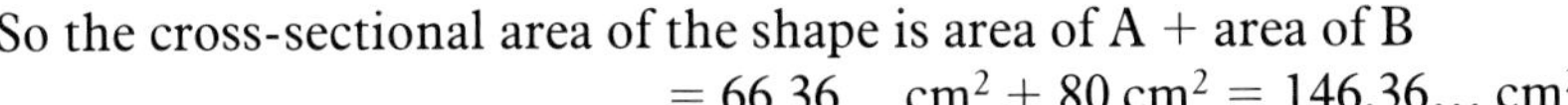
$= 66.36\ldots \text{ cm}^2 + 80 \text{ cm}^2 = 146.36\ldots \text{ cm}^2$

So the volume of the shape is $146.36\ldots \times 12.5 = 1830 \text{ cm}^3$ (3 sf)
Don't round the value for the area. Keep it in your calculator and only round at the end.

Exercise 31:16

Find the volumes of these shapes. Round your answers to 3 sf.

1

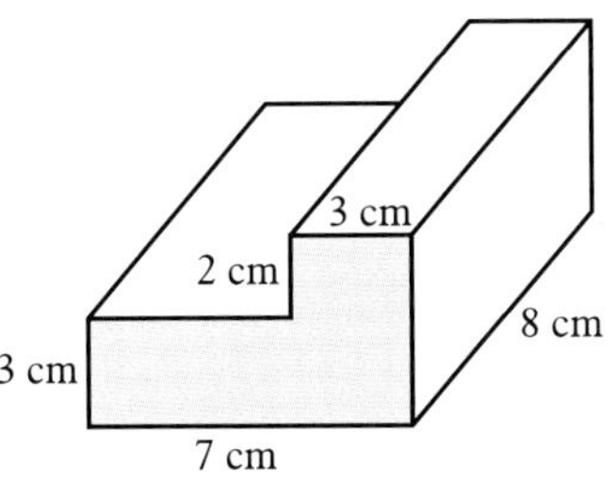

2

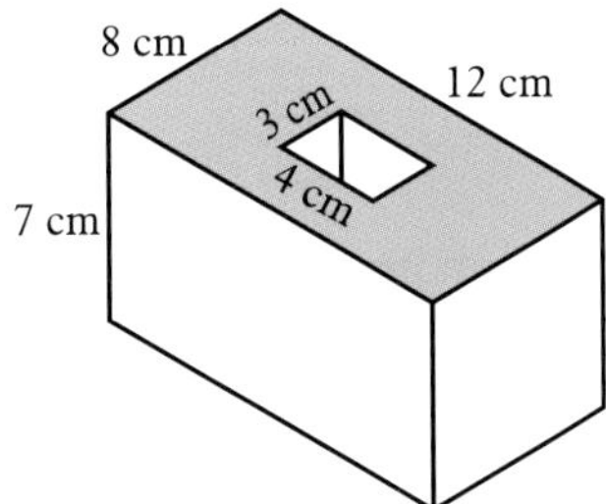

3 47 m, 19 m, 25 m

• 4 45 cm, 16.4 cm, A, 30.8 cm, B, 21.2 cm

This is a cubic millimetre
All the sides are 1 mm.

This is a cubic centimetre

1 cm, 1 cm, 1 cm

There are 10 mm in every 1 cm
So in the cubic centimetre
the width is 10 mm
the length is 10 mm
the height is 10 mm
So there are $10 \times 10 \times 10 = 1000\ \text{mm}^3$ in $1\ \text{cm}^3$

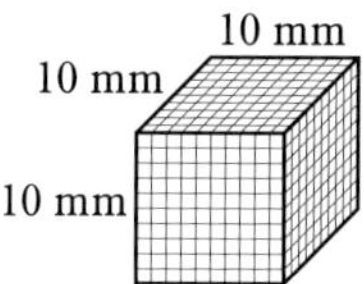

A cubic metre is too big to draw here!
This is a diagram of one.
There are 100 cm in every 1 m.
So in the cubic metre
the dimensions are $100\ \text{cm} \times 100\ \text{cm} \times 100\ \text{cm}$
So there are $100 \times 100 \times 100 = 1\,000\,000\ \text{cm}^3$ in $1\ \text{m}^3$

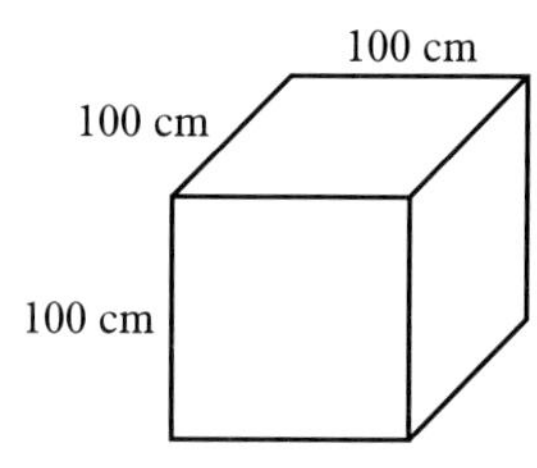

This diagram shows you how to convert cubic units

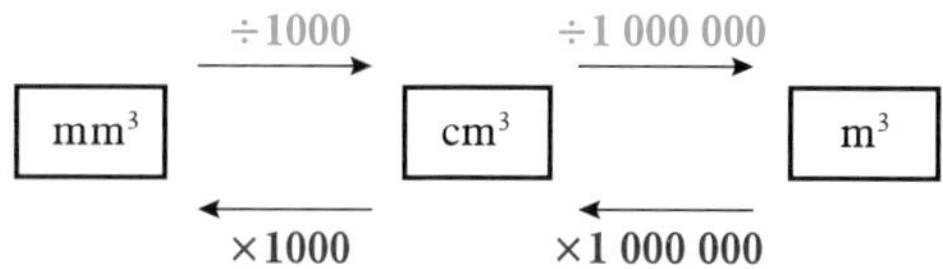

---

5 Draw a sketch of a cube 2 cm by 2 cm by 2 cm. Find the volume in mm^3.

6 Change each of these volumes into cm^3.
a $6\ \text{m}^3$ **b** $0.4\ \text{m}^3$ **c** $12.36\ \text{m}^3$ **d** $2050\ \text{mm}^3$ **e** $672\ \text{mm}^3$

7 Change each of these volumes into m^3.
a $40\,000\,000\ \text{cm}^3$ **b** $7\,900\,000\ \text{cm}^3$ **c** $459\,000\ \text{cm}^3$

4 Density

The density of a neutron star is 10^{14} g per cm^3.
The mean density of the earth is only 5.5 g per cm^3.

The mass of a solid is proportional to its volume.

This is because $\quad \text{Density} = \dfrac{\text{Mass}}{\text{Volume}}$

The units of density are g/cm^3 or kg/m^3.

There is a triangle that can help you to remember how to use this formula.

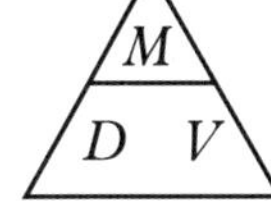

You remember $D = \dfrac{M}{V}$ then write out the triangle.

Cover up the letter you want. Then what you see is the rule.

Example A block of steel has dimensions 2 cm by 3 cm by 4 cm
It has a mass of 187.2 grams.
Work out its density.

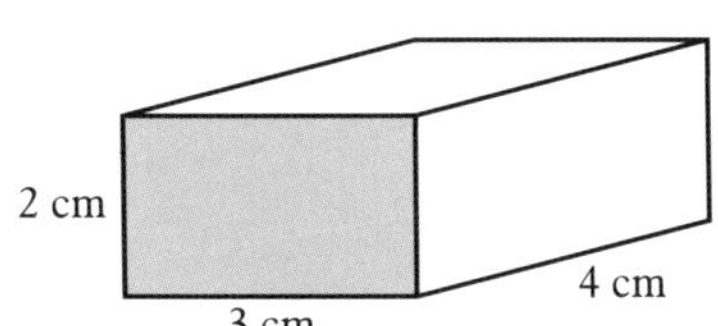

Volume of a cuboid = length × width × height
$= 2 \times 3 \times 4$
$= 24$ cm^3

You need the formula for density:

If you cover D you see $\dfrac{M}{V}$

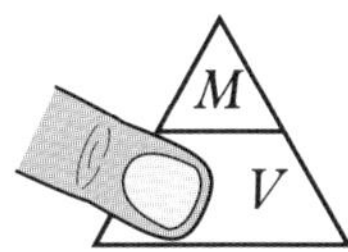

so $D = \dfrac{M}{V}$

$= \dfrac{187.2}{24}$

$= 7.8$ g/cm^3

Exercise 31:17

1 This diagram shows an ordinary house brick.
It has a mass of 2834 grams
Work out its density.

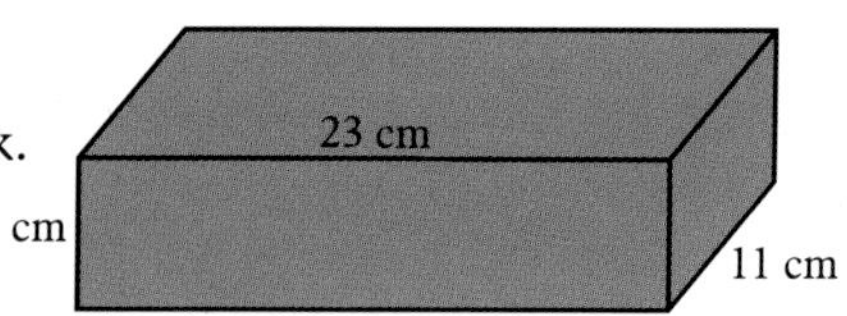

2 Mrs Smowk is a Chemistry teacher.
She has a set of chemical elements. Each of the elements is a cuboid.
Work out (1) the volume and (2) the density of each cuboid.
Give your answers to 3 sf when you need to round.

	Element	Mass (grams)	Dimensions (cm)		
			length	width	height
a	carbon	13.2	3	2	1
b	iron	63.2	2	2	2
c	sulphur	5.3	1.8	1.3	1.1
d	copper	868	3.2	2.3	1.8
e	silver	0.709	0.6	0.45	0.25
f	gold	0.296	0.4	0.24	0.16
g	zinc	121.9	3.7	2.9	1.6
h	lead	10.1	1.4	0.8	0.8

If you know the density and volume of a substance, you can work out the mass.
You need the formula for mass:

If you cover M you see $D\ V$

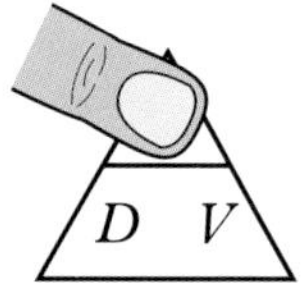

so $M = D \times V$

The density of this piece of glass is 1.8 g/cm^3
It is a cuboid as shown in the diagram.
To find its mass, first you need to work out its volume.
Change all the units to centimetres.

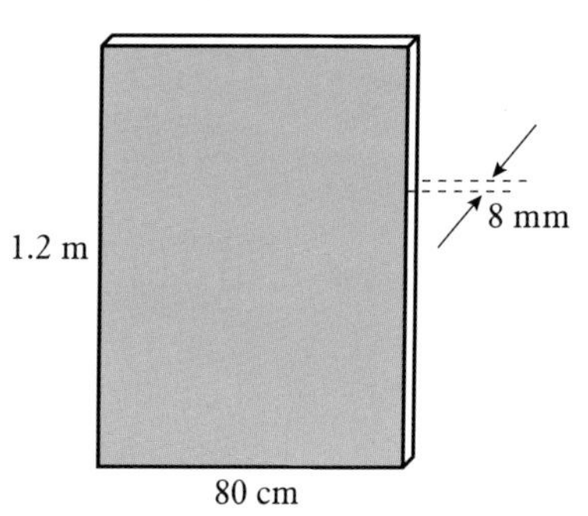

Volume $= 120 \times 80 \times 0.8$
$= 7680\ \text{cm}^3$

Now put these values in $M = D \times V$
so Mass $= 1.8 \times 7680$
$= 13\,824$ g

Now change this to kilograms
$13\,824\ \text{g} \div 1000 = 13.824\ \text{kg}$

---

3 A brass plate has a density of 8.1 g/cm^3
The plate is a cuboid 52 cm by 32 cm by 0.4 cm
Work out the mass of the plate.

● **4** A load of topsoil has a density of 2 g/cm^3.
A lorry is delivering 6 m^3 of topsoil to a new house.
a Change 6 m^3 to cm^3.
b Work out the mass of the soil in grams.
c Work out the mass that the lorry must carry in tonnes.

If you know the mass and density of a substance, you can work out the volume.
You need the formula for volume:

If you cover V you see $\frac{M}{D}$

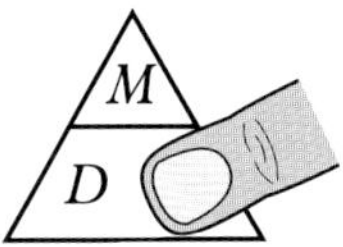

so $V = \frac{M}{D}$

The density of mercury is 13.6 g/cm^3
A mass of 12.8 grams is in the bulb of this thermometer.
Calculate the volume of the bulb.

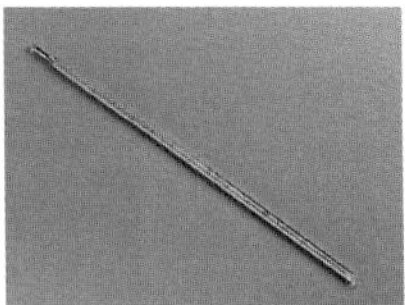

Put these values in $V = \frac{M}{D}$

Volume $= \frac{12.8}{13.6} = 0.941$ cm^3 (3 sf)

---

5 Gold has a density of 19.3 g/cm^3.
This wedding ring weighs 18.4 g.
Work out the volume of the wedding ring.

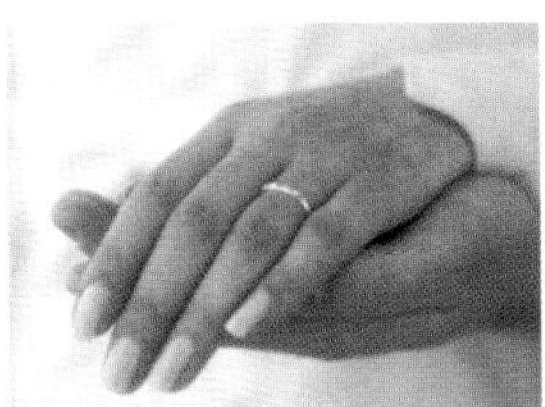

6 George mixes up 30 kg of mortar.
Mortar has a density of 2.2 g/cm^3.
a Work out the mass of the mortar in grams.
b Work out the volume of the mortar in cm^3.
● **c** Work out the volume of the mortar in m^3.

5 Dimensions

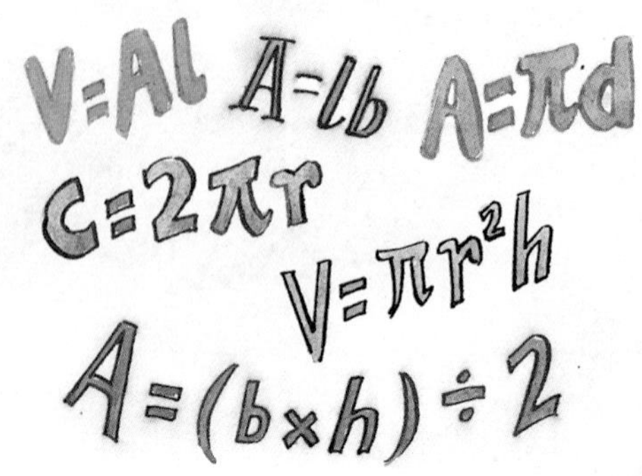

Some of these formulas are for length, some are for area and some are for volume.

You can tell quickly what a formula is for by looking at the dimension of the formula.

Dimension The **dimension** of a formula is the number of lengths that are multiplied together.

Constant A **constant** has no dimension. It is just a number.

Length has one dimension
Any formula for length can only involve constants and length.

$C = \pi d$ is a length formula.
π is a constant.
d is a length.

Area has two dimensions
Any formula for area can only involve constants and length × length.

$A = \pi r^2$ is an area formula.
π is a constant.
$r^2 = r \times r$
which is length × length

Volume has three dimensions
Any formula for volume can only involve constants and length × length × length.

$V = \frac{4}{3}\pi r^3$ is a volume formula.
$\frac{4}{3}$ and π are constants
$r^3 = r \times r \times r$
which is length × length × length

Example Write down the dimension of the expression $\frac{3\pi r^2}{4h}$ where r and h are lengths.

The expression is $\frac{\text{constant} \times \text{constant} \times \textbf{length} \times \textbf{length}}{\text{constant} \times \textbf{length}}$ (one **length** crossed out above and below the line)

This cancels down to give a **length**.
So the dimension is 1.

Exercise 31:18

1 In this question d, e and f are lengths.
Work out the dimension of each of these.

a de **c** $5df$ **e** $34e$ **g** $12e^3$
b $2f$ **d** def **f** d^2 **h** $4e^2f$

2 In this question p, q and r are lengths, c and k are constants.
Work out the dimension of each of these.

a pqr **e** $3kp^2q$ **i** $\frac{3rp}{q}$ • **m** $\frac{r^2p^2}{q^3}$

b $3pq$ **f** $5ckr$ **j** $\frac{3pr^2}{q}$ • **n** $\frac{4c^2krp^3}{q^2}$

c $2rq^2$ **g** $3kpq$ **k** $\frac{7ckp^3}{q^2}$ • **o** $\frac{5ck\pi pq^2r}{p^2q}$

d $4cpq$ **h** $5ckp$ **l** $\frac{ckpqr}{p^2}$ • **p** $\frac{\pi r^3p^2}{ckp^2q}$

3 Sue is trying to find a formula for the volume of a bottle.
She is testing different formulas to see which works best.
The radius of the base of the bottle is r and the height is h.
These are the formulas that she is using.

$V = \frac{3}{5}\pi r^2h$ $V = \frac{3}{5}\pi r^3h$ $V = \frac{3}{5}\pi rh^2$ $V = \frac{3}{5}\pi rh^3$

Explain why Sue should only be testing two of these formulas.

Some formulas have more than one part.
When this happens all of the parts must have the same dimension if the formula is for length or area or volume.
This is a formula for the total surface area of a cylinder.

$A = 2\pi r^2 + 2\pi rh$

The first part is constant × constant × length^2 which is an area.
The second part is constant × constant × length × length which is also an area.

This formula for a volume, V, cannot be right.

$V = 2\pi r^3 + 2rh$

The first part is constant × constant × length^3 which is a volume.
But the second part is constant × length × length which is an area.
So it is impossible for this formula to give you a volume.

---

4 In this question a, b and c are lengths.
Write down what each expression could represent.
If an expression cannot be for length, area or volume, explain why.

a $b + c$

b $3a + 5bc$

c $2ac + 3ab$

d $5ab + 3a^2$

e $5abc + 3b^2c$

● **f** $12a + \frac{bc}{a}$

5 In this question p, q, r, s and t are lengths, c and k are constants.
Write down what each formula could represent.
If an expression cannot be for length, area or volume, explain why.

a $pqr + s^2t$

b $3pq + 5rst$

c $2rq^2 + 4s^2t$

d $4cpq + 2ckr$

e $kp^2q + crst$

f $5ckr + 3cr^2$

g $kp^2q + cr^3$

h $5ckp + cr$

● **i** $\frac{2rp}{q} + \frac{r^2p^2}{q^3}$

● **j** $\frac{\pi pr^2}{qs} + \frac{4crp}{q}$

● **k** $\frac{8ckp^3}{q^2} - \frac{5\pi pq^2r}{s^2t} + \frac{r^2p^2}{q^3}$

● **l** $\frac{ckpqr}{t^2} + \frac{\pi r^3p^2}{cks^2q} - \frac{t^2p^2}{q^3}$

6 Tina is trying to find a formula for the volume of a jar.
r, h and b are lengths.

She thinks that the volume is $V = 3\pi r^2h + \frac{3}{4}\pi rb^2$

Tina's friend Glenda thinks that the volume is $V = 3\pi r^2h + \frac{3}{4}\pi r^2b^2$

Explain why Glenda has to be wrong.

7 Norman thinks that the total surface area of this cylinder is
$A = 2\pi r(r + h)$

a Explain how Norman can show that his formula has the right dimension.

b Does this mean that his formula is correct?

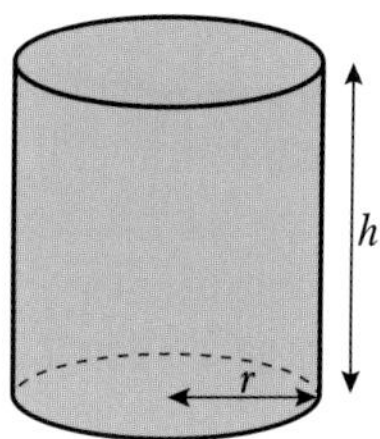

● **8** Cath thinks that the area of material needed to cover this lampshade is
$$A = \pi h(b - a)^2$$
Explain why Cath has to be wrong.

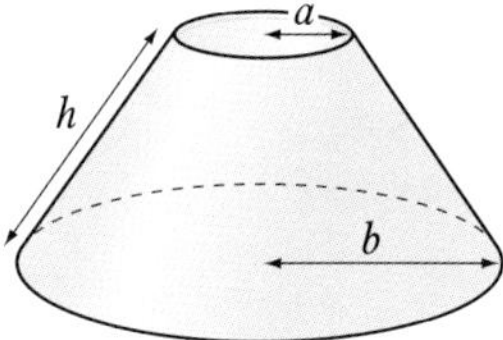

1 Copy each diagram.
Complete it so that it shows a cuboid.

a

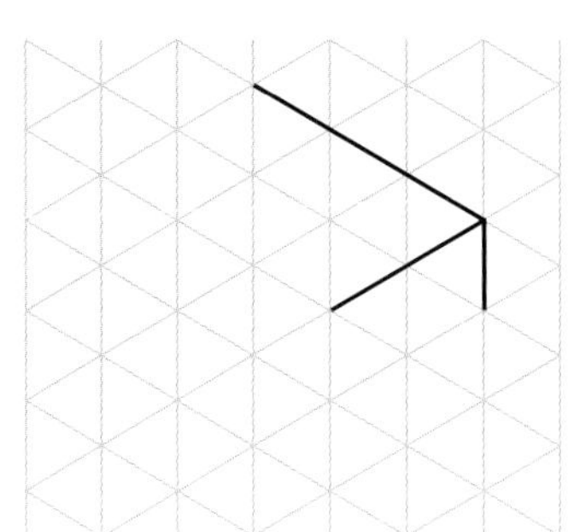

b

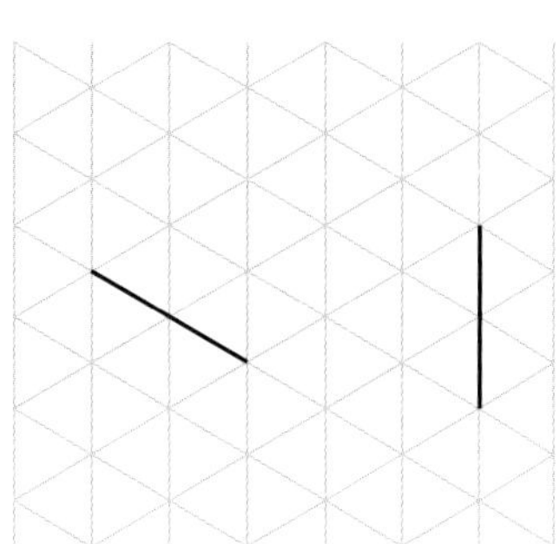

2 Each diagram shows a cuboid with a piece missing.
Draw the missing piece.

a

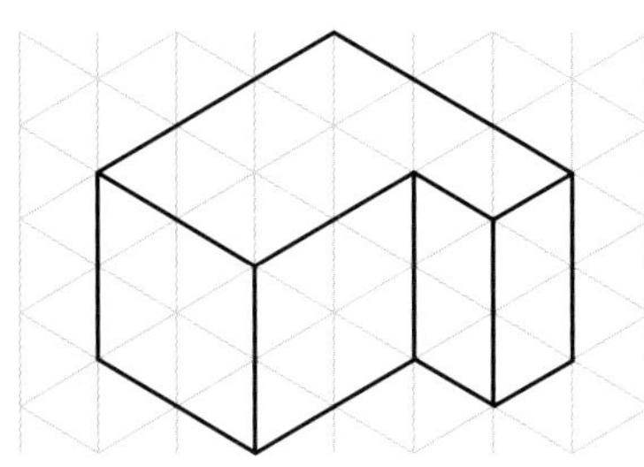

b

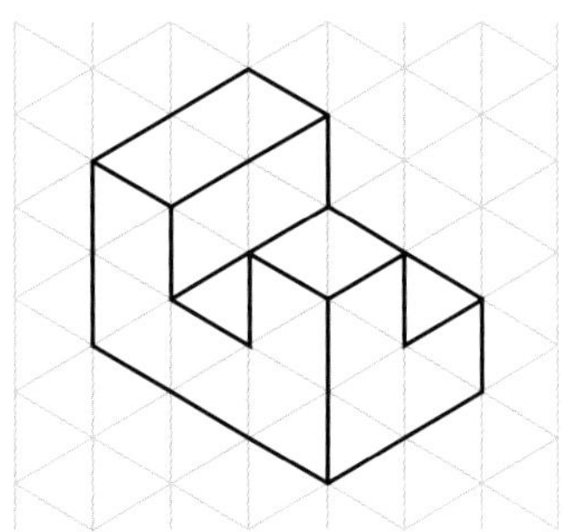

3 **a** Change each of these masses into the units given.
(1) 60 grams into ounces (2) 10 kg into pounds (3) 4 st into kilograms

b Change each of these capacities into the units given.
(1) 5 pints into litres (2) 6 gallons into litres (3) 4500 ml into pints

4 Work out the volume of each of these shapes.

a

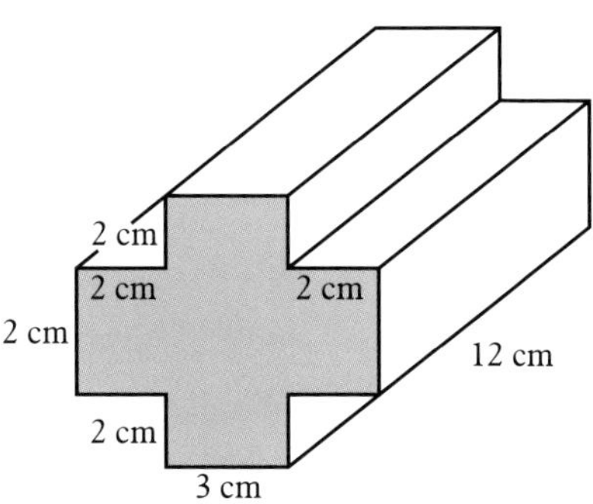

b

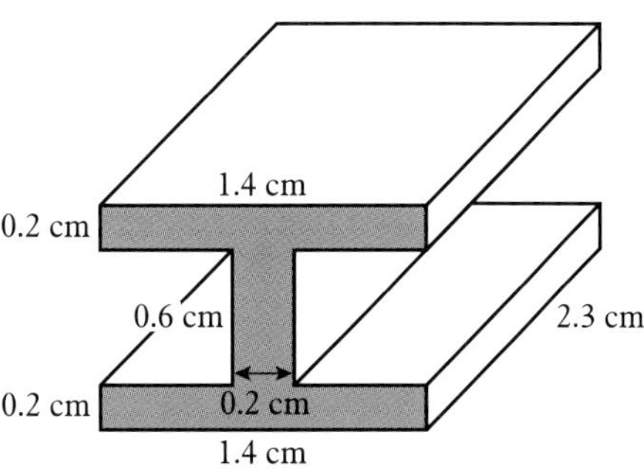

5 Find the volumes of these shapes.
Round your answers to 3 sf.

a

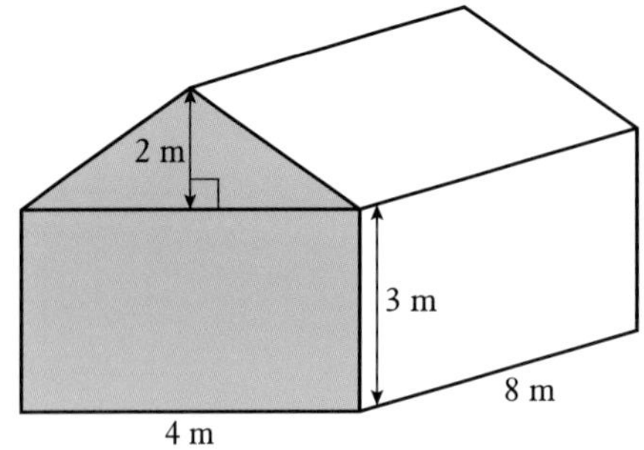

b

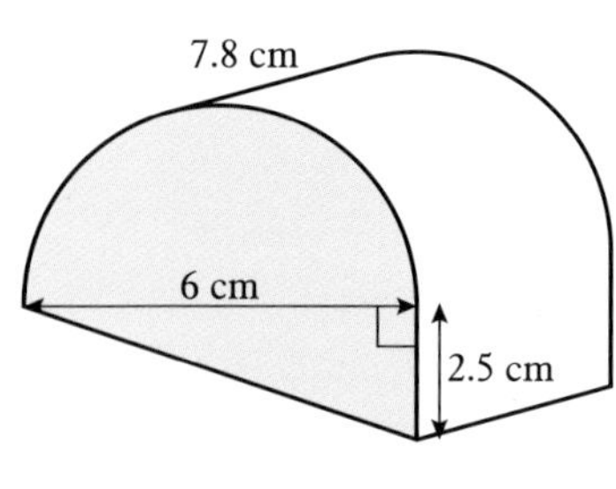

6 The diagram shows a prism made of aluminium.
It has a mass of 48.6 grams.
Work out its density.

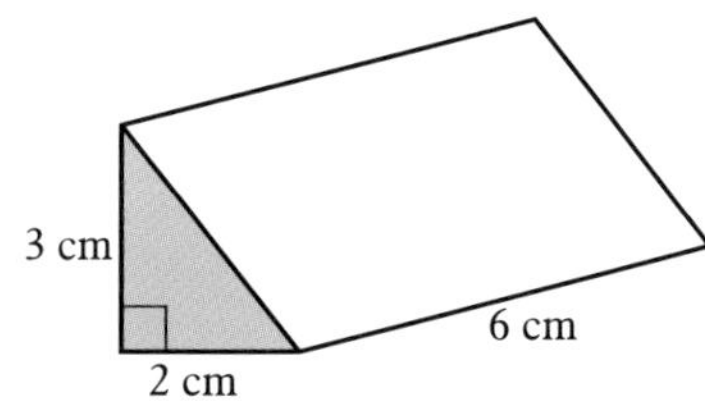

7 A cork float is in the shape of a cylinder.
It has a mass of 784 grams.
Work out its density.

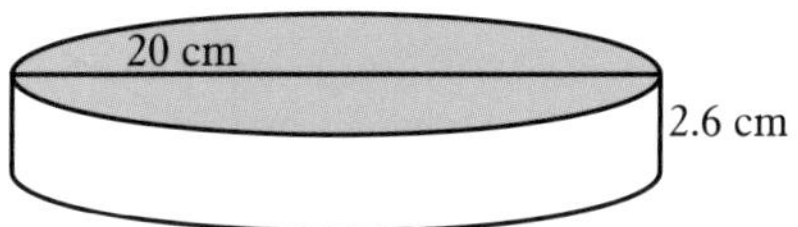

8 A steel girder has a volume of 60 000 cm^3
It has a mass of 462 kg.

a Change the mass from kilograms to grams.

b Work out the density of the girder.

9 In this question a, b, c, d and e are lengths. π and k are constants.
Write down what each formula could represent.
If an expression cannot be for length, area or volume, explain why.

a πab

b kb

c $\dfrac{abc}{k}$

d $\dfrac{\pi a}{b}$

e $\dfrac{4dab}{kc} + \dfrac{2\pi bae}{kc}$

f $\dfrac{\pi c^2 e}{ka}$

g $\dfrac{2a^3}{k} + \dfrac{\pi kb^2 e}{c}$

h $\dfrac{5kc^3d^2}{a^3} - \dfrac{2\pi ka^2 e}{3c}$

i $\dfrac{\pi(kc^2e - 4bd^2)}{a}$

1 A railway tunnel has this cross section.
The tunnel runs in a straight line for $3\frac{3}{4}$ miles.
1 mile = 1760 yards

a Work out the length of the tunnel in yards.

b Find the cross-sectional area.

c Work out the volume of the tunnel in cubic yards.

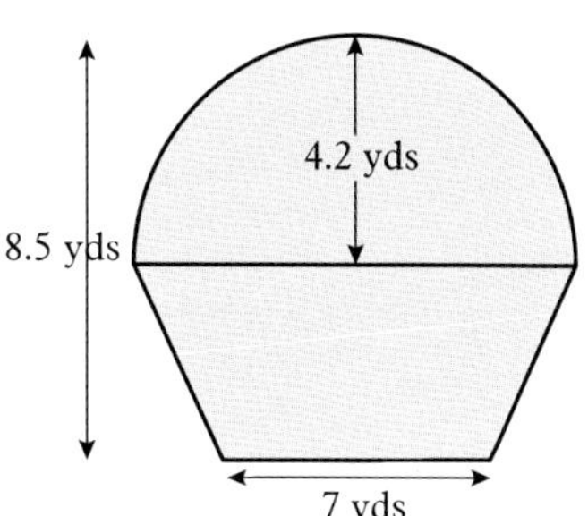

2 Mr Weybridge is moving marble floor tiles in his van.
The floor tiles are cuboids with dimensions 15 cm by 15 cm by 1.4 cm.
The density of marble is 2.7 g/cm^3
He has 3400 tiles to move.
The van can only carry a load of 2.2 tonnes at a time.
How many journeys does he need to make?

3 This is the cross-sectional area of an aircraft hangar.
It is to be built in the year 2020.
The hangar is to be 200 m long.
Find the volume of the hangar.

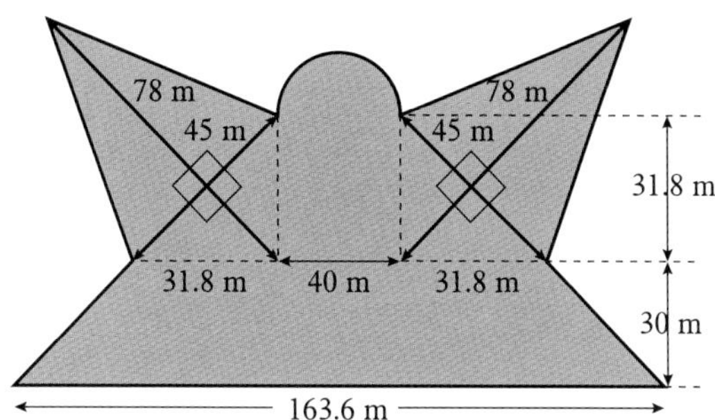

4 A very large concrete pipe has a regular hexagonal cross section.
Within the pipe 4 cylindrical tubes carry liquid gases.
Each tube has a radius of 82 cm.

a Work out the volume of gas in 100 m of 1 tube.

Now split the hexagon into equilateral triangles.

b Use trigonometry to find the height of an equilateral triangle.

c Work out the cross-sectional area of the pipe.

d Work out the volume of concrete in 1 km of pipe.

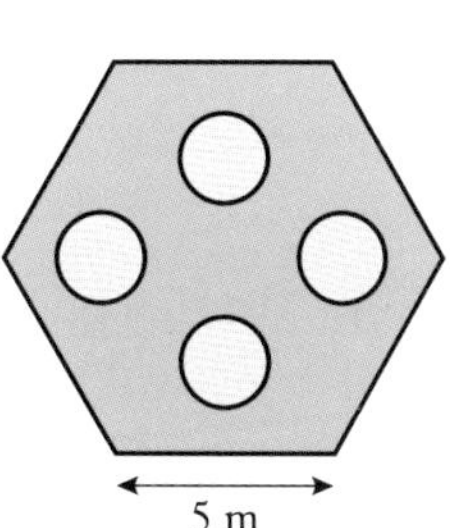

1 Copy and complete the diagram to show a prism.

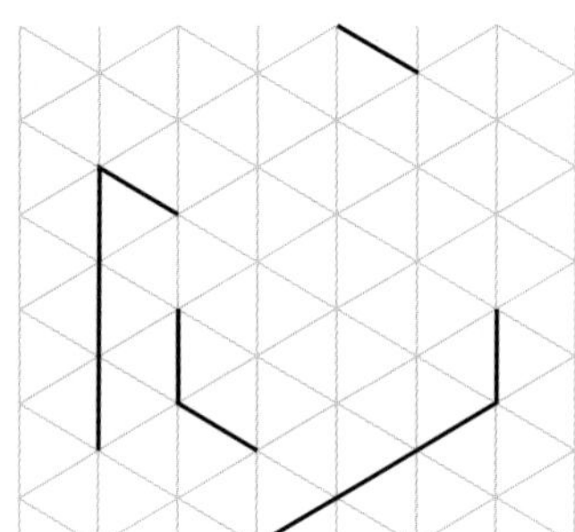

2 Change each of these to the units shown.

a 37 mm to m
b 0.8 km to m
c 7600 kg to tonnes
d 3.08 m to cm
e 3.8 cl to l
f 478 ml to cl

3 Ivan is a weightlifter. He can lift 450 kg.
How many pounds is this?

4 Each side of a cube is 8 cm long.
Find its volume.

5 Find the volume of this prism.

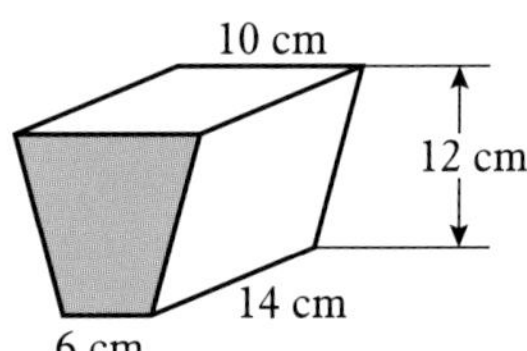

6 This cylinder has volume 86 cm^3.
Find its radius to the nearest mm.

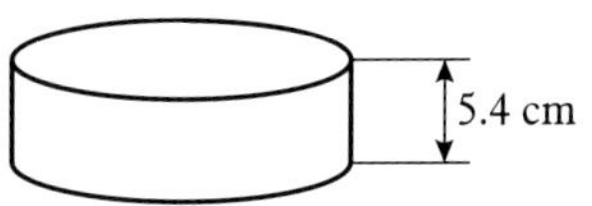

7 In this question l and m are lengths, p and q are constants.
Write down what each formula could represent.
Choose from length, area or volume.

a $pl + qm$
b plm
c pql^2
d pml^2
e $\frac{q(l + m)^2}{l}$
f $(p + q)(l + m)$

32 Inner space

1 Identical shapes

Defining congruence
Looking at congruence
Counting lines of symmetry
Completing patterns with symmetry
Drawing reflections in a line of symmetry
Using planes of symmetry in 3D

CORE

2 About turn

Looking at rotational symmetry
Finding angles inside and outside of polygons
Looking at tessellations

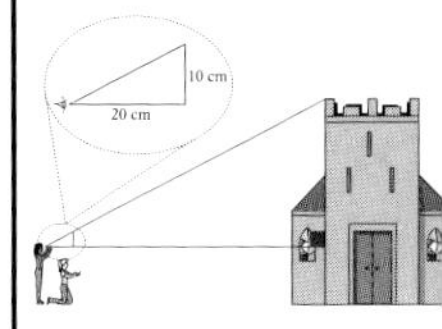

3 Similar triangles

Introducing similar triangles
Using the rules for similar triangles to find missing sides

QUESTIONS

EXTENSION

TEST YOURSELF

1 Identical shapes

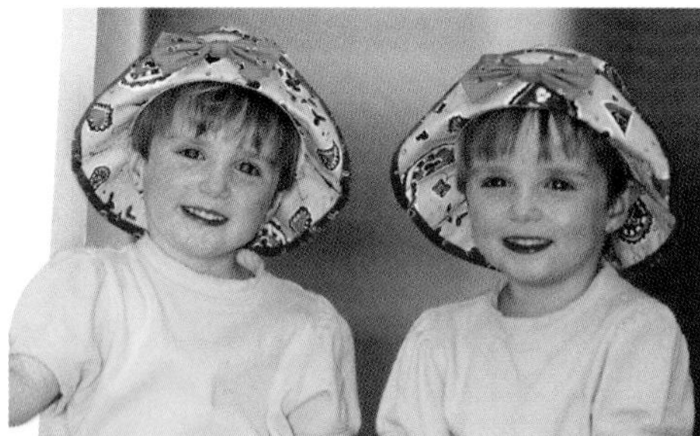

These twins are said to be identical. There may be very small differences but most people can't tell them apart.

In maths, if two shapes are identical they are called congruent.

Congruent Two shapes are **congruent** if they are identical. They have to be the same size *and* the same shape.

Shapes do not have to be drawn the same way round to be congruent. All these triangles are congruent.

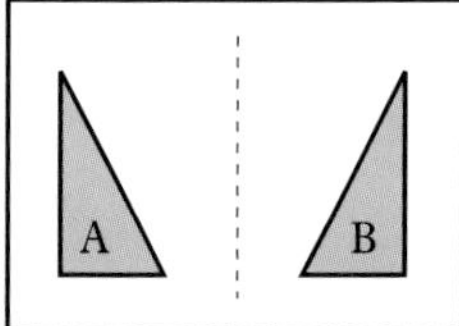

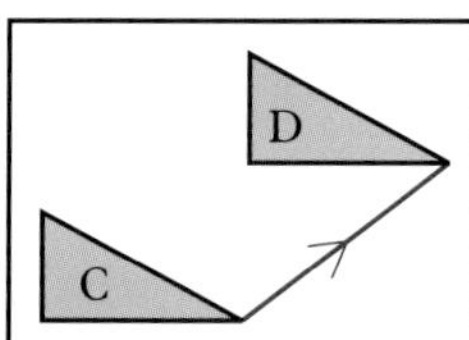

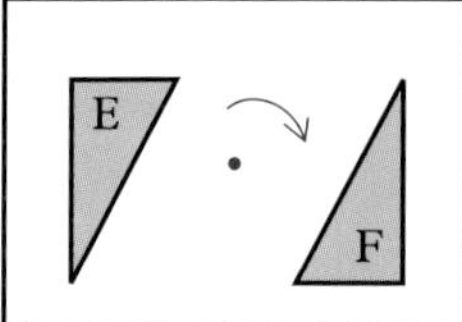

You reflect triangle A to get triangle B.
You translate triangle C to get triangle D.
You rotate triangle E to get triangle F.

Exercise 32:1

1 Look at these shapes. Which shapes are congruent? Write down their letters in pairs.

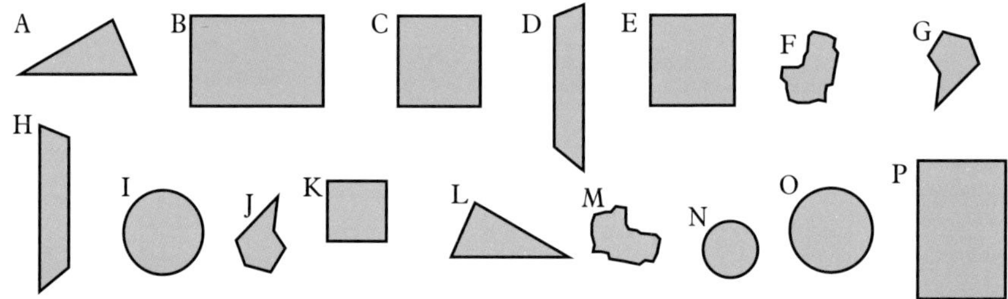

2 Look at these shapes. Which shapes are congruent?
Write down their letters in pairs.

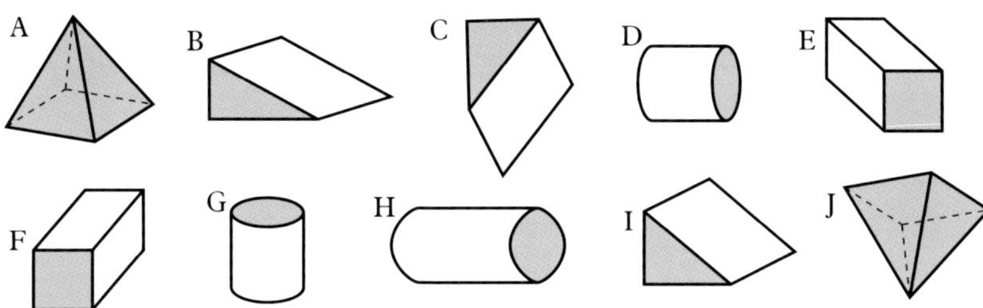

3 You need tracing paper for this question.

a Can shape C be mapped on to shape A by a transformation?

b Can shape D be mapped on to shape A by a transformation?

c Can shape B be mapped on to shape A by transformation?

d Describe fully any transformations you have found in **a** to **c**.

e Which of the shapes are congruent?

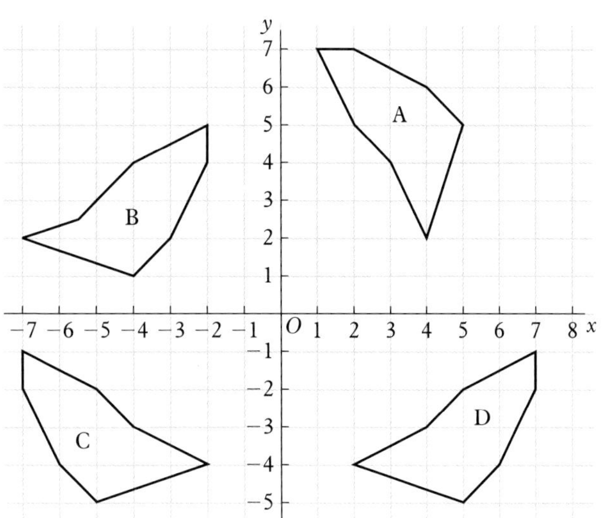

4 Are these shapes congruent? Explain your answer.

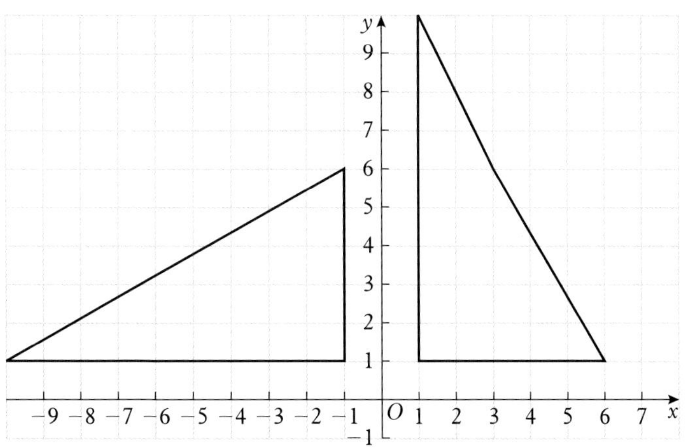

Line of symmetry

A **line of symmetry** divides a shape into two identical halves. Each part is a reflection of the other. If you fold a shape along this line, each part fits exactly on top of the other.

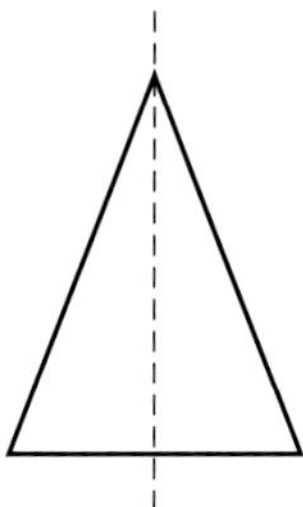

This isosceles triangle has one line of symmetry. You draw a line of symmetry with a dashed line.

Exercise 32:2

1 How many lines of symmetry does each of these shapes have?

a

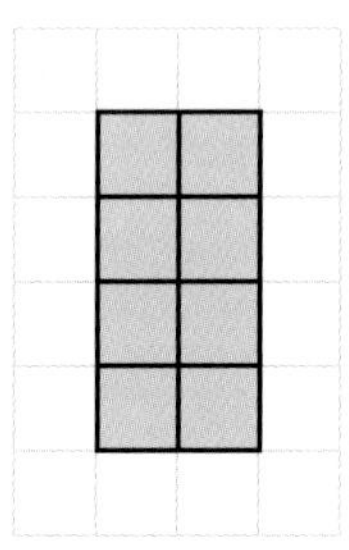

b

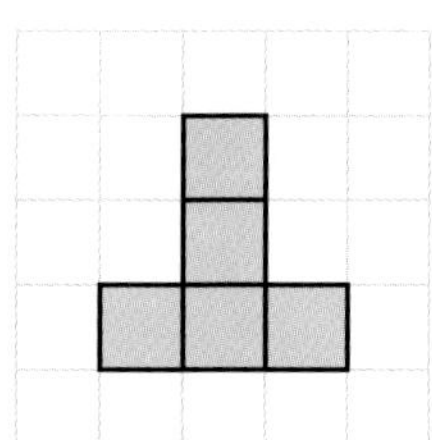

2 Copy these shapes on to squared paper. Mark on all the lines of symmetry.

a

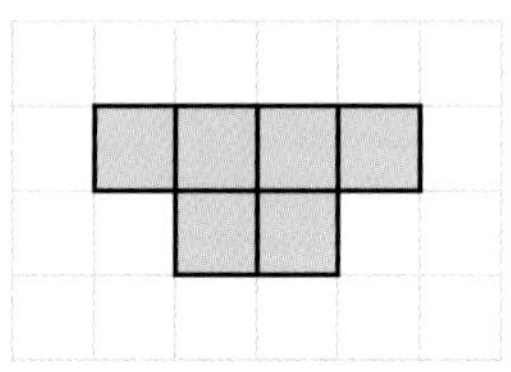

b

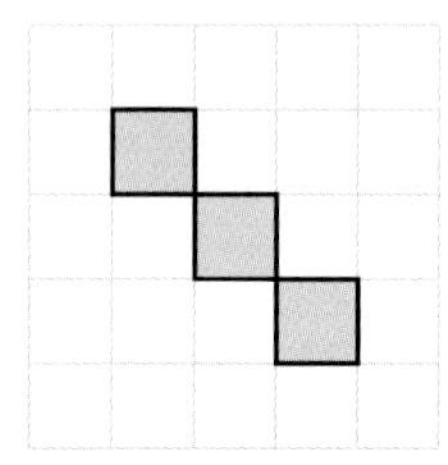

Example

Complete this pattern so that the **red** line is a line of symmetry.

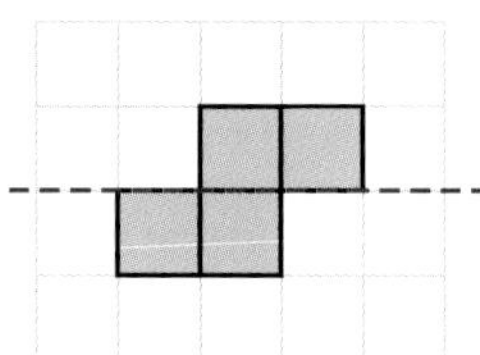

You need to shade in the squares that complete the pattern.
There are two squares needed.

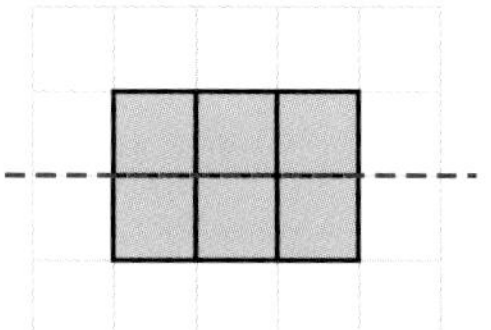

This is the completed pattern.

3 Copy these shapes on to squared paper.
Shade in two more squares so that the **red** line is a line of symmetry.

a

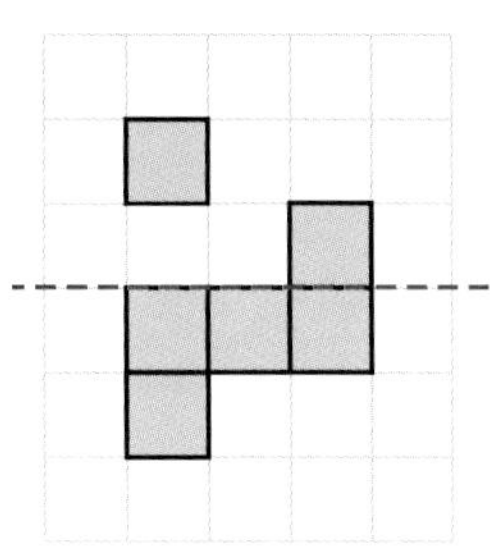

b

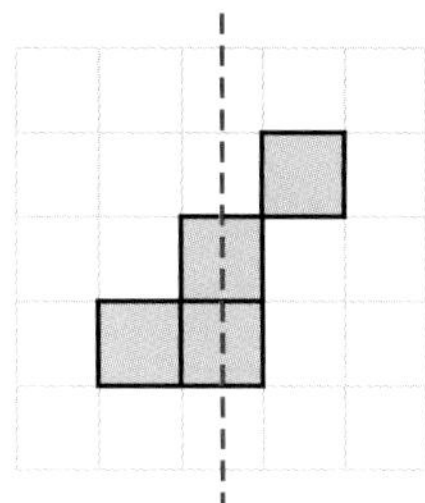

4 Copy these shapes on to squared paper.
Shade in two more squares so that the **red** line and the **blue** line are both lines of symmetry.

a

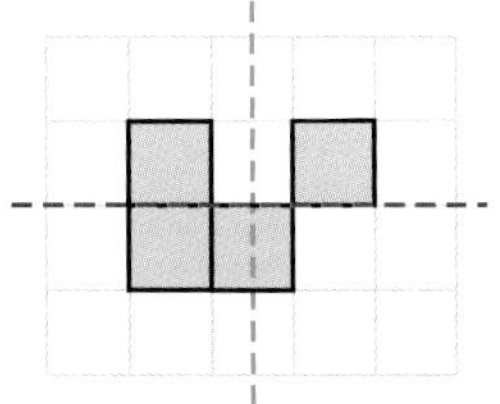

b

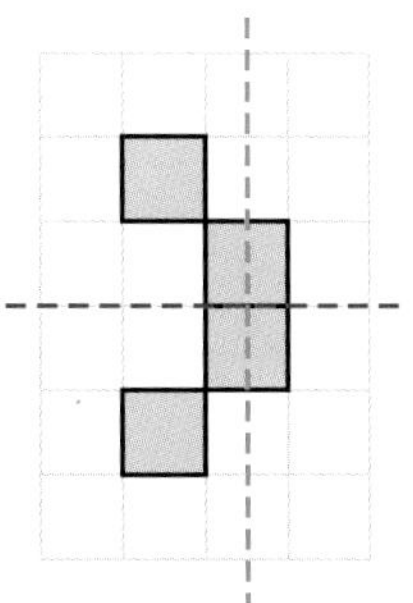

Example Draw the reflection of the shape in the **red** line.

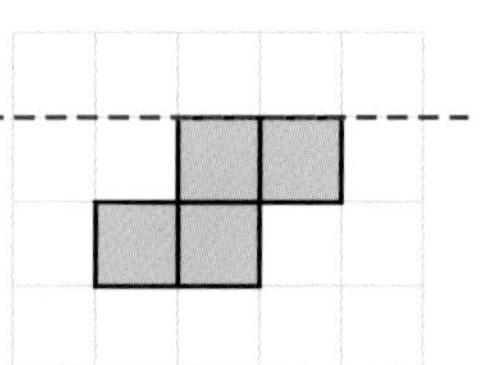

You need to draw what you would see in a mirror if you put a mirror on the red line.
You can use a mirror to help you.

This is the completed picture.
The red line is a line of symmetry.

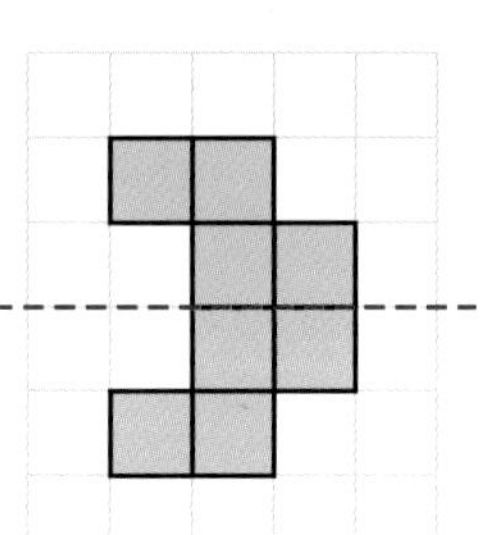

5 Copy these shapes on to squared paper.
Draw the reflection of each shape in the line of symmetry.

a

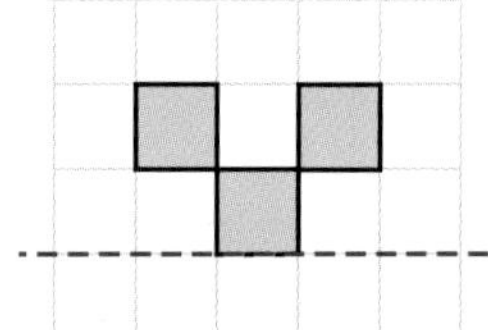

b

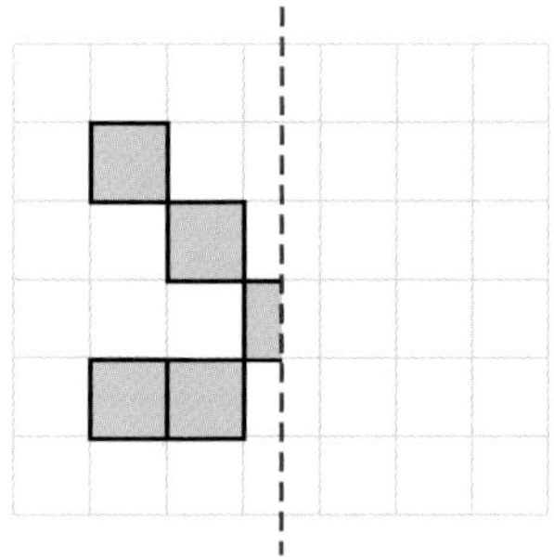

6 Copy these shapes on to squared paper.
Use the **red** lines of symmetry to complete each picture.

a

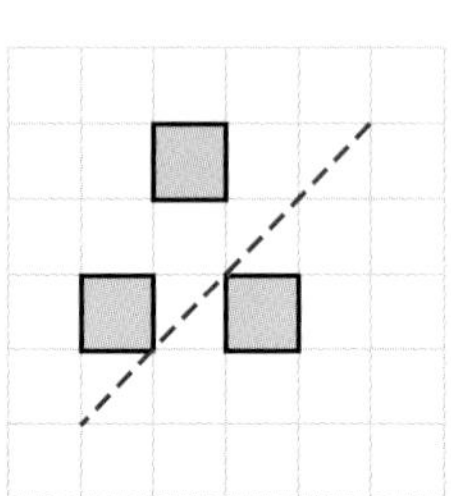

b

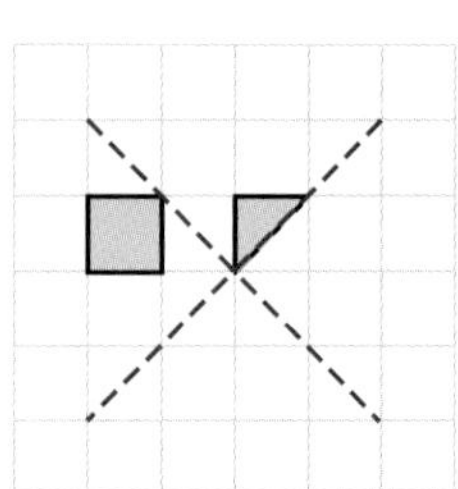

You can also have symmetry in 3 dimensions.

Instead of having a mirror line you can now think about putting a whole mirror into the shape.

This is a cuboid.

You can see the three possible places to put a mirror so that the two halves are symmetrical.

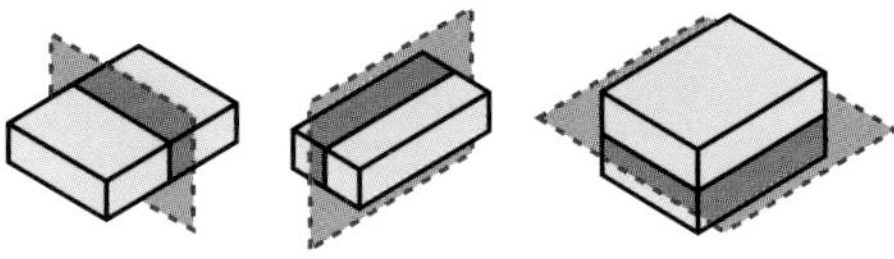

When you can put a mirror into a shape like this the mirror is called a plane of symmetry.

Exercise 32:3

1 How many planes of symmetry does each of these shapes have?

a

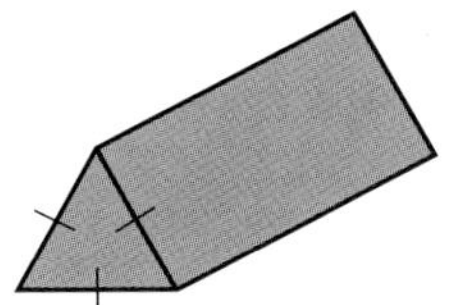

c

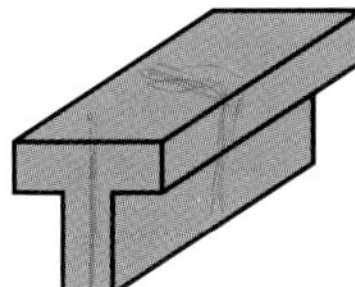

e

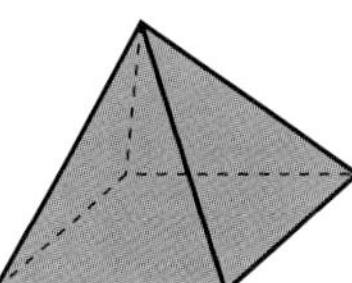

b

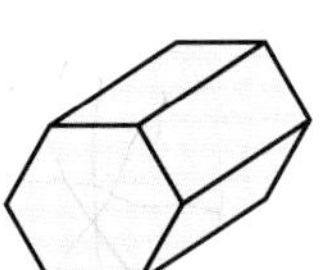

d

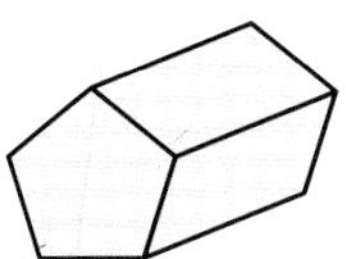

f

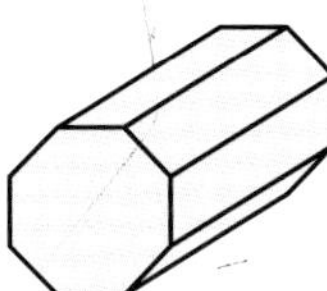

2 How many planes of symmetry does

a a cube have

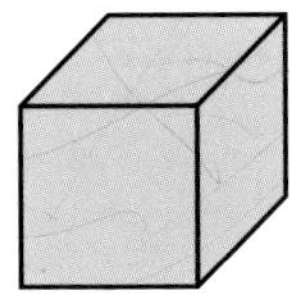

● **b** a sphere have?

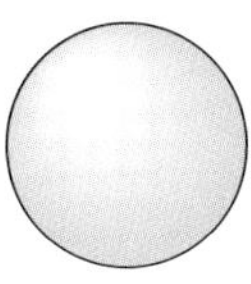

You need worksheet 32:1

2 About turn

The Three Legs of Man is the national symbol of the Isle of Man.

It is based on an earlier design that was a symbol of pagan Sun worship.

Rotational symmetry A shape has **rotational symmetry** if it fits on top of itself more than once as it makes a complete turn.

Order of rotational symmetry The **order of rotational symmetry** is the number of times that the shape fits on to itself. This must be two or more.

Centre of rotation The **centre of rotation** is the point that stays still as the shape makes a complete turn.

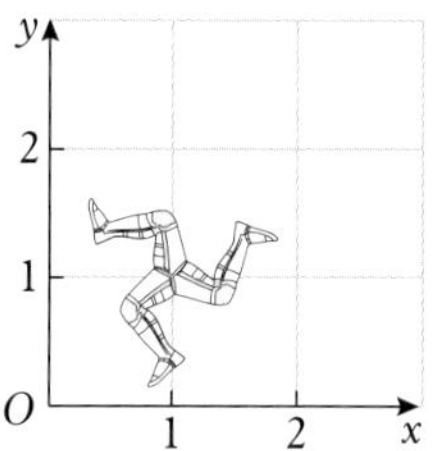

The Three Legs of Man symbol has rotational symmetry of order 3 about its centre at (1, 1).

Exercise 32:4

1 Look at these shapes.
Write down the letter of each one that has rotational symmetry.

a 

b 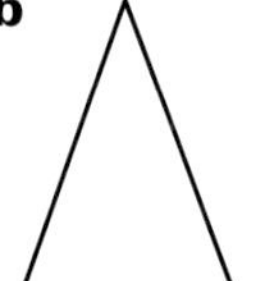

c 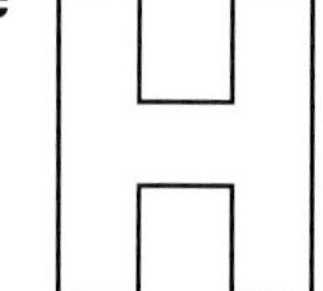

d 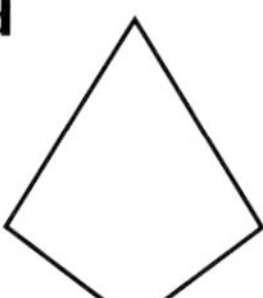

Write down the order of rotational symmetry of each of the shapes in questions **2** and **3**.

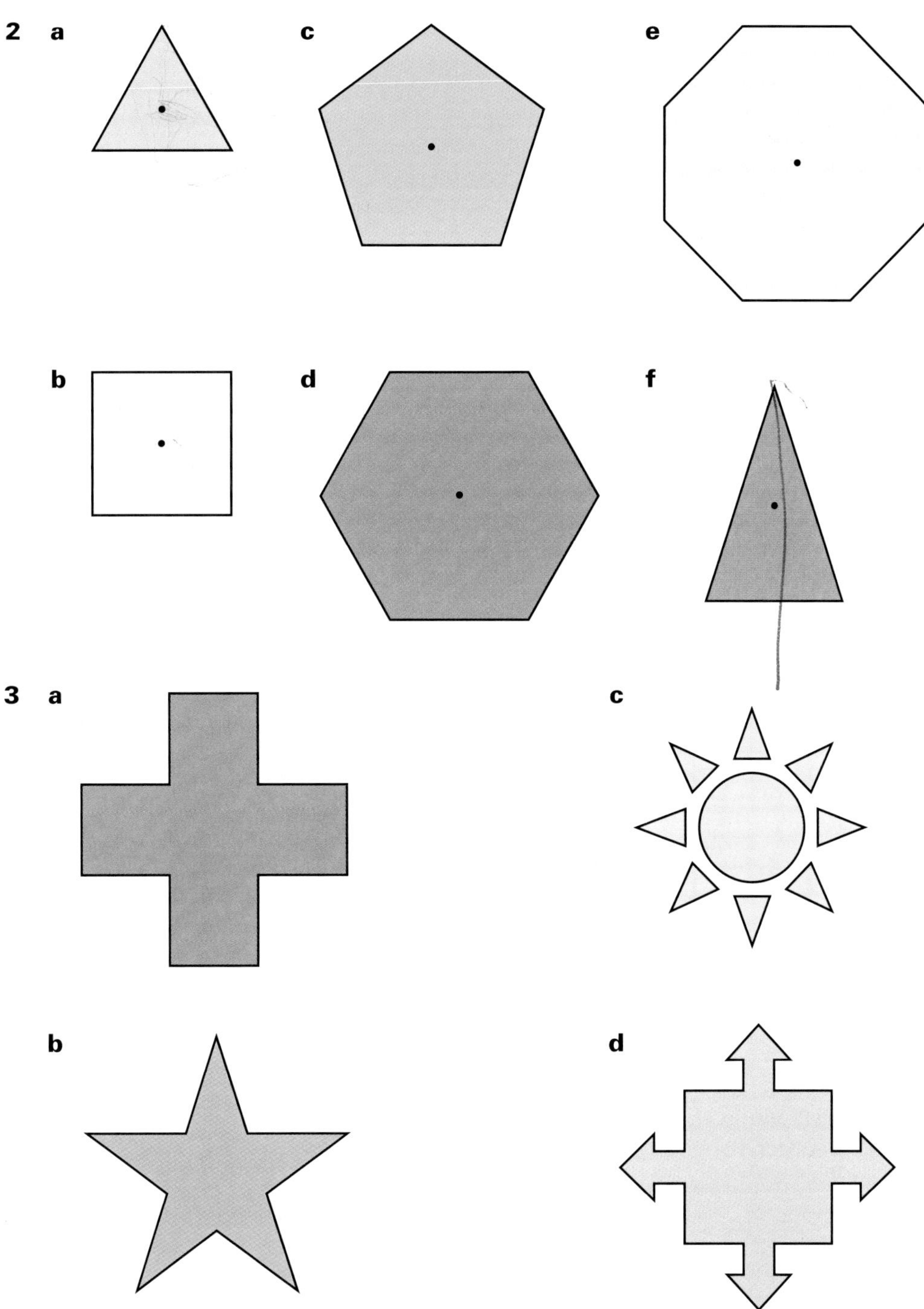

4 Describe the rotational symmetry of each of these graphs.
You will need to give the order of the rotational symmetry and the co-ordinates of the centre of rotation for each one.

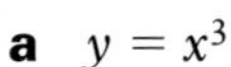

a $y = x^3$

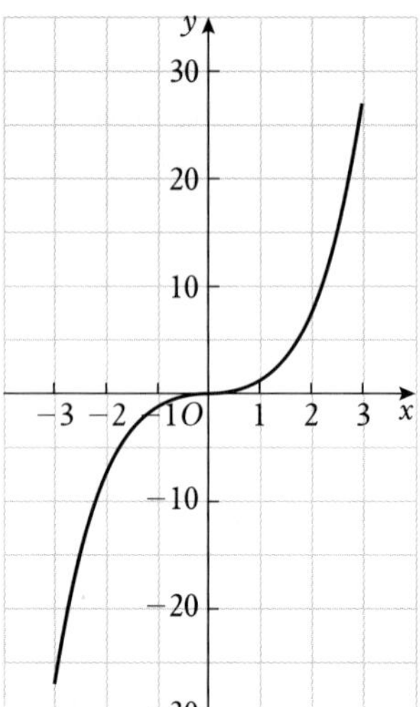

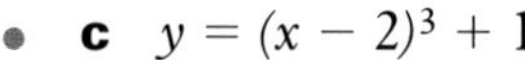

• **c** $y = (x - 2)^3 + 1$

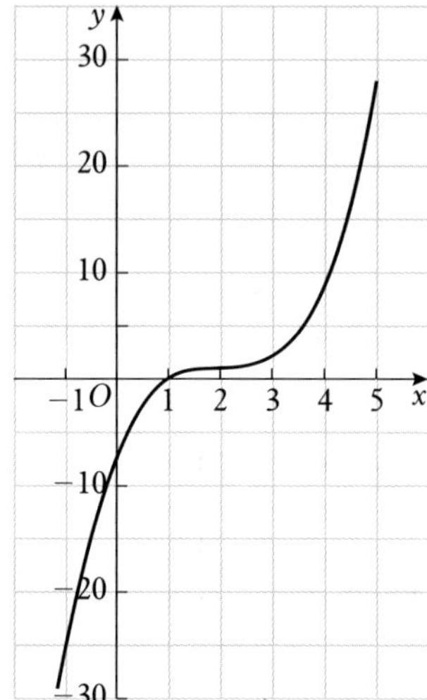

b $y = \dfrac{1}{x}$

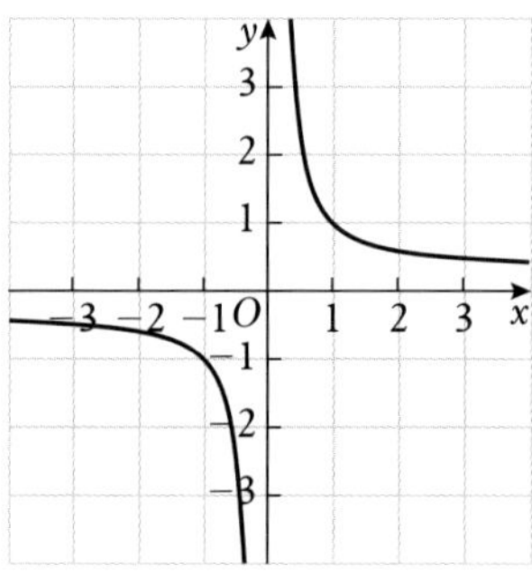

d $y = \dfrac{1}{x - 3} + 2$

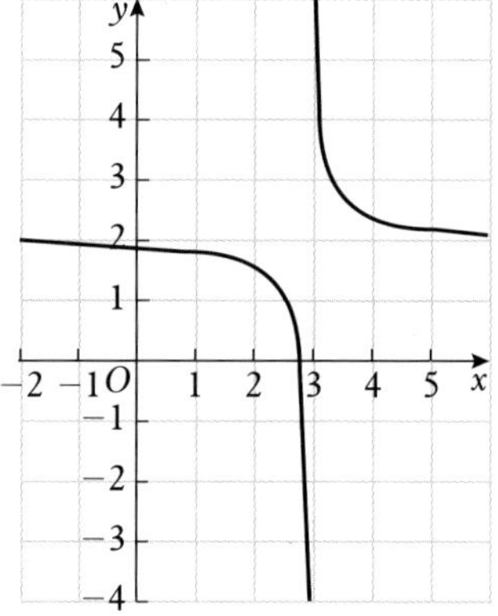

5 Copy the diagram.
Complete it so that it has rotational symmetry of order 4 about C.

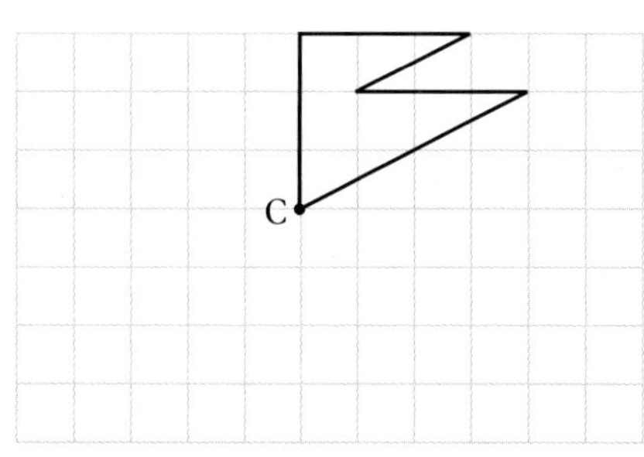

Exterior angles

To find an **exterior angle**:
(1) Make one side longer.
(2) Mark the angle between your line and the next side.
(3) This is the exterior angle. The blue angles are all exterior angles.

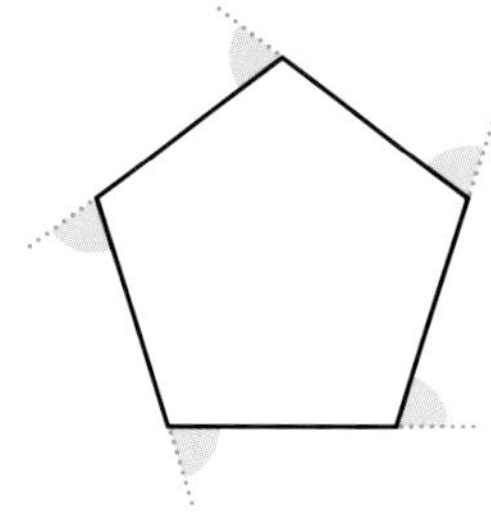

The diagram shows a regular pentagon. It has rotational symmetry of order 5 about the point C.

The pentagon fits onto itself 5 times in one rotation.

The size of each turn is $360° \div 5 = 72°$. This is the size of the exterior angle.

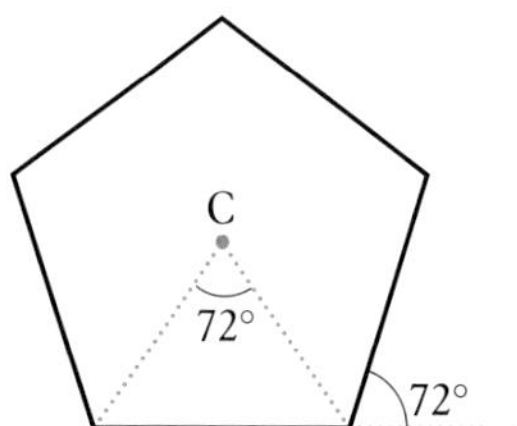

If a regular polygon has n sides then:

1 it has rotational symmetry of order n

2 the exterior angle $= \dfrac{360°}{n}$

3 $n = \dfrac{360°}{\text{the exterior angle}}$

Exercise 32:5

1 Work out the exterior angle of a regular hexagon.

2 Work out the exterior angle of a regular decagon.

3 The exterior angle of a regular polygon is 12°.
How many sides does it have?

4 The exterior angle of a regular polygon is 15°.
How many sides does it have?

5 **a** Write down which of these is not an exterior angle of a regular polygon.
(1) 40° (2) 22.5° (3) 50° (4) 8°
b Explain how you were able to decide.

6 Each diagram shows two sides of a regular polygon.
Work out the number of sides for each one.

a 24°

b 10°

● **c** 140°

● **d** 157.5°

Interior angles

An **interior angle** is the angle inside a shape where two sides meet. The red angles are all interior angles.

The interior angle always makes a straight line with the exterior angle.

This means that interior angle + exterior angle = 180°.

7 Write down the interior angle when the exterior angle is:

a 72° **b** 9° **c** 60° **d** 3°

8 A regular polygon has 30 sides.

a Find the size of the exterior angle.

b Write down the interior angle.

9 The interior angle of a regular polygon is 172°.

a Write down the exterior angle.

b Work out how many sides the polygon has.

You can find the sum of the interior angles of any polygon.

(1) Draw the polygon.

(2) Join one vertex to all the others.
You divide the shape into triangles.
All the interior angles are now inside one of the triangles.

(3) Count the number of triangles.
Multiply by 180° to find the total.

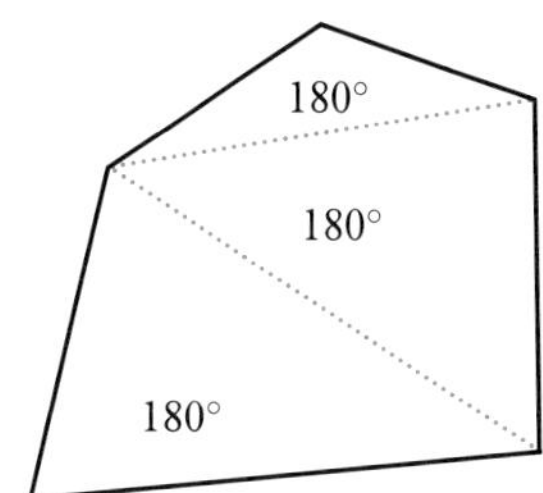

Example Find the sum of the interior angles of a pentagon.
The pentagon splits into **3** triangles.

Total = **3** × 180° = 540°

The sum of the interior angles of a pentagon is 540°.
This is true for all pentagons.

Exercise 32:6

1 Calculate the size of the missing angle in each of these pentagons.

a

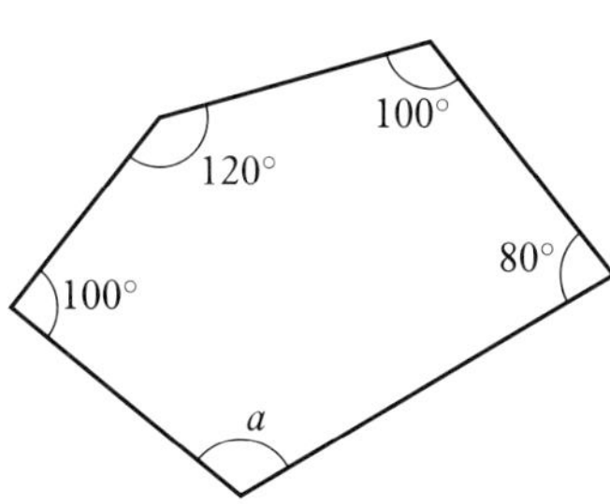

c

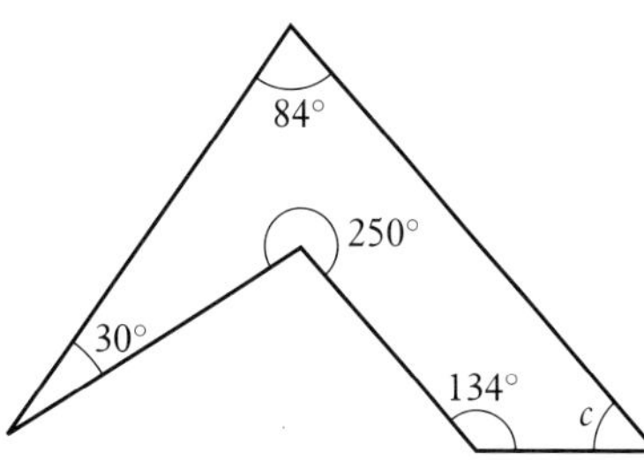

b

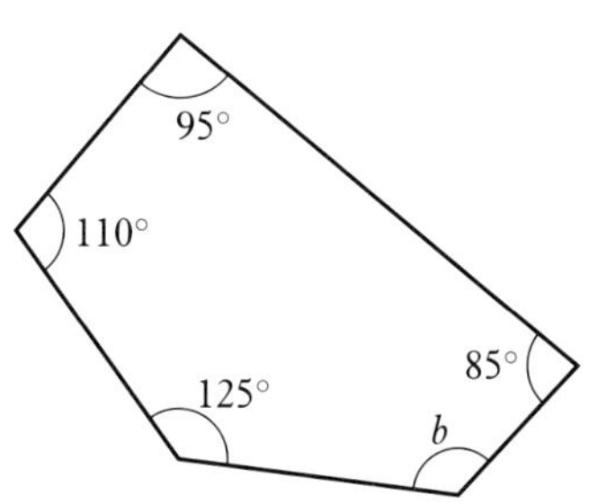

d

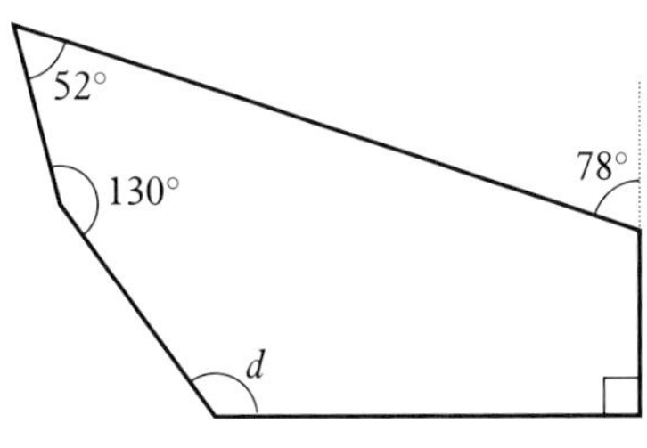

2 **a** A hexagon has 6 sides. Draw a hexagon.
b Join one vertex to all of the others.
c Count the number of triangles.
d Find the sum of the interior angles of a hexagon.

3 **a** A heptagon has 7 sides. Draw a heptagon.
b Join one vertex to all of the others.
c Count the number of triangles.
d Find the sum of the interior angles of a heptagon.

4 **a** An octagon has 8 sides. Draw an octagon.
b Join one vertex to all of the others.
c Count the number of triangles.
d Find the sum of the interior angles of an octagon.

5 **a** A nonagon has 9 sides. Draw a nonagon.
b Join one vertex to all of the others.
c Count the number of triangles.
d Find the sum of the interior angles of a nonagon.

6 **a** A decagon has 10 sides. Draw a decagon.
b Join one vertex to all of the others.
c Count the number of triangles.
d Find the sum of the interior angles of a decagon.

7 **a** Copy the table. Fill it in.

Name of polygon	Number of sides	Number of triangles	Sum of interior angles
	5	3	$3 \times 180°$
	6		
	7		
	8		
	9		
	10		

b Use the results in your table to find a formula for the sum of the interior angles of a polygon with n sides.

The sum of the interior angles of a polygon with n sides is $(n - 2) \times 180°$.

The sum of the exterior angles of any polygon is 360°.

8 The exterior angles of a pentagon are 64°, 78°, 80°, 36° and x°.
Find the value of x.

• **9** The exterior angles of a hexagon are $x°$, $x°$, $2x°$, $2x°$, $3x°$, $3x°$.

a Find the value of x.

b How many of these angles are right-angles?

c How many of the interior angles are obtuse? Explain your answer.

10 Find the sum of the interior angles of a polygon with 22 sides.

• **11** The sum of the interior angles of a polygon is 3240°.

a Use n to stand for the number of sides. Write an equation for n.

b Solve your equation. How many sides does the polygon have?

Tessellation

A **tessellation** is a pattern made by repeating the same shape over and over again.

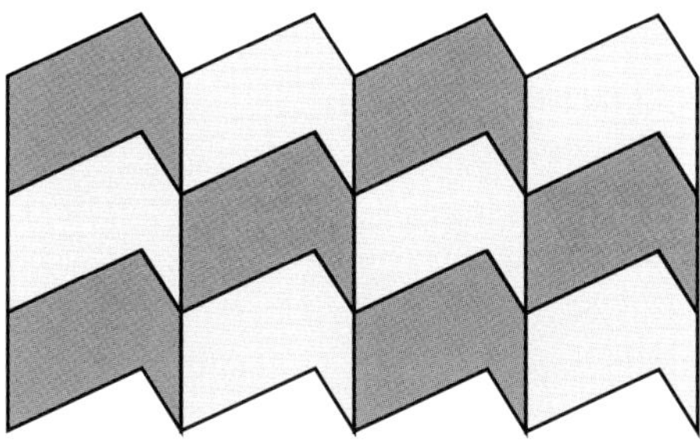

There are no gaps in a tessellation.

Exercise 32:7

1 The diagram shows 2 congruent trapeziums joined along one side.

a Copy the diagram.

b Draw another 10 congruent trapeziums to make a tessellation.

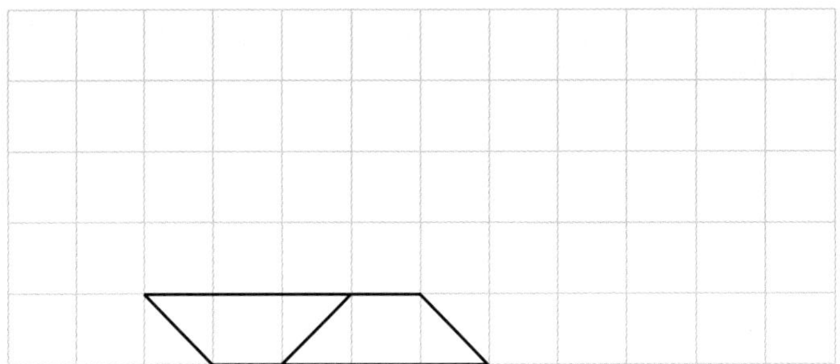

2 **a** Copy the diagram.

b Draw another 10 congruent 'T' shapes to make a tessellation.

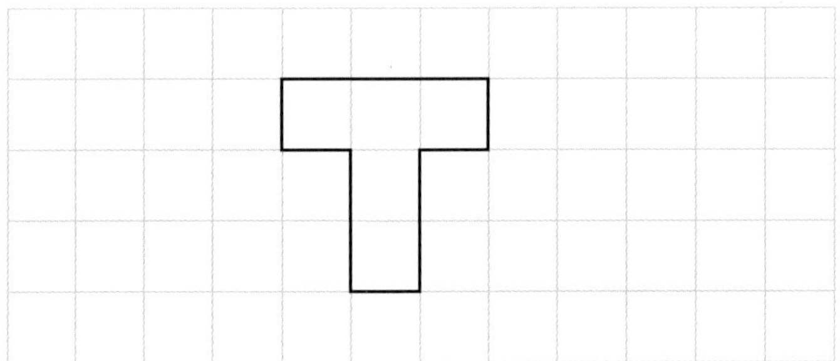

3 Draw a tessellation using congruent triangles.

4 Draw a tessellation using congruent hexagons.

● **5** **a** Find the size of the interior angle of a regular octagon.

b Explain why a regular octagon will not tessellate.

Drawing regular polygons

You can draw a regular polygon by marking equally spaced points around a circle.

To draw a pentagon, start by drawing a circle. If you have an angle measurer you can do this by drawing around it.

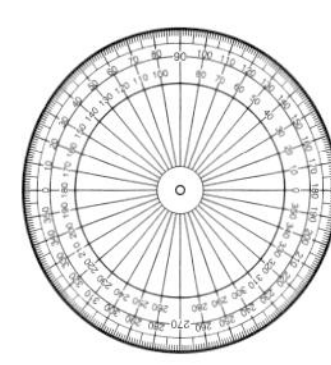

Next, divide the 360° by the number of sides. $360° \div 5 = 72°$.

Mark points around the circumference of the circle at 72° intervals.

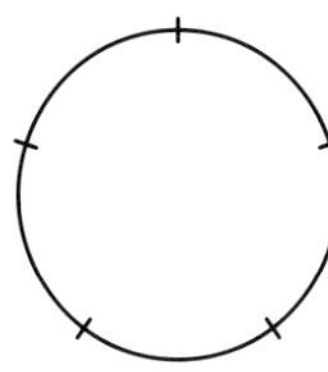

Now join the points with a ruler.

The pentagon is now inscribed in the circle.

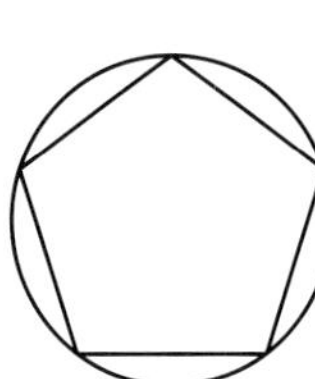

If you are drawing a regular hexagon, you can do this without an angle measurer.

Draw a circle with a pair of compasses. Without changing the compasses, mark points around the circumference of the circle.

You should be able to mark exactly 6 points.

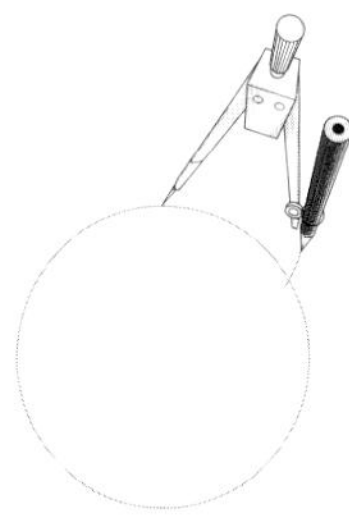

Join these points to form the hexagon.

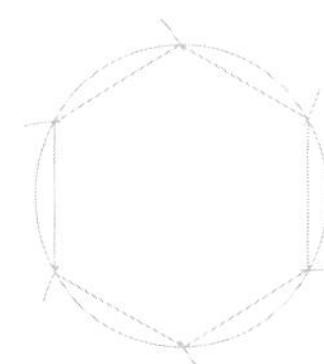

6 Draw the following regular polygons.

a Pentagon

b Hexagon

c Octagon

d Decagon

3 Similar triangles

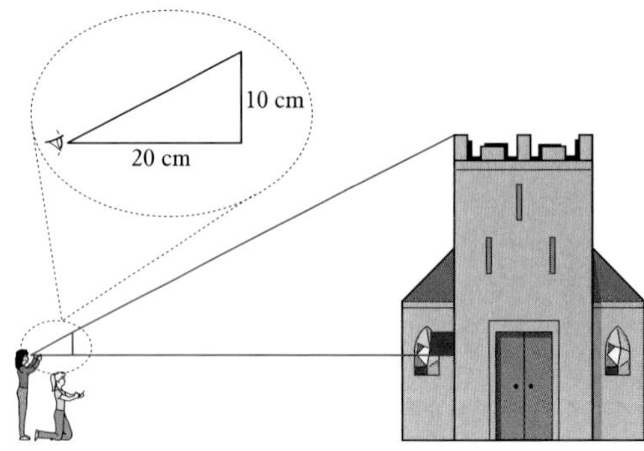

Lin and Karina are finding the height of the church tower.
They haven't got a clinometer to measure the angle.
They are using a triangle made from card.
This section will show you how to find a height like this.

Exercise 32:8

1 **a** You need a piece of 1 cm squared paper.
You will need to draw these triangles accurately.
Start near the bottom left hand corner of your paper.
Draw triangle AB_1C_1 with a right angle at B_1.
$AB_1 = 3$ cm, $B_1C_1 = 2$ cm.

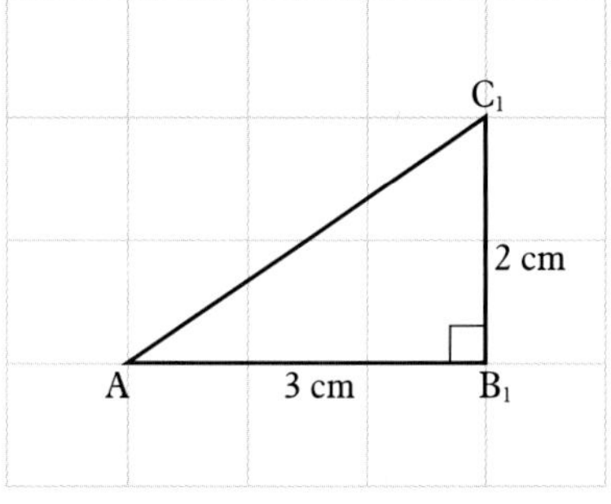

b Now draw AB_2 6 cm long.
Draw another right angle at B_2
and draw in B_2C_2.

c Carry on drawing triangles like this to get this diagram.

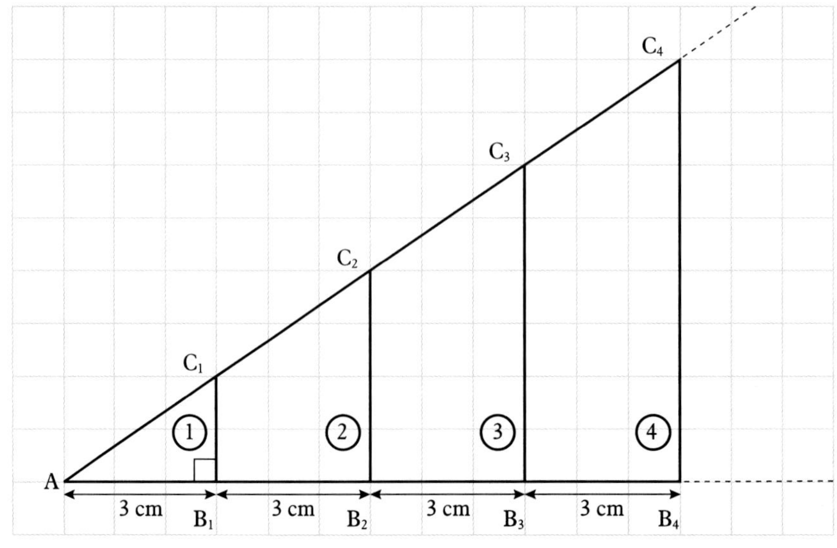

d Copy this table. Measure the sides of the triangles. Fill in the table. The first row has been filled in for you.

Triangle number	Length	Length	Length (2 sf)	Angle (2 sf)	Angle (2 sf)	Ratio	Ratio	Ratio
1	$AB_1 = 3$ cm	$B_1C_1 = 2$ cm	$AC_1 = 3.6$ cm	$C_1\hat{A}B_1 = 34°$	$B_1\hat{C}_1A = 56°$	$\frac{AB_1}{AB_1} = 1$	$\frac{B_1C_1}{B_1C_1} = 1$	$\frac{AC_1}{AC_1} = 1$
2	$AB_2 = \ldots$	$B_2C_2 = \ldots$	$AC_2 = \ldots$	$C_2\hat{A}B_2 = \ldots$	$B_2\hat{C}_2A = \ldots$	$\frac{AB_2}{AB_1} = \ldots$	$\frac{B_2C_2}{B_1C_1} = \ldots$	$\frac{AC_2}{AC_1} = \ldots$

e Continue your table for at least 5 triangles.

2 **a** What do you notice about the angles $C_1\hat{A}B_1$, $C_2\hat{A}B_2$, …?
b What do you notice about the angles $B_1\hat{C}_1A$, $B_2\hat{C}_2A$, …?
c What do you know about the angles at B_1, B_2, B_3, …?
d What do your results to parts **a, b** and **c** tell you about the angles in these triangles?

3 **a** Write down the lengths AB_1, AB_2, AB_3, … as a sequence.
b Copy this. Fill it in.
The lengths are all ………… of 3.
c Write down the lengths B_1C_1, B_2C_2, B_3C_3, … as a sequence.
d Describe this sequence.
e Write down the lengths AC_1, AC_2, AC_3, … as a sequence.
● **f** Describe this sequence.
● **g** What do your results to parts **b, d** and **f** tell you about the sides in these triangles?

4 **a** What do you notice about the ratios $\frac{AB_2}{AB_1}, \frac{B_2C_2}{B_1C_1}, \frac{AC_2}{AC_1}, \ldots$?

b What do you notice about the ratios $\frac{AB_3}{AB_1}, \frac{B_3C_3}{B_1C_1}, \frac{AC_3}{AC_1}, \ldots$?

c What do your results suggest about the ratios of corresponding sides in these triangles?

Similar If two objects are **similar**, one is an enlargement of the other. They have the same shape but different sizes.

Similar triangles

Similar triangles have all 3 pairs of angles equal.
Their three pairs of sides are in the same ratio.

Triangles ABC and DEF are similar. $A\hat{B}C = D\hat{E}F$ and $C\hat{A}B = F\hat{D}E$.
Find the missing length.

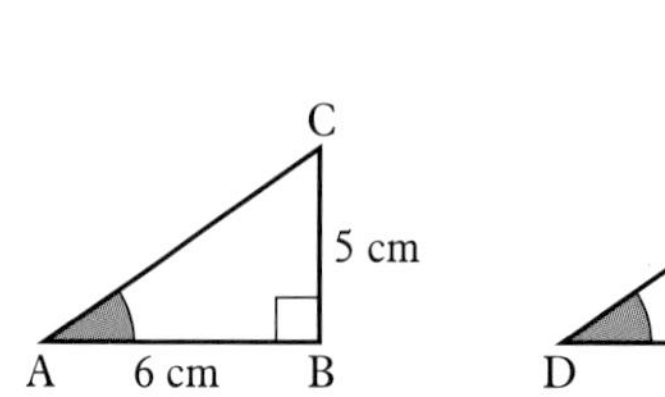

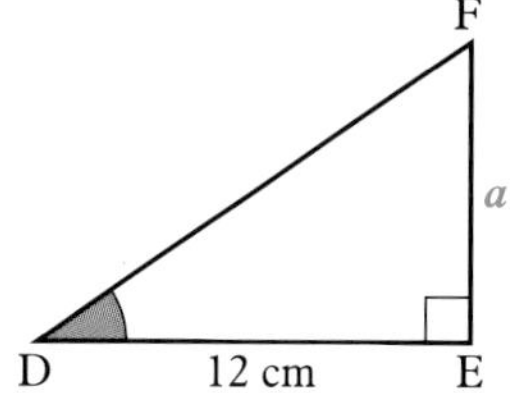

Use common sense. Triangle DEF is bigger than ABC.
So the scale factor going from left to right is **more than 1**

So from triangle ABC to triangle DEF, scale factor $= \frac{DE}{AB} = \frac{12}{6} = 2$

So $a = 2 \times 5 = 10$ cm

Exercise 32:9

Each pair of triangles in questions **1** to **4** are similar.
Find the missing lengths marked with letters.

1

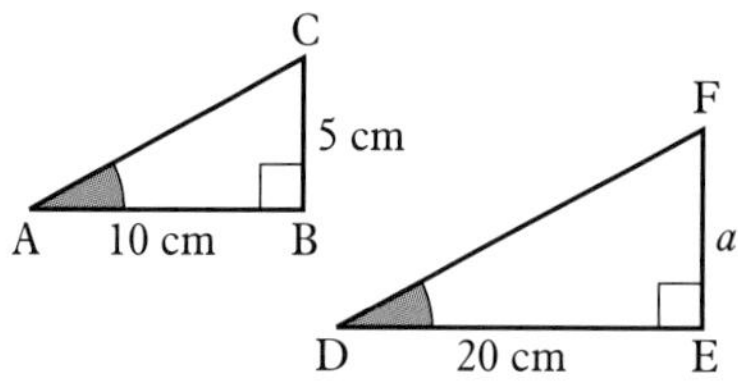

3

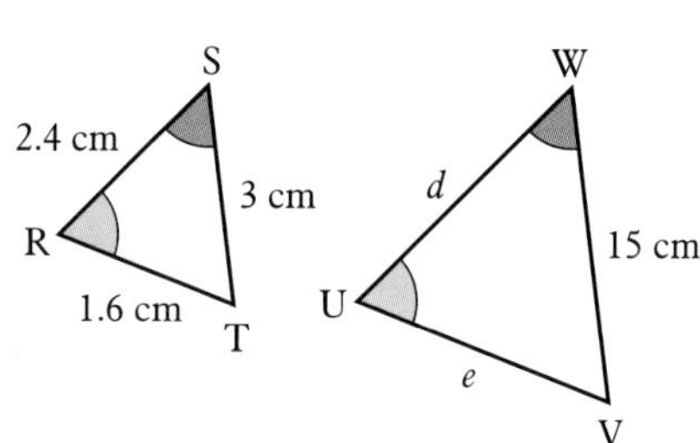

2

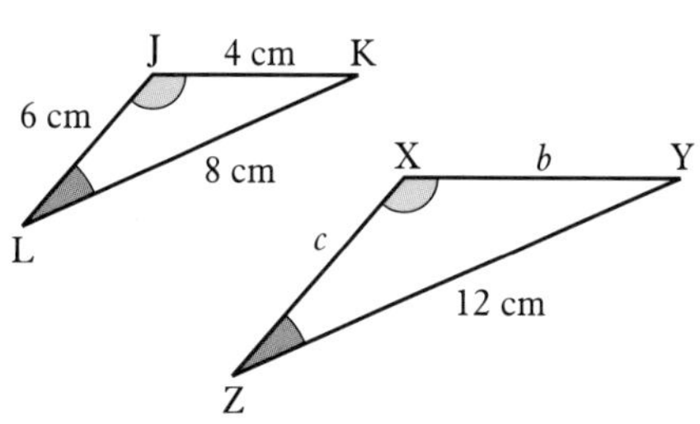

4

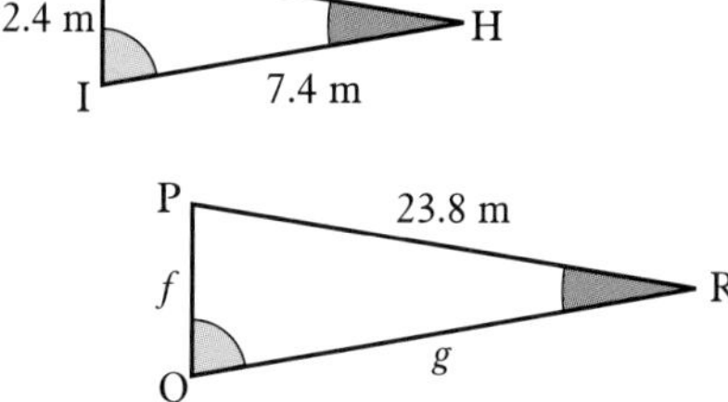

Triangles ABC and FGH are similar. $B\hat{C}A = G\hat{H}F$ and $C\hat{A}B = H\hat{F}G$.
Find the missing lengths.

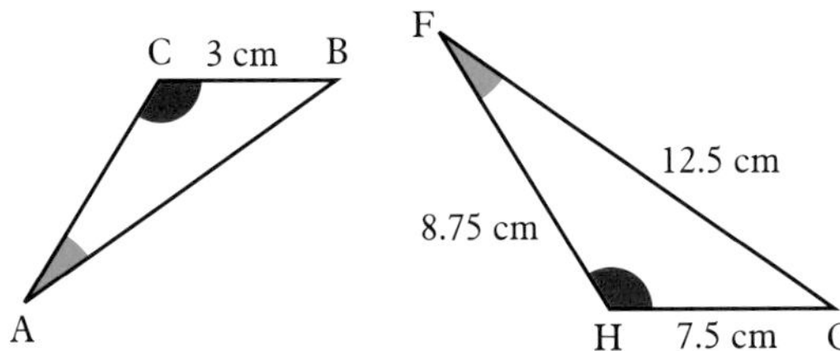

The colours show the pairs of matching angles.
You can trace the triangle on the left.
Rotate it and reflect it so the angles match the positions in the triangle on the right. Your triangles should now look like this.

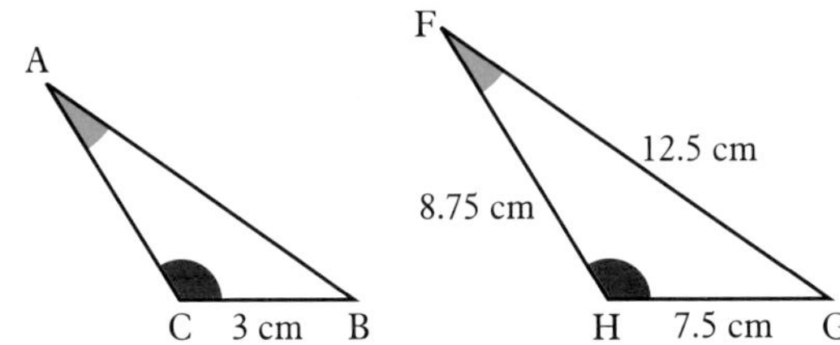

Now use common sense. Triangle BCA is smaller than triangle FGH so the scale factor going from right to left is **less than 1**

So from triangle GHF to triangle BCA, scale factor $= \frac{BC}{GH} = \frac{3}{7.5} = 0.4$

So AC $= 0.4 \times 8.75 = 3.5$ cm and AB $= 0.4 \times 12.5 = 5$ cm

For each pair of triangles in questions **5–12**:

a sketch the diagrams
b write down which pairs of angles are equal
c use tracing paper to show the triangles in matching positions.
d find the lengths marked with letters.

5

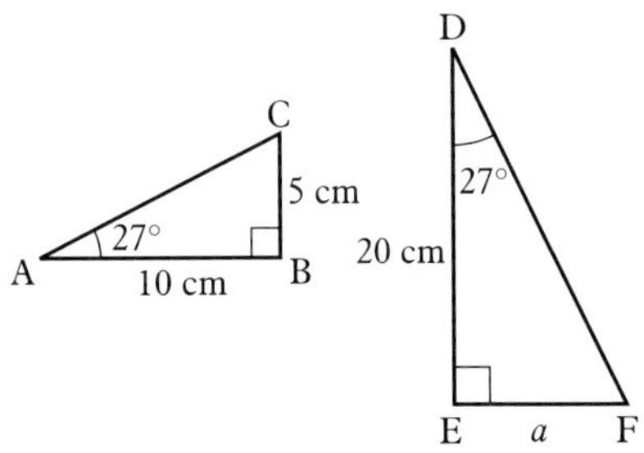

6

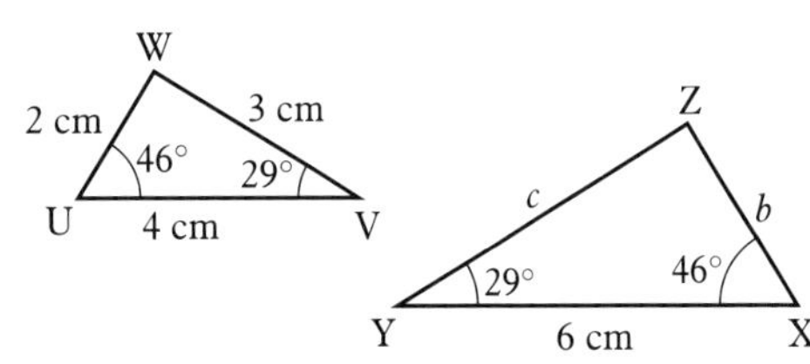

7

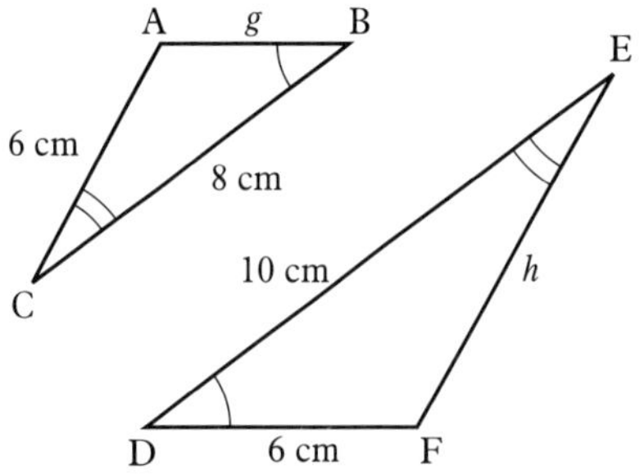

10 You should draw triangles ABC and ADE separately in this question.

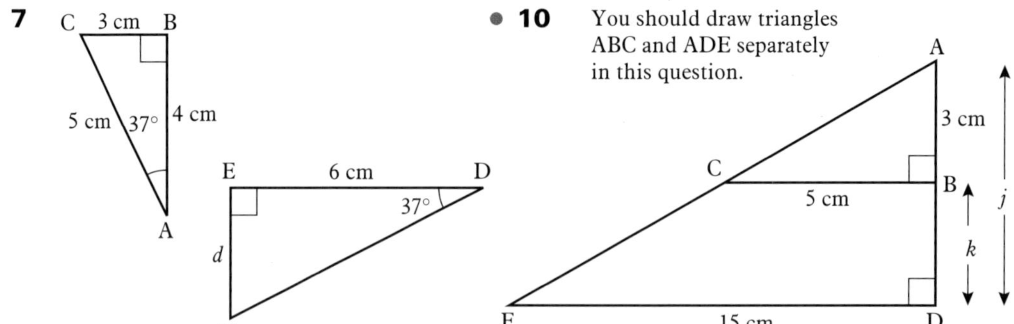

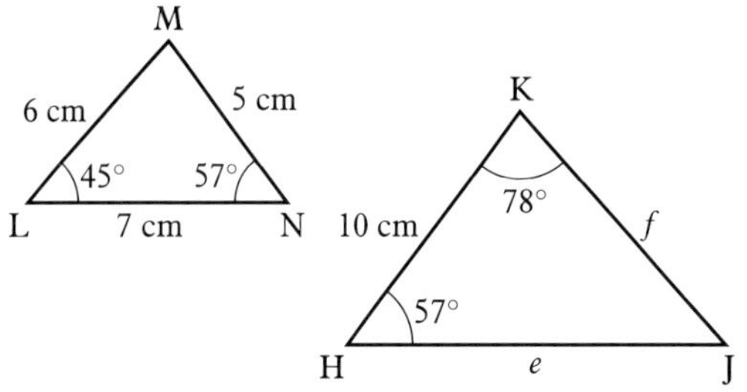

8

11

9

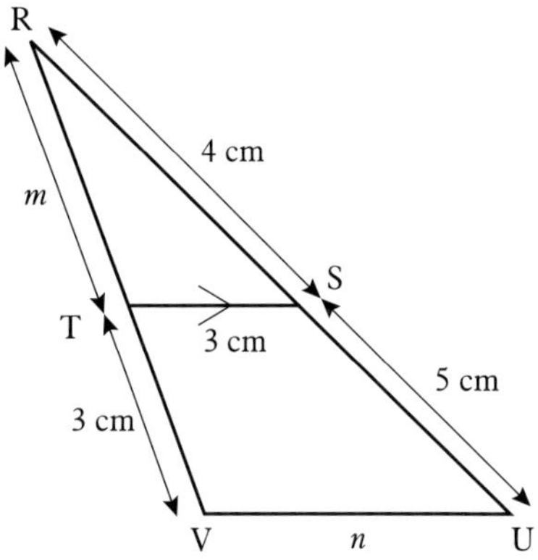

12

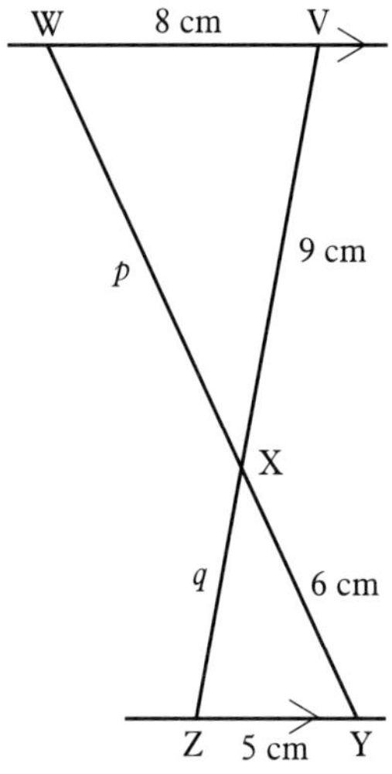

1 **a** Copy the diagram.
b Complete figures B and C so that A, B and C are congruent.

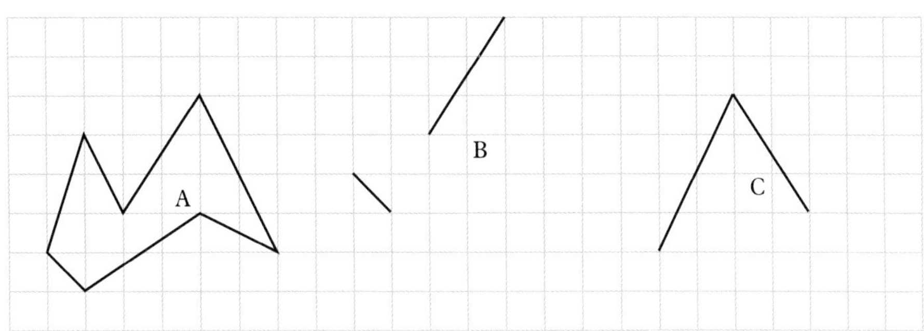

2 These two triangles are similar. Work out the lengths marked with letters.

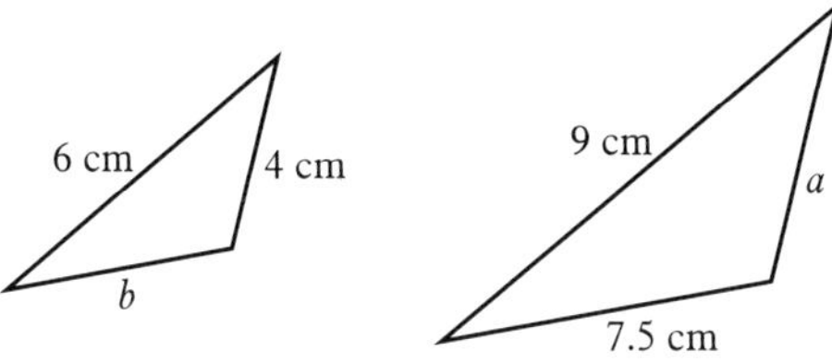

3 **a** Copy these shapes onto squared paper.
b Use the red lines of symmetry to complete each shape.

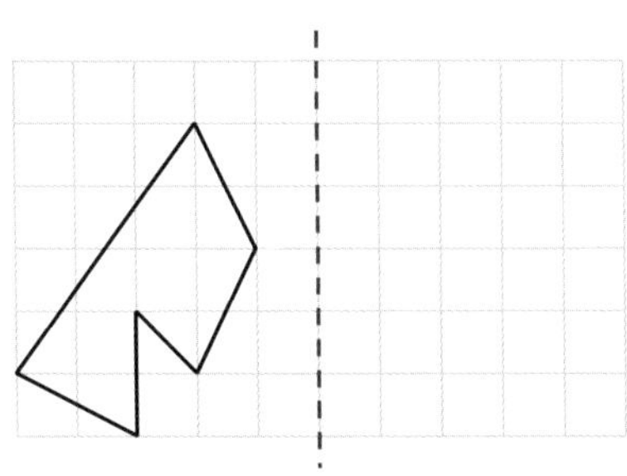

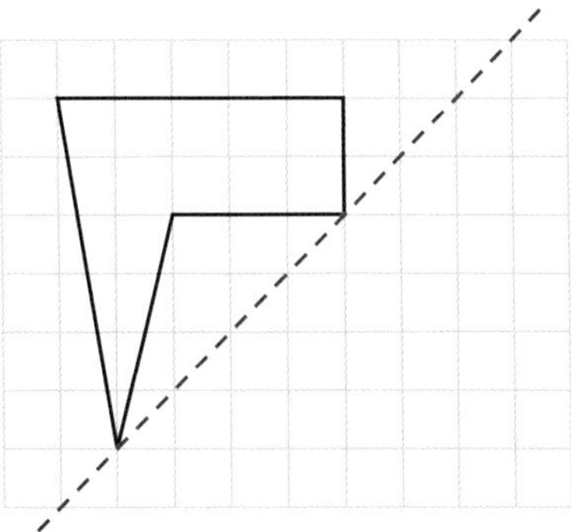

4 **a** Copy the diagram.
b Show the two planes of symmetry on your drawing.

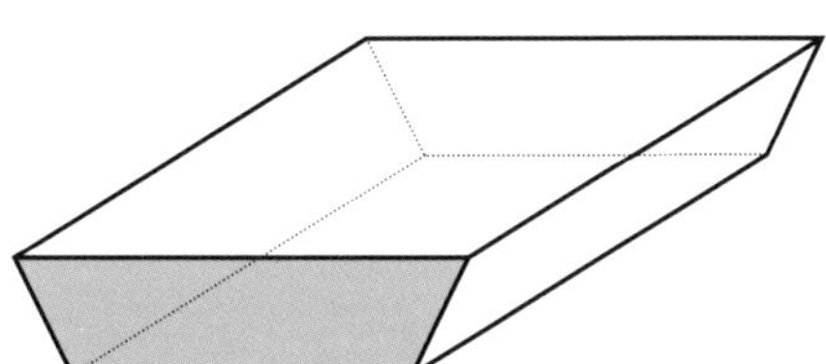

5 **a** Copy the diagrams.
b Complete each figure so that it has rotational symmetry of order 4 with centre at O.

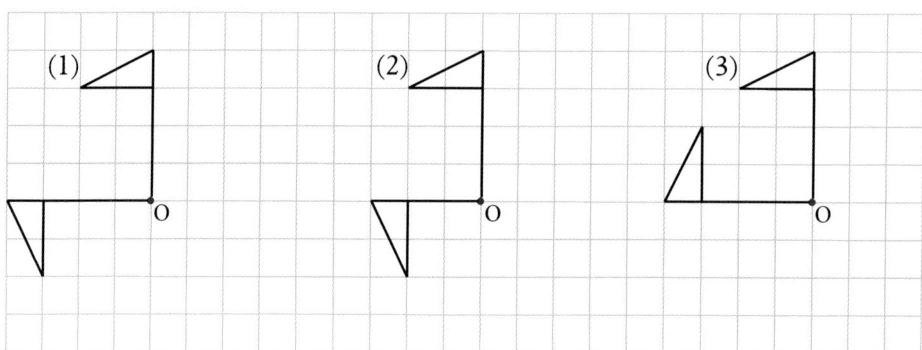

6 Write down the order of rotational symmetry of a:
a parallelogram
b rhombus
c regular decagon.

7 A dodecagon has 12 sides.
a Write down the order of rotational symmetry of a regular dodecagon.
b Find the size of the exterior angle of a regular dodecagon.
c Find the sum of the interior angles of a dodecagon.

8 The diagram shows two of the sides of a regular polygon.
How many sides does the polygon have?

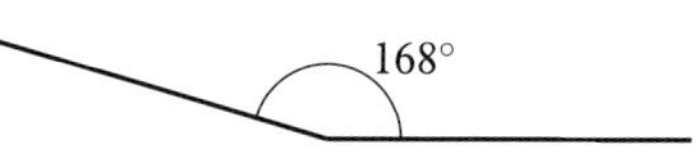

9 Work out the size of the missing angle x in this irregular polygon.

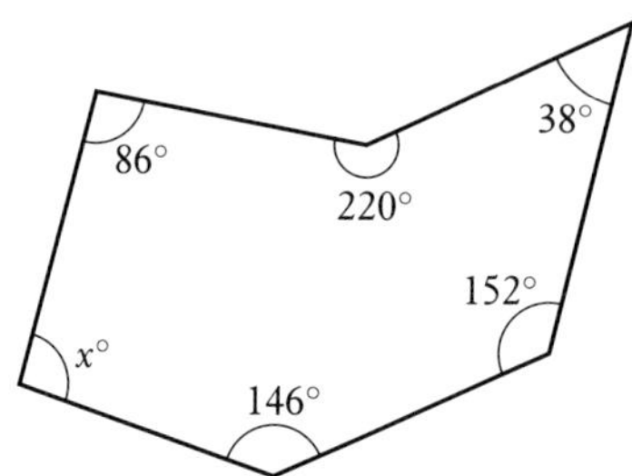

1 **a** Copy the diagram.
b Draw its plane of symmetry.

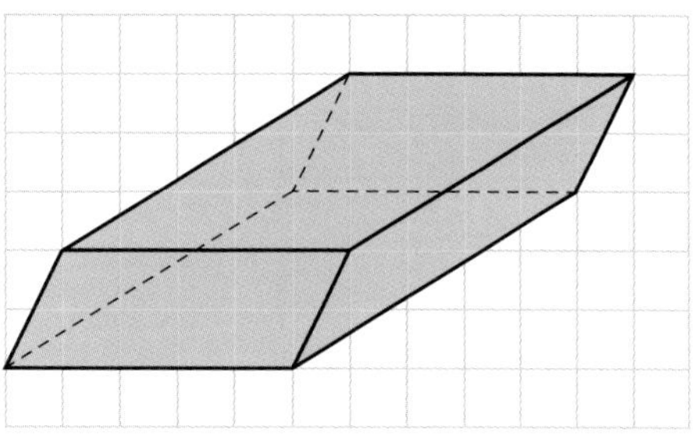

2 The interior angles of a pentagon are $2x°$, $3x°$, $3x°$, $4x°$ and $6x°$.
a Find the value of x.
b Write down the size of each of the interior angles.

3 Only 3 regular polygons will tessellate.
How many sides do they have?

4 These triangles are similar.
Find the value of x.

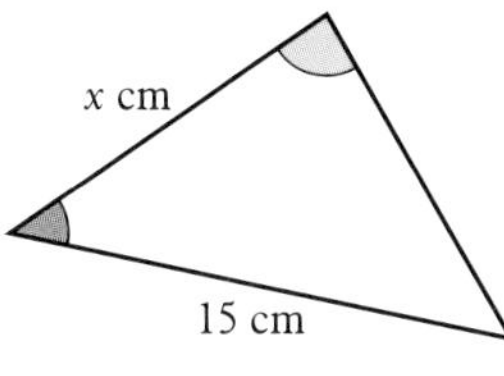

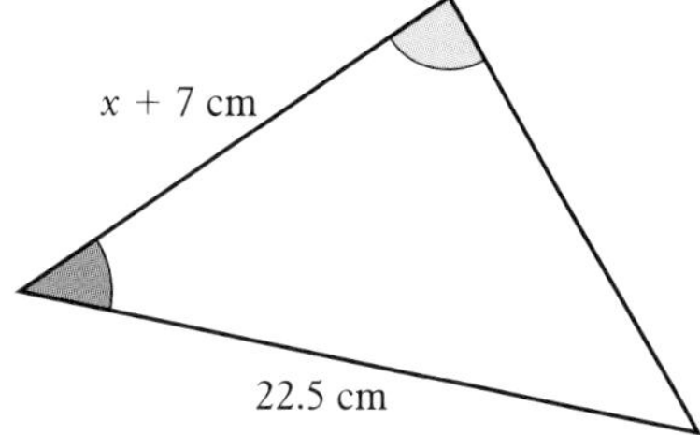

5 **a** Use Pythagoras' theorem to work out the length of CD.

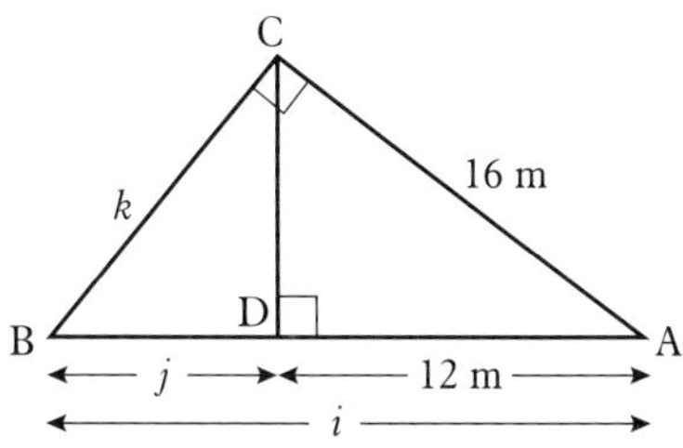

b Write down which pairs of angles are equal in triangles ADC and ABC.
c Find the lengths marked with letters.
d How many similar triangles are there in the diagram?

1 Two of these triangles are congruent. Write down their letters.

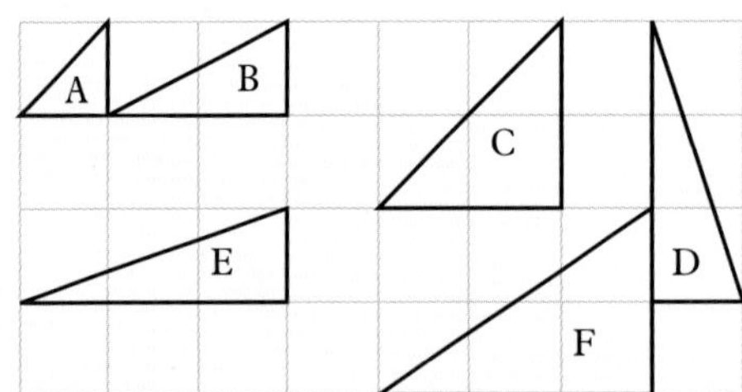

2 Two of the triangles in question **1** are similar but not congruent. Write down their letters.

3 How many planes of symmetry does each of these shapes have?

a

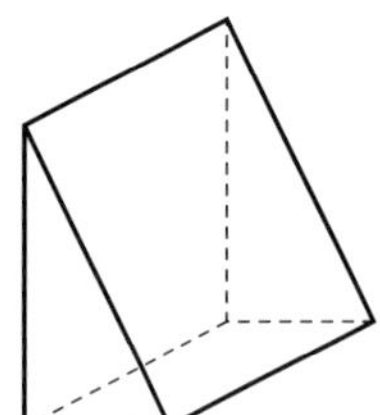

b

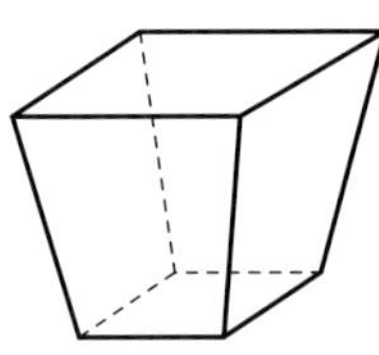

4 Write down the order of rotational symmetry of each of these shapes.

a

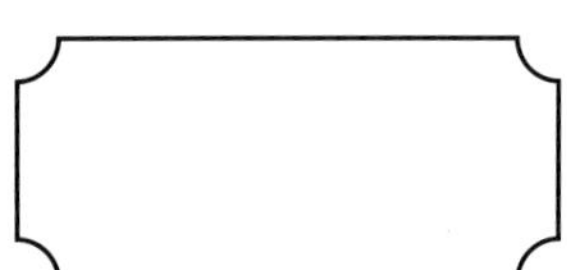

b

5 The interior angle of a regular polygon is 162°.

a Write down the size of the exterior angle.

b How many sides does the polygon have?

6 These two triangles are similar.
Find the value of x.

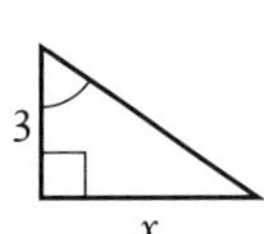

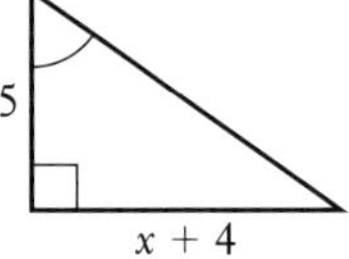

33 Constructions and loci

CORE

1 Constructions
Bisecting an angle
Bisecting a line
Constructing angles

2 Loci
Drawing a locus
Drawing a locus to scale
Looking at boundaries
Solving problems with more than one locus
Investigating goats!

QUESTIONS

EXTENSION

TEST YOURSELF

1 Constructions

Geometrical constructions are used at sea to plan routes.
Ships need to avoid rocks and sandbanks.
They aim to travel in the deepest water.
This chapter looks at how to do these constructions.

Bisecting an angle

Bisecting an angle means splitting it exactly in half.
You do not need an angle measurer to do this.
It is more accurate to do it with compasses.

Exercise 33:1

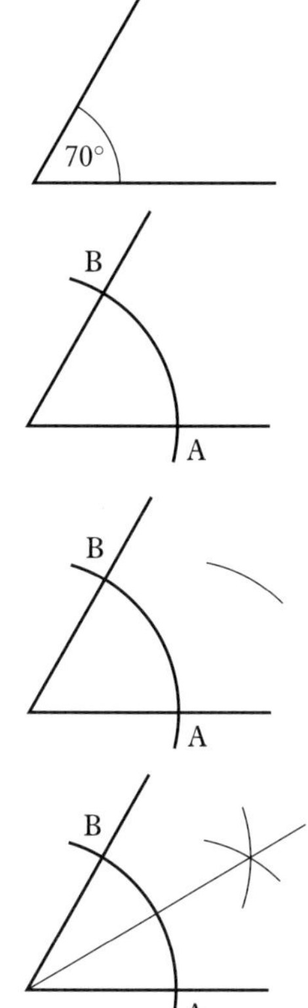

1 **a** Draw a 70° angle.

b Open your compasses a small distance.
You **must** keep your compasses fixed from now on.

c With the compass point on the vertex of the angle, draw a small arc which crosses both arms of the angle. Label these points A and B.

d Place your compasses on point A and draw another arc in the middle of the angle.

e Now place your compasses on point B.
Draw another arc in the middle of the angle.
It should cross the first one.

f Finally, draw a line from the vertex of the angle through the point where your two arcs cross.
This line bisects the angle.

g Measure the two parts of the angle to check that it is correct.

2 **a** Draw a 50° angle.
b Draw an arc crossing both arms of the angle.
Label the points A and B.
c Draw arcs from points A and B.
d Draw the line which bisects the angle.
e Measure the two parts of the angle to check that it is correct.

3 **a** Draw a right angle.
b Bisect the angle.
Use the instructions in question **2** to help you.

4 **a** Draw an angle of 120°.
b Bisect the angle.

Equidistant from two lines

All the points on the line which bisects an angle are **equidistant** from the two arms of the angle.
This means that they are always the same distance from the two lines. Both the red lines marked are the same length. So are both the blue ones.

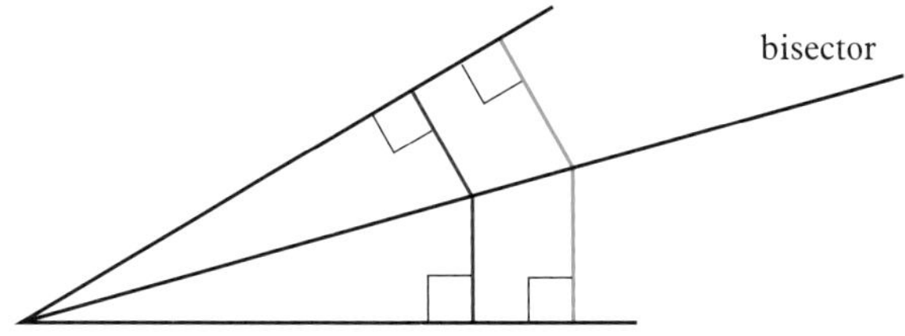

5 **a** Draw two lines AB and AC which are at 66° to each other.
b Draw a line which is equidistant from AB and AC.

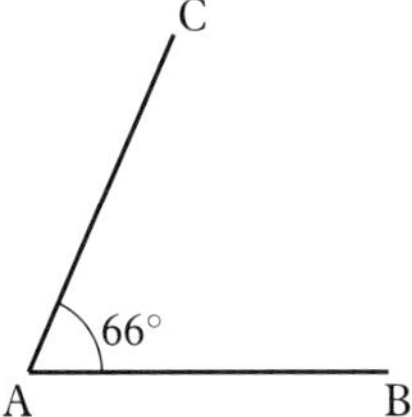

6 **a** Draw two lines PQ and PR which are at 140° to each other.
b Draw a line that is equidistant from PQ and PR.

Exercise 33:2

1 Construct this triangle using a ruler and compasses.
Start by drawing the line AB.

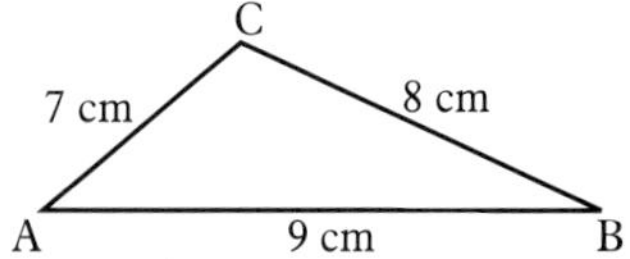

2 **a** Bisect the angle at vertex A of the triangle you have constructed for question **1**.
b Bisect the angle at vertex B of the triangle.
c Bisect the angle at vertex C of the triangle.
The three bisectors should cross at one point.

3 **a** Construct an equilateral triangle with sides 9 cm.
Label your triangle PQR.
b Bisect all three angles of the triangle.
c Mark the point X in the middle of PR.
d Place the point of your compasses on the point where the bisectors cross.
Move your pencil point until it touches point X.

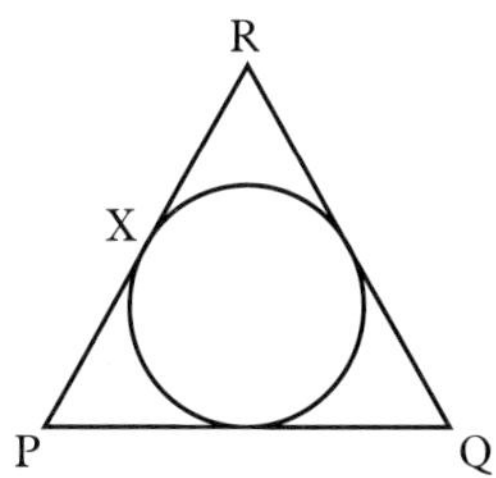

e Draw a circle with your compasses.
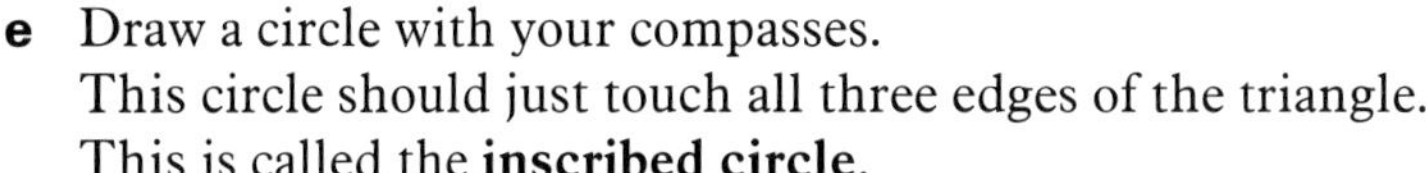
This circle should just touch all three edges of the triangle.
This is called the **inscribed circle**.

4 The sketch shows the path near to the edges of a cliff.
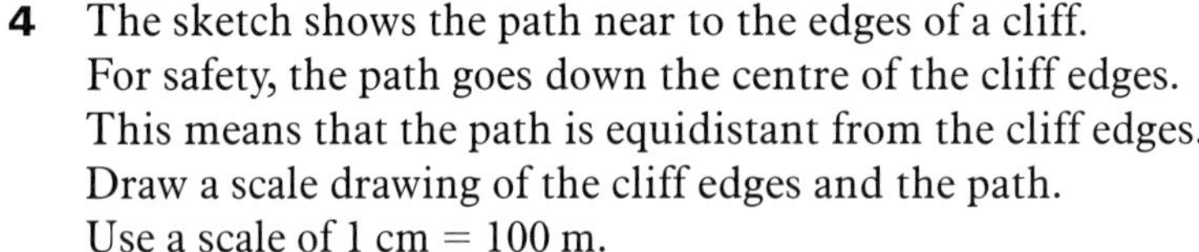
For safety, the path goes down the centre of the cliff edges.
This means that the path is equidistant from the cliff edges.
Draw a scale drawing of the cliff edges and the path.
Use a scale of 1 cm = 100 m.

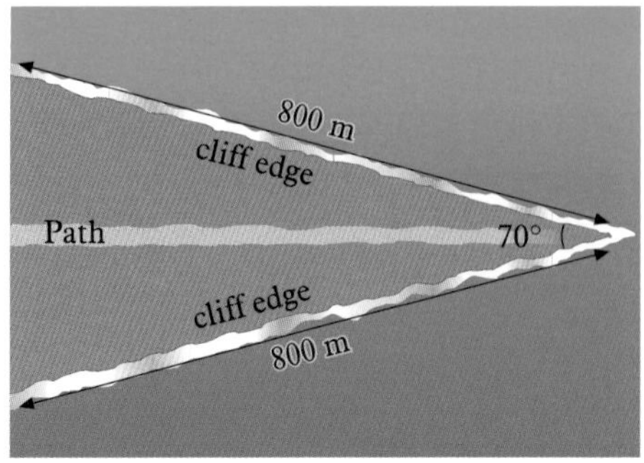

Bisecting a line — **Bisecting a line** means cutting it exactly in half.

Perpendicular — Two lines that are at right angles to each other are called **perpendicular**.

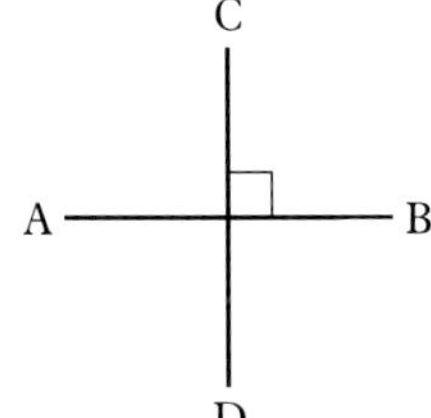

Perpendicular bisector — On this diagram, CD is perpendicular to AB and CD bisects AB. CD is called the **perpendicular bisector** of AB.

Exercise 33:3

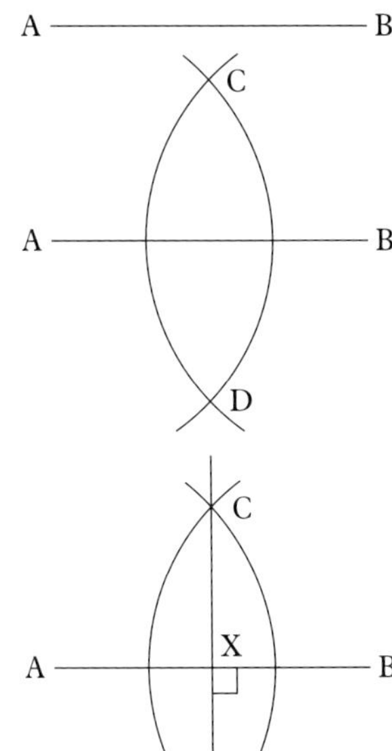

1 **a** Draw a line 10 cm long.
Label the ends A and B.
Put your compass point on A.

b Move your pencil until you can tell it is more than half way along the line.

c Draw an arc from above the line to below it.

d **Without changing your compasses,** move the compass point to B.

e Draw another arc from B.

f Your arcs should cross above and below the line.
Label these points C and D.

g Join C to D. Use a ruler.
Line CD bisects line AB at right angles.
Mark the point of intersection X.
Measure AX and BX with a ruler to check that they are equal.

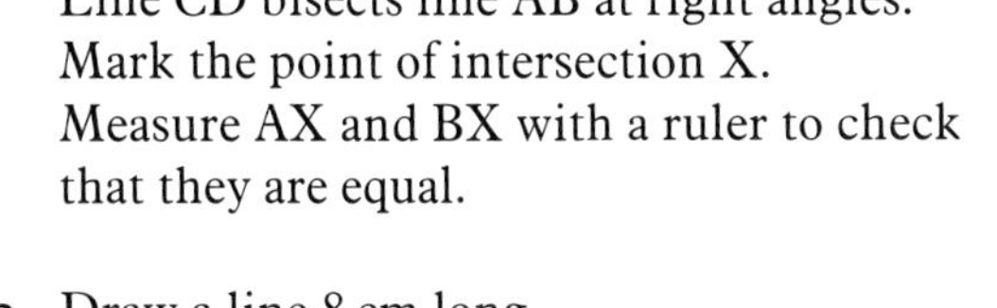

2 **a** Draw a line 8 cm long.
Label your line AB.

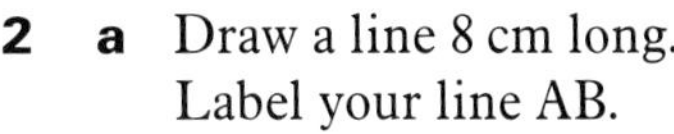

b Draw arcs from A and B.

c Label the crossing points of the arcs C and D.

d Join C to D to bisect the line.

e Check that CD bisects AB by measuring.

3 **a** Draw a line AB 7.4 cm long.

b Bisect the line using ruler and compasses.

Equidistant from two points

All the points on the perpendicular bisector of a line are **equidistant from the two points** at the ends of the original line.

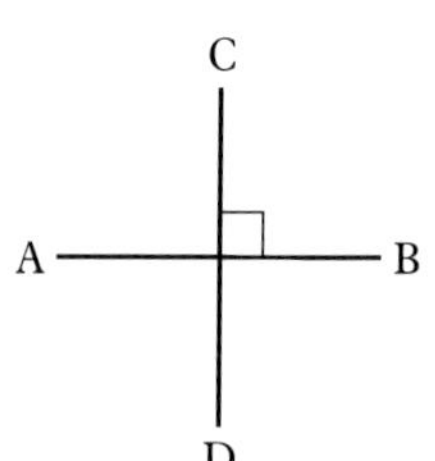

Every point on CD is equidistant from A and B.

In particular, CD passes through the midpoint of AB.

4 **a** Draw points A and B which are 7 cm apart.
b Join the points with a straight line.
c Construct a line that is made up of points that are equidistant from A and B.

5 The diagram shows the position of two buoys near a coastline.
Ships must stay exactly in the middle of the buoys to be in the deepest water.
a Make a copy of the diagram.
It does not have to be exact.
b Draw the path that the ship should take between the buoys.

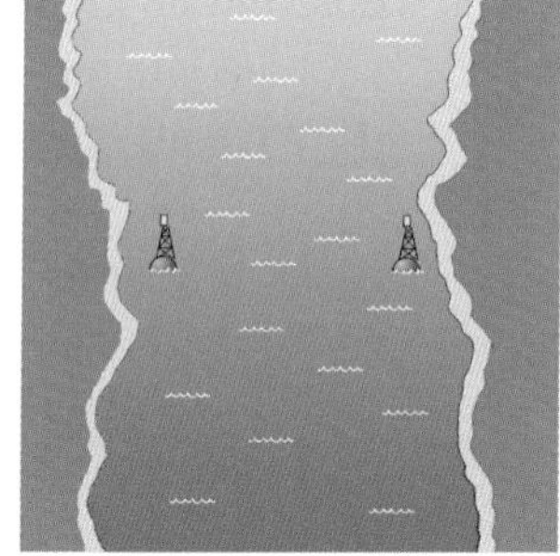

6 The diagram shows a plan of a factory floor.
The red points show the positions of emergency power shutoff buttons A, B and C.
a Make a scale drawing of the factory.
Use a scale of 1 cm = 10 m.
b By constructing a line on your diagram, shade the area of the factory where the workers are closer to button A than button B.
● **c** By constructing another two lines on your diagram, shade the area of the factory where workers are closer to button C than either of the other buttons.

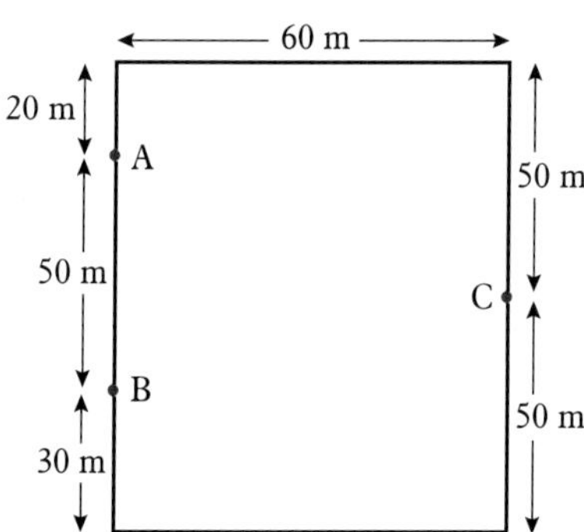

7 **a** Construct an equilateral triangle with sides 10 cm.
Label your triangle PQR.

b Bisect all three sides of the triangle.

c Place the point of your compasses on the point where the bisectors cross.
Move your pencil point until it touches point P.

d Draw a circle with your compasses.
This circle should go through all three points P, Q and R.
This is called **circumscribing the triangle**.

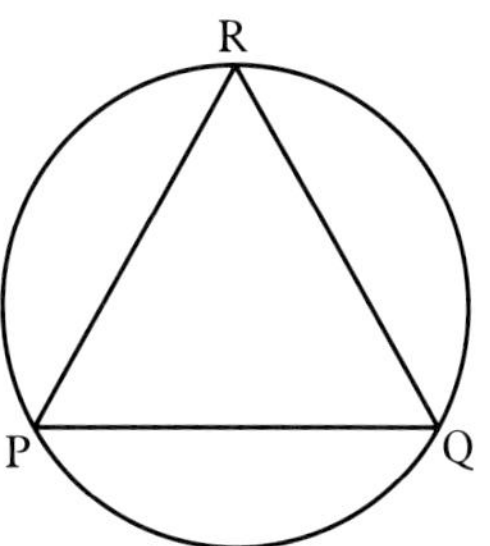

It is possible to construct some angles just using a ruler and compasses.
If you do it carefully, it is more accurate than using an angle measurer.

To construct a 60° angle:

Start with a horizontal line.
Label it AB.

A B

Set your compasses a small distance apart and put the point on A.

Draw an arc from the line upwards until you can see that you have turned through more than 60°

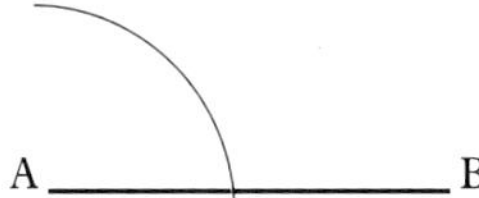

Put the point of your compass on the point where the arc crosses your line.
Draw another arc which crosses the first one.

Join A to the point where the two arcs cross.

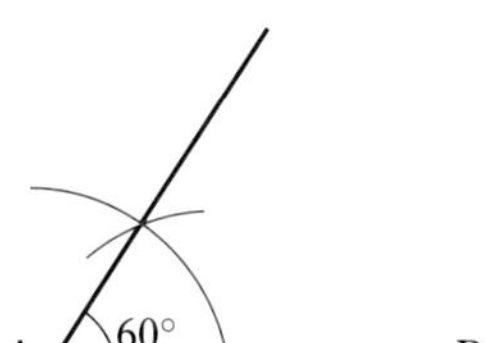

The angle is 60°
You can measure it to check.

Exercise 33:4

1 Construct a 60° angle using ruler and compasses.

2 **a** Construct a 60° angle using ruler and compasses.
b Bisect your angle.
This is how to draw a 30° angle.

3 **a** Construct a 30° angle using the steps in question **2**.
b Bisect your angle.
This is how to draw a 15° angle.

4 **a** Construct a 60° angle using ruler and compasses.
b Bisect your angle.
c Bisect the upper of the two 30° angles you now have.
d Clearly mark a 45° angle.

5 **a** Construct a 60° angle using ruler and compasses.
b Construct another 60° angle using the upper line of the first angle as your base line.
c Clearly mark a 120° angle.

Constructing a 90° angle at a point is the same as drawing the perpendicular from a point on a line.

To draw the perpendicular from X on the line AB:
Set your compasses a small distance apart and put the point on X.

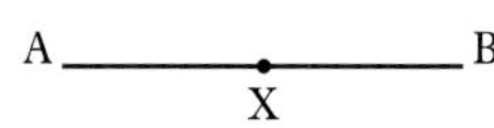

Draw a 180° arc so that it crosses AB either side of X.
Label the points C and D.

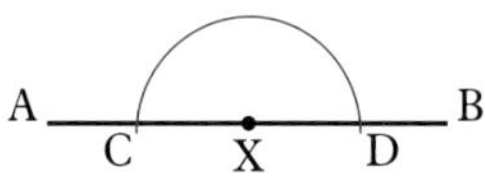

Put the point of your compass on C and draw an arc above X. Put your compass on D and draw another arc. It should cross the first one.
Join X to the point where the two arcs cross.
You now have a 90° angle.

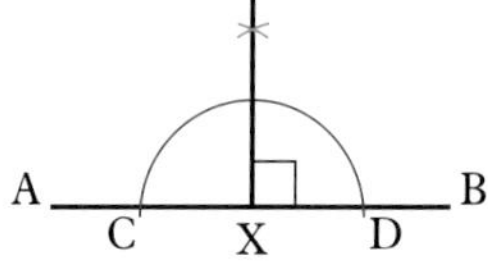

---

6 Construct a 90° angle using ruler and compasses.

7 **a** Construct a 90° angle using ruler and compasses.
b Bisect your angle.
This is another way to draw a 45° angle.

8 **a** Construct a 90° angle using ruler and compasses.
b Bisect your angle.
c Add a 60° angle to your diagram to construct an angle of 105°.

● **9** Use the angle constructions you have seen in the previous questions to construct the following angles.

a 150°
b 75°
c $22\frac{1}{2}°$
d 165°
e 210°
f 330°

● **10** This is a sketch of a regular hexagon.
Make an accurate drawing of this sketch.

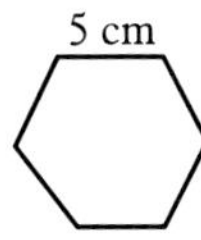

W **11** By bisecting at least two angles of each shape, find the exact centre of each polygon.

W **12** Lawrence has found an old Egyptian treasure map.
Of course, the Ancient Egyptians were excellent mathematicians.
So all the instructions on the treasure map involve maths.
Get your copy of the map and the instructions. Happy hunting!

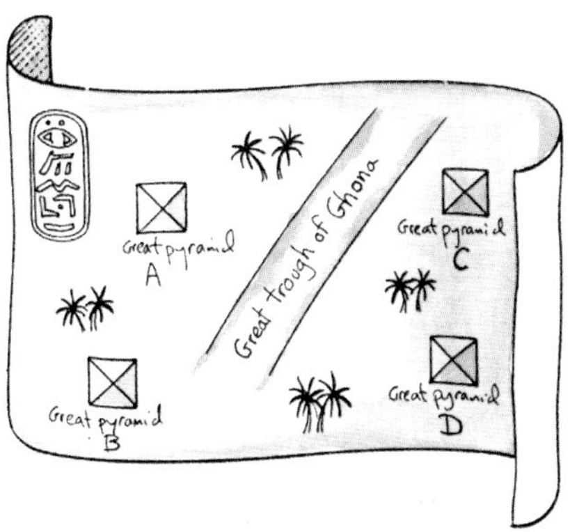

You need to know how to construct a perpendicular from a point down to a line.

•P

To construct the perpendicular from P onto AB

A ——— B

Put your compass point on P and make sure your compasses are open wide enough to be able to draw an arc that crosses AB at two points.
Label the points C and D.

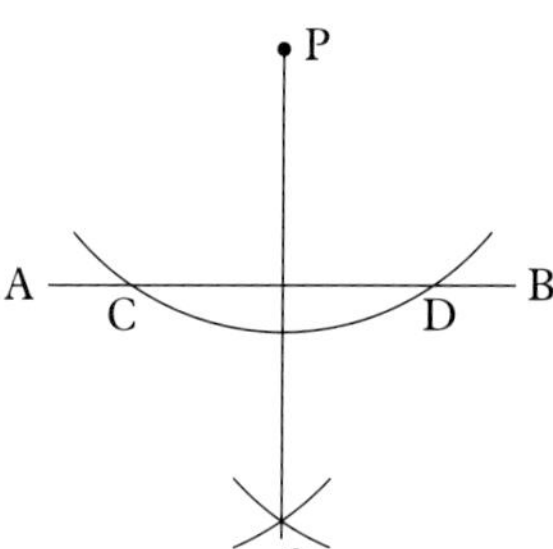

Now put your compass on C and then D and draw two arcs that cross below the line.
Call this point Q.

Now join P to Q.

This line will be perpendicular to AB.

13 Draw the perpendicular from X onto YZ.

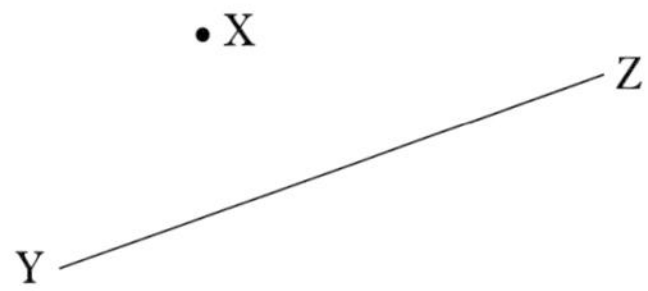

14 Lucy is orienteering.
She sees a road and wants to get there as quickly as possible.
Draw a diagram to show this.
Mark a point for Lucy. Label it L.
Draw a line for the road.
Construct the route that Lucy should take.

2 Loci

In Norway it is not unusual for people to keep animals on the roof!
It is important to keep Sven tied up so that he doesn't fall off.
Sven is attached to a post.
He can eat the grass in a circle.
The radius of the circle is the length of the rope.
The centre of the circle is the post.
Sven can be anywhere inside the circle.

When something can only be on a line or a curve then this line or curve is called a locus.
Loci is the plural of locus.

Locus

The **locus** of an object is the set of all the points which fit a certain condition.
You can describe a locus in words or with a diagram.

The tip of the hour hand on this clock moves in a circle.

The hour hand is 3 cm long.

The locus of the tip of the hour hand is a circle of radius 3 cm.
The centre of the circle is the centre of the clock.

You can also draw the locus.
The locus of the tip of the hour hand is the blue circle.

Exercise 33:5

In questions **1–4**:
- **a** describe the locus in words
- **b** draw a diagram to show the locus.

1 The locus of the tip of the minute hand on a clock. The hand is 5 cm long.

2 The locus of the midpoint of the minute hand in question **1**.

3 The locus of the bob of this pendulum as it swings through a total angle of 80°. The pendulum is 30 cm long. Use a scale of 1 cm to 10 cm.

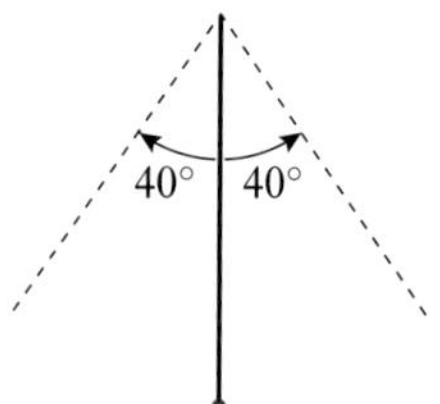

● **4** The locus of a point that is always 4 cm away from a point O.

Example Draw the locus of a point that moves so that it is always 1 cm away from the line AB.

The point can be above or below the line.

A B

The two red lines are part of the locus of the point.
They are both 1 cm from the line.
The red lines are parallel to the original line and are the same length as AB.

Now look at the points at the ends of the line.

If you stay 1 cm away from each point you get a semicircle at each end of the line.
You should use compasses to draw the semicircles.
The blue line is the locus of a point that is always 1 cm away from the line AB.

Exercise 33:6

1 **a** Draw a 7 cm line.
Label it AB.

A B

b Draw the locus of a point that is always 3 cm away from this line.

2 This fence is 10 metres long.

a Draw a line to represent the fence.
Use a scale of 1 cm to 1 m.

b Draw the locus of a point that is always 2 m away from the fence.

3 A wall is 40 metres long.

a Draw a line to represent the wall.
Use a scale of 1 cm to 10 m.

b Draw the locus of a point that is always 10 m away from the wall.

4 **a** Copy this shape.

b Draw the locus of a point that lies outside the shape and 1 cm from the edge of the shape.

c Draw the locus of a point that lies inside the shape and 1 cm from the edge of the shape.

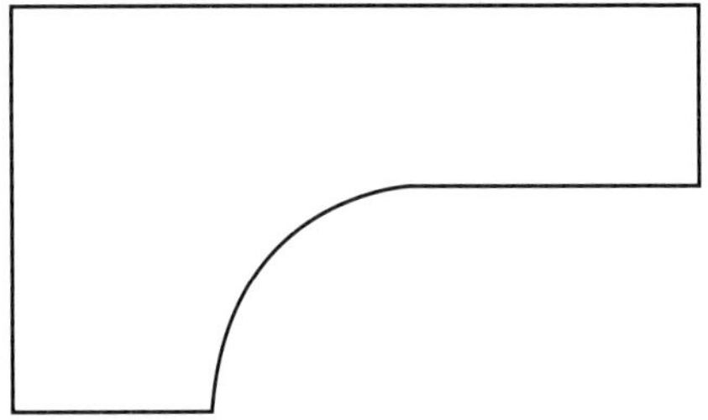

• **5** The rectangle represents a box.

a Copy the rectangle.

b Draw the locus of a point that is 3 cm from the edge of the box.
Remember the locus can be both inside and outside the box.

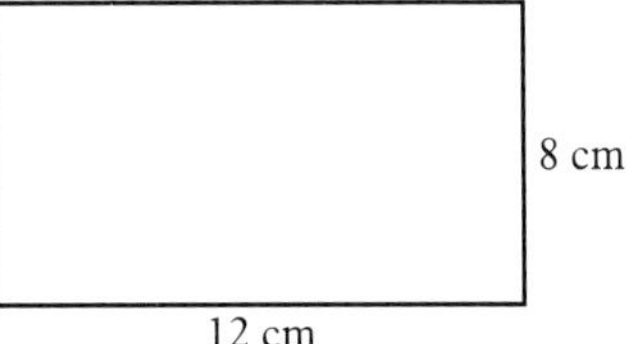

c Copy the rectangle again.

d This coin is rolled around the inside of the box so that is always touching the sides.
Draw the locus of the centre of the coin.

6 **a** Sketch the locus of the centre of this wheel as it rolls along the ground.
b Sketch the locus of the black point on the rim of the wheel.

7 **a** Copy this diagram.
b Draw the locus of a point that moves so that it is always the same distance from the points A and B.
c What is the mathematical name of this locus?

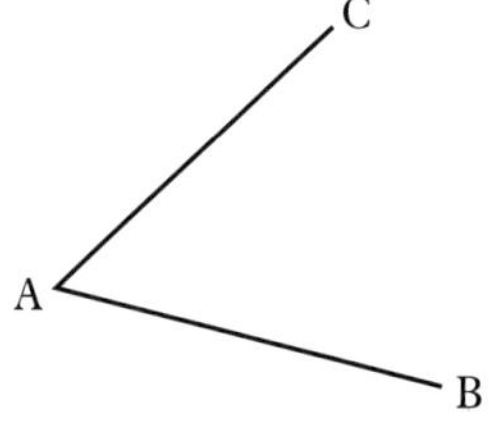

8 **a** Copy this diagram.
b Draw the locus of a point that moves so that it is the same distance from the lines AB and AC in this diagram.
c What is the mathematical name of this locus?

9 **a** Copy this diagram.

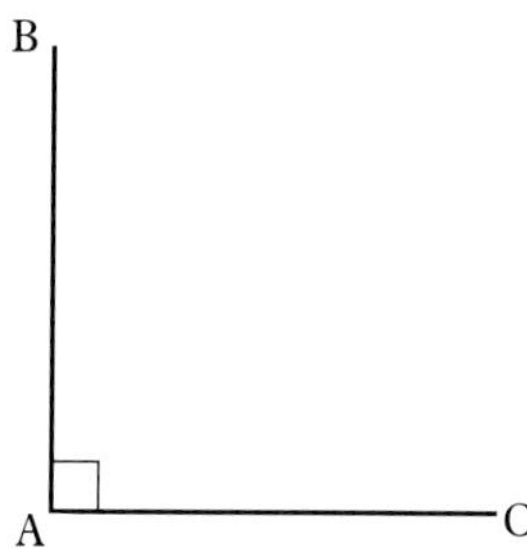

b Construct the locus of a point that moves so that it is the same distance from the lines AB and AC.

You can also use regions to describe where something can be.

Example Sven the goat is tethered to a post in the centre of a roof.

The roof is 8 m long and 7 m wide.
The rope is 3 m long.
Make a scale drawing to show the area where Sven can graze.
Use a scale drawing of 1 cm to 2 m.

You need to draw a rectangle 4 cm by 3.5 cm.
The post, P, is at the centre of the rectangle.
Now draw a circle, centre P, with radius 1.5 cm.

Sven can eat grass anywhere inside the red circle.

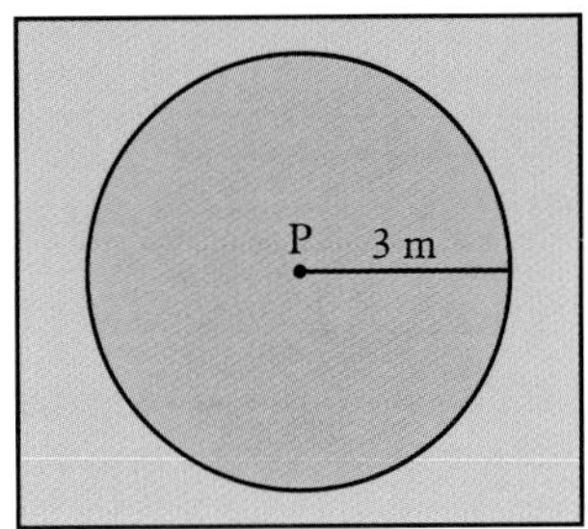

Exercise 33:7

1 **a** Mark a point D in the middle of your paper.
Leave a space of about 8 cm above and below your point.

D is an ambulance depot.
Ambulances answer calls anywhere in a 12 mile radius from the depot.

b Make a scale drawing to show the area covered by the ambulances from this depot.
Use a scale of 1 cm to 2 miles.

2 A horse is tied to a wall at W.
The length of the rope is 3 m.
Make a scale drawing to show where the horse can graze.
Use a scale of 1 cm to 1 m.

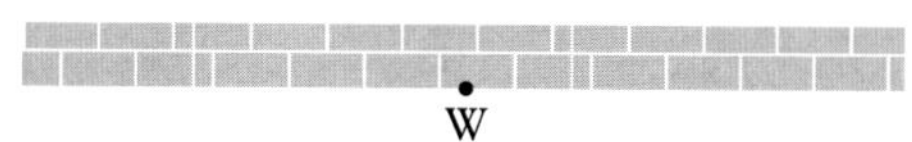

3 A guard dog is on a chain of length 4 m.
The other end of the chain is fixed to a ring.
The ring can move along the rail.
The rail is 5 m long.
Use shading to show the area where the dog can reach.
Use a scale of 1 cm = 1 m.

4 Draw points R and S which are 5 cm apart.

a Construct the locus of the points which are equidistant from R and S.

b Shade on your drawing the region which is closer to R than to S.

5 A bull is chained to a ring in the ground with a 4 m chain.
The ring is in the centre of a yard 10 m by 15 m.
Draw a diagram to show the area of the yard that the bull cannot reach.
Use a scale of 1 cm = 1 m.

You use dotted lines for some boundaries.
This is when the boundary is not included in the region.

Example Show the region where the points are **less than** 2 cm from the point A.

The region is shaded.
The blue circle is dotted because it is not included in the region.

You use a solid line when the line is included in the region.

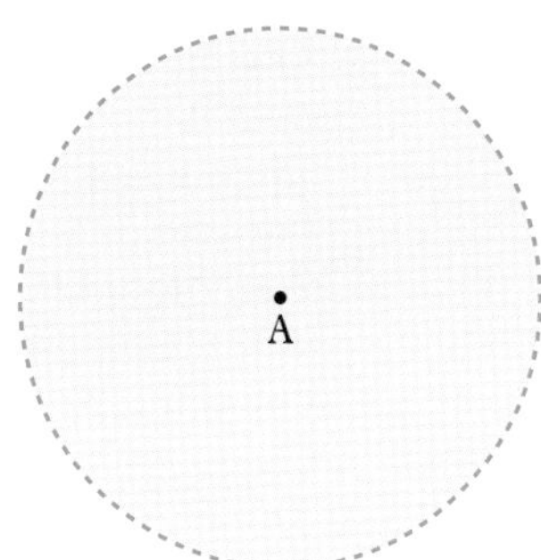

Example Show the region where the points are **at least** 1 cm from the line AB.

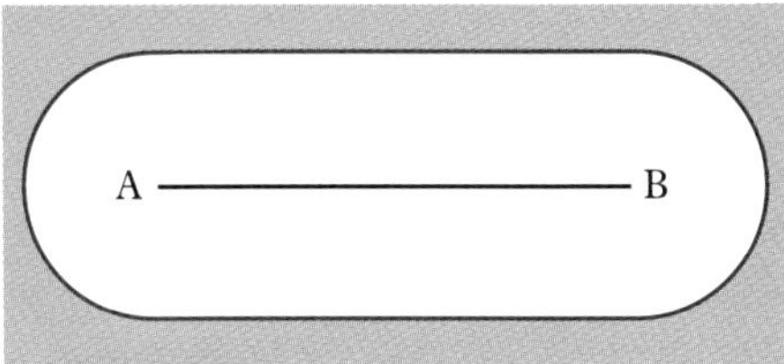

The region is shaded.
The red boundary is a solid line because it is included in the region.

Exercise 33:8

1 Draw a diagram to show the region where the points are less than 5 cm from a fixed point A.

2 Draw a diagram to show the region where the points are 4 cm or less from a fixed point B.

3 Draw a diagram to show the region where the points are at least 3 cm from a fixed point C.

4 T is a radio transmitter.
Transmissions can be received in a region up to 8 km from the transmitter.
Make a scale drawing and shade in the region covered by the transmitter.

5 Simon wants to live more than 5 miles from a pig farm.
Draw a point P to represent the pig farm.
Make a scale drawing and shade in the region where Simon wants to live.

Sometimes there is more than one condition to satisfy.

Example This is a diagram of Kate's garden.
She is going to plant a tree.
The tree must be more than 4 m from the wall of the house.
Kate also wants the tree to be 6 m or less from the gate G.
Where can Kate plant the tree?

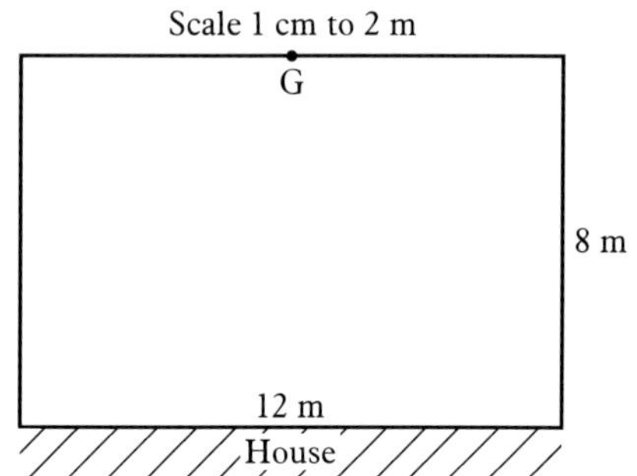

The tree must be more than 4 m from the wall of the house.
The red line is 4 m from the house wall.
The tree can be planted on the opposite side of this line to the wall. The red line is dotted because the tree cannot be planted on the line.

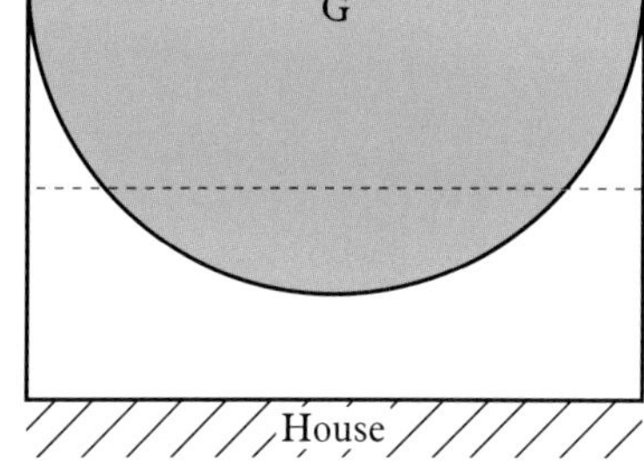

The tree must be 6 m or less from G.
The tree can be planted on the part of the circle centre G and radius 6 m or inside the circle.
This is shown in blue.

Kate can plant the tree where these two regions overlap.
This is shown in green.

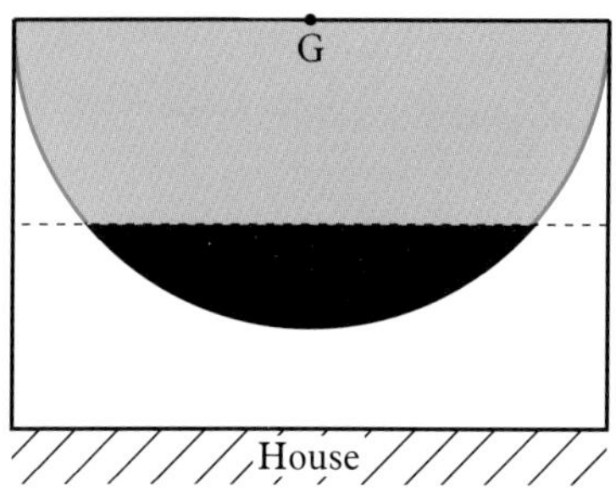

Exercise 33:9

1 A and B show the positions of two radio transmitters. Each transmitter can cover a distance of up to 40 km.

A ———————— B
60 km
Scale: 1 cm to 10 km

a Copy the diagram.
b Draw the boundary of the region covered by transmitter A.
c Draw the boundary of the region covered by transmitter B.
d Use shading and a key to show the region covered by both transmitters.

2 The diagram shows the floor area of a room. The points A and B show the positions of alarm sensors. Each sensor can cover a distance of up to 4 m.

a Copy the diagram.
b Draw the boundary of the region covered by sensor A.
c Draw the boundary of the region covered by sensor B.
d Use shading and a key to show the region covered by both sensors.

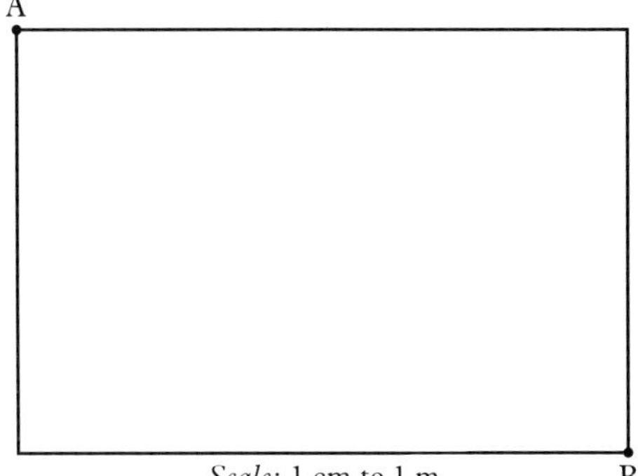

• **3** A company wants to build a storage depot. The depot must be equal distances from Shrewsbury and Birmingham. It must also be less than 30 miles from Hereford.

a Copy the diagram.
b Show on your diagram where the depot can be.

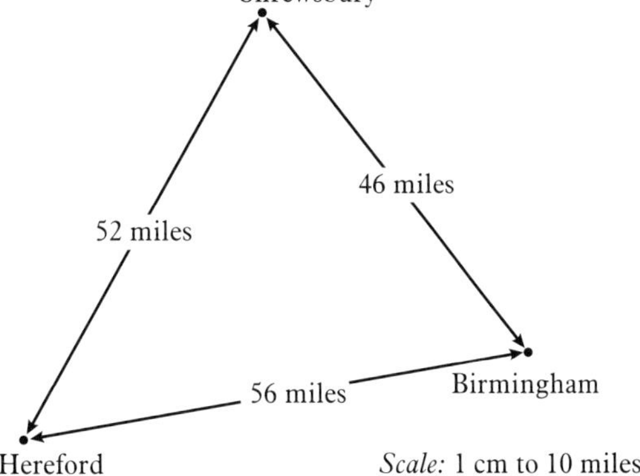

• **4** A television transmitter at Glasgow has a range of 110 miles.
A transmitter at Inverness has a range of 60 miles.
Glasgow and Inverness are 150 miles apart.
Make a scale drawing to show the region covered by both transmitters.

5 **a** Make a rough copy of this treasure map. It does not have to be exact.

b The treasure is buried at a point which is equidistant from A and B. It is also equidistant from C and D. Find the treasure!

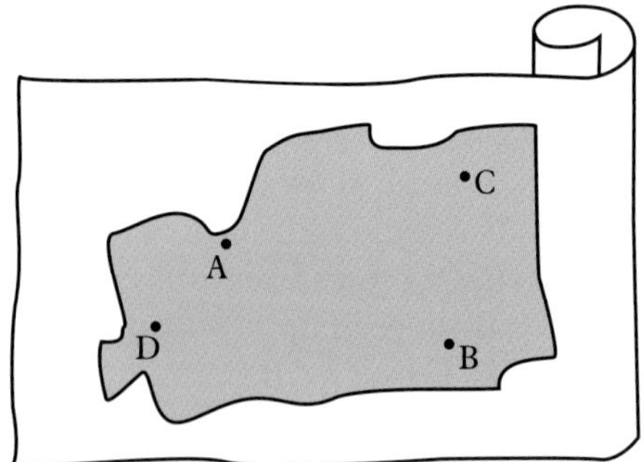

6 Laura plugs her electric mower into the socket on the side of the house. The mower lead is 5 m long.

a Copy the diagram.

b Shade the part of the lawn that Laura can reach with the mower.

c What is the minimum length of lead that Laura would need to cover all the lawn?

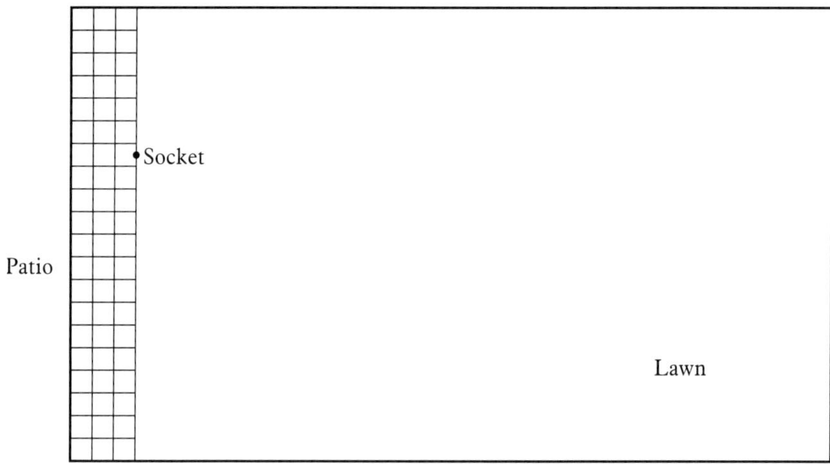

Scale: 1 cm to 1 m

7 The diagram shows the position of two dogs, Shep and Recall, sent out to locate an injured walker. The walker is less than 4 km from Shep and more than 2 km from Recall. The walker is also closer to Recall than to Shep. Draw an accurate diagram to show the region where the walker can be. Use a scale of 1 cm : 1 km

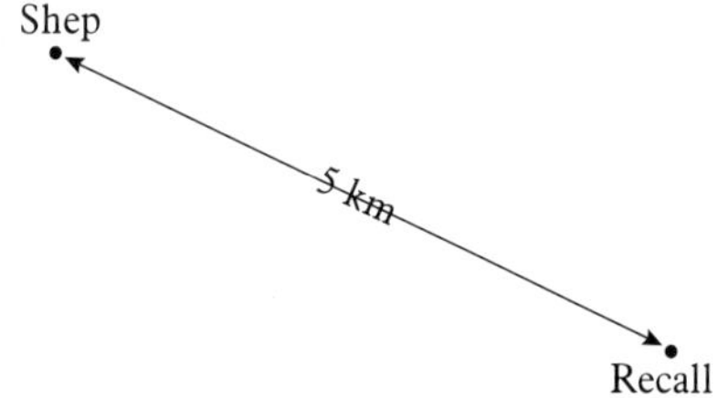

A goat on a lead and where it leads

Billski is a rare type of Russian goat.

He is tied to a post in the centre of his field.
The post is square and with sides of 50 cm.
Billski's rope is 3 m long and is attached to one corner of the post.

Billski is not very bright!
He has a habit of always moving around his field in the same direction.
As it happens this is usually anti-clockwise.

As a result he gets gently wound up (in more ways than one).
He always ends up in the middle of his field, wrapped around his post.

Farmer Gileski always has to go and rescue Billski from his post.

To add some variety into his otherwise dull life, Farmer Gileski often changes the shape of Billski's post. Although he still walks around it in an anti-clockwise direction, at least he takes a slightly different route!

1 Start with Billski's square post.
Assume the rope is fully extended at the beginning of the day.
Draw the area that Billski can reach as he walks around his post.
Think very carefully what happens to the rope as Billski reaches each corner of the post.

2 Change the shape of Billski's post to a rectangle 1 m by 50 cm.
Draw a diagram of the area that Billski can now reach.

3 Invent some post shapes of your own.

You could try:
- different types of triangle
- different types of quadrilateral
- regular polygons
- irregular shapes.

You could try to calculate the area of grass that Billski can reach.

1 **a** Draw a 65° angle.
b Draw an arc crossing both arms of the angle. Label the points A and B.
c Draw arcs from points A and B. They should cross each other.
d Draw the line which bisects the angle.
e Measure the two parts of the angle to check that it is correct.

2 **a** Draw two lines AB and AC which are at 52° to each other.
b Draw the locus of the points which are equidistant from AB and AC.

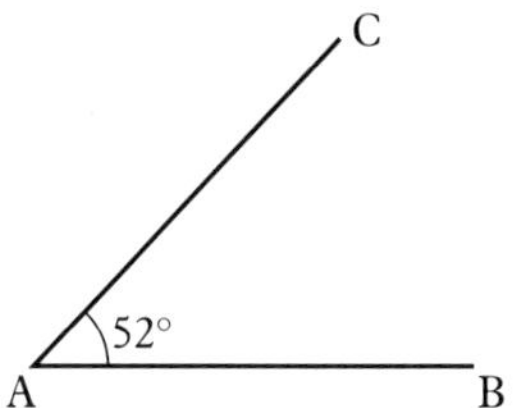

3 **a** Construct this triangle using a ruler and compasses. Start by drawing the line AB.
b Bisect the angle at vertex A of the triangle.
c Bisect the angle at vertex B of the triangle.
d Bisect the angle at vertex C of the triangle. The three bisectors should cross at one point.

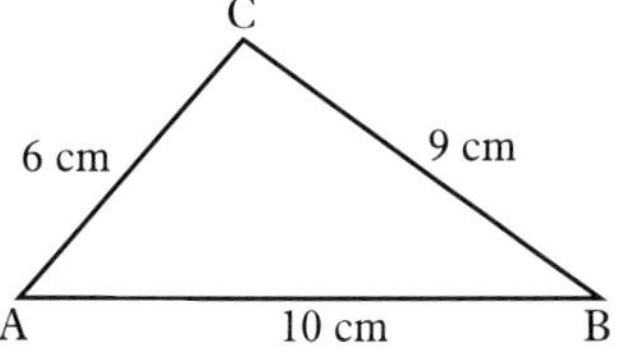

4 **a** Draw two points A and B that are 5 cm apart.
b Join the points with a straight line.
c Construct the locus of the points, which are equidistant from A and B.

5 Construct each of the following angles using ruler and compasses.
a 60° **b** 90° **c** 30° **d** 45° **e** 75°

6 This diagram shows the positions of three emergency telephones. Sharon has broken down. She needs to walk to an emergency phone.
a Make a copy of the diagram. It does not have to be exact.
b By constructing three lines on your diagram, show which areas on the map are closer to each phone.

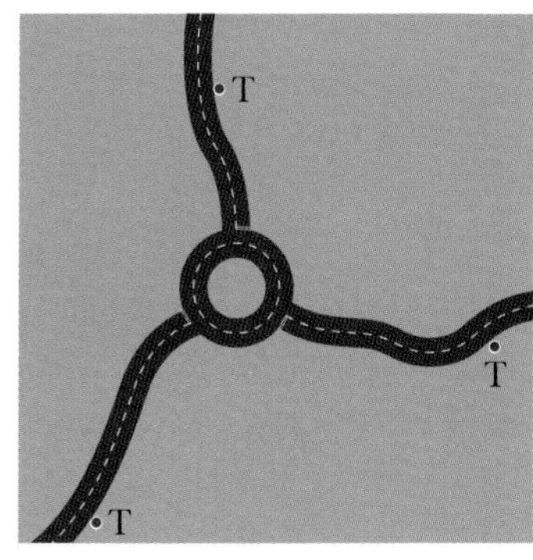

7 **a** Copy this shape. It doesn't have to be exact.

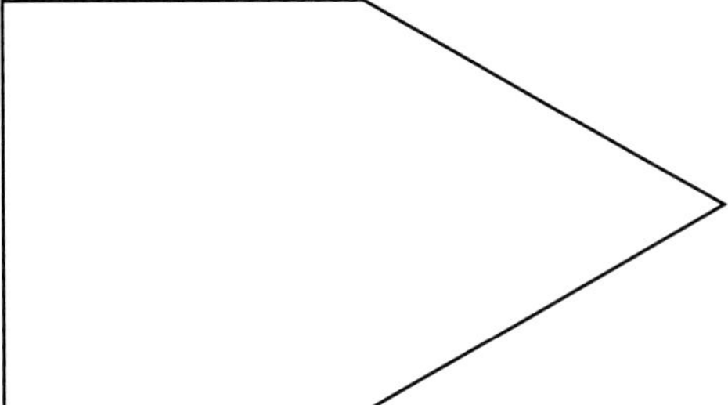

b Draw the locus of a point that is always 3 cm from the edge of the shape and on the outside of the shape.

8 Draw a diagram to show the locus of:

a The midpoint of this ladder as the ladder slides down the wall.

b The lock on this up-and-over garage door as it opens.

c The path of a ball that Richard throws to Thomas.
The ball leaves Richard's hand at $45°$ above the horizontal.

9 A bull is tethered to a ring, R.
The rope is 9 m long.
Make a scale drawing to show where the bull can move.
Use a scale of 1 cm to 2 m.

10 The diagram shows a plan of a rectangular park.
A and B are two drinking fountains.

a Using a scale of 1 cm to 50 m, draw a plan of the park.

b Draw a line on your diagram to help you show the areas of the park which are nearer to fountain A than to fountain B.

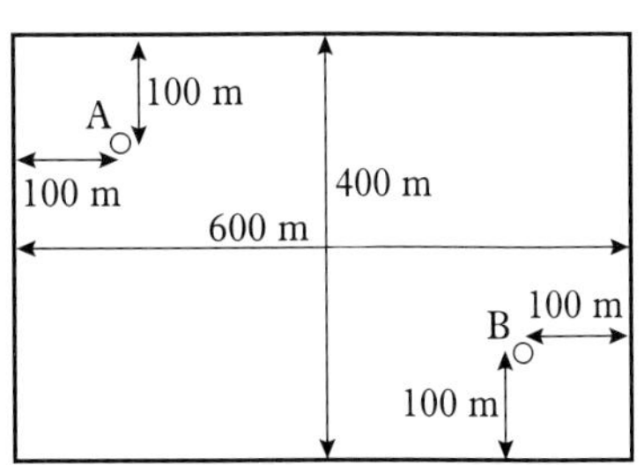

1 This diagram shows three towns in Derbyshire.

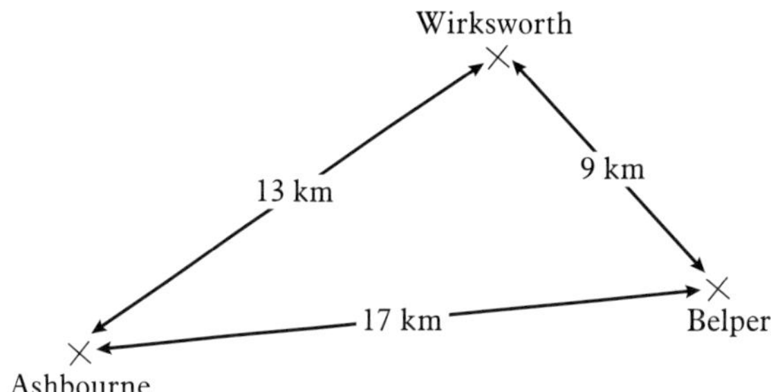

a Make an accurate scale drawing of this diagram.
Use a scale of 1 cm = 2 km.

b A mobile telephone mast is to be placed so that it is equidistant from all three towns. Draw the position of the mast on your diagram.

2 The diagram shows a large room and the position of 3 TV monitors.

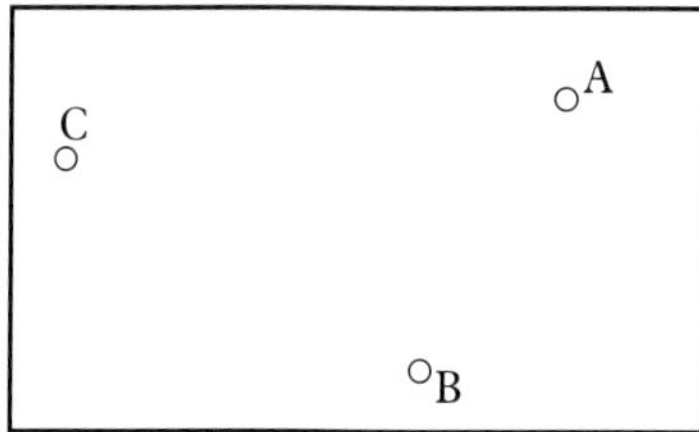

a Make a rough copy of the diagram.

b Lightly shade the area which is nearer to monitor A than monitor B.

c Lightly shade the area which is nearer to monitor A than monitor C.

d Show the area which is closer to monitor A than either of the other 2 monitors.

3 **a** Copy this hexagon.

b Shade the region that is:

closer to AB than DE
and closer to CD than AF
and closer to B than C.

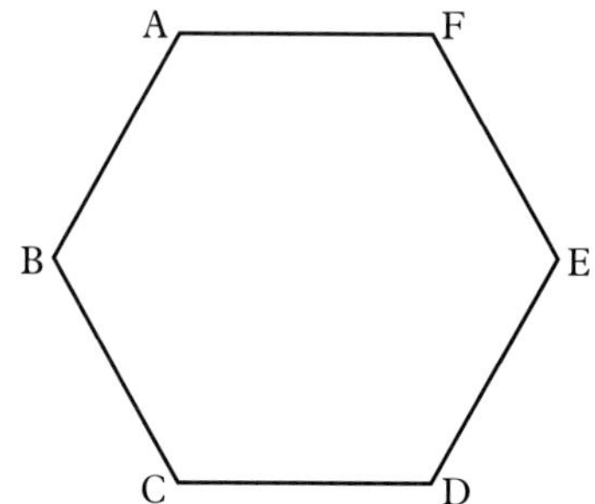

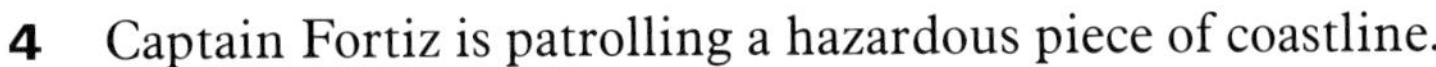

4 Captain Fortiz is patrolling a hazardous piece of coastline.

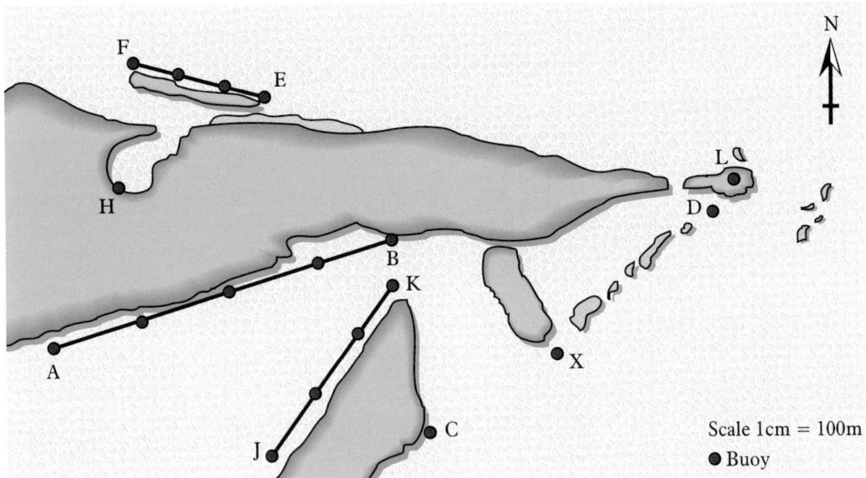

He starts from a point 150 m south of A.
From here he pilots his boat so it is equidistant from the lines of buoys AB and JK.
He continues on this course until he reaches the line BK.
He then steers his boat so that it is always equidistant from buoys C and X.
He continues on this course until he is due east of buoy C.
At this point Captain Fortiz pilots the boat so that it is parallel with the line XD, until he is due south of lighthouse L.
He then travels so that the boat is always 50 m from the lighthouse, until he is due north of it.
Then he sets a course so that he finishes 50 m due north of buoy E.
Now he stays the same distance from the line of buoys EF. He continues on this course until he comes around to the entrance to the harbour north east of H. He then sails directly to a mooring buoy at H.

a Trace the diagram. **b** Draw Captain Fortiz's course.

5 Billy the buffalo is tethered by a rope 28 m long to two posts F and G.
The distance FG is 20 m.
The rope can move freely through a ring on Billy's collar. Billy can then be in a region on either side of the line FG.

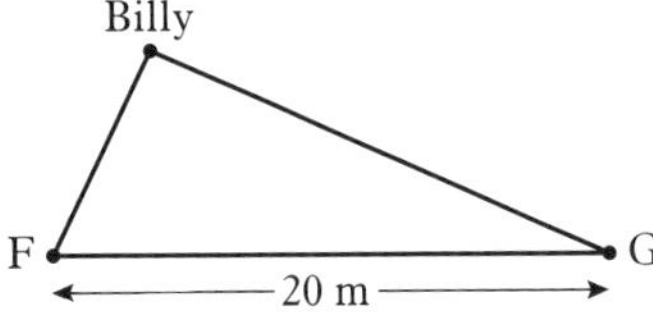

a Draw the locus of the perimeter of the region that Billy can be in.

Billy is then moved.
He is tethered by a rope 28 m long to the point A.

b A is on the outside of a barn that is 20 m long and 10 m wide.
Show the region that Billy can be in.

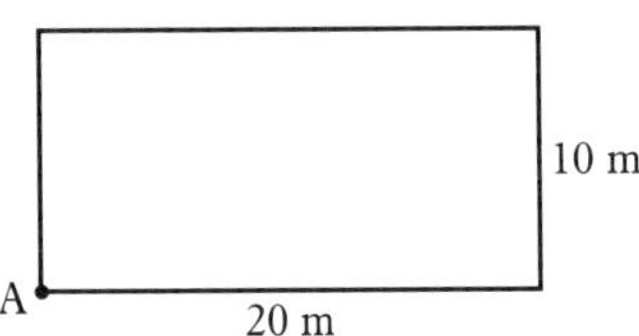

1 Draw two points A and B that are 6 cm apart.
Construct the locus of points that are closer to A than to B.

2 **a** Construct this triangle using ruler and compasses.

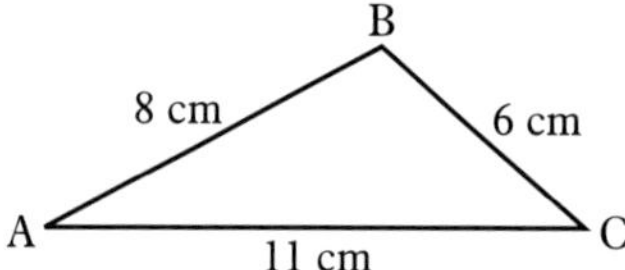

b Measure angle ∠ABC. Give your answer to the nearest degree.

3 Copy the diagram. It doesn't have to be exact.

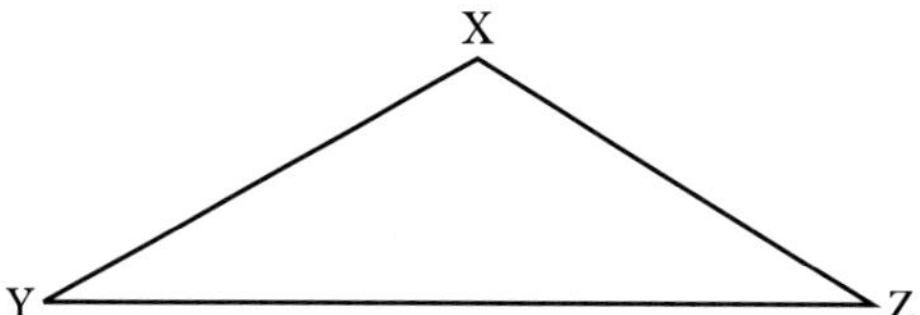

Show the region, inside the triangle, that shows points that are closer to XY than to YZ.

4 **a** Construct this triangle using a ruler and compasses.
Don't remove any construction lines.

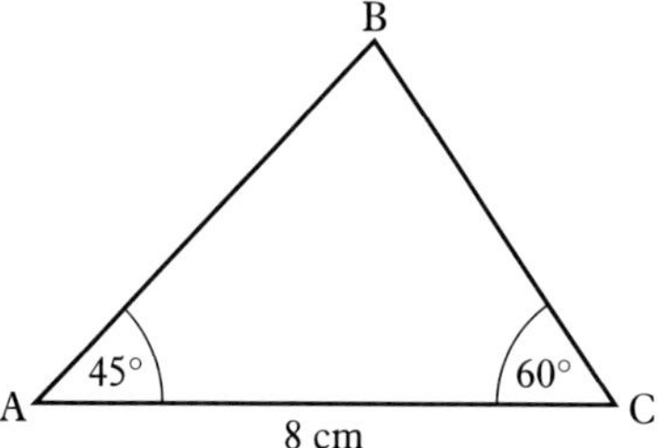

b Measure AB to the nearest mm.

34 Solving equations

CORE

1 Using graphs

Solving quadratic equations using graphs
Changing equations to match your graph
Solving equations using two graphs
Solving equations using more complex graphs

2 Trial and improvement

Revising trial and improvement for whole number answers
Revising solving equations to 1 dp and 2 dp accuracy
Solving numerical problems
Linking this to solving equations using graphs

QUESTIONS

EXTENSION

TEST YOURSELF

1 Using graphs

This rocket needs to dock with the space station.

The trajectory of the rocket must meet the orbit of the space station at exactly the right point.

Timing is all important!

In maths, problems can be solved by looking at the points where two graphs intersect.

Exercise 34:1

In this exercise write all the co-ordinates to 1 dp.
You need to keep all your graphs for the next exercise.

1 **a** Copy and complete this table for $y = x^2 - 3$

x	-5	-4	-3	-2	-1	0	1	2	3	4	5
x^2	25	16			1	0	1	4			
-3	-3	-3			-3	-3	-3	-3			
y	22	13			-2	-3	-2	1			

b Plot the graph of $y = x^2 - 3$ from your table.
Draw your x axis from -5 to 5 and your y axis from -5 to 25.

c Look at the points where the graph crosses the x axis.
Write down the x co-ordinates of the points.

Your graph for question **1** should look like this:

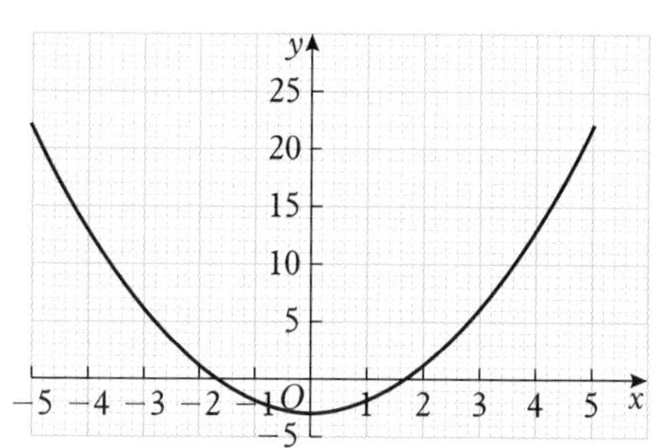

On the x axis, $y = 0$
This means that the points where $y = x^2 - 3$ crosses the x axis are the solutions to $x^2 - 3 = 0$

The points are $\mathbf{x = -1.7}$ and $\mathbf{x = 1.7}$ (1 dp)

You can use graphs to solve lots of different types of equations.
You need to draw your graphs as accurately as possible.
You also need to read off values as carefully as you can.

---

2 **a** Copy and complete this table for $y = x^2 - 10$

x	−5	−4	−3	−2	−1	0	1	2	3	4	5
x^2		16			1	0	1				
−10		−10			−10	−10	−10				
y		6			**−9**	**−10**	**−9**				

b Plot the graph of $y = x^2 - 10$ from your table.
Draw your x axis from −5 to 5 and your y axis from −10 to 15.

c Look at the points where the graph crosses the x axis.
Write down the solutions to the equation $x^2 - 10 = 0$

3 **a** Copy and complete this table for $y = x^2 + 3x - 5$

x	−5	−4	−3	−2	−1	0	1	2	3
x^2	25	16				0			
$+3x$	−15	−12				0			
−5	−5	−5				−5			
y	5	**−1**				**−5**			

b Draw an x axis from −5 to 3 and a y axis from −10 to 15.
c Plot the graph of $y = x^2 + 3x - 5$ from your table.
d Write down the solutions to $x^2 + 3x - 5 = 0$

• **4** **a** Draw a table for $y = 2x^2 + x - 8$
Use x values from −4 to 4.
b Draw an x axis from −4 to 4 and a y axis from −10 to 20.
c Plot the graph of $y = 2x^2 + x - 8$ from your table.
d Write down the solutions to $2x^2 + x - 8 = 0$

You can use graphs to solve equations that are not equal to 0.
To do this you have to draw another line on your graph.

Example

a Draw a graph of $y = x^2 - 3x - 1$
Use x values from -3 to 5.

b Use your graph to solve the equation $x^2 - 3x - 1 = 5$

a Draw a table and plot the values to draw the graph.

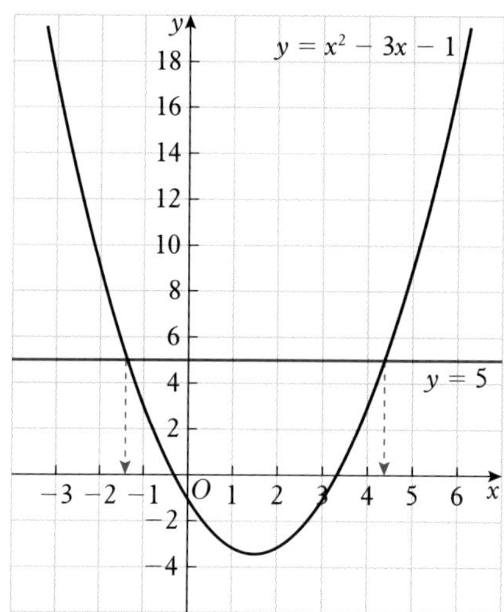

b To solve the equation $x^2 - 3x - 1 = 5$ draw the line $y = 5$ onto the graph. This is the line shown in red.

Next, write down the x co-ordinates of the points where the curve crosses this line. Use the blue dotted lines to help you.
The points are $x = -1.4$ and $x = 4.4$
These x values are the solutions to $x^2 - 3x - 1 = 5$

Exercise 34:2

In this exercise give all the co-ordinates to 1 dp.

1 Find your graph of $y = x^2 - 3$ from Exercise 34:1 question **1**.

a On your graph, draw the line $y = 5$

b Write down the points of intersection between the curve and this line.
These are the solutions to $x^2 - 3 = 5$

2 **a** On your graph of $y = x^2 - 3$, draw the line $y = 10$
b Write down the points of intersection between the curve and this line. These are the solutions to $x^2 - 3 = 10$

3 **a** On your graph draw the line $y = 17$
b Write down the solutions to $x^2 - 3 = 17$

4 Find your graph of $y = x^2 - 10$ from Exercise 34:1 question **2**.
a On your graph, draw the line $y = 5$
b Write down the solutions to $x^2 - 10 = 5$

5 **a** On your graph of $y = x^2 - 10$, draw the line $y = -7$
b Write down the solutions to $x^2 - 10 = -7$

6 Find your graph of $y = x^2 + 3x - 5$ from Exercise 34:1 question **3**.
a Use your graph to find the solutions to $x^2 + 3x - 5 = 2$
b Use your graph to find the solutions to $x^2 + 3x - 5 = -6$

7 This diagram shows the graphs of $y = 3x^2 - 4x - 2$
$y = 8$ and $y = 16$

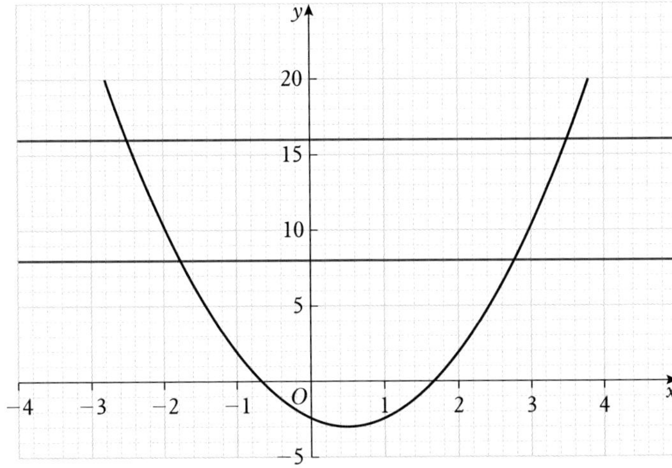

a Use the graph to find the solutions to $3x^2 - 4x - 2 = 8$
b Use the graph to find the solutions to $3x^2 - 4x - 2 = 16$

Sometimes you have to re-arrange an equation to fit the graph you have drawn.

Example Use the graph of $y = x^2 - 3$ to solve $x^2 - 22 = 0$

To solve this problem follow these stages:

1 Write down the equation you want to solve: $x^2 - 22 = 0$

2 Write down the equation of the graph: $x^2 - 3$

3 Add an extra term to make this match the first equation: $(-3 - 19 = -22)$ $x^2 - 3 - \mathbf{19} = 0$

4 Get the extra term onto the RHS of the equation: $x^2 - 3 = \mathbf{19}$

5 Draw the line $y = 19$ on your graph of $y = x^2 - 3$

6 Write down the points of intersection of the curve and the line. The solutions to the equation are $x = -4.7$ and $x = 4.7$ (1 dp).

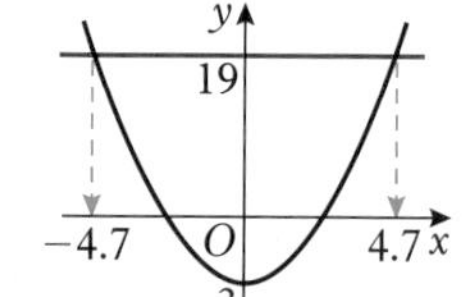

Exercise 34:3

1 **a** Copy and complete this table for $y = x^2 + 4$

x	−5	−4	−3	−2	−1	0	1	2	3	4	5
x^2											
$+4$											
y											

b Plot the graph of $y = x^2 + 4$ from your table.
Draw axes with x from -5 to 5 and y from 0 to 30.

2 Use your graph to solve the equation $x^2 + 4 = 10$
Write your answers to 1 dp.

3 Follow these steps to solve the equation $x^2 - 1 = 0$

a Write down the equation you want to solve: $x^2 - 1 = 0$

b Write down the equation of the graph: $x^2 + 4$

c Add an extra term to make this match the first equation: $x^2 + 4 - \ldots = 0$

d Get the extra term onto the RHS of the equation: $x^2 + 4 = \ldots$

e Draw the line $y = \ldots$ on your graph of $y = x^2 + 4$

f Write down the points of intersection of the curve and the line.

4 Use the method in question **3** to solve the equation $x^2 - 6 = 0$
Write your answers to 1 dp.

5 **a** Copy and complete this table for $y = x^2 - x + 2$

x	-5	-4	-3	-2	-1	0	1	2	3	4	5
x^2											
$-x$											
$+2$											
y											

b Plot the graph of $y = x^2 - x + 2$ from your table.
Draw axes with x from -5 to 5 and y from 0 to 35.

6 Use your graph to solve the equation $x^2 - x + 2 = 5$
Write your answers to 1 dp.

7 Follow these steps to solve the equation $x^2 - x - 8 = 0$

a Write down the equation you want to solve: $x^2 - x - 8 = 0$

b Write down the equation of the graph: $x^2 - x + 2$

c Add an extra term to make this match the first equation: $x^2 - x + 2 - \ldots = 0$

d Get the extra term onto the RHS of the equation: $x^2 - x + 2 \quad = \ldots$

e Draw the line $y = \ldots$ on your graph of $y = x^2 - x + 2$

f Write down the points of intersection of the curve and the line.
Write your answers to 1 dp.

● **8** Use the method in question **7** to solve the equation $x^2 - x - 13 = 0$
Write your answers to 1 dp.

You can solve more complicated equations by plotting graphs.
To solve an equation using graphs:
(1) Draw graphs of both sides of the equation.
(2) Write down the x co-ordinates of the points of intersection.

Example Solve the equation $x^2 - 3x + 4 = 3x + 2$ graphically.

(1) Draw the graph of $y = x^2 - 3x + 4$
(2) Draw the graph of $y = 3x + 2$

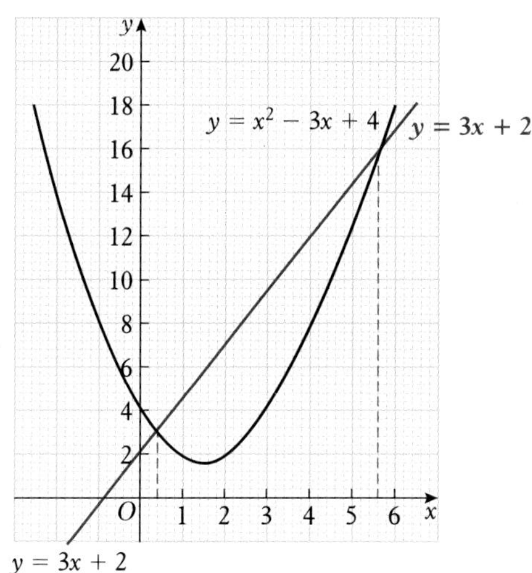

The graphs intersect at $x = 0.4$ and $x = 5.6$
These values are the solutions to $x^2 - 3x + 4 = 3x + 2$

Exercise 34:4

1 **a** Copy and complete this table for $y = x^2 - 2x - 2$

x	-5	-4	-3	-2	-1	0	1	2	3	4	5
x^2			9				1				
$-2x$			6				-2				
-2			-2				-2				
y			**13**				**-3**				

b Plot the graph of $y = x^2 - 2x - 2$ from your table.
Draw axes with x from -5 to 5 and y from -10 to 35.

2 **a** Copy and complete this table for $y = 2x + 2$

x	-5	-4	-3	-2	-1	0	1	2	3	4	5
$2x$			-6			0					
$+2$			2			2					
y			-4			2					

b Draw the graph of $y = 2x + 2$ over the top of your graph from question **1**.

c Write down the x co-ordinates of the points of intersection of the curve and the line to 1 dp.

These are the solutions to the equation $x^2 - 2x - 2 = 2x + 2$
More exact values are $x = -0.83$ and $x = 4.83$

3 **a** Draw a table for the equation $y = x^2 - 4x + 3$
Use x values from -2 to 7.

b Draw a graph of $y = x^2 - 4x + 3$
Draw your x axis from -2 to 7 and your y axis from -5 to 25.

c Use your graph to solve the equation $x^2 - 4x + 3 = 0$

4 **a** Draw a table for the equation $y = x + 2$
Use x values from -2 to 7.

b Draw the line $y = x + 2$ on to your graph from question **3**.

c Use your graphs to solve the equation $x^2 - 4x + 3 = x + 2$

• **5** **a** Draw a table for the equation $y = 3x^2 - 5x - 2$
Use x values from -3 to 4.

b Draw a graph of $y = 3x^2 - 5x - 2$
Draw your x axis from -3 to 4 and your y axis from -5 to 40.

c Draw another line on your graph to solve the equation $3x^2 - 5x - 2 = 3x - 2$

Solving equations using more complex graphs

You can use the same method you have used with quadratic graphs to solve other types of equations.

The next exercise involves cubic graphs and graphs of $\frac{1}{x}$
You plotted these graphs in Chapter 25.

Exercise 34:5

1 **a** Copy and complete this table for $y = x^3$

x	-4	-3	-2	-1	0	1	2	3	4
y		-27			0		8		

b Draw a graph of $y = x^3$
Draw your x axis from -4 to $+4$ and your y axis from -70 to 70.

c Copy and complete this table for $y = 10x + 10$

x	**−5**	**−4**	**−3**	**−2**	**−1**	**0**	**1**	**2**	**3**	**4**	**5**
$10x$			-30				10				
$+10$			10				10				
y			**−20**				**20**				

d Draw the graph of $y = 10x + 10$ over the top of your graph from part **b**.

e Use your graphs to solve the equation $x^3 = 10x + 10$

2 **a** Copy and complete this table for $y = \frac{1}{x}$

x	-5	-4	-3	-2	-1	0	1	2	3	4	5
y	-0.2	-0.25									

b Draw the graph of $y = \frac{1}{x}$. Draw both axes from -5 to 5.

c Copy and complete this table for $y = 0.5x$

x	-5	-4	-3	-2	-1	0	1	2	3	4	5
y		-2				0			1.5		

d Add a line to your graph to solve the equation $\frac{1}{x} = 0.5x$

3 **a** Copy and complete this table for $y = x^3 - 5x + 2$

x	-4	-3	-2	-1	0	1	2	3	4
x^3			-8					27	
$-5x$			10					-15	
$+2$			2					2	
y			**4**					**14**	

b Plot the graph of $y = x^3 - 5x + 2$ from your table.
Draw axes with x from -5 to $+5$ and y from -50 to 50.

c By drawing a suitable straight line on your graph, solve the equation $x^3 - 5x + 2 = 3$. Make sure that you write down all the solutions.

● **d** By drawing a suitable straight line on your graph, solve the equation $x^3 - 5x + 8 = 0$

● **4** This graph shows $y = x + \frac{1}{x}$ and $y = x^2 - 5$

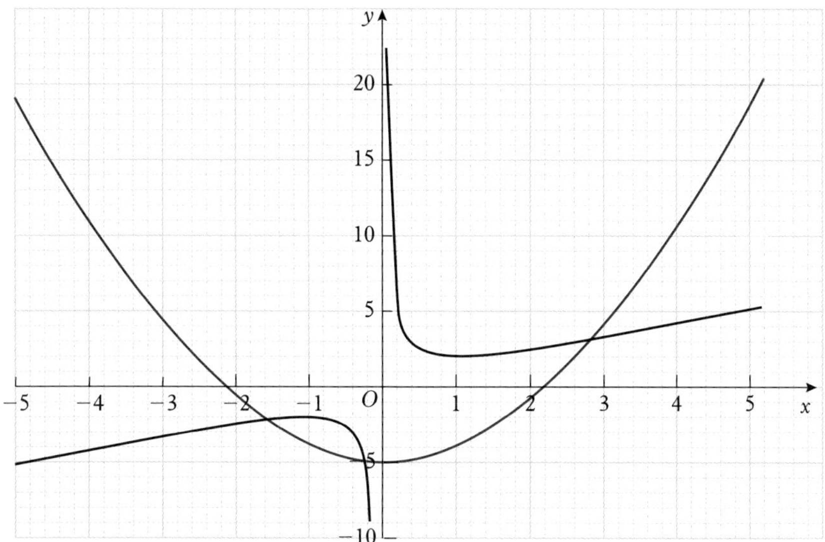

a Which of the two equations is shown by the black graph?

b Use the graph to solve $x^2 - 5 = 0$

c Explain why there are no solutions to $x + \frac{1}{x} = 0$

d Write down the solutions to $x + \frac{1}{x} = x^2 - 5$

e Show that this equation can also be written as $x^2 - x - 5 - \frac{1}{x} = 0$

2 Trial and improvement

Evariste Galois (1811–1832) was a French mathematician who was killed in a duel at the age of only 20. The night before his duel he stayed up and wrote down all of his ideas. It took mathematicians more than 100 years to deal with what he wrote down in one night!

Galois proved that it is impossible to solve equations with x^5 terms and higher powers using an algebraic formula.

You can use trial and improvement to solve these equations.
You can also use trial and improvement for easier equations if you are told to.

Example Solve $x^2 = 1444$ using trial and improvement.

Value of x	Value of x^2	
30	900	**smaller** than 1444
40	1600	**bigger** than 1444
38	1444	correct

Answer $x = 38$
This is only part of the answer.
There may be another answer.
You may need to think about negative values.

Value of x	Value of x^2	
−30	900	**smaller** than 1444
−40	1600	**bigger** than 1444
−38	1444	correct

So $x = -38$ as well.

You can get two answers when you have to solve an equation with an x^2 term. When this happens, you can get two positive answers, two negative answers or one of each.

Exercise 34:6

1 Solve these equations by trial and improvement.
For each part:
(1) copy the table
(2) fill it in
(3) add more rows until you find *two* answers.

a $x^2 + 45 = 670$

Value of x	Value of $x^2 + 45$	
20	...	...
30	...	...
25	...	...

b $x^2 - 41 = 155$

Value of x	Value of $x^2 - 41$	
10	...	...
20	...	...
14	...	...

c $x^2 - 54 = 622$

Value of x	Value of $x^2 - 54$	
20	...	...
30	...	...
...	...	...

d $x^2 + x = 870$

Value of x	Value of $x^2 + x$	
...	...	...

● **2** Solve these equations using trial and improvement.
Draw a table to help you set out your working.
There are two answers for each part.

a $2x^2 + 3x = 5$ **b** $2x^2 + 3x = -1$

3 Solve these equations by trial and improvement.
You only need to find one answer for each part.

a $x^3 = 512$

Value of x	Value of x^3	
...	...	...

b $m^3 + 3m = 1764$

Value of m	Value of $m^3 + 3m$	
...	...	...

4 This Origami crane is made from a square piece of Origami paper.
The area of the square is 324 cm^2.

a Call the length of a side x.
Copy this. Fill it in.
The area of the square is $x \times x = x^2$.
So $x^2 = \ldots$

b Solve the equation in part **a** by trial and improvement to find the length of the side of the paper.

● **5** The length of this rug is 18 inches more than its width.
The area of the rug is 1215 in^2.
Call the width x.

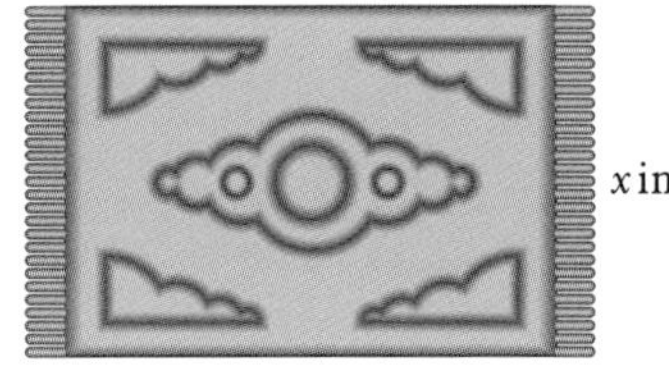

a Copy this. Fill it in.
The length of the rug is ... + ... inches.
The area of the rug is $x \times (\ldots + \ldots)$
So $x \times (\ldots + \ldots) = \ldots$

b Solve the equation in part **a** by trial and improvement to find the length and width of the rug.

Sometimes answers do not work out exactly.
When this happens, you may have to give your answer correct to 1 dp.
Start by trapping the answer between two consecutive whole numbers.
Then look at values to 1 dp.
When your answer is trapped between two 1 dp values you check the value half-way between them.

If this number gives you an answer that is too big then the smaller value is correct to 1 dp.
If this number gives you an answer that is too small then the bigger value is correct to 1 dp.

Example Solve $x^3 = 135$

Value of x	Value of x^3	Bigger or smaller than 135?	
5	125	smaller	
6	216	bigger	x is between 5 and 6
5.5	166.375	bigger	x is between 5 and 5.5
5.1	132.651	smaller	x is between 5.1 and 5.5
5.2	140.608	bigger	x is between 5.1 and 5.2
5.15	136.590 875	bigger	x is between 5.1 and 5.15

This value is half-way between 5.1 and 5.2

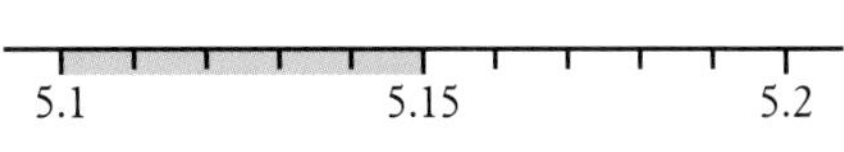

x must be somewhere in the green part of the number line.
Any number in the green part rounds down to 5.1 to 1 dp.

Answer: $x = 5.1$ to 1 dp.

Exercise 34:7

1 Solve these equations by trial and improvement.
Draw a table to help you find each answer.
When the equation has an x^2 term you need to find two answers.
The other equations only have one answer.
Give all of your answers to 1 dp.

a $x^2 = 150$
b $x^2 - 50 = 41$
c $x^3 = 350$
d $x^2 + x = 800$
e $x^3 + x = 67$
f $x^3 + 4x = 50$

You can use trial and improvement to solve number questions too.
You can use it to find square roots and other roots.

2 Find the value of $\sqrt{175}$ using trial and improvement.
Copy this table. Fill it in. Give your answers to 1 dp.

Guess	Value of (guess)^2	Bigger or smaller than 175?
…	…	…

3 Find the value of $\sqrt[3]{146}$ to 1 dp. You need to solve $x^3 = 146$.

4 Find the value of each of these to 1 dp.
You need to decide what equation you need to solve.

a $\sqrt[3]{178}$ **c** $\sqrt[4]{67}$ **e** $\sqrt[4]{563}$

b $\sqrt[3]{456}$ **d** $\sqrt[4]{157}$ **f** $\sqrt[5]{168}$

You can give greater accuracy than 1 dp in your answers.
$x^2 = 135$ gives $x = 11.6$ to 1 dp but you can carry on to get the answer to 2 dp.

Value of x	Value of x^2	Bigger or smaller than 135?	
11.6	134.56	smaller	
11.7	136.89	bigger	x is between **11.6** and 11.7
11.65	135.7225	bigger	x is between **11.6** and 11.65
11.61	134.7921	smaller	x is between **11.61** and 11.65
11.62	135.0244	bigger	x is between **11.61** and 11.62
11.615	134.908 225	smaller	x is between **11.615** and 11.62

this value is half-way between 11.61 and 11.62

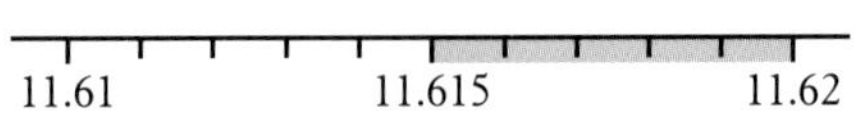

x must be somewhere in the green part of the number line.
Any number in the green part rounds up to 11.62 to 2 dp.

Answer: $x = 11.62$ to 2 dp.

---

5 Solve the equations in question **1** giving your answers to 2 dp.

6 Find the value of each of the roots in question **4** to 2 dp.

You can use the graph of an equation to help you to find a starting value for trial and improvement.

If you have drawn a graph you will be able to see where it crosses the x axis.

This is part of the graph of $y = 5 - x^2$
It crosses the x axis between 2 and 3.

If you are trying to solve $5 - x^2 = 0$ by trial and improvement you can definitely start with $x = 2$ and $x = 3$ before using trial and improvement to get closer to the answer.

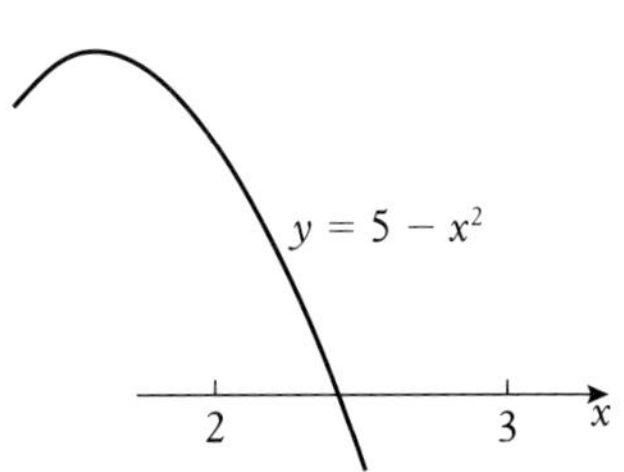

Exercise 34:8

1 This is a sketch of the graph of $y = x^2 - 3x - 5$

The graph crosses the x axis at two points.

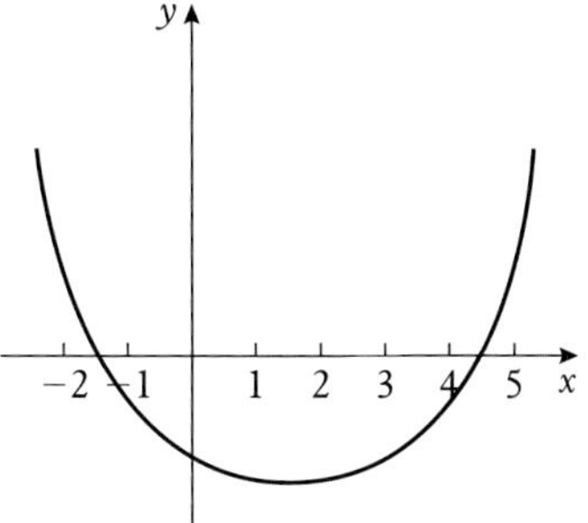

a Write down the whole numbers on each side of both points.

b Copy this table. Fill in the spaces.

Value of x	Value of $x^2 - 3x - 5$	Bigger or smaller than 0?
-2	...	...
-1	...	...

c Add extra rows to your table to find both the answers to $x^2 - 3x - 5 = 0$ using trial and improvement. Give your answers to 1 dp.

2 **a** Copy and complete this table for $y = x^3 - 3x + 5$

x	-3	-2	-1	0	1	2	3
x^3		-8					27
$-3x$		6					-9
$+5$		5					5
y		3					23

b Plot the graph of $y = x^3 - 3x + 5$ from your table.
Draw axes with x from -3 to 3 and y from -20 to 30.

Your graph should cross the x axis once.

c Solve $x^3 - 3x + 5 = 0$ using trial and improvement.
Use your graph to help you find the x values to start from.
Give your answer to 1 dp.

● **3** **a** Draw a graph of $y = x^4 - 2x^2$ using values of x from -2 to 2.

b Solve the equation $x^4 - 2x^2 = 0$ using your graph and trial and improvement.
There are three answers. One of them is exact. Give the other two to 1 dp.

1 **a** Copy and complete this table for $y = x^2 + 2x - 7$

x	−5	−4	−3	−2	−1	0	1	2	3
x^2	25	16				0			
$+2x$	−10	−8				0			
−7	−7	−7				−7			
y	8	1				−7			

b Draw an x axis from −5 to 3 and a y axis from −10 to 15.

c Plot the graph of $y = x^2 + 2x - 7$ from your table.

d Write down the solutions to $x^2 + 2x - 7 = 0$

2 **a** Draw axes with x from −5 to 5 and y from 0 to 30.

b Copy and complete this table for $y = x^2 + x - 5$

x	−5	−4	−3	−2	−1	0	1	2	3	4	5
x^2											
$+x$											
−5											
y											

c Plot the graph of $y = x^2 + x - 5$ from your table.

d Use your graph to solve the equation $x^2 + x - 5 = 5$
Write your answers to 1 dp.

e Follow these steps to solve the equation $x^2 + x - 15 = 0$

(1) Write down the equation you want to solve: $x^2 + x - 15 = 0$

(2) Write down the equation of the graph: $x^2 + x - 5$

(3) Add an extra term to make this match the first equation: $x^2 + x - 5 - \ldots = 0$

(4) Get the extra term onto the RHS of the equation: $x^2 + x - 5 \quad = \ldots$

(5) Draw the line $y = \ldots$ on your graph of $y = x^2 + x - 5$

(6) Write down the points of intersection of the curve and the line.
Write your answers to 1 dp.

3 **a** Copy and complete this table for $y = \frac{6}{x}$

x	-5	-4	-3	-2	-1	0	1	2	3	4	5
y	-1.2	-1.5					6				

b Draw the graph of $y = \frac{6}{x}$. Draw both axes from -5 to 5.

c On your graph draw the line $y = x$

d Write down the solutions to $\frac{6}{x} = x$

4 **a** Copy this table. Allow space to add more rows.

x	x^3	$3x$	$x^3 + 3x$	Bigger or smaller than 6?
0	0	0	0	smaller
1	1	3	4	smaller
2				

b Fill in the missing values in your table.
c Continue your table to solve the equation $x^3 + 3x = 6$ correct to 1 dp.

5 Rod wants to make a circular pond in his garden. He wants the surface area of the pond to be exactly 4 m^2.
Use trial and improvement to find the radius of the pond correct to 1 dp.
You need to solve the equation $\pi r^2 = 4$

6 Aiden wants to solve the equation $x^4 = 56$
a The positive answer lies between two consecutive whole numbers.
Find these two consecutive numbers.
b Use trial and improvement to find the positive solution to 1 dp.

7 The volume of this shape is found

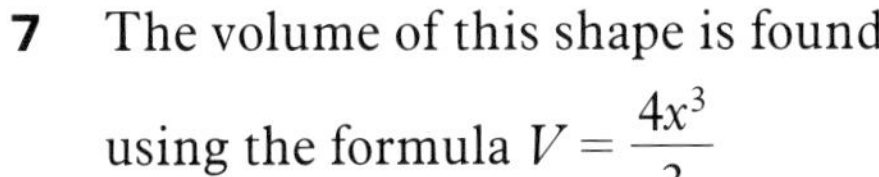

using the formula $V = \frac{4x^3}{3}$

x is the length of the side of the cube and also the height of the pyramid in centimetres.
Find the value of x to 1 dp which will give the shape a volume of 1000 cm^3.

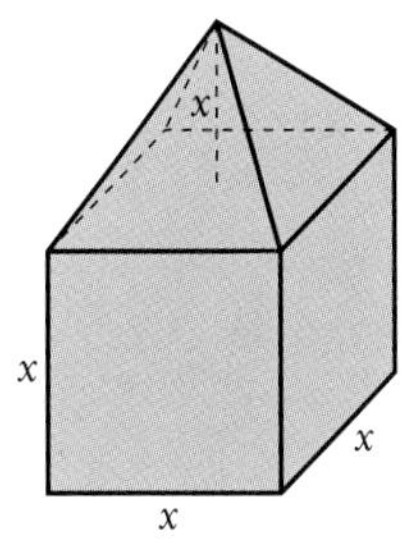

1 **a** Copy and complete this table for $y = x^2 + 2x - 1$

x	−4	−3	−2	−1	0	1	2	3	4
x^2	16				0				
$+2x$	−8				0				
−1	−1				−1				
y	7				−1				

b Draw the graph of $y = x^2 + 2x - 1$ using x values from −4 to 4.
c Use your graph to write down the solutions to $x^2 + 2x - 1 = 4$
d Use your graph to write down the solutions to $x^2 + 2x - 7 = 0$
e On your graph for part **b** draw the line $y = x + 3$
f Use your graphs to solve the equation $x^2 + x - 4 = 0$

2 **a** Draw the graph of $y = 3x^2 - 3x - 3$ using x values from −4 to 4.
b On your graph draw the line $y = 2x - 1$
c Use your graph to write down the solutions to $3x^2 - 5x - 2 = 0$

3 **a** Copy and complete this table for $y = \frac{1}{x^2}$

x	−5	−4	−3	−2	−1	0	1	2	3	4	5
y	0.04	0.06	0.1								

b Draw the graph of $y = \frac{1}{x^2}$ Draw both axes from −5 to 5.

c Copy and complete this table for $y = \frac{1}{x}$

x	−5	−4	−3	−2	−1	0	1	2	3	4	5
y	−0.2	−0.3	−0.3								

d Draw the graph of $y = \frac{1}{x}$ on the same graph as part **b**.

e Write down the solution to the equation $\frac{1}{x^2} = \frac{1}{x}$

4 Solve these equations using trial and improvement.
Give all your answers to 1 dp.

a $x^4 + x^3 + x^2 + x = 100$

b $\frac{12}{x^2 - 5} = 6$

1 The diagram shows the graphs of $y = 2x^2 - 3x - 2$ and $y = 10$

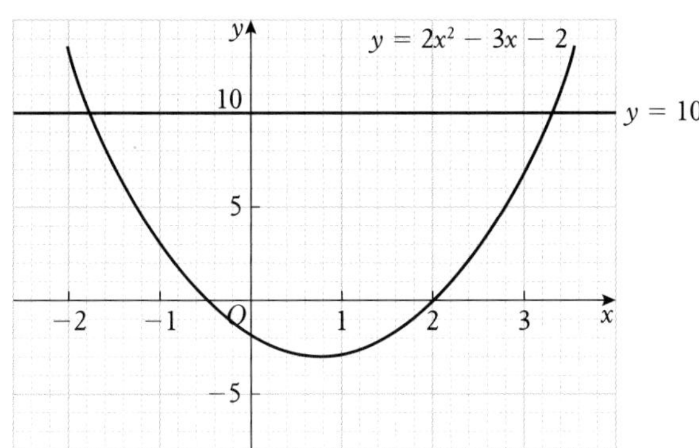

a Use the diagram to write down the solutions of $2x^2 - 3x - 2 = 0$
b Use the diagram to write down the solutions of $2x^2 - 3x - 2 = 10$

2 **a** Copy and complete this table for $y = x^2 - x - 3$.

x	-3	-2	-1	0	1	2	3	4
x^2		4						
$-x$		2						
-3		-3						
y		3						

b Draw the graph of $y = x^2 - x - 3$ from your table.
c Use the graph to write down the solutions of $x^2 - x - 3 = 0$.
d Draw the line $y = 5$ on the same axes.
e Write down the solutions of $x^2 - x - 3 = 5$.

3 **a** Copy and complete this table for $y = x^2 - 3x + 1$.

x	-2	-1	0	1	2	3	4	5
x^2								
$-3x$								
$+1$								
y								

b Draw the graph of $y = x^2 - 3x + 1$ from your table.

c Copy and complete this table for $y = 2x + 3$.

x	-2	-1	0	1	2	3	4	5
$2x$								
$+3$								
y								

d Draw the graph of $y = 2x + 3$ on the same axes.

e Use your graphs to find the solutions of the equation $x^2 - 3x + 1 = 2x + 3$.

4 **a** Copy and complete this table for $y = \frac{1}{x} + 3$.

x	-4	-3	-2	-1	0	1	2	3	4
$\frac{1}{x}$									
$+5$									
y									

b Use your table to draw the graph of $y = \frac{1}{x} + 3$.

c Draw the graph of $y = x + 2$ on the same axes.

d Use your graphs to solve the equation $\frac{1}{x} + 3 = x + 2$.

5 Lisa has drawn a graph of the equation $y = x^3 - x^2 + 5$.
She wants to solve the equation $x^3 = 2x^2 - 4$.
Find the equation of the extra graph she should draw on the same axes.

35 Using trigonometry

CORE

1 Angles and lengths
Revising trigonometry
– finding angles
– finding sides
– working in isosceles triangles

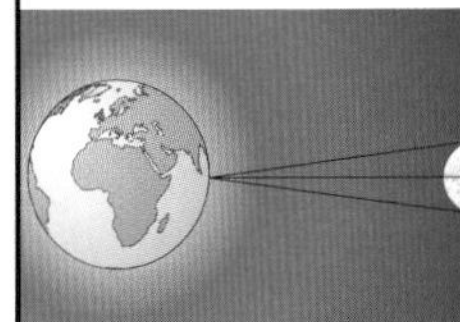

2 Bearing up
Using trigonometry in bearings problems
Looking at angles of elevation and depression

3 Finding the hypotenuse
Using trigonometry to find the hypotenuse

QUESTIONS

EXTENSION

TEST YOURSELF

1 Angles and lengths

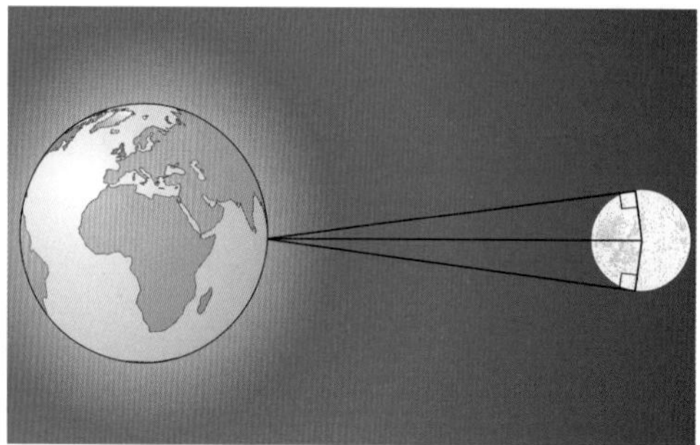

What angle does the moon take up in the sky?

You can use SOH CAH TOA to remember trigonometric formulas.

$$\text{Sin } a = \frac{\textbf{Opposite}}{\textbf{Hypotenuse}} \qquad \text{Cos } a = \frac{\textbf{Adjacent}}{\textbf{Hypotenuse}} \qquad \text{Tan } a = \frac{\textbf{Opposite}}{\textbf{Adjacent}}$$

To find the angle marked a in this triangle.

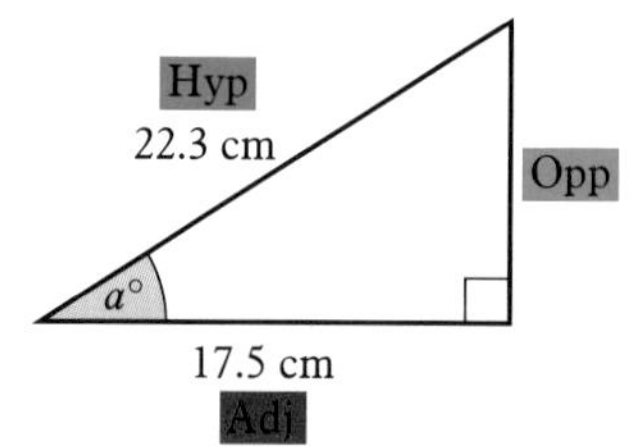

Write out SOH CAH TOA

Cross out the sides that you know.

The formula you need is the one with two sides crossed out.

$$\cos a = \frac{\text{adjacent}}{\text{hypotenuse}}$$

Substitute into the formula:

$$\cos a = \frac{17.5}{22.3}$$

Make sure that your calculator is working in degrees.

Key in:

SHIFT cos (1 7 . 5 ÷ 2 2 . 3) =

to get $a = 38.3°$ (1 dp)
You can use the other two formulas in the same way.

Exercise 35:1

In questions **1–10**:

a Copy the triangle. Label the sides hyp, opp, adj.

b Find the angle marked with a letter. Round your answer to 1 dp.

Check that your answer seems reasonable.

1

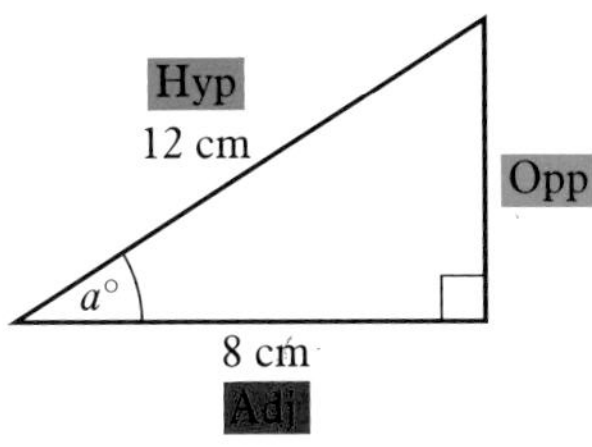

2

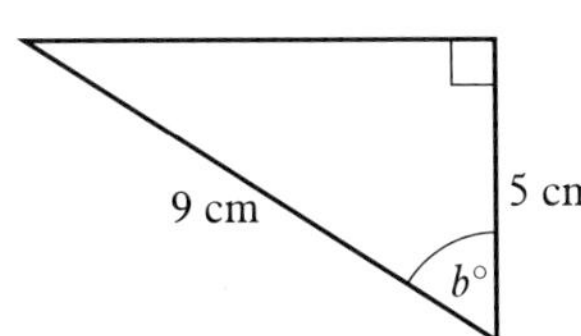

3

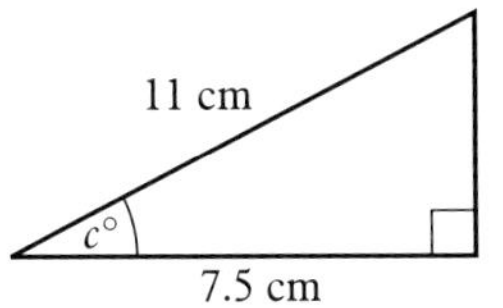

4

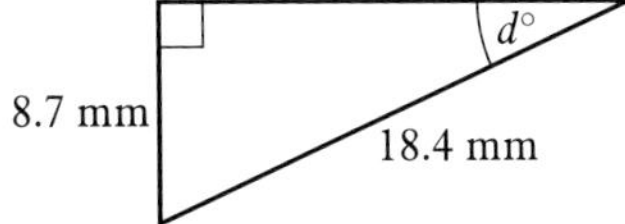

5

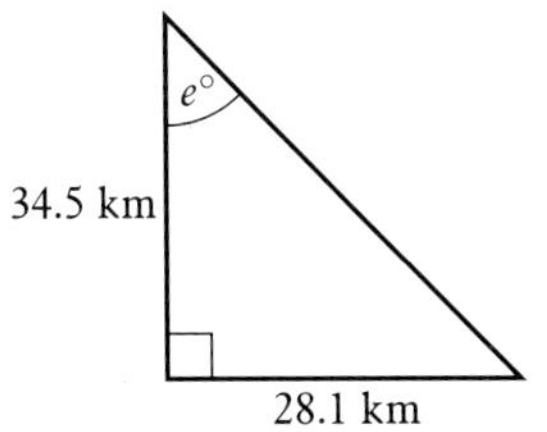

6

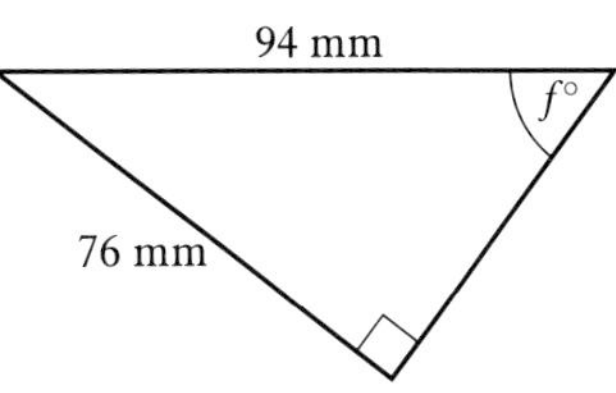

7

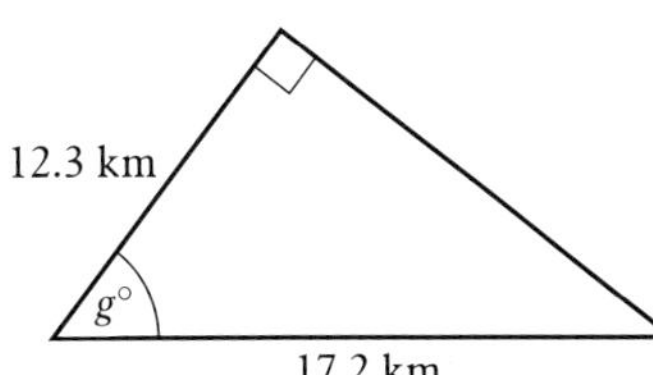

8

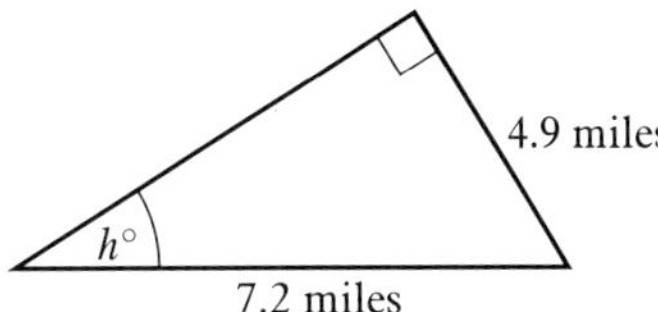

9

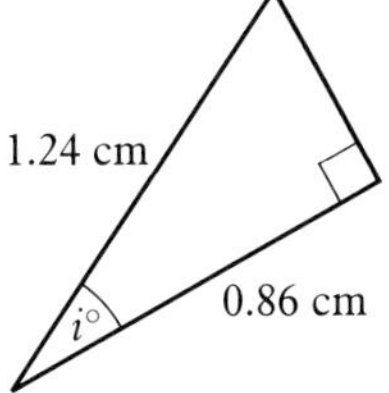

10

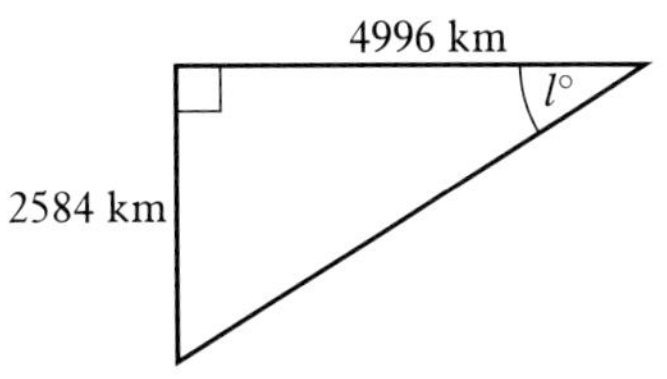

11 John wants to find the angle of slope in one of his fields.
He wants to know if it is safe to drive his tractor.
What is the angle of slope?

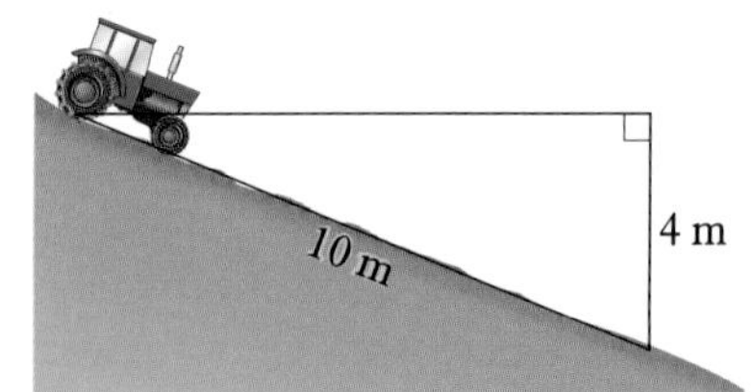

12 Steep roads in Britain have gradients like 1 in 10, 1 in 8, etc.

a Use this diagram to work out the angle of slope of a 1 in 10 road.

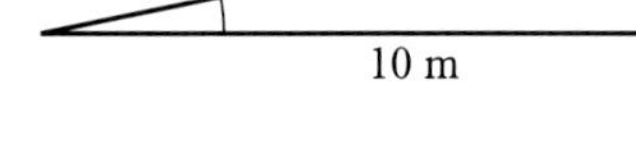

Work out the angle of slope for a road with a gradient of:

b 1 in 7 **c** 1 in 5.

In some questions you have to find more than one angle.
You draw a separate triangle for each angle that you need to find.
In this diagram you need to find angles $x°$ and $y°$.

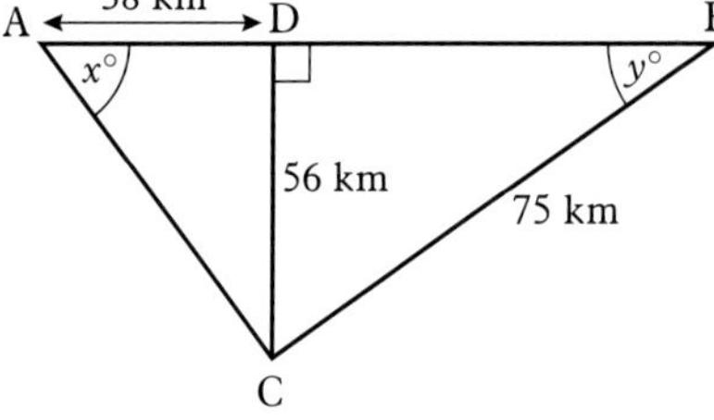

To find x draw triangle ADC separately.
Then you work out $x°$ in the usual way.

Cross out the sides that you know.

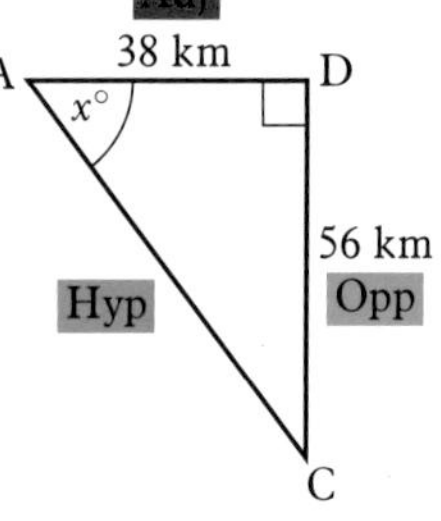

The formula you need is the one with two sides crossed out.

$$\tan x = \frac{56}{38}$$

Make sure that your calculator is working in degrees.

Key in:

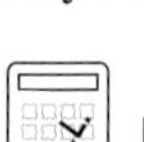

to get $x = 55.8°$ (1 dp)
You then work out y by drawing triangle BCD separately. This gives $y = 48.3°$ (1 dp)

---

13 Find the angles marked with letters.

a

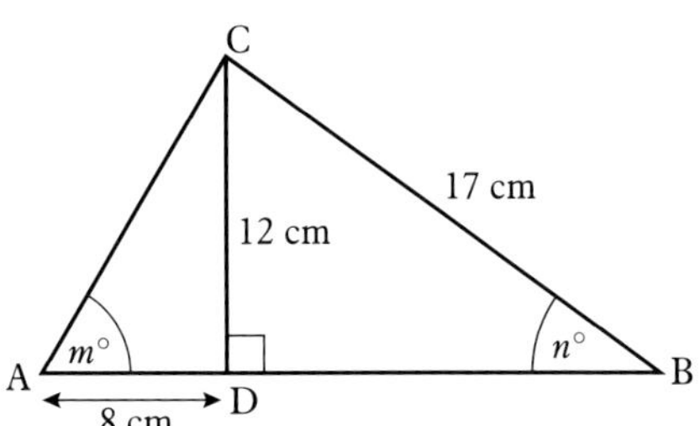

b

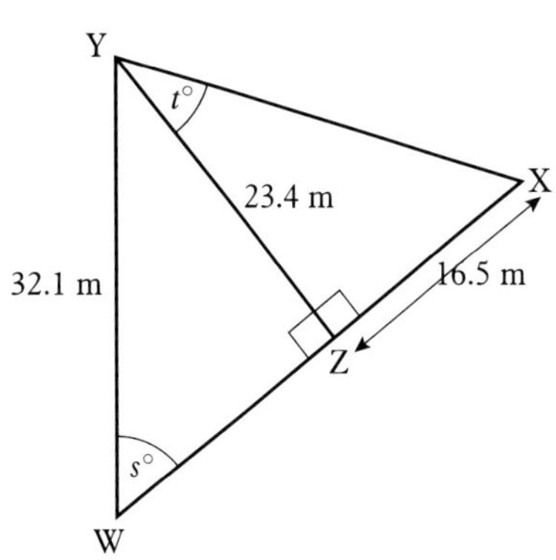

To find the side marked a in this triangle:

Write out SOH CAH TOA.

Cross out the side that you know.
Cross out the side that you need to find.

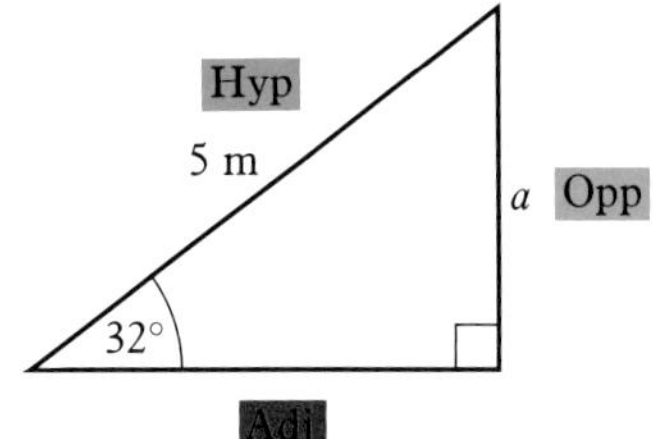

S ~~O~~ ~~H~~ | C A ~~H~~ | T ~~O~~ A

The formula you need is the one with two sides crossed out.

$$\sin 32° = \frac{\text{opposite}}{\text{hypotenuse}}$$

Substitute into the formula:

$$\sin 32° = \frac{a}{5} \qquad \text{So} \qquad 5 \times \sin 32° = a$$

Make sure that your calculator is working in degrees.

Now press:

to get $a = 2.65$ m (3 sf)

You can use the other two formulas in the same way.

Exercise 35:2

In each of questions **1–8**:

a Copy the triangle. Label the sides hyp, opp, adj.

b Find the length of the side marked with a letter. Round your answer to 3 sf.

Check that your answer seems reasonable.

1

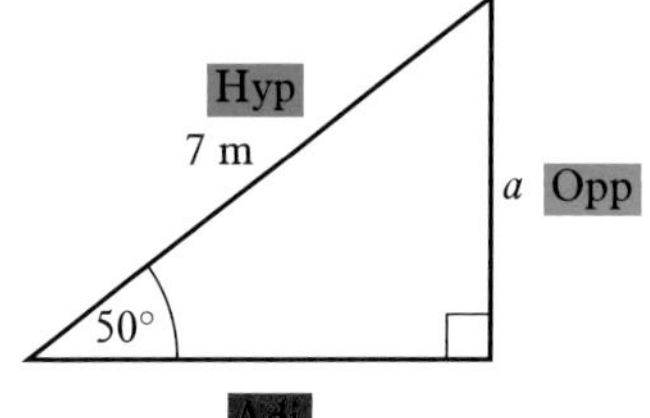

2

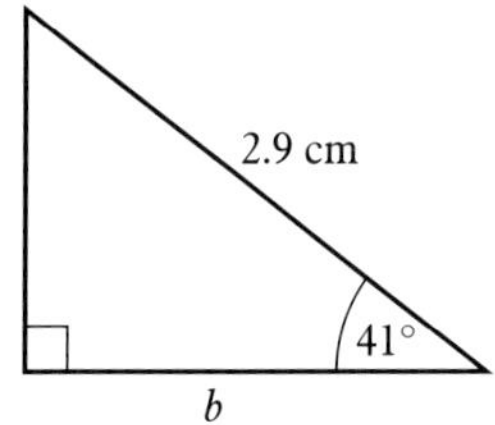

3

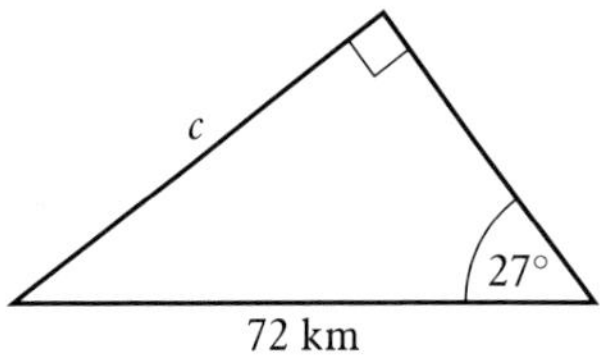

4

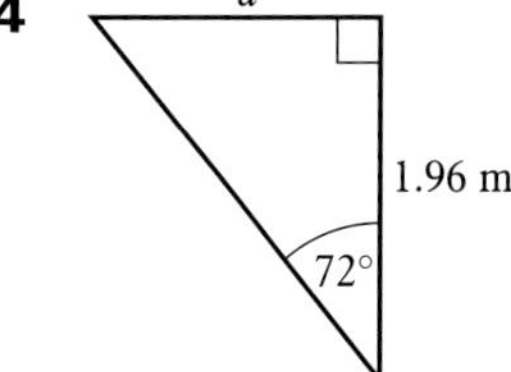

5

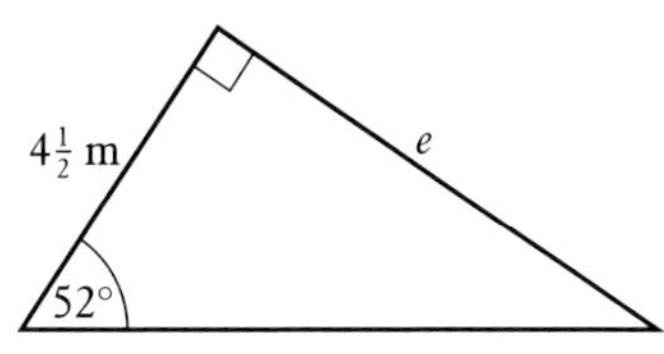

6

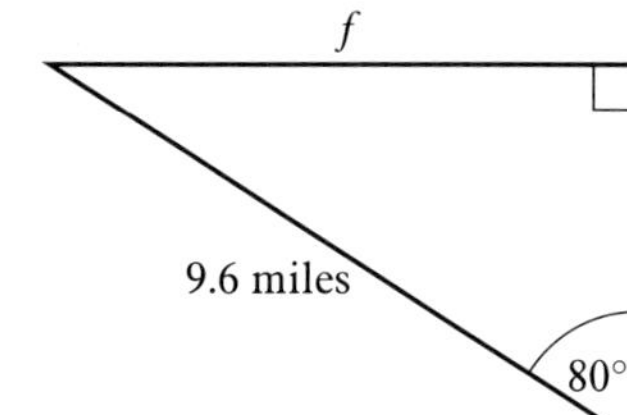

● **7**

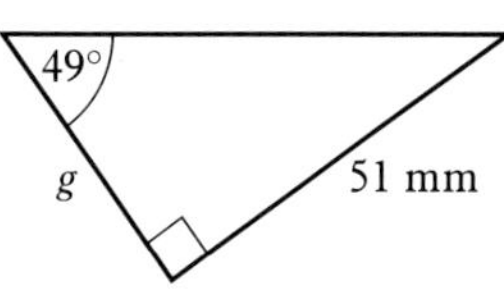

8

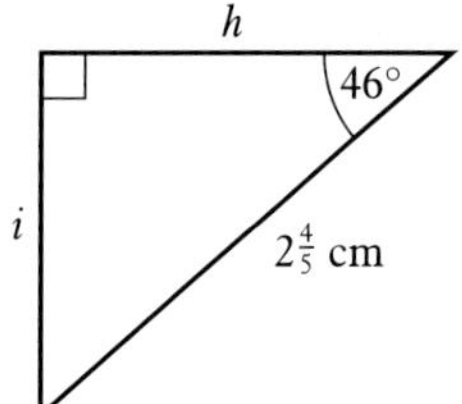

In questions **9** to **14** draw a separate triangle for each length that you need to find.

9

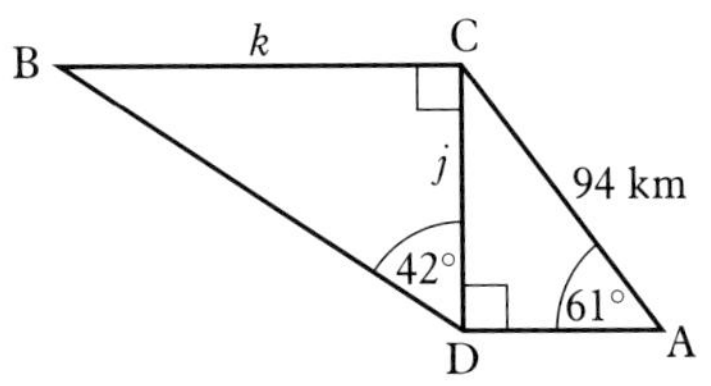

10

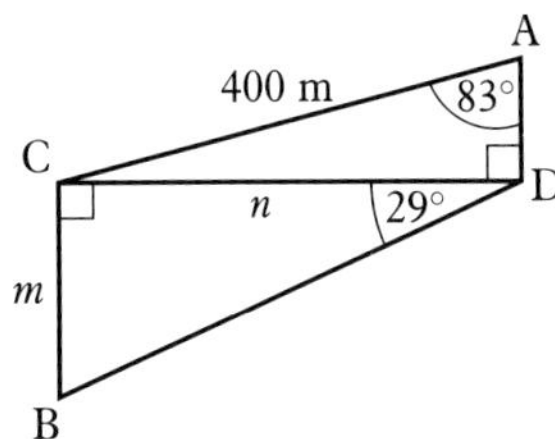

Working in isosceles triangles

You can split an isosceles triangle into 2 right-angled triangles.

To find the base in this triangle split the triangle down the middle.

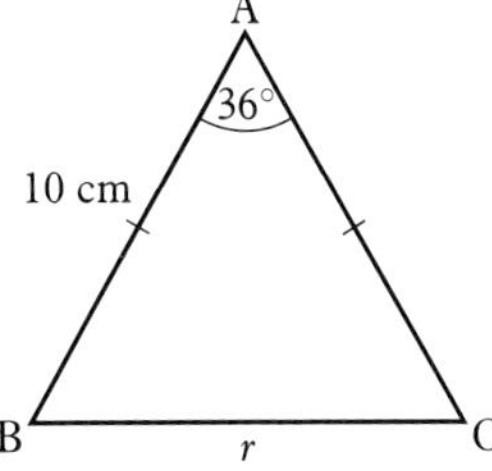

Now you have 2 right angled triangles that are exactly the same.
They are congruent.
Call the base of each triangle a

The angle in each half is $36 \div 2 = 18°$

Look at triangle ABD: $\sin 18° = \dfrac{a}{10}$

Multiply by 10 $10 \times \sin 18° = a$

$r = 2a$ so multiply both sides by 2 to get $20 \times \sin 18° = r$

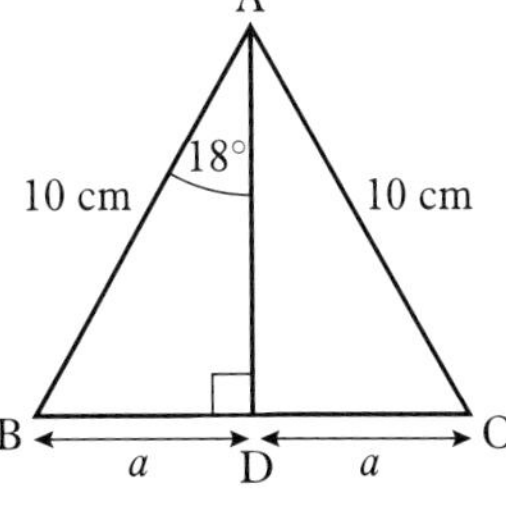

This gives $r = 6.18$ cm (3 sf)

11

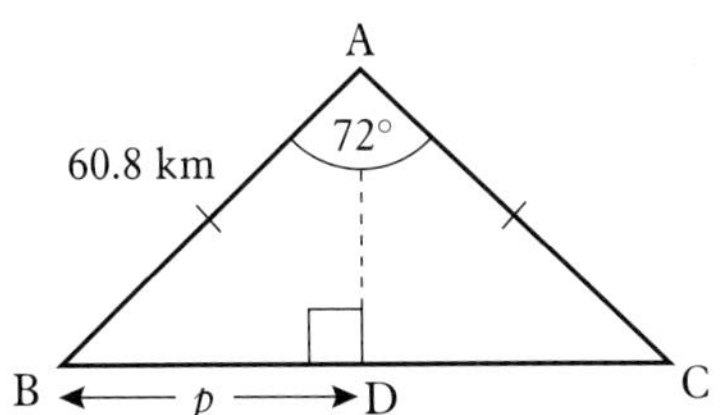

12

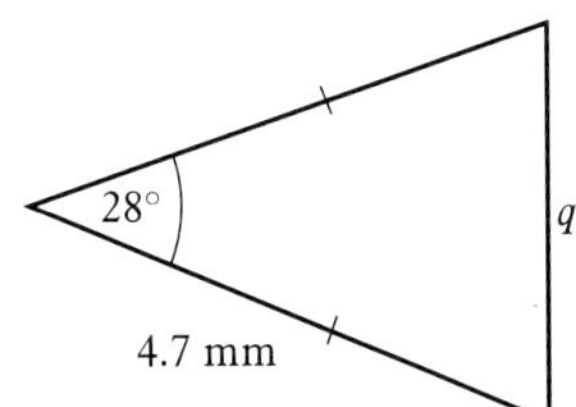

13

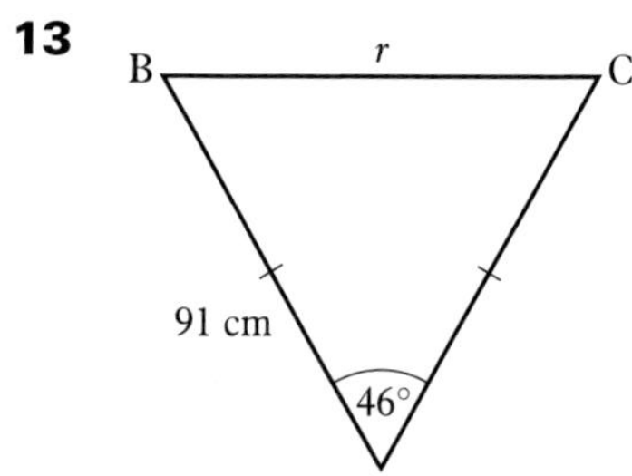

● **14**

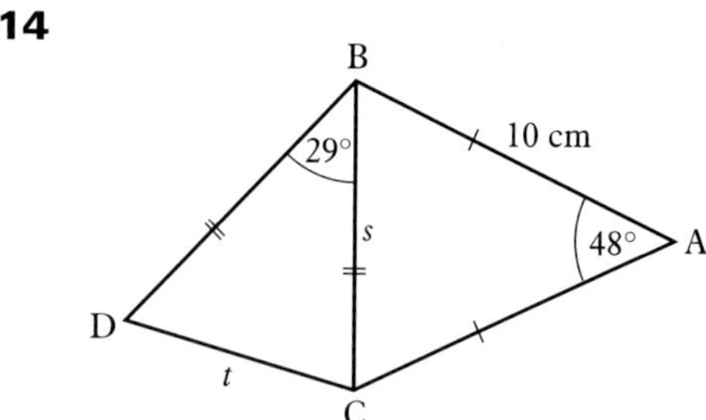

Exercise 35:3

In this exercise you will need to find angles and sides.
Round your answers to 3 sf.

1 Steve is painting the boards on the side of his house.
  a Find the length of the vertical board AB.
  b Find the length of the horizontal board CD.
  He leans his ladder against the side of the house.
  The ladder is 5 m long.
  It makes an angle of 68° with the ground.
  c Find the height of the wall EC.
  d Find the distance of the base of the ladder from the wall.
  e Find the total height of the house if the chimney is 2.1 m tall.
  f Find the angle $\widehat{CED}$.
  g Find the length of the beam DE. Use Pythagoras' theorem.

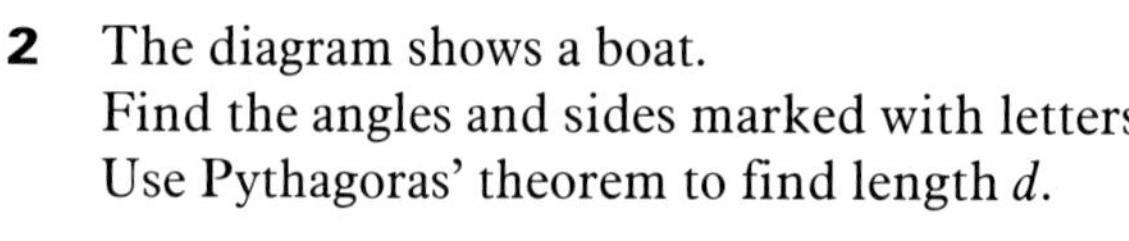

2 The diagram shows a boat.
Find the angles and sides marked with letters.
Use Pythagoras' theorem to find length *d*.

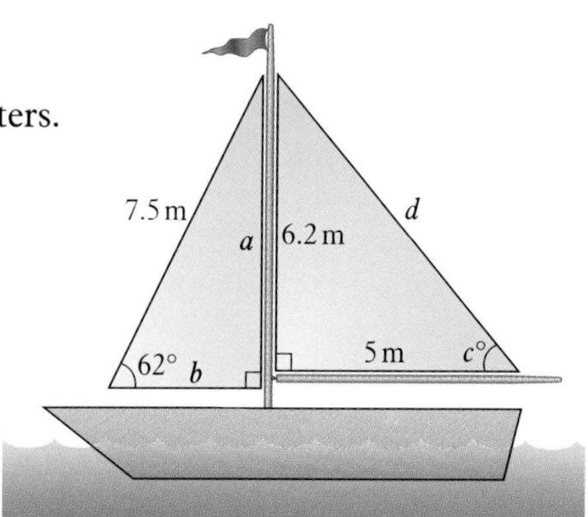

2 Bearing up

Sailing is a sport where you need to know where you are going.

Sailors use bearings to find their way around.

You have seen bearings in Chapter 29. You often need to use trigonometry in questions involving bearings.

Example The diagram shows the positions of two lighthouses, A and B.

The bearing of B from A is 075°.
B is 35 km east of A.
How far north of A is B?

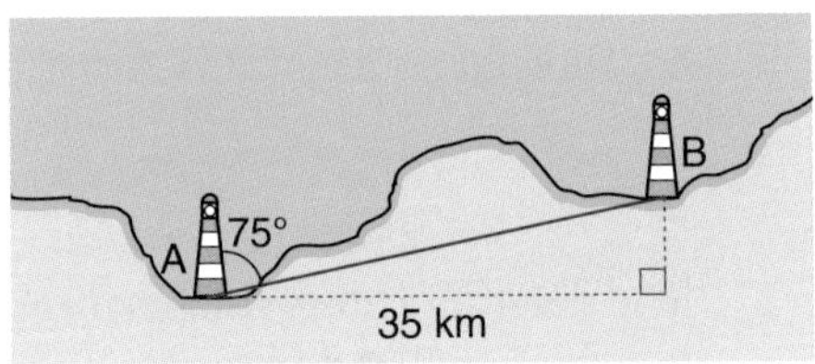

You need to find the length x.
Draw a right angled triangle to help you.

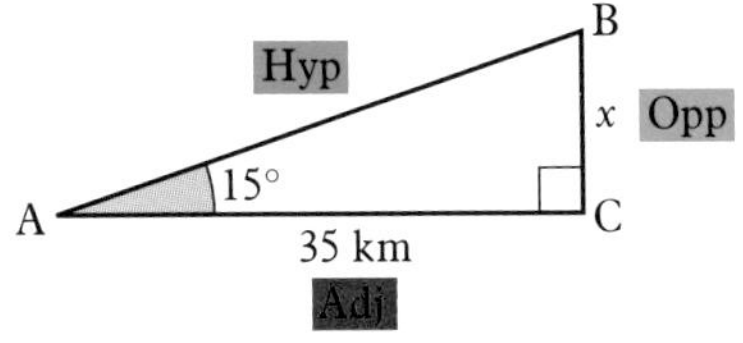

C is the point that is directly east of A and directly south of B
So $A\hat{C}B$ is 90°

In triangle ABC
$C\hat{A}B = 90 - 75 = 15°$

Using trigonometry gives:

$$\tan 15° = \frac{x}{35}$$

$$x = 35 \times \tan 15$$

Make sure that your calculator is working in degrees.

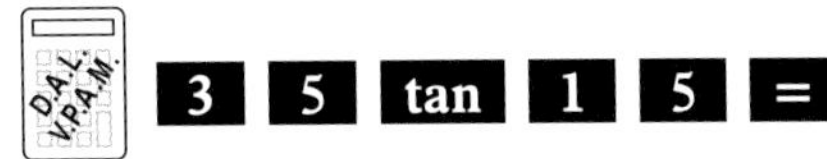

$x = 9.4$ km to 1 dp.
So B is 9.4 km north of A.

Exercise 35:4

1 The diagram shows the position of two ships A and B.
The bearing of B from A is 075°.
B is 25 km east of A.

a Copy the diagram.
Show the information on your diagram.

b How far north of A is B?

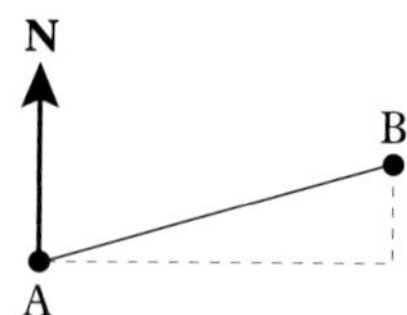

2 The diagram shows the position of two ships A and B.
The bearing of A from B is 244°.
A is 80 km west of B.

a Copy the diagram.
Show the information on your diagram.

b How far south of B is A?

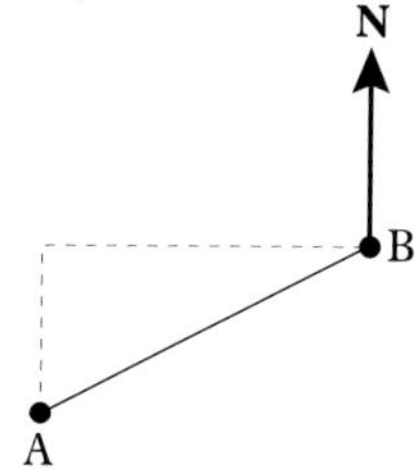

3 The diagram shows the position of two lighthouses P and Q.
The bearing of P from Q is 305°.
P is 63 km west of Q.

a Copy the diagram.
Show the information on your diagram.

b How far north of Q is P?

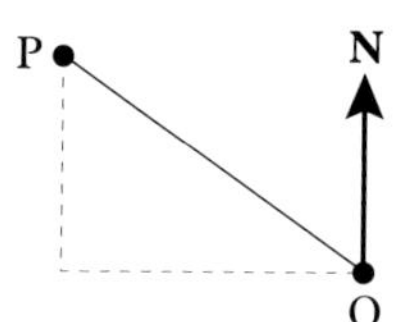

4 The diagram shows the position of two jets Y and Z.
The bearing of Z from Y is 115°.
Z is 377 km east of Y.

a Copy the diagram and fill in the given information.

b How far south of Y is Z?

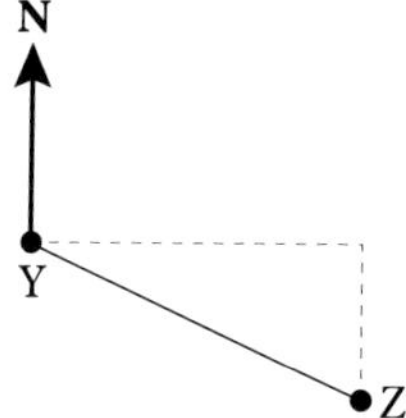

5 The diagram shows the position of two boats A and B.
The bearing of B from A is 122°.
The distance of B from A is 36 miles.

a Copy the diagram and fill in the given information.

b How far south of A is B?

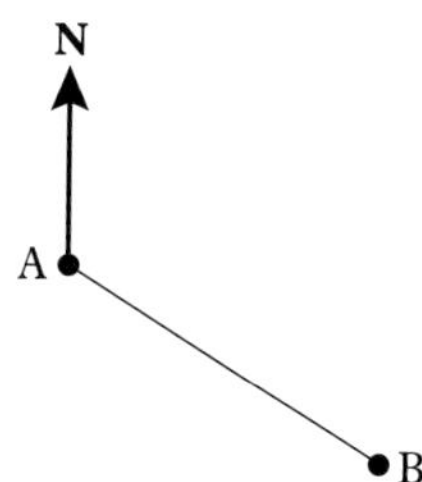

6 A helicopter flies 254 km from Aberdeen on a bearing of 047°.
   a Draw a diagram to show this information.
   b How far east of Aberdeen is the helicopter?
   c How far north of Aberdeen is the helicopter?

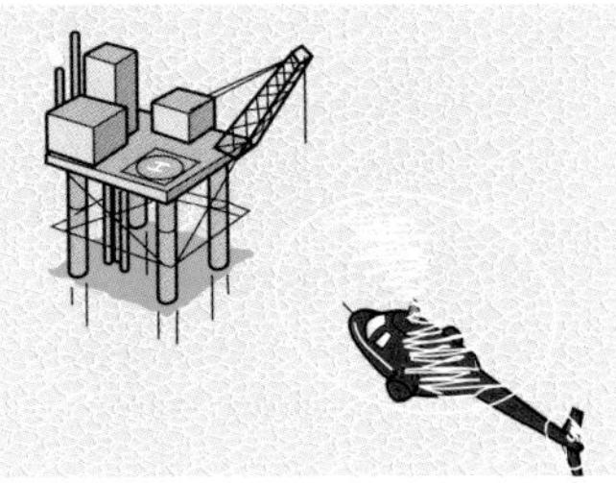

7 A ship sails 40 km from Plymouth on a bearing of 216°.
   a Draw a diagram to show this information.
   b How far west of Plymouth is the ship?
   c How far south of Plymouth is the ship?

8 A jet flies 430 km from its base on a bearing of 315°.
   a Draw a diagram to show this information.
   b How far west of its base is the jet?
   c How far north of its base is the jet?

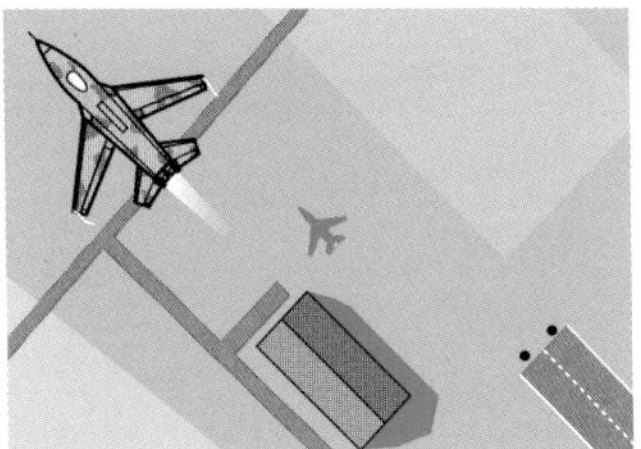

You often need to do bearings questions in stages.

Example A plane flies 20 km from Ampton to Boxford on a bearing of 044°. It then flies 15 km on a bearing of 102° to Canborough.
   a Find the distance from Ampton to Canborough.
   b Find the bearing of Canborough from Ampton.

You need to start by drawing a diagram.
Show all of the information that you are given.
Use A, B and C for the towns. Use extra letters to label all the important points.

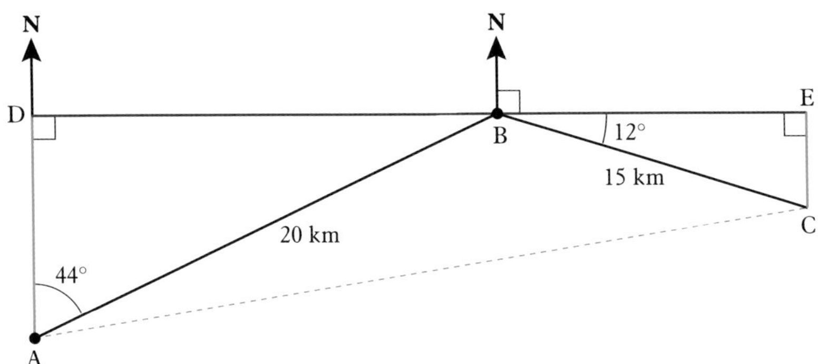

You want to find out about **a** the length from A to C
and **b** the bearing of C from A

First, you need to think about the distances east/west and north/south.

The distance east from A to C is **DB + BE**

In triangle ABD:

$$\sin 44^\circ = \frac{DB}{20}$$

$$DB = 20 \sin 44^\circ$$

In triangle BCE:

$$\cos 12^\circ = \frac{BE}{15}$$

$$BE = 15 \cos 12^\circ$$

So the distance east from A to C is $20 \sin 44^\circ + 15 \cos 12^\circ$
$= 28.56$ km (4 sf)

Give 4 sf in your working if you want to give your final answer to 3 sf.

The distance north from A to C is **AD − EC**

In triangle ABD:

$$\cos 44^\circ = \frac{AD}{20}$$

$$AD = 20 \cos 44^\circ$$

In triangle BCE:

$$\sin 12^\circ = \frac{EC}{15}$$

$$EC = 15 \sin 12^\circ$$

So the distance north from A to C is $20 \cos 44^\circ - 15 \sin 12^\circ$
$= 11.27$ km (4 sf)

Now draw a separate triangle that shows the relevant information.
Label any missing points.

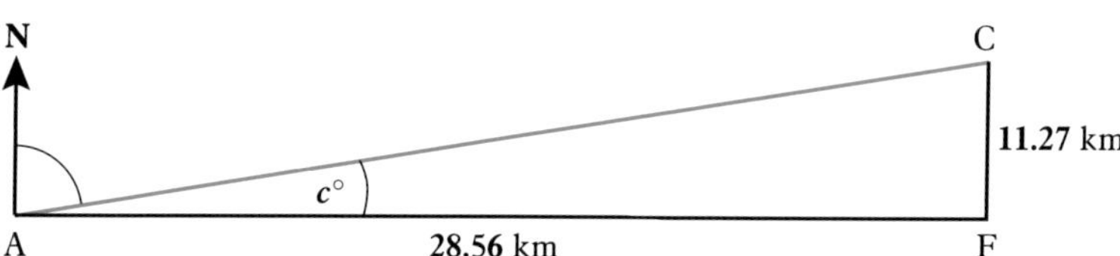

Now you can answer the question!

a In triangle ACF:

$AC^2 = 28.56^2 + 11.27^2$ (by Pythagoras' theorem)

$AC^2 = 942.6865$

$AC = 30.7$ km (3 sf)

b $\tan c = \frac{11.27}{28.56} = 0.3946 \ldots$

$c = 21.53^\circ$

The angle needed for the bearing is $90^\circ - 21.53^\circ = 68.47^\circ$ (2 dp)
So the bearing of C from A is 068° (to the nearest degree).

Exercise 35:5

In this exercise, give all distances to 3 sf and bearings to the nearest degree.

1 A plane flies 13 km from Abingdon to Bampton on a bearing of 285°. It then flies 28 km on a bearing of 260° to Cirencester.

a Draw a diagram to show this information.
b Find the distance from Abingdon to Cirencester.
c Find the bearing of Cirencester from Abingdon.

2 A plane flies 15 km from Harlow to Chelmsford on a bearing of 100°. It then flies 25 km on a bearing of 135° to Southend-on-Sea.

a Draw a diagram to show this information.
b Find the distance from Harlow to Southend-on-Sea.
c Find the bearing of Southend-on-Sea from Harlow.

3 A jet flies 300 km from Manchester on a bearing of 170°. Then it flies 100 km on a bearing of 047° and arrives at Guildford.

a Draw a diagram to show this information.
b Find the shortest distance from Manchester to Guildford.
c Find the bearing of Guildford from Manchester.

4 A jet flies 8100 km from Dover in England on a bearing of 159°. Then it flies 5400 km on a bearing of 123° and arrives at Perth on the coast of Australia.

a Draw a diagram to show this information.
b Find the shortest distance from Dover to Perth.
c Find the bearing of Perth from Dover.

• **5** Frank is repairing lighthouses around the Irish Sea. He flies by helicopter. He sets off from Holyhead in Anglesey and flies for 50 km to Llandudno on a bearing of 089°. Then he flies for 105 km to Douglas in the Isle of Man on a bearing of 330°. His final call is to Fleetwood in Lancashire. He flies 100 km from Douglas on a bearing of 105° to get there.

a Draw a diagram to show this information.
b Find the shortest distance from Holyhead to Fleetwood.
c Find the bearing of Fleetwood from Holyhead.

Angles of elevation and depression

Start by looking horizontally.
When you look *up* at something, the angle is called an angle of *elevation*.
When you look *down* at something, the angle is called an angle of *depression*.

Angle of elevation

If you are at A and you look up to a point B, the **angle of elevation of B from A** is the angle between the horizontal and the line AB. It is the angle *above* the horizontal.

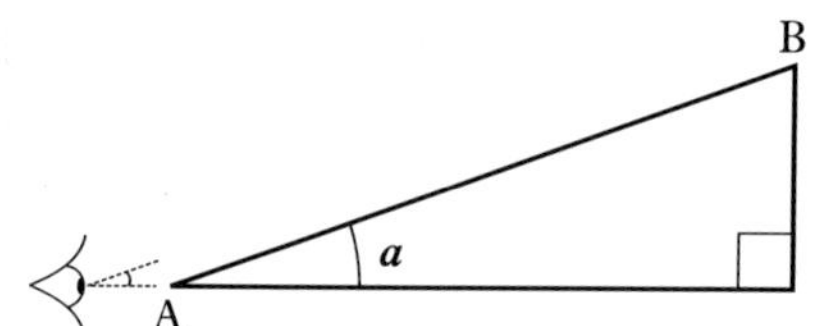

a is the angle of elevation of B from A.

Angle of depression

If you are at P and you look down to a point Q, the **angle of depression of Q from P** is the angle between the horizontal and the line PQ. It is the angle *below* the horizontal.

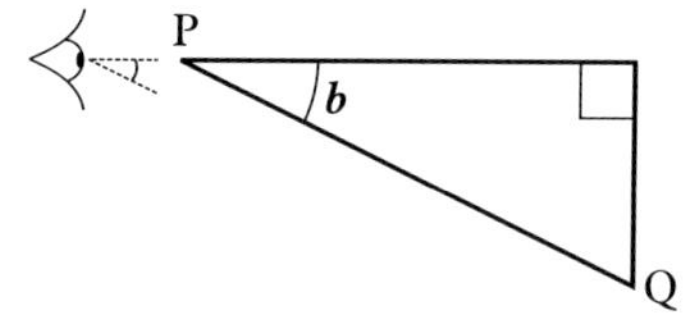

b is the angle of depression of Q from P.

Exercise 35:6

In this exercise round your answers to 3 sf.

1 Sid is standing at point A, 26 metres from the base of a tree.
The angle of elevation of the top of the tree from A is 42°.
Find the height of the tree.

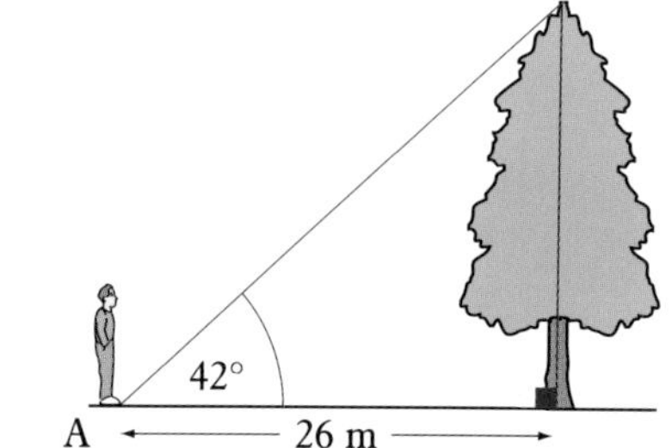

2 Graham is standing at point B, 52 m from a church tower.
The tower is 32 m high.
Work out the angle of elevation of the top of the church tower from B.

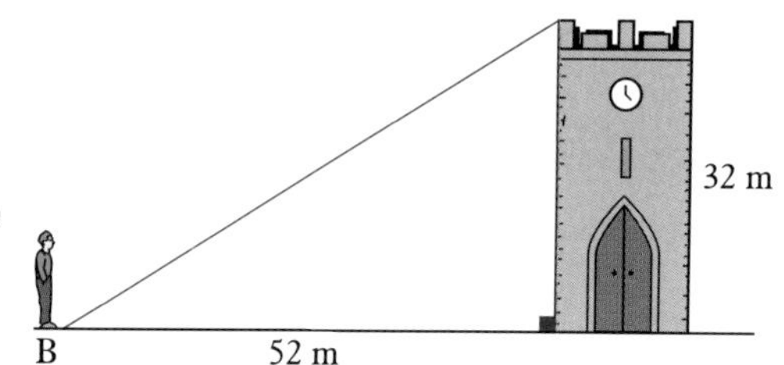

3 Fiona is looking over the edge of a cliff.
She sees a boat on the water below.
The cliff is 105 m high. The angle of depression of the boat from Fiona is 7°.

a Draw a diagram to show this information.

b Work out the distance of the boat from the foot of the cliff.

3 Finding the hypotenuse

Sometimes it helps to know the distance along the hypotenuse.

Look at this triangle. Suppose you need to find the hypotenuse h
You cannot use Pythagoras' theorem, because you only have one side.

To find the side marked h in this triangle:

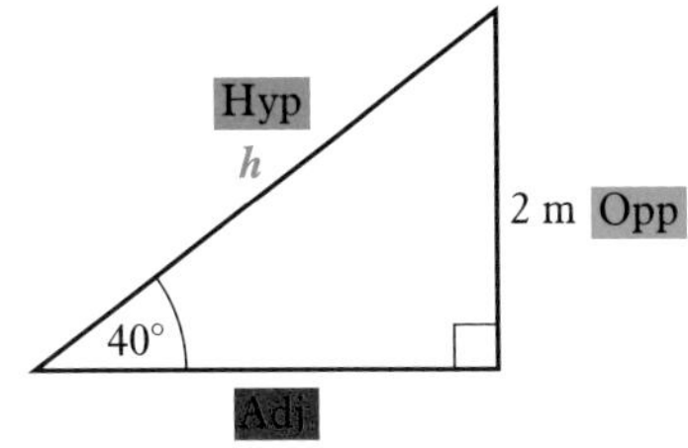

Write out SOH CAH TOA.

Cross out the side that you know.
Cross out the hypotenuse because you want to find it.

The formula you need is the one with two sides crossed out.

$$\sin 40° = \frac{\text{opposite}}{\text{hypotenuse}}$$

Substitute into the formula: $\sin 40° = \dfrac{2}{h}$

You need to make h the subject of the formula.
Here it is a denominator, so multiply by h on both sides.

So $h \times \sin 40° = 2$

Now divide both sides by sin 40° $h = \dfrac{2}{\sin 40°}$

Make sure that your calculator is working in degrees.

Now press:

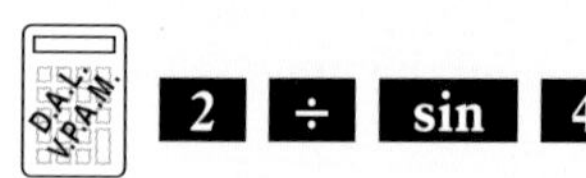

to get $h = 3.11$ m (3 sf)

You can use the formula for cos in the same way.
The formula for tan will also give the unknown in the denominator if you are finding the adjacent.

Exercise 35:7

1 **a** Write out SOH CAH TOA.
Cross out the hypotenuse.
Cross out the side you know.

b Copy this. Fill it in.

$$\sin 32° = \frac{\dots}{h}$$

Hyp h 7 m Opp 32° Adj

c Multiply both sides by h.
Copy this. Fill it in. $h \times \sin 32° = \dots$

d Divide both sides by sin 32°.
Copy this. Fill it in. $h = \frac{\dots}{\dots}$

e Now use your calculator to work out h to 3 dp.

2 **a** Write out SOH CAH TOA.

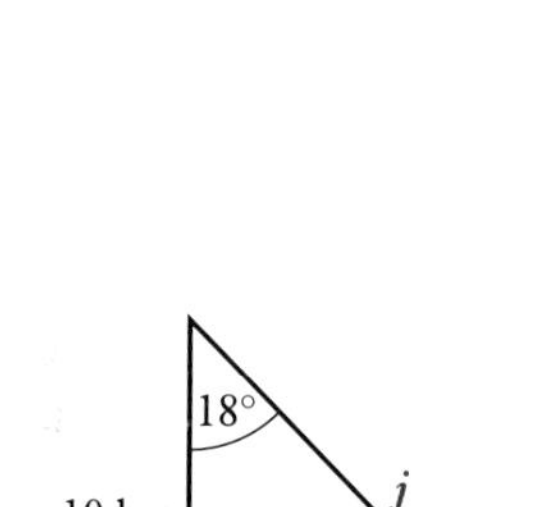

b Cross out the side you want and the side you know.

c Copy this. Fill it in. $\dots\ 18° = \frac{\dots}{j}$

d Rearrange this equation to make j the subject.

e Now use your calculator to work out j to 3 dp.

In questions **3–8** find the lengths of the sides marked with letters. Give your answers to 3 sf.

3

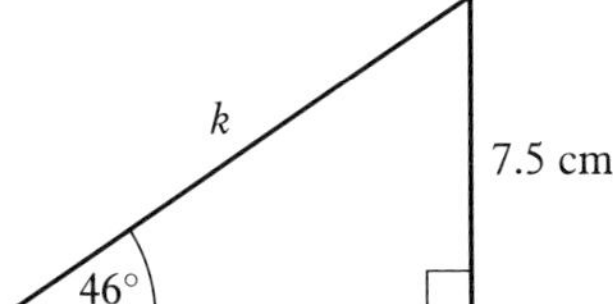

6

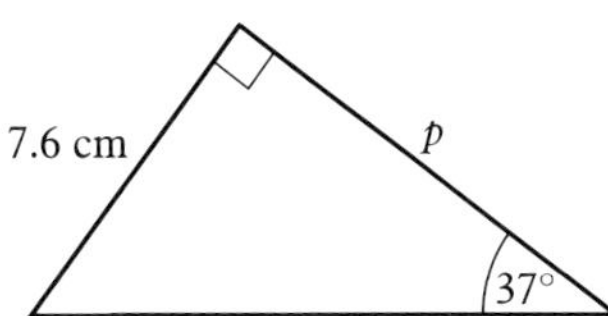

4

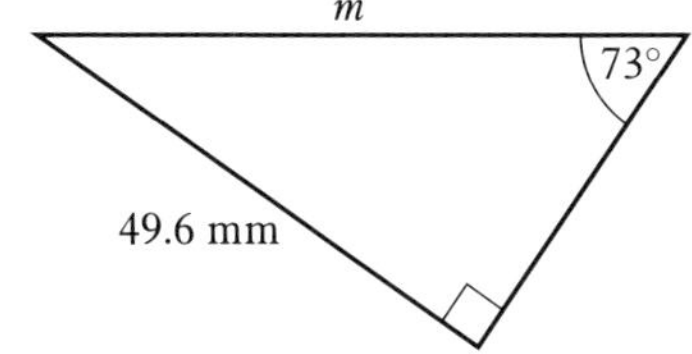

7

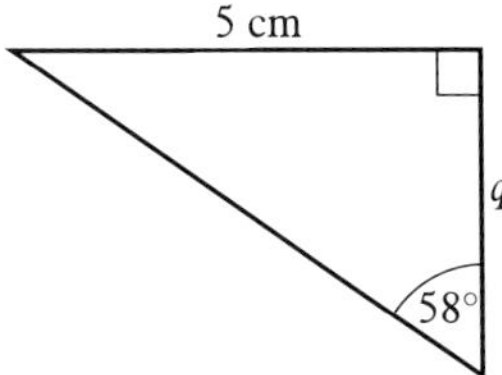

5

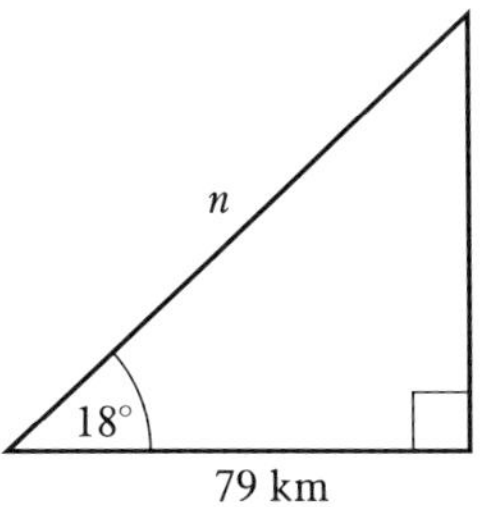

8

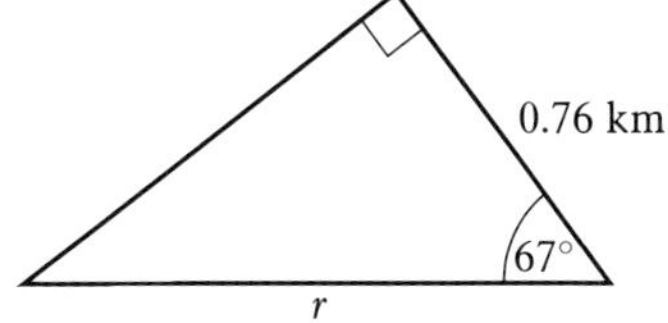

9 Every day Sue and her dog Jumble walk across the diagonal AB of this field. How far does she walk?

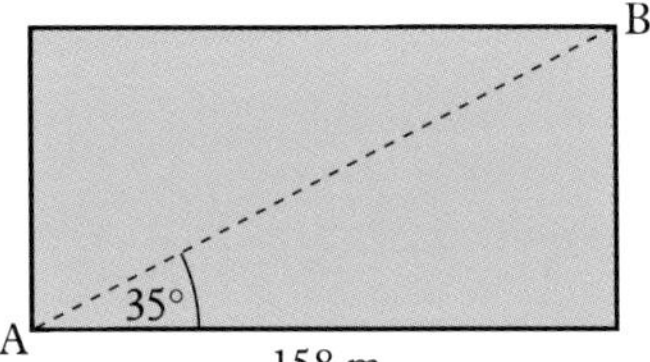

• **10** The Pan Trophy hill climb course goes up the red route shown in the diagram.

a Find the distances AB, BC and CD.

b Work out the total distance of the course.

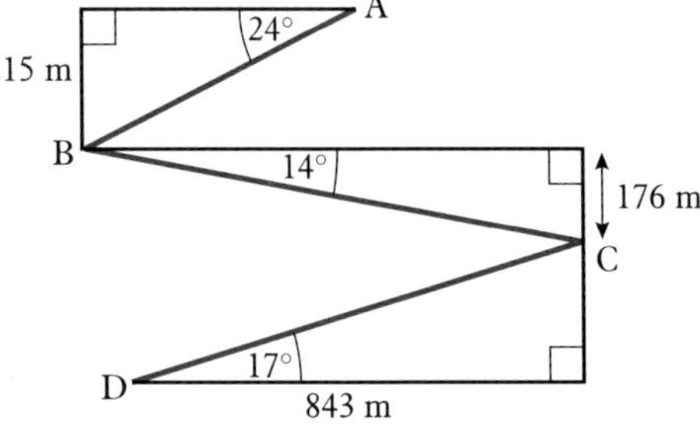

1 Find the labelled angle in each of these triangles.
Give your answers to the nearest degree.

a

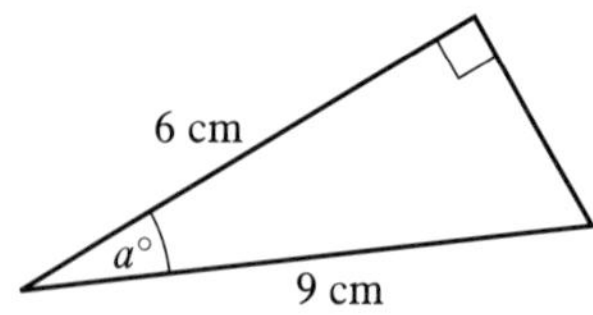

b

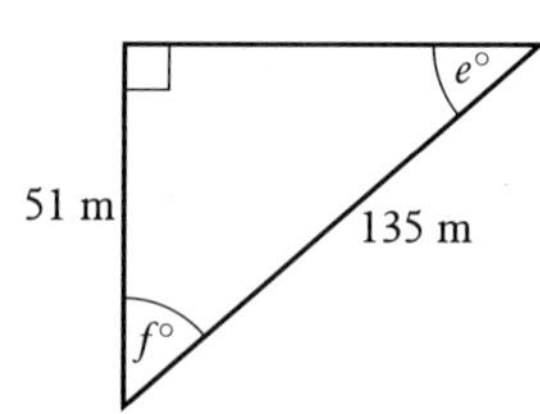

2 Find the labelled side in each of these triangles.
Give your answers to 3 sf.

a

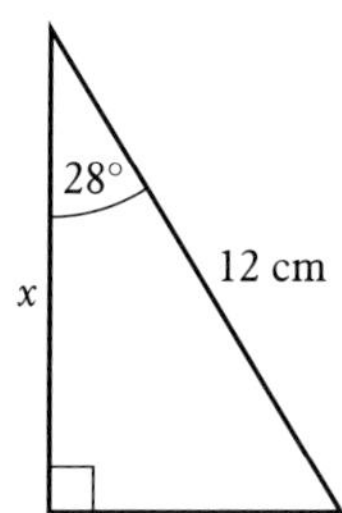

b

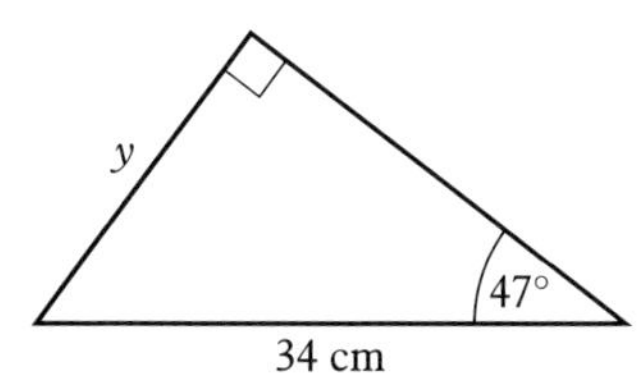

3 This diagram shows a chord in a sector of a circle.
The radius of the circle is 6 cm.
The length of the chord is 10 cm.
Find the angle, x, in the sector to 1 dp.

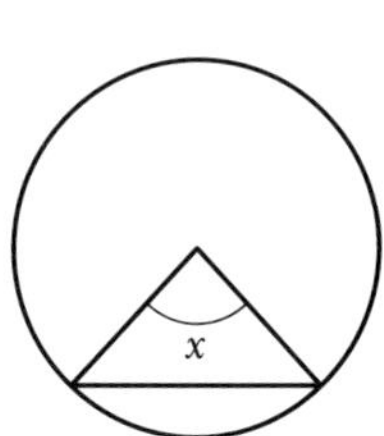

In questions **4–9**, give your answers to 3 sf.

4 The diagram shows two aircraft A and B.
The bearing of B from A is 293°.
B is 615 km west of A.

a Copy the diagram.

b How far north of A is B?

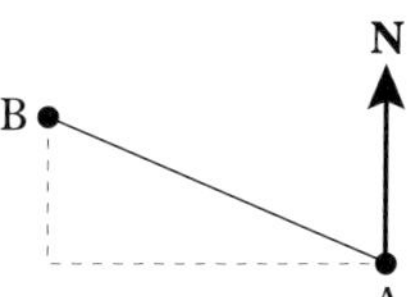

5 A helicopter flies 2500 km from Manchester on a bearing of 130°.

a Draw a diagram to show this information.

b How far east of Manchester is the helicopter?

c How far south of Manchester is the helicopter?

d What is the bearing of Manchester from the helicopter?

6 A ferry leaves a port P and travels 4.7 km on a bearing of 156° to a port Q.
It then travels 8.2 km on a bearing of 054° to a port R.

a Draw a diagram to show this information.

b Show that $P\hat{Q}R$ is 78°.

c Find the shortest distance from P to R.

d Find the bearing of P from R.

7 The diagram shows two buildings.
The distance between the buildings is 80 m.
The smaller building is 34 m high.
The angle of elevation of the top of the taller building from the top of the smaller building is 27°.
Find the height of the taller building.

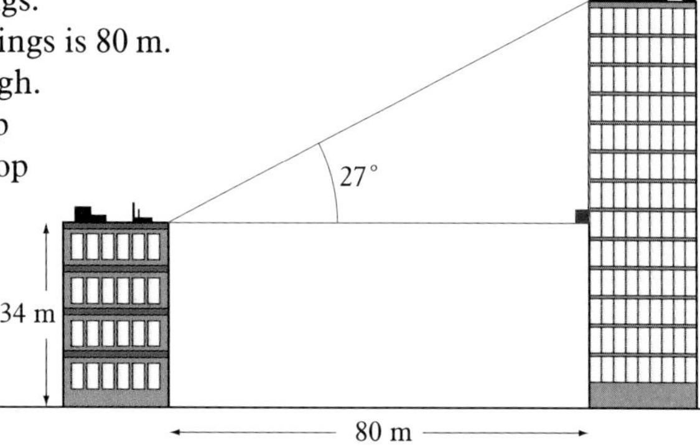

8 Canary Wharf tower in London's docklands is the tallest building in Britain.
Nicki is at the top of the Canary Wharf tower.
She sees a boat on the river below.
The tower is 243.8 m high.
The angle of depression of the boat from Nicki is 37°.

a Draw a diagram to show this information.

b Work out the distance of the boat from the foot of the tower.

9 Find the length of the hypotenuse in each of these triangles.
Give your answers to 3 sf.

a

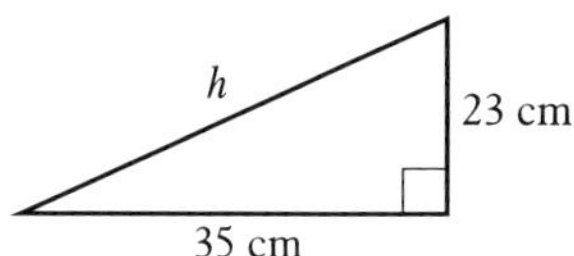

c

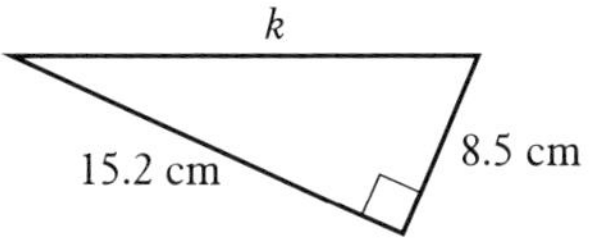

b

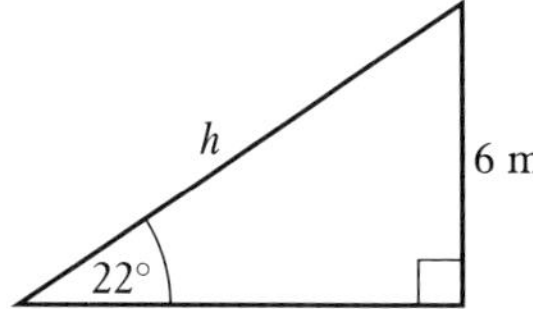

d

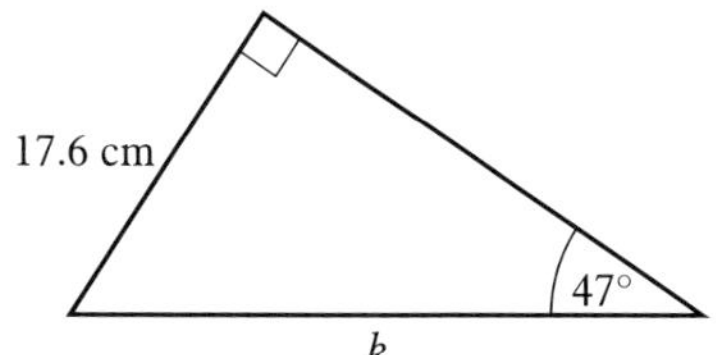

1 Work out the angles marked in this diagram.

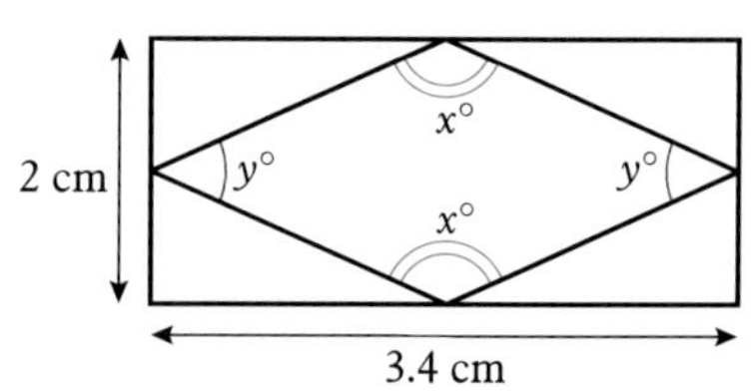

2 **a** Write down the values of sin A, cos A and tan A. in this right-angled triangle.
You only need the letters a and b.
You need to use Pythagoras' theorem.

b Use your answers to part **a** to show that

(1) $(\sin A)^2 + (\cos A)^2 = 1$

(2) $\tan A = \dfrac{\sin A}{\cos A}$

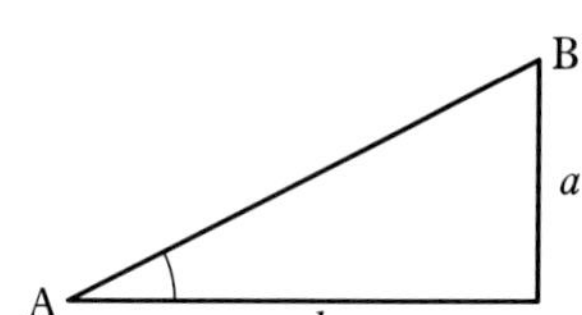

3 Tai is in Paris.
She is looking at the Eiffel tower.
The angle of elevation of the top of the tower from where she is standing is 30°.
She walks 200 m towards the tower.
The angle of elevation of the top of the tower is now 43.2°
Work out:

a the height of the tower

b the horizontal distance of Tai from the tower when she started.

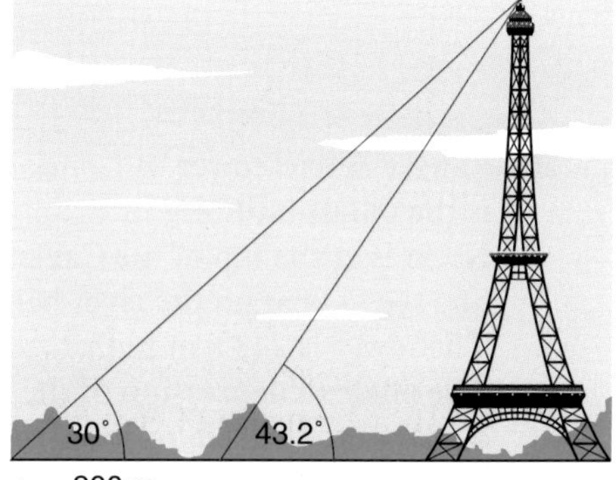

4 Pat is a pylon painter.
One of the sections she has to paint looks like this.

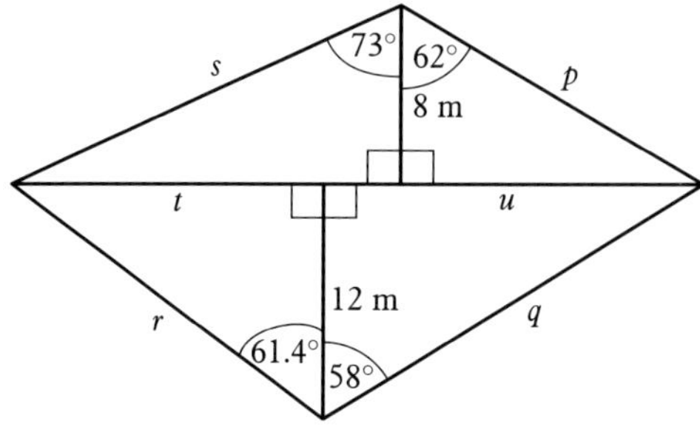

Find the total length of the girders that she paints.

1 Find the size of the angle marked by a letter in each of these triangles.

a

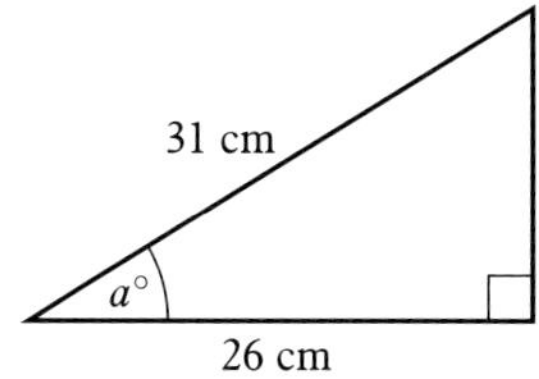

b

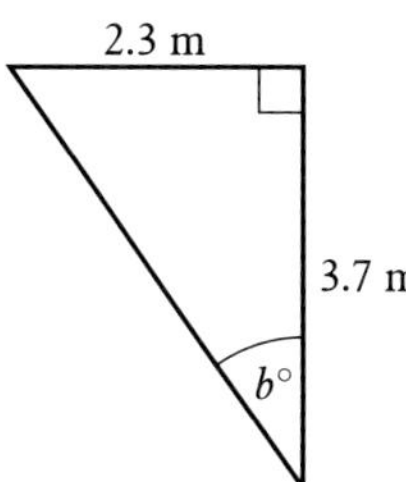

2 Find the length of the sides marked by a letter in each of these triangles.

a

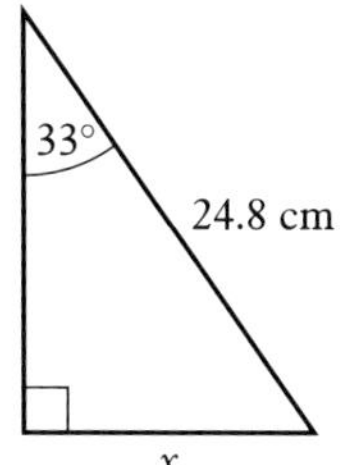

b

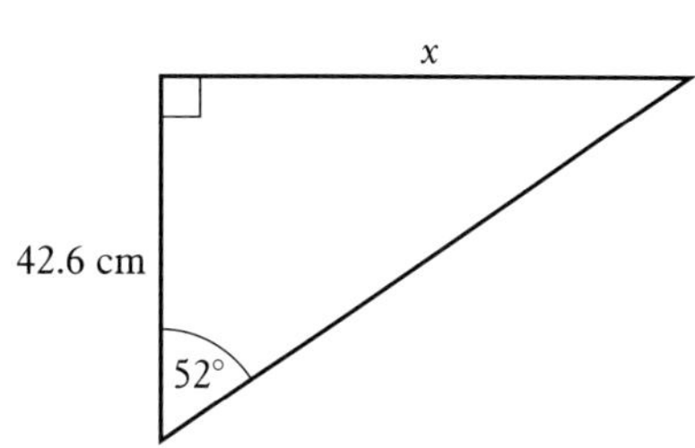

3 A ship leaves a harbour H and travels 9.6 km on a bearing of 072° to reach a port P.

a How far north of H is P?

b How far east of H is P?

c What is the bearing of H from P?

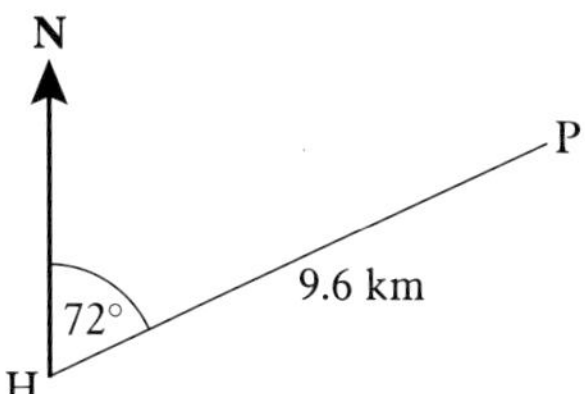

4 Jen is walking in open countryside.
She wants to travel to a village 5 km west and 3 km south of her present position.

a Draw a diagram to show this information.

b Find the bearing that she should take.

5 A helicopter flies 37 km from A on a bearing of 126° to B.
It then flies a further 84 km on a bearing of 238° to reach C.

a Copy the diagram and show this information.
b How far south has the helicopter travelled altogether?
c How far is C to the west of A?
d What is the bearing of A from C?

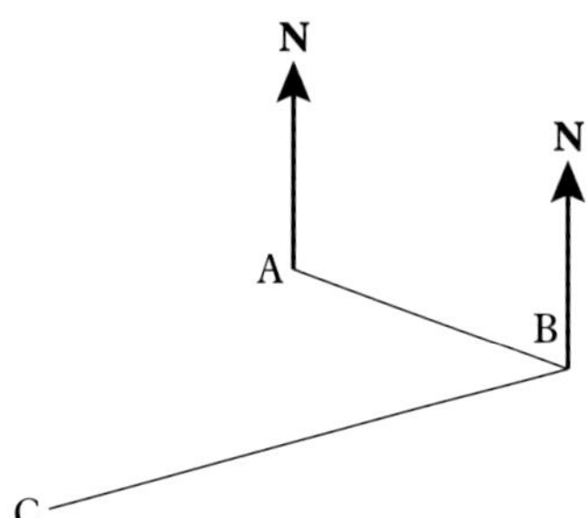

6 Find the length of the hypotenuse in this triangle.

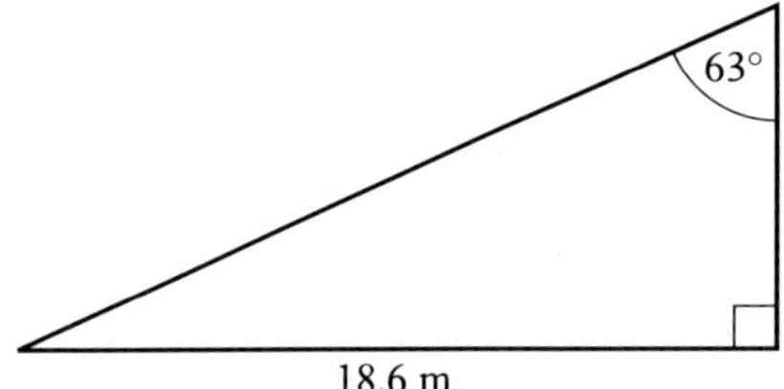

7 The angle of depression of a small boat from the top of a cliff is 18°.
The cliff is 120 m above the sea.

a Draw a diagram to show this information.
b How far is the boat from the foot of the cliff?

8 A ladder leans against a wall at an angle of 60° to the horizontal.
The top of the ladder is 2.6 m above the ground.
Find the length of the ladder to 2 significant figures.

9 Chris measures the angle of elevation of the top of a building as 25°.
He then moves 30 m towards the building.
The angle of elevation is now 40°.
How tall is the building?

36 <Inequalities>

CORE

1 Solving inequalities using algebra

Showing simple inequalities on the number line
Solving linear inequalities
Multiplying and dividing by a negative number
Solving inequalities with several parts
Solving quadratic inequalities

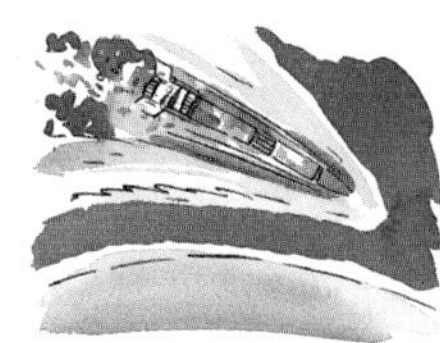

2 Solving inequalities using graphs

Showing inequalities with lines parallel to the axes
Showing two inequalities on the same graph
Graphing inequalities involving both x and y
Showing multiple inequalities on the same graph
Using inequalities to solve problems
Solving more complex inequalities using graphs

QUESTIONS

EXTENSION

TEST YOURSELF

1 Solving inequalities using algebra

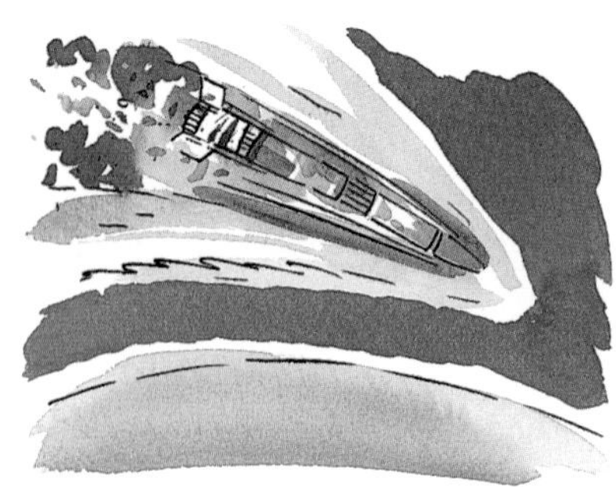

The angle at which a rocket re-enters the earth's atmosphere is critical.

If the angle is too steep then the rocket will travel too quickly.

If it is too shallow, the friction will be too great and the rocket will burn up.

There is only a small range of angles that are suitable.

You use inequalities to describe a range of numbers.

$x > 3$

$x > 3$ means that x can take any value **greater than 3**.
It cannot be 3. On a number line, this is shown like this:

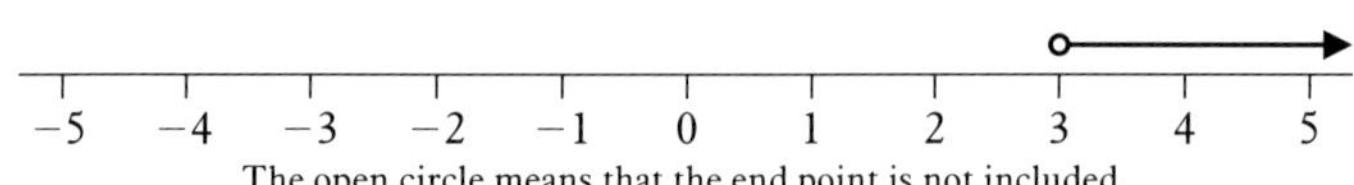

The open circle means that the end point is not included.

$x \leqslant 1$

$x \leqslant 1$ means that x can take any value **less than or equal to 1**.
This includes 1. On a number line, this is shown like this:

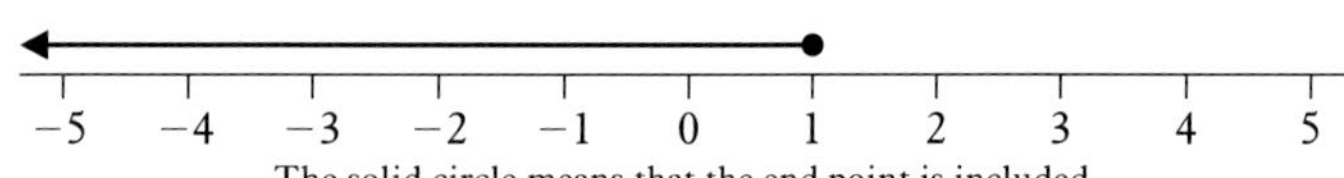

The solid circle means that the end point is included.

$-2 \leqslant x < 4$

$-2 \leqslant x < 4$ means that **x is greater than or equal to -2**.
$-2 \leqslant x < 4$ means that **x is less than 4**.
So $-2 \leqslant x < 4$ means that x is between -2 and 4.
-2 is included, 4 is not.

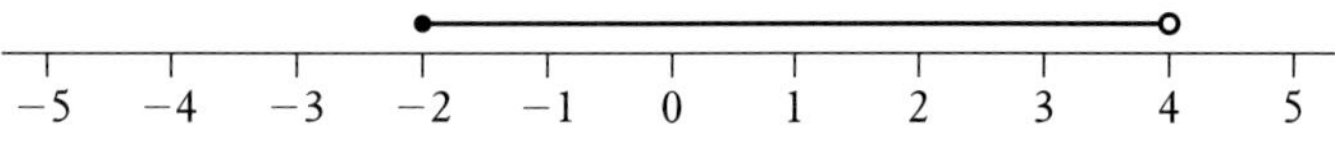

Exercise 36:1

1 Write down inequalities to describe each of these number lines.

a

−5 −4 −3 −2 −1 0 1 2 3 4 5

b

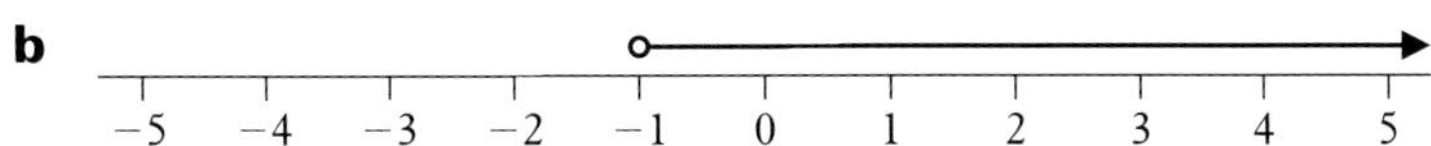

c

−5 −4 −3 −2 −1 0 1 2 3 4 5

d

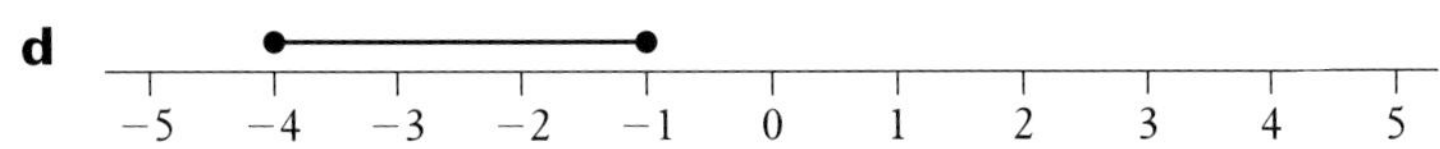

e

−5 −4 −3 −2 −1 0 1 2 3 4 5

f

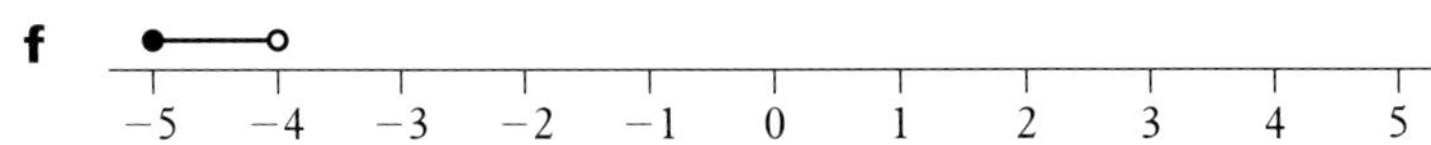

g

−5 −4 −3 −2 −1 0 1 2 3 4 5

2 Draw each of these inequalities on a number line.

a $x > 2$ **c** $x \leqslant -3$ **e** $1 < x < 2$ **g** $-3 \leqslant x \leqslant -1$

b $x < 1$ **d** $x \geqslant -2$ **f** $-1 < x < 4$ **h** $-5 < x \leqslant 4.5$

Integer — An **integer** is a whole number.
Integers are … −4, −3, −2, −1, 0, 1, 2, 3, 4 …

---

3 List the integers that are included in each of these inequalities.

a $1 < x < 4$ **c** $-3 < x < 2$ **e** $-2 \leqslant x \leqslant 6$ **g** $-3 \leqslant x \leqslant -2$

b $1 \leqslant x \leqslant 4$ **d** $-4 < x < 4$ **f** $0 < x < 7$ **h** $-3 < x < -2$

Most inequalities you will see are written in algebra. They are used to solve problems.

Inequalities are solved in a very similar way to equations. This means you can:

- add the same number to both sides of an inequality
- subtract the same number from both sides of an inequality
- multiply or divide both sides of an inequality by any **positive** number.

If you multiply or divide by a **negative** number, there is a new rule that you will see later.

Examples **1** Solve $3x - 5 > 8$

$$3x - 5 > 8$$

Add 5 to both sides: $3x > 13$

Divide both sides by 3: $\boldsymbol{x > \frac{13}{3}}$

2 Solve $5 - x < 2x - 1$

$$5 - x < 2x - 1$$

Add x to both sides: $5 < 3x - 1$

Add 1 to both sides: $6 < 3x$

Divide both sides by 3: $2 < x$

It is better to write this the other way round: $\boldsymbol{x > 2}$

Exercise 36:2

Solve each of these inequalities.

1 $x + 4 < 7$

2 $3x - 3 > 9$

3 $5x - 6 \leqslant 9$

4 $y + 2.4 > 8$

5 $\frac{y}{5} - 6 > 20$

6 $\frac{f}{2} - 7 \geqslant 11$

7 $4(3t + 10) < 20$

8 $\frac{x - 9}{4} \leqslant 6$

9 $6x - 4 > 2x + 6$

10 $3.5g - 2 < 7 - g$

11 $2x - 6 \leqslant x + 7$

• **12** $\frac{5n + 2}{2} \geqslant 2n$

Look at this simple statement:	$14 > 4$	Clearly this is true.
Now add 2 to both sides:	$16 > 6$	It is still true.
Multiply both sides by 3:	$48 > 18$	Still true!
But, dividing both sides by -2 gives	$-24 > -9$	This is **not** true.

-24 is *less* than -9 not greater than it.

This is because of the way negative numbers work.
If numbers go **up** in twos, you can write: $2 < 4 < 6 < 8 < 10$

But if they go **down** in twos,
the inequalities are the other way around: $-2 > -4 > -6 > -8 > -10$

You need a new rule to deal with this.

- If you multiply or divide an inequality by a **negative** number then you must **change the direction** of the inequality sign.

This means that taking an inequality like $14 > 4$
and multiplying both sides by -1 gives $-14 < -4$

Example Solve the inequality $6 - 2x < 12$

$$6 - 2x < 12$$

Subtract 6 from both sides: $-2x < 6$

Divide both sides by -2 **and**
change the direction of the inequality $\boldsymbol{x > -3}$

Exercise 36:3

Solve each of these inequalities.
Be careful if you multiply or divide by a negative number.

1 $4 - x < 7$

2 $-3 > 9 + 6x$

3 $5x - 6 \leqslant 20 + 7x$

4 $6 - 3y > 8 - 5y$

5 $-4(t + 10) < 48$

6 $\dfrac{7 - 2x}{4} \leqslant 6$

7 $3 - 5x > -2x + 6$

8 $6 - 4g < 7 - g$

Some inequalities have three parts to them.

Example Solve $15 < 4x + 7 < 19$

This is the same as the two separate inequalities $15 < 4x + 7$ and $4x + 7 < 19$.
You can solve this by working on both at once.
The aim is to leave a single x in the middle of the inequality.

First remove the +7. $\quad 15 < 4x + 7 < 19$

To do this, subtract 7 from all three parts: $\quad 15 - 7 < 4x + 7 - 7 < 19 - 7$

This gives $\quad 8 < 4x < 12$

Now divide through by 4: $\quad \frac{8}{4} < \frac{4x}{4} < \frac{12}{4}$

This gives the answer $\quad \mathbf{2 <} \; x \; \mathbf{< 3}$

Exercise 36:4

Solve each of these inequalities.

1 $4 < 2x < 8$

2 $12 \leqslant 3t \leqslant 27$

3 $55 \leqslant x + 12 < 74$

4 $24 \leqslant y + 15 \leqslant 38$

5 $3 < \frac{t}{4} < 20$

6 $13 < 2x + 5 < 21$

7 $-7 < 3z + 2 < 20$

8 $3 \leqslant \frac{3x}{4} \leqslant 6$

9 $20 > 6x - 4 > 2$

10 $0 < 10x < 15$

11 $16 > -2x > 24$

• **12** $19 > 6 - 2x > 37$

Solving problems using inequalities

Inequalities can be used to solve problems.
You need to give each item a letter before you write down the inequality.

Example Ben has 30 m of fencing to build a sheep pen.
He wants it to be twice as long as it is wide.
Work out the maximum length of the pen.

Call the width of the sheep pen x.

This is a sketch of the pen.

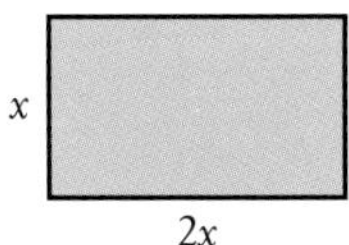

The length of the pen is $2x$.

The total perimeter of the pen is $x + 2x + x + 2x = 6x$
Ben only has 30 m of fencing, so the perimeter must be **less than or equal to 30.**

In algebra this is written: $6x \leqslant 30$
So $x \leqslant 5$
The maximum length of the pen is $2x = 2 \times 5 = 10$ m

Exercise 36:5

Write down an inequality to describe each problem.
Solve the inequality to answer the problem.

1 I think of a number, double it and add 5.
The answer must be less than 70.
What range of numbers can I choose?

2 Howard is given £10 to spend.
He is told that he can buy as many CD singles as he likes but he must keep 75p for his bus fare.
The CDs cost £2.05 each.
What is the maximum number of CDs he can buy?

3 The perimeter of this triangle must not be more than 50 cm.
What is the maximum value x can be?

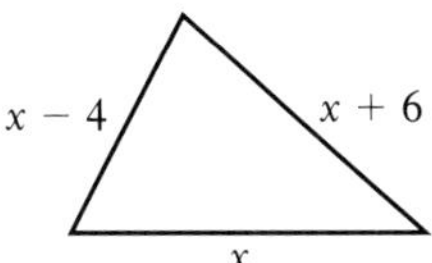

Quadratic inequalities

If you come across an inequality with x^2 in it, you need to be very careful!

Solving the equation $x^2 = 16$
gives two answers $x = -4$ and $x = 4$
This is because $4^2 = 16$ and $(-4)^2 = 16$.

If you start with $x^2 \geqslant 16$
you might be tempted to say $x \geqslant -4$ and $x \geqslant 4$

If you show $x \geqslant -4$ and $x \geqslant 4$ on a number line, it looks like this:

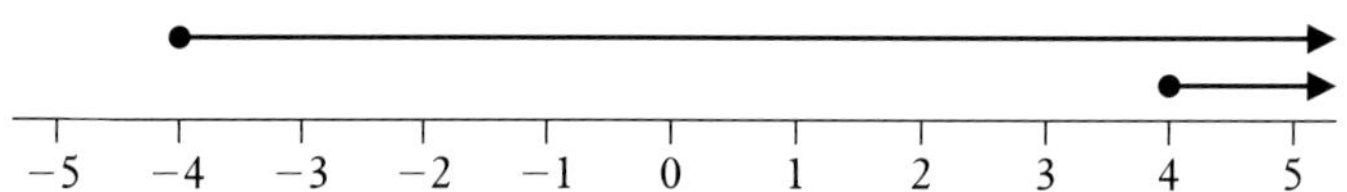

This is the same as just saying $x \geqslant -4$.

But this can't be the right answer to the problem.
Think about $x = -2$.
-2 is greater than -4 so it fits the answer.
But $(-2)^2 = 4$ and 4 is not greater than 16.
So -2 does not fit the inequality.

The $x \geqslant 4$ part of the solution does work.
The other part of the solution should be $x \leqslant -4$.

If you look at these on the number line, it looks like this:

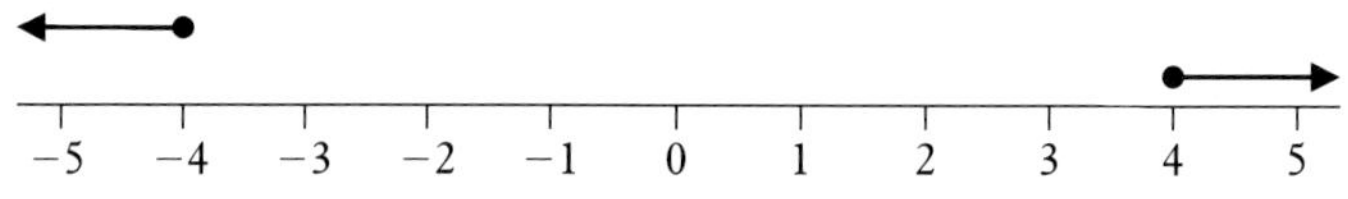

Example Solve the inequality $x^2 + 5 > 30$

$$x^2 + 5 > 30$$

gives $x^2 > 25$

This means that $x > 5$ or $x < -5$

Exercise 36:6

Solve each of these inequalities.

1 $x^2 + 5 > 21$

2 $2x^2 > 32$

3 $x^2 - 6 \geqslant 10$

4 $x^2 + 5 \geqslant 69$

5 $2x^2 - 10 > 190$

6 $x^2 + 5 > 6$

7 $x^2 - 7 > 9$

8 $3x^2 - 9 > 66$

9 $\frac{1}{2}x^2 + 5 > 37$

● **10** $x^2 > 0$

Example

Solve the inequality $3x^2 + 10 \leqslant 37$.
Show your answer on a number line.

$$3x^2 + 10 \leqslant 37$$

Take away 10: $3x^2 \leqslant 27$
Divide by 3: $x^2 \leqslant 9$

This means that you are looking for numbers that are **less** than 9 when they are squared.

The solution is $x \geqslant -3$ and $x \leqslant 3$.
This can be written $-3 \leqslant x \leqslant 3$.

On the number line it looks like this:

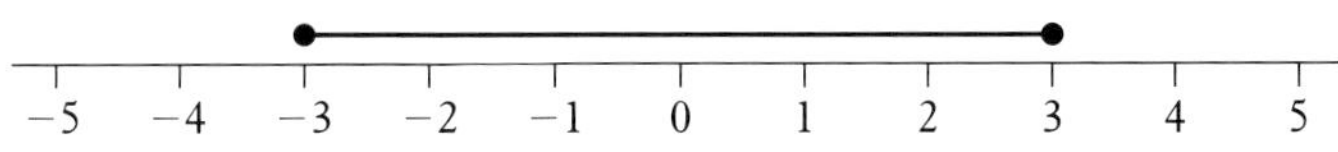

---

11 $x^2 + 10 < 46$

12 $3x^2 + 2 < 5$

13 $x^2 - 6 < 94$

14 $2(x^2 + 5) < 60$

● **15** $3x^2 - 5 < 25$

● **16** $x^2 - 9 < 81$

2 Solving inequalities using graphs

Ali and Graham are visiting a theme park.

They have a maximum of £25 to spend.

They can split their money between rides and food.

There are lots of ways they can do this.

You can use graphs to solve inequalities.
This gives you a 'picture' of the problem which often makes it easier to solve.

The easiest inequalities to show on a graph are those that have a boundary line that is parallel to one of the axes.

Example Show each of these inequalities on a graph.

a $x \geqslant 3$ **b** $y < -2$

a $x \geqslant 3$

The line is $x = 3$.
All the points in the shaded region have an x co-ordinate greater than 3
The solid line shows that the boundary **is** included.

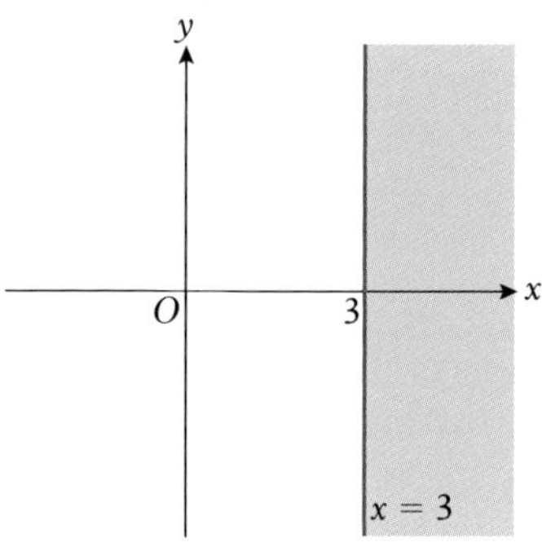

b $y < -2$

The line is $y = -2$.
All the points in the shaded region have a y co-ordinate less than -2
The dashed line shows that the boundary is **not** included.

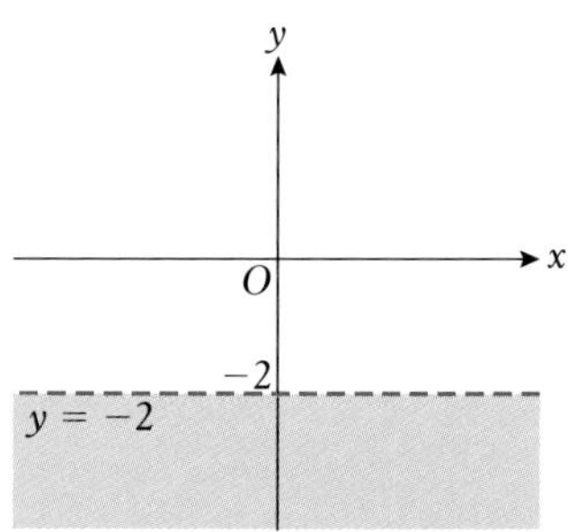

Exercise 36:7

Draw graphs to illustrate each of these inequalities.
Shade the region where each inequality is true.

1 $y \geqslant 3$

2 $x \geqslant 3$

3 $y < 4$

4 $y > 5$

5 $x > 5.5$

6 $x \leqslant -3$

7 $y < -1$

8 $x > -3.5$

9 $y < \frac{1}{2}$

For each of the following graphs, write down the inequality that describes the shaded region.

10

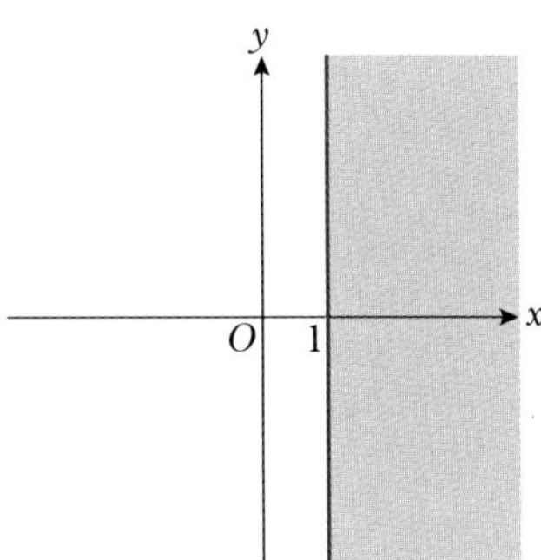

13

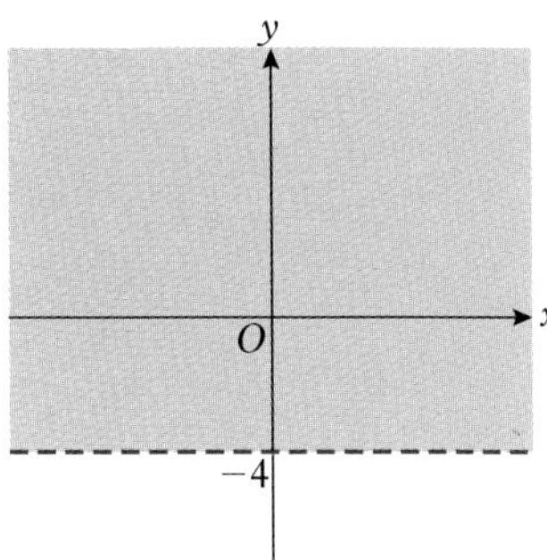

11

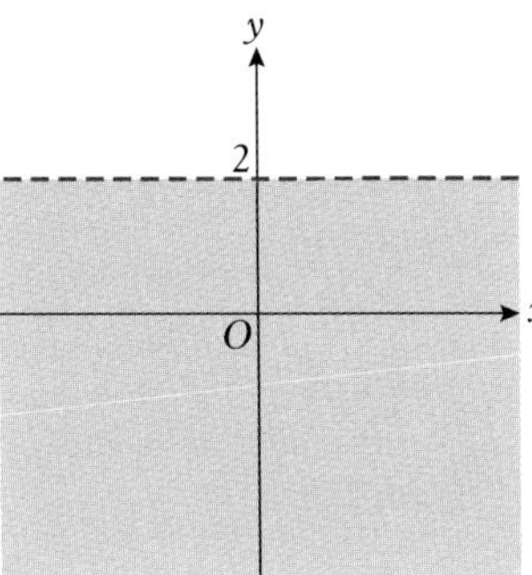

14

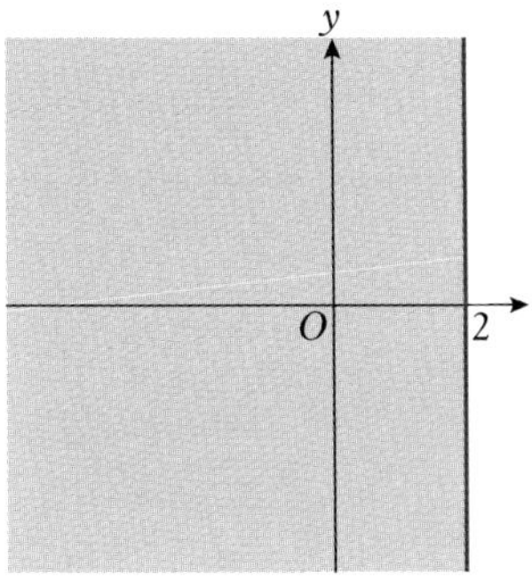

12

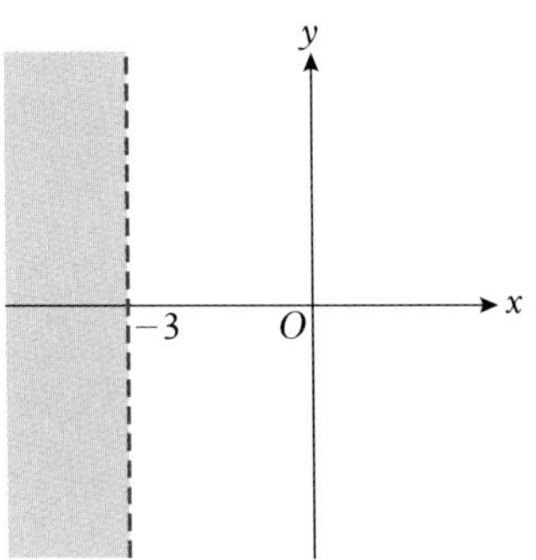

15

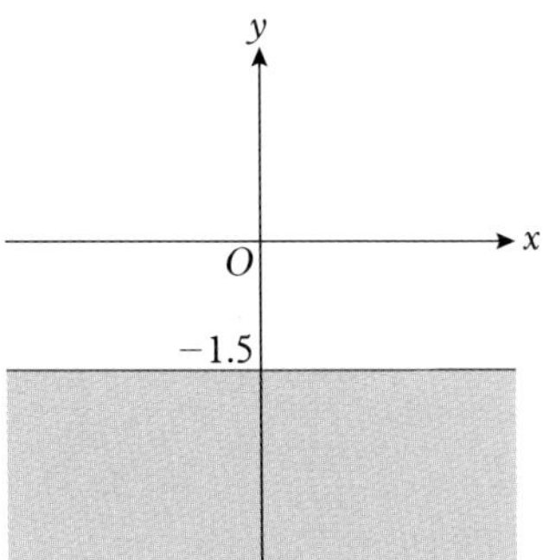

Sometimes a region is sandwiched between two lines.

Example Show each of these inequalities on a graph.

a $-2 < x \leqslant 3$ **b** $-4 \leqslant y < -2$

a $-2 < x \leqslant 3$
The lines are $x = -2$ and $x = 3$
All the points in the shaded region have an x co-ordinate greater than -2 but less than or equal to 3

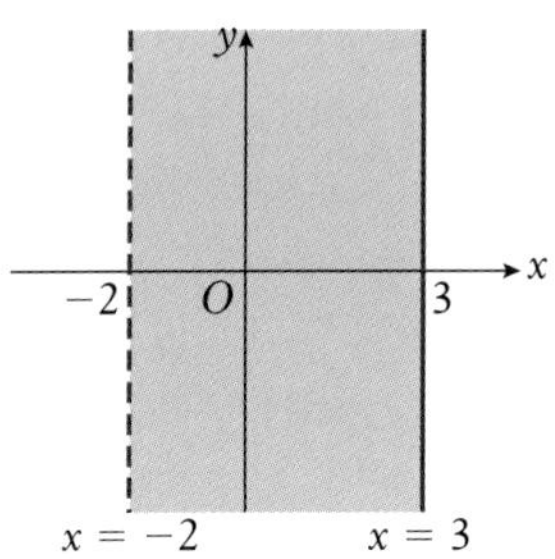

b $-4 \leqslant y < -2$
The lines are $y = -4$ and $y = -2$
All the points in the shaded region have a y co-ordinate greater than or equal to -4 but less than -2

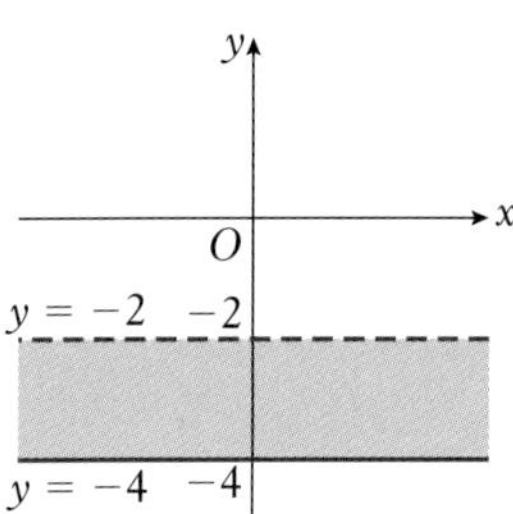

Exercise 36:8

1 Draw graphs to illustrate each of these inequalities.
Shade the region where each inequality is true.

a $2 < x \leqslant 4$ **c** $3 \leqslant y < 5$ **e** $-2 < x \leqslant 0$

b $-1 < x \leqslant 4$ **d** $0 \leqslant y < 2$ **f** $-\frac{1}{2} \leqslant x < \frac{1}{2}$

2 For each of the following graphs, write down the inequality that describes the shaded region.

a

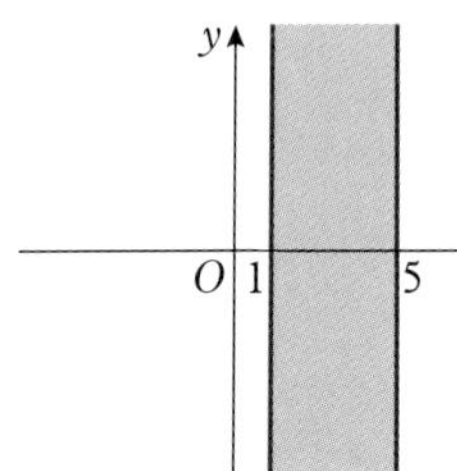

b

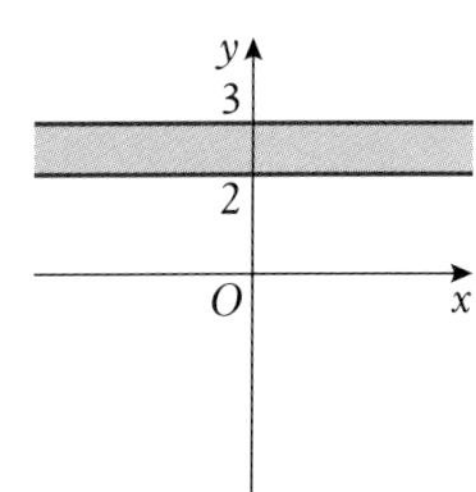

c

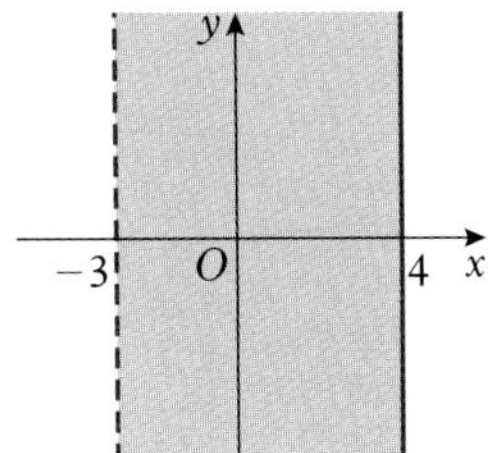

d

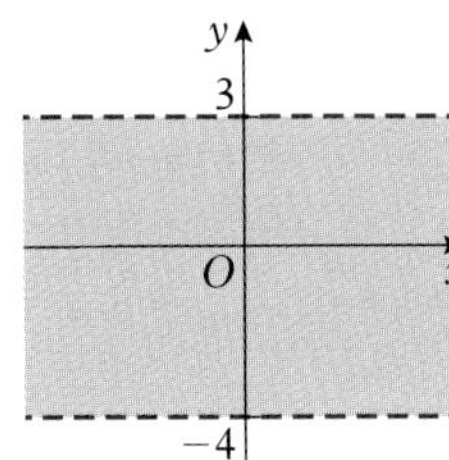

Sometimes you need to use more than one inequality to define a region.

Example Draw a graph to show the region defined by the inequalities $x \geqslant 1$ and $y < 5$

This graph shows $x \geqslant 1$

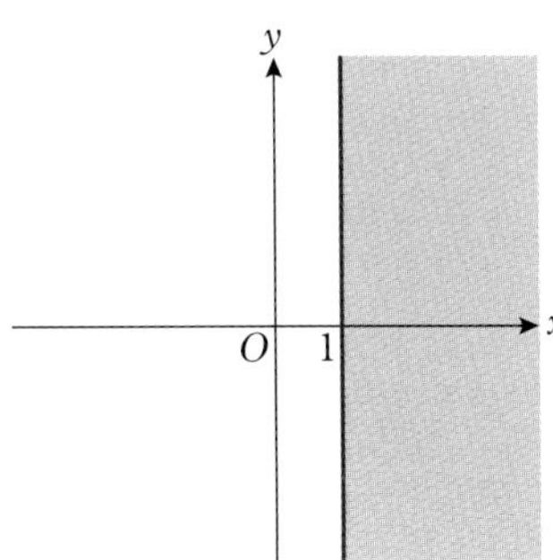

This graph shows $y < 5$

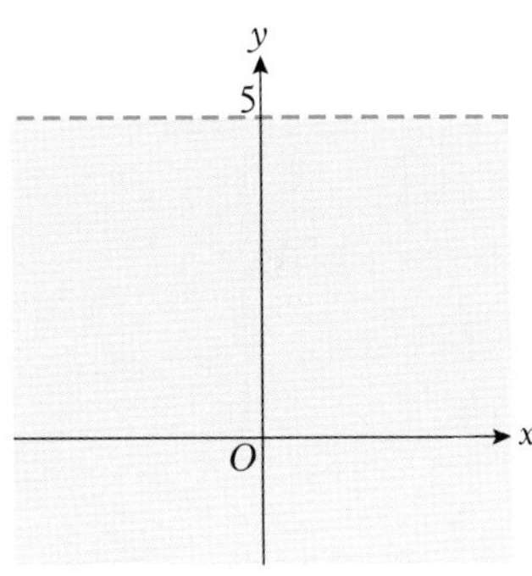

This graph shows both inequalities together.
The purple area shows where both inequalities are true.

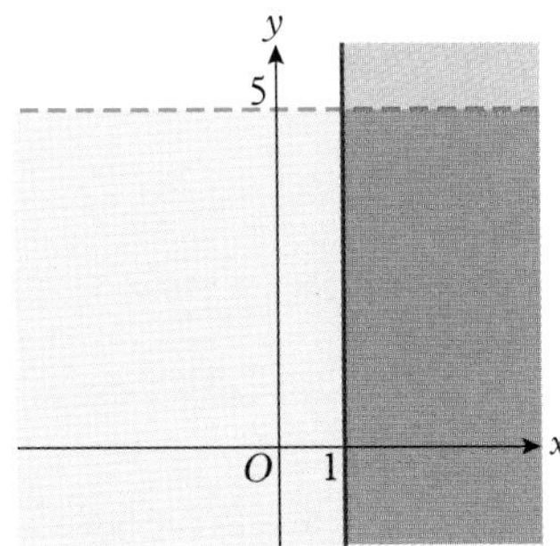

It is important that you label your graphs carefully.
You must say which area represents your answer.
You can use shading in different directions instead of colours.

Exercise 36:9

Draw graphs to show the regions defined by these inequalities.
Label each graph carefully.

1 $y \geqslant 3$ and $x > 3$

2 $x \geqslant 2$ and $y < 4$

3 $y < -2$ and $x > 0$

4 $x \leqslant -2$ and $y > 2$

5 $x > -2$ and $0 \leqslant y \leqslant 3$

6 $x \geqslant -2$ and $2 < y < 3$

● **7** $-2 \leqslant x \leqslant 4$ and $-3 \leqslant y \leqslant 4$

● **8** $-2 < x \leqslant -1$ and $3 \leqslant y \leqslant 4$

For each of the following graphs, write down the inequalities that describe the shaded region.

9

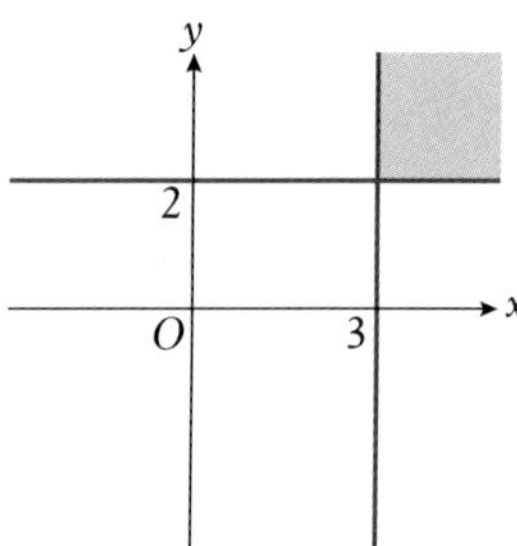

10

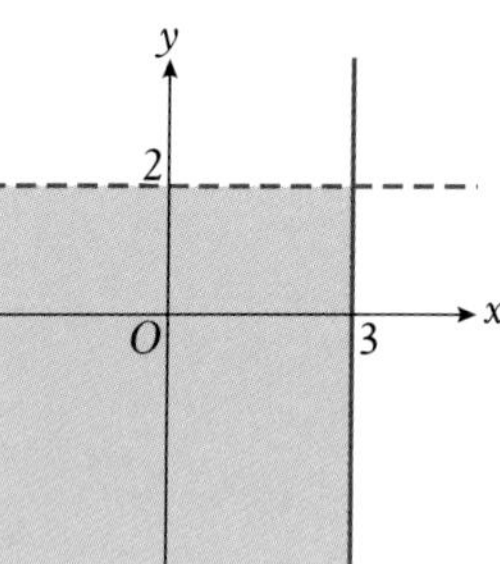

11

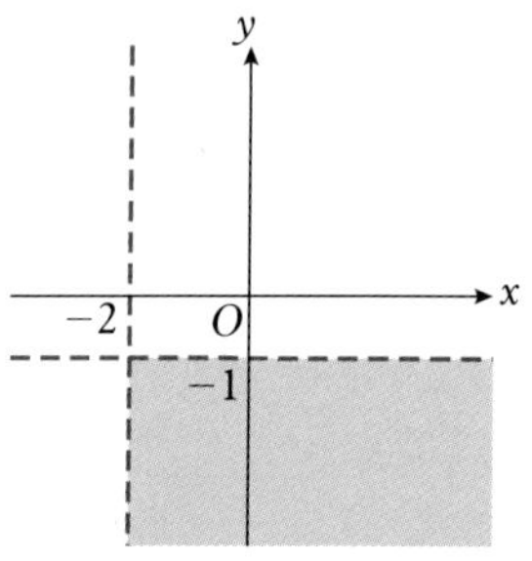

12

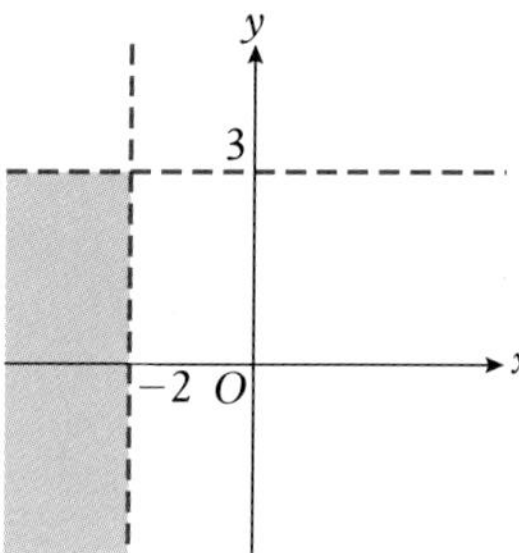

● **13**

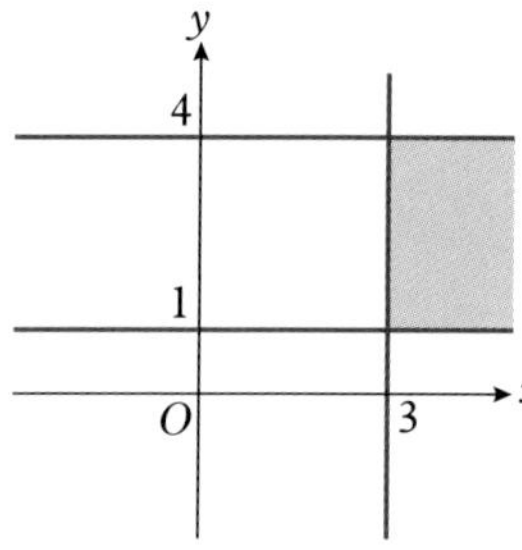

● **14**

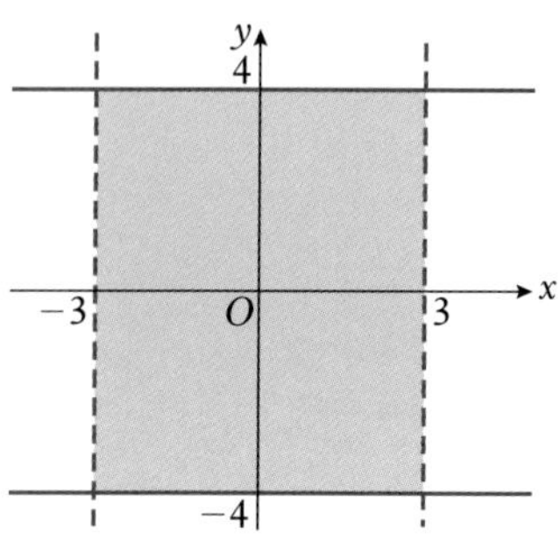

Inequalities with two variables

Sometimes, the lines that form the borders of the regions are not parallel to one of the axes. When this happens, the inequalities will have both x and y in them.

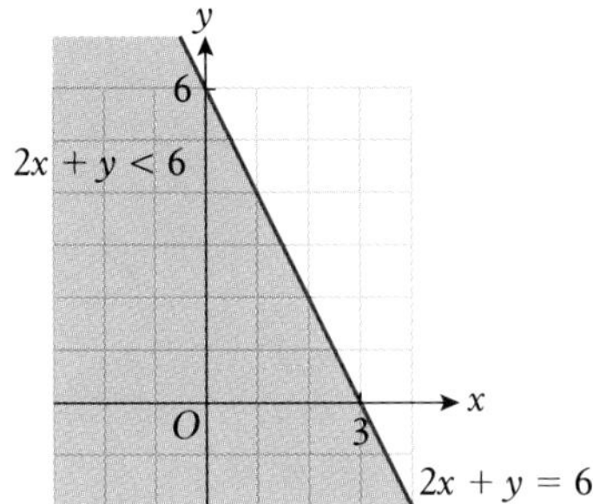

In this type of question, it can be more difficult to decide which side of the line you want. You often have to test a couple of points to help you to decide where to shade.

Example Draw a graph to show the inequality $3x + 2y < 12$

First draw the boundary line on the graph.
This is the line $3x + 2y = 12$

There is a quick way to draw lines when they are written in this way.
There is no need to write out a table of values.
To draw the line, just find the points where it crosses the axes.

The line crosses the y axis when $x = 0$
Putting $x = 0$ gives $2y = 12$ so $y = 6$
So the line crosses at (0, 6)

The line crosses the x axis when $y = 0$
Putting $y = 0$ gives $3x = 12$ so $x = 4$
So the line crosses at (4, 0)

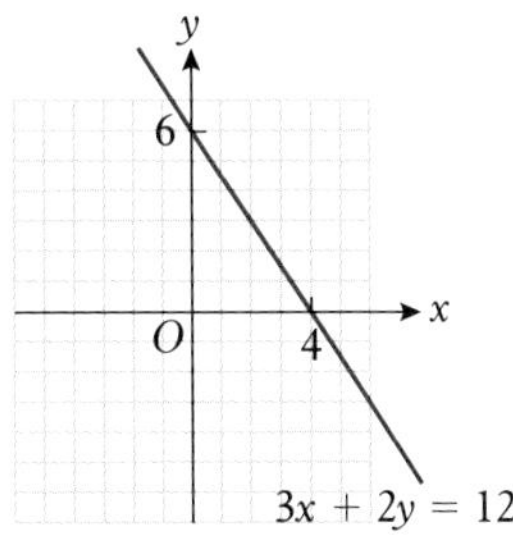

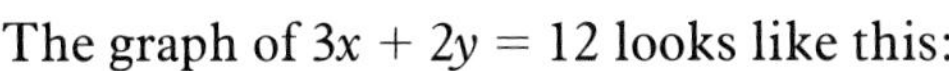

The graph of $3x + 2y = 12$ looks like this:

You now need to check which side of the line you want.
It may seem obvious in this case, but it isn't always!

Pick one point below the line and one point above it. Substitute the co-ordinates into the inequality:

Below the line: (0, 0) $\quad 3x + 2y$
$= 3 \times 0 + 2 \times 0$
$= 0$

This is **less** than 12

Above the line: (6, 6) $\quad 3x + 2y$
$= 3 \times 6 + 2 \times 6$
$= 30$

This is **greater** than 12

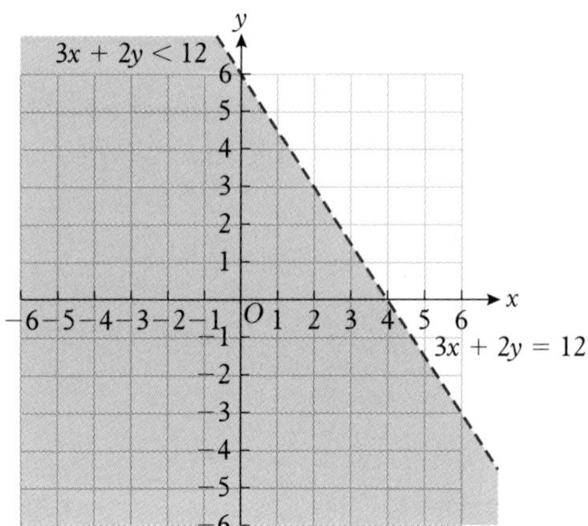

You want $3x + 2y$ to be less than 12 so the required region is **below** the line. The boundary should be drawn with a dashed line as it is not included.

Exercise 36:10

1 Follow these steps to show the region given by $3x + 5y < 15$

a Draw x and y axes from -6 to 6.

b Copy this. Fill it in.

The boundary line is $3x + 5y = 15$
The line crosses the y axis when $x = 0$.
Putting $x = 0$ gives $5y = \dots$ so $y = \dots$
So the line crosses at (…, …).

The line crosses the x axis when $y = 0$.
Putting $y = 0$ gives $3x = \dots$ so $x = \dots$
So the line crosses at (…, …).

c Draw the line $3x + 5y = 15$ onto your graph.

d Copy this. Fill it in.

Point below the line: (…, …) $\quad 3x + 5y$
$= \dots$
$= \dots$

This is … than 15

Point above the line: (…, …) $\quad 3x + 5y$
$= \dots$
$= \dots$

e Shade the required region.

2 Follow these steps to show the region given by $3x + 7y \geqslant 21$
  a Draw x and y axes from -8 to 8.
  b Write down the equation of the boundary line.
  c Find the point where the boundary line crosses the y axis.
  d Find the point where the boundary line crosses the x axis.
  e Draw the boundary line on your graph.
  f Test two points to see which region represents $3x + 7y \geqslant 21$
  g Shade and label the required region.

3 Draw graphs to show the regions defined by these inequalities.
  Label each region carefully.
  a $2x + y > 8$
  b $3x + 2y \leqslant 6$
  c $x + 2y < 10$
  d $3x - 5y \geqslant 15$
  e $2x + 3y - 12 \leqslant 0$
  f $2x + 3y > 18$
  ● **g** $2y > 3x - 9$
  ● **h** $y > x$

4 **a** Draw a graph of the line $y = 2x + 1$
  Use x values from -3 to 4
  b Shade the region where $y > 2x + 1$

5 Draw a graph to show the region $y < 3x - 4$
  Use x values from -4 to 4

Again, you need to be able to draw graphs that show more than one inequality. There can sometimes be three or even four separate inequalities to show on one diagram. It can become rather difficult to find the required region once the diagram is complete.
For this reason, it is sensible to shade the region you do **not** want.
This is called **shading out**.
It means that the region you want is the region left with no shading at all.

Example Show on a graph the region defined by the following set of inequalities: $x \geqslant 0$, $y \geqslant 0$, $x + y < 6$, $x + 3y > 6$

Separately, these inequalities are the unshaded regions shown:

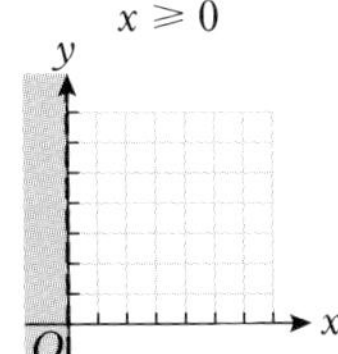

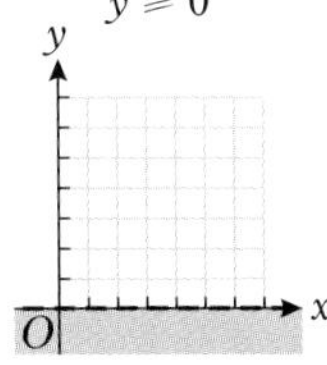

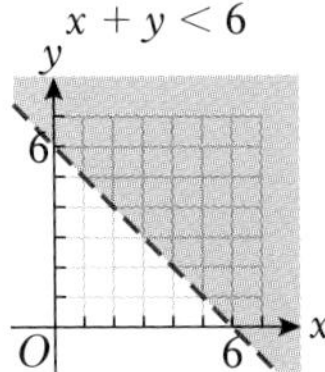

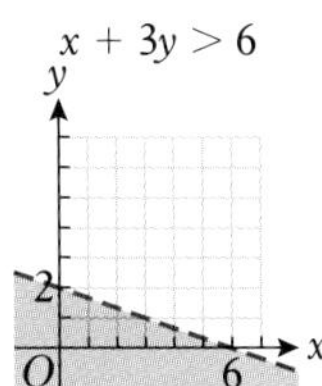

When you draw these on the same diagram, the area left white is the required region.

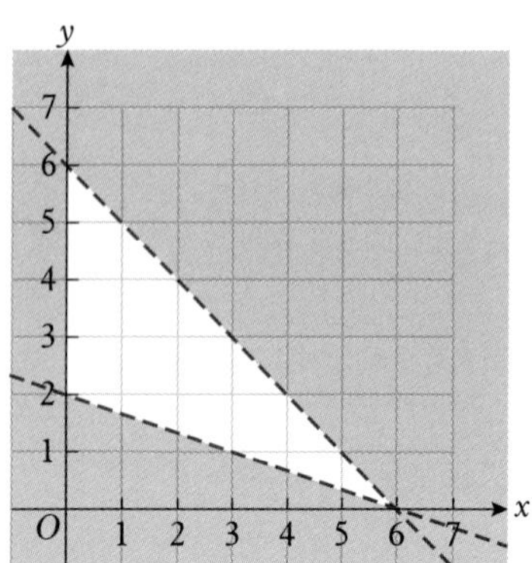

Exercise 36:11

Draw graphs to show the regions defined by these sets of inequalities.
Draw the x and y axes from -10 to 10.
Leave the required region unshaded.
Label each graph.

1	$x \geqslant 0$	$y \geqslant 0$	$x + 2y \leqslant 8$	
2	$x \geqslant 0$	$y \leqslant 0$	$x - 2y \leqslant 8$	
3	$y \geqslant 0$	$x < 6$	$y < x$	
4	$x \geqslant 0$	$y \geqslant 0$	$x + 2y \leqslant 10$	
5	$x + 2y < 6$	$y > x$	$x > -2$	
6	$y > 2x$	$y < 3x$	$x + y > 4$	$x + y < 9$
● **7**	$y > \frac{x}{3}$	$y < 6 - 2x$	$y < 2.5x$	

Solving problems using inequalities

Many real life problems involve the use of limited quantities of materials or resources. These can range from allocating staff to jobs or buying stock from a limited budget. Inequalities can often be used to solve these problems.

In the next exercise, you will see how inequalities can be used to solve problems. You will need the skills you have learnt in the first part of the chapter.

Example A property developer has a plot of land with area 5400 m^2.
He builds two types of house.
The 3 bedroomed Family requires an area of 450 m^2.
The 4 bedroomed Executive requires an area of 600 m^2
He wants to build at least 3 Family houses and at least 4 Executive houses.

a Write down inequalities which describe the restrictions on the builder.
b Draw a graph to show the possible combinations of the two types of house which he can build.
c On your graph, circle all the possible combinations.

a First give letters to each type of house.
Say that the developer builds f Family houses and e Executive houses.
Now write down the inequalities.

He wants to build at least 3 Family houses so	$f \geqslant 3$
He wants to build at least 4 Executive houses so	$e \geqslant 4$
The total area taken up by the Family houses is	$450f$
The total area taken up by the Executive houses is	$600e$
The total area taken up by both types of house is	$450f + 600e$
The builder only has 5400 m^2 so	$450f + 600e \leqslant 5400$
This can be simplified by dividing by 150 to give	$3f + 4e \leqslant 36$

b The graph of these inequalities looks like this:

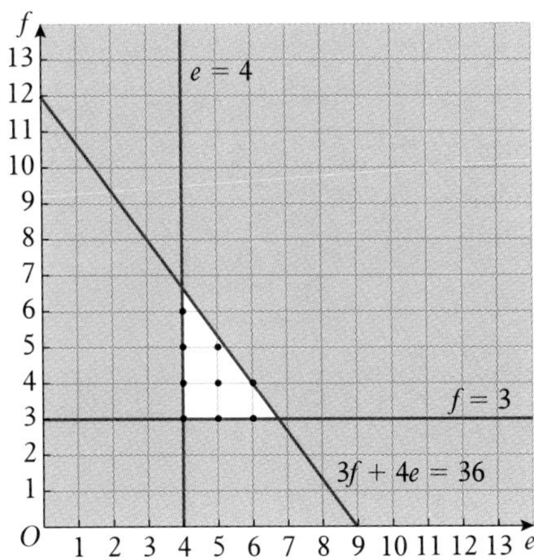

c Each point that is circled shows possible values of e and f as co-ordinates.
The point (5, 4) is circled so the builder could build 5 Executive houses and 4 Family houses.
The maximum number of houses he can build is 10.
He can build 4 Executive and 6 Family houses or 6 Executive and 4 Family houses.

Exercise 36:12

1 Alan wants to buy a combination of chart singles on CD and tape.
CDs cost £4 and tapes cost £3.
He has £24 to spend altogether.
He wants to buy at least one of each type of single.

a Copy each of these. Complete each one with an inequality.
Call the number of tapes t and the number of CDs c.

Alan buys at least one CD so ....
Alan buys at least one tape so ....

The total cost of the CDs is ....
The total cost of the tapes is ....
The total cost of the tapes and CDs must not be more than £24 so ....

b Draw x and y axes from 0 to 8.
Draw a graph showing all of the inequalities you have written down in part **a**.
Put t on the vertical axis and c on the horizontal axis.

c Alan decides to buy 4 tapes.
Write down the possible numbers of CDs he can buy.

2 Fred the farmer needs to re-stock.
He wants to buy at least 30 sheep and at least 12 cows.
Sheep cost £40 and cows cost £70.
He has £5600 to spend altogether.

a Copy and complete these three inequalities that describe the constraints on Fred.

He wants to buy at least 30 sheep so ....
He wants to buy at least 12 cows so ....
He must not spend more than £5600 so ....

b Draw a graph showing all of the inequalities you have written down in part **a**.

c Fred decides he wants to buy as near equal numbers of cows and sheep as possible. He also wants to spend as much of his money as possible. How many of each animal can he buy?

3 A radio DJ has to play a mixture of Chart Hits and Golden Oldies. He can only fit 35 records into his show. He wants to play at least 10 of each. Royalties on Chart Hits are £50 per record but on Golden Oldies are only £30 per record. The budget for the show is £1400.

a Write down four inequalities to describe these constraints.

b Draw a graph showing all of the inequalities you have written down in part **a**.

c What is the largest number of Chart Hits that the DJ can play?

More complex inequalities

It is possible to use graphs to solve inequalities that would be quite difficult to solve using algebra.

These can involve quite complicated functions. You will need to sketch or plot a graph of the function like you did in Chapters 25 and 30.

Example **a** Sketch a graph of $y = x^2 + 5x - 6$
b Use your graph to solve the inequality $x^2 + 5x - 6 > 0$

a First solve $x^2 + 5x - 6 = 0$

$x^2 + 5x - 6 = 0$
$(x - 1)(x + 6) = 0$
$x = 1$ or $x = -6$
This means that the graph cuts the x axis at $x = 1$ and $x = -6$

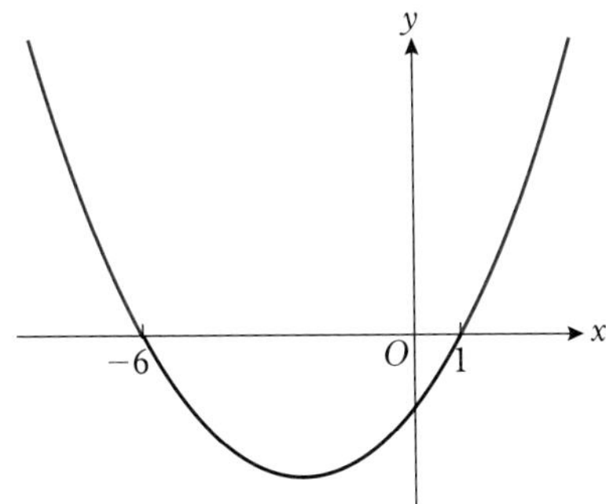

b You want to know when $x^2 + 5x - 6 > 0$
This is when $x^2 + 5x - 6$ is positive.
$x^2 + 5x - 6$ is positive when the **curve is above the x axis.**
So $x^2 + 5x - 6 > 0$ when $x > 1$ or when $x < -6$

Exercise 36:13

1 Look at this sketch graph of $y = x^2 - x - 6$
Use the graph to solve the inequality $x^2 - x - 6 > 0$

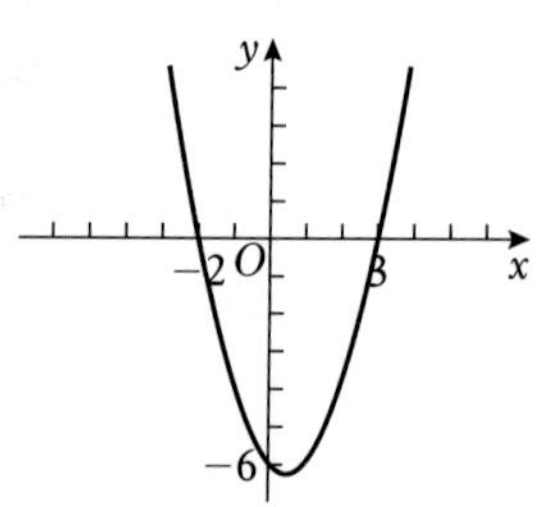

2 Look at this sketch graph of $y = 9 - x^2$
Use the graph to solve the inequality $9 - x^2 > 0$

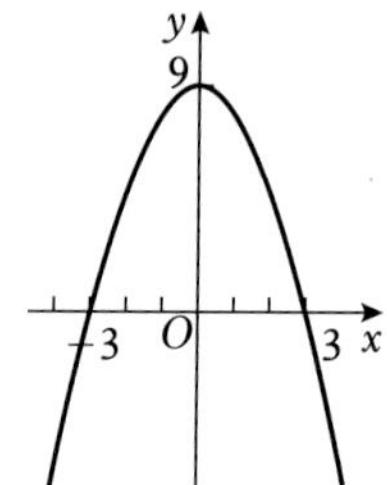

3 Look at this sketch graph of $y = x^2 - 3x$
Use the graph to solve the inequality $x^2 - 3x < 0$

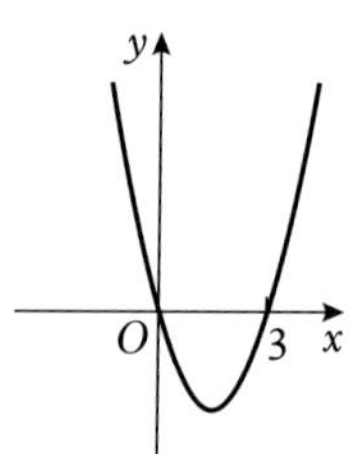

• **4** **a** Copy and complete this table for $y = x^2 - 2x - 2$

x	−5	−4	−3	−2	−1	0	1	2	3	4	5
y											

b Plot the graph of $y = x^2 - 2x - 2$ from your table.
Draw axes with x from −5 to 5 and y from −5 to 30.

c Copy and complete this table for $y = 2x + 2$

x	−5	−4	−3	−2	−1	0	1	2	3	4	5
y											

d Draw the graph of $y = 2x + 2$ over the top of your graph from part **b**.

e Write down the x co-ordinates of the points of intersection of the curve and the line to 1 dp.

f Use your answers to solve the inequality $x^2 - 2x + 2 > 2x + 2$

1 Write down inequalities to describe each of these number lines.

a

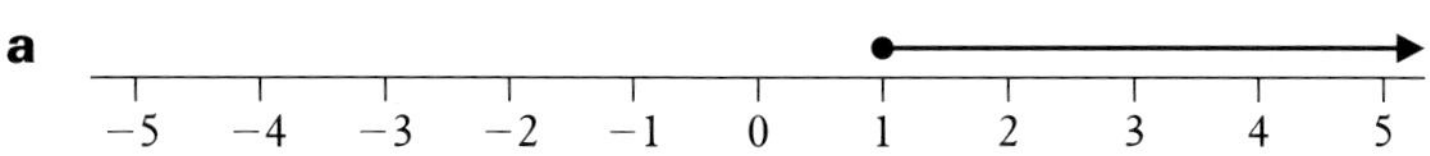

b

−5 −4 −3 −2 −1 0 1 2 3 4 5

2 Solve each of these inequalities.

a $2x < 18$

b $z - 7 > 14$

c $2x - 10 \leqslant 8$

d $2r + 2.8 > 6$

e $5(4t - 10) < 20$

f $\dfrac{8x - 2}{5} \leqslant 6$

g $4x - 7 > 2x + 19$

h $3k - 8 < 7 - 2k$

3 Solve each of these inequalities.

a $4 < x - 4 < 10$

b $18 \leqslant 3p \leqslant 27$

c $63 \geqslant x - 3 > 72$

d $96 \leqslant 8y + 12 \leqslant 108$

e $-15 < 3z + 3 < -6$

f $-2 \leqslant 2(2x + 5) \leqslant 6$

g $18 \leqslant \dfrac{2x - 6}{3} \leqslant 20$

4 Draw a graph to illustrate each of these inequalities.
Shade the region where each inequality is true.

a $y \geqslant 4$ **b** $y > -3$ **c** $-6 \leqslant x \leqslant 1$

5 For each of the following graphs, write down the inequality that describes the shaded region.

a

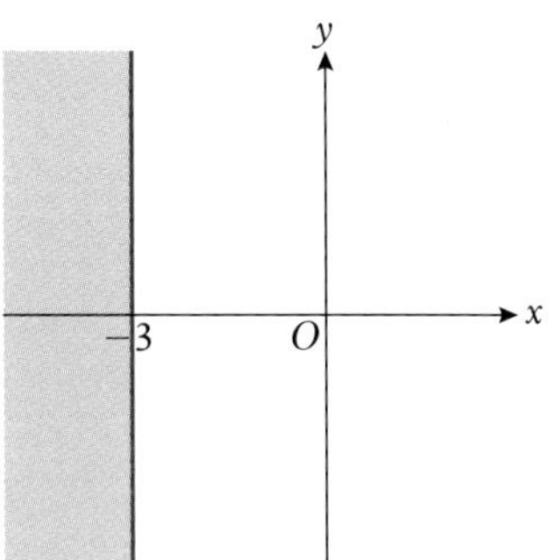

b

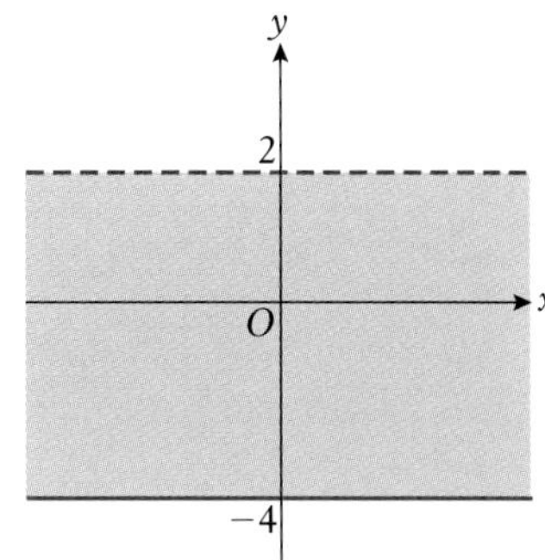

6 Draw graphs to show the regions defined by these inequalities.

a $2x + y > 10$ **c** $2x - 3y - 6 \leqslant 0$

b $3x + 4y \leqslant 12$ **d** $y > 2x + 4$

7 Draw graphs to show the regions defined by these sets of inequalities.
Leave the required region unshaded.
Label each graph.

a $x \geqslant 0$ $y \geqslant 0$ $x + 3y \leqslant 9$

b $x \geqslant 1$ $y \geqslant 2$ $x + 2y \leqslant 10$

c $x \geqslant 2$ $y \leqslant 10$ $x - 2y \leqslant 6$

8 Look at this sketch graph of $y = x^2 + 2x - 15$
Use your graph to solve the inequality $x^2 + 2x - 15 < 0$

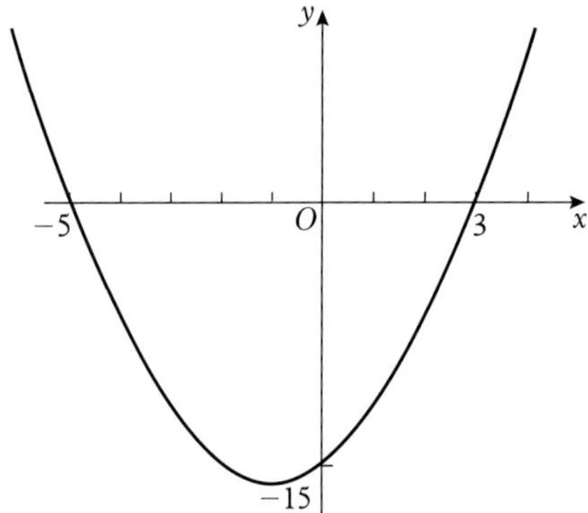

9 Mr Grout is tiling his bathroom.
He is using two types of tiles.
Blank tiles cost £2 each and patterned tiles cost £3 each.
He has a maximum of £600 to spend on tiles.
He has decided to use at least 100 blank tiles and at least 50 patterned tiles.

a Copy and complete these three inequalities that describe the constraints on Mr Grout. Use ***b*** for blank tiles and ***p*** for patterned tiles.

He wants to buy at least 100 blank tiles so ....
He wants to buy at least 50 patterned tiles so ....
He must not spend more than £600 so ....

b Draw a graph showing all of the inequalities you have written down in **a**.

c What is the maximum number of patterned tiles that Mr Grout can buy?

1 A computer company makes two types of laser printer.
The details are given in this table.

	Model DB30	Model DB50
Cost to produce	£120	£90
Worker hours	2	2.5
Machine hours	3	4
Profit	£15	£20

In any one day, the factory has 80 worker hours and 150 machine hours available. They have £3600 to spend on production each day.

a Write down inequalities to describe the constraints described above.

b Draw a graph to show these inequalities.

c What combination of printers should the company make in order to make the most profit?

2 **a** Draw a graph to solve the equation $x^2 + 5x + 6 = 0$
Draw your x axis from -4 to $+2$ and your y axis from -5 to 15.

b Use your graph to solve $x^2 + 5x + 6 > 2$

c By drawing the line $y = -x$ on your graph, solve the inequality $x^2 + 5x + 6 > -x$

3 A lorry is loaded with two different sizes of box. Small boxes have a volume of 2 m^3 whilst large boxes have a volume of 3.5 m^3. The lorry has a maximum capacity of 70 m^3.
The small boxes weigh 30 kg and the large boxes weigh 40 kg. The total weight of the load must not exceed 1225 kg.

a Write down four inequalities to describe these constraints.

b Draw a graph showing all of the inequalities you have written down in part **a**.

c What is the maximum number of large boxes that the lorry can carry?

1 Write down inequalities to describe each of these number lines.

a

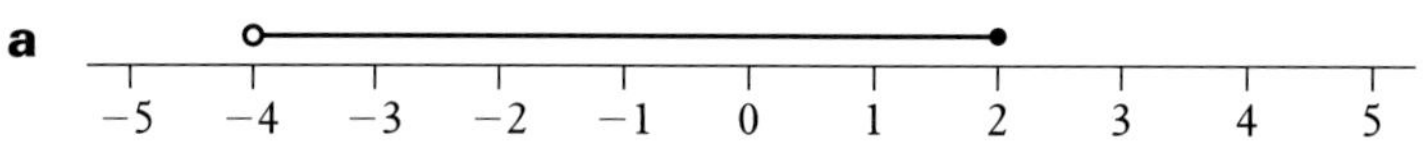

b

−5 −4 −3 −2 −1 0 1 2 3 4 5

c

−5 −4 −3 −2 −1 0 1 2 3 4 5

2 List the integers that are included in each of these inequalities.

a $2 < x \leqslant 5$
b $-3 \leqslant x < 1$
c $-5 \leqslant x \leqslant -1$
d $-3 < x < 3$

3 Solve each of these inequalities.

a $x - 3 < 8$
b $2x + 5 \geqslant 17$
c $4x - 7 \leqslant 12$
d $\frac{x}{4} - 9 > 2.3$
e $\frac{3x + 1}{5} < -4$
f $5x + 11 \geqslant 3x + 7$

4 Solve each of these inequalities.

a $11 - x > 3$
b $\frac{5 - 2x}{7} < -3$
c $3x + 7 \leqslant 8x - 9$
d $10 - 3x \geqslant -2x + 6$

5 Solve each of these inequalities.

a $6 \leqslant 3x < 12$
b $11 < x + 7 \leqslant 19$
c $5 \leqslant 2x - 1 \leqslant 11$
d $-10 < -5x < 0$

6 Write down the inequality that describes the shaded region on each of these graphs.

a

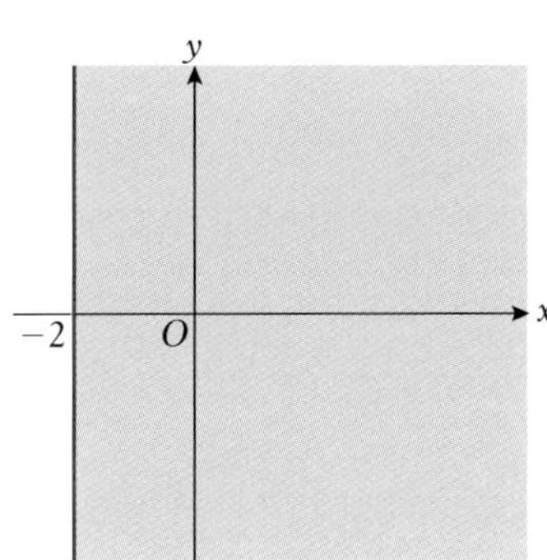

b

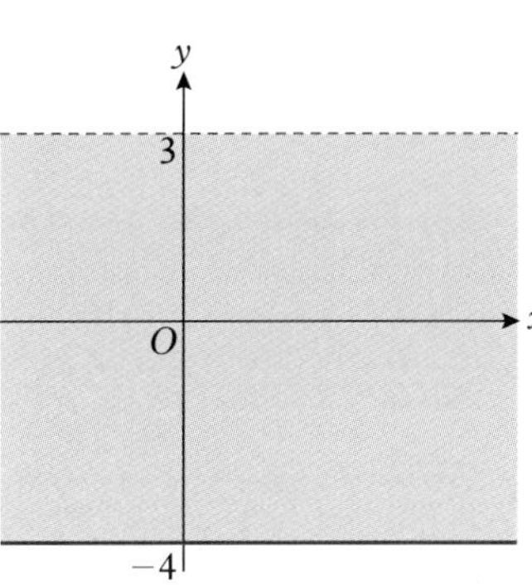

7 Write down inequalities to describe the shaded region on each of these graphs.

a

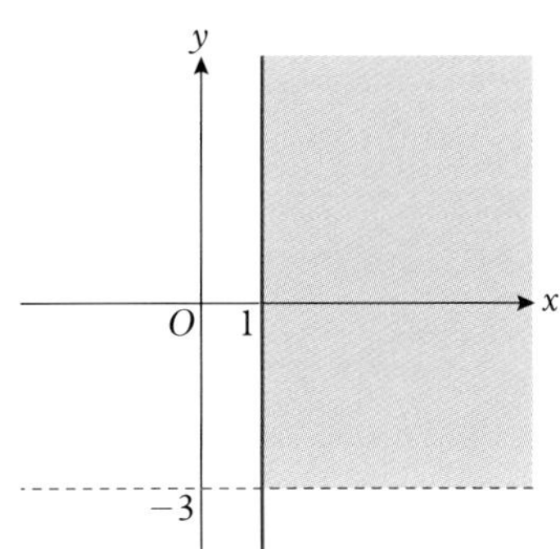

b

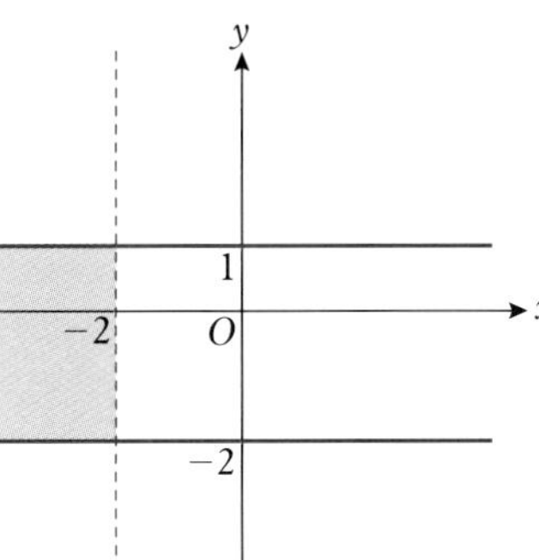

8 Look at this sketch graph of $y = x^2 - 3x + 2$
Use the graph to solve the inequality $x^2 - 3x + 2 > 0$

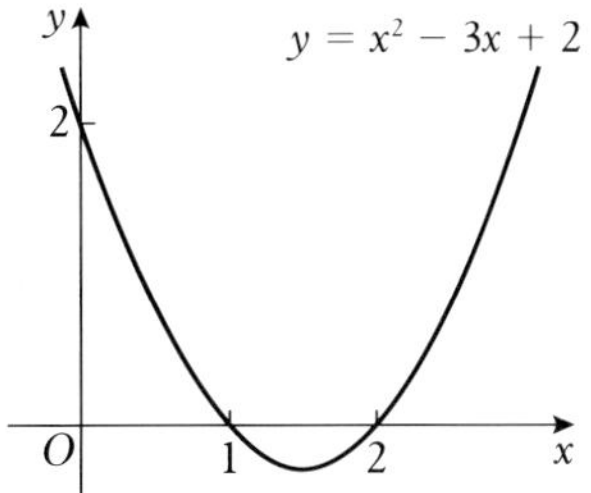

9 A bakery makes both sliced and unsliced loaves of bread. The maximum number of loaves it can make in a day is 800. The number of sliced loaves made is always at least double the number of unsliced loaves. At least 200 unsliced loaves must be made.

a Explain the inequality $s + u \leqslant 800$.

b Write down four other inequalities to describe the situation.

c Draw a graph to show all of the inequalities.

d What is the maximum number of unsliced loaves that can be made?

CHAPTER 16

1 $11 \times 1 = 11$
$11 \times 2 = 22$
$11 \times 3 = 33$
$11 \times 4 = 44$
$11 \times 5 = 55$

The first 5 terms are 11, 22, 33, 44, 55

2 **a** $6n$ **b** $9n$

3 The sequence for $5n$ is 5, 10, 15, 20, 25

a You need to add 1 to each term of the sequence $5n$.
The formula is $5n + 1$.

b You need to subtract 3 from each term of the sequence $5n$.
The formula is $5n - 3$.

4 **a**

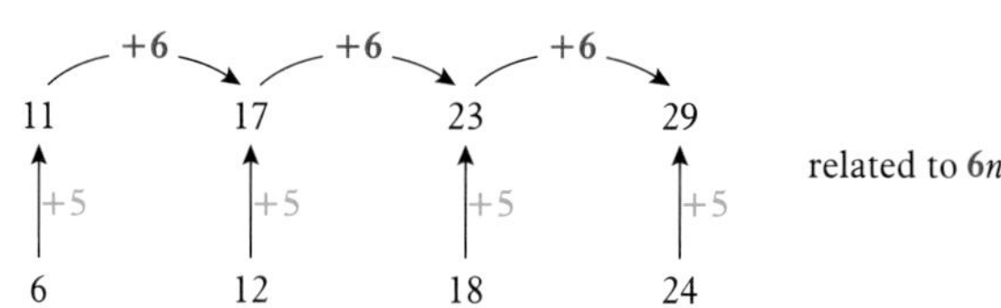

b The formula is $6n + 5$.

5 **a**

b 5, 8, 11, 14

c

+3 +3 +3

5 8 11 14 related to $3n$

+2 +2 +2 +2

Sequence $3n$ 3 6 9 12

The formula is $3n + 2$.

6 **a** $n = 1$ $6 \times 1 - 5 = 1$
$n = 2$ $6 \times 2 - 5 = 7$
$n = 3$ $6 \times 3 - 5 = 13$
The first 3 terms are 1, 7, 13.

b $n = 20$ $6 \times 20 - 5 = 115$

c $6n - 5 = 55$
$6n = 60$
$n = 10$
i.e. the 10th term is 55.

7 **a** $3n + 4 = 10$
$3n = 6$
$n = 2$

b $3n + 4 = 19$
$3n = 15$
$n = 5$

c $3n + 4 = 28$
$3n = 24$
$n = 8$

d $3n + 4 = 304$
$3n = 300$
$n = 100$

8 **a** $4g - 3 = 21$
$4g = 24$
$g = 6$

b $\frac{x}{5} + 6 = 10$
$\frac{x}{5} = 4$
$x = 20$

c $8x = 5x - 12$
$3x = -12$
$x = -4$

d $3a + 13 = 5a$
$13 = 2a$
$6.5 = a$
$a = 6.5$

e $14s - 5 = 9s + 20$
$5s - 5 = 20$
$5s = 25$
$s = 5$

f $\frac{24}{x} = 8$
$24 = 8x$
$3 = x$
$x = 3$

g $6d + 8 = 29 - d$
$7d + 8 = 29$
$7d = 21$
$d = 3$

h $7(3x - 12) = 42$
$21x - 84 = 42$
$21x = 126$
$x = 6$

9 **a** $14 + 2x + 4x - 10 = 6x + 4$
b $6x + 4 = 34$
c $6x = 30$
$x = 5$
d 14 cm, $2x = 2 \times 5 = 10$ cm, $4x - 10 = 4 \times 5 - 10 = 20 - 10 = 10$ cm
e isosceles

10

x	$x^3 - 9x$	
5	80	too small
12	1701	too big
10	910	too big
9	648	too small
9.5	771.9	too small
9.8	853.0	too big
9.75	839.1	too small
9.78	847.4	too small
9.79	850.2	too big
9.785	848.8	too small

so $x = 9.79$ (2 dp)

CHAPTER 17

1 **a** A(−2, 1), B(4, 0), C(3, −4), D(0, −3)
b P: $y = 3$ Q: $x = 2$ R: $y = -2$ S: $x = -4$
c (1) $y = 0$ (2) $x = 0$
d (2.5, 2)

2 **a** 5 squares to the left and 3 squares down or $\begin{pmatrix}-5\\-3\end{pmatrix}$

b

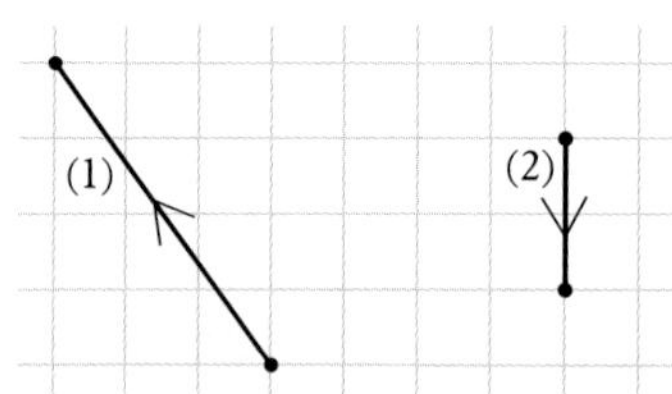

3

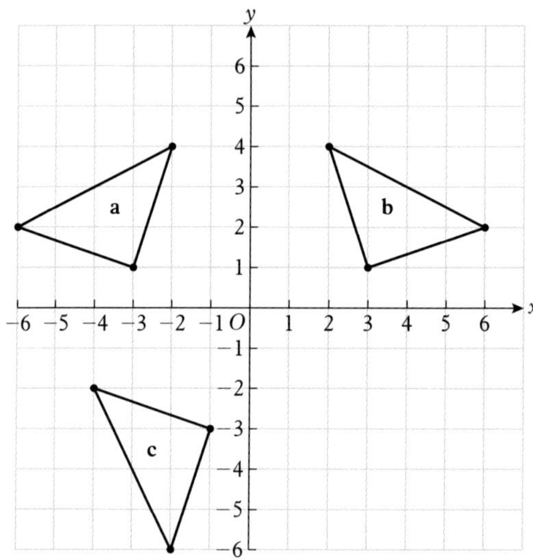

4 **a** a translation 3 squares down and 2 squares to the right

b a translation of $\begin{pmatrix}-3\\4\end{pmatrix}$

c a rotation of 270° anticlockwise about the point (2, −3)

5 **a, b**

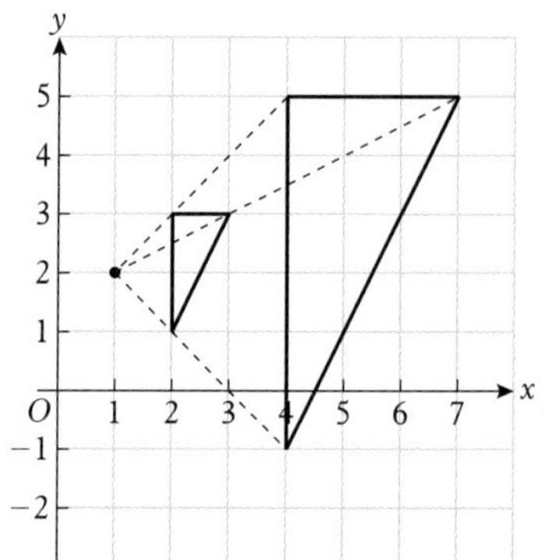

6 a, b, c

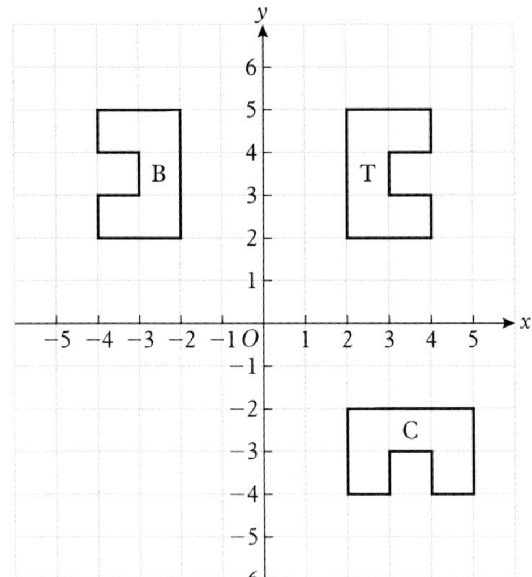

d Reflection in the line $y = x$

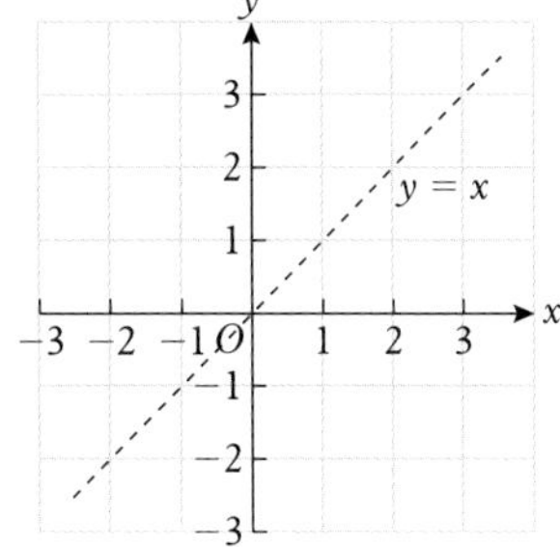

CHAPTER 18

1 a $\text{gradient} = \dfrac{\text{vertical change}}{\text{horizontal change}}$

$= \dfrac{2}{2} = 1$

b $\text{gradient} = \dfrac{-4}{2} = -2$

2 a $\dfrac{11 - 3}{4 - 2} = \dfrac{8}{2} = 4$

b $\dfrac{3 - 9}{2 - 0} = \dfrac{-6}{2} = -3$

3 a $y = 5x - 3$

b $y = -2x$

4 a 3 **b** 1 **c** -6

5 a -7 **b** 1 **c** 0

6 Any line where the number multiplying x is 7
e.g. $y = 7x + 4$, $y = 7x$, $y = 7x - 10$ etc.

7 a $y = 3x + 1$

b $y = -x + 3$

8 a $a = £10$

b $b = \text{gradient} = \dfrac{60 - 10}{25 - 0} = \dfrac{50}{25} = £2$

9 $5x - 2y = 10$

when $y = 0$, $5x = 10$
$x = 2$

when $x = 0$, $-2y = 10$
$y = -5$

$\therefore$ Plot points (2, 0) and (0, −5) and join them to give the line.

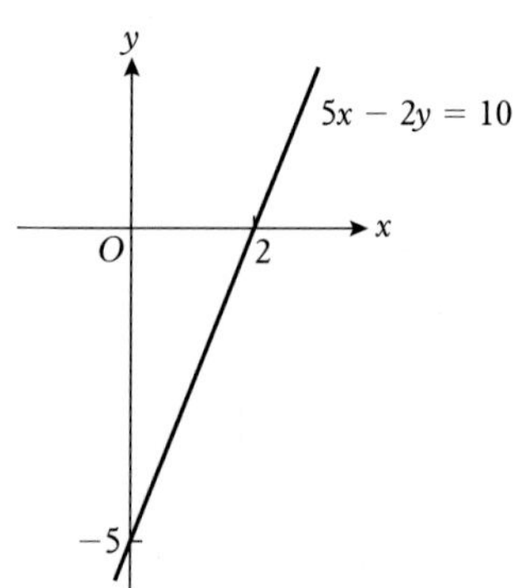

10 **a** not linear (x^2 term) **b** linear **c** not linear $\left(\frac{4}{x} \text{ term}\right)$

CHAPTER 19

1

a

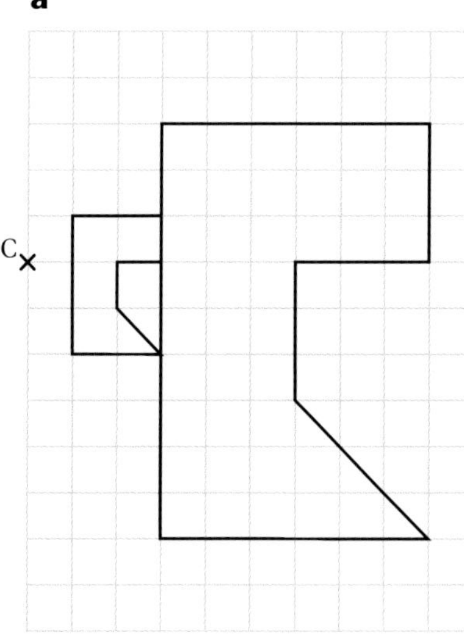

b

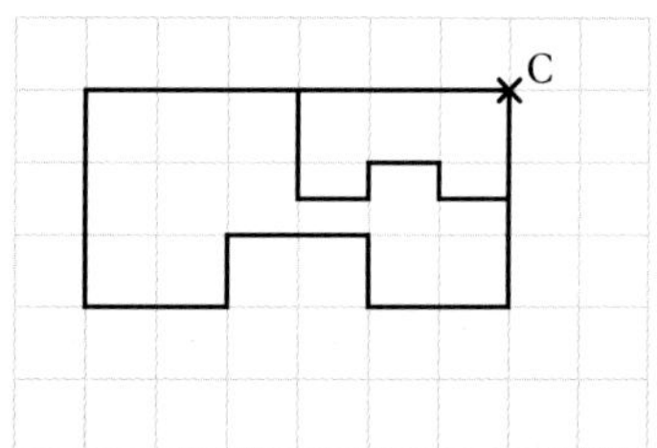

2 Scale factor $= 32 \div 8 = 4$
$a = 5 \times 4 = 20$ cm
$b = 9.5 \times 4 = 38$ cm
$c \times 4 = 48$ cm so $c = 48 \div 4 = 12$ cm

3 $8.5 \text{ cm} \times 5 = 42.5$ cm

4 **a** 30 000 cm = 300 m = 0.3 km

b $7 \times 0.3 = 2.1$ km

5 **a**

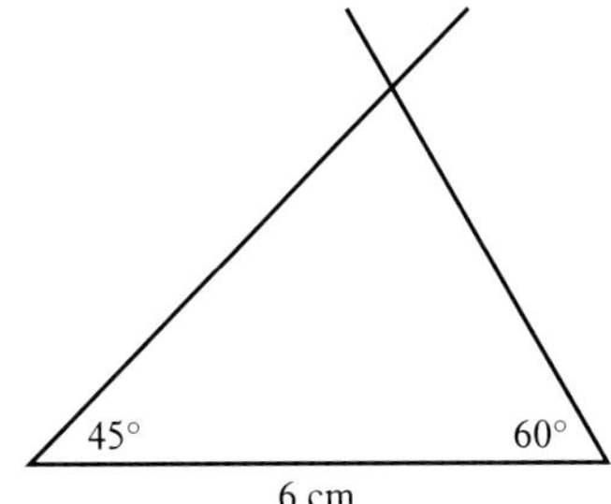

b

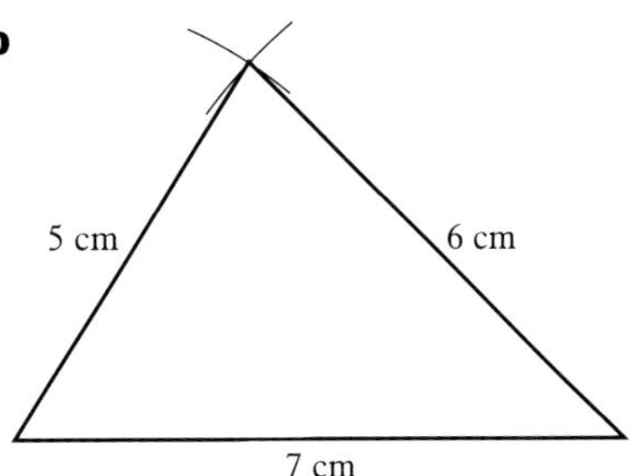

CHAPTER 20

1 **a** 25 min 1 hour

4.35 5 6

1 hour 25 min

b 35 min + 40 min = 75 min = 1 hour 15 min

c 3 hours − 1 hour = 2 hours, 2 hours − 15 min = 1 hour 45 min

2 **a** $200 \times 4 = 800$ km

b $200 \div 2 = 100$ km

c 12 min = $\frac{12}{60}$ hour = $\frac{1}{5}$ hour; $200 \div 5 = 40$ km

3 **a** $\text{Speed} = \dfrac{\text{Distance}}{\text{Time}} = \dfrac{130}{2.5} = 52$ km/hour

b 40 min = $\frac{2}{3}$ hour

$\text{Speed} = \dfrac{\text{Distance}}{\text{Time}} = \dfrac{43}{\frac{2}{3}} = 43 \div \frac{2}{3} = 43 \times \frac{3}{2} = 64.5$ miles/hour

4 **a** 420 chocolates per hour

b 7 chocolates per minute ($420 \div 60$)

c 60 seconds $\div 7 = 8.6$ seconds (1 dp)

5

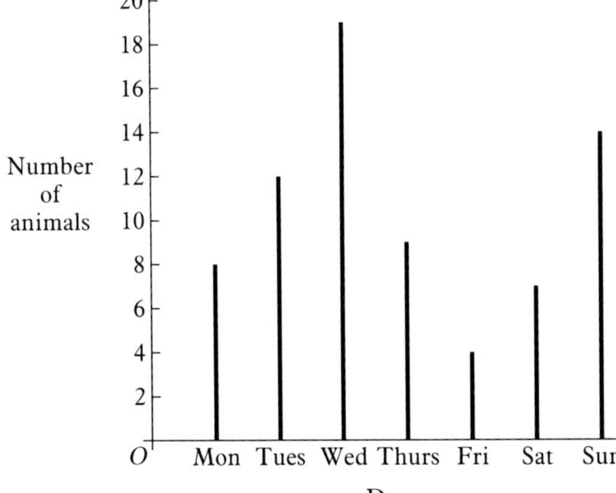

6 **a** 9 km
b 45 min (each square across is 15 min).
c $\frac{1}{2}$ hour (or 30 min)
d $\text{Speed} = \frac{\text{Distance}}{\text{Time}} = \frac{9}{\frac{1}{2}} = 18 \text{ km/hour}$
e $\text{Average speed} = \frac{9+9}{2 \text{ hours } 45 \text{ min}} = \frac{18}{2.75} = 6.5 \text{ km/hour (1 dp)}$

7 **a** £4 **b** Peter lives between 20 and 40 miles from the warehouse.

CHAPTER 21

1 $\tan a = \frac{\text{opp}}{\text{adj}} = \frac{25}{31}$
$a = 38.9° \text{ (1 dp)}$

$\tan c = \frac{\text{opp}}{\text{adj}} = \frac{45}{65}$
$c = 34.7° \text{ (1 dp)}$

$\sin b = \frac{\text{opp}}{\text{hyp}} = \frac{16}{19}$
$b = 57.4° \text{ (1 dp)}$

$\cos d = \frac{\text{adj}}{\text{hyp}} = \frac{4.9}{7.4}$
$d = 48.5° \text{ (1 dp)}$

2 $\sin x = \frac{\text{opp}}{\text{hyp}} = \frac{147}{680}$
$x = 12.5° \text{ (1 dp)}$

3 $\sin 64° = \frac{\text{opp}}{\text{hyp}} = \frac{a}{35}$
$a = 35 \sin 64°$
$= 31.5 \text{ mm (3 sf)}$

$\cos 25° = \frac{\text{adj}}{\text{hyp}} = \frac{c}{156}$
$c = 156 \cos 25°$
$= 141 \text{ m (3 sf)}$

$\cos 74° = \frac{\text{adj}}{\text{hyp}} = \frac{b}{12.5}$
$b = 12.5 \times \cos 74°$
$= 3.45 \text{ cm (3 sf)}$

$\tan 35° = \frac{\text{opp}}{\text{adj}} = \frac{d}{45}$
$d = 45 \tan 35°$
$= 31.5 \text{ cm (3 sf)}$

4 $\tan x = \frac{\text{opp}}{\text{adj}} = \frac{14}{8.5}$
$x = 58.7° \text{ (1 dp)}$

5 $\tan x = \frac{\text{opp}}{\text{adj}} = \frac{15}{21}$
$x = 35.5376\ldots$
$= 36°$ to nearest degree.

Bearing is 036°.

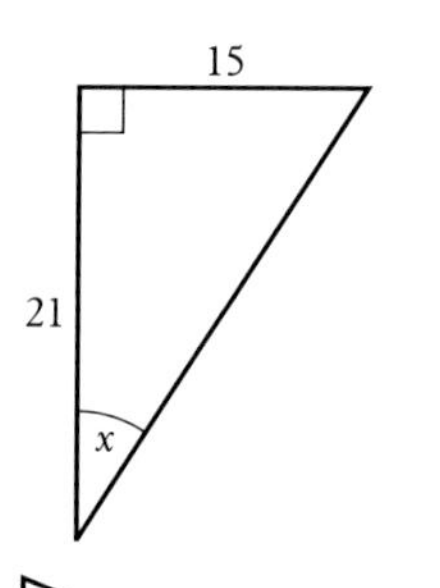

6 $\sin 60° = \frac{\text{opp}}{\text{hyp}} = \frac{x}{35}$
$x = 35 \sin 60°$
$= 30.3 \text{ cm (3 sf)}$

7 $\sin 43° = \frac{\text{opp}}{\text{hyp}} = \frac{h}{532}$

$h = 532 \times \sin 43$

$= 363$ m (3 sf)

8 **a** $\tan x = \frac{\text{opp}}{\text{adj}} = \frac{28}{12}$

$x = 66.8°$ (1 dp)

b $\tan y = \frac{\text{opp}}{\text{adj}} = \frac{12}{6}$

$y = 63.4°$ (1 dp)

532 h 43° P 28 x O 12 y 9 − 3 = 6 14 − 2 = 12

CHAPTER 22

1 **a** $7k$ **b** $13x - 1y = 13x - y$ **c** $5d + 6d^2 - 12$ **d** $3a^2b - 2ab^2$

2 **a** $4y - 20$ **c** $12s^2 - 2s$ **e** $2x^2 + 15x - 8$

b $3x^2 + 6x$ **d** $8b^3 + b^2$ **f** $20x^2 - 41x + 9$

3 **a** $4x - 3 + 2x + 1 + x + 7 + 19 - 3x = 4x + 24$

b $4x + 24 = 38$

$4x = 14$

$x = \frac{14}{4}$

$= 3\frac{1}{2}$

c $4x - 3 = 14 - 3 = 11$; $19 - 3x = 19 - 10\frac{1}{2} = 8\frac{1}{2}$;

$2x + 1 = 7 + 1 = 8$; $x + 7 = 3\frac{1}{2} + 7 = 10\frac{1}{2}$

4 $(4x + 7)(2x - 3) = 8x^2 - 12x + 14x - 21 = 8x^2 + 2x - 21$

5 **a** $2(3t - 2)$ **b** $4y(3y + 1)$ **c** $2ab(12b + 5)$ **d** $3x(4x - 2y + 3y^2)$

6 **a** $\frac{16\cancel{x}}{\cancel{x}} = 16$ **c** $\frac{\overset{1}{\cancel{7}}\cancel{(x^2 - 1)}}{\underset{2}{\cancel{14}}\cancel{(x^2 - 1)}} = \frac{1}{2}$ **e** $\frac{4x + 20}{3(x + 5)} = \frac{4\cancel{(x + 5)}}{3\cancel{(x + 5)}} = \frac{4}{3}$

b $\frac{2a}{5}$ **d** $\frac{\overset{2}{\cancel{6}}(x + 2)\cancel{(x - 1)}}{\underset{1}{\cancel{3}}\cancel{(x - 1)}} = 2(x + 2)$ **f** $\frac{4x - 2}{6x - 3} = \frac{2\cancel{(2x - 1)}}{3\cancel{(2x - 1)}} = \frac{2}{3}$

7 **a** $(x + 4)(x - 3)$ **b** $(a + 1)(a + 7)$ **c** $(y - 2)(y - 8)$ **d** $(x - 9)(x + 9)$

CHAPTER 23

1 **a** diameter = 2 × radius = 2 × 16 = 32 cm

circumference = π × diameter

= π × 32 = 100.53 … cm

= 101 cm (3 sf)

b 4 km = 4000 m = 400 000 cm.

Number of revolutions = 400 000 ÷ 100.53 … = 3978.91 …

Number of **complete** revolutions = 3978.

2 Circumference = $\pi \times 16 = 50.265 \ldots$
arc = circumference ÷ 4 = $50.265 \ldots \div 4 = 12.566 \ldots = 12.6$ cm (3 sf)
Perimeter = 8 + 8 + 12.6
= 28.6 cm (3 sf)

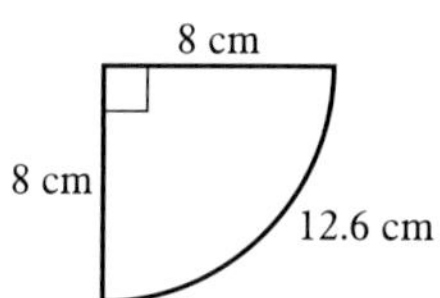

3

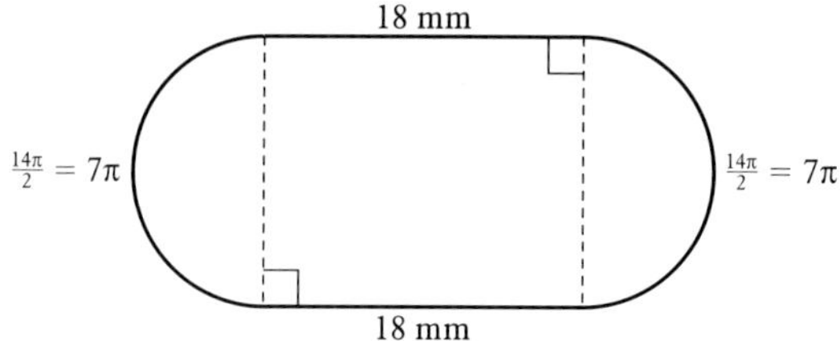

Circumference of circle = $\pi \times 14 = 14\pi$
Circumference of half circle = $14\pi \div 2 = 7\pi$
Perimeter = $7\pi + 18 + 7\pi + 18 = 14\pi + 36$ mm

4 **a** 4.7 cm
b 720 cm
c 36 ÷ 12 = 3 feet
d 4 × 3 = 12 feet
e 7 × 1760 = 12 320 yards
f 6.5 × 3 = 19.5 feet = 19.5 × 12 = 234 inches

5 **a** 1 foot = 12 inches = 12 × 2.54 = 30.48 cm
b 2 yards = 2 × 3 = 6 feet = 6 × 12 = 72 inches = 72 × 2.54 = 182.88 cm
c 20 yards = 60 feet = 720 inches = 1828.8 cm = 18.288 m
d 3 m = 300 cm = 300 ÷ 2.54 inches = 118 inches (3 sf)

CHAPTER 24

1 **a** 27 + 37 = 64 cm^2
b 98 − 40 = 58 m^2

2 **a** By Pythagoras' theorem
$a^2 = 38^2 + 29^2$
$= 2285$
$a = 47.8$ cm (3 sf)

b By Pythagoras' theorem
$42^2 = b^2 + 31^2$
$b^2 = 42^2 - 31^2$
$= 803$
$b = 28.3$ mm (3 sf)

c By Pythagoras' theorem
$c^2 = (\sqrt{7})^2 + (\sqrt{18})^2$
$= 7 + 18$
$= 25$
$c = 5$ cm

d By Pythagoras' theorem
$15^2 = d^2 + 8^2$
$d^2 = 15^2 - 8^2$
$= 161$
$d = 12.7$ cm (3 sf)

3 **a** 5 because $3^2 + 4^2 = 5^2$
b 24 because $7^2 + 24^2 = 25^2$
c 5 because $5^2 + 12^2 = 13^2$
d 15 because $8^2 + 15^2 = 17^2$

4 $\text{OR}^2 = 4^2 + 3^2$
$= 25$
$\text{OR} = 5$

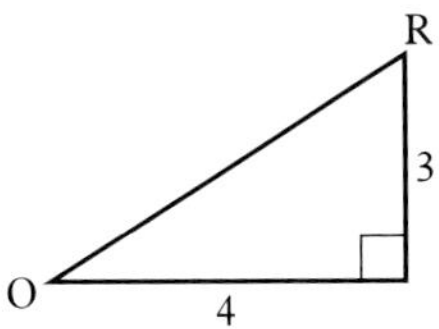

5 $\text{PQ}^2 = 5^2 + 10^2$
$= 125$
$\text{PQ} = 11.2$ (3 sf)

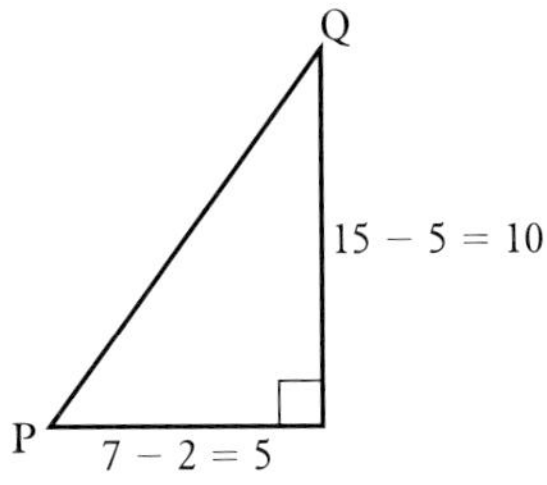

6 $x^2 = 18^2 + 23^2$
$= 853$
$x = 29.2$ cm (3 sf)

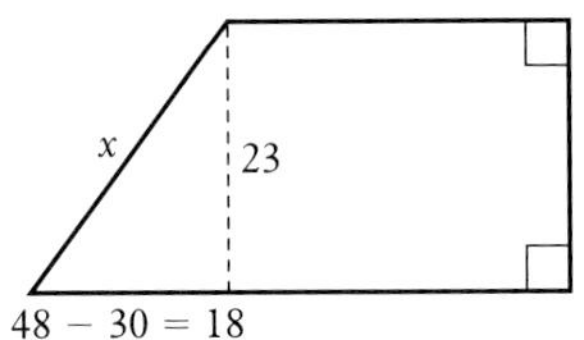

7 $d^2 = 62^2 + 47^2$
$= 6053$
$d = 77.8$ nautical miles (3 sf)

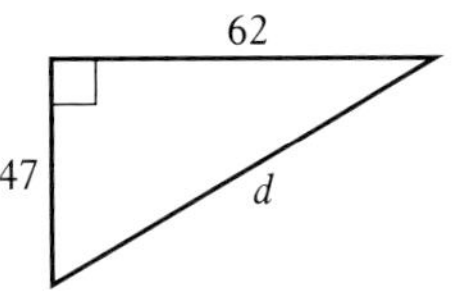

8

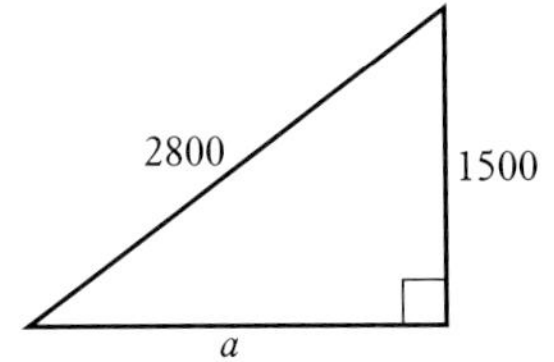

$2800^2 = a^2 + 1500^2$
$a^2 = 2800^2 - 1500^2$
$= 5\,590\,000$
$a = 2364.318\ldots$
$= 2360$ m (3 sf)

$5000^2 = b^2 + 1000^2$
$b^2 = 5000^2 - 1000^2$
$= 24\,000\,000$
$b = 4898.979\ldots$
$= 4900$ m (3 sf)

Horizontal distance $= 2360 + 4900$
$= 7260$ m (3 sf)

CHAPTER 25

1 **a** $y = 2x - 3$

x	-1	0	1	2
$2x$	-2	0	2	4
-3	-3	-3	-3	-3
y	-5	-3	-1	1

b, c, e

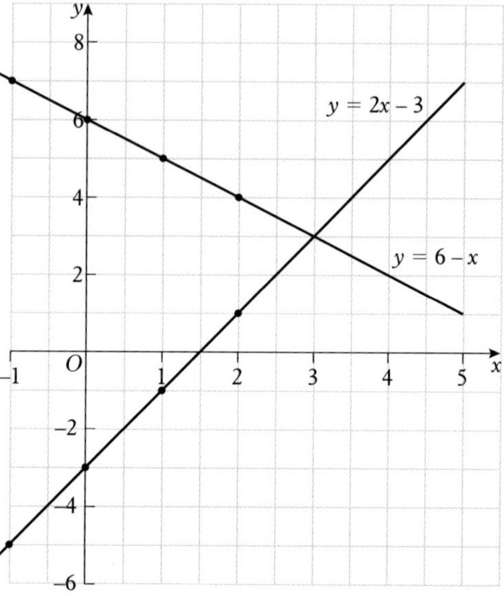

d $y = 6 - x$

x	-1	0	1	2
6	6	6	6	6
$-x$	1	0	-1	-2
y	7	6	5	4

f (3, 3)

2 **A** quadratic **B** linear **C** cubic

3 **a**

x	-2	-1	0	1	2	3	4	5	6
x^2	4	1	0	1	4	9	16	25	36
$-4x$	8	4	0	-4	-8	-12	-16	-20	-24
$+3$	$+3$	$+3$	$+3$	$+3$	$+3$	$+3$	$+3$	$+3$	$+3$
y	15	8	3	0	-1	0	3	8	15

b, c, d

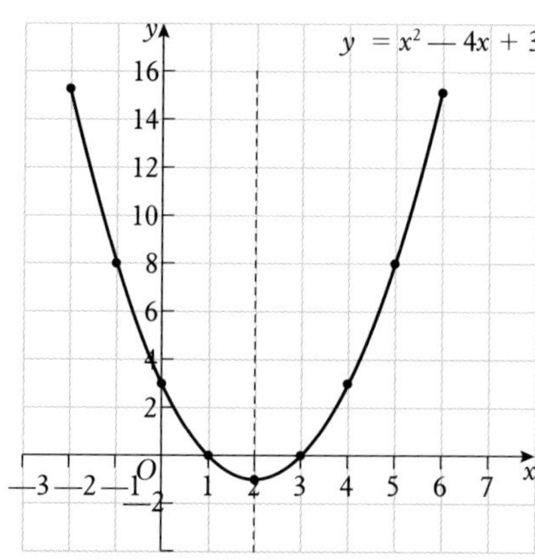

e $x = 2$

f $y = -0.8$ (approximately)

g $x = -1.3$ and 5.3 (approximately)

h $x = 2$

4 a $y = x^3 - x^2 - 6x$

x	**−3**	**−2**	**−1**	**0**	**1**	**2**	**3**	**4**
x^3	−27	−8	−1	0	1	8	27	64
$-x^2$	−9	−4	−1	0	−1	−4	−9	−16
$-6x$	18	12	6	0	−6	−12	−18	−24
y	**−18**	**0**	**4**	**0**	**−6**	**−8**	**0**	**24**

b, c, f

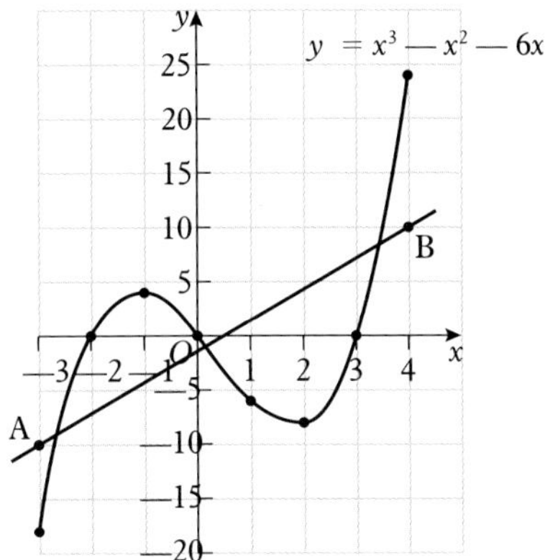

d $y = 3$ (approximately)

e $x = -1.9, -0.1, 3.1$ (approximately)

g

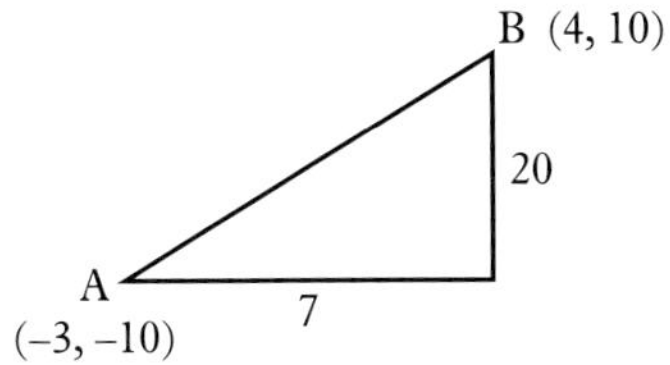

$$\text{gradient} = \frac{20}{7} = 2.9 \text{ (1 dp)}$$

h $(-2.7, -9)$ $(0.1, -1)$ $(3.5, 8.5)$ (approximately)

5 **A** (3), **B** (4), **C** (2), **D** (1), **E** (6), **F** (5)

CHAPTER 26

1 **a, b, c, d, e**

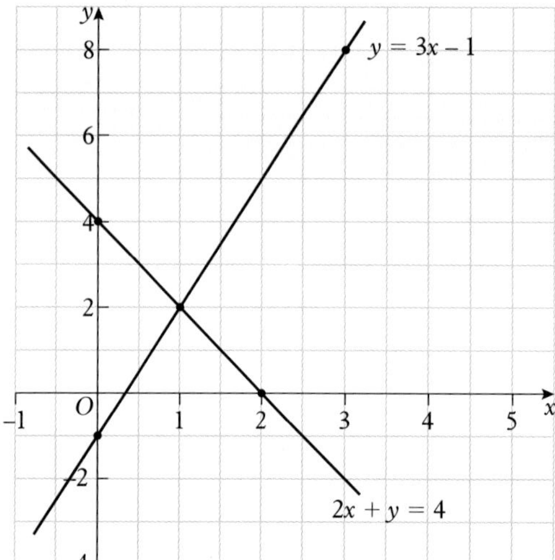

f $x = 1,\ y = 2$

g $y = 3x - 1$; when $x = 1$, $y = 3x - 1 = 3 \times 1 - 1 = 3 - 1 = 2$ ✓

$2x + y = 4$; when $x = 1$ and $y = 2$, $2x + y = 2 \times 1 + 2 = 2 + 2 = 4$ ✓

2 **a**

(1) $3x - 2y = 7$

(2) $x + 2y = 5$

Adding $4x = 12$

$x = 3$

Put $x = 3$ in (2)

$3 + 2y = 5$

$2y = 2$

$y = 1$

Check in (1)

$3x - 2y = 3 \times 3 - 2 \times 1$

$= 9 - 2$

$= 7$ ✓

b

(1) $5x - 2y = 10$

(2) $3x - 2y = 2$

Subtracting $2x = 8$

$x = 4$

Put $x = 4$ in (1)

$20 - 2y = 10$

$20 = 10 + 2y$

$20 - 10 = 2y$

$10 = 2y$

$y = 5$

Check in (2)

$3x - 2y = 3 \times 4 - 2 \times 5$

$= 12 - 10$

$= 2$ ✓

c (1) $3x - y = 13$

(2) $2x + 3y = 5$

$$\begin{aligned}(1)\times 3 \quad 9x - 3y &= 39\\ (2) \quad 2x + 3y &= 5\end{aligned}$$

$$\begin{aligned}\text{Adding } 11x &= 44\\ x &= 4\end{aligned}$$

Put $x = 4$ in (1)

$$\begin{aligned}12 - y &= 13\\ 12 &= 13 + y\\ 12 - 13 &= y\\ y &= -1\end{aligned}$$

Check in (2)

$$\begin{aligned}2x + 3y &= 2 \times 4 + 3 \times (-1)\\ &= 8 - 3\\ &= 5 \quad ✓\end{aligned}$$

d (1) $7x + 2y = 28$

(2) $2x + 3y = 25$

$$\begin{aligned}(1)\times 3 \quad 21x + 6y &= 84\\ (2)\times 2 \quad 4x + 6y &= 50\end{aligned}$$

$$\begin{aligned}\text{Subtracting } 17x &= 34\\ x &= 2\end{aligned}$$

Put $x = 2$ in (1)

$$\begin{aligned}14 + 2y &= 28\\ 2y &= 14\\ y &= 7\end{aligned}$$

Check in (2)

$$\begin{aligned}2x + 3y &= 4 + 21\\ &= 25 \quad ✓\end{aligned}$$

3 **a**

$$\begin{aligned}g &= 4h - 7\\ 4h - 7 &= g\\ 4h &= g + 7\\ h &= \frac{g + 7}{4}\end{aligned}$$

b

$$\begin{aligned}w &= \frac{t}{5} + 2\\ \frac{t}{5} + 2 &= w\\ \frac{t}{5} &= w - 2\\ t &= 5(w - 2)\end{aligned}$$

c

$$\begin{aligned}y &= \frac{3x}{4} - 6\\ \frac{3x}{4} - 6 &= y\\ \frac{3x}{4} &= y + 6\\ 3x &= 4(y + 6)\\ x &= \frac{4(y + 6)}{3}\end{aligned}$$

d

$$\begin{aligned}s &= 10 + 3t^2\\ 10 + 3t^2 &= s\\ 3t^2 &= s - 10\\ t^2 &= \frac{s - 10}{3}\\ t &= \sqrt{\frac{s - 10}{3}}\end{aligned}$$

4 **a**

$$\begin{aligned}A &= \frac{\sqrt{w^2 + 3xy}}{10}\\ &= \frac{\sqrt{(-1)^2 + 3 \times 8 \times 2}}{10}\\ &= \frac{\sqrt{1 + 48}}{10}\\ &= \frac{\sqrt{49}}{10}\\ &= \frac{7}{10}\\ &= 0.7\end{aligned}$$

b $\dfrac{\sqrt{w^2 + 3xy}}{10} = A$

$$\begin{aligned} \sqrt{w^2 + 3xy} &= 10A \\ w^2 + 3xy &= (10A)^2 \\ w^2 &= (10A)^2 - 3xy \\ w &= \sqrt{(10A)^2 - 3xy} \end{aligned}$$

c $w = \sqrt{(10 \times 1)^2 - 3 \times 4 \times 7}$

$$\begin{aligned} &= \sqrt{10^2 - 84} \\ &= \sqrt{100 - 84} \\ &= \sqrt{16} \\ &= 4 \end{aligned}$$

5 **a** (1) $y = 5 - 2x$
(2) $3y + x = 10$

Substitute for y in (2)

$$\begin{aligned} 3(5 - 2x) + x &= 10 \\ 15 - 6x + x &= 10 \\ 15 - 5x &= 10 \\ 15 &= 10 + 5x \\ 5 &= 5x \\ x &= 1 \end{aligned}$$

Put $x = 1$ in (1)

$$\begin{aligned} y &= 5 - 2 \times 1 \\ &= 5 - 2 \\ &= 3 \end{aligned}$$

Check in (2)

$3y + x = 3 \times 3 + 1$

$= 8 \times 1 - 3 \times (-2)$

$$\begin{aligned} &= 9 + 1 \\ &= 10 \ \checkmark \end{aligned}$$

b (1) $x = 4y - 6$
(2) $14 = 8y - 3x$

Substitute for x in (2)

$$\begin{aligned} 14 &= 8y - 3(4y - 6) \\ 14 &= 8y - 12y + 18 \\ 14 &= -4y + 18 \\ 14 + 4y &= 18 \\ 4y &= 4 \\ y &= 1 \end{aligned}$$

Put $y = 1$ in (1)

$$\begin{aligned} x &= 4 \times 1 - 6 \\ &= 4 - 6 \\ &= -2 \end{aligned}$$

Check in (2)

$8y - 3x$

$$\begin{aligned} &= 8 + 6 \\ &= 14 \ \checkmark \end{aligned}$$

CHAPTER 27

1 **a** 20 cm^2 **b** Allow 27 cm^2 or 28 cm^2

2 **a** $(18 \times 14) \div 2 = 252 \div 2 = 126\ \text{cm}^2$

b $\frac{1}{2} \times 13.5 \times 10 = 67.5\ \text{m}^2$

c $\frac{1}{2} \times 7 \times 14 = 49\ \text{cm}^2$

d $\dfrac{(6 + 10)}{2} \times 5 = 8 \times 5 = 40\ \text{cm}^2$

e $20 \times 30 = 600\ \text{cm}^2$

f $15 \times 12 = 180\ \text{m}^2$

3 a

8 × 11 =
88 m²

Diameter = 8 m, radius = 8 ÷ 2 = 4 m

Area of semicircle = (π × radius × radius) ÷ 2

$= (\pi \times 4 \times 4) \div 2$

$= (50.265\ldots) \div 2$

$= 25.1\text{ m}^2$ (3 sf)

Area of shape = 88 + 25.1 = 113.1 m²

b Total area = 372 × 270

= 642 cm²

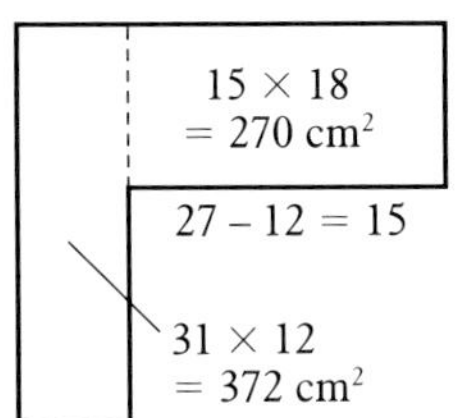

c For triangle, base = 25 − 9 = 16 mm;
height = 18 − 12 = 6 mm

$$\text{Area} = \frac{(16 \times 6)}{2} = \frac{96}{2} = 48\text{ mm}^2$$

Total area = 162 + 48 = 210 mm²

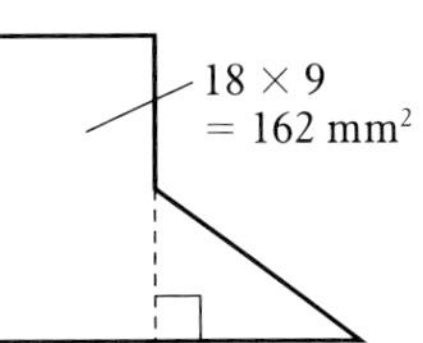

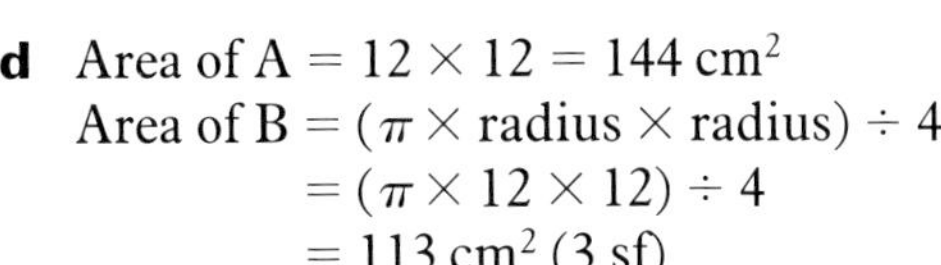

d Area of A = 12 × 12 = 144 cm²

Area of B = (π × radius × radius) ÷ 4

$= (\pi \times 12 \times 12) \div 4$

$= 113\text{ cm}^2$ (3 sf)

Area of D is the same as B

Area C = $(\pi \times 6 \times 6) \div 2 = 56.5\text{ cm}^2$ (3 sf)

Total area = 144 + 113 + 113 + 56.5

= 426.5 cm² (3 sf)

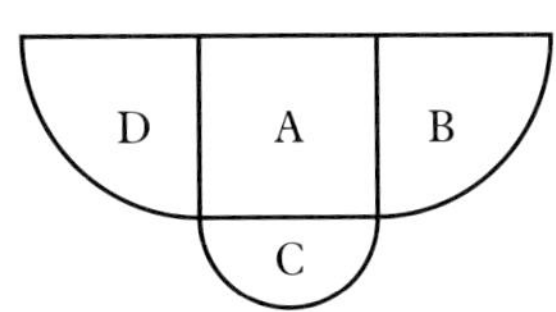

4 a (1)

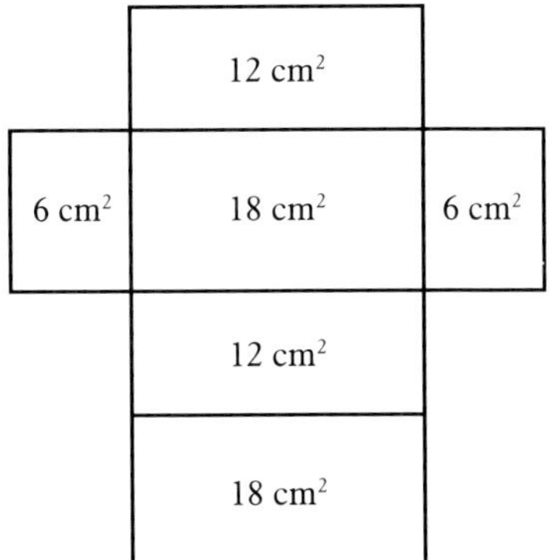

(2) Surface area = 6 + 12 + 18 + 12 + 18 + 6 = 72 cm²

b (1)

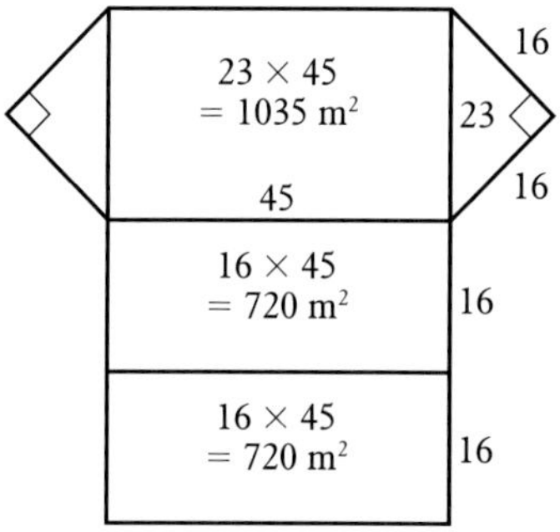

(2) Area of each triangle $= (16 \times 16) \div 2 = 128\ m^2$

Surface area $= 128 + 1035 + 720 + 720 + 128\ m^2$
$= 2731\ m^2$

5 **a** $1\ cm^2 = 100\ mm^2$ so $3\ cm^2 = 300\ mm^2$

b $1\ m^2 = 10\,000\ cm^2$ so $4\ m^2 = 40\,000\ cm^2$

c $1\ cm^2 = 100\ mm^2$ so $750\,000\ mm^2 = 750\,000 \div 100 = 7500\ cm^2$

d $1\ km^2 = 1\,000\,000\ m^2 = 1 \times 10^6\ m^2$
so $5 \times 10^{12}\ m^2 = (5 \times 10^{12}) \div (1 \times 10^6) = 5 \times 10^{12-6}$
$= 5 \times 10^6\ km^2$

CHAPTER 28

1 **a** 5 horses $= 5 \times 2$ guns $= 10$ guns

b 2 cannons $= 2 \times 5$ horses $= 10$ horses
$= 10 \times 2$ guns $= 20$ guns
$= 20 \times 20$ arrows $= 400$ arrows

c 15 archers $= 15 \div 3$ horses $= 5$ horses

d 4 horses $= 4 \times 3$ archers $= 12$ archers
$= (12 \div 2) \times 5$ foot soldiers
$= 6 \times 5 = 30$ foot soldiers

2 1st term $= 10$
2nd term $= 10 \times 2 - 12 = 20 - 12 = 8$
3rd term $= 8 \times 2 - 12 = 16 - 12 = 4$
4th term $= 4 \times 2 - 12 = 8 - 12 = -4$
5th term $= -4 \times 2 - 12 = -8 - 12 = -20$

3 **a** 1st term $= 7 \times 1 + 3 = 7 + 3 = 10$
2nd term $= 7 \times 2 + 3 = 14 + 3 = 17$
3rd term $= 7 \times 3 + 3 = 21 + 3 = 24$
4th term $= 7 \times 4 + 3 = 28 + 3 = 31$

b 10th term $= 7 \times 10 + 3 = 70 + 3 = 73$

4 **a** 50th term = $250 + 27 \times 50 = 250 + 1350 = 1600$

b

Value of n	Value of $250 + 27n$
20	$250 + 27 \times 20 = 790$ too big
15	$250 + 27 \times 15 = 655$ too small
16	$250 + 27 \times 16 = 682$ too small
18	$250 + 27 \times 18 = 736$ too big
17	$250 + 27 \times 17 = 709$ ✓

Or solve the equation

$250 + 27n = 709$

To get $27n = 459$

$n = 17$

The 17th term.

5 **a** (1) 3, 6, 9, 12, 15
(2) 4, 8, 12, 16, 20
(3) 5, 10, 15, 20, 25

b (1) $7n$
(2) $11n$
(3) $15n$

6 **a** $4n + 1$ **b** $4n + 9$ **c** $4n - 3$

7

Term number	1	2	3	4	5
	+6	+6	+6	+6	
Sequence	2	8	14	20	26
	−4	−4	−4	−4	−4
Sequence $6n$	6	12	18	24	30

related to $6n$

You need to take 4 from every term in $6n$ to make the sequence.
So the formula for the nth term of the sequence is $6n - 4$

8 **a**

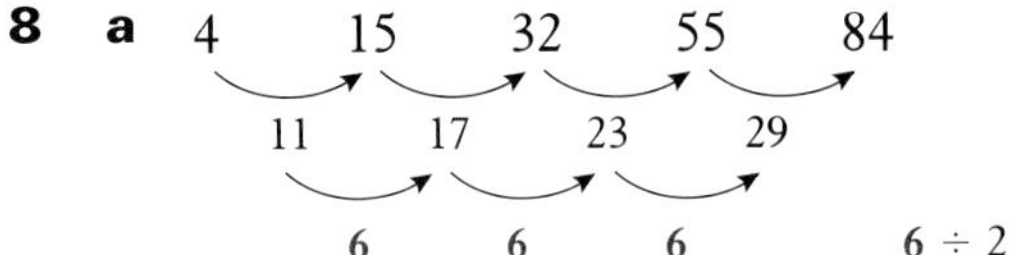

The first part of the formula is $3n^2$

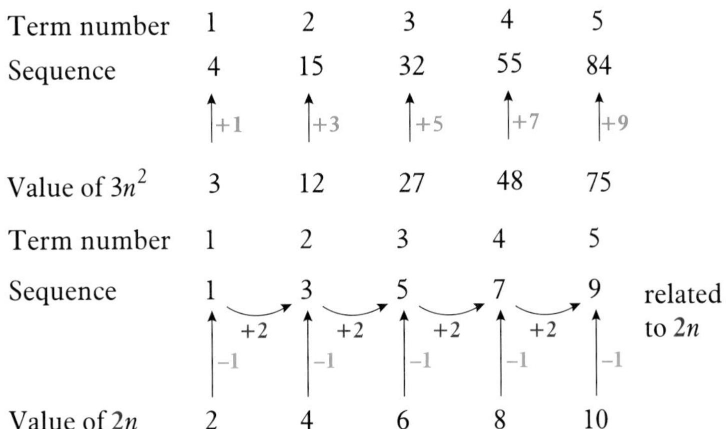

Term number	1	2	3	4	5
Sequence	4	15	32	55	84
	+1	+3	+5	+7	+9
Value of $3n^2$	3	12	27	48	75

Term number	1	2	3	4	5
Sequence	1	3	5	7	9
	+2	+2	+2	+2	
	−1	−1	−1	−1	−1
Value of $2n$	2	4	6	8	10

related to $2n$

The second part of the formula is $2n - 1$

b The whole formula is $3n^2 + 2n - 1$

9 **a** 1st term $= 1^2 - 5 \times 1 + 10 = 6$
2nd term $= 2^2 - 5 \times 2 + 10 = 4$
3rd term $= 3^2 - 5 \times 3 + 10 = 4$
4th term $= 4^2 - 5 \times 4 + 10 = 6$
5th term $= 5^2 - 5 \times 5 + 10 = 10$

b 20th term $= 20^2 - 5 \times 20 + 10 = 400 - 100 + 10 = 310$

c

Value of n	Value of $n^2 - 5n + 10$	
40	$40^2 - 5 \times 40 + 10 = 1410$	too small
42	$42^2 - 5 \times 42 + 10 = 1564$	too big
41	$41^2 - 5 \times 41 + 10 = 1486$	✓

41st term.

10 **a** 1st term $= \dfrac{16 - 2}{1 + 1} = \dfrac{14}{2} = 7$

2nd term $= \dfrac{16 - 4}{2 + 1} = \dfrac{12}{3} = 4$

3rd term $= \dfrac{16 - 6}{3 + 1} = \dfrac{10}{4} = 2.5$

b $\dfrac{16 - 2n}{n + 1} = 1$ means $16 - 2n = n + 1$

(because dividing two expressions to get 1 means they are equal)

$$16 - 2n = n + 1$$
$$16 = 3n + 1$$
$$15 = 3n$$
$$n = 5$$

The 5th term has value 1.

Check $\dfrac{16 - 2n}{n + 1} = \dfrac{16 - 10}{5 + 1} = \dfrac{6}{6} = 1$ ✓

CHAPTER 29

1 **a** $a = 180 - 47 - 52$ (angles in a traingle)
$a = 81°$

$b = 180 - 81$ (angles on a straight line)
$b = 99°$

b $c = 36°$ (alternate angles)

c $d = \dfrac{180 - 40}{2}$ (base angles of isosceles triangle)

$d = 70°$

$e = 180 - 2 \times 70$ (missing angle is 70° base angle of isosceles triangle)
$e = 40°$

d $f = 360 - 123 - 119 - 70$ (angles in a quadrilateral)
$f = 48°$

e $g = \frac{180}{3}$ (angles in an equilateral triangle)

$g = 60°$

$h = 180 - 60$ (angles on a straight line)

$h = 120°$

f $i + 3i = 180°$ (angles on a straight line)

$4i = 180$

$i = 45°$ $3i = 3 \times 45° = 135°$

2 **a** $a = 43°$ (alternate angles)

b $b = 110°$ (corresponding angles)

c $c = 128°$ (alternate angles)

$d = 34°$ (alternate angles)

$e = 180° - 128° - 34°$ (angles in a triangle)

$= 18°$

d $f = 119°$ (corresponding angles)

$g = 119°$ (corresponding angles with f)

Angle above $g = 61°$ (angles on a straight line)

Angle on the right of $125° = 55°$ (angles on a straight line)

$h = 180° - 61° - 55°$ (angles in a triangle)

$h = 64°$

3 **a** $a = 70°$ (angle at the centre = 2 × angle at the circumference)

b $b = 90°$ (angle in a semi circle)

$c = 48°$ (angles in the same segment)

c $e = 18°$ (angles in the same segment)
$f = 36°$ (angle at the centre = 2 × angle at the circumference)
$g = 18°$ (base angles isosceles triangle)
$h = 18°$ (angle in the same segment as g)

d Angle on left of centre of circle

$= 2 \times (180° - 90° - 34°)$ (twice the angle in the triangle from tangent, radius and across the middle of the diagram)

$= 112°$

$m = 56°$ (angle at the centre = 2 × angle at the circumference)
$n = 180° - 56°$ (opposite angles in a cyclic quadrilateral)
$= 124°$

4 **a** (1) 065°
(2) 180 + 65 = 245°

b (1) 110°
(2) 180 + 110 = 290°

c (1) 180 + 155 = 335°
(2) 155°

5 **a**

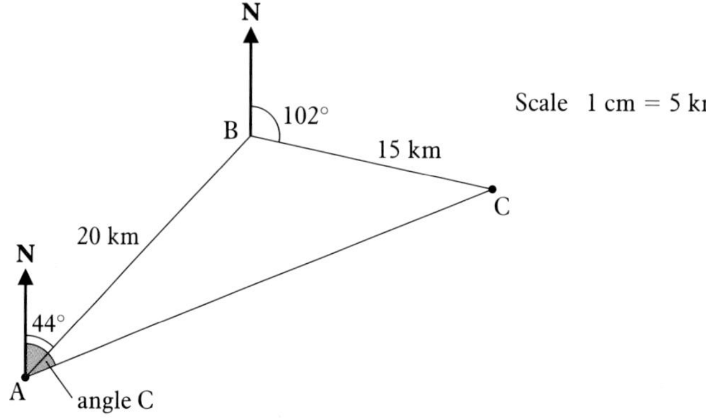

b AC = 6.1 cm
∴ Distance from A to C is 30.5 km (allow ±0.5 km)

c Angle C = 70°
∴ Bearing of C from A is 070° (allow ±2°).

CHAPTER 30

1 **a** $3x + 12$
b $x^2 - 7x$
c $-15x + 15$
d $6x^3 + 2x^2$

2 **a** $x^2 + 7x + 12$
b $x^2 - 5x - 14$
c $6x^2 - 21x + 15$
d $42x^2 - 10x - 8$

3 **a** $3(x + 2y)$
b $x(x + 3)$
c $3t(x - 3y)$
d $3xz(5y - 2)$

4 **a** $(x + 2)(x + 3)$
b $(x + 3)(x + 7)$
c $(x - 7)(x + 4)$
d $(x + 10)(x - 3)$

5 **a** $x^2 + 8x + 15 = 0$
$(x + 3)(x + 5) = 0$
$x = -3, x = -5$

b $x^2 - 8x + 12 = 0$
$(x - 2)(x - 6) = 0$
$x = 2, x = 6$

c $x^2 + 2x - 3 = 0$
$(x + 3)(x - 1) = 0$
$x = -3, x = 1$

d $x^2 - 4x - 12 = 0$
$(x - 6)(x + 2) = 0$
$x = 6, x = -2$

6 **a** $y = x^2 - 2x - 15$
$= (x - 5)(x + 3)$

b $y = x^2 + 5x - 14$
$= (x - 2)(x + 7)$

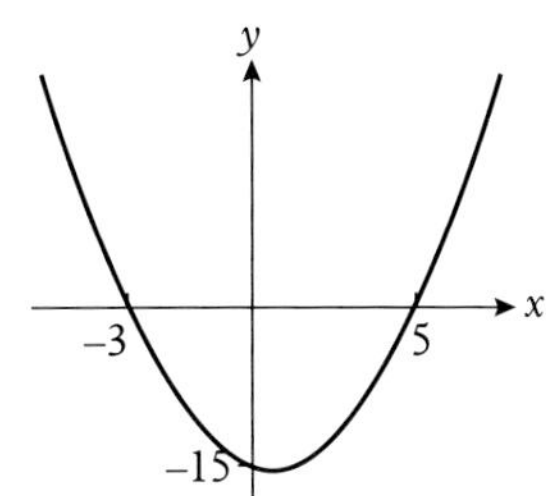

7 **a**
$$\begin{aligned} 6r &= 3rt + 4 \\ 6r - 3rt &= 4 \\ r(6 - 3t) &= 4 \\ r &= \frac{4}{6 - 3t} \end{aligned}$$

b
$$\begin{aligned} 7x + 3y &= 3xt \\ 7x - 3xt &= -3y \\ x(7 - 3t) &= -3y \\ x &= \frac{-3y}{7 - 3t} \end{aligned}$$

c
$$\begin{aligned} t &= \frac{r + 4}{r} \\ rt &= r + 4 \\ rt - r &= 4 \\ r(t - 1) &= 4 \\ r &= \frac{4}{t - 1} \end{aligned}$$

d
$$\begin{aligned} 3z &= \frac{4y - 3}{y} \\ 3yz &= 4y - 3 \\ 3yz - 4y &= -3 \\ y(3z - 4) &= -3 \\ y &= \frac{-3}{3z - 4} \end{aligned}$$

CHAPTER 31

1

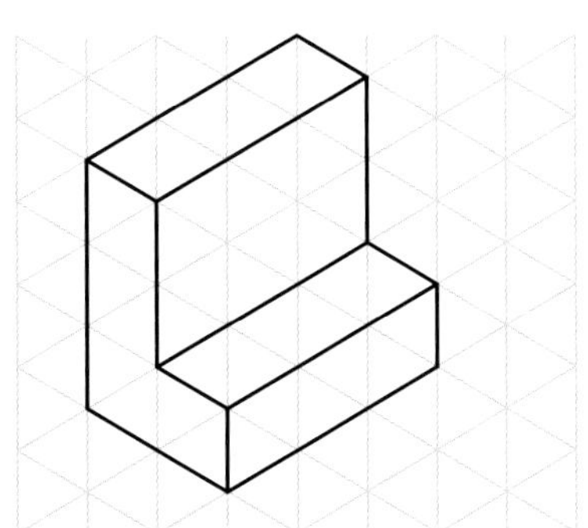

2 **a** 0.037 m **b** 800 m **c** 7.6 tonnes **d** 308 cm **e** 0.038 *l* **f** 47.8 cl

3 $450 \div 0.45 = 1000$ pounds

4 $8^3 = 512\ \text{cm}^3$

5 Area of end $= (10 + 6) \div 2 \times 12 = 8 \times 12 = 96\ \text{cm}^2$
Volume $= 96 \times 14 = 1344\ \text{cm}^3$

6 Area of end $= 86 \div 5.4 = 15.925\ldots\ \text{cm}^2$ so $\pi r^2 = 15.925\ \ldots$

$r^2 = 15.925\ \ldots$

$$r = \sqrt{\frac{15.925}{\pi}} = 2.3 \text{ cm to the nearest mm.}$$

7 **a** length **c** area **e** length
b area **d** volume **f** length

CHAPTER 32

1 D and E

2 A and C

3 **a** 1
b 4 only if top and bottom are square. Otherwise 2.

4 **a** 2 **b** 4

5 **a** $180° - 162° = 18°$
b $360 \div 18 = 20$ sides

6 $\frac{x}{3} = \frac{x+4}{5}$ $\left(\text{or } \frac{5}{3} = \frac{x+4}{x}\right)$

$5x = 3(x + 4)$
$5x = 3x + 12$
$2x = 12$
$x = 6$

CHAPTER 33

1

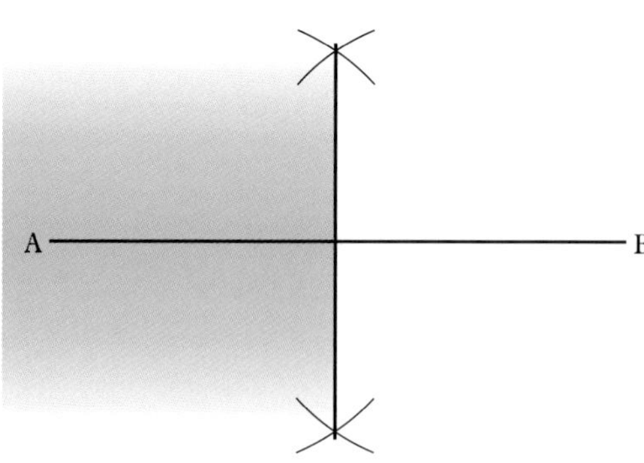

Points on the shaded side of the line are closer to A than to B.

2 **a**

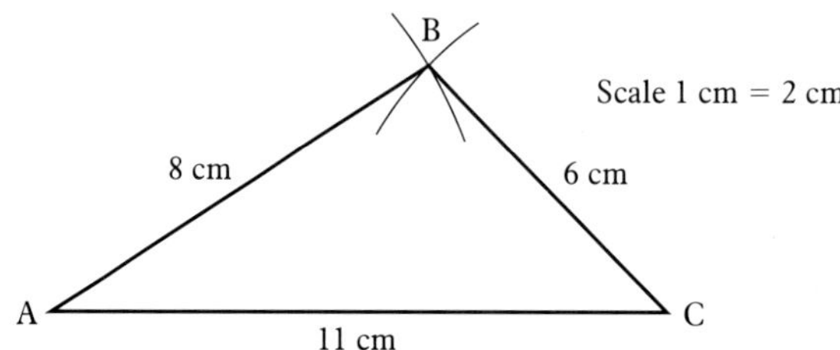

Scale 1 cm = 2 cm

b 102° (allow ±1°)

3

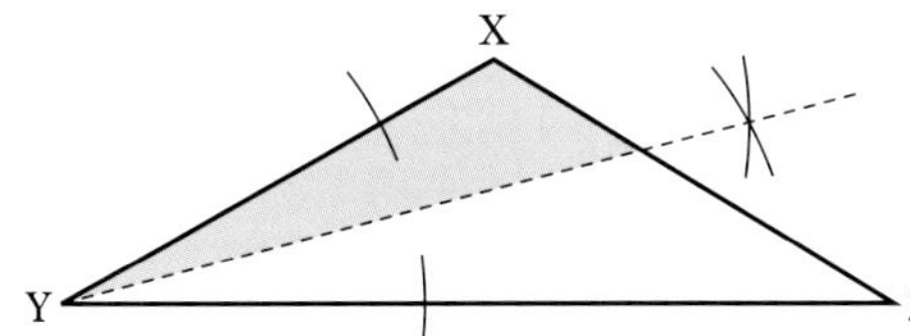

The shaded area shows the points closer to XY than YZ

4 **a**

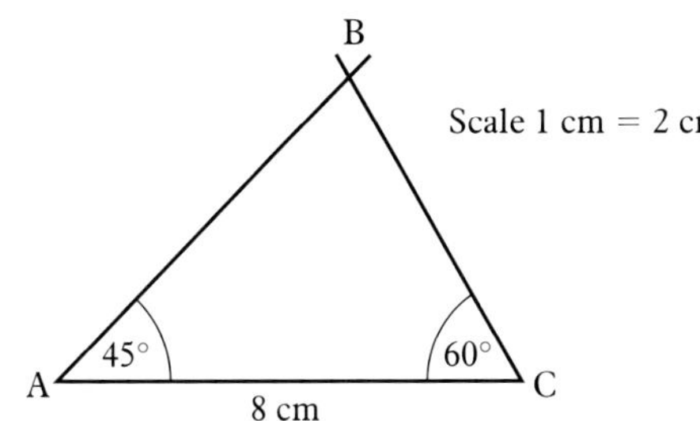

b AB = 7.2 cm to the nearest mm (allow ±1 mm)

CHAPTER 34

1 **a** −0.5, 2 **b** −1.8, 3.3

2 **a**

x	**−3**	**−2**	**−1**	**0**	**1**	**2**	**3**	**4**
x^2	9	4	1	0	1	4	9	16
$-x$	3	2	1	0	−1	−2	−3	−4
−3	−3	−3	−3	−3	−3	−3	−3	−3
y	**9**	**3**	**−1**	**−3**	**−3**	**−1**	**3**	**9**

b, d

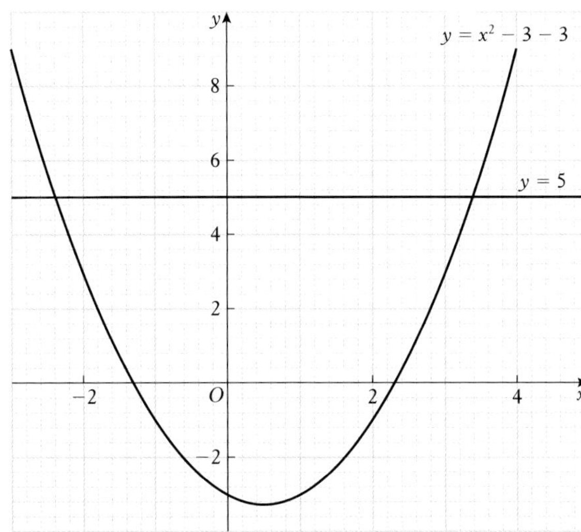

c −1.3, 2.3 **e** −2.4, 3.4

3 a

x	**−2**	**−1**	**0**	**1**	**2**	**3**	**4**	**5**
x^2	4	1	0	1	4	9	16	25
$-3x$	6	3	0	−3	−6	−9	−12	−15
$+1$	1	1	1	1	1	1	1	1
y	**11**	5	**1**	**−1**	**−1**	**1**	5	**11**

c

x	**−2**	**−1**	**0**	**1**	**2**	**3**	**4**	**5**
$2x$	−4	−2	0	2	4	6	8	10
$+3$	3	3	3	3	3	3	3	3
y	**−1**	**1**	**3**	**5**	**7**	**9**	**11**	**13**

b, d

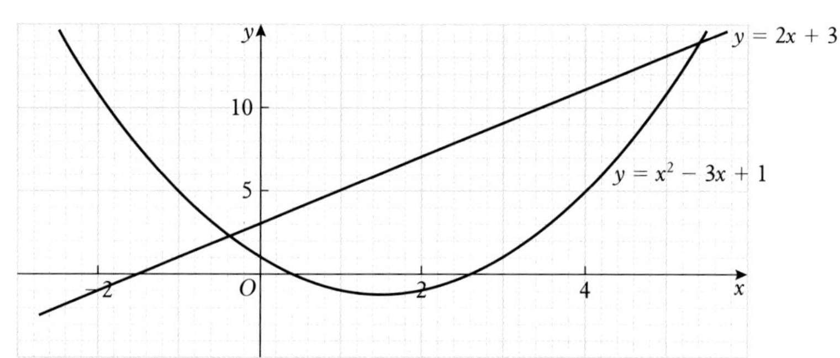

e −0.4, 5.4

4 a

x	**−4**	**−3**	**−2**	**−1**	**0**	**1**	**2**	**3**	**4**
$\frac{1}{x}$	−0.25	−0.33	−0.5	−1		1	0.5	0.33	0.25
$+3$	3	3	3	3		3	3	3	3
y	2.75	2.67	2.5	2		4	3.5	3.33	3.25

b, c

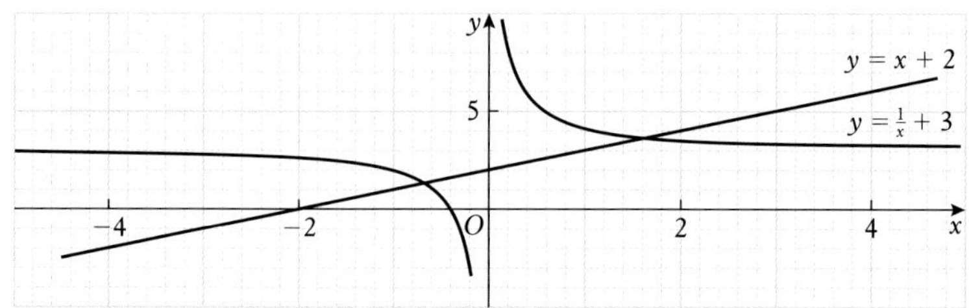

d −0.6, 1.6

5 $$\begin{aligned} x^3 &= 2x^2 - 4 \\ x^3 - x^2 &= x^2 - 4 \\ x^3 - x^2 + 5 &= x^2 - 4 + 5 \\ x^3 - x^2 + 5 &= x^2 + 1 \end{aligned}$$

$y = x^2 + 1$ is needed. She would then find the x values where the curves cross.

CHAPTER 35

1 a $\cos a = \dfrac{26}{31} = 0.8387 \ldots$

$a = 33.0°$ (1 dp)

b $\tan b = \dfrac{2.3}{3.7} = 0.6216 \ldots$

$b = 31.9°$(1 dp)

2 a $\sin 33° = \dfrac{x}{24.8}$

$x = 24.8 \sin 33°$

$= 13.5$ cm (3 sf)

b $\tan 52° = \dfrac{x}{42.6}$

$x = 42.6 \tan 52°$

$= 54.5$ cm (3 sf)

3 a $9.6 \cos 72°$
$= 2.97$ km (3 sf)

b $9.6 \sin 72°$
$= 9.13$ km (3 sf)

c $180° + 72° = 252°$

4 a

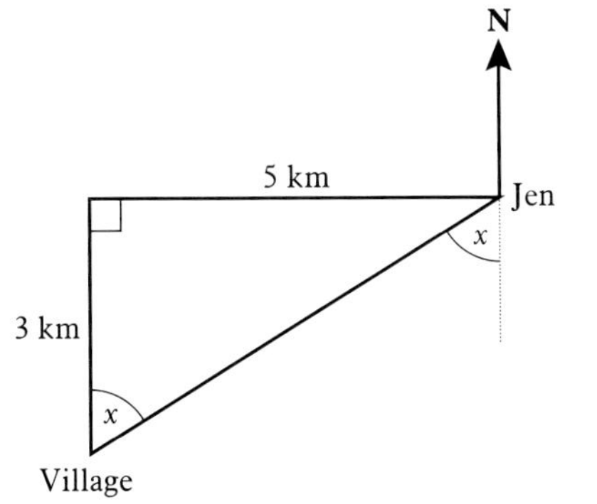

b $\tan x = \frac{5}{3} = 1.666 \ldots$

$x = 59.0°$ (1 dp)

Bearing $= 180° + 59°$

$= 239°$

5 a

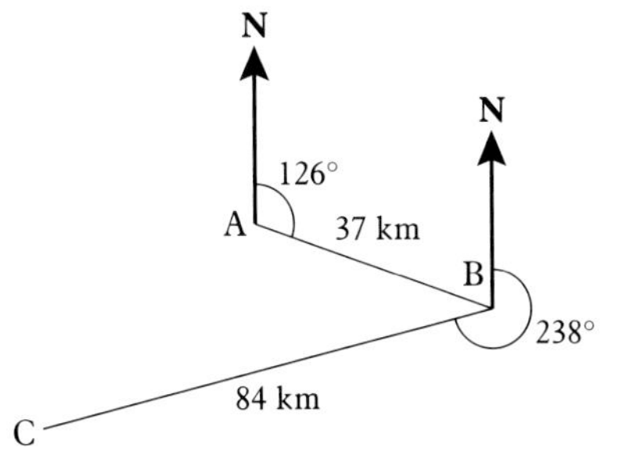

b $37 \cos 54° + 84 \cos 58°$

$= 21.748 \ldots +$
$44.513 \ldots$

$= 66.261 \ldots$

$= 66.3$ km (3 sf)

c $84 \sin 58° - 37 \sin 54°$

$= 71.236 \ldots - 29.933 \ldots$

$= 41.30 \ldots$

$= 41.3$ km (3 sf)

d

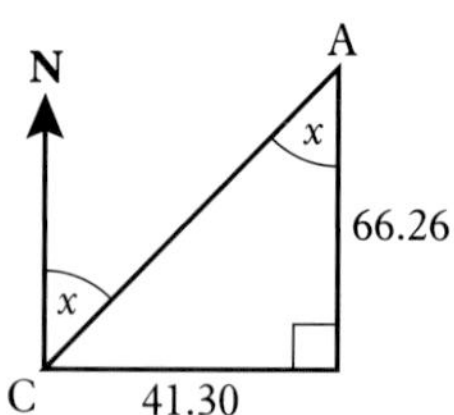

$$\tan x = \frac{41.30}{66.26} = 0.6233$$

$$x = 31.9° \text{ (3 sf)}$$

Bearing of A from C is 032°.

6 $\sin 63° = \dfrac{18.6}{h}$

$$h = \frac{18.6}{\sin 63}$$

$$= 20.9 \text{ m (3 sf)}$$

7 **a**

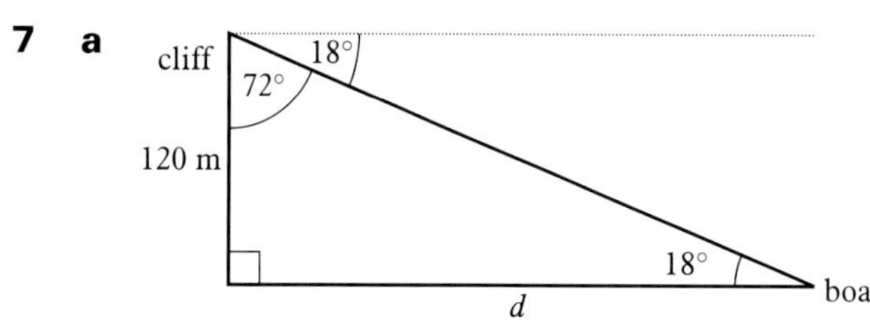

b $\tan 72° = \dfrac{d}{120}$ or $\tan 18° = \dfrac{120}{d}$

$d = 120 \tan 72°$ $\qquad d = \dfrac{120}{\tan 18°}$

$= 369$ m (3 sf) $\qquad = 369$ m (3 s.f.)

8 $\sin 60° = \dfrac{2.6}{l}$

$$l = \frac{2.6}{\sin 60}$$

$$= 3.0 \text{ m (2 sf)}$$

9

25°
40°
30 m
x
h

$h = (30 + x) \tan 25°$

$h = x \tan 40°$

$x \tan 40° = 30 \tan 25° + x \tan 25°$
$x(\tan 40° - \tan 25°) = 30 \tan 25°$
$x = \dfrac{30 \tan 25°}{(\tan 40° - \tan 25°)}$
$x = 37.525 \ldots$ m
$h = x \tan 40° = 31.5$ m (3 sf)

CHAPTER 36

1 **a** $-4 < x \leqslant 2$ **b** $-5 \leqslant x < 1$ **c** $x > -2$

2 **a** 3, 4, 5
b $-3, -2, -1, 0$
c $-5, -4, -3, -2, -1$
d $-2, -1, 0, 1, 2$

3 **a** $x < 11$
b $2x \geqslant 17 - 5$
$2x \geqslant 12$
$x \geqslant 6$
c $4x \leqslant 12 + 7$
$4x \leqslant 19$
$x \leqslant 4.75$
d $\dfrac{x}{4} > 11.3$
$x > 45.2$
e $3x + 1 < -20$
$3x < -21$
$x < -7$
f $2x + 11 \geqslant 7$
$2x \geqslant -4$
$x \geqslant -2$

4 **a** $-x > -8$
$x < 8$
b $5 - 2x < -21$
$-2x < -26$
$2x > 26$
$x > 13$
c $7 \leqslant 5x - 9$
$16 \leqslant 5x$
$3.2 \leqslant x$
$x \geqslant 3.2$
d $10 \geqslant x + 6$
$4 \geqslant x$
$x \leqslant 4$

5 **a** $6 \leqslant 3x < 12$
$2 \leqslant x < 4$
b $11 < x + 7 \leqslant 19$
$4 < x \leqslant 12$
c $5 \leqslant 2x - 1 \leqslant 11$
$6 \leqslant 2x \leqslant 12$
$3 \leqslant x \leqslant 6$
d $-10 < -5x < 0$
$-2 < -x < 0$
$2 > x > 0$
$0 < x < 2$

6 **a** $x \geqslant -2$ **b** $-4 \leqslant y < 3$

7 **a** $x \geqslant 1, y > -3$ **b** $x < -2, -2 \leqslant y \leqslant 1$

8 $x < 1$ or $x > 2$

9 **a** s represents the number of sliced loaves
u represents the number of unsliced loaves
The total number of loaves is less than or equal to 800.
b $s \geqslant 0, u \geqslant 0, u \geqslant 200, s \geqslant 2u$

c

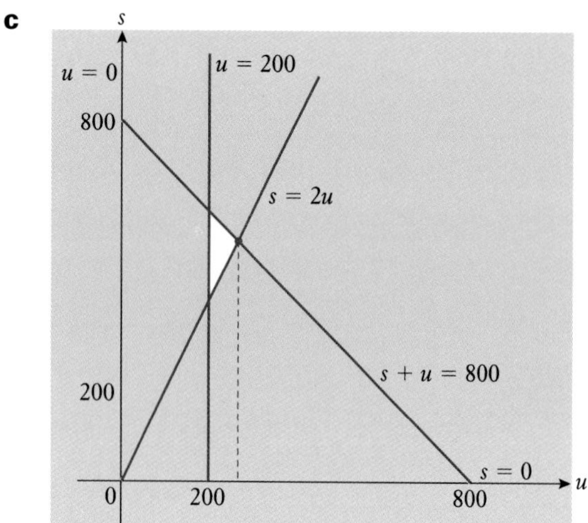

d The red point on the graph shows the furthest point along the u axis which satisfies all the inequalities. This gives the most unsliced loaves that can be made as 266.